OXFORD
THE CHRISTIAN CHURCH

Edited by

HENRY AND OWEN CHADWICK

THE
ORTHODOX CHURCH
IN THE
BYZANTINE EMPIRE
—

J. M. HUSSEY

CLARENDON PRESS · OXFORD

Oxford University Press, Walton Street, Oxford OX2 6DP

Oxford New York
Athens Auckland Bangkok Bombay
Calcutta Cape Town Dar es Salaam Delhi
Florence Hong Kong Istanbul Karachi
Kuala Lumpur Madras Madrid Melbourne
Mexico City Nairobi Paris Singapore
Taipei Tokyo Toronto
and associated companies in
Berlin Ibadan

Oxford is a trade mark of Oxford University Press

Published in the United States by
Oxford University Press Inc., New York

First published 1986
First published as a Clarendon Paperback 1990

British Library Cataloguing in Publication Data
Data available

Library of Congress Cataloging in Publication Data
Hussey, J. M. (Joan Mervyn)
The Orthodox Church in the Byzantine Empire.
(Oxford history of the Christian Church)
Includes bibliographical references and index.
1. Orthodox Eastern Church—Byzantine Empire.
2. Byzantine Empire—Church history. I. Title. II. Series.
BX300.H87 1985 281.9'09'02 85–13821
ISBN 0–19–826456–9

3 5 7 9 10 8 6

Printed in Great Britain on acid-free paper by
Biddles Ltd., Guildford and King's Lynn

PREFACE

I SHOULD like to express my grateful thanks to the Trustees of the Leverhulme Foundation for the award of an Emeritus Research Fellowship and to the Trustees of the Bethune-Baker Fund for a grant towards the cost of typing. A good deal of the work for this book was done in the Gennadius Library and in the British School at Athens and more especially in the University of Cambridge Library where I have to thank hard-pressed assistants for their generous help.

This book is built on the work of past and present scholars too numerous to thank individually. But I should like to say in gratitude how much I owe to the late Norman Baynes who introduced me to the thought-world of East Rome. And it is a pleasure to acknowledge my special indebtedness over the years to three living scholars—Jean Darrouzès, Herbert Hunger, and Paul Lemerle—whose distinguished work has opened avenues leading to a more constructive view of an often changing Byzantine society. I am also most grateful to Julian Chrysostomides and Henry Chadwick both of whom read the typescript and made valuable suggestions.

J.M.H.

5 June 1984

NOTE TO PAPERBACK EDITION 1990

I am grateful to reviewers for pointing out misprints and errors which I have tried to put right. It has not been possible to cover bibliography for the years 1984–9 though one or two items have been inserted, but I have added lists of Byzantine Emperors, Popes and Patriarchs of Constantinople, and maps.

J. M. H.

CONTENTS

Abbreviations   xi

List of Rulers, Popes, and Patriarchs   xxi

List of Maps   xxviii

Introduction   1

PART I

CHALLENGE AND RESPONSE WITHIN
THE HISTORICAL FRAMEWORK

I. The Christological Problem in the Early Middle Ages   9

   1. The seventh-century watershed in the Byzantine Empire   9

   2. The theological background to seventh-century
     monotheletism   10

   3. Monenergism and monotheletism against a background
     of imperial crisis   13

   4. The Quinisext council (691–692)   24

II. The Iconoclast Controversy 726–843   30

   1. The North Syrian rulers: the first phase 726–787   30
     The background to the eighth-century crisis
     The opening conflict under Leo III
     Constantine V and the council of 754

   2. The first restoration of the icons   44
     The Empress Irene and the council of Nicaea (787)
     Conflicting currents 787–843
     Irene and Constantine VI
     Nicephorus I, Michael I, and the Patriarch Nicephorus
     (802–813)

   3. The second phase of iconoclasm   55

   4. The restoration of orthodoxy in 843: the Synodicon   62

   5. The significance of the controversy over icons   65

III. The Age of Photius 843–886   69

  1. Patriarch Methodius (843–847): the first patriarchate of Ignatius (847–858)   69

  2. Photius's first patriarchate (858–867)   72

  3. Ignatius's second patriarchate (867–877); the council of Constantinople (869–870)   79

  4. Photius's second patriarchate (877–886): the council of 879–880: the alleged second Photian schism   83

  5. Photius—churchman and humanist   86

  6. Byzantine missionary activities in the early middle ages   90

IV. Leo VI's Dilemma: Nicholas Mysticus and Euthymius 886–925   102

  1. Leo VI: the Emperor's fourth marriage   102

  2. Nicholas I's second patriarchate (912–925): the interdependence of church and state   108

V. The Patriarchate (925–1025): The Predominance of Constantinople   111

  1. Co-operation and criticism 925–970   111

  2. The imperial advance in the East: the Muslims and the non-Chalcedonian Churches   114

  3. Caucasian and North Pontic regions: Russia   116

  4. Byzantium and South Italy   119

VI. Increasing Pressures on Constantinople and the Widening Gap 1025–1204   124

  1. Impending threats   124

  2. Patriarchs (1025–1081)   127

  3. 1081: a new era or continuity?   141

  4. Philosophers and theologians: individual heretics: ecclesiastical currents   142

  5. The dualist heresies   156

  6. Relations with the West   167

VII. The Effects of the Fourth Crusade 1204–1261   184

    1. The patriarchate of Constantinople 1204–1261: the
       Latins in occupation   184

    2. Ecclesiastical organization within the various
       Latin conquests   192
         (i) Greece and the Cyclades
         (ii) Venetian conquests: Crete
         (iii) Cyprus

    3. Thirteenth-century rival Byzantine churches: Nicaea
       and Epirus   206

    4. The Nicaean Empire and Rome   211

VIII. Contacts: Failure and Achievement 1258–1453   220

    1. Michael VIII Palaeologus and the papacy: Byzantine
       doubts concerning union 1258–1274   221

    2. Michael VIII and the council of Lyons (1274)   229

    3. Byzantine reaction to the union 1274–1282   235

    4. Andronicus II and Andronicus III: internal problems:
       Josephites and Arsenites: repudiation of the union   243

    5. Patriarch Athanasius I and his immediate successors   249

    6. Renewed contacts with the West under Andronicus II
       and Andronicus III   255

    7. Palamite problems   257

    8. John V Palaeologus and John VI Cantacuzenus:
       Constantinople and the West   260

    9. Manuel II: the council of Ferrara–Florence and after   267

   10. The authority of the Byzantine Church in the later
       middle ages (*c.* 1334–1453)   286

PART II

ORGANIZATION AND LIFE OF
THE ORTHODOX CHURCH IN BYZANTIUM

    1. Collegiality: the emergence of the pentarchy; the
       position of Constantinople   297

    2. The patriarchate of Constantinople and the Emperor   299

    3. Canon law: the nomocanons   304

4. The *Notitiae Episcopatuum*: the higher clergy and
   imperial ceremonial   310

5. The oecumenical Patriarch and his election   312

6. Patriarchal administration: the major officials of the
   Great Church   314

7. The patriarchal synod: the metropolitans   318

8. Secular clergy in the provinces (eparchies) and in the
   dioceses   325

9. Monks and monasteries   335

10. The spiritual life of the Orthodox in Byzantium   349

Bibliographical Note   369

Glossary   381

Index   385

Maps   409

ABBREVIATIONS

AHR	*American Historical Review* (New York, 1895–)
Alexander, *Patriarch Nicephorus*	P. J. Alexander, *The Patriarch Nicephorus of Constantinople: Ecclesiastical Policy and Image Worship in the Byzantine Empire* (Oxford, 1958); see review by J. Gouillard, *BZ*, 51 (1958), 403–5
Angold	M. Angold, *A Byzantine Government in Exile: Government and Society under the Laskarids of Nicaea (1204–1261)* (Oxford, 1975)
Anna Comnena	Anna Comnena, *Alexiad*, ed. B. Leib (Budé with French trans., Paris, 1937–45), 3 vols.
ASS	*Acta Sanctorum Bollandiana* (Brussels, etc., 1643–)
B	Byzantion (Paris and Liège, 1924–9; Brussels etc., 1930–)
Barker, *Manuel II*	J. W. Barker, *Manuel II Palaeologus 1391–1425: A Study in late Byzantine Statesmanship* (New Brunswick, 1969)
Beck, *Geschichte*	H.-G. Beck, *Geschichte der orthodoxen Kirche im byzantinischen Reich* (Göttingen, 1980)
Beck, *Kirche*	H.-G. Beck, *Kirche und theologische Literatur im byzantinischen Reich* (Munich, 1959); useful reference work but bibliography only goes to about 1957
Bornert, *Commentaires*	R. Bornert, *Les Commentaires byzantins de la divine liturgie du VIIe au XVe siècle* (Paris, 1966)
Bréhier	L. Bréhier, *Le Monde byzantin*, I–III(Paris, 1947–50)
Browning, *Byzantine Empire*	R. Browning, *The Byzantine Empire* (London, 1980)
BS	*Byzantinoslavica* (Prague, 1929–)
Bury, *Eastern Roman Empire*	J. B. Bury, *A History of the Eastern Roman Empire from the Fall of Irene to the Accession of Basil I (AD 802–867)* (London, 1912)
BZ	*Byzantinische Zeitschrift* (Leipzig, 1892–)
CB	*Corpus Scriptorum Historiae Byzantinae* (Bonn, 1828–97)
Cedrenus	*see* Scylitzes

CFHB	*Corpus Fontium Historiae Byzantinae* (Berlin, etc., 1967–)
CMH	*Cambridge Medieval History*, vol. IV, pts 1 and 2 (Cambridge, 1966–7)
Corpus	*Corpus Iuris Civilis*, III, *Novellae*, ed. R. Schoell and W. Kroll (Berlin, 1895); II, *Codex Justinianus*, ed. P. Krueger (Berlin, 1895)
Dagron, 'Le Christianisme dans la ville byzantine'	G. Dagron, 'Le Christianisme dans la ville byzantine', *DOP*, 31 (1977), 1–25
Darrouzès, 'Documents byzantins'	J. Darrouzès, 'Documents byzantins du XII⁰ siècle sur la primauté romaine', *REB*, 23 (1965), 42–88
Darrouzès, *Documents inédits*	J. Darrouzès, *Documents inédits d'ecclésiologie byzantine* (*Archives de l'Orient chrétien*, 10, Paris, 1966)
Darrouzès, *Offikia*	J. Darrouzès, *Recherches sur les ὀφφίκια de l'Eglise byzantine* (*Archives de l'Orient chrétien*, 11, Paris, 1970)
Darrouzès, *Registre*	J. Darrouzès, *Le Registre synodal du patriarcat byzantin au XIV⁰ siècle: Étude paléographique et diplomatique* (*Archives de l'Orient chrétien*, 12, Paris, 1971)
DDrC	*Dictionnaire de droit canonique* (Paris, 1935–65)
De Cerimoniis	Constantine VII Porphyrogenitus, *De Cerimoniis Aulae Byzantinae*, ed. J. J. Reiske (*CB*, 1829–40) and ed. in part by A. Vogt (Budé, Paris, 1935, 1939–40)
Demetrius Cydones	Démétrius Cydonès, *Correspondance*, ed. R.-J. Loenertz, I–II (*ST* 186 and 208, Vatican, 1956 and 1960)
Dennis, *Manuel II in Thessalonica*	G. T. Dennis, *The Reign of Manuel II Palaeologus in Thessalonica 1382–1387* (*OCA*, 159, Rome, 1960)
DHGE	*Dictionnaire d'histoire et de géographie ecclésiastique* (Paris, 1912– , in progress)
DOP	*Dumbarton Oaks Papers* (Cambridge, Mass., 1941–)
Dossier grec	V. Laurent et J. Darrouzès, *Dossier grec de l'Union de Lyon (1273–1277)* (*Archives de l'Orient chrétien*, 16, Paris, 1976)
DR	F. Dölger, *Regesten der Kaiserurkunden des ostromischen Reiches*, pts. 1–5 (Munich and Berlin, 1924–65); pt. 3, 2nd edn. by P Wirth (Munich, 1977, essential to use this edn.); entries are cited here by number which is continuous throughout
DS	*Dictionnaire de spiritualité* (Paris, 1937–)
Dvornik, *Byzantine Missions*	F. Dvornik, *Byzantine Missions among the Slavs: SS. Constantine-Cyril and Methodius* (New Brunswick, 1970)

Dvornik, *Légendes*	F. Dvornik, *Les Légendes de Constantin et de Méthode vues de Byzance* (with trans. of the Old Church Slavonic *Vitae Constantini et Methodii* (Prague, 1933))
Dvornik, *Photian Schism*	F. Dvornik, *The Photian Schism* (Cambridge, 1948)
EB	*Études byzantines*, I–III (Bucharest, 1943–5) (continued as *REB*)
ECR	*Eastern Churches Review* (London, 1966–78)
EEBS	Ἐπετηρὶς Ἑταιρείας Βυζαντινῶν Σπουδῶν (Athens, 1924–)
Every, *Byzantine Patriarchate*	G. Every, *The Byzantine Patriarchate 451–1204*, 2nd edn. (London, 1962)
Fedalto, *Chiesa latina*	G. Fedalto, *La Chiesa latina in oriente*, I, 2nd edn. essential (Verona, 1981); II, *Hierarchia Latina Orientis* (Verona, 1976)
FM	A. Fliche and F. Martin (gen. eds.), *Histoire de l'église depuis les origines jusqu'à nos jours* (Paris 1934–); needs revision but still useful, see vol. V, L. Bréhier (590–757) and vol. VI, E. Amann (757–888)
Festal Menaion	*The Festal Menaion*, trans. Mother Mary and K. Ware (London, 1969)
Franchi, *Concilio II di Lione*	A. Franchi, *Il Concilio II di Lione (1274) secondo la Ordinatio Concilii generalis Lugdunensis* (Rome, 1965); supplements Mansi from a Vatican MS
Franchi, *La svolta*	A. Franchi, *La svolta politico-ecclesiastica tra Roma e Bisanzio (1249–54): La legazione di Giovanni da Parma. Il ruolo di Federico II. Studio critico sulle fonte* (Rome, 1981)
Geanakoplos, *Michael Palaeologus*	D. J. Geanakoplos, *Emperor Michael Palaeologus and the West 1258–1285: A study in Byzantine–Latin Relations* (Cambridge, Mass., 1959)
Gero, *Constantine V*	S. Gero, *Byzantine Iconoclasm during the Reign of Constantine V: With particular Attention to the Oriental Sources* (*Corpus Script. Christ. Orient.*, 384, Subsidia, 52, Louvain, 1977)
Gero, *Leo III*	S. Gero, *Byzantine Iconoclasm during the Reign of Leo III: With particular Attention to the Oriental Sources* (*Corpus Script. Christ. Orient.*, 346, Subsidia, 41, Louvain, 1973)
Gill, *Byzantium and the Papacy*	J. Gill, *Byzantium and the Papacy 1198–1400* (New Brunswick, 1979)
Gill, 'Church	J. Gill, 'The Church Union of the Council of Lyons

Union'	(1274) portrayed in Greek documents', *OCP*, 40 (1974), 5–45
Gill, *Conciles*	J. Gill, *Constance et Bâle-Florence* (*Histoire des conciles œcuméniques* 9, Paris, 1965)
Gill, *Council of Florence*	J. Gill, *The Council of Florence* (Cambridge, 1959)
Gill, *Personalities*	J. Gill, *Personalities of the Council of Florence and other essays* (Oxford, 1964)
Golubovich, *Biblioteca*	G. Golubovich, *Biblioteca bio-bibliografica della Terra Santa e dell'Oriente francescano*, I–V (Quaracchi, 1906–27)
Gouillard, 'L'Hérésie'	J. Gouillard, 'L'Hérésie dans l'empire byzantin des origines au XIIe siècle', *TM*, 1 (1965), 299–324
Gouillard, 'Synodikon'	J. Gouillard, 'Le Synodikon de l'Orthodoxie, édition et commentaire', *TM*, 2 (1967), 1–316
GR	*Les Regestes des Actes du Patriarcat de Constantinople*, V. Grumel, fasc. 1–3 (Paris, 1932–47; fasc. 1, 2nd edn. Paris, 1972, essential to use this); V. Laurent, fasc. 4 (Paris, 1971); J. Darrouzès, fasc. 5–6 (Paris, 1977–9, in progress); acts are cited here by number which is continuous throughout the series
Grabar, *Iconoclasme*	A. Grabar, *L'Iconoclasme byzantin: Dossier archéologique* (Paris, 1957)
Greek Acta	*Quae supersunt actorum graecorum Concilii Florentini*, ed. J. Gill (Rome, 1953)
Gregory Palamas, *Triads*	Grégoire Palamas, *Défense des saints hésychastes*, introduction, critical text, French translation and notes by J. Meyendorff, 2 vols. (Louvain, 1959, 2nd edn., 1973); there is an English trans. of the *Triads* by N. Gendle (London, 1983)
Hamilton, *Latin Church in the Crusader States*	B. Hamilton, *The Latin Church in the Crusader States: The Secular Church* (London, 1980)
Hammond, *The Waters of Marah*	P. Hammond, *The Waters of Marah: The present State of the Greek Church* (London, 1956)
Hefele	C. J. Hefele, *Histoire des conciles*, trans. H. Leclercq (Paris, 1907 ff.)
Hunger, *Literatur*	H. Hunger, *Die hochsprachliche profane Literatur der Byzantiner*, 2 vols. (Munich, 1978)
Hunger, *Register*	H. Hunger and O. Kresten (eds.), *Das Register des Patriarchats von Konstantinopel*, I, *Edition und Übersetzung der Urkunden aus den Jahren 1315–1331*

(*CFHB* XIX/1; separate index vol. by C. Cupane, Vienna, 1981)

Hunger, *Studien* H. Hunger (ed.), *Studien zum Patriarchatsregister von Konstantinopel*, I, Beiträge (Öst. Ak. d. Wiss., phil.-hist. Kl., Sitzungsber. 383, Vienna, 1981)

Hussey, *Church and Learning* J. M. Hussey, *Church and Learning in the Byzantine Empire 867–1185* (London, 1937)

Iconoclasm *Iconoclasm*, ed. A. Bryer and J. Herrin (Birmingham, 1976)

Janin, *Églises et monastères*, II, III R. Janin, *La Géographie ecclésiastique* . . . II, *Les Églises et les monastères des grands centres byzantins* (Paris, 1975); III, *Les Églises et monastères de Constantinople* (Paris, 1953, 2nd edn., 1969)

JEH *Journal of Ecclesiastical History* (London, 1950–)

Joannou, *Discipline générale* P.-P. Joannou, *Discipline générale antique* (*II*^e*–IX*^e *s.*), I–II (*Pont. comm. per la redaz. del Cod. di diritto can. orient. Fonti*, fasc. IX, Grottaferrata, 1962–3)

JÖB *Jahrbuch der österreichischen byzantinischen Gesellschaft* (Vienna, 1951–68), continued as *Jahrbuch der österreichischen Byzantinistik* (Vienna, 1969–)

JRS *Journal of Roman Studies* (London, 1911–)

JTS *Journal of Theological Studies* (London, 1900–)

Jugie, *Le Schisme byzantin* M. Jugie, *Le Schisme byzantin: Aperçu historique et doctrinal* (Paris, 1941); see review by A. Michel, *BZ*, 45 (1952), 408–17

Kirchengeschichte als Missionsgeschichte *Kirchengeschichte als Missionsgeschichte* (gen. ed. H. Frohnes *et al.*), vol. II, ed. K. Schaeferdiek (Munich, 1978)

Kitzinger, 'Cult' E. Kitzinger, 'The Cult of Icons before Iconoclasm', *DOP*, 8 (1954), 83–150

Kotter B. Kotter (ed.), *Die Schriften des Johannes von Damaskos*, vol. II, *Expositio Fidei*; vol. III, *Contra Imaginum Calumniatores Orationes Tres* (Berlin and New York, 1973, 1975)

Laiou, *Andronicus II* A. E. Laiou, *Constantinople and the Latins: The Foreign Policy of Andronicus II 1282–1328* (Cambridge, Mass., 1972)

Lamma P. Lamma, *Comneni e Staufer: Ricerche sui rapporti fra Bizanzio e l'Occidente nel secolo XII*, 2 vols. (Rome, 1955–7)

Lemerle, *Cinq études* P. Lemerle, *Cinq études sur le XI*^e *siècle byzantin* (Paris, 1977)

Lemerle, Humanisme byzantin	P. Lemerle, *Le Premier Humanisme byzantin. Notes et remarques sur enseignement et culture à Byzance des origines au Xe siècle* (Paris, 1971)
Lenten Triodon	*The Lenten Triodon*, trans. Mother Mary and K. Ware (London and Boston, 1978)
Leo Grammaticus	Leo Grammaticus, *Chronographia*, ed. I. Bekker (*CB*, 1842)
Leo the Deacon	Leo the Deacon, *Historia*, ed. C. B. Hase (*CB*, 1828)
Liber Pontificalis	*Liber Pontificalis*, ed. L. Duchesne, 2 vols. (Paris, 1886–92)
Loenertz, I–II	*see* Demetrius Cydones
Longnon	J. Longnon, *L'Empire latin de Constantinople et la principauté de Morée* (Paris, 1949)
Mansi	J. D. Mansi, *Sacrorum Conciliorum Nova et Amplissima Collectio*, 31 vols. (Florence and Venice, 1759–98)
Manuel II, *Letters*	*The Letters of Manuel II Palaeologus*, text, trans, and notes by G. T. Dennis (*DOP* Texts 4 = *CFHB* 8, Washington, DC, 1977)
Mendham	J. Mendham, *The Seventh General Council* (London, 1850)
Meyendorff, Byzantium and the Rise of Russia	J. Meyendorff, *Byzantium and the Rise of Russia: A Study of Byzantino-Russian relations in the Fourteenth Century* (Cambridge, 1981)
Meyendorff, Christ	J. Meyendorff, *Christ in Eastern Christian Thought* (Washington and Cleveland, 1969; 2nd edn. New York, 1975)
Meyendorff, Introduction	J. Meyendorff, *Introduction à l'étude de Grégoire Palamas* (Paris, 1959; trans. London, 1962)
MGH	*Monumenta Germaniae Historica*, ed. G. H. Pertz, T. Mommsen *et al.* (Hanover, 1826– ; new edns. in progress (Hanover and Berlin))
MGH SS	*Monumenta Germaniae Historica: Scriptores*
MM	F. Miklosich and J. Müller, *Acta et Diplomata Graeca Medii Aevi Sacra et Profana*, 6 vols. (Vienna, 1860–90)
Murphy–Sherwood	F. X. Murphy and P. Sherwood, *Constantinople II et Constantinople III* (*Histoire des conciles œcuméniques* 3, Paris, 1973)
Nicholas Mysticus	Nicholas I Patriarch of Constantinople: *Letters*, text, and trans. by R. J. H. Jenkins and L. G. Westerinck (CFHB 6, Washington, DC, 1973)

Nicol, *Epiros I*	D. M. Nicol, *The Despotate of Epiros* (Oxford, 1957, goes to about 1267 and needs some revision)
Nicol, *Epiros II*	D. M. Nicol, *The Despotate of Epiros 1267–1479* (Cambridge, 1984)
Nicol, *Meteora*	D. M. Nicol, *Meteora: The Rock Monasteries of Thessaly* (London, 1963)
Norden, *Papsttum*	W. Norden, *Das Papsttum und Byzanz: Die Trennung der beiden Mächte und das Problem ihrer Wiedervereinigung bis zum Untergange des byzantinischen Reichs (1453)* (Berlin, 1903)
Obolensky, *Bogomils*	D. Obolensky, *The Bogomils: A study in Balkan Neo-Manichaeism* (Cambridge, 1948)
Obololensky, *Commonwealth*	D. Obolensky, *The Byzantine Commonwealth: Eastern Europe, 500–1453* (London, 1971)
OCA	*Orientalia Christiana Analecta* (Rome, 1935–)
OCP	*Orientalia Christiana Periodica* (Rome, 1935–)
Ostrogorsky, *History*	G. Ostrogorsky, *History of the Byzantine State*, 2nd English trans. based on the 3rd German edn. with some additions (Oxford, 1968)
Ostrogorsky, *Studien*	G. Ostrogorsky, *Studien zur Geschichte des byzantinischen Bilderstreites* (Breslau, 1929); the fragments are reprinted in H.-J. Geischer, *Der byzantinische Bilderstreit* (Gütersloh, 1968), pp. 41–3
Percival, *Nicene and Post-Nicene Fathers*, 14	H. R. Percival, *A Select Library of Nicene and Post-Nicene Fathers of the Christian Church*, 2nd ser., vol. 14 (Oxford and New York, 1900)
PG	J.-P. Migne, *Patrologiae Cursus Completus: Series Graeco-Latina*, 161 vols. in 166 (Paris, 1857–66)
Pitra, *Analecta Sacra*	J.-B. Pitra, *Analecta Sacra et Classica*, VI (Paris and Rome, 1891)
PL	J.-P. Migne, *Patrologiae Cursus Completus: Series Latina*, 221 vols. (Paris, 1844–55)
PLP	*Prosopographisches Lexikon der Palaiologenzeit*, ed. E. Trapp (Vienna, 1971–)
Podskalsky, *Theologie*	G. Podskalsky, *Theologie und Philosophie in Byzanz* (Munich, 1977)
Pseudo-Codinus	Pseudo-Kodinos, *Traité des offices*, ed. J. Verpeaux (Paris, 1966)
Raynaldus	O. Raynaldus, *Annales Ecclesiastici ab anno 1198* (Rome, 1646–1727); ed. A. Theiner (Bar-le-Duc, 1870–83)
REB	*Revue des études byzantines* (Bucharest and Paris, 1946–)
REG	*Revue des études grecques* (Paris, 1888–)

Roberg, *Union*	B. Roberg, *Die Union zwischen der griechischen und der lateinischen Kirche auf dem II. Konzil von Lyon (1274)* (Bonn, 1964)
Roncaglia	M. Roncaglia, *Les Frères Mineurs et l'église grecque orthodoxe au XIIIe siècle (1231–1274)* (Cairo, 1954)
RP	G. A. Rhalles and M. Potles, Σύνταγμα τῶν θείων καὶ ἱερῶν κανόνων κτλ, 6 vols. (Athens, 1852–9)
Runciman, *Crusades*	S. Runciman, *A History of the Crusades*, 3 vols. (Cambridge, 1951–4)
Runciman, *Eastern Schism*	S. Runciman, *The Eastern Schism: A Study of the Papacy and the Eastern Churches during the XIth and XIIth Centuries* (Cambridge, 1955)
Runciman, *Sicilian Vespers*	S. Runciman, *The Sicilian Vespers: A History of the Mediterranean World in the late Thirteenth Century* (Cambridge, 1958)
Sathas	K. N. Sathas, Μεσαιωνικὴ βιβλιοθήκη. *Bibliotheca Graeca Medii Aevi*, 7 vols. (Venice and Paris, 1872–94)
SBN	*Studi bizantini e neoellenici* (Rome, 1924–)
SC	*Sources Chrétiennes* (Paris, 1924–).
Schreiner, *Kleinchroniken*	P. Schreiner, *Die byzantinischen Kleinchroniken*, I, Introduction and Text; II, Historical Commentary (*CFHB* 12 (1) and 12 (2), Vienna, 1975 and 1977)
Scylitzes	*Ioannis Scylitzae Synopsis Historiarum*, ed. J. Thurn (*CFHB* 5, Berlin and New York, 1973)
Scylitzes Cont.	*Ioannes Scylitzes Continuatus*, ed. E. T. Tsolakes (Thessalonica, 1968)
Setton, *Crusades*	K. M. Setton (ed.-in-chief), *A History of the Crusades*, I–IV (Wisconsin, 1969–77, in progress)
Setton, *Papacy and the Levant*	K. M. Setton, *The Papacy and the Levant (1204–1571)*, I—II (Philadelphia, 1976–8)
Ševčenko, 'Intellectual Repercussions'	I. Ševčenko, 'Intellectual Repercussions of the Council of Florence', *Church History*, 24 (1955), 291–323
Speck, *Konstantin VI*	P. Speck, *Kaiser Konstantin VI. Die Legitimation einer fremden und der Versuch einer eigenen Herrschaft*, 2 vols. (Munich, 1978)
ST	*Studi e Testi* (Rome and Vatican, 1900–)
Stein, *Der Beginn*	D. Stein, *Der Beginn des Bilderstreites und seine Entwicklung bis in die 40er Jahre des 8. Jahrhunderts* (*Miscellanea Byzantina Monacensia*, XXV, Munich, 1980)
Stiernon	D. Stiernon, *Constantinople IV* (*Histoire des conciles œcuméniques*, 5, Paris, 1967)

Symeon the New Theologian, *Catecheses*	Syméon le Nouveau Théologien, *Catéchèses*, ed. B. Krivocheine, I–III (*SC* 96, 104, 113, Paris, 1963–5)
Syropoulos, *Mémoires*	V. Laurent (ed. and trans.), *Les 'Mémoires' du Grand Ecclésiarche de l'Église de Constantinople Sylvèstre Syropoulos sur le concile de Florence (1438–1439)* (Rome, 1971 = *Concilium Florentinum: Documenta et Scriptores*, Series B, 9)
Theophanes	Theophanes, *Chronographia*, ed. C. de Boor, 2 vols. (Leipzig, 1883–5)
Theophanes Cont.	Theophanes Continuatus, *Chronographia*, ed. I. Bekker (*CB*, 1838)
Thiriet, *Romanie vénitienne*	F. Thiriet, *La Romanie vénitienne au moyen âge: Le développement et l'exploitation du domaine colonial vénitien (XIIᵉ–XVᵉ siècles)* (Paris, 1959)
TM	*Travaux et Mémoires* (Paris, 1965–)
Traversari	Ambrogio Traversari, *Latinae Epistolae . . .*, ed. L. Mehus, 2 vols. (Florence, 1759)
Van Dieten	J. L. Van Dieten, *Geschichte der Patriarchen von Sergios I. bis Johannes VI. (610–715)* (Amsterdam, 1972)
Vavřínek-Zástěrová, 'Byzantium's Role'	V. Vavřínek and Zástěrová, 'Byzantium's Role in the Formation of Great Moravian Culture', *BS*, 43 (1982), 161–88
Vita Euthymii	*Vita Euthymii Patriarchae Cp*, text, trans., and commentary by P. Karlin-Hayter (Brussels, 1970; the notes to this admirable edition are a depository of information on Leo VI's reign though the arrangement makes it difficult to disinter this)
Vlasto, *Entry*	A. P. Vlasto, *The Entry of the Slavs into Christendom* (Cambridge, 1970)
Vryonis, *Decline*	S. Vryonis, *The Decline of Medieval Hellenism in Asia Minor and the Process of Islamization from the Eleventh through the Fifteenth Century* (Los Angeles and London, 1971)
VV	*Vizantiiskii Vremennik* (St Petersburg and Leningrad, 1894–)
Wellesz, *Byzantine Music and Hymnography*	E. W. Wellesz, *A History of Byzantine Music and Hymnography*, 2nd edn. (Oxford, 1961)
Will	C. J. C. Will, *Acta et scripta quae de controversiis ecclesiae graecae et latinae saeculo undecimo composita extant* (Leipzig and Marburg, 1861)

Wilson, *Scholars*	N. G. Wilson, *Scholars of Byzantium* (London, 1983)
Wolff, 'Politics in the Latin Patriarchate'	R. L. Wolff, 'Politics in the Latin Patriarchate, 1204–1261', *DOP*, 8 (1954), 225–303
Wolfson	H. A. Wolfson, *The Philosophy of the Church Fathers*, I, 3rd edn. (Cambridge, Mass., 1970)
Wolter–Holstein	H. Wolter and H. Holstein, *Lyon I et Lyon II* (*Histoire des conciles œcuméniques*, 7, Paris, 1966)
Zepos	J. and P. Zepos, *Jus Graeco-romanum*, vols. 1–8 (Athens, 1931; contains reprints of works edited by Zachariae von Lingenthal, Heimbach, and others)
ZRVI	*Zbornik Radova Vizantološkog Instituta* (Belgrade, 1952–)

LIST OF RULERS, POPES, AND PATRIARCHS

LATE ROMAN AND BYZANTINE EMPERORS

Diocletian	285–305	Theodosius III	715–17
Constantine I	324–37	Leo III	717–41
Constantius II	337–61	Constantine V	741–75
Julian	361–3	Leo IV	775–80
Jovian	363–4	Constantine VI	780–97
Valens	364–78	Irene	797–802
Theodosius I	379–95	Nicephorus I	802–11
Arcadius	395–408	Stauracius	811
Theodosius II	408–50	Michael I Rangabe	811–13
Marcian	450–7	Leo V	813–20
Leo I	457–74	Michael II	820–9
Leo II	474	Theophilus	829–42
Zeno	474–5	Michael III	842–67
Basiliscus	475–6	Basil I	867–86
Zeno (again)	476–91	Leo VI	886–912
Anastasius I	491–518	Alexander	912–13
Justin I	518–27	Constantine VII	913–59
Justinian I	527–65	Romanus I Lecapenus	920–44
Justin II	565–78	Romanus II	959–63
Tiberius II Constantine	578–82	Nicephorus II Phocas	963–9
Maurice	582–602	John I Tzimisces	969–76
Phocas	602–10	Basil II	976–1025
Heraclius	610–41	Constantine VIII	1025–8
Constantine III and Heraclonas	641	Romanus III Argyrus	1028–34
Constans II	641–68	Michael IV the Paphlagonian	1034–41
Constantine IV	668–85	Michael V Calaphates	1041–2
Justinian II	685–95	Zoe and Theodora	1042
Leontius	695–8	Constantine IX Monomachus	1042–55
Tiberius III	698–705		
Justinian II (again)	705–11	Theodora (again)	1055–6
Philippicus Bardanes	711–13	Michael VI Stratioticus	1056–7
Anastasius II	713–15		

Isaac I Comnenus	1057–9	Theodore I Lascaris	1204–22
Constantine X Ducas	1059–67	John III Ducas	1222–54
Eudocia	1067	Vatatzes	
Romanus IV Diogenes	1068–71	Theodore II Lascaris	1254–8
Eudocia (again)	1071	John IV Lascaris	1258–61
Michael VII Ducas	1071–8	Michael VIII	1259–82
Nicephorus III	1078–81	Palaeologus	
Botaneiates		Andronicus II	1282–1328
Alexius I Comnenus	1081–1118	Palaeologus	
John II Comnenus	1118–43	Michael IX	1294–1320
Manuel I Comnenus	1143–80	Palaeologus	
Alexius II Comnenus	1180–3	Andronicus III	1328–41
Andronicus I	1183–5	Palaeologus	
Comenenus		John V Palaeologus	1341–91
Isaac II Angelus	1185–95	John VI Cantacuzenus	1347–54
Alexius III Angelus	1195–1203	Andronicus IV	1376–9
Isaac II (again) and	1203–4	Palaeologus	
Alexius IV Angeli		John VII Palaeologus	1390
Alexius V Murtzuphlus	1204	Manuel II Palaeologus	1391–1425
(ruling from Nicaea, 1204–61)		John VIII Palaeologus	1425–48
Constantine (XI)	1204	Constantine XI (XII)	1449–53
Lascaris		Palaeologus	

EPIRUS AND THESSALONICA

(i) *Rulers of Epirus*

Michael I (without the title of Despot)	1204–c. 1215	[conquered in 1339 by the Byzantine Emperor	
Theodore (probably without the title of Despot)	c. 1215–25	Andronicus III and then in 1348 by the Serbian Stephen Dušan]	
[Constantine?	1225–c. 1230]	Symeon Uroš Palaeologus	1349–56
Michael II	c. 1230–?before 1268	Nicephorus II (again)	1356–9
Nicephorus I	? before 1268–c. 1290	[various Serbian, Albanian	
Thomas	c. 1290–1318	and Italian rulers in Arta	
Nicholas Orsini	1318–23	and in Joannina 1359–	
John Orsini	1323–35	1460, followed by the	
Nicephorus II	1335–9	Turkish conquest]	

(ii) *Rulers of Thessalonica*

Theodore (Emperor)	1225–30	Demetrius (Despot)	1244–46
Manuel (Despot)	1230–37/40	[Conquered by John III	
John (Emperor until 1242, then Despot)	1237/40–44	Vatatzes of Nicaea in 1246]	

POPES, 314–1455

Sylvester I	314–35	Honorius I	625–38
Mark	336	Severinus	640
Julius	337–52	John IV	640–2
Liberius	352–66	Theodore I	642–9
(Felix II	355–65)	Martin I	649–55
Damasus I	366–84	Eugenius I	654–7
(Ursinus	366–7)	Vitalian	657–72
Siricius	384–99	Deusdedit II	672–6
Anastasius I	399–401	Domnus	676–8
Innocent I	401–17	Agatho	678–81
Zosimus	417–18	Leo II	682–3
Boniface I	418–22	Benedict II	684–5
(Eulalius	418–19)	John V	685–6
Celestine I	422–32	Conon	686–7
Sixtus III	432–40	(Theodore	687)
Leo I the Great	440–61	(Pascal	687)
Hilary	461–8	Sergius I	687–701
Simplicius	468–83	John VI	701–5
Felix III (II)	483–92	John VII	705–7
Gelasius I	492–6	Sisinnius	708
Anastasius II	496–8	Constantine I	708–15
Symmachus	498–514	Gregory II	715–31
(Laurence	498, 501–5)	Gregory III	731–41
Hormisdas	514–23	Zacharias	741–52
John I	523–6	(Stephen II	752)
Felix IV (III)	526–30	Stephen III (II)	752–7
Boniface II	530–2	Paul I	757–67
(Dioscorus	530)	(Constantine	767–9
John II	533–5	(Philip	768)
Agapetus I	535–6	Stephen IV	768–72
Silverius	536–7	Hadrian I	772–95
Vigilius	537–55	Leo III	795–816
Pelagius I	556–61	Stephen V	816–17
John III	561–74	Pascal I	817–24
Benedict I	575–79	Eugenius II	824–7
Pelagius II	579–90	Valentine	827
Gregory I the Great	590–604	Gregory IV	827–44
Sabinian	604–6	(John	844)
Boniface III	607	Sergius II	844–7
Boniface IV	608–15	Leo IV	847–55
Deusdedit I	615–18	Benedict III	855–8
Boniface V	619–25	(Anastasius	855, d. *c.* 880)

Nicholas I	858–67	John XIX	1024–32
Hadrian II	867–72	Benedict IX	1032–44
John VIII	872–82	Sylvester III	1045
Marinus I	882–4	Benedict IX (again)	1045
Hadrian III	884–5	Gregory VI	1045–6
Stephen VI	885–91	Clement II	1046–7
Formosus	891–6	Benedict IX (again)	1047–8
Boniface VI	896	Damasus II	1048
Stephen VII	896–7	Leo IX	1049–54
Romanus	897	Victor II	1055–7
Theodore II	897	Stephen X	1057–8
John IX	898–900	(Benedict X	1058–9)
Benedict IV	900–3	Nicholas II	1059–61
Leo V	903	Alexander II	1061–73
(Christopher	903–4)	(Honorius II	1061–72)
Sergius III	904–11	Gregory VII	1073–85
Anastasius III	911–13	(Clement III	1080–1100)
Lando	913–14	Victor III	1086–7
John X	914–28	Urban II	1088–99
Leo VI	928	Pascal II	1099–1118
Stephen VIII	928–31	(Theodoric	1100, d. 1102)
John XI	931–5	(Albert	1102)
Leo VII	936–9	(Sylvester IV	1105–11)
Stephen IX	939–42	Gelasius II	1118–19
Marinus II	942–6	(Gregory VIII	1118–21)
Agapetus II	946–55	Calixtus II	1119–24
John XII	955–64	Honorius II	1124–30
Leo VIII	963–5	(Celestine II	1124)
Benedict V	964–6	Innocent II	1130–43
John XIII	965–72	(Anacletus II	1130–8)
Benedict VI	973–4	(Victor IV	1138)
(Boniface VII	974, and 984–5)	Celestine II	1143–4
Benedict VII	974–83	Lucius II	1144–5
John XIV	983–4	Eugenius III	1145–53
John XV	985–96	Anastasius IV	1153–4
Gregory V	996–9	Hadrian IV	1154–9
(John XVI	997–8)	Alexander III	1159–81
Sylvester II	999–1003	(Victor IV	1159–64)
John XVII	1003	(Pascal III	1164–8)
John XVIII	1004–9	(Calixtus III	1168–78)
Sergius IV	1009–12	(Innocent III	1179–80)
Benedict VIII	1012–24	Lucius III	1181–5
(Gregory	1012)	Urban III	1185–7

Gregory VIII	1187	Benedict XI	1303–4
Clement III	1187–91	Clement V	1305–14
Celestine III	1191–8	John XXII	1316–34
Innocent III	1198–1216	(Nicholas	1328–30)
Honorius III	1216–27	Benedict XII	1334–42
Gregory IX	1227–41	Clement VI	1342–52
Celestine IV	1241	Innocent VI	1352–62
Innocent IV	1243–54	Urban V	1362–70
Alexander IV	1254–61	Gregory XI	1370–8
Urban IV	1261–4	Urban VI	1378–89
Clement IV	1265–8	Boniface IX	1389–1404
Gregory X	1271–6	Innocent VII	1404–6
Innocent V	1276	Gregory XII	1406–15
Hadrian V	1276	(Clement VII	1378–94)
John XXI	1276–7	(Benedict XIII	1394–1423)
Nicholas III	1277–80	(Alexander V	1409–10)
Martin IV	1281–5	(John XXIII	1410–15)
Honorius IV	1285–7	Martin V	1417–31
Nicholas IV	1288–92	Eugenius IV	1431–47
Celestine V	1294 (d. 1296)	(Felix V	1439–49)
Boniface VIII	1294–1303	Nicholas V	1447–55

PATRIARCHS OF CONSTANTINOPLE, 381–1456

Nectarius	381–97	Menas	536–52
John I Chrysostom	398–404	Eutychius	552–65
Arsacius	404–5	John III Scholasticus	565–77
Atticus	406–25	Eutychius (again)	577–82
Sisinnius I	426–7	John IV the Faster	582–95
Nestorius	428–31	Cyriacus	595–606
Maximian	431–4	Thomas I	607–10
Proclus	434–46	Sergius I	610–38
Flavian	446–9	Pyrrhus	638–41
Anatolius	449–58	Paul II	641–53
Gennadius I	458–71	Pyrrhus (again)	654
Acacius	472–89	Peter	654–66
Fravitas	489–90	Thomas II	667–9
Euphemius	490–6	John V	669–75
Macedonius II	496–511	Constantine I	675–7
Timothy I	511–18	Theodore I	677–9
John II Cappadox	518–20	George I	679–86
Epiphanius	520–35	Theodore I (again)	686–7
Anthimus I	535–6	Paul III	688–94

Callinicus I	694–706	John VIII Xiphilinus	1064–75
Cyrus	706–12	Cosmas I	1075–81
John VI	712–15	Eustratius Garidas	1081–4
Germanus I	715–30	Nicholas III Kyrdi-	1084–1111
Anastasius	730–54	niates Grammaticus	
Constantine II	754–66	John IX Agapetus	1111–34
Nicetas I	766–80	Leo Stypes	1134–43
Paul IV	780–4	Michael II Curcuas	1143–6
Tarasius	784–806	(Oxeites)	
Nicephorus I	806–15	Cosmas II Atticus	1146–7
Theodotus Melissenus	815–21	Nicholas IV Muzalon	1147–51
Cassiteras		Theodotus II	1151–4
Antony I Cassimatas	821–37	(Neophytus I	1153–4)
John VII Grammaticus	837–43	Constantine IV	1154–7
Methodius I	843–7	Chliarenus	
Ignatius	847–58	Luke Chrysoberges	1157–70
Photius	858–67	Michael III of	1170–8
Ignatius (again)	867–77	Anchialus	
Photius (again)	877–86	Chariton Eugeniotes	1178–9
Stephen I	886–93	Theodosius Boradiotes	1179–83
Antony II Cauleas	893–901	Basil II Camaterus	1183–6
Nicholas I Mysticus	901–7	Nicetas II Muntanes	1186–9
Euthymius I	907–12	Dositheus of	1189
Nicholas I Mysticus	912–25	Jerusalem	
(again)		Leontius Theotokites	1189
Stephen II	925–7	Dositheus of Jerusalem	1189–91
Tryphon	927–31	(again)	
Theophylact	933–56	George II Xiphilinus	1191–8
Polyeuctus	956–70	John X Camaterus	1198–1206
Basil I Scamandrenus	970–4	Michael IV	1208–14
Antony III the	974–9	Autorianus	
Studite		Theodore II	1214–16
Nicholas II	979–91	Irenicus	
Chrysoberges		Maximus II	1216
(unoccupied 991–6)		Manuel I Sarantenus	1217–22
Sisinnius II	996–8	Germanus II	1222–40
Sergius II	1001–19	Methodius	1240
Eustathius	1019–25	Manuel II	1244–54
Alexius the Studite	1025–43	Arsenius Autorianus	1255–9
Michael I	1043–58	Nicephorus II	1260
Cerularius		Arsenius Autorianus	1261–4
Constantine III	1059–63	(again)	
Leichudes		Germanus III	1265–6

Joseph I	1266–75	Macarius	1376–9
John XI Beccus	1275–82	Nilus	1379–88
Joseph I (again)	1282–3	Antony IV	1389–90
Gregory II (George of Cyprus)	1283–9	Macarius (again)	1390–1
		Antony IV (again)	1391–7
Athanasius I	1289–93	Callistus II	1397
John XII Cosmas	1294–1303	Xanthopulus	
Athanasius I (again)	1303–9	Matthew I	1397–1410
Niphon I	1310–14	Euthymius II	1410–16
John XIII Glykys	1315–19	Joseph II	1416–39
Gerasimus I	1320–1	Metrophanes II	1440–3
Isaias	1323–32	Gregory III	1443–50
John XIV Calecas	1334–47		(when he
Isidore I	1347–50		left Con-
Callistus I	1350–3		stantinople;
Philotheus Coccinus	1353–4		d. 1459)
Callistus I (again)	1355–63	Gennadius II Scho-	1454–6
Philotheus Coccinus (again)	1364–76	larius (first term of office)	

LIST OF MAPS

at end

Map 1   The Byzantine Empire c. 1025

Map 2   The Aegean World c. 1214–1254

Map 3   The Orthodox Church in the Byzantine Empire
c. 1050

INTRODUCTION

In accordance with the plan of this series this book deals with the Church of the Byzantine Empire from the re-shaping of the polity in the post-Justinianic period of the seventh century to the downfall of Byzantium in the fifteenth century. It was within this framework that one of the main branches of Orthodox Christianity developed and was enabled to give its religion to the neighbouring Slav peoples. When John Meyendorff published his *Byzantine Theology* in 1974 a reviewer took exception to his title on the ground that the truths of Orthodoxy were not related to any historical period.[1] This may be so, but it is also a fact that Orthodox theology was Byzantine theology. Universal truths have to be articulated in a temporal milieu and this articulation however imperfect is that of its generation. The historian cannot therefore discard the world in which medieval eastern Orthodoxy developed, nor ignore the ecclesiastical framework of the Church, and indeed the spirituality of its people is often better understood in the light of the contemporary background.

In the present state of our knowledge a book on the Byzantine Church must necessarily be in the nature of an interim report since much pioneer work remains to be done. Probably the most significant result of the research of this generation is a change of emphasis. Byzantine life is now seen as marked by constant change though at the same time there was loyal adherence to certain traditions governing the outlook of both Church and Empire. It has also become increasingly clear that Byzantium had its own creative contribution to make not only in art (that at least had been allowed), but in other fields and most vital of all in its many-sided religious life. The Church was not a department of state. But it was closely integrated into the daily life of an empire which was regarded as being ideally the mimesis or copy of the heavenly kingdom. Yet in the last resort the Church maintained its own responsibility for the things which were not Caesar's.

[1] P. Sherrard in *JEH*, 26 (1975), 430.

This book is written primarily for the non-specialist layman wishing to know something of a Church which was one of the main vitalizing forces in the East Roman Empire. It attempts to trace the medieval history of Greek Orthodoxy in terms of challenge and response; to outline the organization of the Byzantine Church, indicating its essential role in the imperial polity and in Christendom; and finally to suggest that way in which its members tried to achieve what was, and still is, the heart of Orthodoxy, that is, the gradual *theosis* or deification of each individual Christian.

A recurrent challenge to the Greek Orthodox Church running through its medieval history and beyond came both from the western Latin Church and from the (all too often forgotten) eastern non-Chalcedonian Nestorian and monophysite Churches. This challenge largely turned on the interpretation of Trinitarian and Christological doctrine. In the case of the West it also concerned ecclesiastical authority because the eastern conception of the equality of all bishops and a collegial authority clashed with the Latin development of a single supreme bishop of Rome. The gap between Greek and Latin was there long before the aggravation of 1204. Primarily rooted in theological differences this gap was further widened by cultural, political, and linguistic problems, due in part—as far as Latins and Greeks were concerned—to the differing fortunes of the eastern and western halves of the Roman Empire. But as far as theology went it was also to be found within the eastern provinces and beyond, as the non-Chalcedonian Churches show.

Factual evidence reveals the increasing extent to which the differences between Greek and Latin contributed to a rift which became the concern of all circles in Byzantium, making increasing demands upon diplomats as well as churchmen. For in the later middle ages the restoration of union between the Greek and Latin Churches was closely linked to the pressing need for a united Christian front in the face of a rapidly advancing Islam. Neither Lyons II (1274) nor Ferrara–Florence (1438–9) could provide an acceptable solution. But failure does not mean that these abortive negotiations can for that reason be omitted or watered down. They were significant for various reasons. They underlined the tenacity with which the Orthodox Church maintained its doctrinal and ecclesiological traditions. And they throw light on many aspects of the Byzantine world particularly in the post-1204 years. Behind the more formal diplomatic exchanges many, often conflicting, cross-currents can be discerned—the mediating Latin friars going backwards and forwards between the papal and imperial courts or on other missions, the dead weight of Greek anti-union opinion, the agony and frustration of Manuel II and his family, the false hopes of Patriarch Joseph and the Emperor John VIII—all this comes out and contributes to a picture of life balanced on a knife-edge, often perforce pessimistic and yet able to produce a Nicholas Cabasilas with his *Life in Christ*, or a Symeon of Thessalonica urging his people not to count economic gain as more important than supporting the Orthodox episcopate. And in the background the often unfortunate role of the monks in the capital must be balanced by the stabilizing influence of the widely scattered monastic foundations ranging at various times from the Studite house and Athos to the Meteora or the Patir of Rossano and St Saviour of Messina.

East–West ecclesiastical relations also reveal how little the Greeks knew of Latin theology (using 'theologia' in the western doctrinal sense, for to the Greeks it meant the spiritual contemplation of God). The Church, despite differences between its members, was regarded as being one, but it early ceased to draw on its common heritage, at least as far as the Greeks were concerned. The major Greek fathers of the fourth and fifth centuries were rapidly translated into Latin, as was the seventh-century Maximus the Confessor. But the Latin father Augustine of Hippo was not known in Greek until the late middle ages and then only in part, for instance the translation of the *De trinitate* by the fourteenth-century Manuel Calecas who also translated other later Latin works, as Boethius and Anselm of Canterbury, while his contemporaries the Cydones brothers made Aquinas available. Thus for most of the middle ages the Greeks knew little of the western tradition. It was partly that they had long tended to regard the Latins as 'barbarians' using a language which was in the Greek view ill-suited to express doctrinal truths. It was also partly due to a certain antagonistic undercurrent of political rivalry and hostility, for instance in the earlier period in Italy and the Balkans and then later on over the crusades. Further, the Greeks on the whole did not gravitate much to the West, though there were frequent contacts in Italy. But it was otherwise with the westerners who came East for various reasons. There was always the incentive of a pilgrimage to Jerusalem or the journey on crusade which could mean travelling through Byzantine lands, and finally there was the opportunity of actually settling in the conquered Aegean lands. It was only in the late middle ages that the Greeks were brought up against some of the more acceptable aspects of Latin culture (together it must be said with much which they disliked). It was then that the Latin theological works, such as Augustine or Aquinas, began to be translated, though not on a large scale. Much remained unknown and might indeed have been found to be out of line with Greek doctrinal teaching. The Greeks were also in disagreement with the western use of the scholastic method, as they showed when debates took place, particularly in the fourteenth-century disputes. They regarded logic as a useful, indeed an essential, tool, but considered that dialectic could not be applied to the mysteries of faith. Much as some Greeks in the later period might admire individual Latins whom they got to know, with few exceptions (as for instance Demetrius Cydones) they probably felt that their own rich patristic heritage provided for their doctrinal and spiritual needs and for the most part they had no desire to explore western thought.

Thus during the 800 years and more from Heraclius to the end of the Empire the Orthodox Church went its own way. Closely integrated with the daily life of the East Romans, it was able to perfect and adapt its central administration, to organize its provinces and dioceses to meet changing needs, and to introduce its religion and way of life to its Slav neighbours. Above all it deepened its spiritual life which was centred in a developing liturgical round, particularly in the eucharist. This service kept its original character and purpose, but during the course of the middle ages it was gradually enriched by additional actions, responses, hymns, and ceremonies. The Byzantines had a strong feeling for dignified ceremony and symbolism and this left its mark in ecclesiastical as well as imperial developments, bringing out and enhancing the meaning of the liturgy and indeed of the Christian faith. But it did not obscure the purpose of the sacramental life as is evidenced by the writings of the more spiritually minded members of the Church, often monks, but by no means always so.

The vigilance with which the Church guarded doctrinal belief was seen not only in its relations with the Latin Church but in its treatment of heresies which cropped up within the Empire, particularly adherence to ancient Greek thought conflicting with Christian teaching as well as various forms of widespread and recurrent dualism. Such challenges were brought to light and met in public trials and by synodal rulings. Then there was a whole range of dubious superstitions, belief in portents and wonders, demonology, magical practices, to be found at all levels of society. These were to some extent ingrained in human nature and were frequently pin-pointed by official condemnation. But often there was a very thin line between superstition and more harmless folklore much of which has survived into modern times.[2] Superstitions did not however make up the essential life of Greek Orthodoxy (or of any other Christian Church) and it is therefore not expatiated on here as in some more modern treatments of Byzantium. What mattered was the liturgical life and faithful adherence to the traditions of the Church.

[2] See G. A. Megas, Ἑλληνικαὶ ἑορταὶ καὶ ἔθιμα τῆς λαϊκῆς λατρείας (Athens, 1963).

PART I

CHALLENGE AND RESPONSE
WITHIN THE HISTORICAL
FRAMEWORK

I

THE CHRISTOLOGICAL PROBLEM IN THE EARLY MIDDLE AGES[1]

1. *The seventh-century watershed in the Byzantine Empire*

THE emergence of the medieval Roman Empire is often placed in the fourth century AD. This is because the foundation of Constantinople as the capital of what was then the eastern—and senior—half of the Roman Empire and the acceptance of the Christian religion by the ruling dynasty shaped the destiny of East Rome throughout the middle ages. But from the political, and to some extent the ecclesiastical, point of view it was the seventh century which saw the two major changes which subsequently influenced the whole tenor of Byzantine life. The rise of Muhammad and the subsequent victories of the Muslims in the south and east brought a contraction of the physical boundaries of the Christian Empire and a religious challenge which was never fully met. At the same time the South Slavs were advancing into the Balkan provinces with in some ways more propitious results for Byzantium. It is true that this penetration eventually brought the establishment of independent, and on occasion menacing, principalities within the Roman provinces south of the Danube, but at the same time it provided a much-needed infusion of fresh blood and manpower into the Byzantine polity for many Slavs settled within the Empire and became integrated into its multiracial society. In contrast to the Muslim Arab and Turkic invaders, the Slavs accepted Christianity and learnt much from Hellenic civilization and Graeco-Roman statecraft.

That this challenging situation was to some extent brought under control and the Empire thus spared complete disintegration was largely due to the quality of Byzantine rulers during both the seventh and eighth centuries. So in spite of mistakes in their religious policy they managed to halt the Muslim advance into Asia Minor, thus retaining the indispensable Asian core of Empire, and

[1] I am greatly indebted to Henry Chadwick for help with this and the succeeding chapter.

they appear to have set in motion far-reaching administrative and military reforms well suited to meet the needs of a rapidly changing situation. And, as will subsequently emerge, in their different ways both Slav and Muslim radically altered the ecclesiastical situation in the Christian world. Slav acceptance of Christianity brought an enlargement and enrichment of the Christian family, as well as welcome additional manpower to the East Roman Empire. Muslim domination of some of the oldest Christian regions meant a change of emphasis in the administrative framework of the Church. Alexandria and Antioch, formerly powerful advocates of their differing interpretations of Christian doctrine and leaders in the Christian world, were now in infidel territory, likewise Jerusalem which by reason of its associations had always been—and was to remain—a special centre of Christian devotion. This threw into high relief the claims of Rome long associated with St Peter and St Paul and of Constantinople, the New Rome, with its growing prestige as the imperial capital.

2. The theological background to seventh-century monotheletism

The theological problems of the seventh century did not mark the opening of any new era. Throughout the late Roman and early medieval periods the Church had been concerned with the gradual formulation of basic Christian doctrine. It was necessary to define its teaching on the Trinity and the Incarnation, on cosmology and soteriology, not only in order to instruct the faithful but to meet the challenge of successive heretical interpretations. The continuity and constructive nature of this work should be stressed and the Byzantines themselves frequently emphasised the extent to which they were carrying on the tradition of 'the Fathers'. This tradition was built up by men of vision who dominated the early centuries, but it did not end with the fourth-century Cappadocians or the first four general councils from Nicaea I (325) to Chalcedon (451). For instance, Chalcedon left problems only partly solved; certain of Origen's heretical views lingered on in the sixth century and beyond; and there was need to enlarge the Christian theological vocabulary in order to explain more clearly the full implications of the Incarnation, particularly in so far as this was related to man's place in the Divine economy.

Thus the seventh and eighth centuries saw the Church still

concerned with Christological problems. It saw too the positive contribution of an outstanding Christian thinker, the seventh-century Maximus the Confessor. All too often historians convey a negative impression of the work of the early Byzantine Church, implying that it was dominated by complicated conciliar arguments and fruitless attempts to placate dissident elements, such as the monophysites or the Nestorians, particularly in the sixth and seventh centuries. This is not really true, and the failure of apparent political aims should not obscure doctrinal achievement.

The seventh-century theological controversies can be traced back to the problems arising out of the council of Chalcedon (451). This council had stated that Christ had two natures, the divine and the human, but one person or hypostasis. Its definition that Christ is known 'in two natures' had tended to offend the Alexandrians and in particular the followers of Cyril, Patriarch of Alexandria (d. 444), and was regarded by some as having a pro-Nestorian bias in its treatment of the two natures of Christ. Its supporters were regarded as dyophysites in contrast to those who stressed a single nature, the monophysites.

As was the practice in the Byzantine Empire, Emperor and churchmen both took part in ecclesiastical affairs. The greater part of the sixth century was dominated by Justinian (527–65). Perhaps more than any other Byzantine Emperor he interpreted his imperial mandate as including theological as well as the administrative problems of the Church. He obviously desired to find some solution to current doctrinal controversy which would be acceptable to Rome and the West and would quiet the dissenting voices of monophysites and Nestorians. But it should be noted that the imperial provinces in which monophysite views predominated, Egypt and Syria for instance, were not at first hostile towards the central government and separatist in outlook. This only developed when they had abandoned hope (after Jacob Baradaeus had provided a rival episcopate) of gaining a monophysite Emperor, that is, until after Theodora's death. It was for reasons of prestige that Alexandria certainly resented the rise to power of Constantinople and the increasingly decisive part which the imperial capital took in ecclesiastical as well as secular affairs. But the political element should not obscure the primary importance of the theological problem.

The Alexandrians took their stand on Cyril of Alexandria's

formula, 'one nature incarnate of God the Word'. Strict dyophysites, a minority, could not accept the implications of Cyril's
teaching, but the majority of the Chalcedonians interpreted Cyril's
word 'nature' (φύσις) as the equivalent of 'hypostasis' (ὑπόστασις) or
'person' (πρόσωπον), thus preserving the unity of the Persons in
whom there were two natures each retaining its own special
properties or characteristics. Thus it was possible for Cyrillian
Chalcedonians to accept the theopaschite formula which arose as a
subject of controversy when the Patriarch of Antioch, Peter the
Fuller (d. 488), began to chant the *Trisagion*, the 'Thrice-holy'
chant, addressing God the Son as 'Holy God, holy Mighty, holy
Immortal', with the additional words 'who was crucified for us'.
Extreme dyophysites maintained that the human Christ and not the
Logos suffered on the cross, a view which would deny the unity of
the two natures forming one person. At Constantinople the *Trisagion* was commonly understood as referring to the Trinity, in which
case the addition was not orthodox. But the use of the phrase
'crucified for us' as applied to God the Son was vital. The Word, the
Son of God, and not just the human Christ, had to suffer in the flesh
if man was to fulfil his destiny in the divine economy through his
deification. As Gregory of Nazianzus put it 'In order that we may
live again, we need a God who was incarnate and suffered death.'[2]

This question of the nature of the hypostatic union with the
soteriological implications was faced in the sixth century. Justinian
supported by his Patriarch and by the Fifth general council
(Constantinople II, 553) drew out the intentions of Chalcedon in
making it clear that the human Christ and the eternal Logos had a
single hypostatic identity. Thus theopaschism was acceptable in the
sense that one of the Trinity, the Son of God, was crucified and
buried. At the same time certain teachings of the Nestorians were
condemned in Justinian's censure of the Three Chapters (that is
excerpts from Theodore of Mopsuestia, Theodoret, and Ibas of
Edessa favouring a strongly two-nature Christology), which was
confirmed by the council of 553 with the reluctant assent of the
Pope Vigilius. Though the Edict of Union (the *Henoticon*), an
attempt to compromise with the monophysites sponsored by the
Emperors Zeno (476–91 and Anastasius(491–518) had been repudiated under Justinian's uncle, Justin I (518–27), the recognition in

---

[2] Gregory of Nazianzus, Hom. 45, 28, *PG* 36, col. 661 C, cited Meyendorff,
Christ, 51.

553 of the Cyrillian position, provided it was interpreted 'as the holy Fathers have taught',[3] should have gone some way towards winning over the monophysites. The standing council in Constantinople (*synodos endemousa*) had already condemned certain heretical views on the creation and on the nature of man deriving from Origen (d. *c*.254) and Evagrius of Pontus (d. 399) which were current in monastic circles.[4] This censure of Origenism was confirmed by the council of 553.

3. Monenergism and monotheletism against a background of imperial crisis

Though of first importance for Orthodox theology the strenuous efforts of Justinian and the Fifth general council (553) did not win over the monophysites. In the following century once again their differences with the Chalcedonians came to a head over the distinction or otherwise of the divine and human nature in Christ. Following Chalcedon it had been officially emphasized in 553 that there was a single person in two natures. The problem now centred in a question which had not yet been specifically dealt with by a general council, that is, whether there were one or two operations or activities and one or two wills in the incarnate Christ. It was therefore not clear whether it was possible to believe in two natures with a single activity (ἐνέργεια) and a single will (θέλημα). This question was vital to the controversy because to have agreed on one *energeia* or one will would have answered one of the principal monophysite objections to the Chalcedonian definition, and therefore should have gained monophysite support. But it should be recognized that in exploring this problem monothelites and monenergists remained Chalcedonians (and not compromising monophysites as was the case under Cyrus in Egypt for a short time).

This question of the human and divine natures of Christ would in any case have needed formal examination and pronouncement, but it unfortunately arose in the seventh century against a particularly disturbed background. The Empire was then facing a serious and prolonged crisis. The Italian lands were being eaten away by the Lombard invaders, though Ravenna and the South were still held and there was strong Greek influence within Rome itself. The

---

[3] Mansi, IX. 367–75; Hefele, III (1). 105–32 (see Anathema 8).
[4] GR[2] 245.

Asian, Syrian, and Egyptian provinces were being attacked by Persia with considerable success and the loss of Jerusalem and the Holy Cross (614) was a blow to Christian and to imperial morale. The northern frontier seemed to be collapsing before the sustained Avar and Slav penetration. And at one point the Persians even encamped on the Asian shore of the Bosphorus, though their plan to capture Constantinople with Avar aid in 626 failed. It did however seem that the very existence of the Empire was being threatened. It was therefore all the more necessary to promote the traditional imperial policy of unity within the polity. Unfortunately there were now two main bodies of Christian dissidents—the monophysites whose strength lay in Egypt and Syria, and the Nestorians who had established their non-Chalcedonian Church on Persian territory. For their part, the Persians fully realized the advantages of favouring these separatists, whether within their Empire or in their newly-conquered regions, and the Chalcedonians suffered accordingly. In the Byzantine Empire there was a close alliance between the Emperor Heraclius and Sergius, the Patriarch of Constantinople, and they both realized that their position would be strengthened if they could win over at least the monophysites. Heraclius, a man of considerable military and administrative capability, succeeded in driving back the Persians and may have been responsible (though this is disputed) for inaugurating some kind of reorganization of the Asia Minor provinces into regions (themes) in which military needs were given precedence. The move to support him in the religious sphere seems to have come from the Patriarch Sergius of Constantinople (610–38) who, like the Emperor Heraclius, was greatly concerned to pacify the monophysites, particularly the Copts of Egypt and the Jacobites of Syria and the Armenian provinces. The Jacobites were so called from the monophysite bishop Jacob Baradaeus who had ensured the succession of the monophysite episcopate in Syria by his underground consecrations during Justinian's reign. The Nestorian Church in Persia did not pose so obvious a threat to Byzantine imperial recovery and in any case was now somewhat removed from its jurisdiction.

During the early years of his patriarchate Sergius sounded various ecclesiastics for their views on a single activity (ἐνέργεια) in Christ. Much of the evidence comes from references in Maximus the Confessor's dialogue with Pyrrhus (the *Disputation*).[5] Sergius saw good hope of reconciling the monophysite critics of Chalcedon's 'in two natures' by the formula 'one activity and one will'. From 618 he began to circulate a (forged) memorandum to Pope Vigilius ascribed to the Patriarch Menas of Constantinople in which this formula occurred and he asked for a verdict on its reconciling potentialities. The theologians he sounded included Theodore Bishop of Pharan in Sinai[6] who admired the recently published writings of Pseudo-Dionysius the Areopagite; a monophysite bishop called Paul the One-eyed; a half-hearted Chalcedonian at Alexandria named George Arsas[7] (whose zealously Chalcedonian bishop John the Almsgiver was furious when the secret correspondence with Sergius was disclosed); and above all Cyrus bishop of Phasis (Poti) in Lazica in the Caucasus, a region thrown into prominence by Heraclius' wars against Persia.

Approaches in the eastern provinces, Syria, Armenia, and Mesopotamia were made, partly through the mediation of the Emperor Heraclius who was engaged in re-establishing Byzantine authority in the lands recently occupied by the Persians. He hoped that the doctrine of a single activity would win over the strongly entrenched monophysites who had been so markedly favoured by the Persians and were largely in control of the Churches in these regions. Thus, with the assistance of Sergius, in 626 Heraclius discussed the question of the single activity with Cyrus of Phasis, and Sergius subsequently wrote to him defending a single activity in Christ.[8] The Emperor also attempted to promote monenergism in Armenia where Ezra had become Catholicos. Greek, Syrian, and Armenian sources vary in their accounts of relations between Byzantium and the Armenian Church but it is likely that Armenian opposition to Chalcedon arose not so much from doctrinal dissent from a council where they had not been present as from hostility towards the subordination of Armenia to the ecclesiastical jurisdiction of Constantinople. In Syria and Palestine Heraclius did rather better in

---

[5] *PG* 91, col. 332 BC; Mansi, X. 741 E–744 A; and see also the Lateran Council of 649 and the General Council of Constantinople III (680) and Murphy–Sherwood.

[6] *GR* I[2]. 281; see also Murphy–Sherwood, 141 ff. and 303 (French trans. of Theodore of Pharan).

[7] *GR* I[2] 280 (ex. 279).

[8] *GR* I[2]. 285.

getting support, and monotheletism was to survive under Muslim domination.

More tangible results were achieved in Egypt. Here there had been conflict between the Chalcedonian and monophysite parties. But in 631 Cyrus of Phasis was made Patriarch of Alexandria and the Coptic Patriarch Benjamin fled. Cyrus published his pact of union consisting of nine chapters or statements on the Christology which it was hoped would be acceptable to both Chalcedonians and monophysites under pain of anathema. The seventh attempt deals with the single activity of Christ by anathematizing those not confessing that 'this one and the same Christ and Son worked both the divine and human by one theandric activity as St Dionysius says'.[9] There seems to be a certain deliberate ambiguity in this formula and indeed, in trying to conciliate the monophysites without antagonizing the Chalcedonians, Cyrus spoke of having used 'a flexibility (*oeconomia*) pleasing to God' in the wording without in any way sacrificing orthodoxy.[10]

The first significant opposition to the doctrine of monenergism came from Sophronius. He had been born in Damascus and was a Palestinian monk who had travelled widely. He knew the famous exponent of orthodoxy, Maximus the Confessor, who had acquired his title 'Confessor' as a result of his sufferings in the defence of Chalcedonian purity against monothelete compromises and had been head of the imperial chancery before becoming a monk and dedicating himself to the Chalcedonian cause. Sophronius was in Alexandria at the time of Cyrus' declaration and begged him to desist. A year later in 634, old as he was, he became Patriarch of Jerusalem (the Arab invasion of that year having removed Palestine from Byzantine control). In the customary systatic, or synodal, letter to the other patriarchs and the Pope announcing his enthronement Sophronius made clear his position by stressing the two natures of Christ, divine and human, and the two activities in a single person, asserting that a single activity would imply a single nature and would therefore be contrary to dyophysite belief. He also pointed out Cyrus' substitution of 'one' for 'new' in his use of

---

[9] Mansi, XI. 565 D; Hefele, III (1), 341. The Pseudo-Dionysius speaks however of a 'new' and not 'one', theandric activity (*PG* 3, col. 1072 C).

[10] Quoted by Patriarch Sergius in his letter to Pope Honorius, *GR* 291; Hefele, III (1). 344 (from the acts of the Sixth General Council).

the phrase from Pseudo-Dionysius which he quoted in support of his argument.[11]

Before his election as patriarch Sophronius had also visited Constantinople to remonstrate with the Patriarch Sergius, who tried to temporize by issuing an instruction (the *Psephos*, June 633) stating that the terms 'one activity' and 'two activities' were not to be used. The doctrinal position was elaborated by Sergius in a letter to Pope Honorius. He tended to minimize the whole controversy as an unnecessary dispute over words,[12] though it seems that his own leaning was towards 'one activity'. The Latin original of Honorius' reply is not extant, but the Greek translation was used at the Sixth general council where Honorius was specifically condemned (with the then Pope's concurrence). In his letter he agreed with Sergius that the dispute was one of words and that it was wiser to avoid using the terms either one or two activities, but though he speaks of one will, 'We confess one will of our Lord Jesus Christ', it is in the sense of two wills in harmony, that is, he was apparently not a monothelete, though he has been criticized as such[13] and he was cited by the monotheletes in support of their cause.

Against the threat of further invasion and the knowledge that the enforced doctrinal unity in the eastern provinces was only too precarious, Heraclius, at the instigation of Sergius, took the controversy to its logical conclusion (as he saw it) by asserting that Christ had a single will, as was implied in monenergism. An *Ecthesis* or exposition of faith, based on Sergius's *Psephos* was drawn up with the help of Pyrrhus (subsequently his successor) and was set up in the narthex of Hagia Sophia (autumn 638). This restated Chalcedonian teaching on the Trinity and Incarnation, forbade discussion concerning either one or two activities in the incarnate Saviour, and asserted that Christ had a single will but without confusion of his two natures, each keeping its own attributes in a single person, the Incarnate Logos.[14]

Sergius died on 8 December 638 and Pyrrhus became Patriarch of Constantinople. At this stage Pyrrhus supported the monotheletes

[11] Mansi, XI. 532 D; cf. 572 B.
[12] See Hefele, III (1), 343 ff.
[13] Cf. Wolfson, 480 (favourable) and Murphy–Sherwood, 162 (critical).
[14] Murphy–Sherwood, 306 ff., gives a French translation of the text of the *Psephos* and *Ecthesis* in parallel columns. See Hefele, III (1), 387 ff. (text in the acta of Lateran 649, 3rd session; in Mansi, X. 991–8).

and in late 638 or early 639 the *Ecthesis* was approved by the standing synod in Constantinople. The next five years saw a confused political and ecclesiastical situation. The old Emperor Heraclius died in 641, having failed to drive back either the Arabs who were pouring into Syria, Palestine, and Egypt, or the Slavs crossing the Danube into the Balkans. He also left a succession complicated by rival family claims. Opposition to the official ecclesiastical policy was growing in both orthodox and monophysite circles. Anti-Chalcedonian Armenia and monophysite Egypt were almost ready to come to terms with their new Muslim masters. Orthodox opposition, centred in the person of Maximus the Confessor, was steadily growing in North Africa. In Rome Pope John IV (640–2) was also protesting against imperial policy. He tried to clear Honorius of any acquiescence in this and he anathematized monotheletism. The immediate successors of Heraclius, the Emperors Constantine III and then Constans II, seem to have been orthodox and the *Ecthesis* was said to have been removed, as Pope John had asked. Patriarch Pyrrhus who had been associated with the *Ecthesis* fled to Africa. Paul became Patriarch (641–53), though Pyrrhus had not been canonically deposed, as Pope Theodore (John IV's successor) was to point out in his answer to Paul's synodal letter to him announcing his consecration. Pyrrhus subsequently had a curious career which illustrates the uncertainty many felt concerning the controversy over monenergism and monotheletism. He went to North Africa and in July 645 held a public debate with the orthodox Maximus the Confessor in Carthage.[15] Pyrrhus pleaded for the use of either phrase—two wills, and one will, on the ground that since complete harmony existed between the two wills it was possible to speak of 'one common will consisting of two individual wills'. Maximus refuted this on the ground that there can be a composite person or hypostasis but not a composite single nature. Pyrrhus professed himself convinced. 'You have shown that we cannot properly speak of one activity in any way whatsoever.'[16] He then went to Rome where he was received by Pope Theodore and now recognized as the legitimate Patriarch of Constantinople, though subsequently he recanted, fled to Ravenna, and was then

[15] Mansi, X. 709–60; *PG* 91, 288–353; Hefele, III (1), 405–22 (translation of the debate).
[16] Mansi, X. 757; Hefele, III (1), 421.

excommunicated by Theodore. Theodore had also written a letter of protest to Patriarch Paul which is no longer extant, but is known from Paul's reply, in which he defended 'a single will of our Lord, in order not to ascribe to the one Person a conflict or a difference of wills, so as not to be forced to admit two willers'[17] whereupon Paul was deposed by Theodore. An attempt to still the controversy was made in 648 by issuing the Type, or Rule of faith (*Τύπος περὶ πίστεως*).[18] Though in the form of an imperial edict, Paul was most probably behind this. It stated briefly the two sides of the controversy and then commanded the cessation of further discussion and the removal of the *Ecthesis* from Hagia Sophia. The faithful should henceforth follow 'the Holy Scriptures and the traditions of the five oecumenical councils and the utterances and confessions of the Fathers'. Penalties for infringement were appended. The defect in the eyes of the orthodox was the failure to come down in their favour by specifically denouncing the monotheletes. On the contrary, the Type laid down that none of those who had previously taught one will and one activity, or two wills and two activities, should ... be exposed to blame or accusation.

If the Type was meant to appease papal opposition it failed. Pope Theodore had died on 14 May 649 and on 5 July 649 Martin I, who had been apocrisiarius in Constantinople, was consecrated without waiting for imperial approval which could have been given through the exarch of Ravenna. He immediately called a synod which met in the Lateran on 5 October 649. It was attended by some hundred bishops mainly from the West, Italy, Africa, though others such as Stephen of Dor in Palestine also took part, and there were as well refugee monks and clerics from the East in Rome (including Theodore of Tarsus). Maximus the Confessor was there, urging return to orthodoxy. The Type had been issued in the form of an imperial edict and the sanctions mentioned in its closing paragraph would have been implemented by imperial authority. But its critics put the onus for it squarely on Patriarch Paul of Constantinople and were careful not to criticize the Emperor. Perhaps they hoped to win him over, for it was clearly in imperial interests that harmony should be restored, since ecclesiastical discord could only weaken resistance to both internal revolts and increasing

[17] Mansi, X. 1024; Hefele, III (1), 431; cf. GR^2 300 and Van Dieten, 88 ff.
[18] Mansi, X. 1029–32; *DR* 225; Hefele, III (1), 432–4.

external pressures from Muslims and Slavs. The monotheletes tried to discredit the orthodoxy of Martin I and of the West by drawing attention to another issue, the addition of the filioque to the creed, the earliest instance of this accusation being brought against the West.[19]

The Lateran synod in Rome was not an oecumenical council but one of the normal bi-annual provincial synods as visualized by Nicaea I (canon 5). As was customary when doctrinal problems were discussed, both the statements being questioned and the supporting evidence from the Bible and the fathers were read out by a notary, in this case the chief notary Theophylact. Both sides would usually prepare this material in the form of a florilegium or anthology of appropriate passages. Interventions were made by the various members of the synod, on this occasion chiefly by Pope Martin and Bishops Maximus of Aquileia and Deusdedit of Cagliari in Sardinia. As always, great stress was laid on fidelity to patristic tradition. The strong Greek element among the clergy of Rome may have had something to do with the fact that there was a Greek as well as a Latin version of the acta,[20] both of which were authenticated by Pope Martin. The Greek was said to have been at the request of the Greek monks as it was intended that the proceedings should be digested by Greek-speaking regions. It would seem that Greek modes of thought naturally prevailed and Maximus the Confessor may have had a major hand in this. The greater part of the time was taken by the notarial reading of the evidence produced by both sides. The synod ended by affirming Chalcedon, with an addition on the two natures and an elaboration in twenty canons dealing more explicitly with the controversial Christology, condemning by name Theodore of Pharan, Cyrus of Alexandria, Sergius of Constantinople, and his successors Pyrrhus and Paul, as well as the 'impiissimam Ecthesim' and 'scelerosum Typum', but carefully avoiding criticism of the Emperor.[21] Pope Martin evidently thought it proper that in matters of heresy he should take the lead. He sent an encyclical with the acta of the council to rulers and bishops of both East and West, including the patriarchates of Jerusalem and Antioch, despite the fact that they

[19]   Maximus the Confessor, *PG* 91, col. 136.
[20]   *PG* 90, col. 153 B.
[21]   Mansi, X. 1151 ff.; Hefele, III (1), 434 ff.

were the findings of a provincial, and not an oecumenical, council (as Maximus the Confessor would have liked to think).[22] Paul, Archbishop of Thessalonica (whose vicarate of Illyricum came under papal jurisdiction) was deposed and excommunicated until he should accept the acta.[23]

A special letter was also sent to the Emperor Constans from the Pope and synod with the Greek acta, asking for his support in rooting out heresy. Constans reacted with hostility to Martin's conciliar activities. He also took exception to Martin's failure to get imperial approval of his election from the exarch of Ravenna. Olympius, the exarch originally sent to Rome in 649 to call the Pope to account, himself rebelled and subsequently died in 652. It was not until June 653 that another exarch was able to act on his instructions and arrest Martin who was taken prisoner to Constantinople where he was tried, partly for an irregular election, but mainly for treason on the ground that he had supported the rebel Olympius, charges which he refuted, showing throughout both dignity and humility under cruel treatment. No discussion of what was ostensibly the real reason for his arrest, that is the religious controversy and the unilateral actions of the Lateran council of 649, was permitted during his interrogation. He was exiled to Cherson in March 654 and died on 16 September 655.

The monk Maximus the Confessor, a powerful force behind the orthodox position, was also arrested, probably in 654 though the exact date is uncertain. He was brought to Constantinople and imprisoned and tried on both political and religious grounds. At his first trial, probably in May 655, he was accused of treasonable activities in North Africa at the time of the exarch Gregory's revolt and the Arab invasion, and of holding heretical Origenist tenets. But the real charge against him was his support of the Lateran council of 649 and his refusal to recognize the Type. The Emperor shrewdly recognized the powerful influence of Maximus and attempted for several years to win him over by persuasive means. After his first trial he was exiled to Bizya in Thrace and there are extant accounts of his discussions with Theodosius, archbishop of Caesarea in Bithynia.[24] Maximus maintained the validity of synodal rulings whether or not a

[22] *PG* 91, col. 137 D.
[23] Mansi, X. 833.
[24] *PG* 90, cols. 136–60; Hefele, III (1), 466 ff.

synod had been called by the Emperor, and took his stand on the two wills and activities and the rulings of the Lateran council of 649. Finally, persuasion and clemency having failed, Maximus was retried in Constantinople in the spring of 662 and condemned to mutilation and banishment to the fortress of Schemarium in Caucasian Lazica, where he died on 13 August 662. Constans II had good reason to fear Maximus who was a far more able protagonist than anyone in the monothelete camps, and was indeed the outstanding theologian of the seventh century.

The condemnation and death of Pope Martin and Maximus the Confessor somewhat paradoxically saw the orthodox triumph. Martin's successors, Popes Eugenius (654–7) and Vitalian (657–72), were on better terms with the Emperor Constans, who was by now so heavily pressed by the Arabs and Slavs that he even thought of transferring his seat of Empire to Italy. In 663 he himself came first to Rome, and then to Sicily, where he made Syracuse his centre. When he visited Rome he was apparently on amicable terms with Vitalian. The religious controversy seemed to have been dropped, and indeed Constans must have realized the need for internal unity in view of the dangerous situation of the Empire.

After Constans II's assassination in 668, his son and successor Constantine IV began by devoting himself to countering the Arab and Avar attacks which culminated in a bid to take the City itself, effectively defeated in 677–8. This was certainly one of the decisive events in the long drawn-out struggle between Christendom and Islam. It was followed by a move towards peace in the Church when in 678 Constantine approached the Pope, asking him to send twelve bishops and representatives of the Greek monasteries in the West to Constantinople to discuss the doctrinal misunderstandings which had arisen. The Pope, then Agatho (678–81), consulted his bishops throughout the West, even as far distant as the aged Theodore of Tarsus, 'archbishop of the great island of Britain and philosopher', and then sent the Emperor Constantine a letter and a profession of faith condemning monotheletism. The delegates arrived in Constantinople on 10 September 680 and the Emperor gave orders to his Patriarch George to convoke his bishops, and likewise to the titular Macarius of Antioch, and the ecclesiastics of Alexandria and the patriarchal vicar of Jerusalem.

The proposed discussion thus turned into a general council, the Sixth, or Constantinople III (680–1), called by the Emperor, and presided over by him or his representatives (the Emperor himself was present for the first eleven sessions and for the last). The council held eighteen sessions, from 7 November 680 to 16 September 681.[25]

In the first session the papal legates, addressing the Emperor, asked who had introduced 'the new doctrine of one activity and one energy in the incarnate Lord Jesus Christ', and the Emperor invited the Patriarchs George of Constantinople and Macarius of Antioch and others to reply to the papal legates. Throughout it was really Macarius who was the defender of monotheletism and monenergism, attempting to base his defence on the tradition of the fathers and the five general councils, as well as the pronouncements of the Patriarchs of Constantinople Sergius, Pyrrhus, Paul, Peter, and also Pope Honorius of Rome and Patriarch Cyrus of Alexandria. Macarius, when in the second session he was confronted with Pope Leo's 'Agit enim utraque forma', maintained that Leo had not actually spoken of two activities and that he himself did not specify any number but simply followed Pseudo-Dionysius the Areopagite in speaking of 'theandric activity', moreover he refused to attempt to give any definition of 'theandric activity.[26] But later at the eighth session he admitted that he spoke only of 'one will and a theandric activity', not two natural activities and two natural wills.[27] The council in its various sessions considered the patristic and conciliar evidence collected by both sides and the dyothelite doctrine was accepted. Macarius was condemned in the ninth session and deposed 'from all priestly dignity and function', as was his follower Stephen.[28] In succeeding sessions there was considerable discussion particularly concerning patriarchal and papal offenders. Attempts to soften any condemnation, or at least publicity, failed. After lengthy discussions and prolonged raking through the patriarchal archives for all available material, those, living or dead, who had supported the heretical doctrine on the single activity and the single will were anathematized and a statement was issued, thus summarizing Christological belief:

Completely preserving that which is without confusion or division we briefly state the whole; believing that after his incarnation our Lord Jesus

[25] On this council see Murphy–Sherwood.
[26] Mansi, XI. 217 ff.; Hefele, III (1), 488 ff.
[27] Mansi, XI. 345 E; Hefele, III (1), 492 ff.
[28] Mansi, XI. 377–87; Hefele, III (1), 497 ff.

Christ, our true God, is one of the Trinity, we state that he has two natures shining forth in his one hypostasis. In this, throughout the whole course of his incarnate life, he made manifest his sufferings and miracles, not simply in appearance but in reality. The difference of the natures is recognised in one and the same hypostasis because each nature wills and works what is proper to it in communion with the other. Thus we proclaim two natural wills and two natural activities working together for the salvation of the human race.[29]

The minutes of the sessions of the Sixth general council were prepared by hand of Agatho, the archivist or chartophylax of the Great Church and six copies were made (for the Emperor, the Pope, and the four patriarchs). They were read, approved, and signed by the Emperor and those present, and were received and accepted by Pope Conon in Rome (who before he became Pope had taken part in the council as a papal legate). Thus the re-establishment of orthodoxy and the rejection of monenergism and monotheletism had brought Constantinople and Rome together again. The attempt to meet the monophysites had failed, and, like the Nestorians, they were not reconciled to the main body of Christendom and continued to build up their separate Churches mainly in what were by now Muslim-dominated territories.

4. The Quinisextum council (691–692)[30]

Relations between Rome and Constantinople were soon disturbed again due to differences raised by the Quinisextum council, known as the council in Trullo because it was held in the domed hall of the imperial palace in Constantinople. This council was called as was customary by the Emperor (then Justinian II) but without consultation with Rome. It opened some time after 1 September 691. Neither the Fifth (553) nor the Sixth (680–1) general councils had passed disciplinary canons since they had concentrated on dogma, and after a span of more than two hundred years there were outstanding problems concerning discipline and morals, apart from

---

[29] Mansi, XI. 639 A–640 B; Hefele III (1), 509–10.

[30] GR I².317; see also S. Salaville, *REB*, 2 (1944), 278 (on the date) and V. Laurent, 'L'Œuvre canonique du concile in Trullo (691–92), source primaire du droit de l'église orientale', *REB*, 23 (1965), 7–14; Laurent, p. 17, note 42, comments on the term 'Quinisext', or in the original πενθέκτη, which seems to appear for the first time in the twelfth-century canonist Balsamon.

the additional difficulties caused by Muslim and Slav incursions. In this, as in other respects, Justinian II may too have wished to emulate his more famous namesake in his care for the good ordering of the polity. At the council the opening address by the Emperor stated that the decay of general moral standards demanded urgent attention and stressed the need to eliminate Jewish and pagan elements.[31] The 102 canons are significant on various counts. A number deal with the old perennial problems of the early middle ages, such as clergy discipline and the difficulties caused by barbarian incursions. Clerics forced to leave their churches or unable to reach them because of invaders were to return as soon as political conditions allowed (can. 18) and in any case should avoid being absent for too long. The tendency to linger in the capital shown by all ranks was in fact by no means only due to enemy occupation, and was indeed found throughout the Byzantine period since a country appointment was often regarded as virtual exile. Bishops who could not even get to their sees because they were in enemy hands were urged to exercise the authority of their office from other bases (can. 37). As reflected in earlier councils, monastic life posed continual problems. Pseudo-hermits in black clothes and with long hair who lived a worldly city life were either to enter a cenobitic house or to be expelled to the desert (can. 42). Genuine hermits were first to spend three years probation in a monastery, submitting to the abbot's discipline, followed by a further year outside the monastery before final enclosure (can. 41). Women were not to wear a display of fine clothes and jewels when approaching the altar to be clothed (can. 45). Once they had committed themselves to the monastic life they were not to leave their house without the superior's consent and then only if accompanied by an elder nun (can. 46).

Certain popular pastimes were forbidden to lay and cleric alike under pain of excommunication or deposition respectively: gambling (can. 50), attending horse-racing, mimes and their presentation, or theatrical dances (can. 51). The consultation of soothsayers, use of incantations and amulets, so common in the late Roman Empire, were all prohibited (can. 61). Certain pagan festivities and survivals were to be rooted out from the life of the

---

[31] Mansi, XI. 933 E; Hefele, III (1), 560 ff.; English trans. by Percival, *Nicene and Post-Nicene Fathers*, 14. 356 ff.

faithful, such as the festivals in honour of Pan (the Bota) and Bacchus (the Brumalia), public dancing, men dressed as women and vice versa, the use of the comic, satyrical, and tragic masks, the invocation of Bacchus at vintage time (can. 26), jumping over bonfires lit in front of houses and shows at new moon (can. 65). Such folk customs were however too deeply ingrained to be rooted out by conciliar decree and there is evidence that some of these long survived. Whenever possible folklore was incorporated into the life of the Church but it did not always lend itself to this, hence the prohibitions laid down in such canons as these. Various rulings also reflect on general everyday conduct, such as the canon against stabling animals in churches except in cases of dire need (can. 88); love-feasts in church were forbidden (can. 74), as also were pornographic pictures (c. 100), and abortions were condemned as murder (can. 91); those who had to sing the psalms were to do so in a proper manner without any noisy shouting (can. 75).

Wise care in regulating the normal daily life of lay and cleric was unlikely to offend the devout laity and clergy. There were however two groups of rulings to which exception was taken by Churches outside the patriarchate of Constantinople. The Armenians were called to order for using only wine at communion and not wine and water (can. 32), for appointing to clerical orders only from certain priestly families (regarded as a Jewish custom; can 33); and for not abstaining from eggs and cheese (that is animal produce) on Saturdays and Sundays in Lent (can. 56). The Armenian Church, always touchy in its relations with Constantinople, did not accept those canons in a co-operative spirit. Still more serious was the opposition from Rome which, like Armenia, was reproved for usages differing from those of Constantinople. The Quinisextum had followed up its opening affirmation of the first six general councils (can. 1) with a general statement of its belief in the 85 'Apostolic' canons, 'accepted by the Fathers and handed down in the name of the holy and glorious Apostles' (can. 2), thus ignoring the fact that Rome only recognized the first fifty of these late-fourth-century canons, which had been translated by Dionysius Exiguus and were probably all his copy had. 'Traditional ecclesiastical observance' was also required which meant giving up fasting on Saturdays in Lent in accordance with 'apostolic' canon 65 (one of those not accepted by Rome) under pain of clerical deposition and excommunication for the laity (can. 55). Further, an important series of canons (especially 3, 6, 13) laid down rulings on clerical marriage which were at variance with the proclaimed (but at that time not always practised) Roman usage.

Another canon to which Rome took exception was a statement on the position of Constantinople in the ecclesiastical hierarchy. 'Renewing the rulings of the 150 Fathers assembled in the God-guarded and imperial city[32] and those of the 630 who met at Chalcedon[33] we decree that the see of Constantinople shall have equal privileges to the see of Old Rome and shall enjoy equal esteem in ecclesiastical matters and shall be second after it (can. 36)', that is, Constantinople had equal privileges with Rome, and came after it only 'in time but not in honour'.[34] Rome had not yet accepted Chalcedon canon 28, and primacy, and to a lesser extent, clerical marriage and fasting in Lent, were points of difference which continued to arise from time to time in polemic and which soured relations between Constantinople and Rome, particularly the question of primacy.

Justinian II obviously desired and expected the Pope to confirm the acta of the Trullan council which was regarded as a continuation of the Sixth general council, and therefore fully oecumenical, a view which continues to be held by the Orthodox Churches. Of the 228 fathers at the council (220 of whom signed acta), 10 came from eastern Illyricum, still under papal jurisdiction (1 from Hellas, 4 from Crete, 4 from Macedonia, and 1 from Epirus). The council was also attended by the resident papal apocrisiarius, Basil bishop of Gortyna in Crete, who signed the minutes. According to the *Liber Pontificalis*, the Pope subsequently disavowed the signatures of the Roman legates.[35] The papal signature was however necessary in order to confer oecumenicity. A special place of honour in the copy of the acta was left for this purpose, as also for the signatures of the absent prelates of Ravenna, Thessalonica, and Corinth. Pope Sergius I (687–701) refused on the ground that he could not accept all the disciplinary rulings. The Byzantine protospathar Zacharias, sent soon after the council[36] to fetch him to Constantinople, was himself

---

[32] Second general council, Constantinople I (381), can. 3.
[33] Fourth general council, Chalcedon (451), can. 28.
[34] The twelfth-century canonist Aristenus, cited Percival, *Nicene and Post-Nicene Fathers*, 14. 382.
[35] *Liber Pontificalis*, I. 372–4 with note 14, p. 378.
[36] DR 259 (*c.*692).

attacked and ironically only escaped with the help of papal assistance, and even then the Roman army and populace thronged round
the Lateran palace until he had left the City. Justinian II was at that
time unable to pursue the matter, as he had to meet disaffection at
home which shortly afterwards drove him from the throne in 695.
When he returned from exile in 705 he took up the question of
Roman recognition of the council in Trullo with the Pope, then
John VII (705–7), and was milder in his demands. He sent two
metropolitans to Rome suggesting that the Pope should call a
council of bishops to look at the canons and draw up a list of those
which were not acceptable to Rome.[37] Apparently the Pope made
no changes in the document and returned it to the Emperor, the
Liber Pontificalis implying that he signed it.[38] It was John's successor
Pope Constantine I who was summoned to Constantinople in 710[39]
and courageously went. After a journey by way of South Italy and
Chios he was royally received in Constantinople, and then went to
Nicomedia to meet the Emperor, returning in October 711 with an
imperial renewal of the privileges of the Roman Church.[40] The
Liber Pontificalis, the only extant source, is brief on this episode, but
appears to indicate that the Pope and the Emperor resolved their
differences over the disputed canons.

The council in Trullo was a telling comment on seventh-century
Christendom. The canons on the disrupted diocesan life, the
monastic disorder, the pagan survivals, speak for themselves. The
Emperor, in accordance with established tradition, regarded himself
as responsible for the right ordering of Christian life and he
naturally assumed that this task should be carried out in conciliar
collaboration with the episcopate. He clearly wished to ensure
uniformity in ecclesiastical usage, hence the comment in canon 56
on Armenian Lenten fasting. 'It therefore seems good that the
whole Church of God, which is throughout the world, should
follow the same rule.' His position had indeed been strengthened by
the recent engulfing of the ancient patriarchates of Antioch and
Alexandria in a Muslim sea. But though Constantinople, the
imperial capital and bulwark of Christendom, had strengthened its

[37] DR 264 (after 1 Mar. 705).
[38] *Liber Pontificalis*, I. 385–6; cf. Murphy–Sherwood, 246–7, who consider that
he did not sign in spite of the evidence of the *Liber Pontificalis*.
[39] DR 266 (before 5 Oct. 710).
[40] DR 269.

already strong claims to leadership, its authority did not go unchallenged. The position of Rome was noticeably stronger *vis-à-vis* Constantinople than it had been in the days of Justinian I, as is shown by its rejection of the imperial emissary Zacharias and its successful refusal to accept rulings at variance with its own usage. Medieval Christendom with its two great Christian centres of Constantinople and Rome was in process of emerging.

II

THE ICONOCLAST CONTROVERSY
726–843

1. The North Syrian rulers: the first phase 726–787

The background to the eighth-century crisis

The position of Constantinople in Christendom was for a time weakened by its eighth and early ninth-century crisis concerning icons,[1] in one sense a continuation of the Christological problem. The long drawn-out dispute in the Eastern Church over the use of icons had deep roots. The early Church avoided figural representation of Christ for various reasons. The second commandment (Exodus 20:4) forbade graven images and there was the strong desire to avoid any kind of idolatry such as was associated with the pagan world. Then both Old and New Testaments stressed that true worship was not concerned with material sacrifices but should be in spirit and in truth. And so in the catacombs Christ was portrayed by means of symbols. But by the fourth century it was clear that special material objects, such as the Cross and other holy relics, were being widely venerated. Gregory of Nyssa for instance extols the joy of those who touch the very relics of a martyr whom they address with a prayer of intercession just as though he were alive before them. At the same time the pagan cult of the imperial portrait was accepted and integrated into the normal practice of the Christian Empire. It was understandable that this was carried into the practice of the religious world. By the early fifth century the worship of religious images was being practised in the Church, as St Augustine noticed. It was opposed by Epiphanius of Salamis (d. 403) in Cyprus whose works were later cited by the iconoclasts. The authenticity of certain passages in his writings has been questioned by some scholars because of his refutation of a Christological argument which was thought to point to a later date. But there is in fact nothing unusual in such a point of view at this date (cf. Eusebius of Caesarea when

---

[1] The word 'icon' (εἰκών), or 'image', is used here, as by the Byzantines in its widest sense, i.e. as a representation in the round or flat in any medium.

dealing with the Empress Constantia's request for a picture of Christ), and opinion now favours the acceptance of these passages as genuine.[2]

The late sixth and seventh centuries saw a marked intensification in the use of images. Such practices were not unchallenged, which perhaps accounts for the fact that those giving evidence about their use, pilgrims from the Holy Land for instance, seem to be somewhat on the defensive. Images now performed miracles, were worshipped and honoured, prayed to, set up as objects of devotion in private houses and workshops, as well as being used on public and official occasions. When in 656 a debate was held in Bithynian Bizna in an attempt to convert Maximus the Confessor to the officially supported monotheletism, the two protagonists were reported at its close to have kissed not only the Gospels and the Cross but also the icons of Christ and the Theotokos.[3] The image was regarded as being so closely connected with its prototype as to possess supernatural (some would say magic) efficacy. Hence the role of the icon in times of crisis, as at the Persian siege of Edessa in 544, though it has been pointed out that in the original account the use of the icon was not so much that of a palladium as a secretly worked miracle.[4] But in the minds of the Byzantines there was no doubt about the palladian qualities of the icon of St Demetrius of Thessalonica, or of the Mother of God in the various sieges of Constantinople. Thessalonica was never taken by the Slavs. The City beat off its attackers for nearly five hundred years.

The explanation of the growing cult of the icon in the late sixth and seventh centuries and the beginning of its firm rooting in the life of the Orthodox Church has been found in the need for additional security. It was a time when external forces seemed to be disrupting the life of the Empire, though in the end this time of crisis proved to be one of transformation rather than complete disruption. Justinian I's reconquest in North Africa and in Spain was lost to the Muslims, as were certain of the East Mediterranean provinces; part (but by no means all) of Italy went to the Lombards;

---

[2] See S. Gero, 'The True Image of Christ: Eusebius' Letter to Constantia Reconsidered', *JTS*, n.s., 32 (1981), 460–70; cf. also Kitzinger, 'Cult', 93, note 28, where this question of authenticity is discussed.

[3] Cited by Kitzinger, op. cit 99.

[4] See Kitzinger, op. cit. 103 ff. for further references; S. Runciman, 'Some remarks on the Image of Edessa', *Cambridge Historical Journal*, 3 (1931), 238 ff.

Slavs and some of the Hunnic peoples spread through the Balkans, even into Greece. People living in the seventh century could not foresee Byzantium's remarkable recovery, ironically much of it to come under the able leadership of heretical iconoclast emperors. For them, the enemy was overrunning their countryside and pressing at the gates of their two finest cities, Constantinople and Thessalonica, and it was a life or death struggle in which the supernatural qualities of the holy icon could offer protection.

Thus the change in attitude to figural representation is understandable. To the unlettered peasant or soldier the icon simply seemed to afford protection in times of trouble, but the more articulate could go further and explain why it had such charismatic qualities. At a practical level it had also long been recognized that the picture was a means of educating the illiterate. The sixth-century Hypatius of Ephesus, though not himself taking pleasure in icons, pointed out this use: 'We allow simpler and immature folk to have these as being fitted to their natural development, that they may learn through the eye by means adapted to their comprehension.'[5] But the icon was more than this because it could bring the beholder into contact with God. As the Pseudo-Dionysius visualized, it could lead the Christian through the various hierarchical stages to the Deity. Bishop Hypatius of Ephesus had also stressed this, 'some will thus be led to spiritual beauty'.[6] Then, in reverse, there was the relation of the icon, not to the beholder, but to its prototype. Since man was created in the image of God through the indwelling of the Holy Spirit, he had in him something of God, and this was reflected in his portrait, particularly that of the saint. And how much more of Christ, who, since he became man, could be portrayed. By the late seventh century Christian apologetic on this theme had reached the point of regarding it as a tenet of Orthodox teaching. At the Quinisextum council in Constantinople in 691–2 canon 82 stated:

---

[5] Hypatius of Ephesus, bk. I, ch. 5, cited by N. H. Baynes, 'The Icons before Iconoclasm', *Harvard Theological Review*, 44 (1951), 94–5. A fragment of Hypatius, *Diverse Questions*, bk. I, ch. 5, is preserved in the Paris codex gr. 1115 and printed by A. Diekamp, *Analecta Patristica* (= *OCA* 117, 1938), 127–9. Part of the same fragment is cited by Theodore Studites, Ep., bk. II, no. 171, *PG* 99, col. 1537.
[6] Cited by Baynes, op. cit. 94.

In certain paintings of holy icons a lamb is represented being pointed out by the figure of the Forerunner, a lamb which is the prefiguration of grace, prefiguring for us in the Law the true Lamb which is Christ our God. Though we venerate the old prefiguration and shadows as symbols and announcements of truth given to the Church we prefer the grace and the truth which we have received in fulfilment of the Law. And so in order that that which is perfect may be made clear to the eyes of all, even in paintings, we decree that in future instead of the ancient Lamb, 'he who taketh away the sin of the world', Christ our God, shall be portrayed on icons in human form. And by means of this we shall understand the depth of the humiliation of the Word of God and think on his life in the flesh and his passion and death for our salvation whence came the redemption of the world.[7]

Opposition to figural portrayal came long before the bitter controversy of the eighth century. Within the Church many had doubts which grew with the spread of superstitious practices associated with icons. From the fourth century onwards various objections were voiced. The Spanish synod of Elvira in the early fourth century had urged caution in the use of icons lest they should be painted on the walls of churches. Doubts had been expressed, for instance by Eusebius of Caesarea and Epiphanius of Cyprus, and by a sect within the Armenian Church (the first group-protest the members of which eventually seceded to the heretical Paulicians), but contrary to the condemnation of the sixth-century Severus at the fifth session of Nicaea II there is evidence that the monophysites did use icons.[8] The opponents of icons in the pre-iconoclastic period usually derived support from the Mosaic prohibition against graven images (Exodus 20:4–5) and stressed the Christian emphasis on worship in spirit and in truth. Obviously use of material media could, and did, lead to idolatry, and the tenacious survival of pagan and non-Jewish practice is vividly illustrated by the golden bull set up and worshipped by a group of peasant monks in Egypt as late as

---

[7] Mansi, XI. 977–980; Joannou, *Discipline générale* I, 218–20 (with Latin and French trans.).

[8] For instance Sophronius tells how the Alexandrian monophysites venerated an icon of the Theotokos, and Severus in his sermon (which survives in the Syriac) only condemns the impropriety of representing the archangel Michael in the insignia of a praetorian prefect. I am grateful to Henry Chadwick for drawing my attention to this evidence. See also H. Chadwick, 'John Moschus and his friend Sophronius the Sophist', *JTS*, n.s., 25 (1974), 67, note 3, and S. Brock 'Iconoclasm and the Monophysites', in *Iconoclasm*, 53–7.

the fourth century. But the Christological argument for and against icons was not really developed until the eighth century and then not in the opening stages of the conflict.

The opening conflict under Leo III

The reasons for the flare-up of the controversy in the eighth century are still disputed and to such an extent that assessments vary from considering it as the most significant event in Byzantine history to regarding it as of almost only peripheral importance. In examining the causes (and course) of the struggle interpretations to some extent seem to reflect the individual interests of scholars, the more secular-minded historian regarding the movement as part of wider imperial policies while to the Orthodox the fight for icons was so closely related to the basic Christological position as to involve the presentation of an integral part of their belief. Lossky even went as far as to say that icons were the expression of Orthodoxy as such. Moreover it is difficult to get a fair picture of the iconoclasts partly because their writings were destroyed except in so far as extracts were preserved because refuted in Orthodox councils, and partly because they understandably had a bad press in Orthodox chronicles and histories, though surviving oriental sources have done some-thing to correct the Greek bias.[9]

In attempting to discover why the movement against icons took official form under the eighth-century North Syrian (mistakenly called Isaurian) Emperors, Leo III and his son Constantine V, scholars have noticed a similar tendency among Muslims whose power was increasing so rapidly at this time. The two religions, Islam and Christianity, were now face to face. To some extent they shared common ground and had common roots and their relations were marked by more than perpetual antagonism, as the fruitful cross-fertilization in the long history of Byzantino-Arab relations was to reveal. It is therefore necessary to consider contacts, and debts if any, between Byzantium and Islam in initiating the policy of banning the use of icons.

Leo III, originally called Conon, was himself of North Syrian origin, born at Germaniceia (Marash). Thus he began life in a Jacobite milieu, though he must later have professed himself a supporter of Chalcedon since he held official positions in Byzan-

[9] See especially Gero, *Leo III* and id., *Constantine V*.

tium. Armenian sources seem to show him as a protector of Chalcedonian Orthodoxy, something that iconophile Byzantine sources would hardly stress.[10] Whether or not he was transplanted to Mesembria in Thrace by Justinian II in the late seventh century, as the Greek chronicler Theophanes says,[11] appears to be uncertain and is not supported in the Patriarch Nicephorus' writings or in the oriental sources. Germaniceia was the scene of Byzantino-Arab warfare and it is probable that in his early years Leo may have been open to Muslim influence and he probably spoke Arabic.

It has often been claimed that there is a more direct link than this rather general early influence and that when Leo III made his first open move against icons in 726 he was motivated by the example of the Muslim ruler Yazid (720–4). But in fact very little is known about the Muslim edict against images. Theophanes makes brief mention of an edict promulgated in the year in which Yazid died (that is, between the beginning of the year, 1 September 723 and his death on 27 January 724), and he then adds 'Most people had not heard of his devilish edict'.[12] It is unlikely that this little-known edict sparked off the action of Leo III, though he was known to have had a renegade Syrian, Beser, as one of his advisers. Yazid seems to have been engaged in a 'smear campaign' against the Christians and was subsequently made a scapegoat for Byzantine iconoclasm, as shown by John of Jerusalem's somewhat exaggerated account of the iconoclast movement at the council of Nicaea II in 787. But in the early Syriac and Arabic sources Leo III is not linked with Yazid's policy.[13] There is in fact eighth and ninth-century evidence that the Byzantines attributed iconoclasm to Jewish rather than Muslim influence, and with a good deal of legendary accretion, such as the introduction of an odd figure called Tessaracontapechys (forty cubits).[14] The connection between the Old Testament prohibition and the Jewish religion was understandably stressed in iconophile polemic and is found in a work attributed to Germanus,[15] as also in

---

[10] See Gero, *Leo III*, 141–2.
[11] Theophanes, I. 391, 6–8; cf. Gero, *Leo III*, 25 ff.
[12] Theophanes, I. 402.
[13] See Gero, *Leo III*, 81 ff.
[14] See O. Grabar, 'Islamic Art and Byzantium', *DOP*, 18 (1964), 83–4, note 40; Lemerle, *Humanisme byzantine*, 31 ff.; Gero, *Leo III*, 59 ff.
[15] Stein, *Der Beginn*, pp. 262 ff., thinks it was anonymous, probably written between 730 and 754. Germanus I was Patriarch of Constantinople 715–30.

John of Damascus.[16] In this connection a Jewish soothsayer was said to have promised Leo a long reign if he banned images. It is this Jewish theme which was elaborated in John of Jerusalem's *Narratio* which he produced at the fifth session of Nicaea II,[17] only here he specifically described the Jew as a magician from Tiberias called Tessaracontapechys who made the promise not to Leo but to Yazid, and who thus caused the heresy to arise whereby the pseudo-bishop of Nacoleia imitated the lawless Jews and the impious Arabs. This variation was in keeping with the understandable desire of the council of Nicaea to avoid casting any kind of official blame on Leo III, who was after all the founder of the reigning house and the great-grandfather of the young Constantine VI.

Even so, the legendary embroidery in iconodule literature was already obscuring the motives and influences behind the controversy, though some corrective of this can now be found in the less biased oriental sources which also do justice to the North Syrian rulers' military achievements, even representing them as defenders of the faith. Added to this, the comparative paucity of sources and the survival of iconoclast material only in an iconophile setting must inevitably increase the difficulties of fair appraisal. The possibility of cross-currents of general Semitic influence, particularly on the eastern borders, if not proven, at least cannot be ruled out. But there is no evidence of direct contact between Leo and Yazid. There is however sufficient internal evidence to account for the movement on two grounds: popular practice and imperial policy. The growing use of icons, and particularly its abuse, had increasingly concerned churchmen, as has already been shown, and is reflected in the measure of support which the iconoclasts Leo III and Constantine V received. And the imperial aspect of the policy is revealed in an analysis of the two main phases of the movement in the eighth century.

Some of the few surviving documents of the very early phase refer to disquiet in Asia Minor. Patriarch Germanus of Constantinople (715–30) wrote to three prelates, Metropolitan John of Synnada, Bishop Constantine of Nacoleia (both of Phrygia), and Bishop Thomas of Claudiopolis (one of Leo III's close advisers), reproaching them with iconoclast views and, in the case of Thomas, with the

---

[16] *De Imaginibus, Oratio* I, ed. Kotter, III, and *PG* 94, col. 1236 D.
[17] Mansi, XIII. 197 ff.; Gero, *Leo III*, 67; Hefele, III (2), 770.

actual destruction of icons.[18] These bishops were known to have visited Constantinople but there is no evidence as to whether they did, or did not, discuss their problem with the Emperor. All that can be said is that certain churchmen in Asia Minor held iconoclastic views. In the *De Haeresibus et Synodis* attributed to Germanus the author makes Constantine of Nacoleia the main leader of those departing from the traditions of the Fathers.[19] He regards supporters of such views as undesirable innovators rather than heretics and there is no hint of any kind of doctrinal implication. Nor is there any assertion of ecclesiastical independence, or outspoken criticism of the Emperor, though there is a suggestion that certain people (unspecified) at court[20] are also acting against the devout. This attitude may have been politic on the author's part and was later stressed at the council of Nicaea (787) by Patriarch Tarasius who also castigated Constantine of Nacoleia as the originator of the movement. Such writings and letters, whether by Germanus or not, certainly indicate that there was local iconoclast feeling and action in Asia Minor, but the authoritative lead was to come from the Emperor.

Leo III's first dramatic action against icons was to order the removal of the mosaic image of Christ above the Chalce entrance to the complex of imperial palace buildings. This was in the early autumn of 726 after a volcanic eruption which threw up a small island off Thera (Santorin) and Therasia, an event regarded by some as an expression of divine displeasure (presumably at the use of icons). The chronicler Theophanes says that Leo had already begun to speak out against icons,[21] but just how far his iconoclast views had previously been publicized is unknown, or whether such pronouncements (if made) did in fact cause the rebellion in the Helladic theme and the Cyclades which some historians attribute to purely economic reasons. The Chalce episode of 726 certainly provoked violent opposition from the Constantinopolitans. It has been suggested that there is evidence that an edict was also issued in

[18] Mansi XIII, 100 B–128 A; Gero, *Leo III*, 87 ff., Stein dates these between 726 and 730.

[19] PG 98, col. 77 A; Stein challenges Germanus's authorship, see *Der Beginn*, App. I, pp. 262–8.

[20] PG 98, col. 77 B.

[21] Theophanes, I. 404, 3–4.

this year,[22] in which case the Patriarch Germanus presumably temporized from 726 to 730 (the year of his deposition), which might account for his being described as 'two-faced' by the iconoclast council of 754. But on the whole the consensus of opinion supports 730 as the date of the first formal edict. On 17 January a silentium or imperial council was held in the palace in the Hall of the Nineteen Divans and a decree issued for the destruction of the icons of the saints. Germanus, who had hoped to change Leo's views, refused to put his signature to any decree of this kind and he therefore had to retire from office and went to live on his private estates where he died in 733. He was succeeded by his syncellus, Anastasius (730–54) who supported Leo. Something of the ravages of the iconoclasts at this time is known from the *De Haeresibus et Synodis*. These despoilers not only broke up and burnt images but destroyed or removed altar furniture and cloths and stripped relics of their valuable reliquaries, all of which was later condemned and forbidden by the iconoclast council of 754, thus confirming the account in the tract. On the nature of persecution against iconophiles there is relatively little information for Leo III's reign, and also very little on early iconoclast tenets. The infringement of the second commandment, the cult of icons with burning of candles and incense, worship rather than veneration of the saints, were all condemned. Christ was to be represented not in human form but by the Cross, and it is possible that the series of short iambic poems on the Cross by iconoclasts, preserved because they were commented on by the iconophile Theodore Studites, can be dated to this early period.[23]

Constantine V and the council of 754

Under Leo III's son and successor Constantine V (741–75) the struggle was intensified both in action and in theory. Persecution if spasmodic, could be severe and the iconoclasts greatly widened their field of argument. No longer content with the charge of idolatry, they reinforced their position by developing a much more sophisticated theological approach recognizing that the relationship of icons to Christological teaching must be taken into account. The out-

[22] See M. V. Anastos, 'Leo III's Edict against the Images in the year 726–727 ...', *Byzantinische Forschungen*, 3 (1968, reprinted Variorum, 1979), 5–41 and Gero, *Leo III*, 106, note 55.

[23] Thus argues Gero, *Leo III*, 113ff, but this date is questioned by L. Lamza, *Patriarch Germanos I* (Würzburg, 1975), p. 178f.

standing champion of the iconophiles, John of Damascus (†749) had already launched a defence of icons on Christological grounds, though, writing as he did from Muslim territory, it is not clear whether his work was known to Constantine V, the theologian of the iconoclasts.

Constantine V was an able ruler who has been maligned in iconophile sources. Like his father he was a good general and administrator, but in temperament he was something of a contrast, passionately fond of horses (probably the origin of his nickname Copronymus rather than Germanus' murky baptismal story—he was also called Caballinus' or 'Horsey'), much addicted to music and theatrical displays, more sophisticated and bolder in his metaphysical ventures than Leo had been, and opposed to monasticism as a way of life. In the early years of his reign he was faced with a major rebellion from his brother-in-law Artabasdus and he had to undertake continual campaigns against the advances of Muslim and Slav. It was understandable that he found it difficult to face additional commitments in Italy where both Pope and Byzantine governor were being pressed by the aggressive Lombards, hence the fateful papal request to the Franks for help in 753.

Thus the political pressures of his early years left Constantine little time for any iconoclast policy and there may even have been a temporary relaxation. Stephen the Younger's *Life* mentions confiscations and white-washed walls, but there was clearly nothing like the more severe persecution of the years after 754. Like his father, Constantine seems to have organized a certain amount of propaganda by holding meetings in the provinces and he got his episcopate to help him in looking out relevant iconoclast passages in patristic texts. But he took his father's work a stage further by attempting to get synodal approval for an iconoclast policy. A council was therefore summoned and it met in the imperial palace in Hieria on the Asian shore opposite Constantinople from 10 February to 8 August 754, and then on 8 August it moved to the church of the Blachernae in the capital for the final session. No patriarch was present until the last session. Anastasius, who had died early in 754 was only replaced on 8 August when Constantine II (754–66) was installed; the three eastern patriarchs, all now living in Muslim territory, had been unable to send legates; nor had any come from the Pope, embroiled as he was with the Lombards and then forced to flee to Frankish territory. But 338 bishops were present so that it was hardly an unrepresentative assembly, though subsequent events seemed to indicate that a number of the bishops could scarcely have been dedicated iconoclasts and probably merely found it politic to conform. An avowed iconoclast, Theodosius, bishop of Ephesus, presided, assisted by two vice-presidents, Sisinnius, bishop of Perge in Pamphylia, and Basil, bishop of Pisidian Antioch.

The minutes of the council have not survived, though it is known that the three iconophiles specifically anathematized were Patriarch Germanus, 'the two-faced, the worshipper of wood', Mansur 'the Saracen-minded' (John of Damascus), and George of Cyprus (the author of the *Nouthesia*, or *The admonition of an old man concerning the holy icons*, written under Constantine V).[24] The *Definition*(ὅρος) can however be reconstructed as it was cited and refuted section by section in the sixth session of Nicaea II which restored Orthodoxy in 787. On that occasion each section was read out by Gregory, bishop of Caesarea and was then answered by Epiphanius, a patriarchal official, under the heading 'The refutation of the patched-up and falsely so-called Definition of the disorderly assembled crew of the Christianity-detractors.'[25]

The iconoclasts, who held that their council of 754 was the seventh oecumenical council, began with the traditional profession of belief in the apostolic and patristic traditions and in the preceding six general councils. The arguments of the iconoclasts, set out at length with supporting evidence and summed up at the end in the Anathemas,[26] were directed against idolatry (condemned by the Bible and the fathers) and against the material nature of images. It was stressed that an image of Christ either circumscribed an uncircumscribable Godhead and confused the two natures (monophysite), or divided the human from the divine Person (Nestorian).

---

[24] Mansi, XIII. 356 CD; Theophanes, I. 427 f.; *Nouthesia*, ed. M. B. Melioransky, 'Georgii Kiprianin i Ioann Ierusalimlianin, dva maloizvestnych bortsa za pravoslavie v VIII v. ('Two little-known champions of Orthodoxy in the eighth century'), *Zapiski Istor.-Filolog. Fak. Imp. S. Peterburgskago Univ.* 59 (1901).

[25] Mansi, XIII. 204–364; Percival, *Nicene and Post-Nicene Fathers*, 14, gives only a brief summary of what are described as the 'verbose' proceedings of Nicaea II. Mendham translates almost the whole of Nicaea II (with occasional inaccuracies; he left out for instance lists of bishops).

[26] See M. V. Anastos, 'The Argument for Iconoclasm as presented by the Iconoclastic Council of 754', *Studies in Honour of A. M. Friend* (Princeton, NJ, 1955, reprinted Variorum, London, 1979), 177–88, with trans. of Anathemas 8–20 and the closing acclamations.

To the iconoclasts the only true image of Christ was the eucharist. They maintained that the true image of a saint was the reproduction of his virtue, that is, an ethical image within the believer and not any kind of material representation.[27]

In certain respects the council toned down Constantine V's more extreme views which were evident in his theological writings probably produced before the council met. Surviving evidence has had to be reconstructed from fragments cited in iconophile works refuting his views.[28] Some of Constantine's wording on the two natures of Christ seems to indicate monophysite tendencies, and this gains support from Michaël the Syrian's praise of him as 'orthodox' (that is, monophysite). Nor were his views on the Mother of God and the saints and relics those accepted by the six general councils. Hence explicit statements correcting these views in the definitions of the 754 council. For instance *Definition* 15 confessed Mary to be rightly and truly the Theotokos, our mediator with God. Constantine had not forbidden the cult of relics, though he was evidently opposed to this and was unwilling to use the title of 'saint' or 'holy', for instance thus speaking simply of the Church 'of the Apostles'.

In spite of the ruling in the council of 754 that forbade burning, looting, and misuse of sacred buildings, in the post-conciliar years these and other measures against icons and iconophiles were eventually stepped up. As a class the prelates were to some extent open to imperial pressure and on the whole they evidently gave support—at least outwardly—to official policy, and the measure of this is shown by the petitions for readmission to the Church from penitents on the restoration of icons, and by the difficulty of staffing the Church without the clergy whom the iconoclast bishops had ordained. In assessing the extent of the persecution and the distribution of the rival parties, whether on a geographical, a social, or ethnical basis, extreme caution is necessary because of the fragmentary nature of surviving evidence. The army was not predominantly iconoclast as such; most soldiers would be unlikely to be swayed by theological arguments, but on the other hand they would tend to support successful generals, such as the two first North Syrian rulers, and to that extent were iconoclast. There seems

[27] See M. V. Anastos 'The Ethical Theory of Images formulated by the Iconoclasts in 754 and 815', *DOP*, 4 (1954, reprinted Variorum, London, 1979), 151–60.

[28] See Ostrogorsky, *Studien*, and Alexander, *Patriarch Nicephorus*.

to be no evidence that Leo III deliberately won over Anatolian soldiery or appeased an Asian populace by an iconoclast policy. Regional support for iconoclasm is hard to identify and the old contention that the European provinces were for, the Asian against, icons breaks down before contradictory fragments of evidence. Perhaps the *Life* of Stephen the Younger gives some clue when the saint was reported as having advised his monks to disperse in view of imperial threats. He himself was imprisoned and his house on Mount Auxentius in Bithynia became virtually depopulated, and he suggested that his monks should seek a refuge in remote regions likely to be friendly, which he named as the maritime coasts of South Italy and the northern Black Sea or the southern coast of Asia Minor and Cyprus, that is, areas at a distance from Constantinople. But not all monasteries were iconophile as the change to non-figural decoration in some of the chapels in the Cappadocian rock monasteries shows. Some monks even held office as iconoclast prelates. Persecution or otherwise depended very much on the inclinations of the provincial governors.

With the formal ecclesiastical condemnation of the icons in 754 those refusing to abandon them could be punished as heretics, clerics degraded, monks and laity excommunicated. There were some spectacular instances of persecution going beyond the prescribed punishment, but these were spasmodic and were probably played up in the reports of iconodule literature. From 760 onwards Constantine's anger seems to have been directed against the monks. These had not, as often stated, been the object of iconoclast venom from the outset in Leo III's reign and the suggestion that they were persecuted for economic reasons or because they manufactured icons cannot be accepted. It is more probable that their obstinate refusal to abandon icons, together with a clash of outlook due to the secular-minded Constantine's failure to understand the ascetic way of life, accounts for the disbandment and appropriation of certain monasteries and the imprisonment or public ridicule of their inmates during the latter part of his reign. Under Leo III the movement in the Empire had only begun to get under way and there was relatively little persecution. It is true that what was to become the classic defence of icons was voiced by a monk, but it was from one living outside the Empire in Muslim territory—John of Damascus (the 'Saracen-minded Mansur' of the 754 anathemas).

From Constantine V's reign onwards the home ranks began to close. For instance the treatise *Ad Constantinum Caballinum* (wrongly attributed to John of Damascus and perhaps by John of Jerusalem) was a violent attack on the Emperor.[29] In certain monastic centres opposition to iconoclasm was to harden. In particular the Studite house in Constantinople, led by its abbot Theodore, played an important role in the ninth century during the later stages of the controversy.

With the death of Constantine V in 755 iconoclasm died down, however long traces of it may have lingered, and the ninth-century revival was temporary and even at times somewhat half-hearted. In examining the causes for the eighth-century movement direct Jewish and Islamic influences must be rejected, though this is not to deny that they may have indirectly contributed to create the atmosphere which generated an iconoclast outlook.[30] Within the Byzantine Empire there was an age-long undercurrent of anxiety concerning the growing popular use—and abuse— of icons and this was used to support what was essentially an imperial initiative owing its effectiveness to Leo III and Constantine V. It may have been for reasons of policy that the importance of Bishop Constantine of Nacoleia in the early stages of the movement was exaggerated both by the Second council of Nicaea and in early iconophile literature; he later peters out and is not found in the non-Greek sources. This is not to say that there was no genuine iconoclast feeling in the Asian provinces, but there seems to have been no systematic local organization of eighth-century iconoclasm (either then or subsequently), though there were cruel outbursts in some regions, as that promoted by Michael Lachanodracon, the governor of the Thracesian theme in western Asia Minor. It depended on the Emperor and it was he who initiated the prohibition, though it is true that Constantine V thought it desirable to get the backing of a church council and even had to suffer it to modify certain of his more radical views. In the legal code, the *Ecloga*, promulgated just before his iconoclast measures, Leo III made clear his views on his

[29] *PG* 95, cols. 309–44. This exists in two versions, the longer one written after Constantine V's death, presumably before 787 as there is no reference in it to the condemnation of iconoclasm; see Gero, *Leo III*, 13 and 62 ff.

[30] Cf. P. Crone, 'Islam, Judeo-Christianity and Byzantine Iconoclasm', *Jerusalem Studies in Arabic and Islam*, 2 (1980), 59–95 (to the present writer not altogether convincing).

own position. He was acting in the Byzantine tradition as the Viceroy of God. He had been handed the power of sovereignty and had been commanded, in the words of St Peter, to 'tend the faithful flock'. This applied not only to the promotion of justice in the spirit of a Moses or a Solomon but equally to matters of faith, and Leo, like other Byzantine rulers, felt responsible for the good conduct of ecclesiastical as well as secular affairs. This Byzantine conception of the ruler's divinely appointed mission was further reinforced by the Graeco-Roman tradition of an Emperor cult which had been adapted within the Christian framework, again stressing the Emperor's direct relationship to God. It is unlikely that the icon with its charismatic powers was really seen as a serious challenge to the imperial portrait. Constantine, even more than his father, certainly committed himself to the removal of the image from religious life and it was he who reinforced his position by building up theological support for iconoclasm. His reign is the high watermark of the movement.

2. The first restoration of the icons

The Empress Irene and the council of Nicaea (787)

Leo IV (775–80) who succeeded his father Constantine V was not an outstanding personality. He was also much more moderate than Constantine, even indifferent, and the more violent aspects of the iconoclast movement seem to have been suspended, evidence of the extent to which this depended on the ruler's outlook. It is true that iconoclasm itself was not repudiated, but the harshness of Constantine V's last years was greatly abated. Irene, the vigorous Athenian wife of Constantine's son and heir Leo, was herself known to be a supporter of icons. On Leo IV's death in 780 he left as successor his ten-year-old son Constantine VI and this gave Irene her opportunity. As well as being an ardent iconophile she was also an ambitious and forceful character. In the face of some opposition she asserted her right to act as regent for her son, who had been crowned Emperor during his father's lifetime. In certain respects she was to prove an unwise ruler, though not entirely so.[31] She managed to organize affairs so as to bring the restoration of icons, though this was not achieved in an instant, just as icons were not

---

[31] Cf. Speck, *Konstantin VI*, 108 ff.

immediately thrown overboard at the onset of the attack on them. There must always have been a certain amount of overlap, even of turning a blind eye. After all both the Emperors Leo IV and Theophilus had iconophile wives.

The Patriarch of Constantinople, Paul IV (780–4), was old and infirm and apparently filled with remorse for his earlier iconoclast views when he had sworn to oppose icon veneration. Now after having urged the calling of a general council to reconcile the Byzantine Church with the rest of Christendom, he retired to a monastery and resigned. Tarasius (784–806), an able layman and administrator, the protoasecretis (first secretary), was elected Patriarch in his place and on this occasion, as earlier in the case of Patriarch Germanus, he was acclaimed by 'all the people'[32] of Constantinople who had been invited to the Magnaura palace for this purpose. He was consecrated on 25 December 784. This was open to criticism from Tarasius' enemies and others who objected to the uncanonically rapid promotion from lay status to the highest ecclesiastical office. It was however a judicious choice, as was shown by Tarasius' moderation towards repentant iconoclasts and his adroit handling of the Second council of Nicaea in 787. He only accepted office on condition that a general council should be called to annul the decrees of the Hieria council of 754, which had itself claimed to be the Seventh oecumenical council. When Tarasius harangued the crowd in the Magnaura in a speech reported in the *acta* of Nicaea, he stressed the pressing need for this general council, whatever might be the opposition.

The co-operation of the Pope was essential. The Empress Irene may already have written one letter to Hadrian I announcing the council and asking for his presence.[33] After Tarasius' consecration he himself wrote to the Pope, as well as Irene in what was probably a second letter. He gave news of the patriarchal election and renewed the invitation to a general council. He also sent the usual synodica, or profession of faith (which went as well to the three oriental patriarchs),[34] and he explained the reasons for his rapid elevation from lay status to the office of Patriarch. His profession of faith included an express statement of his adherence to icon

---

[32] Theophanes, I. 458.
[33] DR 341 (29 August 784) and 343 (second letter after Tarasius' consecration).
[34] GR 351–2.

veneration and to orthodox teaching on the Theotokos and saints.[35] Pope Hadrian replied both to Irene and to Tarasius. As might be expected, he was critical of Tarasius' uncanonical elevation and also of his use of the title 'oecumenical'; but he applauded the projected council as a means of restoring orthodoxy and he agreed to send to Constantinople two legates, his oeconomus the arch-priest Peter and Abbot Peter of the Greek monastery of St Sabas in Rome, who were given wide powers. Further, a point which regularly reappeared in papal communications, he brought up the question of the restoration of papal patrimonies in the Byzantine Italian provinces and of the ecclesiastical jurisdiction over Sicily, Calabria, and Illyricum which had been transferred from the papacy to Constantinople in the mid-eighth century.[36] This item and other unpalatable points in Hadrian's letter were suppressed in the Greek translation presented to the council of Nicaea and are only known from the Latin version of Anastasius the Librarian. Tarasius' letters sent to the three eastern patriarchs never got through to their recipients and the most that the couriers achieved was a meeting with certain eastern monks. As a result two monks, Thomas and John, the syncelli of Alexandria and Antioch, were sent to the council to explain the difficult situation of the Christian Church under Muslim rule; they were apparently not properly appointed legates. Jerusalem did not seem to have even this measure of representation, though in signing the acta Thomas was said to have represented the three patriarchates.

The council was convened by traditional imperial order and it met in August 786[37] in the church of the Holy Apostles in Constantinople in the presence of Irene and Constantine. But the imminent restoration of the icons was obviously going to present a problem to the iconoclast bishops and those ordained by them, presumably by now the majority of the clergy. Tarasius had already

[35] GR 351 (exact date unknown but after 25 Dec. 784; the papal reply was dated 26 Oct. 785).

[36] Views differ as to precisely when this took place. See M. Anastos, 'The transfer of Illyricum, Calabria and Sicily to the Jurisdiction of the Patriarchate of Constantinople in 732–33', *SBN* (= *Silloge bizantina in onore di S. G. Mercati*), 9 (1957), 14–31, (reprinted Variorum, 1979) who opts for Leo III; V. Grumel, 'L'Annexation de l'Illyricum oriental, de la Sicile et de la Calabre au patriarcat de Constantinople', *Recherches de science religieuse* (= *Mélanges Jules Lebreton*, II), 40 (1952), 191–200, puts the case for Constantine V and the pontificate of Stephen II (752–7).

[37] On the date see GR 355; 'the beginning of August', according to Tarasius.

been forced to forbid official meetings among iconoclast bishops which were being held without his knowledge and directed against him. There was also support for iconoclast policy in certain secular circles. This erupted in the opening sessions of the council when imperial guards burst in to stop proceedings and were supported by some of the bishops present. Tarasius was shouted down and the assembly dispersed. Irene then organized the re-posting of the suspect troops and brought in from Thrace others on whom she could rely. A second summons to a general council went out in May 787, this time to meet in nearby Nicaea in Bithynia which had venerable associations with Constantine the Great and in all probability would be freer from the tumults of the capital.

The council opened in the church of the Holy Wisdom on 24 September 787. Though the ruler or his representative was present, by tradition the presidency belonged to Rome, but on this occasion, at the request of the Sicilian bishops, Tarasius opened the council. From the outset the pressing problem which was to heighten the underlying antagonism between the moderates and the stricter monastic element was present. This turned on the treatment to be accorded to the iconoclast bishops and by implication involved the clergy whom they had ordained. In addition to the bishops, a number of distinguished monks were present at the council, such as Plato, abbot of Saccudium, and Nicephorus, later Patriarch, from Medicium. Moved by inflexible principles rather than by common sense, they were implacably opposed to any leniency. Many of the bishops present had obviously accepted the regime imposed at the imperial command and with the wind of change in 780 they had presumably returned to orthodoxy. A few had not done so, though they were now ready to express penitence and make their profession of faith. Three, Ancyra, Amorium, and Myra, were accepted on this basis. Seven others, including Nicaea, Rhodes, Iconium, and Pisidia, presented a more serious case as they had held illegal meetings and then joined the opposition when the earlier council of 786 was disrupted. After considerable discussion and prolonged reference to works of the fathers, and in the face of various monastic accusations, most of the penitents were received back by the council. It was agreed that the only exceptions would be those who had maltreated iconophiles and here proof, not mere accusation, was required. During these first sessions the correspondence between Tarasius, the Pope (whose letter was truncated by the

Byzantines, as already mentioned), and the eastern patriarchates was read out and discussed, and general agreement expressed in the second session with Hadrian's statement concerning the difference between the veneration of the icons and the worship to be given to God alone.

A more prolonged discussion of the iconophile position and the refutation of iconoclast tenets took place in the fourth, fifth, and sixth sessions. The fathers of this council might well have been dismayed had they known that posterity was to some extent to regard as the most valuable part of these sessions, the contribution which their discussions preserved in the acta made towards an understanding of the iconoclast theology which was being refuted. And it must be admitted that the iconoclast *Definition* or *Horos* (ὅρος) condemned by the council at least presented a well-reasoned point of view in contrast to the anecdotal ramblings of the iconophile members of the council. It is necessary to look elsewhere for any definitive and deeper elaboration of the iconophile position, such as is found in the writings of John of Damascus or Theodore Studites or the Patriarch Nicephorus. On the other hand Tarasius showed obvious diplomacy in allowing the iconophiles to indulge their reminiscences on the subject of icons, though this was probably not what Pope Hadrian had in mind when in his letter he hoped that all would speak out freely without fear. Nevertheless the *Definition*, drawn up presumably by Tarasius, was succinct and went to the heart of the matter. This was read by Bishop Theodore of Taurianum in the seventh session on 13 October 787. After the usual profession of faith in the creed and in the six general councils, it went on to decree that, following the traditions of the Church,

We define with all certainty and accuracy that just as the representation of the venerable and life-giving Cross, so the venerable and holy icons, in painting or mosaic or any other appropriate medium, should be set up in the holy churches of God, and on the sacred vessels and vestments, on walls and on panels, both in houses and by the way-side, and also the image of our Lord God and Saviour Jesus Christ, our undefiled Lady, the holy Theotokos, the angels worthy of honour and all holy and devout people. For the more often they are seen in figural representation, the more readily men are lifted up to remember their prototypes and long for them, and these should be given honourable veneration (προσκύνησις), but not that true worship (λατρεία) of our faith which belongs to the Divine Nature alone. But we should offer them incense and candles, as we do to the representation of the venerable and life-giving Cross and to the books of the Gospels and to other holy objects, according to ancient custom. For the honour which is given to the icon passes to that which the icon represents, and in venerating the icon we venerate the prototype.[38]

In conclusion, anyone violating icons or relics or monasteries was condemned to degradation if a cleric, to excommunication if a layman or monk. Iconoclast writings were to be destroyed and their tenets were condemned as heretical.

For its eighth and final session at the imperial request the council moved from Nicaea to the Magnaura palace in Constantinople and on 23 October 787 the definition was read in the presence of Irene and Constantine and duly signed, the rulers being acclaimed as a new Helena and a new Constantine. In addition to the minutes and the *Horos* there were also twenty-two disciplinary canons, apparently drawn up in Constantinople and not at Nicaea.[39] These dealt partly with specific problems arising out of the recent unhappy times, such as secular appropriation of ecclesiastical property.

After the close of the synod Tarasius sent a letter to the Pope giving a brief account of the proceedings, but it is not clear whether he asked for ratification. The full proceedings were taken back to Rome by the two Peters, the papal legates, but the Latin translation which was made was so poor that the Nicaean council almost seemed to have perpetrated those very errors which it sought to eradicate. It was in this inaccurate form that the conciliar acta reached Charlemagne and Frankish circles which perhaps gave Charlemagne his opportunity to assert himself *vis-à-vis* both Byzantium and the papacy. He got theologians to draw up a detailed refutation of both iconoclast and iconophile tenets, taking a midway stance on the theological issue. But his attitude was also certainly motivated by politics, and he may already have had in mind the coronation of 800. Constantinople was attacked in the *Libri Carolini*, Constantine V called merely a 'rex', Irene and Constantine VI regarded as blasphemous in claiming to rule with God, and it was stressed that a woman (Irene) had no place in a synod.[40] These *Libri Carolini*, or the *Capitulare de Imaginibus*, went to Rome. Hadrian I (though he had his own points of disagreement

---

38 Mansi, XIII. 377 DE.
39 Hefele, III (2), 775 ff. (text given).
40 *PL* 98, cols. 1247–92; Mansi, XIII. 759–810; *MGH*, Ep., V, no. 2, pp. 5–57.

with Constantinople) certainly supported Nicaea II. He sent a long letter to Charlemagne in which he stressed his own authority and defended the veneration of icons.[41] He did not however manage to prevent the rejection of Nicaea II by a council of Frankish clergy at Frankfurt in 784, though his own representatives were present. The papacy was in fact in an awkward situation in Italy. Since the mid-eighth century Byzantine occupation with troubles elsewhere had forced the Popes to rely on Carolingian help against the Lombard kingdom and the unruly Roman factions. Hence the embarrassment in which Hadrian I found himself on this occasion.

Conflicting currents 787–843

The restoration of icons under Irene in 787 did not immediately provide a universally acceptable solution to the controversy which had rent the East Roman Empire under the North Syrian rulers. Whether from conviction or expediency a number of churchmen had obviously accepted iconoclasm; many people had long felt that the popular use of icons was giving rise to much superstition; and above all the military successes of Leo III and Constantine V had endeared them to the army and indeed to the general public. The troubled years 787–843 saw an uneasy acceptance of orthodoxy followed by a short-lived and milder form of iconoclasm before the final restoration of the icons in 843. Throughout this period were to be seen the often conflicting currents which were to determine the future course of East Roman fortunes. Monasticism was eventually to grow in strength as foreshadowed by the activities of the intimidating Abbot Theodore Studites (759–826) who was sternly opposed to ecclesiastical moderation or imperial intervention in church affairs. Then relations with the West began to take a different turn and the emergence of a powerful Frankish kingdom was to pose a challenge to Byzantine imperial claims to universal supremacy in the Christian world. This vigorous western political growth affected papal relations with Constantinople and to some extent pointed the way to future misunderstandings between the two great Christian centres. Within the Byzantine Empire the very success of iconoclasm, though of a temporary nature, had shown the

[41] See *Libri Carolini*, ed. H. Bastgen, *MGH, Legum Sectio* III, *Concilia*. t. II Supplementum, and *PL* 98, discussed by S. Gero, 'The Libri Carolini and the Image Controversy', *Greek Orthodox Theological Review*, 18 (1973), 7–34.

strength of the imperial authority which was able for a time to maintain this unorthodox policy fortified by the prestige engendered by effective leadership in the face of Arab and Bulgar attacks.

Irene and Constantine VI

These conflicting tendencies can be seen during the reign of Irene and her immediate successors. The council of Nicaea II may have restored orthodoxy but there remained an undercurrent of iconoclasm ready to exploit for political purposes what was probably a family struggle for power. When the young Emperor Constantine VI attempted to oust his dominating mother, the Empress Irene, and assume control of the government it was the iconoclast party and the Asian troops who backed him, though he himself was not an iconoclast. But he lacked military ability and political adroitness and his mother returned to power. His second attempt to assert himself over the question of his marriage also failed and this time proved his final undoing. His divorce from his wife Mary the Paphlagonian and subsequent second marriage to Theodote in 795 created the so-called adultery, or 'moechian', controversy. The grounds for the divorce were debatable and in any case second marriages were frowned on in Byzantine canon law. The Patriarch Tarasius only penalized the priest Joseph who had been persuaded to perform the marriage, exercising *oeconomia* towards the Emperor. Both the offence and the temporizing patriarchal attitude gave the extreme monastic element grounds for opposition to Tarasius and the Emperor. But the loudly-voiced criticism of the monks only resulted in the exile of Abbot Plato of Saccudium (a house on Mount Olympus in Bithynia) and his followers, including Theodore (later of the Studite monastery in Constantinople). But their exile was short-lived, as in 797 the Emperor was blinded by his mother who recalled the monks. The priest Joseph's fortunes went up or down according to the imperial wish. He was excommunicated under Irene, reinstated by her opponent and successor Nicephorus I, and finally in 812 in response to Studite pressure was degraded under the pro-monastic Michael I. *Oeconomia*, even when prompted by humane motives, was outside the severe monastic code, an attitude which was to cause endless rifts between moderates and extremists throughout the history of Byzantium.

In the difficult post-787 period of readjustment an even more tricky problem than Constantine VI's second marriage was the question of the episcopate, since this affected the good government of the whole Byzantine Church. The extremists wished the Patriarch Tarasius to depose all iconoclast bishops, even if repentant, as well as those who had been guilty of any kind of simony, interpreting simony in an impossibly wide sense to include ordination fees and offerings normally made to a bishop. Patriarchal decrees witness to the prolonged struggle between Tarasius and the monks[42] during which there was even recourse to Pope Hadrian I,[43] not that much satisfaction was obtained from papal sources. This split between extremists and moderates within the orthodox ranks inevitably weakened any concerted orthodox stand against lingering iconoclasm itself. It was moreover an indication of the growing strength of the monastic party that it was able to challenge patriarchal policy in this way. The final word however usually lay with the Emperor and when Tarasius died in 806 the monks did not on this occasion succeed in placing their nominee on the patriarchal throne.

Irene may have been orthodox in belief and instrumental in restoring the icons but in certain other respects her reign was disastrous. Apart from the uneasy ecclesiastical equilibrium as well as political opposition centred in her son Constantine VI, there was squandering of economic resources and repeated military failures against external enemies such as the Arabs and Bulgars. There was loss of prestige due to western territorial encroachment in Italy, followed by Charlemagne's imperial coronation in St Peter's in 800. Then Rome had realized that the Franks (though often overbearing, as in their attitude to Nicaea II) were likely to be more effective allies than the Byzantines and in any case the papacy was perpetually irritated by its failure to get back its ecclesiastical jurisdiction in southern Italy, Sicily, and Illyricum which had been transferred to Constantinople in the mid-eighth century. Irene was by no means unaware of the problems posed by Charlemagne and the papacy, but in the event these were left for her successors to deal with. Her over-ambition, arrogance, and on the whole poor statesmanship created such havoc in the Empire that in October 802 she was ousted without difficulty by Nicephorus, a former treasury official.

---

[42] *GR* 360 ff.
[43] *GR* 364 (Tarasius to Hadrian I, end of 790).

Nicephorus I, Michael I, and the Patriarch Nicephorus (802–813)

Nicephorus I (802–11) was a tough ruler. He had to restore an economy ruined by Irene's foolishly lavish grants and to secure the military defences in the Balkans and Asia Minor. He was orthodox, but evidently not pro-monastic. When the moderate Patriarch Tarasius died in 806, the Studite monks saw an opportunity for one of their own persuasion. Theodore Studites was their obvious candidate. Nicephorus I however secured the appointment of another Nicephorus. He came from an iconophile family and, like Tarasius, was a layman at the time of his election though by no means divorced from ecclesiastical affairs.[44] He had worked under Tarasius in the imperial secretariat and in 787 he went with him to the council of Nicaea as an imperial official. He subsequently led a retired life near the Bosphorus and then at the imperial command he took charge of a large poorhouse in Constantinople. After hesitation he accepted imperial nomination and on 5 April became a monk. On 9 and 10 April he was ordained deacon and presbyter and was enthroned in Hagia Sophia on Easter Day 12 April. At this period he seemed to fall in with imperial policy. Apparently bowing to the wishes of the Emperor, who was furious at the papal coronation of Charlemagne, he did not send the Pope his customary synodical announcing his election and setting out his profession of faith. He also had to call a synod to reinstate Joseph the priest who had conducted Constantine VI's second marriage.[45] This enraged the monastic party and Theodore Studites' vociferous opposition brought him another period of exile.[46] At this time Theodore regarded the Patriarch Nicephorus as the betrayer of high ecclesiastical principles and was markedly hostile towards him, contemptuously describing him as 'Caesar's steward'.[47]

The Emperor Nicephorus I had shown no desire to reverse the moderate orthodox religious policy which had on the whole prevailed during Tarasius' patriarchate. But after his disastrous defeat and death in battle against the Bulgar Krum in 811 there were quick changes in policy varying from support for the extreme monastic party to the revival of iconoclasm. Nicephorus I's successor Michael I

[44] For sources and detail see Alexander, *Patriarch Nicephorus*.
[45] GR 377 (cf. GR 368).
[46] GR 378–81.
[47] Theodore Studites, Ep., bk. I, no. 26 (*PG* 99, col. 992 D), cited Alexander, *Patriarch Nicephorus*, 73.

(811–13) was an ineffective ruler who did not continue the states-manlike economic and military policies of his predecessor. The Studites were recalled from exile and their influence was reflected in Michael's religious outlook. The Patriarch Nicephorus was induced to reverse the reinstatement of the priest Joseph (812)[48] and he stated moreover that his earlier action in 809 had been due to imperial pressure.[49] This was in effect a victory for the Studites. Then the church authorities were urged to act against Manichaeans or Paulicians and other heretics.[50] This was in contrast to the policy of Nicephorus; he had valued the fighting qualities of the Paulicians and had enrolled them in his army, promising them religious freedom. Relations with the papacy and the West also took a different turn. The Patriarch Nicephorus was now able to send his synodal letter to the Pope, Leo III, apologizing for the delay due to hindrance from 'the powers that be'.[51] The western imperial coronation, which had so infuriated the Emperor Nicephorus, was accepted by Michael I. He tried to stem Carolingian advance into Byzantine Adriatic territory by recognizing Charlemagne's title, though conceding only 'Emperor and Basileus', not 'Emperor of the Romans' which was reserved for East Roman rulers. Later Byzantine emperors did not accept this concession to the West and liked to taunt the German rulers by deliberately calling them 'rex' and not 'imperator'. Subsequent Byzantine repudiation could not however root out Germanic assumption of imperial authority which, though differing from the Byzantine conception, was nevertheless to constitute a continuing challenge to the universal claims of Constantinople. As far as Michael I was concerned renewed links with Rome and Aachen and strong monastic support at home could not compensate for his unstatesmanlike rule. Appar-ently relying on foolish advice given him by Theodore Studites, Michael was crushingly defeated by the Bulgars at Versinicia (813). In the face of the menacing Bulgarian advance on Constantinople hostility to the iconodules grew. The military failures of the Byzantines seemed to reflect divine displeasure at their iconophile religious policy. The tomb of the great general Constantine V was

---

[48] GR 387.

[49] GR 388; for a detailed analysis of the underlying currents in the moechian affair and their relation to the conflict between secular clergy and monks see Alexander, *Patriarch Nicephorus*, 80 ff.

[50] GR 383 and 384.

[51] GR 382; cited by Alexander, *Patriarch Nicephorus*, 106–7 with translation.

besieged by iconoclasts in the capital and they called on the dead ruler to arise and help them (June 813). Shortly afterwards, with the support of the army, Leo the Armenian, commander of the Anatolicon theme, gained the throne (10 July 813).

3. The second phase of iconoclasm

Leo V (813–20) hoped to emulate the military successes of the North Syrian iconoclast emperors whose memory was so revered in military circles and among many of the people. He kept the Bulgars at bay and was able to conclude a long-term treaty with them. He then set about reintroducing the religious policy which in the popular mind was closely linked with the victories of the eighth-century iconoclast leaders. It was clear that the decisions of Nicaea II had by no means succeeded in rooting out the heresy. The efforts of the orthodox towards this end had indeed been weakened by schism within their ranks caused by the violent feuds of the monks with the Patriarch over his policy of compromise or *oeconomia*. Meanwhile the not inconsiderable party of iconoclasts were awaiting their opportunity. Their earlier attempts in the late eighth century to oust Irene with the help of the late Emperor Leo IV's brothers, and then the young Emperor Constantine VI, had failed. But now was their opportunity and in Leo V they had a leader of very different calibre.

Backed by the army and soon to be fortified by a comparatively successful foreign policy, Leo V intended to revert to the iconoclasm of the North Syrian emperors. Something of the strength of iconoclast support may have been suspected by the Patriarch Nicephorus who appears to have approached Leo in 813 before he was yet in the capital, asking him to affirm his orthodoxy. Leo, wishing to put no obstacle in the way of his coronation, evidently temporized. Nicephorus then seems to have drawn up a more detailed profession of faith which the Emperor, once crowned, did not sign.[52] In the following year 814 Leo set up a small commission of iconoclasts headed by John Hylilas (John the Grammarian). They worked in the imperial palace in over-luxurious conditions (so the anti-iconoclast press alleged) and their task was the compilation of a florilegium from biblical and patristic sources in order to refute the

---

[52] GR 389, '10 July or shortly before', with comments on apparent discrepancies in the sources; cf. DR 386.

claims of the iconophiles. According to Nicephorus[53] and the
Scriptor Incertus de Leone Bardae Armenii filio[54] their work was based
on that of Constantine V and they used the acta of the iconoclast
council of Hieria of 754 (not always identical with the more
extreme views of Constantine V). At the same time Leo tried to win
over the Patriarch Nicephorus. He pointed out that icon veneration
was widely regarded as a reason for military disasters and indicated
divine displeasure. He suggested that an acceptable solution would
be to remove those icons which were hung low (and could
therefore be venerated and kissed by the devout) while retaining
those placed higher up but solely for purposes of edification and
instruction.

Nicephorus rejected the Emperor's proposal and refused to enter
into any discussion (though a number of bishops and abbots
evidently did so). He gathered together his supporters to oppose the
Emperor's designs and just before Christmas they all met in the
patriarcheion. The iconoclast florilegium was read out and rejected
and those present signed a promise to stand firm in their opposition.[55] An all-night service was then held in Hagia Sophia. The
Emperor countered this by summoning the Patriarch to the palace.
At first they met alone and when the Emperor tried to convert
Nicephorus to his point of view Nicephorus (according to his *Vita*)
replied with a learned exposition of the iconophile theology. Then
the Patriarch's party and the Emperor's armed supporters waiting in
the wings were admitted and iconophile sources report strong
words on either side. Aemilianus, the bishop of Cyzicus, stated that
it was customary for ecclesiastical enquiries to be held in church and
not in the imperial palace. Theodore Studites, like John of Damascus before him, denied the imperial right to intervene in ecclesiastical questions. 'Your responsibility, Emperor, is with affairs of state
and military matters. Give your mind to these and leave the Church
to its pastors and teachers.'[56] Thus the monastic party challenged
the traditional relationship between church and state in Byzantium.

At the Epiphany services Leo omitted the usual icon veneration.
He had already succeeded in winning to his side many of the

[53] *Refutatio et Eversio*, 236ʳ, cited Alexander, *Patriarch Nicephorus*, 128.
[54] *PG* 108, col. 1025 B (*CB*, with Leo Grammaticus, p. 350).
[55] *GR* 391.
[56] Theosterictus, *Vita Nicetae Mediciensis, ASS*, April I (3 Apr., App., p. xxx;
the passage recounting this episode is translated in Alexander, *Patriarch Nicephorus*,
130–3.

Patriarch's supporters and he openly demanded that Nicephorus should either agree to remove low-hanging icons or else resign. Nicephorus himself had also been trying to plead his cause in influential quarters by appealing to the Empress[57] and to high officials.[58] Though by now a sick man, he stood firm and refused to resign.[59] Without his consent and while he was still ill and virtually under house arrest, the permanent (endemousa) synod of Constantinople met. It sent a deputation to Nicephorus to summon him to appear before it to answer for his crimes and urged him to accept iconoclasm. Nicephorus refused and evidently retaliated by condemning the bishops and clergy involved in this exercise.[60] His name was then removed from the diptychs. Finally under pressure he resigned on or about 13 March and went into exile on the Asian side of the Bosphorus. Though an exponent of moderation, and where possible compromise (oeconomia), when his basic principles were opposed to those of the Emperor no one could taunt him with being 'Caesar's steward'.

On Easter Day (1 April 815) a new patriarch, Theodotus Mellissenus Cassiteras, was enthroned. He was reputed to be of some virtue though of unclerical habits, and he was inevitably an iconoclast. Leo would have liked to appoint John the Grammarian but was dissuaded on the grounds that he was not old enough nor of sufficiently distinguished lineage. Soon after Easter a synod was held in Hagia Sophia. The acta of this council were destroyed on the restoration of orthodoxy but something of the content can be gathered from the detailed refutation made by the Patriarch Nicephorus in his Refutatio et Eversio.[61] The synod reaffirmed the iconoclast council of Hieria-Blachernae (754) and annulled the act of Nicaea II (787) specifically censuring the folly of the Empress Irene and the Patriarch Tarasius. The florilegium of the iconoclast committee was read and accepted. The dogmatic Definition (Horos) drawn up by the council had a florilegium appended, but it is not clear whether this was identical with that of the committee. The

---

[57] GR 395.
[58] GR 396–7.
[59] GR 398–9.
[60] GR 400.
[61] This was to have been edited by Alexander; see Patriarch Nicephorus, 180 ff. and 242 ff. (summary of the text); see also D. Serruys, 'Les Actes du concile iconoclaste de l'année 815', Mélanges d'archéologique et d'histoire, 23 (1903), 345–51 and G. Ostrogorsky, Studien. The treatise remains unprinted.

Horos condemned the untraditional veneration and the unedifying manufacture of icons, but abstained from calling them idols, 'for there are many degrees of evil'.

This ninth-century revival of iconoclasm was in effect less harsh and uncompromising than that of Leo III and Constantine V. Unlike the council of 754 it did not introduce the argument from idolatry. But to judge from the content of Nicephorus's *Refutatio* the Christological implications raised by Constantine V were still important, since he deals with these at some length. The ninth-century iconoclasts also set store by the 'ethical theory of icons'[62] linked with the 'argument from holiness',[63] again not a new line of thought. It was maintained that the only real and living icon of the saint was the reproduction of his virtues in the soul of the individual, rather than some meaningless figure in material colours which could only express the mortal body and not the saint's real inner holiness. Dead matter could not reveal the glorious state of the saint enjoying eternal life with God. The revived iconoclasm may have provided more precise, or fuller, references for sources cited at the 754 council, but it was essentially based on the eighth-century movement.[64]

It is difficult to assess to what extent obstinate iconophiles suffered persecution in the ninth century because accounts of this derive from partisan and probably exaggerated sources, such as the *Vita Nicephori* or the letters of Theodore Studites. In the 815 council an attempt was made to win over certain orthodox bishops and when this failed they were then and there subjected to unseemly physical assault and then exiled. The ex-Patriarch Nicephorus persistently refused discussion with heretics and he remained across the Bosphorus in exile until he died in 828. He was comparatively

[62] Se M. V. Anastos 'The Ethical Theory of Images formulated by the Iconoclasts in 754 and 815', *DOP*, 8 (1954), 151–60 (reprinted Variorum, London, 1979), where he points out the derivative nature of the arguments of the 815 iconoclasts.

[63] See Alexander, *Patriarch Nicephorus*, 138 ff.

[64] Alexander began by overemphasizing the originality of the 815 council; see his 'The Iconoclast Council of 815 and its Definition', *DOP*, 7 (1953), 35–66. He subsequently modified some of his views, as he admits in his 'Church Councils and Patristic Authority: The Councils of Hiereia (754) and St Sophia (815)', *Harvard Studies in Classical Philology*, 63 (1958), 493–505. His book, though published in 1958, was apparently completed several years before this (see his preface, ix) and it does not altogether reflect his later views and his acceptance of criticism on certain points (cf. Ostrogorsky, *History*, 203, note 1).

unmolested. He stood his ground but was far less belligerent than Theodore Studites. Leo V had evidently hoped to inaugurate a policy which, though iconoclast, would make as few demands as possible upon its opponents. He did win over a substantial number of bishops, as well as abbots who were increasingly being appointed to bishoprics. Support for iconoclasm was not confined to Constantinople but ranged from Otranto in South Italy to the cities and monasteries of Asia Minor. The acceptance of iconoclasm by a number of monastic houses was in contrast to the earlier eighth-century movement. There were instances of monasteries which defected in Constantinople, on Bithynian Mount Olympus, and among the Cappadocian rock pinnacles. This may have been due to the minimal nature of the demands made. Provided that they did not teach or assemble, and accepted the Patriarch Theodotus, the monks were unmolested.

But for Theodore Studites it was an obligation to proclaim orthodox views openly, loudly, and unceasingly.[65] He and his hard core remained a constant source of irritation; hence the increasing severity of the conditions imposed on the Studite leader who was moved from prison to prison in Asia Minor. Theodore nevertheless managed to maintain an excellent system of underground communication. His letters show him encouraging his followers, lamenting desertions, rallying support from Palestinian monasteries and from the orthodox Patriarchs of Jerusalem and Alexandria (possibly also from Antioch though no letter has survived). He also did not hesitate to seek help from Rome. Here in the old capital there were Greek monasteries and Greek communities as well as a number of iconodule refugees, including the future Patriarch, Methodius. Theodore wrote both to the archimandrite of the Greek house of St Sabas and to the Pope asking for help.[66] With his excellent intelligence service he was evidently aware of proposed missions to Rome from the capital, hence his hurried approach to the Pope putting his case and possibly hoping for a formal synodal condemnation of the heresy. The banning of icon veneration and the forced resignation of Patriarch Nicephorus had created a rift between Rome and Constantinople and in keeping with his desire for unity and reconciliation Leo V also tried to win over the Pope. An

---

[65] Cf. Theodore, Ep., bk. II, no. 2, *PG* 99, cols. 1120–1.
[66] Ibid., Ep., bk. II, no. 12, *PG* 99, cols. 1152–3.

imperial embassy appears to have gone to Rome, probably with the other mission from Theodotus with the Patriarch's synodica.[67] In Theodore's second letter to the Pope he praises him for refusing to receive the Patriarch's legates (apocrisiarii) and thanks him for meeting his own two envoys, who seem to have arrived soon after the iconoclast deputation. The Emperor evidently wished to maintain that he was essentially orthodox and that the use to which icons were put was not a cause for general discussion, but a matter for each church to decide for itself. He may also have made the point that the ex-Patriarch Nicephorus had resigned of his own free will. The embassy probably went some time after the death of Pope Leo III (16 June 816) since this Pope had recognized the Patriarch Nicephorus and the orthodox Byzantine predecessors of Leo V and would hardly be sympathetic to the intruded Patriarch Theodotus and the iconoclast Emperor. The most likely time would have been the late autumn of 816 or spring of 817, that is after Stephen's short pontificate and during Pascal I's time. It was Pascal who turned down Emperor Leo's overtures, as noted in Theodore's second letter to the Pope[68] and in Pascal's own letter to Leo. He might refuse to meet the ecclesiastical envoys but he had to receive those from the Emperor, and it was to the Emperor and not to the Patriarch that a papal embassy was sent. The Patriarch Nicephorus described how the legates demanded the restoration of the icons and obstinately refused to eat at the imperial table since the heretical Byzantine churchmen were also invited.[69] The firm papal stand did not succeed in altering Leo V's policy but it did give moral support to the iconophiles and dashed any hopes that Leo might have had of a general council which would set aside Nicaea II and propound a more flexible policy with regard to the use of icons.

Leo was murdered on Christmas Day 820. His successor, Michael II, was a vigorous but uneducated soldier from Amorium in Phrygia. He tried to eliminate dissension by forbidding discussion and adopting a policy of conciliation. He recalled the iconophile exiles. Led by Theodore Studites, they still protested vehemently.

---

[67] *GR* 410, dated 815–16, but in his more recent work Grumel puts it later. On this whole question see V. Grumel, 'Les Relations politico-religieuses entre Byzance et Rome sous le règne de Léon V l'Arménien', *REB*, 18 (1960), 19–44.

[68] Ep. bk. II, no. 13, *PG* 99, cols. 1153–6; see Grumel, op. cit., pp. 32–5.

[69] *12 Chapters against the Iconoclasts*, ed. A. Mai, *Spicilegium Romanum*, vol. X, pt. 2 (Rome, 1844), p. 156, cited Grumel, op. cit. 38–9.

When they approached Michael he made it clear that they could do what they liked provided that they were outside the capital, but he himself was not prepared to venerate icons and would leave the Church as he found it. Finally, since the Emperor would not make any further concessions or consider the reappointment of Nicephorus as patriarch, there was deadlock and all further discussion on icons was prohibited.[70] As Theodore Studites remarked early on in Michael's reign, 'The winter is past, but spring has not yet come'.[71] When Theodotus died Michael chose as patriarch Antony Cassimatas (*c.* January 821) who as bishop of Syllaeum in Pamphylia had been a leading member of the commission which drew up the florilegium for the 815 synod of Hagia Sophia. The ex-Patriarch Nicephorus still stood firm or he might possibly have been reinstated as a conciliatory gesture. He won the grudging praise of his old enemy Theodore Studites and he died in exile in 828. He had made a twofold contribution to the Church, first by his moderate policy in the days of orthodoxy, and then by his steadfast opposition to heresy supported by his theological writings.[72] Theodore never really gave Nicephorus the credit due to him, whatever belated tributes he paid. He certainly recognized him as 'the true Patriarch' who had shown courageous resistance,[73] but it was not in rallying round the ex-Patriarch that he thought peace and orthodoxy would be found, but rather through the action of the Elder Rome. The old lurking mistrust between Theodore the monk and the secular clergy seemed to poison relations even in adversity. The significance of Theodore's appeals to Rome has been much debated, but it was a move which did not necessarily imply any more than the recognition of the value of support from the see which had always been accorded primacy of honour. Pope Pascal I reacted to Michael II as he had to Leo V. He sent a document defining orthodox doctrine and asking for the restoration of the Patriarch Nicephorus and of orthodoxy. His demands were refused and his legate, the Greek iconodule Methodius, was imprisoned.[74] Michael did however attempt to solicit the good offices of the western Emperor, Louis the Pious, explaining his views and asking Louis to support the

---

[70] *Vita Theodori Studitae*, ch. 60, PG 99, col. 317 and *Vita S. Nicolai Studitae*, PG 105, col. 892 B.

[71] Ep., bk. II, no. 121, PG 99, col. 1397 B.

[72] See below p. 66.

[73] Ep. bk. II, no. 1, PG 99, col. 1116 C.

[74] *Vita Methodii*, PG 100, col. 1243 ff.

Byzantine embassy which was going to Rome.[75] Louis however merely took the view of Charlemagne and the council of Frankfurt which was no help to Michael. In any case Michael had other pressing problems and could not allow the question of the icons to over-dominate his programme. Early in his reign with Bulgarian help he had successfully foiled the dangerous revolt in Asia Minor led by Thomas the Slav, joined by many dissident elements. But he had been unable to prevent the strategic islands of Crete and Sicily from falling to Muslim forces from Africa and Spain.

Michael II died in 829 leaving as his successor his son Theophilus who had been associated with him as co-Emperor from 821. Theophilus was a contrast to his father. Educated by the learned John the Grammarian (who later became Patriarch in 837), he was a cultured man, greatly attracted to Muslim civilization. As an iconoclast and an Amorian he did not receive fair appraisal in pro-Macedonian sources. Theophilus was rather more extreme than his father in his support of iconoclasm and he inflicted some cruel and much publicized punishments. But in general iconophiles could go their own way outside Constantinople. It was however significant that icon veneration evidently went on unchecked within the imperial household. Theophilus was aware of his wife Theodora's proclivities but he seems to have taken no effective steps to counter such tendencies. This was symptomatic of the general weakening of the iconoclast movement and though traces of iconoclasm probably lingered for some time there was no obstinate or widespread resistance when the death of Theophilus in 842 left a minor and a regency headed by the iconodule Empress Theodora who was bent on the restoration of orthodoxy.

4. *The restoration of orthodoxy in 843: the* Synodicon

In directing the regency for the two-year-old Michael III (842–67) his mother Theodora was assisted by a small council of which Theoctistus, the logothete of the drome, was the most influential member. Theodora's personal religious views were well known, though possibly she may have hesitated to introduce any immediate reversal of her husband's policy. Iconoclasm seemed to have been accepted in a quiet way by the army and the civil service as well as

---

[75] *DR* 408, dated 10 Apr. 824.

by many bishops and some monasteries. The able Patriarch John the Grammarian was a dedicated iconoclast. On the other hand it was likely that many who had accepted iconoclasm under pressure as a matter of expediency, particularly in its more tolerant and modified form, would be ready to reverse their allegiance. As previously, the restoration of icons was strongly supported by outstanding and powerful monastic leaders, such as Joannices, doyen of the communities on Bithynian Mount Olympus, and though Theodore Studites had died in 826 the movement had not weakened. The steps whereby orthodoxy was restored are variously described in the different sources.[76] There seemed to be two elements on the iconodule front—the regent's party and the monastic party. Theodora (no doubt fortified by Methodius) was supported by the logothete Theoctistus and possibly her uncle Manuel, her brothers Bardas and Petronas, and another relative, Sergius Nicetiates.[77] But already there could be perceived that latent antagonism between Theoctistus and Bardas which was to erupt later in the reign. Personal and political ambitions were closely interwoven with religious policy, and the underlying rift between seculars and monks and their respective partisans long remained, despite the return to orthodoxy.

It was more than a year before orthodoxy was formally restored on the first Sunday of Lent 843, to be known in future as Orthodoxy Sunday. Unlike the restoration of 787 no general council was held. After preliminary discussions, a local ecclesiastical assembly having no claim to oecumenicity met in Constantinople.[78] This took place in the Kanikleion, the palace of Theodora's minister Theoctistus. It appears to have been attended by clergy, monks, and laymen. John VII the Grammarian, who was then still Patriarch, was summoned, but refused to attend and remained entrenched in the patriarcheion. He was deposed on 3 March 843 and was only with difficulty dislodged from his apartments. His successor was Methodius (843–7), elected the next day and enthroned a week later on Sunday, 11 March 843. Methodius, for a time an iconodule refugee in Rome, had been imprisoned and ill-treated by Michael II, apparently because he happened to be the bearer of

[76] Detailed analysis in Gouillard, 'Synodikon', 120 ff.
[77] See C. Mango, 'The Liquidation of Iconoclasm and the Patriarch Photios', in *Iconoclasm*, 134.
[78] See Gouillard, 'Synodikon', 125 ff.

an unwelcome letter to the Emperor from Pope Pascal I. Theophilus later on had somewhat inconsistently restored him to favour, iconophile though he was. Theophilus admired his learning and allowed him to live in the imperial palace.[79]

There are few details on the procedure of the council of 843. The acta are not extant and it is doubtful whether documents can be assigned to this council.[80] There appeared to be general agreement on the confirmation of Nicaea II and the restoration of the icons, and florilegia supporting the traditional veneration were at hand. The only obstacle, according to a persistent tradition, which may or may not be legendary, was the Empress Theodora's desire to avoid any slight on her husband's memory. Various devices to get round this problem are recorded, ranging from a supposed deathbed repentance to Theophilus' appearance in a dream to one Symeon appealing from the next world for mercy. If Theodora did press this point it is easy to appreciate at least one of her motives: she desired to remove any taint of heresy from the father of her son, the reigning Emperor. It may have been for this reason that, though in practice an iconodule, she was, as Bury thought, hesitant about overturning iconoclasm. Bury considered that the sources suggested Theoctistus, possibly with the magister Manuel, as the driving force.[81] In the event, there was no mention of Theophilus: the iconoclast councils were abrogated and Nicaea II restored.

The first formal celebration of the return to orthodoxy took place on the day of Methodius's enthronement, the first Sunday of Lent, 11 March 843, and there are varying accounts as to what happened on this occasion. In the tenth-century *De Cerimoniis* of Constantine VII protocol was described 'as it used to be', and then 'as it is now'. In the first part of the ceremony no change is noted and this account may well represent what actually occurred in 843. 'On the Saturday evening the Patriarch goes to the church of the all-holy Theotokos in Blachernae. And with him are the metropolitans, archbishops and bishops who happen to be in the City then, as well as the clergy of the Great Church and of the churches outside,

---

[79] On his ability, good judgement, and eloquence see *Vita Methodii*, PG 100, col. 1253 B.

[80] Cf. Beck, *Kirche*, 56 with his three possible documents (his 'vielleicht' is however a very shaky one) and GR 416–17; Gouillard, *BZ*, 51 (1958) 404, regards GR 417 as suspect.

[81] Bury, *Eastern Roman Empire*, 145–6.

together with all those leading the solitary monastic life within the God-guarded City, and all those who are to celebrate the mid-night office in the holy church.' The next day the Patriarch and all with him leave the church which was situated near the north-west land walls and process through the city to Hagia Sophia on the eastern side. There they would meet (on this first occasion) the Empress Theodora and the little Emperor and the court who enter the church from the palace.[82] Then the festival is celebrated, the statement read out with its anathemas and also its remembrances for the orthodox dead and its acclamations for the orthodox living.[83] Afterwards Theodora gave a banquet, but, as the *De Cerimoniis* recounts, this subsequently became the privilege of the Patriarch.

The core of the Synodicon was probably written by Methodius for the first anniversary of the event.[84] The commemoration appears to have taken definite shape by the last quarter of the ninth century at latest. It is attested for the year 899 in the *Cletorologion* of Philotheus and by then had become part of the annual liturgical cycle. Its place in the office varies: for instance, it might be proclaimed from the ambo before or after the Epistle during the Divine Liturgy, or during or after Orthros.[85] As the festival of Orthodoxy took root throughout the Empire many variant practices arose and many different recensions, according to the individual needs of the Great Church in the capital or the smaller churches in the provinces. Further, as later generations met new problems of heresy, the original Synodicon had to be expanded to deal with these. So there came into existence the three main groups described as the Macedonian, the Comnenian, and the Palaeologan versions.[86] In this way the Synodicon became a living witness to the orthodox life of the Church.

5. *The significance of the controversy over icons*

The controversy itself was by no means a frustrating waste of time. it did at least clarify certain issues and it stimulated lively discussion

---

[82] *De Cerimoniis*, CB, I, bk. 1, ch. 28, pp. 156 ff. (= Vogt, vol. I, bk. I, ch. 37, pp. 145 ff.).
[83] See Gouillard, 'Synodikon', 93 and 97.
[84] Ibid. 158.
[85] Ibid. 13 ff. On the office of Orthros see below pp. 351 ff.
[86] Ibid. 3 ff.

on a subject which was to be of importance in Orthodox church life. As the support for the icons moved from Germanus and John of Damascus's traditional defence to the Christological challenge of Constantine V's reign, and then to the more 'scholastic' approach of Theodore Studites and Patriarch Nicephorus,[87] there was an increasing emphasis on the meaning of the Incarnation in relation to the Christian view of matter and it was not without a struggle that this was given its true value (monastic spirituality had to face the same problem). Moreover the quality of the protagonists, for instance men such as Theodore Studites or Nicephorus who had their roots in the eighth century, bore witness to the availability of educational opportunities at that time.[88]

It is often maintained that monastic opposition formed the backbone of the iconodule opposition and was henceforth a strong element in public life. It certainly had outspoken leadership and both Theodore Studites and John of Damascus protested against imperial interference in ecclesiastical affairs. Certain centres, notably the communities on Bithynian Mount Olympus and in the Studite house in Constantinople, offered recognized resistance. But some houses appear to have swum with the tide. The strengthening of widespread monastic influence on the actual policy of the Byzantine state really took place rather later, after the development of the powerful houses on Mount Athos and particularly as the state weakened after 1204. Probably the guidance of Theodore Studites in the conduct of monastic life was a more important factor in the development of monasticism than in the actual iconoclast controversy. This is not to deny the influence of the individual holy man at all times as a potent but occasional factor, or the temporary troubles caused by mobs of monks liable to gather in the capital and whip up trouble at times of crisis. Nor is it to detract from the varied contributions made by monastic houses in the daily life which went on after the controversy as it had done before: this was not an effect of iconoclasm. As far as the iconoclast controversy is concerned it is in fact almost impossible to identify classes or territorial regions which were consistently for or against.[89] For the ordinary man much depended on the lead given by the ruling power of the

[87] Alexander, *Patriarch Nicephorus*, especially ch. 8.
[88] Lemerle, *Humanisme byzantin*, 130 ff. and 302 ff.
[89] Cf. H. Ahrweiler, 'The Geography of the Iconoclast World', in *Iconoclasm*, 21–7.

moment, and for the soldier the success or otherwise of military leadership was the telling factor.

In matters concerning Rome and the West it was not iconoclasm which was the primary factor in loosening ties with the papacy or provoking the imperial pretensions of the Carolingian rulers. Here a far more important part was played by political factors, though an exception might be made for the transference of ecclesiastical jurisdiction over South Italy, Sicily, and part of the Balkans to the patriarchate of Constantinople in so far as it was provoked by religious difference between an iconoclast Emperor and an iconophile Rome. This action was certainly an abiding irritant in papal and Byzantine relations, but it was in no sense responsible for anything approaching a rift. This was yet to come.

The most important and permanent result of the controversy was the firm establishment of icons in the daily life of the orthodox. But at first it was only gradually that they were restored to full use in churches. On 29 May 867 when Photius preached in Hagia Sophia to inaugurate the mosaic of the Theotokos and Child he made it clear that this was the first icon to replace those which had been 'scraped off' the walls, though it is known that at least some had already been placed in certain imperial buildings.[90] During the later ninth century literary evidence testifies to the splendour of the new figural decoration. An epigram in the Greek Anthology praises the glories of the figures in the Chrysotriclinus in the imperial palace. 'The ray of truth is radiant once more . . . For see how once again Christ in his icon shines above the ruler's thrones and drives out dark heresies. Above the entrance the Theotokos rises up like a divine gate and guardian. Near her are the ruler and the patriarch who with her help have put an end to heresy.'[91] The Empress Theodora was no longer in power and therefore did not stand with Michael III and Patriarch Methodius. Thus the iconophile victory certainly gave a stimulus to religious art, though it must be remembered that the iconoclast period was by no means devoid of art, but it made use of it in a different way and with a different purpose.[92] Now with Nicaea II icons became a regulated part of

[90] C. Mango, *The Homilies of Photius Patriarch of Constantinople* (Cambridge: Mass., 1958), Homily 17, ch. 4, pp. 283 and 291.

[91] *Anthologia Palatina*, I, no. 106, pp. 12–13 (Paris, 1864).

[92] See A. Grabar, *Iconoclasme*, particularly on the use of art by the iconoclast Emperors and earlier.

liturgical and architectural developments. So there came into being an accepted iconography which laid down the pattern of ecclesiastical representation (though not to the exclusion of other styles elsewhere, both classical and realist, and for different purposes). Such figural representation was usually either in mosaic, or, especially as expense became a factor, in fresco.

These icons in churches and monasteries, as well as those in private devotional use, had a sacramental value to the beholder. They were held to be possessed of special graces. Their presence stressed the strongly held belief in the sanctity of matter, a belief that found its fulfilment in theosis or the deification of human beings. In his three apologies on the divine icons John of Damascus wrote 'I worship the Creator of matter who became matter for my sake, who was willing to dwell in matter, who worked out my salvation through matter';[93] and 'Although the mind wears itself out with its efforts it can never cast away its bodily nature (τὰ σωματικά).[94] This was a conception not unknown in the West (and found in writings ranging from St Augustine to Teilhard de Chardin), but in general it was not so much emphasized by western modes of thought. This may be one reason why icons never played so powerful a role in Latin worship as in that of the Orthodox Churches, nor was deification generally so stressed in the West.

[93] John of Damascus, *De Imaginibus Orationes*, I, ch. 16, *PG* 94, col. 1245 A; ed. Kotter, III. 89.
[94] Ibid., II, ch. 5, col. 1288 B; ed. Kotter, III. 72.

III

THE AGE OF PHOTIUS (843–886)

1. Patriarch Methodius (843–847):
the first patriarchate of Ignatius (847–858)

Methodius was faced with the problem caused by those who had lapsed during the second period of iconoclasm. Here he began by acting with some severity. He deposed those bishops who had returned to iconoclasm under Leo the Armenian and his successors and likewise all who had been ordained by such bishops after their lapse.[1] At the same time he had to provide the Church with an adequate episcopate in order to ensure the continuity of its daily life. He evidently had difficulty in finding sufficient candidates of moderate outlook who could satisfy all the canonical requirements and in some cases he appears to have relaxed these, thus incurring the criticism of his extremist opponents. A policy of this kind, regarded by Methodius as being in the best interests of the Church, inevitably roused the rigorist monastic element whose firm antagonism to any kind of *oeconomia* was accompanied by an equally firm conviction that they were called upon to play a leading, even a decisive, role in ecclesiastical affairs. They no doubt felt that they themselves could provide excellent candidates better fitted for episcopal office. The acute difficulties experienced by Methodius are reflected in his unhappy relations with the followers of Theodore Studites during the years 845–6. Certain bishops and abbots in the extremist party evidently voiced publicly their criticism of the Patriarch's appointments and were penalized for this.[2] Methodius then asked the Studites to repudiate Theodore's writings against the Patriarchs Tarasius and Nicephorus and their policy of compromise, as indeed Theodore himself in the end seems to have done. They refused. They were therefore anathematized, and possibly cursed (the formal ecclesiastical *katathema*). It was pointed out that the fourth canon of Chalcedon required monks to live apart from the

---

[1] GR 422, spring or summer 843
[2] GR 433.

world and to refrain from meddling in ecclesiastical or temporal affairs.[3] A schism resulted.

This action was apparently still unresolved at Methodius's death, even though just before he died the Patriarch tried to make his peace with the recalcitrant monks. He explicitly stated in his testament that he forgave those who had flouted the patriarchal authority and he desired to receive them back into the Church, but again only on condition that they repudiated Theodore Studites' criticism of Tarasius and Nicephorus.[4] Methodius, like his more moderate predecessors, had had to face the growing challenge, not so much of the authority of the isolated holy man, but of an increasingly powerful monastic party. These monks regarded themselves as the guardians of the Orthodox faith and as watch-dogs to ensure the rigorous observance of canon law. This was an element that was to persist within the Byzantine polity. Originally led by the Studites, in the later middle ages this movement was to some extent centred in the monastic communities of Mount Athos. It was not always victorious, but it could certainly not be ignored.

On Methodius's death both the monastic party and their opponents had their candidates. The choice rested with the Empress Theodora who opted for Ignatius, a son of the Emperor Michael I Rangabe. From an early age Ignatius had been a monk and at the time of his election was abbot of a house on one of the Princes Islands. Theodora did not however observe the normal procedure of receiving from the synod three nominations from which to select and to this extent Ignatius's election might be considered irregular. Though a monk, Ignatius had not so far shown himself to be a strong Studite partisan and it might have been hoped that he would take a midway stance and conciliate the two opposing parties. But this was not so. Ignatius proved to be neither wise nor tactful. He was drawn into the monastic party and at the same time also became involved in imperial politics on the side of the Empress Theodora whose authority was being challenged by her brother Bardas and the young Emperor Michael III. Ignatius's anti-Methodian feelings were evidenced by his public and ill-judged antagonism towards the friend of Methodius, the Sicilian Gregory Asbestas, archbishop of Syracuse. Gregory had been accused of canonical irregularity in

[3] *GR* 429 and 434.
[4] *GR* 436, with a discussion of the motives underlying the schism; cf. Dvornik, *Photian Schism*, 15.

consecrating the bishop of Taormina and his case was still *sub judice*. It was possibly for this reason that Ignatius declared that his status was suspended, but this is not clear.[5] When Gregory took his place in the procession at the patriarchal enthronement in Hagia Sophia Ignatius told him that he had no right to be there and with such rudeness that Gregory flung out in a rage, declaring that the Church had been given a wolf instead of a pastor. He was followed by some of his supporters. Gregory and two of his friends were subsequently condemned, possibly for continued opposition to Ignatius, and they were deposed by the Constantinopolitan synod,[6] whereupon both sides appealed to Rome. Evidence on both the cause and the sequence of events in this episode seems conflicting, but there can be no doubt that the Methodians and the Ignatians were now bitterly opposed.[7]

Ignatius's own downfall was closely related to the fate of his supporter, the Empress Theodora. In 856 she was displaced and her chief minister, the logothete Theoctistus, was assassinated. Her son, Michael III, was declared of age and her brother, the influential Bardas, took control. He was a cultivated, urbane, and ambitious man, the very antithesis of Ignatius, the monk who despised secular learning. Ignatius, no doubt aware of Bardas's scorn of him, unwisely tried to undermine his authority by bringing various apparently unproved charges against him, including incest. In late 857 or early 858 he forbade him to enter Hagia Sophia for the usual Epiphany services.[8] Further, he refused to support the Empress Theodora's forced entry into monastic life. In 858 it was said that he had been involved in an anti-Bardas plot. For this alleged treason he was exiled to Terebinthus, an island two miles east of Principo in the sea of Marmora.

Negotiations, and almost certainly some pressure, resulted in Ignatius's resignation,[9] but only on terms[10] which were interpreted by the Ignatians as implying that the new Patriarch would not

[5] GR 445, end of 847 or first quarter of 848; Dvornik, *Photian Schism*, 19 ff. with reason suggests a later date.

[6] See P. Karlin-Hayter, 'Gregory of Syracuse, Ignatios and Photios', in *Iconoclasm*, 141 ff.

[7] On the various ambiguities of this episode see Dvornik, *Photian Schism*, 18 ff.

[8] GR 449.

[9] GR 455 with a discussion of the conflicting evidence on the nature of the resignation.

[10] GR 456.

repudiate any of Ignatius's patriarchal actions and would remain in communion with him. This would mean in practice the recognition of the legitimacy of Ignatius's ordinations, despite the irregularity of his election, and might be supposed to include approval of his pro-monastic policy, in so far as this had favoured the extremists. The new Patriarch, Photius, appears to have agreed to certain conditions and he was enthroned some time before 25 December 858.

2. Photius's first patriarchate (858–867)

The protoasecretis Photius was a layman and civil servant at the head of the imperial chancery. His father was related to Patriarch Tarasius and he himself may have been connected by marriage with the ruling house. He also had a well-founded reputation as one of the leading scholars of his day which was likely to commend him to Bardas. His lay status was not necessarily a bar to his rapid elevation to the patriarchate since there was precedent for ecclesiastical dispensation on this point, as in the earlier case of Tarasius. After being tonsured, Photius was quickly ordained reader, subdeacon, deacon, and priest, in time to be enthroned just before the Christmas festivities. He was certainly not the kind of man to be a puppet in the hands of the Ignatian party and at the outset he plainly indicated his attitude by appointing Gregory Asbestas to be one of his consecrating bishops, even though Gregory's case was still being considered by Rome (to whom he had appealed when he was condemned by the Ignatian synod). The Ignatians were clearly disappointed and friction was further aggravated by considerable misunderstanding as to the interpretation of the conditions agreed to by Photius in return for Ignatius's retirement. They evidently expected Photius to follow their line of policy and to do nothing which Ignatius (and by implication his followers) did not approve, treating Ignatius as if he was 'his own father'.[11] They therefore claimed that Photius had broken his word. They were also pro-Theodora and hostile to the new regime which accounted for the severity (unjustly attributed to Photius) with which some of them were treated by the government. The refusal to acknowledge Photius soon came to a head when a meeting was held by the rebels in the church of St Irene. Here Photius was declared deposed and

[11] Theognostus, *Libellus* to Nicholas I, Mansi, XVI. 300, cited Dvornik, *Photian Schism*, 54.

Ignatius restored as legitimate Patriarch. Shortly afterwards in the early spring of 859 Photius retaliated by calling a synod of bishops in the church of the Holy Apostles. In the presence of 170 bishops Ignatius was declared deposed.[12] Certain of the extremist leaders, including Metrophanes of Smyrna and Antony of Cyzicus, were also removed from office, possibly at the same synod.[13]

Photius then prepared to consolidate his position. He sent to Rome the customary letter announcing his enthronement and containing his profession of faith (his synodica).[14] This also went as usual to the eastern patriarchates of Alexandria, Antioch, and Jerusalem.[15] In this he mentioned in discrete terms the 'retirement' or 'departure' of Ignatius,[16] and pointed out that he himself had been raised to his high office somewhat against his will. At the same time Michael III wrote to the Pope asking for legates to be sent to a council to be held in Constantinople, ostensibly to clear up iconoclasm but in reality to confirm Ignatius's deposition. In his reply to Michael III Pope Nicholas I stressed his surprise that he had not been consulted in the affair of the Patriarch Ignatius whom Michael had reported as having already given up his see of his own free will. He was therefore charging his legates, Radoald bishop of Porto and Zacharias bishop of Anagni, with the task of looking into, rather than merely confirming, Ignatius's resignation. The Pope added that his two legates were to make a careful enquiry in the synod which was to be held as to whether canonical procedure had been observed and were to report to him. He would then give his apostolic pronouncement as to the best course of action for the Church of Constantinople. This was an approach that was hardly likely to be acceptable to the Byzantines, implying as it did that the deposition of Ignatius was not necessarily valid. Further, Nicholas made what was by now becoming a perennial papal demand. He asked for the restoration of the lost papal jurisdiction in Illyricum (that is, most of the Balkans) with its vicariate in Thessalonica, as well as the return of its patrimonies in Sicily and Calabria.[17] This

---

[12] GR 459.
[13] GR 460.
[14] GR 464.
[15] GR 465.
[16] GR 464; ὑπεξελθόντος, PG 102, Ep., bk. I, no. 1, col. 588 C.
[17] Nicholas's first letter to Michael III, 25 Sept. 860, MGH, Ep., VI, no. 82, pp. 433–9, French trans. in Stiernon, 249–53.

insistence on Rome's claim to jurisdiction in Illyricum was no doubt all the more urgent now in view of the growing rivalry between the Roman and Byzantine Churches over responsibility for the conversion to Christianity of the young Bulgarian principality. A letter was also sent to Photius in which the Pope reproached him for his rapid and uncanonical ascent through the clerical grades. For this reason he wrote that he could not at once confirm Photius's consecration as patriarch, but if his legates reported favourably on the ecclesiastical situation in Constantinople he hoped then to be able to honour him as befitted the prelate of so great a see.[18] Thus in this letter too Nicholas implied that he had the right to the final decision, though he carefully left his options open.

The papal legates duly reached Constantinople and the council, presided over by the Emperor in its first session, was held in the church of the Holy Apostles in April 861. The records of its proceedings are incomplete because the acta were destroyed by the pro-Ignatian council of 869–70 and what has survived comes from a Latin extract in the canonical collection of Cardinal Deusdedit. This can be supplemented by material from Ignatius's partisans even though this is rather one-sided and in any case probably represents 'Ignatian' policy rather than the views of Ignatius himself. At the council Ignatius was declared rightly deposed because he had been appointed by a secular ruler thus infringing 'Apostolic' canon 30 (= 29).[19] The Roman legates formally approved the deposition. This was not what Nicholas I had intended. The legates however were under considerable pressure in Constantinople and the Byzantines had indeed only agreed to bring up the case again on the understanding that a final decision would be given and the matter not referred back to the Pope for his ruling. But at least the legates had asserted the Roman right to intervene in a matter of this kind.

At some time after the deposition of Ignatius, the council of 861, at which the Roman legates were still present, registered its condemnation of the iconoclast heresy. This was a problem which had been specifically mentioned in the letters of Michael III and Photius to Nicholas I. Opinions vary on the importance which should be attached to this. It may have been a diversionary move by

[18] *MGH*, Ep., VI, no. 83, pp. 439–40; French trans. in Stiernon, 253–4.
[19] *GR* 466.

Photius, but even so it is reasonable to suppose with Dvornik that the heresy had not disappeared overnight in 843.[20] Another topic considered before the legates left Constantinople in September 861 concerned monastic and episcopal abuses. These are dealt with in 17 disciplinary canons signed by 130 bishops.[21] They included a ruling which would make it impossible in future for a layman or monk to pass *per saltum* to the episcopacy, as Photius and others before him had done.[22]

After the council letters were sent to the Pope by Photius[23] and by Michael III with the acta of the 861 council.[24] Photius's apologia was a moving appeal for charity and understanding. He contrasted the idyllic tranquillity of his life as a scholar and tutor with the troubles which he knew would beset him if he became patriarch. Hence his reluctance to accept this office. He defended himself from the charge of having violated canonical procedure by his rapid ascent from lay status to the episcopate, since the canons of Sardica forbidding this were not recognized by the Byzantine Church. He pointed out that it was indeed quite legitimate for the two Churches to maintain traditions which differed in discipline and rite. He did however add that the 861 council had now decided that in future Constantinople would adopt the Roman usage on the particular point at issue. The problem of rooting out iconoclasm was referred to. Then—most important of all both to the papacy and to Byzantium—Photius broached the question of papal jurisdiction in Illyricum. He affirmed that he himself would willingly have acceded to Rome's demands, but ecclesiastical affairs involving imperial territory were matters of state outside his competence. Finally, the Pope was asked not to give credence to those who came from Constantinople without patriarchal letters of introduction, since under pretence of being on pilgrimage to Rome such people were in fact only interested in stirring up trouble. This last was an attempt to counter the intrigues of the Ignatians, notably abbot

[20] See Dvornik, *Photian Schism*, *passim* and 'The Patriarch Photius and Iconoclasm', *DOP*, 7 (1953), 69 ff.; and cf. C. Mango, 'The liquidation of iconoclasm and the Patriarch Photios', in *Iconoclasm*, 133 ff.

[21] *GR* 468.

[22] *GR* 468, 17.

[23] *GR* 469, Aug. or Sept. 861; *PG* 102, Ep., bk. I, no. 2, pp. 593–617; French trans. by Stiernon, 254–8.

[24] *DR* 460 (*c*.Aug. 861; partial reconstruction from Nicholas I's letters).

Theognostus who was only too likely to engage in anti-Photian propaganda in Rome.

However clearly he might profess his own willingness to meet Nicholas's demands, Photius knew very well that there was no possibility of imperial concessions in the question of papal authority in the Balkans. The Byzantine ambassador Leo who brought the imperial letter to Rome must have made this clear and it is probably the reason why Nicholas I changed his ground between the autumn of 861 and the spring of 862. Thus in letters of 18 March 862 to Photius[25] and Michael III[26] he repudiated his legates' action in deposing Ignatius at the council of 861 and he declared that the case was still open. Meanwhile in view of this he could not recognize Photius, though he did not rule out the possibility of this later on, should he find that Ignatius had been rightly condemned. At the same time he went even further in a letter to the three eastern patriarchs, Alexandria, Antioch, and Jerusalem,[27] calling Photius a most wicked intruder. He made it clear that by reason of his position in Christendom the final decision was his alone. As Photius had foreseen, the situation may well have been aggravated by the arrival in Rome of the pro-Ignatian abbot Theognostus to present a *Libellus* to the Pope on Ignatius's behalf, though at the council of 861 Ignatius himself had expressly refused to appeal to the papacy.

In the event, a council was held in Rome, either in April or possibly during the summer, 863. Ignatius was declared to be still the legitimate Patriarch and Photius was deprived of his title and degraded to lay status; Gregory Asbestas was likewise degraded. The papal legates were declared to have exceeded their mandate at the council of 861. The legate Zacharias of Anagni, who was at hand, was deposed and excommunicated. Radoald was out of reach in Frankish territory. Then there was a brief reference to the traditional use of icons, but no mention of the council of Nicaea II. It was made clear that the holy apostolic see reserved to itself the right of final judgement.[28] Nicholas evidently expected that if he

---

[25] *MGH*, Ep., VI, no. 86, pp. 447–51.
[26] *MGH*, Ep, VI, no. 85, pp. 442–6, French trans. in Stiernon, 258–61.
[27] *MGH*, Ep., VI, no. 84, pp. 440–2.
[28] On the council see *MGH*, Ep., VI, no. 91, pp. 517–23 and no. 98, pp. 556–61.

backed Ignatius he would in return get control over Bulgaria, as the papacy later admitted.[29]

But the Byzantines made no concessions to Rome. They went ahead with an attack on Bulgaria thus inducing the khan Boris to capitulate and receive baptism at the hands of the Greeks in 864. When Michael III did write to Nicholas I in the late summer of 865 he firmly denied Nicholas's right to intervene in the internal affairs of the Byzantine Church and he asked for the return of the pro-Ignatian monks who had given Rome such false information. He pointed out that the retrial of Ignatius by the papal legates in Constantinople had been (as was asserted at the time) merely out of courtesy to the Pope. This letter is not extant but it can be reconstructed from the Pope's answer. It evidently caused offence by its aggressive tone; Michael even attacked the Latin language as 'barbaram et scythicam'.[30] Nicholas's reply (28 September 865)[31] defended the papal primacy, as Gelasius I and Leo I had done before him, stressing that Rome, unlike Constantinople, had an unassailable apostolic tradition. He even said that only the Pope could summon a council, which was against accepted Byzantine usage. Nevertheless, as a conciliatory gesture, Nicholas expressed his willingness to reconsider the rival claims of Ignatius and Photius and they were invited to come to Rome themselves, or to send proxies for this purpose.

While this letter was on its way to Constantinople the newly converted Bulgarian Boris (now baptized 'Michael', with Michael III as his godfather) was pressing Constantinople to grant him a patriarch for his Church. When he failed to get his way, he turned to Rome (August 866) and Nicholas seized the opportunity. He did not provide the desired Patriarch, but he dealt adroitly with Bulgarian religious problems in such a way as to belittle Byzantine ecclesiastical usage and status.[32] Consequently Boris then turned to the Latin Church.

Enraged by Nicholas's policy Photius and Michael III were in no mood to consider any of the Pope's proposals. Photius set about

---

[29] *MGH*, Ep., VII, nos. 37–40, pp. 294–6.
[30] *MGH*, Ep., VI, no. 88, p. 459.
[31] Ibid. 454–87; French trans. H. Rahner, *L'Eglise et l'Etat* ... (Paris, 1964), 338–61. Nicholas was ill at the time so this long letter may owe something to his secretary, Anastasius the Librarian.
[32] On the Pope's *Responsa ad Consulta Bulgarorum* see below, ch. IV, section 6.

defending his Church's discipline and usage from the criticisms made by the Pope and by the western missionaries in Bulgaria. On one particular point he opened the way to future trouble in Byzantino-papal relations. Western Frankish missionaries in Bulgaria had introduced the creed with the addition of the filioque. This was a western innovation and was not sanctioned by any general council, nor was it at that time papal usage. It was attacked by Photius who went as far as to mention that it was heretical since to make the Holy Spirit proceed from both the Father and the Son was to admit of two principles. This was all set out at length in an encyclical to the eastern patriarchs.[33] They were invited to send representatives to Constantinople to deal with the troubled situation. The detailed criticisms of Latin theology contained in this letter were to feature constantly in future polemic between Rome and Constantinople.

Photius then held a synod about which there is little detailed information. It is however clear that Nicholas I was deposed and anathematized.[34] Both before and after the council Photius had approached the Frankish ruler Louis II and his wife asking for support against Nicholas[35] and evidently their reward was to be Byzantine recognition of the western imperial title. In making this move, and indeed throughout, Photius must have had the support of Michael III and the issues were never purely ecclesiastical but had strong political undertones. The target was Pope Nicholas, not the Latin Church as a whole which Nicholas seemed to imply when he appealed to Hincmar of Rheims to mobilize western help against Byzantium.[36] Nicholas himself died on 13 November 867 before the news of his deposition by the Byzantine synod reached Rome. In any case the deposition was an unwise move and one of Photius's few errors of judgement. It roused the enmity of Rome and made reconciliation more difficult. Of more immediate importance for Photius was the fact that it played into the hands of Basil the Macedonian, the favourite of Michael III and by now co-Emperor. He assassinated Michael on 23–4 September 867. Bardas, another of Photius's supporters had already been killed on 21 April 866. The

---

[33] *GR* 481, spring or summer 867.
[34] *GR* 482 (Aug. or Sept. before 24 Sept. 867).
[35] *GR* 479 (beginning of 867) and *GR* 483 (Sept., before 24 Sept. 867).
[36] *MGH*, Ep., VI, no. 100, pp. 600–9.

new Emperor needed recognition and was ready to sacrifice Photius to the Ignatians and the papacy.

3. Ignatius's second patriarchate (867–877): the council of Constantinople (869–870)

In Basil I's day (as indeed at other times) there was certainly a dividing line between the monastic point of view and the liberal and humanist outlook of a man such as Photius, but it is probably misleading to speak of an 'extremist' and a 'moderate' party.[37] Much was determined by opportunist political aims and personal expediency, though not necessarily to the exclusion of the needs of the Byzantine Church. Basil, who had attained the throne through certainly one, and probably two murders, needed to strengthen his position. He was well aware that he had participated in the council of 867 which had taken the extreme step of deposing Pope Nicholas I. He therefore hastened to rectify this by denouncing Photius and recalling Ignatius who was reinstalled on 23 November 867. Imperial letters were promptly dispatched to Rome. The first letter appears to have been lost, but is referred to in the second letter of 11 December 867.[38] In these letters Basil deplored the state of the Byzantine Church and explained that this was due to the iniquities of Photius. He asked the Pope to set matters right. He hoped for the recognition of Ignatius's legitimate claim to the patriarchate and for the repudiation of the 867 and certain earlier synods. In the case of Photius's ordinations, he made a special plea for leniency in dealing with clerics who had offended but later repented. Basil had no option but to replace Photius if he wanted papal support. But obviously he had no wish to perpetuate a discontented clerical party in opposition or to ignore the need for an adequate supply of clergy. At the same time Ignatius sent a letter to the Pope asking for a ruling on the pressing question of the Photian clergy.[39] Both Ignatius and Photius also sent representatives to put their respective cases (as Nicholas I had already suggested), though in the case of Photius this could only be a formality. Basil asked in his letter that legates should

---

[37] Dvornik, *Photian Schism*, uses these rather misleading terms very freely, as do other historians.

[38] DR 474 (no mention of first letter); French trans. of second letter in Stiernon, 261–3.

[39] GR 499.

be sent to Constantinople to report on the papal investigation, for he planned to hold a council there. In December 867 an invitation to attend was sent to Jerusalem.[40] The locum tenens of Antioch was included in this letter, and presumably Alexandria was also informed since its representatives turned up in time for the ninth session.

Pope Nicholas I had been succeeded by the benevolent elderly Hadrian II (867–72). It was therefore under Hadrian that the enquiry took place at St Peter's in Rome on 10 June 869 when a synod was held which condemned the Photian council of 867. It deposed clergy ordained by Photius and would only recognize Ignatian bishops who had subsequently supported Photius if they signed a statement (*Libellus satisfactionis*) anathematizing all heresies, as well as Photius and his activities, and specifically recognizing the authority of the apostolic see[41]

In the autumn of 869 the papal decisions and the *Libellus* were taken to Constantinople by the Roman legates, Donatus, bishop of Ostia, Stephen, bishop of Nepi, and the deacon Marinus. The council met in the spacious galleries of Hagia Sophia and was presided over by the imperial representative, the patrician Baanes, as custom demanded, not by the Roman legates as the Pope had intended. Significantly only five metropolitans and seven bishops came to the first session, and even by the tenth and last session there were only about 103 present. As the legates pressed home Hadrian's unpalatable demands, Basil's conciliatory attitude rapidly changed to hostility. He was supported by the clergy who found the contents of the *Libellus* very hard to swallow; some refused outright to sign and many boycotted the council.

The strong Photian party felt itself hardly done by; even if its members submitted and did penance they were then only to be admitted to communion as laity. Further their condemnation was presented by the papal legates as a *fait accompli*. Even Basil objected to this and insisted that Photius be heard. In fact Photius was given the opportunity of appearing before the council. He was pressed to do so and came reluctantly on 20 and 29 October[42] but he refused to plead saying that his kingdom was not of this world. He and his followers were formally excommunicated in the seventh session and

[40] GR 500.
[41] Mansi, XVI. 27–8; French trans. in Stiernon, 270–2.
[42] Mansi, XVI. 75–81 and 97; French trans. in Stiernon, 272–6 and 277–8.

the offending Photian *acta* were burnt in a copper bowl at the eighth session.

Between the eighth and last sessions there was a long and unexplained gap (5 November 869–12 February 870). Apart from the imposition of penalties in the Ignatian–Photian controversy, a number of other canons were drawn up and approved at the tenth and last session at which the Emperor presided.[43] These mainly dealt with abuses of a disciplinary or administrative nature. There was also a clear statement on the inviolable position in the Church of the five patriarchates, the pentarchy of Rome, Constantinople, Alexandria, Antioch, and Jerusalem, in that order, with primacy of honour to the Elder Rome (can. 21), and a warning about lay interference in higher ecclesiastical elections, though with a loophole making possible normal Byzantine procedure in this respect (can. 22).

Throughout this council the growing antagonism between Rome and Constantinople was very near the surface. The *Libellus* was particularly resented. An attempt was even made surreptitiously to get back the bishops' signed statements from the Roman legates' rooms in the capital. Possibly the noticeably high-handed behaviour of the legates was due to their fear of deviating in any way from papal instructions, mindful of the fate of the more pliable legates Radoald and Zacharias on an earlier occasion.

The situation could hardly have been eased by the arrival of a Bulgarian embassy during the last session of the council. The Bulgarian ruler Boris wished to bring up once more the question of his ecclesiastical allegiance—was it to Rome or to Constantinople? The immediate problem had arisen because Rome had refused to grant him the archbishop of his choice, namely, the Latin Formosus. This clearly created an opportunity for Constantinople. A separate meeting was held under the Emperor's chairmanship. The matter was to be decided by the oriental patriarchs, to the fury of the papal legates. As might have been foreseen, the verdict was in favour of the patriarchate of Constantinople.[44] A momentous but not unreasonable decision.[45] The Roman legates however then produced a papal letter to Ignatius forbidding him any share in Bulgarian ecclesiastical affairs. The papal claims were later emphasized by

[43] GR 502; Mansi, XVI. 397–406; French trans. in Stiernon, 278–99.
[44] DR 486.
[45] See also below, p. 99.

Pope John VIII in a letter to Boris,[46] avowing that Bulgaria was within Roman ecclesiastical jurisdiction, threatening to excommunicate Ignatius if he persisted in intruding and implying that his recognition had been conditional on non-interference in Bulgaria.

During the years of Ignatius's second patriarchate relations between Rome and Constantinople were scarcely more harmonious than under Photius. Ignatius was in difficulties because of lack of clergy, since so many pro-Photians had been put out of action. Both Ignatius and Basil wrote to Hadrian asking for some relaxation of the penalties imposed on Photian clergy, but without success.[47] Rivalry over the Bulgarian Church was proving a constant irritant and it was hardly edifying for the new converts to see Greek and Latin missionaries literally chasing each other out of the country.[48] By reason of scarcity of approved men, Ignatius seemed to have been driven to send clergy ordained by Photius to Bulgaria, which was an added papal grievance against him. Both Hadrian II and John VIII (872–82) threatened Ignatius on this score and also complained to the Emperor and to Boris but without result.[49] A further problem was posed within the Byzantine Empire by the strength of the pro-Photian party. It was clear that some *modus vivendi* must be devised in order to avoid a continuing split within the Greek Church. Following the council of 869–70 the offending clergy had had a hard time. Photius was exiled to a monastery near the Bosphorus where he lamented his difficulties and particularly the lack of access to his books. But gradually a blind eye was turned on the conciliar condemnation. Photius was recalled and became tutor to Basil's sons. His condemnation by Hadrian II and the 869–70 council was ignored, and in any case Ignatius himself was hardly on very good terms with Rome. Photius's reconciliation with Ignatius followed some time after 872, possibly in 876. There are various accounts of this, describing Photius's frequent visits to Ignatius who was now old and ill. In the funeral oration on his father Basil I, Leo VI emphasized the disastrous impact which the schism had made on the Church, and he even spoke of the whole Church being in exile with its archbishop before the recall of Photius and the end of dissension and the holy kiss of peace.[50]

[46] *MGH*, Ep., VII, no. 7, p. 277 (between Dec. 872 and May 873).
[47] GR 504; DR 488.
[48] Cf. GR 505.
[49] GR 504; DR 488.
[50] A. Vogt–I. Hausherr, 'L'Oraison funèbre de Basile Iᵉʳ', *Orientalia Christiana*, 26 (1932), 62–9.

4. Photius's second patriarchate (877–886): the council of 879–880: the alleged second Photian schism

It appeared to have been understood that when Ignatius died Photius would be reinstated as Patriarch. This inevitably involved a new council to revoke the former conciliar condemnations, and with this in mind Basil I wrote to Rome in 877 before the death of Ignatius.[51] As the papacy needed imperial help against the Saracens attacking Italy, the moment was propitious. The papal legates, Eugenius, bishop of Ostia, and Paul, bishop of Ancona, were dispatched to Constantinople. They travelled by way of Bulgaria and as they went exhorted the Bulgarians to expel 'the perfidious Greeks'. Ignatius was also threatened with excommunication and deposition. As it happened, Ignatius had died on 23 October 877 and on 26 October Photius reascended the patriarchal throne. Faced with this situation when they arrived in Constantinople, the legates were at a loss and felt that they could not act. Fresh letters were then sent to John VIII by Basil and Photius and the clergy of Constantinople. The Pope was asked to recognize Photius and to take part in a new council to annul anti-Photian measures.[52] If only for political reasons, the Pope did not wish to antagonize the Byzantine Emperor and he wisely recognized the strength of the support for Photius among the clergy. He discussed the problem with a small committee and then dispatched the cardinal-priest Peter to Constantinople with his terms. He also circularized all relevant parties — the Emperor and the Patriarch Photius, the oriental patriarchs and the clergy in Constantinople, particularly the small but hard-core group of pro-Ignatians.[53] By reason of his position as head of the universal Church the Pope claimed the authority to release Photius and his clergy from penalties previously imposed. He would recognize Photius as Patriarch, but only on condition that he apologized for his earlier offences in the forthcoming council and refrained from any activity in Bulgaria. Photius's opponents were enjoined to recognize him and if they did so they were not to be further penalized. Thus unity was to be restored within the Byzantine Church and between Rome and Constantinople. It was emphasized that the Pope had the right to bind and to loose.

The Byzantines did not see it quite in this light and the

[51] *DR* 496.
[52] *GR* 513 (autumn 878 or winter 878–9); *DR* 497.
[53] *MGH*, Ep., VII, nos. 207–10, pp. 166–87.

Commonitorium which the legates brought was somewhat altered in the Greek version which was read in the fourth session of the council and signed by those present. In the face of John VIII's firm assertion that Photius should not have reascended the patriarchal throne without papal permission, Photius consistently maintained that he had never been rightfully deposed. Further it was made clear to the legates that each of the patriarchates was accustomed to chose its patriarch without interference from another patriarchate (a hit at the papacy). Photius therefore naturally refused to offer any public apology and it was understandable that the papal demand for this did not appear in the Greek version of the *Commonitorium*. The Latin text is not extant, but Dvornik has shown that most of the Greek contents correspond to passages on the subject to be found in papal letters and that, apart from the apology and a watering down of the Bulgarian request, there appeared to be no drastic changes. It would therefore be unfair to charge Photius and his advisers with wholesale fabrication, as has been done in the past.[54] The legates must have been aware that an exact translation had not been produced, but they had already been censured by John VIII for their lack of initiative on their arrival in Constantinople and they probably realized that inflexible opposition would only result in a further rift which was the last thing that the Pope desired.

The council opened in Hagia Sophia with 383 bishops present, a testimony to the strength of Photius's support. It met under the presidency of Photius, probably because Basil I was in mourning for the death of his son Constantine and therefore was not appearing in public. The choice of Photius, a former imperial official, as president was not unprecedented; Tarasius, also an ex-civil servant, had done the same at Nicaea II, on that occasion because the ruler was a woman. Acts against Photius, including the Roman council of 867 under Hadrian II and almost certainly the Ignatian council of 868–9 (Constantinople IV), were annulled. Nicaea II was declared a general council and reference was made to the use of icons and the elevation of laymen to the episcopate. One session, with a limited membership, was held in the imperial palace under the Emperor's presidency. As customary, a symbol of faith (*Horos*) was agreed on: and it was emphasized that there was to be no change in the tradition of the fathers or in the creed. On the filioque Rome and

----

[54] See Dvornik, *Photian Schism*, 175 ff.

Constantinople still seemed to be at one: this had not yet been added
to the creed in use in Rome, though it was found elsewhere in the
West, notably in Spain and in the Carolingian Empire. The *Horos*,
signed by the Emperor together with the acta was then presented at
the last and full session of the council and accepted.

The question of Bulgaria had been raised when the pontifical
letters were read in the second session. Here Photius pointed out
that he had made no ecclesiastical appointments there since he had
come to the patriarchal throne and he referred to his previous letter
to Nicholas I where he had expressed his willingness to restore the
sees claimed by Rome had this been within his power. It was
however then, as previously, a matter for 'imperial decision and
other canonical considerations', which really meant that any ecclesiastical readiness to compromise had to be endorsed by the
Emperor, and it was suggested in the council that there might even
be agreement in the Church over future diocesan redistribution. At
this point the matter was however ruled out of order and promptly
dropped. In fact Greek missionaries already in Bulgaria stayed there
despite Basil's alleged willingness 'to allow St Peter to take possession again of the Bulgarian diocese' (according to John VIII's
letter to Basil).[55] In any case the Bulgarian ruler, anxious to
establish an autonomous Church, made his own decision, which in
the end favoured Constantinople and not Rome.[56]

John VIII did not react altogether favourably to the proceedings
of the 879–80 council. In his reply to the Emperor he certainly
expressed gratitude for the concession over the Bulgarian diocese
and he hoped for continuing help in the defence of the Holy Roman
Church. He did however add that though supporting Photius's
reinstatement he could only approve his legates' actions as long as
they were not against 'apostolic instructions'.[57] To Photius he
expressed astonishment that so much that he had expressly laid
down had been altered and changed.[58] But John VIII was sufficient
of a diplomat and a realist to understand that Photius was firmly
established with the Byzantine Church behind him. He may also
have become aware of the misleading nature of the information fed

[55] *MGH*, Ep., VII, no. 259, pp. 228–30.
[56] See below p. 99.
[57] *MGH*, Ep., VII, no. 259, pp. 228–30.
[58] *MGH*, Ep., VII, no. 258, pp. 226–8.

to the papacy by dissidents such as Theognostus. In any case he did genuinely desire to promote church unity.

It was for long maintained that John VIII changed his mind and condemned Photius and that this second schism was continued by his successors, Marinus I (882–4), always hostile to Photius, Stephen VI (885–91), and Formosus (891–6), another enemy. But Dvornik has shown that the evidence found in the Anti-Photian Collection appended to the acts of the 869–70 council is unreliable and that in fact no second schism took place.[59] This view did however become part of the gradual Latin build-up of the legend whereby Photius was regarded in the West as a schismatic villain and arch-heretic, though as early as the seventeenth century the protestants had their doubts about this. But the historical vindication of Photius really only took place during the last hundred years and it was the work of a number of scholars investigating independently. Of these, Dvornik in particular has greatly strengthened the case for Photius.[60]

Though it is now generally accepted that Photius's second term of office was not marked by schism with Rome, there still remained difficulties for him within the Byzantine Church. Led by Stylianus of Neocaesarea and Metrophanes of Smyrna, a small group of Ignatians obstinately refused to recognize him. It is not clear how far they were implicated in Photius's resignation (29 September 886).[61] It is more likely that political factors were involved, since the retirement, allegedly on the ground of old age and illness, coincided with the accession of Leo VI (30 August 886). The new Emperor had had an unhappy boyhood and he had reason to regard with suspicion Theodore Santabarenus, one of Photius's friends. He also wished to provide for his younger brother Stephen who was chosen by the standing synod of Constantinople to become the new Patriarch (18 December 886). Photius was exiled to a monastery. He died in communion with Rome.

5. *Photius—churchman and humanist*

As well as the controversies with the Ignatians and Rome there were certain other aspects of the work of Photius and his near contemporaries. Photius himself, like his friend Nicholas Mysticus, was

---

[59] Dvornik, *Photian Schism*, 216 ff.
[60] See ibid. for details; cf. *DS* 79, cols. 1397 ff. (Stephanou).
[61] *GR* 536.

active in the mission field, not only in Great Moravia where Byzantine and Frankish interests clashed, or in the Balkans where both Constantinople and Rome sought to win over Bulgaria, but also in the Black Sea and Caucasian regions where the Rus and the Khazars were involved.[62] The patriarchal duty in this respect was made clear in the *Epanagoge*, a document with which Photius was concerned, designed as an introduction to legal works, though never officially issued as such.[63] Here the Patriarch was exhorted to win over all unbelievers. Apostolic activity of this kind was also in accordance with the Byzantine conception of its world role, a view which seemed all the more justified during the period of its triumphant expansion from the mid-ninth to the mid-eleventh centuries. Other specifically patriarchal duties laid down in the *Epanagoge* were the promotion of orthodoxy and the elimination of heresy. Photius himself never had to face the full flood of a major official confrontation with heresies such as monophysitism or iconoclasm, though his family suffered from the latter. But where there were differences of belief and custom, as with the Franks, he supported Orthodox doctrine and usage. In his encyclical to the three eastern patriarchs he strongly condemned certain Latin usages and particularly the Frankish insertion of the filioque into the creed.[64] He set out Orthodox teaching on the filioque at length in his *Mystagogia*. This was not at the time a specific attack on Rome since the addition to the creed was not yet being used there. But the work was to provide material for future polemicists from the late twelfth century onwards when the filioque had become a burning issue between Rome and Constantinople.[65] The question of different usages which arose in Photius's day in connection with rival activities in the mission field did not really spring into prominence again until the patriarchate of the pugnacious Cerularius. A more deep-rooted and persistent problem of heresy was that of dualism. Here Photius took a stand against the 'Manichaeans' who in various guises were insidiously infiltrating into the Church throughout its medieval life.[66]

---

[62] See below pp. 92 ff.
[63] See Ostrogorsky, *History*, 240–1 (with bibliography); text in Zepos, II. 236–368, see Tit. III. 2.
[64] GR 481 (spring or summer 867).
[65] PG 102, 263–392; on its later use see Dvornik, *Photian Schism*, 400–1.
[66] See below ch. VI, section 5.

Yet however excellently Photius fulfilled the many demands of his patriarchal office, there was quite another equally, if not more, important side to him. He was a scholar of far-ranging interests and considerable intellectual power, and he was a key figure in the history of classical studies in Byzantium.[67] His philological bent was reflected in his *Lexicon*, a work which was used by later compilers and writers, as in the Suda, or by Eustathius of Thessalonica. He explored secular and religious topics alike, as can be seen from two of his major works, the *Bibliotheca* (*Myriobiblon*) and the *Amphilochia*.

The *Bibliotheca* is a remarkable literary history, the only one of its kind to be found in Byzantium.[68] It was written at the request of his brother Tarasius who wanted to have notes on the books read by Photius while he was away. Photius said in his opening address to Tarasius that he was going on an embassy to the 'Assyrians' (Arabs). It has been suggested that this was in 838, but it is not clear where in Baghdad Photius would have found all the books commented on in the *Bibliotheca*; presumably he had access to them somewhere in Constantinople before 838.[69] The 279 entries in the *Bibliotheca* vary from a few lines to a full-length study. The authors chosen are both pagan and Christian, ranging from Demosthenes and Plutarch to Eusebius and Chrysostom. In some cases, as the fifth-century historian Olympiodorus, Photius gives the only available information on an author now completely lost. His excellent judgement is shown by forthright and penetrating comment. His powers of criticism enabled him to detect *spuria* sheltering, as often happened, under some famous name, for instance that of Chrysostom.[70] The *Amphilochia*, written later in life, was in the form of answers to questions apparently put by Photius's friend Amphilochius, metropolitan of Cyzicus. Here there were many religious topics and the

[67] For an assessment of his influence see Lemerle, *Humanisme byzantin*, ch. 7 and Wilson, *Scholars*, ch. 5.

[68] Ed. with trans. by R. Henry, 8 vols. (Budé, Paris, 1959–77); J. H. Freese, *The Library of Photius* (London, 1920), gives an English trans. of nos. 1–165 with notes. The work appears originally to have had no specific short title, but in a fourteenth-century manuscript it is called the *Myriobiblon*, and late in the sixteenth century became known in the West as the *Bibliotheca*. Cf. W. T. Treadgold, *The Nature of the Bibliotheca of Photius* (Dumbarton Oaks Studies 18, Washington, DC, 1980).

[69] See Lemerle, *Humanisme byzantin*, 37 ff. and 179 ff.

[70] See for example no. 274, ed. R. Henry, vol. 8, p. 114, rejected by Photius on grounds of style and content, a verdict in which later scholars appear to concur.

answers often drew on Photius's powers as philologist and biblical exegete. But, as in his other works, he never discarded secular learning which in his view had its proper place as an aid to Christian understanding.

Photius's literary activities and his preferences witness to the availability of texts and the use which could be made of non-Christian material in a Christian society. With his lively intellectual curiosity, his critical sense and his use of so many classical authors, he may seem something of an innovator. He was certainly a prominent figure in promoting the humanist, and to some extent patristic and biblical, studies which were to characterize the post-iconoclastic period—witness his *Bibliotheca* and *Amphilochia* and commentaries.[71] Like his near successor Nicholas Mysticus he did not share the more ascetic and detached attitude of the monastic world of his day towards scholarship in general and Hellenism in particular. He became a churchman against his inclination, though nevertheless retaining his humanist interests and independent outlook. But he was by no means the only scholar in the field.

Photius's career and writings underline two striking facts—the number of available texts, and the pleasure which people took in using them, as he himself stresses. His brother Tarasius is known because the *Bibliotheca* was written for him. But in assessing the intellectual climate of the day it is equally important to remember the unknown friends and younger men who enjoyed discussion with him and met in his house. In a letter to Nicholas Mysticus he describes how they eagerly awaited his return as he hurried back from his ministerial duties in the palace[72]—he did in fact for a time hold high government office as protoasecretis before he became patriarch. Though not a professional teacher at a patriarchal school as Dvornik suggested, he obviously gave freely of his spare time both to beginners and to the more advanced, all of whom remain anonymous.

But there are certain names besides that of Photius which come to mind—Leo the Mathematician, or Nicholas Mysticus. Then there was Photius's near contemporary Arethas, archbishop of Caesarea

---

[71] Full justice to Photius as a humanist has at last been done by Lemerle in his study *Humanisme byzantin*; for the range of Photius's writings see Beck, *Kirche*, 520 ff.

[72] *PG* 102, col. 597 A–D, trans. and discussed in Lemerle, *Humanisme byzantin*, 197–8.

in Cappadocia, a cantankerous and difficult man, continually changing sides in the ecclesiastical controversies of his day. Arethas was a bibliophile with lively intellectual interests and is famed for the manuscripts which he copied or had copied. These embrace a wide range of works from the classical world and they have an added value in that Arethas liked to fill the wide margins on which he insisted with his own comments. Evidence still remains to be explored but enough has emerged to illuminate the work of the ninth and early tenth centuries of which Photius was a leading exponent. Ignatian and papal quarrels were of vital concern to their own day and have significance for later generations in that they heralded the course which the future would take. But it may be suggested that they have unfairly overshadowed more constructive interests and developments involving both churchmen and laity which resulted in what Paul Lemerle has called 'le premier humanisme byzantin'.

6. *Byzantine missionary activities in the early middle ages*

The adoption of Christianity by Constantine the Great and then towards the end of the fourth century the proscription of other religions within the Roman Empire led to that interdependence of church and state which was to characterize medieval Byzantium. This inevitably meant that missionary work would be closely associated with imperial diplomacy rather than individual effort as was more often the case in the Latin West.[73] At first the Empire was necessarily occupied with its own internal religious problems and the conversion of neighbouring countries, such as Georgia, Armenia, or Ethiopia, was not the result of deliberate imperial policy. But by the end of the sixth century Constantinople had demonstrated its awareness of its responsibilities in the mission field, as well as the

---

[73] See H-G. Beck, 'Christliche Mission und politische Propaganda im byzantinischen Reich', *Settimane di studio del Centro italiano di studi sull'alto medioevo*, XIV (Spoleto, 1967), and in *Ideen und Realitäten in Byzanz* (Variorum, London, 1972). On Byzantine missions in general see C. Hannick in *Kirchengeschichte als Missionsgeschichte*, gen. ed. H. Frohnes *et al.*, vol. II, ed. K. Schaeferdiek (Munich, 1978).

political advantages which such a policy could bring.[74] But such advantages were by no means one-sided. Here Byzantium was heir to the traditions of Greece and Rome. The Empire was regarded as the repository of civilization in contrast to a 'barbarian' world beyond its frontiers. In East Roman eyes the gift of Christianity which they brought offered at the same time an introduction to a more highly developed way of life. Thus their converts integrated into the civilized *oecumene* and Byzantine statecraft and culture were introduced to young and vigorous societies who were able to combine what they had learnt from East Rome with their own native originality.

From the seventh century onwards the loss of Egypt and Syria to the Muslims and the failure to convert them and to bring them within the Byzantine orbit made it all the more vital to have some measure of understanding first with the Turkic peoples already established to the north-east of the Black Sea and in the northern Caucasus and then with the Bulgars and Slavs settling in the Balkans. Already before the seventh century there were long-established links with the Crimea. As early as 325 there was a bishop of Bosphorus in the peninsula where the Goths were living. From this base contacts were made with the Hunnic–Turkic migrants in the area between the Danube and the Caucasus. Justinian I had won over the Lazi in the eastern Black Sea region. Likewise by the seventh century Abasgia was an ecclesiastical province. Thus Byzantium had established a foothold in the Caucasus. The Alans in the north-eastern Caucasus appear to have known Christianity early on, but evidence is scanty as to how they fared. By the late ninth century they were known to have renewed contacts under Patriarch Nicholas Mysticus and by the early tenth century a bishop travelled thence, though with some reluctance. Episcopal lists and archaeological finds suggest that missionary work was also active north of the Black Sea among the Turkic Bulgars, some of whom were to migrate to the Balkans when the Khazar expansion took place in the late seventh century. This work appeared to be done by non-resident missionary bishops as befitted

[74] On pre-seventh-century mission work see vol. I in the series *Missions-geschichte*. This volume also contains several general essays including one by Karl Holl in which he contrasts Byzantine missionary work with that of the medieval West.

those toiling among semi-nomadic peoples. Thus both the Bulgars settling in Bulgaria and the Magyars in Hungary would already have met Christianity and some of them would have been converted.[75]

This work included the powerful Khazar kingdom which by the eighth century was established to the north-east of the Black Sea. Khazaria was particularly important to Byzantium both for economic reasons (trade routes into Asia) and as a barrier to any Arab advance through the Caucasus to the north. Justinian II, who took refuge in Khazaria during his exile, and Constantine V, son of the Emperor Leo III, both married Khazar princesses. Byzantium may at the time have had hopes of converting Khazaria and the Crimea had already proved itself an obvious base for work in this area. But any permanent development of this kind was halted by successful Jewish activities from the eighth century onwards and by the Khazar adoption of full Judaism in the course of the ninth century. Nevertheless the Byzantines usually had good relations with the Khazars and certainly attempted to put the case for Christianity. In 860 under Michael III a Byzantine diplomatic mission went to the Khan's residence at Samandar, for both powers then had a common problem of defence against 'barbarians', perhaps the Viking Rus, or Ros ('Pῶς) as they were known to the Greeks. The Khan had mentioned that he hoped that the embassy would include a Christian theologian among its diplomats. It was in fact headed by Constantine and Methodius, two brothers from Thessalonica, both distinguished in their different ways.[76]

Constantine (his later monastic name was Cyril) was an outstanding scholar, a philologist and linguist. He was a friend of Photius sharing with him that vigorous interest in intellectual pursuits

---

[75] See G. Moravcsik, 'Byzantinische Mission im Kreise der Türkvölker an der Nordküste des Schwarzen Meeres', *Proceedings of the XIIIth International Congress of Byzantine Studies, Oxford 1966* (Oxford, 1967), 15–28, and 'Byzantine Christianity and the Magyars in the period of their migration', *American Slavic and East European Review*, 5 (1946), 29–45, reprinted in *Studia Byzantina* (Amsterdam and Budapest, 1967), 245–59.

[76] There is a considerable literature on Constantine (Cyril) and Methodius. See F. Grivec and F. Tomšič, *Constantinus et Methodius Thessalonicenses. Fontes* (with Latin trans.) (Zagreb, 1960); F. Grivec, *Konstantin und Method, Lehrer der Slaven* (Wiesbaden, 1960); F. Dvornik, *Les Slaves, Byzance et Rome au IXᵉ siècle* (Prague, 1933; 2nd edn., 1969); id., *Légendes*; id., *Byzantine Missions*; Vlasto, *Entry*; see also the bibliography cited in Beck, *Geschichte*, 103–6; and the general account in Obolensky, *Commonwealth*, and in *CMH* IV (1).

which was a feature of ninth-century life in the capital.[77] Constantine, who was called the 'Philosopher', benefited from the unofficial educational opportunities available at this time. He may also have been the patriarchal librarian. He was ordained deacon (not priest, nor was he later consecrated bishop as is sometimes asserted).[78] In the 850s he may have been employed in an embassy to the Caliph Mutawakkil and taken part in debates with Muslim theologians.[79] His brother Methodius had been for a time governor of a region near Thessalonica, perhaps Strymon. Then Methodius abandoned this post and entered one of the monasteries on Bithynian Mount Olympus near Brusa. When the question of the embassy to the Khazars arose (860), with the request for a theologian, Constantine was an obvious choice and his brother went with him. The mission travelled to Khazaria by way of the Crimea. While spending several months at Cherson Constantine learnt some Hebrew. This was likely to be useful since the Khazars were monotheists under Jewish influence and Hebrew was the language of the court. As so often in Byzantine diplomacy the mission had a double purpose. It was to strengthen the alliance between the Khazars and Constantinople against 'barbarian' attacks[80] and at the same time it stressed the divine source of imperial claims to universal authority.[81] And then it was ready as always to present the case for Christianity, though on this occasion it was recognized that the Jewish faith was already firmly entrenched. But even at this late date the Khan appeared to take an interest in Christianity and in the *Vita Constantini* he did in fact say that he would turn to the Christian faith if a Byzantine theologian could refute the arguments of the

[77] I. Ševčenko, 'The Definition of Philosophy in the Life of Saint Constantine', *For Roman Jakobson* ... (The Hague, 1956), 449–57, admirably analyses the nature of Constantine's 'philosophia' and its relation to Christian teaching.

[78] Darrouzès, *Offikia*, 431–2, considers it unlikely that a young deacon of 23 years would hold so important a post as chartophylax as Dvornik supposed; cf. Dvornik, *Byzantine Missions*, 57.

[79] This is controversial; see Vlasto, *Entry*, 329, note 91 and Dvornik, *Byzantine Missions*, Appendix I.

[80] On the possible identification of the 'barbarians' with the Rus see H. Ahrweiler, 'Les Relations entre les Byzantins et les Russes au IXᶜ siècle', *Ass. Internat. des Études Byzantines, Bulletin d'Information et de Co-ordination*, 5 (Athens and Paris, 1971), 57–61.

[81] See M. V. Anastos, 'Political theory in the Lives of the Slavic saints Constantine and Methodius', *Harvard Slavic Studies*, 2 (1954), 11–38 (reprinted Variorum, London, 1979).

Jews and the Muslims.[82] At the official opening banquet the Khan drank to the One God, Constantine to 'the Trinity whom the Christians glorify'. Then, according to the *Vita Constantini*, a series of theological debates on the Incarnation and Mosaic law followed, as well as discussions with the Muslim experts who were also courting the Khazars.[83] But the Khazars were not won over, though the alliance was confirmed, and a certain number of Christian prisoners released. It is noticeable that Byzantine propaganda was entrusted to a professional and sophisticated advocate. This was normal practice and was essential when facing equally well-informed adversaries, as the Jews or the Arabs.

In their eastern missions Constantine and Methodius were not successful in converting their Khazar hosts to Christianity. Their major achievement was eventually to lie elsewhere among the Slavs. The movement of peoples in the early middle ages had brought the Slavs filtering across the Danube into the East Roman provinces in the Balkans and even as far as the Peloponnese. Some settled in eastern Europe and with the Scandinavian Vikings were to form the principality of Kiev. Other migrants were of Turkic origin, as the Magyars who were to move into central Europe in the early tenth century, breaking up Great Moravia to form the kingdom of Hungary. Then some of the Onogur Turks or Bulgars from Great Bulgaria on the Volga joined the Slavs south of the Danube to form the powerful kingdom of Bulgaria. In central Europe the Slavs set up the kingdoms of Great Moravia (Bohemia, Moravia, Slovakia, and part of later Hungary) and Pannonia. It was here that the main work of Constantine and Methodius themselves lay.[84]

In the ninth century Great Moravia had come up against the expanding East Frankish kingdom and had received its Christianity mainly from this source. It is true that the *Vita Constantini* speaks of the presence in Moravia of Italians and Greeks as well as Germans and according to archaeological evidence Irish monks may also have been active.[85] But most of the work had been done by the East Franks (Germans) and technically Great Moravia was under the

[82] *Vita Constantini*, ch. 8, Dvornik, *Légendes*, 358.
[83] Ibid., ch. 9–11, Dvornik, ibid. 361 ff.
[84] See G. Ostrogorsky, 'The Byzantine Background of the Moravian Mission', *DOP*, 19 (1965), 1–18.
[85] See Vavrínek-Zásterová, 'Byzantium's Role', on archaeological findings.

ecclesiastical jurisdiction of the archbishop of Salzburg; certainly the Franks thought this to be the case. There was then no question of converting a pagan people. But the church services were in Latin and therefore unintelligible to the majority. At that time the Slavs had no written language. Even if they had, it was widely held that there were only three permissible liturgical languages—Hebrew, Greek, and Latin. But in 862 Rastislav, the ruler of Great Moravia, sent to Michael III asking him for 'a teacher capable of instructing us in the true Christian faith in our language'.[86] He evidently knew that Constantinople had close contacts with the Slav world and had teachers who could speak his tongue. Whether he had in mind anything more than oral instruction is not clear. In fact the *Vita Constantini* spoke of a demand for a 'bishop' as well as a 'teacher',[87] in which case Rastislav may have envisaged a Church under Constantinople rather than a Frankish archbishop. Politics must certainly also have concerned his embassy. At this time an understanding between Moravia and Byzantium would be to their mutual advantage in view of the alliance between the ambitious East Franks and an expanding Bulgaria. Moravia lay dangerously vulnerable between these two powers while Byzantium was only too aware of Bulgaria's growing strength. It would be a triumph as well as a safeguard for Constantinople if Moravia could be brought within the Orthodox orbit.

Rastislav's request was met by sending the best that Constantinople had—Constantine, a distinguished philologist and theologian (who was then probably a deacon), and Methodius, an experienced provincial administrator and then at the time of his departure to Moravia hegumenus of the monastery of Polychron.[88] But no bishop. Coming as they did from Thessalonica, a city where Slavonic was spoken almost as often as Greek, situated in the neighbourhood of Slav settlers, the two bilingual brothers were admirably fitted to deal with Moravian needs. Constantine had already realized the futility of trying to lay any lasting foundations in working with the Slavs without a written language. It was his genius which invented a Slav alphabet based on the south

---

[86] *Vita Constantini*, ch. 14, Dvornik, *Légendes*, 372.
[87] Ibid.
[88] After Methodius returned from Khazaria he was made head of the monastery of Polychron; but it is not clear where this was; see Janin, *Églises et monastères*, II. 208–9.

Macedonian dialect with which he was familiar. It is generally agreed that this was the Glagolitic script, known as Old Church Slavonic. Later towards the end of the ninth century a second alphabet following Greek letters as far as possible was produced in Bulgaria. This was known as Cyrillic (though it was not the work of Constantine-Cyril). Eventually it was to replace Glagolitic nearly everywhere.

Constantine and Methodius went to Great Moravia in 863. Some translations had been made before they went, others were undertaken as time permitted in Moravia and after, particularly later on in Bulgaria. The liturgical offices—the divine liturgy and the hours, the psalter and those parts of the New Testament (Gospels, Acts, Epistles) which were used in the services, were basic essentials. There were a number of liturgical books used during the cycle of the Church's year and almost all these were to be found in Slavonic in the tenth century. Often they were not literal translations but were adapted for Slav use. The Latin mass which was already widely in use was also translated. The Byzantine liturgy which was translated was probably that of St John Chrysostom.[89] Excerpts from the church fathers and various homilies were also made. At Rastislav's request a code of law, the *Ecloga*, was provided.

The Byzantines not unnaturally met with opposition from the Frankish clergy who regarded them as unauthorized intruders. But with Rastislav behind them they stood their ground and continued to train their followers for church work in the Slav tongue. They were at first supported by the papacy. When it became necessary to ordain some of their followers they could hardly approach any Frankish bishop so they travelled south. In Venice their use of the Slavonic tongue in the liturgy was sharply criticized by the Latin clergy there, the 'trilinguists', but it was defended by Constantine who pointed out the use made of the vernacular in church services in various, mostly eastern, churches. 'It is better', he said, 'to speak five words which can be understood than ten thousand in a foreign tongue.'[90] The use of the vernacular by those 'orthodox in every respect' was even admitted later on in certain circumstances by the canonist Balsamon, provided that 'the holy prayers are accurately

[89] See A. Dostál, 'The Origins of the Slavonic Liturgy', *DOP*, 19 (1965), 67–87.
[90] *Vita Constantini*, ch. 16, Dvornik, *Légendes*, 375–8.

translated from a clearly written Greek text'.[91] But it was not normal Byzantine policy.

The two brothers had been invited to Rome by Nicholas I. They reached Rome probably in late December 867 or early 868 and were greeted by Nicholas's successor, Hadrian II. They were particularly welcome as the bearers of the alleged relics of Pope Clement I which they had found earlier on during their stay in Cherson while travelling to Khazaria. The use of Slavonic in the services was formally approved by papal bull and the liturgy celebrated in certain Roman churches in Slavonic. On the Pope's instructions some of the brothers' followers were ordained by Roman bishops. The papacy had its reasons for its policy. In this way it could support the young Slav Church in Moravia as a means of strengthening its authority in the face of Frankish encroachment. It would also have had in mind its constant concern to recover direct papal jurisdiction over Pannonia as well as the lands lost to Constantinople in the eighth century. It was still hoping to win back Bulgaria and here a Slavonic liturgy might be a useful enticement.

Constantine died while in Rome on 14 February 869 after entering a monastery and taking the name of Cyril. He expressly charged his brother not to return to his former monastic life in Byzantium but to go on with their work in Great Moravia. The papacy supported this and continued to promote these plans. Methodius was sent back to the rulers of Moravia and Pannonia to put forward the suggestion of a church hierarchy independent of the Franks. This was followed by the consecration of Methodius as bishop and his appointment—perhaps rather unwisely as it turned out—as archbishop of Pannonia with his see at Sirmium and as papal legate to the Slavs with jurisdiction over Moravia and Pannonia. This roused the Franks. Further, Rastislav was supplanted by the then pro-Frankish Svatopluk. With the support of the ruler withdrawn Methodius was easily attacked and tried by a Frankish synod. He was charged with encroachment on Frankish episcopal rights and also with not using the filioque in the creed as the Franks did. He was imprisoned, but in 873 was released at papal insistence. His title was then altered to archbishop of Moravia. He continued

---

[91] RP IV. 452–3; (Resp. 6 to Mark of Alexandria); *PG* 138, col. 957 B. He is speaking here of 'orthodox Syrians and Armenians and other regions', and it is not clear how far 'other regions' was meant to imply an open invitation.

his work, training clergy and translating into Slavonic, but he was greatly harassed by the Frankish clergy and by the Moravian ruler Svatopluk. After his death in 885 his followers were driven out. Some managed to get into Bulgaria. Others, sold into slavery, were redeemed in Venice and went to Constantinople where they joined a group working for the Slav mission to the Balkans. At the opening of the tenth century Great Moravia itself was broken up by the Magyars, while the Germans steadily encroached eastwards throughout the middle ages.

But the Slavonic liturgy lingered on, certainly until the twelfth century in Bohemia, possibly in southern Poland, and it was long used in Dalmatia. In Hungary where there were close contacts with Constantinople Byzantine ecclesiastical influence was strong until the end of the twelfth century. Originally the migrant Magyars had met with Greek Christianity when moving north of the Black Sea. Once they settled within the Carpathian horseshoe they were open to influences from both east and west. The territories which they occupied at the end of the ninth century had long been subjected to Christian influences both from Rome and from Byzantium. During the tenth century they were brought into contact with Constantinople in various ways. Their raids left prisoners and hostages in the Empire who thus got to know Orthodox Christianity. Their ambassadors visited the capital and there are records of baptisms, all the more impressive since the converts would be given an imperial godparent. Byzantium never lost an opportunity for making its neighbours feel that they were being initiated into a splendid and powerful imperial world, taking their place in the illustrious 'family of kings' with the Emperor at its head. In the mid-tenth century the monk Hierotheus was consecrated bishop of Turkia (Hungary) by the Patriarch Theophylact. But Frankish missionaries were also at work and it was from this source that the ruler Géza and his son Stephen were baptized. In 1000 Stephen, who became the first king of Hungary, accepted his crown from Pope Sylvester II. But as Moravcsik has emphasized there was at this time no schism between the two Churches and, despite the formal strengthening of the Hungarian link with Rome, Byzantine influence remained throughout the eleventh and twelfth centuries. There were obvious geographical reasons for diplomatic ties between Constantinople and Hungary. In the twelfth century the Emperor Manuel I (himself half Hungarian) even thought for a time before his own son was born that a Hungarian prince might marry his daughter and succeed to the imperial throne. In addition to close political relations, architecture, archaeological remains, literary and documentary evidence all attest to the powerful influence of Byzantium in ecclesiastical and cultural spheres. It was from Hungary that the first Latin translation from the Greek of St John of Damascus was made.[92] But with the Fourth Crusade and the virtual break-up of the old medieval Byzantine Empire as well as the growing rift between the Orthodox and Latin Churches Hungary looked increasingly West and was encouraged to do so by Rome.

Thus plans for an Orthodox Church in central Europe ultimately failed. But the outstanding contribution of Constantine and Methodius to Europe remained.[93] This was the creation of a literary language which opened to the southern and eastern Slavs the cultural and religious world of Byzantium and at the same time offered them an indispensable tool for their own creative output. The immediate effect of this was seen in Bulgaria where the ruler Boris welcomed some of Methodius's most experienced colleagues who had been expelled from Moravia, including Clement and Naum. After weighing up where the greatest political advantage lay Bulgaria had finally opted for Orthodox Christianity which meant throwing in its lot with the Byzantine world. So far this had meant for Bulgaria Greek clergy and the Greek liturgical language. But with the creation of written Slavonic and the arrival of men trained in the work of translation the situation changed, though not without protest from the Byzantine clergy already in Preslav and from some of the Turkic boyars there. Boris I's successor Symeon (893–927) had spent some years in Constantinople and had a strong appreciation of Byzantine culture. But despite his admiration for Greek letters he realized that Slavonic was the tongue of his people and he may have visualized a Slavonic hierarchy and liturgy as a means of unifying his kingdom with its two distinct ethnic elements Slav and Bulgar. In a sense this was running contrary to strongly held Byzantine views which a 'half-Greek' (as Symeon was known) with imperial pretensions might have been expected to uphold. In

[92] See G. Moravcsik, 'The Role of the Byzantine Church in Medieval Hungary', *American Slavic and East European Review*, 6 (1947), 134–51 (reprinted) in his *Studia Byzantina*, Amsterdam and Budapest, 1967).
[93] The paradoxical nature of the Byzantine contribution is discussed by Vavřínek-Zásterová, 'Byzantium's Role', 176–88.

Byzantine eyes Greek was the language *par excellence* in the civilized world. When expedient a vernacular might be tolerated, but it was noticeable that the numerous Slavs settled in the Peloponnese were integrated into the Greek population and not encouraged to retain their native tongue.[94]

It was not so in the once-Roman Balkan provinces. With the support of the ruler, Clement and his fellow-workers settled in Bulgaria. Centres for training clergy and especially for continuing the works of translation were established at Ochrida in southern Macedonia and at Preslav in the north-east. Although missions from both Rome and Constantinople had been active in the country for some time, there still remained much need for pastoral work among the pagan population of the countryside. Here Clement took the lead in organizing both missionary and educational work. After he had become the first Slav bishop, Naum who had been at Preslav was sent to assist him in this work. Clement had done much to help his struggling Slav clergy by adapting and translating for them suitable material from Greek homilies and by continuing the translation of the liturgical book the *Triodion*. He himself composed hymns and prayers. Thus he laid the foundations for a religious and cultural centre which throughout the middle ages was to influence not only Bulgaria but neighbouring Slav countries as well as Mount Athos. Clement used the Glagolitic script of his master Constantine, but at the same time a simpler alphabet was developed in Preslav in eastern Bulgaria, the Cyrillic, based mainly on Greek letters, and it was this which for the most part eventually superseded the Glagolitic, both in the Church and at court and as the general literary language. The school of Preslav was responsible for a vast literary output geared mainly to the needs of religious life and drawing on Byzantine sources.[95]

The influence of this vernacular culture in Slavonic spread from Bulgaria to neighbouring regions, Serbia, Bosnia, Croatia—sometimes in Glagolitic as in Croatia.[96] But its most significant beneficiary was Russia.[97] It was through Bulgarian channels that

---

[94] I. Ševčenko, 'Three Paradoxes of the Cyrillo-Methodian Mission', *Slavic Review*, 23 (1964), 220–36.
[95] G. C. Soulis, 'The Legacy of Cyril and Methodius to the Southern Slavs', *DOP*, 19 (1965), 19–43 (with bibliography).
[96] See Soulis, op. cit. 38–43.
[97] See below pp. 117 ff.

the gift of a literary medium was passed to Kievan Russia. But Kiev also owed much to the direct interest of Byzantium whose missionary work here was closely linked to the need for political understanding with this powerful principality. The first Russian attack on Constantinople in 860 had alerted Constantinople to the danger. Following closely on this was the mention by Photius of a bishop sent to the Russians about 867.[98] He was followed by an archbishop.[99] There is no evidence as to whether they were to permit the use of Slavonic, or indeed as to what happened to them. It is known from a treaty of 944 that there were Christians in Russia. According to the Russian *Primary Chronicle* the princess Olga was baptized in 954 or 955 in Kiev, that is before her state visit to Constantinople in 957.[100] The fact that she did not understand Greek may point to the use of Slavonic in the services in Kiev. This usage could have come from Moravia in the late ninth century, or more probably from Bulgaria which was enjoying the full benefit of the Moravian heritage.[101] But the real starting point is in 989 with the baptism of Vladimir, the only way in which he could get delivery of the imperial bride promised by Basil II as a reward for military help in a political crisis. This meant the official Kievan acceptance of Christianity and the establishment of an Orthodox Church under the jurisdiction of the Patriarch of Constantinople. Thus Russia was linked to the cultural and religious world of Byzantium and was eventually to regard itself as the heir of Constantinople.

[98] *GR* 481; *PG* 102, Ep., bk. I, no. 13, cols. 736–7.
[99] *DR* 493 (dated *c.*874?).
[100] See Ostrogorsky, *History*, 283, note 1. See below, p. 117.
[101] See D. Obolensky, 'The Heritage of Cyril and Methodius in Russia', *DOP*, 19 (1965), 45–65; L. Müller, 'Byzantinische Mission nördlich des Schwarzen Meeres vor dem elften Jahrhundert', *Proceedings of the XIIIth International Congress of Byzantine Studies, Oxford 1966* (Oxford, 1967), 29–38.

IV

LEO VI's DILEMMA: NICHOLAS MYSTICUS AND EUTHYMIUS (886–925)

1. Leo VI: the Emperor's fourth marriage

During Photius's lifetime and throughout the tenth century Byzantine prestige steadily grew and the Empire became once more a dominating factor in Balkan and East Mediterranean politics, successfully meeting the challenge of the Slav world, and to some extent of the Muslims. The patriarchate, though on occasion its activities reflected Byzantine addiction to controversy, continued to promote the interests of Orthodoxy.

In the early years of Leo VI's reign the Church was occupied in allaying the opposition which still lingered after Photius's forced resignation and relegation to a monastery (he eventually came back to favour though not to office). The Ignatian party held that his ordinations were invalid and that he had not been recognized by Pope John VIII. But his second fall was really instigated by Leo's minister Stylianus Zaoutzes for political reasons. He was suspected of working against Leo VI during his father's lifetime. He may also have been considered too powerful a figure with unacceptable views on the authority of the Church (if the ideas of church and state expressed in the *Epanagoge* are his, perhaps significantly the *Epanagoge* did not become an official publication).

Photius was followed in the patriarchate by Stephen (18 December 886–17/18 May 893), presumably a more acceptable candidate since he was Leo VI's brother. But Stephen had been ordained to the diaconate by Photius and was therefore not recognized by the Ignatians led by Stylianus of Neocaesarea, though to their discomfiture he was recognized by Rome. After a brief and comparatively uneventful term of office Stephen was succeeded by Zaoutzes' candidate, Antony II Cauleas (August 893–12 February 981). He was a monk from Mount Olympus, a pro-Studite, who had been ordained by either Ignatius or Methodius and was therefore not suspect to the Ignatians. By now the opposition which had had no support from Rome had virtually petered out[1] and it was said that by his death in 901 Antony had achieved 'the union of the whole Church'.[2] In any case it was to be swept into the background by the major internal controversy which arose over Leo's marriages in the early decades of the tenth century.

The brunt of this problem fell upon Antony Cauleas's successor in the patriarchate, Nicholas I Mysticus (1 March 901–February 907; 15 May 912–15 May 925) He had been private secretary to Leo VI. Like Photius he had an outstanding personality. He was one of the few Byzantine patriarchs to leave a full corpus of letters in which he is revealed not only in his better-known political activities but also as a much occupied churchman and pastor, yet with true and generous concern for supplicants and for his many personal friends.[3]

Nicholas was inevitably closely involved in Leo's marriage problems and to a lesser extent so was the abbot Euthymius who for a time supplanted him in the patriarchate (February 907–15 May 912). The dispute, known as the affair of the tetragamy, arose when circumstances impelled the Emperor to override the canonical prohibitions against third and fourth marriages. The rulings of the state and of the Orthodox Church concerning marriage were well established and had indeed been reinforced by Leo VI himself. Second marriages were frowned on, third and fourth prohibited, and indeed fourth marriages were counted invalid and any offspring illegitimate.[4] Like the English Henry VIII, Leo VI (886–912) understandably wished for a legitimate male heir to succeed him. The controversy certainly illustrated the way in which Byzantines unhesitatingly used Rome if it suited them to do so. Leo VI was unlucky in his wives—hence his 'great matter'. His first wife, the devout Theophano died in 893 without giving him a male heir. In 898 he took a second wife, Zoe, the daughter of his minister Stylianus Zaoutzes, and she died in 899, also leaving no son. His

---

[1] See *GR* 596; V. Grumel, 'La Liquidation de la querelle Photienne', *EO*, 33 (1934), 257–88; and P. Karlin-Hayter, 'Le Synode à Constantinople de 886 à 912 et le rôle de Nicolas le Mystique dans l'affaire de la tétragamie', *JÖB*, 19 (1970), 59–101.

[2] *Vita Euthymii*, ch. 10, p. 65, and on the meaning of this phrase, pp. 184 ff.

[3] Cf. 'Nicholas Mysticus'. *passim*.

[4] Cf. P. Noailles and A. Dain, *Les Novelles de Léon VI le Sage* (Paris, 1944), Nov. 90, pp. 296–9 and *GR* 595.

third wife, the ravishing beauty Eudocia Baïane, died in childbirth (12 April 901). This third marriage had been tolerated, but only just. Leo then took a mistress, Zoe Carbonopsina, and it was in the palace itself that in 905 her son Constantine was born in the purple. To Leo it was vital that the infant should be legitimated and his position further strengthened by the marriage of his mother and father.

Rome might show a measure of economy over fourth marriages, but the Byzantine Church was horrified at such a suggestion which contravened all the canons. And after all, as one of the most violent leaders of the opposition, Arethas, said, God only thought it necessary to create one wife for Adam.[5] Still, it was recognized that Leo's desire for a son was only human,[6] but even so there was opposition to any ceremonial baptism of the child. The near-contemporary life of Euthymius, the monk from Mount Olympus who became the friend of Leo VI and a familiar figure in Constantinopolitan circles, abounds in detail showing the Emperor's anxious efforts to solve the dilemma and further secure his dynasty. Apart from attempts to influence the Patriarch and bishops at imperial dinner parties, according to the *Vita Euthymii* and other sources Leo had some evidence that Nicholas had been engaged in treasonable activities connected with the rebellion of Andronicus Ducas and could therefore bring further pressure to bear on the Patriarch.

In the event Nicholas agreed to the imperial baptism of the baby, possibly to conciliate the Emperor. There was strong opposition from the metropolitans. The ceremony was performed by the Patriarch himself in the Great Church at Epiphany (6 January 906) with Euthymius's support. He acted as godfather, though he was too old and weak to carry the child.[7] Nicholas, in a letter to Pope Anastasius III setting out his position in the tetragamy, said that he only performed the baptism on condition that Leo immediately separated from his mistress Zoe Carbonopsina. But on the third day after the baptism 'the mother was introduced into the palace with

---

[5] *Arethae Scripta Minora*, ed. L. G. Westerink (Leipzig (T), 1968), I. 129. Arethas became archbishop of Caesarea in Cappadocia in 902 or 903. This forceful personality also had an important place in the history of scholarship; for an assessment of his work see Lemerle, *Humanisme byzantin*, 205–41, Wilson, *Scholars*, 120–35, and above, pp. 89 ff.

[6] Nicholas Mysticus, Ep. 32, p. 216.

[7] *Vita Euthymii*, op. cit. 71 ff.

an escort of imperial guards, just like an emperor's wife'.[8] Subsequently, probably around Easter 906, Leo and Zoe were married by the priest Thomas. She was crowned Augusta by the Emperor himself.

The Byzantine hierarchy stood united in condemnation. Leo was forbidden the usual ceremonial imperial entry to the Great Church through the royal gates and was only permitted to enter as far as the sacristy (*metatorion*) and then only by a side door. His wife was not proclaimed Empress in church, her name was not in the diptychs. In view of Byzantine ceremonial activities (apart from other considerations) this was an impossible situation. Leo appealed to Rome and the three eastern patriarchs[9] for a dispensation which he obtained. The papal legates came to Constantinople in early 907. But the Byzantine bishops, though willing to bless the child when he was brought in to them after the banquet in the palace on St Trypho's day, remained obdurate. Likewise the Patriarch after much vacillation. According to the *Vita Euthymii* Leo castigated Nicholas, once his fellow student, as an inveterate schemer. The metropolitans were then immediately exiled. Likewise Nicholas who was rushed off to his monastery in Galacrenae without even a shirt or a book, so he says. His letter to the Pope stating his view of the situation was aflame with indignation both at his own treatment and at the papal dispensation concerning the fourth marriage.[10]

It was the abbot Euthymius who followed Nicholas as patriarch in February 907. He was the friend and confessor of Leo who had built him the monastery of Psamathia and had the habit of dropping in unexpectedly to visit the community. But Euthymius's close relations with the Emperor did not incline him to condone the fourth marriage. He deposed the priest who had performed the ceremony[11] and the synod probably in 907 came out against the dispensation.[12] Euthymius resolutely refused ever to proclaim the 'head-strong and high-handed' Empress Zoe in church or to put her name in the holy diptychs.[13] This attitude did nothing however to

---

[8] Nicholas Mysticus, Ep. 32, pp. 218–9.

[9] *DR* 545.

[10] Nicholas Mysticus, Ep. 32, written soon after his reinstatement, i.e. during the second half of 912; *GR* 635; *DR* 571. Cf. Theophanes Cont., 371.

[11] *GR* 625.

[12] *GR* 626.

[13] *Vita Euthymii*, ch. 17, pp. 109 ff.

appease the deposed Patriarch Nicholas. The bitterness felt by Nicholas and his followers is reflected in the atrocious maltreatment given to Euthymius when on the death of Leo VI in 912 Nicholas returned to office under Leo's brother the Emperor Alexander. In the struggle to turn him out Euthymius lost two teeth and was pummelled into unconsciousness.[14] This vindictiveness even extended to his small foal which was to be drowned; in the end it was turned loose to die and was rescued by a wandering peasant who fled by night with the animal. Euthymius's nominees were ejected, his name was removed from the diptychs, and the Nicholaites restored. Once again the Byzantine Church was divided.

According to the *Vita Euthymii*, Nicholas and Euthymius were eventually reconciled before the latter died on 20 August 917. Some would have liked to have seen Euthymius back as patriarch but he resolutely refused to consider leaving his 'long-desired' way of life.[15] But as so often in Byzantium, underlying antagonisms lingered on. There were problems over Euthymius's burial. There was even strong feeling later in the century when Patriarch Polyeuctus restored his name to the diptychs.

With Nicholas's return to the patriarchate in 912, soon to be followed by the death in 913 of the ineffective Emperor Alexander, the situation changed. As the most powerful of the regents for the young Constantine VII Porphyrogenitus Nicholas's authority was in the ascendant, despite the antagonism of the Dowager Empress Zoe. She cast off the nun's habit forced on her by Nicholas and returned to the palace and her small son, claiming the regency and for a short term ousting Nicholas. But failure to deal with foreign policy, particularly the Bulgarian offensive, or to control those manœuvring for power, brought her rule to a speedy end. Nicholas again took charge only to give way (to some extent) to the competent and ambitious Grand Admiral of the Fleet, Romanus Lecapenus. With the blessing of Nicholas he was crowned co-Emperor as Romanus I (920–44) thus providing the strong secular control needed during the minority in the established dynasty.

Nicholas remained in the patriarchate until he died on 15 May 925. In the circumstances he was too useful (and perhaps too dominant) a figure to be relegated to the background by Romanus I.[16] The

---

[14] *Vita Euthymii*, ch. 19, pp. 121 ff.
[15] *Vita Euthymii*, ch. 21–22, pp. 135 ff.

difficulties caused by the fourth marriage and particularly by Rome's part in the affair were smoothed over early in Romanus's reign. The acquiescence of the three eastern patriarchs does not seem to have roused strong feeling in Constantinople. Rome was another matter as the vehement protest of Nicholas's letters show. In the event the legality of Leo VI's fourth marriage was tacitly accepted, if under protest. As Nicholas later wrote to Pope John X, 'It was done at that time out of regard for the imperial status, but it was improper and not in accord with the canons of the Church.'[17] The principles of the Orthodox Church were made clear in the *Tome of Union* of 9 July 920. Discreetly avoiding particular cases, a synodical ruling laid down the strictest penalties for third marriages (allowing that here there might just conceivably be mitigating circumstances), but for the future it utterly forbade fourth marriages.[18] Euthymians were to be reinstated in their sees if they wished, though understandably there were many problems in so doing, as Nicholas's later letters show.

Nicholas made a strong appeal to Rome to support the Constantinopolitan synod's ban on fourth marriages. He asked for legates to be sent to end the troubles which had arisen partly by reason of the attitude of the heads of the Roman Church. Thus schism would be eliminated and the normal commemoration of the Pope could be made in the diptychs.[19] Nicholas was writing after the *Tome of Union* and in the end Roman legates did arrive in the spring of 923 and some kind of peace between Rome and Constantinople seems to have been restored, though dissidents within the Byzantine Church continued until well towards the end of the tenth century.[20] The position of Rome in the tetragamy dispute contrasts sharply with the attitude of the papacy towards Constantinople in the post-1204 period. In the late middle ages Rome was constantly

---

[16] For the political background of Romanus I and Constantine VII see A. Rambaud, *L'Empire grec au X° siècle; Constantin Porphyrogénète* (Paris, 1870) and S. Runciman, *The Emperor Romanus Lecapenus and his Reign* (Cambridge, 1929, repr. 1963); both are useful but in need of revision. A. Toynbee, *Constantine Porphyrogenitus and his World* (London, 1973) is uneven. An excellent though brief account is given by Ostrogorsky, *History*.

[17] Nicholas Mysticus, Ep. 53, p. 290.

[18] *GR* 669.

[19] Nicholas Mysticus, Ep. 56, 53, 77 (all to Pope John X); *GR* 671, 675, 711.

[20] Cf. *GR* 803. See also Nicholas Mysticus, pp. xxv–xxvi, on the Euthymian hierarchy.

exerting pressure on the Byzantine Church, assuming that it was the highest authority acting as of right. In the days of Patriarch Nicholas Constantinople certainly accorded primacy of honour to Rome. Both Leo VI and Nicholas had understandably been anxious to consult Rome (though for different reasons). But Constantinople tended to resent unilateral action by Rome. It clearly wished to act within the framework of the pentarchy and therefore thought it desirable to settle the principles involved in the tetragamy on the basis of the consensus of the five ancient patriarchates, which meant in practice by agreement with Rome after discussion as between equals. Leo VI had appealed to all four in order to strengthen his position. But the three eastern patriarchates did not carry the same weight as Rome. Hence Nicholas's pressing appeals to the papacy to support him in his stand against Leo.

2. Nicholas I's second patriarchate (912–925); the interdependence of church and state

The drama and the vital dynastic issues of the tetragamy so dominate the lively (if one-sided) *Vita Euthymii* that they tend to overshadow other aspects of Nicholas Mysticus's work. A man of dominating personality and great energy, fierce in defence of the Church, yet no less active in affairs of state, he was an admirable exponent of Byzantine tradition which stressed the interdependence of church and state, the two interdependent aspects of the polity. During the minority of Constantine VII Nicholas had acted as head of state except for the disastrous period when the jealous and aggressive Dowager Empress Zoe had managed to drive him out of the palace, advising him to confine himself to purely ecclesiastical matters. The emergence of Romanus Lecapenus, the Grand Admiral of the fleet, and his subsequent coronation as co-Emperor, still saw Nicholas as senior minister. His value was well demonstrated in the struggle with the ambitious Bulgarian ruler Symeon who had for some years resolutely refused to have any direct contact with the Byzantine Emperor himself.

The vigorous and expanding Bulgarian principality posed a major problem for Constantinople in the tenth century. During the regency before Romanus Lecapenus took control, Nicholas Mysticus had attempted to solve the problem by peaceful means. His opponent Symeon was no uncultured barbarian. He had been educated in Constantinople, he enjoyed Greek literature and was, so Nicholas himself says, 'a keen student and a reader of books',[21] and was even described as 'half-Greek'.[22] He had for a time been a monk but rejected this way of life for the throne. Nicholas may well have known him in Constantinople. So when in 913 after ill-judged provocation from the Byzantines Symeon advanced towards Constantinople Nicholas tried to stave off an attack on the Empire by negotiating. He met Symeon outside the city walls. He promised renewal of the customary tribute (payment of which was a well-known Byzantine device) and offered the betrothal of the young Constantine VII to one of Symeon's daughters. Such a marriage would have given Symeon the position of authority in Constantinople which he coveted. It has been suggested that had Symeon taken control Bulgaria might possibly have been integrated into the Byzantine Empire, thus constituting a more effective barrier to invaders such as the Muslims and Franks than was possible when the recurrent resurgence of a hostile Bulgaria had to be coped with. It would also have ensured the dependence of the Bulgarian Church on Constantinople, an important consideration for the Patriarch of Constantinople. But whether Nicholas had in mind long-term policy of this kind is unknown.[23] In any case his negotiations with Symeon were repudiated by Zoe when she temporarily ousted him from the regency. The Bulgarian affair was so mismanaged that Zoe brought about her own downfall and worse still provoked military retaliation from Symeon that continued until his death in 927.

Nicholas returned as regent, and then as Romanus I's adviser. But the harm had been done and Symeon was now set to realize his aims by force. Nicholas Mysticus's part in the affair was obviously not a military one. His letters on Bulgarian affairs, some quite lengthy, are mostly to Symeon. These reflect the moving concern of the ageing Patriarch for his spiritual son and they continually stress the common faith of the two nations, 'Romans and Bulgars are the Body of Christ', he wrote.[24] But the letters also indicate the nature

---

[21] Nicholas Mysticus, Ep. 26, p. 184.

[22] Liutprand, *Antapodosis*, ed. J. Becker (Hanover and Leipzig, 1915), ch. 29, p. 87.

[23] This is suggested by Browning, *Byzantine Empire* 82–3; the opposite view is taken by S. Runciman, *The First Bulgarian Empire* (London, 1930), pp. 157–8. Subsequent events tend to refute Browning's optimism.

[24] Nicholas Mysticus, Ep. 26, p. 184.

of Symeon's ambitions and provide the official response to his requests. Nicholas rejects Symeon's demand that Romanus I should abdicate in his favour. 'If God means you to sit on the Roman throne, then he will accomplish this, so desist from fighting and leave it to him.'[25] He points out that Romanus would be willing to accept an alliance between his family and that of Symeon, which would in effect be an imperial marriage, since Romanus was by then co-Emperor.[26] Eventually the old and ailing Patriarch wrote his last letter in 925 before his death on 15 May, reproaching Symeon for his broken promises (and his futile sarcasms), not knowing that the sudden death of the Bulgar in 927 was soon to afford at least a temporary respite. Bulgaria may have been brought within the Byzantine orb, but it was by no means tamed as can be seen from Nicholas's flow of letters.

Major problems, as the tetragamy or Bulgaria, did not prevent Nicholas from dealing with innumerable diocesan and other matters, nor did he grudge advice to individuals in need. A number of short and mostly unrhetorical letters are full of beneficent advice or instruction for the alleviation of hardship (as in the case of obstreperous soldiers billeted on a defenceless widow). It is through the survival of collections of letters such as those of Nicholas Mysticus, or of the fourteenth-century Athanasius, that the patriarchal daily routine comes to life.

[25] Ibid., Ep. 18, p. 126 (spring/summer 921).
[26] Ibid., Ep. 16, pp. 108–10 (after 17 Dec. 920).

V

THE PATRIARCHATE 925—1025: THE PREDOMINANCE OF CONSTANTINOPLE

1. Cooperation and criticism 925–970

Perhaps Romanus I desired a respite from a dominating and outstanding Patriarch such as Nicholas I had been. He was known to have in mind the appointment of his eunuch son Theophylact who had been ordained deacon at an early age. When Nicholas I died the boy was probably too young[1] for even Byzantine 'economy' to allow his promotion. Nicholas was therefore replaced, first by Stephen II of Amasea (29 June 925–18 July 928) and then by the monk Trypho (14 December 928–August 931). Neither could compare with Nicholas in ability or character. It was supposed to have been agreed that Trypho would resign when Theophylact was considered by Romanus I to be old enough to take his place. For some reason not clearly understood Trypho gave up, or was ousted from, his office in 931 when Theophylact was only fourteen years old. The youth was not however enthroned until 933,[2] possibly because of controversy concerning the legality of a promotion contrary to canon law, and more probably to allow time for communication with Rome. However much Romanus I might emphasize that the patriarchal appointment was wholly the concern of the Byzantine Church, in this case it was evidently considered worth while getting papal legates to come to the consecration, as they did.[3] At this juncture it suited the tangled politics of the then dominant Crescentii family in Rome to be on good terms with the Byzantine Emperor, though (as was often stressed in the sources) Theophylact could hardly be regarded as an ideal candidate for the patriarchate. But his initial lack of experience and his continuing secular interests did not necessarily mean that ecclesiastical administration was neglected. His senior metropolitans, of Cyzicus and

---

[1] Scylitzes, p. 242 (*CB*, II, p. 332).
[2] GR 786.
[3] DR 625.

Heracleia, for instance, saw to that, in fact only too well if remarks about the dangers of encroachment on patriarchal authority are to be believed.[4]

During the years between the accession to office of Theophylact (933) and Alexius Studites (1025) the Empire steadily met its challenges and its prestige was at its peak. The quality of its patriarchs may have varied but the Church gave to the Emperors co-operation and on occasion criticism. The patriarchal register—as far as it is possible to reconstruct this—gives at least a hint of the range of ecclesiastical activities.

Polyeuctus (3 April 956–5 February 970), though ageing, was a man of spirit and took his stand on matters of principle, but he left no corpus of letters to reveal the details of his personality as Nicholas Mysticus had done. It may have been a tribute to a too forceful character that during the early years of his patriarchate the Macedonian Constantine VII (sole Emperor from 944–59) tried to dislodge him and failed.[5] After the short reign of Romanus II (959–63) Constantine's two sons Basil II and Constantine VIII succeeded as minors. Guardianship and direction of policy were seized by members of powerful military families, who became successive co-Emperors, first Nicephorus II Phocas (963–9), and then John I Tzimisces (969–72). Both were men of authority and successful generals, but Polyeuctus did not hesitate to challenge what he regarded as imperial infringements of canon law and encroachments on the rights of the Church.

Since Nicephorus Phocas had acted as godparent to the imperial children he was regarded as a spiritual relative of Theophano the Dowager Empress and therefore canonically debarred from marrying her. This difficulty was surmounted, but Polyeuctus remained bitterly critical of the Emperor Nicephorus's ecclesiastical policy. Nicephorus was a devout and even austere man and had earlier on been inclined towards the monastic life. He was criticized when he abandoned this and chose instead the role of statesman and general. He had a keen eye to the needs of imperial defence. He even went as far as to declare that men who fell in battle against the Muslims should be counted as martyrs. This was categorically turned down

[4] Cf. J. Darrouzès, 'Un Discours de Nicétas d'Amasée sur le droit de vote du patriarche,' Ἀρχεῖον Πόντου, 21 (1952), 162–78, and *Epistoliers byzantins du X⁶ siècle* (Paris, 1960), 30–2 on administration during Theophylact's patriarchate.

[5] Scylitzes, p. 247 (*CB*, II, pp. 337–8).

by a synodal protest citing St Basil as the authority for rejecting such a pronouncement.[6] Though a friend of monks and patron of the recently founded Lavra on Mount Athos, Nicephorus unhesitatingly condemned the abuse of the monastic way of life, and he thought it right to limit the erection of new houses.[7] Here he had in mind not only the maintenance of standards but the financial and military needs of the state, since taxation suffered when land was donated to monasteries and then left uncultivated. The same restrictions were to apply to metropolitan and episcopal foundations.[8] He also emphasized his right to control episcopal appointments.[9] Polyeuctus disapproved of such encroachments on ecclesiastical freedom as he saw it, but was unable to effect any change during Nicephorus's short reign.

There had been continuing rivalry among the powerful families over the guardianship of the young princes and Nicephorus was assassinated in 969. Much of this intrigue was at the instigation of the powerful general John Tzimisces. He proposed to marry the fascinating and by now twice-widowed Empress Theophano, who had also been involved in the conspiracy, and he planned to become co-Emperor. In such a situation patriarchal support was important and this was Polyeuctus's opportunity. He laid down his terms for entry to Hagia Sophia and the imperial coronation. The Augusta Theophano was to be expelled from the palace (she was in fact dispatched to Prote, one of the Princes Islands in the sea of Marmora); the murderers of Nicephorus were to be punished; and measures against the freedom of the Church, described as Nicephorus's 'tome', were to be referred to the synod.[10] Tzimisces thought it wise to agree and he was then crowned as John I. He made an unexciting but acceptable marriage with Theodora, one of Constantine VII's daughters. These were politic concessions and did not necessarily mean that John I would grant a free hand to property-owners, ecclesiastical or otherwise. It was in a way a reassertion of the Byzantine principle that church and state must work together in unity, though in matters affecting the temporal well-being of the state, the Emperor usually got his way. That is probably what is

[6] GR 790.
[7] See below p. 346.
[8] DR 699.
[9] DR 703.
[10] GR 793 and GR 794; DR 726 and 727.

implied in Tzimisces' often-quoted statement on the priesthood and Empire rather than any implication that the priesthood had overruling control. 'I acknowledge two powers in this life: the priesthood and the empire. The Creator of the world has entrusted to the former the cure of souls and to the latter the care of bodies. If neither part is damaged, the well-being of the world is secure.'[11] What is being emphasised in this passage is interdependence.

2. *The imperial advance in the East: the Muslims and the non-Chalcedonian Churches*

The close co-operation between church and state during the years 933–5 was in general exemplified in the frontier conquests though on occasion modified by political needs. In the east, it was a period of steady advance against the Muslims bringing the Christian forces into contact with various ecclesiastical problems. First the conversion of the Muslims and here Byzantium, in contrast to its work in other fields,[12] had no real success. There were of course individual or group conversions but that could work both ways often as a matter of expediency. When Curcuas captured Melitene in 934 whole Muslim families turned Christian because they did not wish to be deported. There was inevitably considerable cross-fertilization in the eastern marcher lands. The fortunes and activities of the Christian marcher lords are well illustrated in the epic poem *Digenis Acritas*, the frontier warrior of 'dual origin', the son of a Christian mother and a converted Muslim emir father. But in general the failure of the Orthodox Church to make genuine conversions on any large scale among Muslims was a feature of Byzantine history (in contrast to its success with the South Slavs and Russia). On the contrary during the course of the middle ages the tenacity with which the Islamic world clung to its faith intensified. As it extended its conquests it continually drew the conquered native Christians into its fold,[13] though some (as the Church recognized) maintained a kind of crypto-Christianity beneath apparent acceptance of Islam.

The advance in the east inevitably brought renewed contacts with the separated Christian monophysite Churches. The achievements of the Byzantines in extending the eastern frontiers into

---

[11] *Leo the Deacon*, bk. 6, ch. 7 (*CB*, pp. 101–2).
[12] See above, ch. III, section 6.
[13] See Vryonis, *Decline*.

Mesopotamia, North Syria, and Armenia during the tenth and early eleventh centuries are much lauded. But ultimately disastrous consequences are scarcely recognized.[14] The fertile Mediterranean coastal strip with its citrus trees below the rugged Cilician Gates was ruthlessly devastated to facilitate the capture of Tarsus. This scorched earth policy applied everywhere, and together with the panic flight eastward of Muslims, and the forced transportation into slavery of captives, meant the depopulation of the frontier regions. To make good this situation the Syrian Jacobites (monophysites) were encouraged to expand into the newly instituted themes, and they overflowed into the regions around Melitene, Marash, and Edessa. This influx of wealthy Syrian families and merchants brought back prosperity to the devastated regions. The establishment of the separated non-Chalcedonian Jacobite Church was accompanied by the foundation of new bishoprics as well as monasteries which became flourishing centres of activity. The Syrian migration seems to have been buoyed up by a promise of religious toleration from Nicephorus II. Such an attitude towards heterodoxy was a matter of urgent political expediency. Even so, it was entirely contrary to the deep-rooted Byzantine conception of the Emperor as a pillar of orthodoxy. It roused continual opposition both from ecclesiastical circles in Constantinople and from the local Chalcedonian minorities. Nevertheless this policy was generally continued by Nicephorus's powerful successors John Tzimisces and Basil II (†1025). It was reversed by the weaker and less-able eleventh-century rulers from 1028 onwards with disastrous results. It was however noticeable that this tolerance was not uniformly applied. Again for political reasons, further south in the key city of Antioch orthodoxy was strictly enforced and the consequent diversion of Syrian Jacobites to northern regions was welcomed as reducing heretical influence in a particularly sensitive political area.[15]

A migration similar to that of the Syrians took place among the Armenians. The eastward expansionist policy of Constantinople involved the gradual absorption of Armenia. Ani, the last

[14] For a salutary corrective see the analysis of G. Dagron, 'Minorités ethniques et religieuses dans l'orient byzantin à la fin du Xe au XIe siècles: L'Immigration syrienne', *TM*, 6(1979), 177–216.

[15] See V. Grumel, 'Le Patriarcat et les patriarches d'Antioche sous la seconde domination byzantine, 969–1084', *EO*, 33 (1934), 129–47.

independent region fell to Constantine IX in 1045. As various areas were conquered or acquired, leading families were offered privileges and estates in Cappadocia, or in south-east Asia Minor where in the later eleventh century the kingdom of Lesser Armenia was to emerge and become an important factor in crusader politics. This Armenian migration introduced a monophysite element into orthodox regions, though not in so powerful and compact a form as in the case of the Jacobite Church. But it meant friction. Though for centuries individual Armenians had held high positions in Byzantine service (presumably paying lip-service to orthodox belief), they were disliked by the Greeks. The presence of considerable numbers of monophysite Armenians in the Asia Minor themes was felt to be a challenge to the Byzantine Church and was to lead to an unwise religious policy in the critical years after 1025.

3. Caucasian and North Pontic regions: Russia

Rather more successful was the consolidating missionary work begun much earlier in the Caucasus and the North Pontic areas.[16] This had already been much in the mind of patriarchs such as Nicholas I Mysticus. He was particularly assiduous in supporting Peter the metropolitan of Alania in the central Caucasus, an area converted at the end of the ninth and beginning of the tenth centuries. Like many other metropolitans Peter felt keenly his isolation from the capital. The Patriarch wrote on his behalf to the ruler of Abasgia and also sent Peter a series of sympathetic but bracing letters assuring him that he was not forgotten but adding that he knew quite well that he had been sent not to luxury but to 'labours and toils and difficulties'.[17] Problems concerning the outlying rights of the metropolitan of Alania continue to figure in the late tenth- and early eleventh-century registers of Sisinnius II and Eustathius. Metropolitan Nicholas of Alania had problems of maintenance when he was detained by stormy seas on returning to his diocese and had to put up for a time in Cherson seeking help from the monastery of the Holy Epiphany at Kerasontus.[18] During

---

[16] See also above ch. III, section 6.

[17] Nicholas Mysticus, Ep. 135, p. 438; see also Ep. 52, 134, 135.

[18] *GR* 806 (997–9) and 827 (1024) concerning rations of cheese and wine to be provided by the monastery for the bishop and his companion (accommodation specifically excluded).

this period the area in and around the Crimea, long firmly committed to Christianity and to Byzantium, provided valuable bases from which missionaries could work and was too an important political asset in controlling changing factors on the northern borders. Here the Khazars (converted not to Christianity but to Judaism) had by the tenth century declined and the two rising powers were the nomadic Turkic Pechenegs and the principality of Kiev dominated by the Scandinavian Northmen or Rus. The Pecheneg tribes, who in the late ninth century were moving westward into the steppe lands north of the Black Sea, were courted by Byzantine diplomats and their value to the Empire is stressed in the mid-tenth-century handbook of the foreign office, the *De Administrando* of Constantine VII. But though they figure prominently in the tenth and eleventh-century Byzantine foreign policy they do not appear to have been converted to Christianity. Perhaps their mobility militated against ecclesiastical organization if any such attempts were made.

It was otherwise with Russia. Here as usually the case political and religious considerations were closely linked. During the ninth and early tenth centuries Constantinople had been made aware of new dangers which threatened from the north-east. Varangian desire for plunder and then for regular trade agreements and the growth of the Kievan principality had evoked diplomatic and ecclesiastical approaches from Emperor and Patriarch. But though by the mid-tenth century there were evidently Christians in Russia there was no established link with the Orthodox Church.

In 957 the Kievan princess Olga, regent for her son Svyatoslav, made a spectacular visit to Constantinople. Here she was accepted as the spiritual daughter of Constantine VII and his wife Helena and was accorded a spendid reception and received into intimate imperial circles. Whether she was baptized in Constantinople on this occasion or previously in Kiev in 955 seems undecided[19] but she certainly must have had Christian contact in Kiev before she came south. Her links with Constantinople did not however prevent her from turning to the German Otto I in 959 shortly after her return

---

[19] Obolensky, *Commonwealth*, 195, suggests that a solution to apparently conflicting evidence would be the recognition of two stages to Olga's conversion, preliminary acceptance and then formal baptism which in the case of Olga took place in Constantinople in 957; see also *Kirchengeschichte als Missionsgeschichte*, 2 (4), 340 ff.

home asking him to send a bishop and priests to Kiev. This he apparently did though without permanent results. But once again rival claims of Christian power in East and West had demonstrated to central and east European rulers that they had a choice of alignment.

In the event the Rus remained on the whole pagan until towards the end of the tenth century until political events forced Constanti-nople to realize the urgent need to bring Kiev within the Christian 'family of kings'. The threat had arisen in connection with Bulgaria. With the death of the ambitious Symeon in 927 and the succession of a more compliant ruler Bulgaria had for a time been under Byzantine influence. But the atmosphere changed to one of hostility in the 950s. Nicephorus II unwisely provoked the Bulgarians further by refusing customary tribute. He then called on Svyatoslav to suppress their attacks, only to find that by 969 the Kievan ruler was exercising his own control over Bulgaria to the exclusion of Byzantium. This would have meant the presence on Constantino-ple's northern borders of an unacceptably powerful neighbour. Nicephorus's successor John I Tzimisces was left with the double task of expelling Syvatoslav and subduing Bulgaria. He incorpor-ated Bulgaria into the Empire and put an end to the highly-prized independent Bulgarian patriarchate. In 971 his victory over Svya-toslav (who was to perish on his way home) was sealed by a treaty with Kiev which secured an ally and provided a valuable source of mercenaries.

Despite his mother's baptism Svyatoslav, like many of his subjects, had been pagan. The formal conversion of the Kievan ruler and his state was to come a few years later. In 988–9 Kievan military aid saved the situation for Basil II who was fighting for his throne against powerful rebels. Some of the Varangians stayed on to form the core of the imperial bodyguard. The Kievan ruler, Olga's grandson Vladimir, was rewarded for this aid with the Emperor's sister Anna as bride, a mark of great favour as imperial princesses 'born in the purple' were not at that time normally betrothed to foreigners. A condition of the marriage was the acceptance of Christianity by Vladimir and by his subjects.[20] In fact Anna seems only to have arrived after Vladimir had threatened Constantinople by attacking Cherson, though the precise sequence of events seems

[20] *DR* 771 (end 987/8); *DR* 776 and 777 (989).

uncertain. But it is clear that this time the acceptance of Christianity by the Kievan ruler meant that his state, and later on other Russian regions, were firmly linked to the Orthodox Church under the guidance of the patriarchate of Constantinople. This momentous decision was given prominence in the Russian *Primary Chronicle* where the Kievan ruler is described as weighing up the merits of various faiths—Muslim, Jewish, and Christian, both Roman and Greek. Finally he decided for the Greek Church after the deep impression made on his envoys by the splendid liturgical rites in Hagia Sophia where he felt that God surely dwelt among men. It is generally agreed that much of this is legendary, but even so there are strands of truth. The Kievan ruler was not alone in being impressed by the splendour of Orthodox worship. Nor was he unaware of the political strength afforded to the ruler of a polity based on such close interdependence of church and state as prevailed in Byzantium. Conversion also meant close relations with a Christian world which offered more than statecraft and economic advantages. It opened the gateway to the civilization of the Hellenic world whose scholars had already provided the linguistic means whereby liturgical and theological works in a Slav language could be made available. While preserving its own ethnic characteristics Russia could thus share in the cultural riches of the Byzantine world particularly its art and its theological literature, its chronicles and its legal works.[21] It meant moreover that when the Greek and Balkan Churches were submerged for three centuries and more beneath Muslim rule, Orthodoxy could serve as a 'universal' force outside the bounds of the old Byzantine Empire.

4. Byzantium and South Italy

Byzantine extension of its influence in the north-east, the subjugation of Bulgaria begun by John I Tzimisces and completed by 1014 by Basil II, and the successful drive against the Muslims in the eastern reaches and in the Aegean all combined to give Constantinople a commanding position. The next step was to consolidate the Byzantine position in South Italy and to win back Sicily from the Muslims, and this was the intention of the last great Macedonian

---

[21] See Meyendorff, *Byzantium and the Rise of Russia*, 9–28, on Byzantine civilization in Russia and also certain differences in political ideology.

ruler Basil II (†1025). It is understandable that the attitude of Constantinople towards the western powers was one of disdain. The Byzantines were quite unaware of rising forces in the West which were eventually to contribute to the downfall of the East Roman Empire in the later middle ages. This is particularly true of the many-sided reform movement stirring within the tenth-century Latin Church, though as yet not touching papal personnel to any great extent. It was to be a contributory factor in stimulating an upsurge of devotion which was one of the forces behind the fatal crusading movement from the late eleventh century onwards.

In the tenth century on the whole Byzantium controlled its south Italian provinces, though Sicily was lost to the Muslims and the mainland was still troubled by them. The Greek Church was strong in the south and Greek monasticism deep-rooted there, particularly on the 'Holy Mountain' up in the hills above Rossano whence came St Nilus in 1004 to found the still active house of Grottaferrata near Rome. There were Greeks and Greek monastic houses in Rome itself.[22] Latin houses such as Monte Cassino drew freely on Byzantine expertise in matters of craftsmanship and in other fields, and there were political links between Constantinople and Italian principalities, as for instance Capua.[23] In Rome itself the political and ecclesiastical situation in the second half of the tenth century reflected little credit on the papacy and afforded opportunity for outside interference. Leading families were struggling for control and for the appointment of their own nominee as Pope. The situation also posed a problem for Byzantium by reason of the ambitions of the Saxon ruler Otto I, a mere 'rex' in the eyes of Constantinople. Otto took over the North Italian Lombard king-dom which was being misgoverned by his vassal Berengar and he then adopted the imperial policy of the Carolingians. In 962 he was crowned Emperor in Rome by Pope John XII. He allied with the house of Tusculum against the Roman family of the Crescentii and was to exercise far stricter control over Pope and City than Charlemagne had done. Further, Otto I had designs on Byzantine South Italian lands. Had he succeeded these regions would no doubt

[22] See B. Hamilton, 'The City of Rome and the Eastern Churches in the Tenth Century', *OCP*, 27 (1961), 5–26 (reprinted Variorum, 1979).

[23] See H. Bloch, 'Monte Cassino, Byzantium and the West in the Earlier Middle Ages', *DOP*, 3 (1946), 163–224; much of this is based on eleventh-century evidence.

have been withdrawn from the ecclesiastical jurisdiction of the Patriarch of Constantinople and returned to Rome. Though taken over at least 200 years earlier their transference to Constantinople had remained a permanent grievance with the Curia, as was evidenced in Liutprand's provocative anti-Byzantine propaganda piece, the *Legatio*.[24]

Otto I did attack South Italy, but with only temporary success. In 972 he achieved something of a truce by negotiating for his son Otto II, a Byzantine bride Theophano, not a 'born-in-the-purple' Macedonian princess as requested but probably a relative of the general and co-Emperor John I Tzimisces. Both Otto II and Otto III retained their interest in Italy as did their successors. The half Byzantine Otto III (†1002) even hoped to make Rome the centre of a western Empire in the East Roman tradition and he was betrothed to a genuine Byzantine princess, presumably Zoe, the niece of the powerful Emperor Basil II, but this came to nothing by reason of Otto's early death.

Intervention in Italian affairs and western imperial claims were from now onwards to be a permanent feature of German politics to the detriment of Byzantine interests. During the late tenth and first half of the eleventh centuries German attempts to control the papacy were resisted by the Roman Crescentii with whom the Byzantines had an understanding. From time to time 'Roman' popes dislodged by the German party appealed to Constantinople for help. Throughout this period Constantinople showed its determination to maintain its hold on South Italy. In 968 Patriarch Polyeuctus affirmed his right to control the South Italian Church when he elevated the archbishop of Otranto to the rank of metropolitan with one or more suffragans (the sources are not agreed as to the number).[25] It is understandable that the see-saw of politics in Rome made it difficult for Constantinople always to be sure who was in possession of the papal throne at any given time and therefore there may have been gaps in the registration of the

---

[24] See *Relatio de Legatione Constantinopolitana*, 3rd edn., ed. J. Becker (Hanover and Leipzig 1915), ch. 17, pp. 184–5. Liutprand of Cremona was twice ambassador to Constantinople, first from the North Italian ruler Berengar II, then from Otto I (968). In spite of his deliberately sour outlook on Byzantine life and resentment at the close watch kept on his every movement, even when he is trying to stir up Latin feeling against Constantinople he reveals (enviously and against his will) the high prestige and sense of security then enjoyed by the capital.

[25] *GR* 792.

current papal name in the diptychs. This intermittent absence of the usual recognition was not necessarily an indication of formal schism and there is indeed no reason for thinking that any such state of affairs existed at this time. Polemic on the procession of the Holy Spirit attributed to Patriarch Sisinnius II has now been shown to belong to a later period.[26] Likewise Sergius II's alleged use of Photius's encyclical against the Latin Church addressed to the eastern patriarchs and his supposed concern with the filioque and schism have been discounted.[27]

Far from being unduly troubled by the relations with the Latins, the Byzantines in 1025 could look with some satisfaction on the extent of their influence. In conquered Bulgaria the patriarchate had been suppressed and an archbishopric dependent on the Byzantine Emperor set up. The Kievan ruler and his subjects had been won for Orthodoxy and the higher ecclesiastics in Russia were Greek appointed, though the lower clergy were native using the Slavonic vernacular in their services. The conquests on the eastern borders had added to prestige but had also certainly created ecclesiastical problems by bringing closer contact with the separated monophysites, though there was also compensation in the restoration of Byzantine control over the deeply venerated Christian city of Antioch. Both within and without the Empire the Orthodox tradition was being greatly enriched by an upsurge of monastic foundations, particularly on Mount Athos, the Byzantine Holy Mountain. Confident in its widespread influence and growing prestige the Empire might well consider that it was equipped to extinguish heresies, such as the dualism deep-rooted in the newly-formed Bulgarian themes, or the tenacious monophysitism of the Armenian immigrants, or even to exact recognition of their position from Rome. It was reported by the western Rudolf Glaber that in 1024 the Emperor Basil II and the Patriarch Eustathius sent an embassy to Pope John XIX asking him to recognize the Church of Constantinople as universal in its own sphere (*in suo orbe*) as the Pope was in the world (*in universo*).[28] Presumably the Byzantine 'sphere' would have included the disputed South Italian dioceses.

[26] GR 814.
[27] GR 818 and 819; see also Dvornik, *Photian Schism*, 393–4.
[28] GR 828 and DR 817.

To judge from sharp criticism of him from north of the Alps the Pope appeared to have considered granting the request,[29] but nothing further seems to be known about this, except that it was wholly unpalatable to the western church reformers. It does however reflect the spirit of Constantinople at this time, confident, but mistakenly so.

[29] See V. Grumel, 'Les Préliminaires du schisme de Michel Cérulaire ou la question romaine avant 1054', *REB*, 10 (1953), 5–23.

VI

INCREASING PRESSURES ON
CONSTANTINOPLE AND
THE WIDENING GAP 1025–1204

1. Impending threats

The Byzantine Empire had weathered many crises ever since its inception in the fourth century. It had adequate military and naval defences; its reservoir of manpower was replenished by immigrant Slavs settling south of the Danube; and it produced a series of able leaders, either rulers usually from an established house or generals taking control as co-Emperors for minors or weaklings. During this time the Church, while maintaining its normal everyday life, had succeeded in overcoming challenges to its tradition and had moreover made a major contribution in bringing the South Slavs and the Russians within the orbit of the Orthodox Church and to some extent the Byzantine Empire. But with the eleventh century came the parting of the ways for Byzantium. During the later middle ages any pre-eminence in East Mediterranean politics was gradually lost until the Empire was finally submerged in a Muslim Ottoman world. The Orthodox Church on the contrary, not exclusively a Byzantine preserve, held its own and survived the political downfall.

When the powerful Macedonian ruler Basil II died in 1025 latent internal weaknesses and external pressures were not immediately apparent. But the kind of leadership which had previously served Byzantium so well was not forthcoming. The Macedonian successor was the Empress Zoe, a foolish elderly woman. The able and popular George Maniaces who might have been another Tzimisces was killed in 1043 while on his way to Constantinople to challenge the Emperor Constantine IX. For the rest, possible, though not outstanding, candidates, such as the Emperor Isaac Comnenus (1057–9) or Romanus Diogenes (1068–71) were pushed off the throne by cliques in Constantinople. The dominating feature of politics during the years 1025–81 was the constant manœuvring for the throne. The military claimants were from leading Byzantine families owning considerable estates in Asia Minor and in Europe. But they had to contend with rivals from a ministerial milieu who had gained the ear of the court. It was not until 1081 that a member of a military landed family, Alexius Comnenus, managed to outwit his rivals and to establish a dynasty which lasted a century, and rather belatedly gave some stability to the government. He was an able ruler, if also an adroit opportunist, but the odds were against him and his house.

In 1025 Byzantium may understandably have felt secure in its pre-eminence but relaxation in vigilance and changes in methods of defence were to prove fatal and demonstrated the weakness of its political system. Resting on the prestige and pre-eminence accruing from successful expansion during the years 843–1025, it was considered safe to replace the old system of military service by taxation (which was by no means always devoted to other methods of defence upkeep). Buffer states, such as Armenia, were taken into the Empire without establishing adequate frontier protection. Newly-acquired provinces, such as Bulgaria, were treated so un-wisely that latent nationalism was fomented. The fleet was neg-lected (geography alone demanded adequate sea power) and reliance on Venice's naval resources was to exact a fatally high price in the form of trade concessions. Mercenaries, expensive and often unreliable, now formed the core of what had once been largely a force of native soldiers. And so Byzantium was at a loss when overtaken in the political field by circumstances unforeseen and beyond its control.[1]

For set against such inadequacies were dangerous outside pres-sures. In the East Turkish tribes were establishing themselves in Mesopotamia, North Syria, and the former Armenian Kingdoms, areas ill-disposed towards Constantinople, an attitude aggravated by an unwise religious policy. At intervals Turkish raiders were penetrating into Asia Minor strongholds. Some landed families at least were aware of the crisis in the east. Recently-acquired estates disappeared as the eastern frontier was breached. Military leaders protested at the central government's comparative unconcern with defence measures. But when from 1068–71 Romanus IV took

---

[1] On the eleventh-century developments see the interpretation of Lemerle, 'Byzance au tournant du son destin (1025–1118)', *Cinq études*, 251–312.

control and went on campaign his efforts were treacherously
undermined in Constantinople and he was deposed. The failure to
drive back the Seljuk Turks resulted in the firm rooting of the
Muslim kingdom of Iconium in central-southern Asia Minor.

There were further complications in the north and west. The
Slavs under Byzantine rule were growing more restive. Indepen-
dent principalities, such as Zeta or Croatia, were crystallizing.
Though in fact most of the Balkans were firmly aligned to the
Orthodox Church there was always readiness—as in the Bulgarian
Boris's day—to play off Greek against Latin ecclesiastical authority.
Discontent with both Byzantine overlordship and with the established Church was finding its outlet in the widespread dualist
Bogomil heresy. Further threats came from across the Danube and
north of the Black Sea where Turkic nomads, the Pechenegs and
then the Cumans, were on the move. Beyond the Balkans in
Hungary, now settled by the Magyars, a new political factor was
emerging. Hungary was a country with obvious interests in the
north-west Balkans and, though by no means immune from the
influence of the Orthodox Church, it was however to throw in its
lot with Latin Christianity and the West in spite of twelfth-century
overtures from Constantinople where the Comneni recognized its
value as an ally.

It was doubtful whether anyone in Byzantium really appreciated
the changes taking place in the West, the Greek Church still less
than the government. And yet it was from fellow Christians in the
Latin world that one of Byzantium's greatest dangers, the crusading
movement, was to come. The Byzantines had always rather looked
down on the West, particularly its emperors who (despite the
efforts of Charlemagne) were regarded as usurpers outside the
genuine imperial tradition. The Pope, it is true, had always been
accorded primacy of honour in Christendom but the rapid succession of popes and anti-popes in the tenth and first half of the
eleventh centuries had hardly inspired respect. Further the attempt
to control papal elections by the Germans, even if crowned as
western emperors, only aroused suspicion in Byzantium, just as the
efforts of Frankish missionaries had done earlier on in the Carolingian period. The mild contempt of Constantinople for the West
came to the surface when the tenth-century Emperor Nicephorus II
taunted the German Emperor's legate Liutprand of Cremona about
the youthfulness and inexperience of the Saxon Church. And yet it

was in Frankish and German lands that the pre-Gregorian reform movement was already under way, something undreamt of, and indeed never appreciated, in Constantinople.

In 1025 Byzantium still had two provinces in South Italy, Calabria and Apulia, which were under the ecclesiastical jurisdiction of the Patriarch of Constantinople, though this was perpetually disputed by Rome. After Basil II's death his plans to strengthen the Byzantine position in Italy and to wrest Sicily from the Arabs never successfully materialized. The whole political situation was moreover radically altered by the infiltration of the Northmen into Italy and Sicily from the early eleventh century onwards. At first they were useful mercenaries in the service of both Latin and Byzantine, but they soon turned into aggressive and permanent settlers, first in South Italy and then in Sicily. The German Emperor, bent on controlling the papacy and Rome, was drawn into the struggle to evict them. The Byzantines were equally concerned, not only the Emperor but the patriarchate, since the loss of the South Italian provinces to the Normans would almost certainly mean the predominance of the Latin Church already strengthening its position in those regions. Nevertheless the dangers inherent in the impending conflict in Italy, the continuous losses in the east and rising nationalist feeling in the Balkans were hardly appreciated in ecclesiastical circles in Constantinople where unwise and intolerant policies, particularly towards the non-Chalcedonians, often aggravated an already threatening situation.

2. Patriarchs (1025–1081)

During the years 1025–81 none of the five patriarchs in office could be considered a nonentity. In their different ways they reflect something of the strength and weakness of Byzantine ecclesiastical life. Alexius Studites (12 December 1025–20 February 1043),[2] the abbot of the Studite house in Constantinople, was appointed by Basil II shortly before his death. Basil however did not observe the usual practice of asking the metropolitans for nominations from which to select a candidate. Later in 1037 when Alexius came up against the ambitions of the minister John the Orphanotrophus, the

---

[2] On Alexius Studites see *DHGE*; G. Ficker, *Erlasse des Patriarchen von Konstantinopel Alexios Studites* (Kiel, 1911); and FM, VII. 136–8.

brother of the Emperor Michael IV the Paphlagonian, his election
was declared invalid by a group of metropolitans mustered by John.
Alexius adroitly foiled the plot by offering to resign provided that
all his metropolitan ordinations were also declared invalid and
anathemas pronounced against the emperors whom he had
crowned.[3] Understandably Alexius was among the opponents of
the Paphlagonian house and supported the Macedonian party who
produced as Empress the reluctant Theodora, an elderly nun and the
last of that dynasty. The patriarchal register though sparse indicates
the range of Alexius's interests and activities. He was much
concerned with settling individual marriage problems as well as
with the general rules governing the complicated laws of kindred
and affinity. But he was no Nicholas Mysticus. Despite his Studite
upbringing and the canonical rulings his attitude to imperial
infringements was somewhat flexible, though in the case of the old
Empress Zoe's forbidden third marriage to Constantine IX Monomachus at least he himself did not perform the ceremony or give the
blessing, but simply offered the kiss of peace after the marriage. It
was one of those political dilemmas which constantly involved the
Church and demanded the exercise of *oeconomia* or expediency. For
Zoe had the disposition of a mule and was unlikely to be dissuaded
from the marriage. It was also obvious that the Empire needed some
kind of male guidance. As the contemporary historian Psellus
cynically remarked 'It might be said that the Patriarch recognised
the problem and accepted the will of God in the matter'.[4]

Patriarch Alexius's rulings on matters of discipline concerning
both lay and ecclesiastical circles point to old problems. He was
much concerned with the misuse of monasteries and strict rules
were laid down to prevent illegal hiring out or handing over to lay
control either the house or its property. In a synodal ruling he
attempted to provide means for regulating clerical disputes and
eliminating uncanonical acts. In particular all clerics and monks
were forbidden to resort to secular judges, evidently a frequent
practice and already condemned before Alexius's day.[5]

Most important of all was Alexius's attitude towards heresy. Here
Alexius and his eleventh-century successors seemed obsessed with a

---

[3] *GR* 842.
[4] *Chronographia*, Constantine IX, ch. 20, ed. E. Renauld (Paris, 1926), I. 127.
[5] *GR* 833 (Nov. 1027) and 835 (Jan. 1028).

desire to bring non-Chalcedonian Armenians and Jacobites into the Orthodox Church, unlike Basil II who had wisely allowed some latitude, certainly in Mesopotamia though not in Antioch. In 1029 the Jacobite Patriarch John VIII Bar Abdoun was called to Constantinople where he spent some months. But all attempts to convert him failed and he was excommunicated by the synod there and exiled.[6] Similarly charges were brought against Jacobites in the region of Melitene and the leaders of the heresy were questioned before the synod. Many members of the senate were also present for a drive against heresy in Byzantium was a combined operation of church and state. The Jacobite Patriarch was inflexible, but some bishops abjured their errors and were received back into office (with certain restrictions).[7] Evidently the non-Chalcedonians continued to prosper in Melitene and its environs. A few years later a number of synodal rulings were issued penalizing mixed marriages, debarring heretics from testifying against the Orthodox and limiting their right of inheritance.[8] The continued antagonism roused by such restrictions, even though they were clearly largely ineffective, did not make for loyalty towards Constantinople in the face of the Turkish advance. Thus for Byzantium the problem was not purely a religious one. The significant ethnic changes caused by the immigrant Syrians and Armenians affected the recently conquered eastern regions as well as eastern Asia Minor. These were the very provinces which were under attack in the eleventh century and it would have been politic to pursue a policy of religious toleration. As it was, religious dissidents must have felt that they were probably better off in the long run under Muslim than Orthodox rule.[9]

Alexius Studites' successor was Michael Cerularius (25 March 1043–2 November 1058).[10] Apart from Photius he is probably (and

---

[6] GR 838 (Oct. 1029).

[7] GR 839 (May 1030).

[8] GR 846 (Sept. 1039).

[9] G. Dagron, 'Minorités ethniques et religieuses dans l'orient byzantin à la fin du Xe et au XIe siècle: L'Immigration syrienne', *TM*, 6 (1976), 177–216; Vryonis, *Decline, passim* and 'Byzantium: the Social Basis of Decline in the Eleventh Century', *Greek, Roman and Byzantine Studies*, 2 (1959), 159–75.

[10] By reason of the significance which was later attached to the episode of 1054 there is considerable literature on Cerularius. See L. Bréhier, *Le Schisme oriental du XIe siècle* (Paris, 1899); Jugie, *Le Schisme byzantin*; E. Amann, 'La Rupture du XIe siècle', in FM, VII; Runciman, *Eastern Schism*, all in need of some revision; F. Dvornik 'Constantinople and Rome', *CMH* IV(1); Beck, *Geschichte* (brief, with more recent bibliography).

undeservedly) the best known of the Byzantine patriarchs because he was associated by later generations with a supposed formal schism between Rome and Constantinople. He did not come from the learned circles then flourishing in the City, nor did he appear to have any genuine monastic vocation though he was a monk at the time of his enthronement. He had been involved in a conspiracy against Michael IV and may have become a monk to avoid paying the penalty for his treason. The Empress Zoe's third husband, Constantine IX Monomachus, had been a fellow conspirator and was his friend. After Constantine's marriage to Zoe, Cerularius was in favour at court and he became the Patriarch Alexius's protosyncellus. When Alexius died Constantine raised Cerularius to the patriarchal throne. If the Emperor thought that he now had a co-operative ally as patriarch he was mistaken. Throughout his long office under three Emperors and an Empress Cerularius proved arrogant and overbearing, though it should be said that in his private life he did at least show some better feelings and took care to arrange for the education of his two young nephews. He entrusted them to the scholar Michael Psellus, though even this was probably directed towards his own interests.

Michael Cerularius's patriarchal register shows the usual activities, such as dealing with the complicated rulings on marriage, with episcopal difficulties and disputes, and monastic problems as the reopening of Nea Mone, the house on Chios which had been temporarily closed by reason of alleged occult practices. Apart from such daily routine carried out by his secretariat, his patriarchate was characterized by his attempt to exalt the position of the Byzantine Church. Following his predecessor's policy he tried to bring the separated Churches of the monophysites under his control. He evidently considered that he was the superior of the three eastern patriarchates, Antioch, Alexandria, and Jerusalem. He regarded himself as the equal of the Pope and censured Latin practices where these differed from those of the Greek Church. Further, and Byzantine sources seem to regard this as his worst offence, he criticized imperial policy, stressing the superiority of his own position. All four rulers during his patriarchate, Constantine IX, Theodora, Michael VI, and Isaac I, found his attitude and many of his activities often disruptive and even intolerable.

With the annexation of Ani in 1045 the last remaining kingdom of Armenia had fallen to Byzantium. It no doubt seemed undesirable to Orthodoxy to have an independent non-Chalcedonian Church within the Empire and, however unwise from the political angle, Byzantine religious policy towards the Armenians was in accordance with usual practice. The Armenian Church did not recognize the council of Chalcedon, and many of its customs differed from those of Constantinople, such as its use of unleavened bread in the Divine Liturgy, or fasting on Saturdays. It was probably with conformity in mind that in 1048 Constantine IX invited Peter I, Catholicus of the Armenian Church, to Constantinople.[11] The meeting in 1048 was amicable but negative in result and subsequent relations were to deteriorate as attacks on the monophysites were intensified later on during Constantine X's reign. The Armenian Church had always been the symbol of its people's nationalism. Annexation and dispersal could not extinguish this spirit, as the successful establishment of Lesser Armenia in south-east Asia Minor was soon to demonstrate.[12] It was unfortunate that Byzantium's eleventh-century ecclesiastical policy towards Armenia should have exacerbated the long-standing antagonism between Greek and Armenian, provoking endless friction in Asia Minor just at a time when a united front against Turkic invaders was needed.

In their Armenian policy Constantine IX and Cerularius were at one. It was otherwise with western affairs. Throughout Constantine IX's reign the political situation in Italy presented increasing problems. Under the leadership of the Hauteville family the Normans were eating into the central Italian Lombard principalities as well as the remaining Byzantine provinces in South Italy. The Byzantine governor Argyrus had the strong support of Constantine. But he was a Lombard belonging to the Latin rite and was greatly disliked by Cerularius. Argyrus tried to strengthen his position by allying with Pope Leo IX who had been appointed in 1048 by the German Emperor Henry III. Leo was from Lorraine where the pre-Gregorian reformers had long been active. Though in a sense owing his position to Henry (who supported church reform) Leo quickly showed that the papacy was going to be independent of secular control. And the whole reform movement tended to exalt the position of the Pope, as Leo's friend Hildebrand

[11] DR 891.
[12] See Sirarpie Der Nersessian, *Armenia and the Byzantine Empire* (Cambridge, Mass., 1945), for a brief account of the Armenian point of view.

made clear when he became Pope as Gregory VII in 1073. Leo was not the man to be browbeaten by an arrogant eastern Patriarch, and like his predecessors he never forgot the lost jurisdiction in South Italy and Illyricum and took every opportunity to encourage Latin churches in the disputed areas. But he was anxious to check the aggressive Normans and was willing to join forces with Argyrus. Both the Pope and the Byzantines also hoped for support from Henry III, but this did not effectively materialize. In the event Argyrus was defeated by the Normans in February 1053 and later in June Leo was captured by them. He was well treated and was able to continue to deal with ecclesiastical matters.

At this juncture when it was still hoped that a coalition between eastern and western powers might halt the Normans a provocative letter from Leo, archbishop of Ochrida, to John, the Greek bishop of Trani in Apulia, reached the Pope by hand of Humbert, cardinal bishop of Silva Candida, who had translated it into Latin. In the Latin version it purported to come from Michael, 'universalis patriarcha Novae Romae', as well as from Leo of Ochrida.[13] Whether the insertion of Michael's name was due to Humbert or not, the document certainly reflected the Patriarch's views and he no doubt stirred up Archbishop Leo to send it regardless of the difficult political situation. In this letter John of Trani was charged to see that it reached 'all Frankish bishops and priests and peoples and the most reverend Pope himself' so that they might correct their errors. The letter selected minor differences of usage, as rules for fasting in Lent, or the shaven versus the bearded face for clerics as well the much disputed use of unleavened bread at mass. It was offensive and all the more so in that it followed on the closing of the Latin churches in Constantinople by Cerularius. The Pope responded, assisted by Humbert who was throughout most unconciliatory. But before his reply was sent off two letters from Constantinople reached him. One was from Constantine IX who had been informed of the worsening situation in Italy by John of Trani who came in person to see the Emperor. The other letter was from Michael Cerularius, evidently more conciliatory in tone but still unacceptable to Rome. These letters are known only from the papal replies.[14] To Constantine, 'his beloved son, the glorious and

---

[13] *PL* 143, cols. 793–8; Will (better edition), 56–64.
[14] *PL* 143, cols. 773–81; Will, 85–92.

devout Emperor of New Rome', the Pope was graciously encouraging, hoping for action against the Normans from Argyrus and Henry III as well as from the Byzantine Emperor, but he strongly condemned Cerularius's recent activities. In contrast to his letter to Constantine there was a studied coldness in his reply to 'the archbishop of Constantinople' who was particularly admonished for his offer to see that the papal name was commemorated in all the churches 'in toto orbe terrarum' provided that his own name was equally recognized in the Roman Church. Evidently here Leo had misunderstood the use of '*oecumene*' which to the Greeks meant only 'throughout the Empire'. In this and other correspondence it was made clear to the Greeks that the Roman Church was the '*caput et mater ecclesiarum*'; there was no question of *primus inter pares*. Thus the views of the western reformed Church and those of the Byzantine Patriarch were diametrically opposed.

The two papal letters were taken to Constantinople by legates sent to deal with the political and ecclesiastical situation. This embassy was headed by Humbert who had played a major part in formulating the papal replies. He was a prominent leader in the campaign for purifying the Latin Church, particularly from simony, and was a staunch supporter of the papal claim to plenitude of power. He was as intolerant and overbearing as Cerularius and not the man to promote conciliation and understanding. The legates reached Constantinople in April 1054 and were well received by the Emperor but virtually boycotted by Cerularius. Evidently there was a public debate on the ecclesiastical points at issue. Nicetas, a Studite monk and disciple of the distinguished abbot Symeon the New Theologian, supported the Greek side, but was induced to withdraw his advocacy and his works were burnt. All this was under imperial, and not patriarchal, auspices.

Then, exasperated beyond bearing at the failure to draw Michael Cerularius and perhaps aware of the hostility of the clergy and populace of Constantinople, on 16 July Humbert took final action and excommunicated the Patriarch and his close associates in a bull which was left on the altar of the Great Church at the morning liturgy. A subdeacon tried to return the bull but it was flung to the ground and eventually reached the Patriarch. The legates left Constantinople on 18 July, parting on friendly terms with the Emperor. But they were recalled to the capital by Constantine that they might meet the synod to discuss the bull. The Emperor then discovered that he was not to be allowed to attend this meeting. He realized that Cerularius was fomenting popular fury at the excommunication and fearing for the safety of the legates he hurriedly sent them off again. When the synod met it drew up a statement refuting the charge of heresy brought against Cerularius and included in this an accurate Greek translation of the bull.[15] Cerularius argued that the legates were impostors and that the papal letters were forged by Humbert in consultation with the Patriarch's alleged enemy Argyrus. He pointed out that Humbert had visited Argyrus *en route* and that the seals of the letters had been tampered with. Thus the embassy ended leaving a seemingly triumphant Michael Cerularius and an unreconciled papacy. Leo IX had died on 19 April 1054 when the embassy had just reached Constantinople but the actions of his emissaries during the interregnum were probably valid. In any case they represented views acceptable in western ecclesiastical circles.

These contrasting points of view are to some extent reflected in the correspondence of the Pope and the Patriarch with Peter III, Patriarch of Antioch. Peter was on friendly terms with Pope Leo IX and had sent him the usual synodica announcing his appointment and containing his profession of faith. Leo reciprocated,[16] exhorting him to resist any encroachments on the ecclesiastical jurisdiction of Antioch, a reference to Michael Cerularius who had already had to apologize to Antioch for interfering in its affairs.[17] But, as in his letters to Constantinople, the Pope particularly emphasized the position of the apostolic see as head of all Churches, a view which ran counter to the eastern conception of ecclesiastical government through the pentarchy of the old patriarchates. For his part Cerularius was anxious to justify his actions to the eastern patriarchs. In two letters to Peter of Antioch he pressed his case too far and made false statements concerning the points at issue between Rome and Constantinople.[18] His accuracy was challenged by Peter. For instance, his assertion that the name of the Pope had been

---

[15] *Edictum Synodale*, PG 120, cols. 735–48; Will, 155–68. The original bull is in the Latin account of the episode, *Brevis et Succincta Commemoratio*, PL 143, cols. 1001–4; Will, 150–4. There is a translation in Jugie, *Le Schisme byzantin*.

[16] PL 143, cols. 769–73; Will, 168–71.

[17] GR 860 and 861.

[18] GR 866 and 870; PG 120, cols. 816–20 and 781–96 (the probable order of the letters); Will, 184–8, 172–84.

omitted from the diptychs since Justinian I's day was untrue. Peter himself had heard it commemorated in the liturgy when he was in Constantinople forty-five years earlier. Further Cerularius had unfairly implied that the bull had excommunicated the whole Orthodox Church. In fact both Humbert and Cerularius had been careful to limit their censures. Humbert praised the most Christian and Orthodox City, its rulers, clergy, senate, and people and specifically anathematized only Cerularius and his close associates.[19] Likewise the Patriarch hurled anathemas only against the authors of the impious bull and of the letters, which he believed to be a forgery concocted by impostors and not coming from the Pope. In fact since neither Church was attacked as such the way was open for reconciliation. Peter of Antioch, like Archbishop Theophylact of Bulgaria, was one of the more tolerant Greek ecclesiastics and he urged Cerularius to show forbearance and understanding. He stressed the relative unimportance of many of the differences. The filioque and unleavened bread he thought mattered, but, he said, if only Rome would omit the added filioque in the creed a blind eye might be turned to the rest, including the unleavened bread.[20] But, tolerant as he was, like other eastern churchmen he stood by the traditional form of government through the pentarchy and general councils.[21]

It was partly this fundamental conflict between the western view of the papacy and Byzantine tradition which contributed to the failure of the papal mission of 1054. No effective political alliance was formed. The Norman position in Italy was further consolidated when the papacy was forced to make the best bargain open to it and in 1059 had to recognize the new settlers as its vassals. In the papal view the Normans were at least of the Latin Church and to that extent strengthened the papal position at the expense of the Greek churches in Italy.

Viewed in their historical framework the events of 1054 have in a sense been magnified out of all proportion. It is true that at the time there was great strength of feeling on both sides. One only has to look at the documents to realize the deliberate provocation and discourtesy towards each other of both Humbert and Cerularius, as

[19] GR 869 (*Edictum Synodale*).
[20] PG 120, cols. 795–816; Will, 189–204.
[21] See his letter to Dominic of Grado, PG 120, cols. 755–82; Will, 208–28.

well as the insistence of the Pope on claims which seemed to go far beyond accepted tradition in the eastern Churches. Posterity has however read into this dramatic episode 'a formal schism' which did not then exist. What the quarrel did was to bring to the surface once again differences in doctrine and custom which had long been recognized and which were to be exaggerated and worked over in the bitter polemic of the later middle ages. But that time had not yet come. Once the Roman legates had left in July 1054 it was no doubt thought that normal relations between Constantinople and the curia would eventually resume—particularly vital at this time as the Pope could be an important factor in a difficult political situation. And this is in fact what happened. What Constantinople had not yet really grasped were the implications and problems inherent in the western concept of the Pope as *caput et mater* of all Churches. That was to come together with the intensified embitterment engendered by the Latin crusading movement and its culmination in 1204. That was when the real schism occurred.[22]

The Humbert–Cerularius quarrel made virtually no impact at the time on Byzantine society and gets hardly a mention in contemporary writings. Cerularius may well have been congratulating himself on his firm assertion of his position as leading churchman in the Aegean and Middle East. In fact his downfall was impending and for quite another reason.

Constantine IX died in 1055 soon after the affair with Humbert. Though he had originally been the friend of Michael Cerularius their relations had become strained. Succeeding rulers were to find the Patriarch's ambitions equally unacceptable. The old Empress Theodora, the last of the Macedonian dynasty, ruled from 1055–6. The contemporary historian Psellus, who was immersed in court activities, said that the Empress detested Cerularius once she came to power because he openly expressed his dislike of a woman on the throne. This may not be entirely unrelated to criticism of Cerularius's interest in a suspect prophetess who was exiled. Psellus hints that Theodora was preparing to depose him when she died. Theodora's successor was Michael VI, an indecisive elderly civilian. Cerularius and others intrigued against him and forced him to resign in favour of Isaac Comnenus who came from a prominent

[22] See the analysis of P. Lemerle, 'L'Orthodoxie byzantine et l'œcuménisme médiéval: Les Origines du "schisme" des Églises', *Bull. de l'Assoc. Budé* (1965), 228–46.

landed family, one of a group of military men concerned at the neglect of imperial defences. Isaac I (1057–9) needed money for defence purposes and the Church was not exempt. He was charged by Cerularius with ignoring the rights of church property and soon the two men came into open conflict. It is not clear exactly what authority Cerularius was claiming. Psellus, who was at the centre of the crisis, wrote to him 'You despise emperors and oppose all authority.'[23] Another historian alleged that the Patriarch maintained that there was no difference between the priesthood and the Empire, or very little, and implied that the priesthood was the more important.[24] Cerularius certainly wore the purple shoes then regarded as an imperial prerogative. This time he had gone too far. Isaac exiled him and called a synod to depose him. The chief charges against him were drawn up by Psellus in a document known as the *Accusation*. But the indictment remained undelivered because on 2 November 1058 the Patriarch suddenly died on his way to attend the synod, which had been summoned at a place well away from Constantinople for fear of popular support for him in the capital. Psellus's *Accusation* is an informative document.[25] The main charges were treason and heresy. Cerularius was accused of trying to supplant the Emperor, but it is not clear whether he meant to combine the imperial and patriarchal offices. If so, he was attacking the basic structure of the Empire and was unlikely to succeed. He evidently thought the priesthood superior to secular office and here again he was stressing something alien to the established interdependence of church and state each essential to the other and with different functions. Cerularius was also charged with heresy and accused of dabbling in occult mysteries and consulting unsavoury soothsayers whom he allowed into the Great Church. Many details bring to life his character and activities. For instance in his colourful arrogance he set up looms in the vaults of Hagia Sophia to spin the exclusive imperial gold cloth for his own use. Had he lived he would certainly have been deposed, though there was some risk in this because of his following in the capital and his links with the influential Ducas family to whom he was related by marriage. Isaac probably later paid the penalty for his attack on Cerularius which

---

[23] Ep. 207, Sathas, V. 511.
[24] Scylitzes Cont., p. 105 (*CB*, II, p. 643).
[25] Ed. E. Kurz, *Michaelis Pselli Scripta Minora*, I. 232–328 (Milan, 1936); see also L. Bréhier, *REG*, 16 (1903), 375–416 and 17 (1904), 35–76.

would certainly have roused the antipathy of the Ducas and may have contributed to his own somewhat sudden and unexplained abdication in 1059.

After such a firebrand as Cerularius the next two patriarchs must have proved a welcome relief. Constantine III Lichudes (2 February 1059–9/10 August 1063) had been a distinguished and valued minister, proedrus, and protovestiarius. He was one of several candidates and was chosen for his statesmanlike and virtuous qualities. Scylitzes Continuatus spoke of an election by 'clergy and people' as well as the synod,[26] unusual if so, but perhaps a sop allowed by the Emperor to compensate for his unpopular attack on the late Patriarch. Before his ordination and enthronement were permitted the Emperor (always in financial difficulties) made him give up the administration (and revenues) of the Mangana which he had received from Constantine IX before he became patriarch.[27] The most significant aspect of Lichudes' patriarchate was the continued persecution of the monophysites, all the more disastrous in view of defence problems and the possibility that if driven too far the Syrians and the Armenians would join, or at any rate tolerate, the Turkic invaders, which was in fact what happened. Michael the Syrian reported two edicts in Constantine Ducas's reign under an unnamed Patriarch whose sudden death he considered to be a sign of divine displeasure. This must have been Lichudes. All non-Chalcedonians were to be evicted from Melitene and their sacred books burnt.[28]

John Xiphilinus (1 January 1064–2 August 1075), who followed Lichudes, belonged to the same circle of intellectuals as Psellus.[29] He had been nomophylax in charge of the Law School set up by Constantine IX in 1045 and then later in the reign fell into disfavour at court, the victim of an intrigue. Like his friend Psellus he went into a monastery on Bithynian Mount Olympus. Unlike Psellus he found his vocation there, stayed on and became head of the house. With reluctance he agreed to take up the patriarchal office, in his eyes no promotion but a descent from a higher form of divine service. During the first year of Xiphilinus's patriarchate the drive

[26] Scylitzes Cont., p. 106 (*CB*, II, p. 644).
[27] Scylitzes Cont., p. 106 (*CB*, II, pp. 644–5); see Lemerle, *Cinq études*, 280–2.
[28] *GR* 890 and 891.
[29] On Xiphilinus see W. Fisher, *Studien zur byzantinischen Geschichte des elften Jahrhunderts* (Plauen i. V., 1883), pp. 2–49 (now in need of some revision).

against the monophysites continued. The Jacobite Patriarch Athanasius and some of his bishops were imprisoned for a time in the
monastery of the Greek metropolitan of Melitene. Then they were
summoned to Constantinople, as well as Ignatius, the Jacobite
metropolitan of Melitene. Athanasius died *en route* but Ignatius
arrived and was exiled by the synod to Mount Ganos in Gallipoli.[30]
Later in 1065 the Armenians, ecclesiastics and princes, were summoned to Constantinople and pressed to agree to ecclesiastical
union but without success. Their hatred of the Greeks was only
intensified and the Armenians living in Asia Minor vented their
fury on their Greek neighbours. The Greek metropolitan of
Caesarea was seized and cruelly killed by Kakig the ex-king of Ani.
But this was not merely a religious problem; it reflected deep-
rooted racial antipathy of long standing which was only exacerbated
by Constantinople's religious policy. As usually the case in Byzantium, orthodoxy was more important than political expediency and
here Xiphilinus was in the normal Byzantine tradition.

Xiphilinus's expertise as a jurist served him well in dealing with
intricate marital problems of canon and civil law, as is seen in the
synodal rulings of 1066 and 1067.[31] From Psellus's eulogy on him
he is revealed as a man of compassion, aware of the needs of the
poor, as in his organization of a daily distribution of bread behind
the phiale of Hagia Sophia.[32] His attitude towards the state was
firm rather than aggressive. He did not hesitate to uphold ecclesiastical prerogative against imperial claims, as for instance in his
rejection of an imperial attempt to appoint a bishop in a way
contrary to canon and civil law.[33] Towards the end of his
patriarchate he was closely involved in matters of state. Constantine
X died in 1067 leaving three minors. It was Xiphilinus who acted
with the senate in absolving their mother Eudocia from her promise
to Constantine not to marry again. It was obviously in the interests
of the Empire to have a military man in charge and in 1068 Eudocia
chose as her second husband the general Romanus Diogenes
(1068–71). Xiphilinus lived on into the succeeding reign of the
young Ducas Michael VII (1071–8) and supported his attempt to
ally with the Norman Robert Guiscard and to betroth his son

[30] GR 893.
[31] GR 896 and 897.
[32] GR 905.
[33] GR 900.

Constantine to Guiscard's daughter Helen.[34] Xiphilinus was the finest of the eleventh-century patriarchs, humane, a philosopher as well as a jurist, balanced in outlook, a spiritually-minded man with a strong sense of duty.

Cosmas I of Jerusalem (8 August 1075–8 August 1081) had a reputation for sanctity. His term of office covered the troubled period preceding Alexius Comnenus's successful *coup* of 1081. Michael VII had been deposed in 1078; he became a Studite monk and was subsequently elected by the synod to be metropolitan of Ephesus.[35] Cosmas could not approve the third marriage of Michael's successor, Nicephorus III Botaneiates, to the Alan princess Maria, Michael's ex-wife, though he went no further than degrading the priest who married them.[36] But Cosmas did successfully oppose Alexius Comnenus's attempt to repudiate his wife Irene Ducaena when he wanted to marry the fascinating already twice-wed ex-Empress Maria Alania. Alexius even had himself crowned without Irene which alarmed the Ducas family. Alexius's mother, the redoubtable Anna Dalassena, hated Irene and the Ducas connection. Moreover she had in mind to replace Patriarch Cosmas (who was pro-Ducas) with her own favourite monk Eustratius Garidas. According to the historian Anna Comnena, Cosmas agreed to abdicate provided that he was first allowed to crown Irene Empress. This he did and then went. The most significant synodal act during his office was the condemnation of certain heretical views connected with the teaching of the scholar John Italus who was a friend of the Ducas family. This was during the period 1076–7.[37] At this time the Ducas family were still in power. John Italus was not then mentioned by name and the more important sequel to this action took place in the succeeding reign of Alexius Comnenus, the rival of the Ducas family whose protégé the Emperor was not inclined to favour. Thus when Patriarch Cosmas departed from office the issue of the philosophers versus the theologians was left largely unresolved. This is only one of various pointers indicating that in many respects the year 1081 did not really mark a break in continuity for the Empire.

[34] *GR* 901.
[35] *GR* 909.
[36] *GR* 910.
[37] *GR* 907; see below pp. 142 ff.

3. 1081: a new era or continuity?

By April 1081 the Comnenian family in the person of Alexius I had secured the throne. For nearly a hundred years (1081–1180) three able rulers—Alexius I, his son John II, and his grandson Manuel I—gave an apparent measure of stability to Byzantium. They came from the military aristocracy whose previous attempts to take control, first by Isaac I Comnenus, then by Romanus IV Diogenes, had been short-lived. Now with the Comnenian dynasty the ascendancy of the civil aristocracy was overthrown. It was not until 1185 that the Comnenian dominance was ended, first by the brief minority of Manuel I's young son Alexius II (1180–3), and then by the unacceptable autocracy of Andronicus I the erratic and unstable cousin of Manuel, whose growing tyranny brought him a cruel death in 1185. The throne fell to the less competent Angeli family (1185–1204) and the way was open for an avaricious Venice bent on enlarging her economic empire and a Roman Church anxious to assert the overall supremacy of the papacy.

It is true that under the Comneni there were certain changes which contrast with the regime during the years 1025–81. Alexius I pursued a close-knit family or 'clan' policy where key (and other) positions were assigned to his relatives. Alterations in hierarchical arrangements and in administration strengthened the ruling house at the expense of the previously powerful civil bureaucracy. There are certainly also other contrasts. Dynastic continuity and the undoubted ability of the Comneni did bring about a consistent (if not always successful) stand against internal weakness and external pressures. Nevertheless all this only afforded a breathing space. Whether ruled by eleventh-century mediocrities or competent Comnenian diplomats, in both political and ecclesiastical fields—often inseparable—the years 1025–1204 were characterized by certain trends spanning the two centuries and pointing to the future. The ambitions of the Normans occupying South Italy and Sicily and coveting Byzantium itself; the growing independence of the Balkan principalities who were also to stake a claim to Constantinople; the vigorous reform movements of the western Church and the claims of the papacy; the growing polemic on differing points of doctrine and discipline within the two Churches; the Latin concern over lack of access to the Holy Places; the building up of western crusading fervour and colonial ambitions; and above all the growth of flourishing communities in Italy, such as Venice and Genoa, with the drive to push their way still further into eastern markets thus eroding the Byzantine economy—all these factors were coming to the boil throughout the eleventh century, only to be intensified during the twelfth century as the West grew in strength and battened on an Empire fighting with inadequate weapons to keep back, or at least to come to terms with, the Turks, as well as having to deal with the aggressive Pecheneg and Cuman tribes on the north-east frontiers.

Continuity is also found in certain more specifically internal developments, despite some change of emphasis. These were mainly intellectual and religious activities. For instance philosophical studies were vigorously pursued in both eleventh and twelfth centuries often leading, albeit inadvertently, to charges of heresy. Then on a rather different level there were various forms of dualist heresy, especially the widespread Bogomilism which also tended to be dangerous to the government since it readily led to attacks on the establishment. This popular movement was particularly active in both centuries, and indeed persisted in some form or other throughout the middle ages. Here as in many other ways the eleventh and twelfth centuries foreshadow the Palaeologan period.

4. Philosophers and theologians: individual heretics: ecclesiastical currents

Cosmas, the last of the five notable eleventh-century patriarchs, was succeeded by Eustratius Garidas (May 1081–July 1084), the candidate of Alexius Comnenus's formidable mother Anna Dalassena. His appointment may have been some compensation to her for having to swallow the Ducas connection forged by the marriage of Irene Ducaena to her son which Cosmas had so unaccommodatingly refused to sever. Eustratius seemed to have had none of the qualities of his immediate predecessors and the highlight of his brief and troubled patriarchate, the trial of John Italus and his followers, was not initiated by him and was an episode in which he played a comparatively minor role. It was in fact even thought that he was partial to the accused.

This first heresy trial in Alexius's reign was directed against a pupil of Michael Psellus.[38] He was John Italus who had finally

---

[38] Gouillard, 'Synodikon', provides an indispensable guide to the heresy trials (texts and commentary).

succeeded his master in the post of head (hypatus) of the philoso-phers. The attack must be viewed against the background of contemporary intellectual activity. The humanist approach with its interest in classical antiquity, an approach seen so clearly from the days of Photius onwards,[39] continued in the eleventh century and was particularly reflected in an interest in philosophical studies. Here the lead was taken by Psellus. He was a remarkably vigorous and many-sided man, a scholar whose career included nearly forty years of usually successful intrigue at court as well as a major share in promoting higher education in Constantinople. He was particu-larly occupied with Plato and the neoplatonists and had a large, and according to him, international, following of students. The views of Plato and his interpreters, for instance Proclus, often differed from Christian teaching on certain subjects, as the origin of the world or the future of the soul, and it was therefore necessary for scholars to take great care to dissociate themselves from such teaching. Ortho-doxy thus regarded pagan philosophy as an ancillary to theology which could be used only as long as it did not conflict with Christian doctrine. After all even the revered John of Damascus had extensively drawn on Aristotelian logic in the first part of his *Fount of Knowledge*. Evidently Psellus was suspected of going beyond the permitted bounds and of holding heretical views, but he refuted any such charge and defended himself in a short profession of faith.[40] He did not have to face a trial, though he did absent himself from court for a while, entering a monastery in Bithynian Mount Olympus in Asia Minor which (as might be expected) he found highly uncongenial. The feeling which had been roused against him may have been reflected in his correspondence with John Xiphili-nus, his old colleague. The two men had been engaged in teaching in the capital, Psellus more interested in rhetoric, philosophy, and the arts, Xiphilinus in law, though evidently in each case not exclusively so. To what extent they were rivals in the scholastic arena is not clear,[41] but they certainly did not agree in their philosophical priorities. Xiphilinus bitterly reproached Psellus for

[39] See Lemerle, *Humanisme byzantin*, *passim*.
[40] See A. Garzya, 'On Michael Psellus's Admission of Faith', *EEBS*, 35 (1966–7), 41–6 (text and English summary).
[41] For a revision of long accepted interpretations see Lemerle, ' "Le Gouver-nement des philosophes": Notes et remarques sur l'enseignement, les écoles, la culture', *Cinq études*, 195–248; he is not in agreement with the suggestions of W. Wolska–Conus, 'Les Écoles de Psellos et de Xiphilin sous Constantin IX Monomaque', *TM*, 6 (1976), 223–43.

his championship of Plato. In his reply to Xiphilinus Psellus stressed that the church fathers had found much of value in the old philosophers and had used their methods. He passionately emphasized that much as he revered Plato, in the last resort his hope was in Christ. You say that Plato is mine, he wrote, but it is Christ who is mine.[42]

Criticism of Psellus did not prevent the continued study of the neoplatonists and the use of dialectic, as the career of John Italus showed. He went on lecturing and in the eyes of some authorities he was regarded as perverting his students. The fears of the conservative, and particularly the monastic, element came to a head in the heresy trial of 1076–7, renewed in 1082 under Alexius I. The first protest was during Michael VII's reign. At that time Italus had imperial support. He was a friend of the reigning Ducas family and certain of his discussions on philosophical and theological topics were dedicated to the Emperor Michael and his brother Andronicus.[43] There was obviously general discussion about Italus's views and the matter came to the standing synod in Constantinople. Nine errors contrary to orthodoxy were condemned. These errors can be summed up as the use of human reason to explain divine mysteries such as the Incarnation and the hypostatic union, the acceptance of specific views contrary to Christian teaching, and the assumption that philosophy was a valid study and source of truth in its own right. The minutes of the trial have not survived but the errors are listed in the later 1082 trial and appear in the nine anathemas of the Synodicon which are read out on the first Sunday of Lent together with one or two further errors (tradition varies).[44] On the occasion of the 1076–7 trial the synod compromised. Italus was not mentioned by name, but it must have been clear that the popular teacher with his crowded lecture room was the main objective. Italus

[42] See U. Criscuolo, *Epistola a Giovanni Xifilino*, critical text, introduction, translation, and commentary (Naples, 1973); Greek text also in Sathas, V.

[43] Some of Italus's writings have been edited. See G. Cereteli (ed.), *Opuscula Selecta*, 2 vols. (Tiflis, 1924–6, lithograph), re-edited by N. Ketschakmadze, *Ioannis Itali Opera* (Tiflis, 1966), with brief introduction in Russian and Georgian and notes in Latin; P. Joannou (ed.), *Ioannes Italos, Quaestiones Quodlibetales* (Ἀπορίαι καὶ λύσεις) (Ettal, 1956); J. Gouillard, *TM*, 9 (1985), 133–74.

[44] There is some confusion over the details of the condemnations of the 1076–7 and 1082 trials and the traditions of the Synodicon vary; see Gouillard, 'Synodikon', 188–202; see also *GR* 907; P. E. Stephanou, *Jean Italos, philosophe et humaniste* (=*OCA* 134, Rome, 1949); Hussey, *Church and Learning*, 89–94; P. Joannou, *Christliche Metaphysik in Byzanz*, I (Ettal, 1956).

protested his innocence and affirmed his Christian faith to Patriarch Cosmas asking for a full enquiry. Cosmas however let the matter drop and Italus continued his lecture courses, no doubt employing dialectic as before but without necessarily subscribing personally to unorthodox views.

With the accession of Alexius Comnenus in 1081 the situation changed. Genuine apprehension continued among the more conservative whose views on learning were certainly not the same as those who wished freely to explore the resources of philosophy and evidently did so. It was noticeable however that neither Patriarch Cosmas nor his successor Eustratius took the lead in the protest against the intellectuals. This was left to the Emperor Alexius. For on this occasion there was a significant political element involved and the offender was named. The fact was that John Italus, who had been suspect during Michael VII's reign, was himself a Latin from South Italy and probably of partly Norman blood. Moreover in 1077 he had acted as envoy to Robert Guiscard on behalf of Michael when it was hoped to come to an understanding between the Normans and the Byzantines. Now in 1081 a rival Byzantine dynasty was on the throne. Guiscard had become a dangerous enemy. In open alliance with the anti-Comnenian faction he was attacking Byzantine territory and challenging Alexius's authority. Italus was an obvious target. In defending himself he had none of Michael Psellus's elegance of style or adroitness of argument even though his bold dialectic had held his student audience. Anna Comnena gave Italus a bad press in her history. She significantly stressed that he was stirring up dangerous trouble, presumably of a political nature, a reference to the opposition to the accession of Alexius. She also deplored his clumsy use of the Greek tongue, a defect attested by others and a fault which may have led him inadvertently to make statements open to misinterpretation.

Probably with political motives in mind, it was Alexius rather than ecclesiastics who really took the initial move against Italus in 1082.[45] A mixed court of laity and clergy summoned by the Emperor found him guilty on the charges already anonymously anathematized in 1077, with two other charges added. Italus had no chance of defending himself; at one point he was almost lynched by a threatening mob, perhaps stirred up by the monks. He disappeared

[45] DR 1078–9.

into monastic life. But the study of philosophy and theological discussion did not cease.

It may however be no mere coincidence that at this time more formalized educational arrangements for the clergy emerged, though without creating an institution in the modern sense of the term. Alexius I himself paid considerable attention to the training of the clergy which he considered to be often wanting both in the capital and elsewhere. In his novel of 1107 he tried amongst other things to stimulate suitable clergy to teach by creating a special class or grade (with remuneration) for them and in this way he hoped to ensure that future clerks received a sound education and were fitted to undertake their pastoral responsibilities.[46] Further there is evidence that schools or centres of education under patriarchal authority developed during the twelfth century. There were evidently certain leading teachers, one for the Gospels (also called 'oecumenical', an honorary title of secular origin)[47] and two others for the Epistles (the 'Apostle') and the Psalter respectively, as well as a fourth, the Master of the Rhetoricians (the Rhetor).[48]

Care for teaching and pastoral work really lay with the Patriarch and episcopate, but Alexius never hesitated to intervene in ecclesiastical matters whether concerning heresy or church organization. His activities were not always well received. In fact general statements often made about Alexius's devotion to orthodoxy and the Church need some qualification. Anna Comnena's picture of her father as the popular protector of orthodoxy is no doubt true up to a point— this was in any case part of accepted imperial responsibility. But her description of her parents as the 'holy pair' poring over the works of the church fathers day and night gives only part of the story. Alexius was not the only Emperor to expound the truths of orthodoxy and to enjoy theological discussion. On the other hand he was no unfailingly benign friend of the clergy. He came from a military milieu whose ranks, unlike those of the civil aristocracy, did not proliferate high-ranking clerics or show any special

---

[46] DR 1236; Darrouzès, *Offikia*, 72–5.

[47] DR 1236; Darrouzès, *Offikia*, 67–8.

[48] Ibid., 75–9, who points out that many relevant texts are still unpublished and therefore only provisional comment can be made; R. Browning, 'The Patriarchal School at Constantinople in the Twelfth Century', *B*, 32 (1962), 167–202 and 33 (1963), 11–40, mainly on the location of 'schools' and identification of teachers.

partiality for ecclesiastical office.[49] But his steps seemed dogged by disputes and problems linked to some doctrinal question or concerned with control of ecclesiastical administration.

Surviving evidence points to a conflict between the vested interests of Emperor and higher clergy, with the Patriarch and metropolitans opposing the Emperor and the high office-holders of the Great Church. According to the critic John Oxites there was little to choose between any of these and his outspoken views afford a salutary corrective to the uninhibited praise which Anna Comnena gives her father. John V Oxites, Patriarch of Antioch (1089–1100), was a friend of the Patriarch of Constantinople, Nicholas III. He left his see in 1098 after the conquest of Antioch by the Latin crusaders and came to Constantinople, the usual refuge of clergy in exile. In 1100 he resigned his patriarchate, pleading administrative difficulties, ill health (he had gout), old age, and a desire for quiet and opportunity for study. He retired to a monastery on the island of Oxeia in the sea of Marmora. He was a vigorous and forthright man and he left various writings, including anti-Latin polemic and suggestions for the reform of church administrations. Among his works, as well as a short advisory memorandum to the Emperor, there was an address to the Emperor Alexius in which he unleashed biting invective, hurling against the Emperor accusations of widespread ecclesiastical spoliation (not simply the affair of the church treasure), injustice, maladministration, oppression, and on the moral side he stressed the Emperor's lack of genuine repentance which had invoked divine displeasure resulting in disastrous attacks on the Empire. He also boldly referred to the illegal seizure of the throne. Added to this he linked with Alexius the higher clergy who were accused among other things of being as rapacious as 'the wolves of Arabia'. He added that instead of robbing churches the very wealthy might have been made to contribute to the needs of state.[50] All this may have an element of exaggeration but on the whole it rings true and it reflects as it were the accumulative effect not only of a dangerous political situation

---

[49] See A. P. Kazhdan, *Social'nyj sostav gospodstvujuščego klassa Vizantii XI–XII vv.* (*The social structure of the ruling class in Byzantium during the XIth and XIIth centuries*) (Moscow, 1974), summarized by I. Sorlin, 'Bulletin Byzantino-Slave', TM, 6 (1976), 367–80.

[50] See P. Gautier, 'Diatribes de Jean l'Oxite contre Alexis Ier Comnène,' REB, 28 (1970), 5–55 (text, trans. and commentary).

but also of the various problems and clashes which make it difficult to ignore the underlying struggle between the Emperor and certain ecclesiastical elements.

Indeed throughout Alexius's reign underlying tension and conflicting interests came to the surface. Alexius offended the powerful clergy of the Great Church by his pointed edict on their need for reform; his upgrading of certain bishoprics was resented by the parent metropolitans; his confiscation of church treasure to deal with an acute crisis met with opposition within the synod and elsewhere (though there was precedent for such action). His views on relations with Rome seemed on occasion to conflict with those of his Patriarch as well as many of his subjects, a situation frequently repeated in the years to come. In fact within the polity there was increasing ecclesiastical tension. This gathered force during the later middle ages as political need for western help (to be bought only at the price of church union) intensified, while Orthodox tradition, pulling in a different direction, was tenaciously adhered to by most churchmen and laity. It was a tribute to Alexius's ability and determination that, though he did not always get his way and had to face bitter criticism such as that of John Oxites, he did on the whole maintain some control over conflicting and constantly changing church affairs.

Alexius found that heretical issues were by no means settled with the condemnation of Italus and his followers (some of whom were deacons of the Great Church and were acquitted). He had to deal with other cases of alleged heresy, as well as the rather different problem of the rapidly spreading popular dualist sects.

The case of Leo, the metropolitan of Chalcedon, plagued the early years of Alexius's reign and was closely linked to political opposition to the Comnenian regime. Leo had violently opposed the requisitioning of ecclesiastical treasure in late 1081 and early 1082. He was supported by the stricter clergy and by Italus and his followers (soon to be tried on different charges and known to be pro-Ducas). Leo also accused the Patriarch Eustratius of diverting part of the appropriated treasure to his own secular use, though he refused to bring positive written proof of this. Subsequently in 1086 under his successor Nicholas III by order of the Emperor the ex-Patriarch was cleared of this charge.[51] Leo was deposed from his

---

[51] *GR* 940 (Jan. 1086) and *DR* 1130.

bishopric,[52] but he went on agitating and he was exiled to Sozopolis on the Black Sea.[53] This did not settle the controversy. Leo continued to develop his view that it was in effect iconoclastic to melt down and convert to secular use the precious metals to be found on the icon frames and perhaps (as later became the usage) on part of the actual icon itself. He maintained that this was to attack the sanctity of the icon. Nevertheless Alexius wished to heal the rift and to settle the troubled question of his seizure of church treasure. He made it clear that there would be no further such acts of appropriation.[54] At a council convened at the Blachernae Palace in 1091 or 1092 it was pointed out that in accordance with the rulings of Nicaea II, which were read out at the meeting, relative veneration was given to the icon and only the prototype worshipped, while the relative veneration was not transferred to the actual material of the icon. Leo, who had been allowed to return to Constantinople, made his peace and accepted the decisions of Nicaea II on the right veneration of icons and was restored to his see.[55] Though he was difficult and obstinate and, according to Anna Comnena,[56] no canonist, a man with more zeal than knowledge, he was all the same a virtuous, courageous, and likeable person with a certain dry sense of humour and friends did not desert him. In the end Alexius won him over.

There were other problems of heresy during the reign of Alexius, some of which involved the monophysite Armenians many of whom were now within the Empire. Such was the affair of Nilus the Calabrian and his monastic associates. This followed closely on the trial of Italus and it concerned unorthodox teaching on the relation between the two natures of Christ, that is whether the assumed human nature of Christ was deified by nature ($\varphi \acute{\upsilon} \sigma \iota \varsigma$), or by participation or adoption ($\theta \acute{\varepsilon} \sigma \iota \varsigma$). Nilus thought that it was by nature. Nilus had a considerable following and the Emperor himself tried to reason with him but failed. In the early years of Nicholas III's patriarchate he was condemned and the hypostatic union reaffirmed. Anna Comnena considered that Nilus was simply a case

[52] *GR* 941 (Feb. or Mar. 1086).
[53] *GR* 955 (*c*.1089, but see P. Stephanou, 'Le Procès de Léon de Chalcédoine', *OCP*, 9 (1943), 27, who puts it in late 1087 or early 1088.
[54] *DR* 1085 and discussion on date.
[55] *GR* 967 and 968; opinion differs as to the year; see Stephanou, op. cit. 57–64.
[56] Anna Comnena, VII. 4.

of a well-meaning but ignorant monk who did not understand theological terms. But the episode was not without significance as Anna was quick to note, since the point at issue had a dangerous attraction for the Armenians who were thronging the capital.[57]

The Armenians were an ever-present concern to Emperor and Church. Alexius, always ready for theological disputation, set himself the task of winning them over while he was at Philippopolis in 1114 and he asked for the help of his friend Eustratius, metropolitan of Nicaea, who was with him. Alexius was in fact at that time dealing himself with dualist heretics but there were also a number of Armenians in the region.[58] As Patriarch John IX was to point out in defence of Eustratius later on in 1117 it was all too easy to fall into doctrinal error. In addition Eustratius also appeared to have been caught up in cross-currents of jealousy and conflicting interests, while his friendship with Alexius was a hindrance rather than a help.

Eustratius had been a pupil of John Italus, but he had specifically dissociated himself from the heretical views ascribed to his master. But like Italus he used Proclus and the other neoplatonists. He was a commentator on Aristotle, on the *Nicomachean Ethics* and the second book of the *Analytics*. As a leading theologian with anti-Latin views he had taken part in discussions in Constantinople with the Italian Peter Grossolanus on the controversial topics of the filioque and azymes. In response to Alexius's request he set out to write on the two natures of Christ using dialectic—Anna remarked that he prided himself on his use of this method even more than those who had frequented the Stoa and Academy. In dealing with this sensitive issue he laid himself open to the charge of unorthodoxy—the Armenians as well as the Orthodox found his views unacceptable. Eustratius himself appeared to have said that his writings on this subject were circulated by his enemies in an unrevised draft unknown to him and he admitted that he had once been led astray by pseudo-Cyrillic work. The case against Eustratius was set out at length by Nicetas, metropolitan of Heracleia.[59] Despite Alexius's efforts the charge was pressed and came before the synod in 1117. Opinions were divided and Eustratius's opponents only just got their condemnation through. A second session was held to discuss

[57] Anna Comnena, X. 1; *GR* 945; Gouillard, 'Synodikon' 202–6.
[58] Anna Comnena, XIV. 8.
[59] Text, trans, and commentary in Darrouzès, *Documents inédits*.

the appropriate penance. The Patriarch urged *oeconomia* and *philanthropia* and suggested the minimum, that is the retention of rank but suspension of office until the synod should decide otherwise. Considerable animosity was shown in the discussions which ensued, some urging the insertion of Eustratius's name in the Synodicon as a heretic, some even wishing to break off communion with the Patriarch and with those bishops who spoke on Eustratius's behalf. Contrary to the hopes of Alexius and the Patriarch those who vigorously opposed the use of dialectic in considering doctrinal questions won. Eustratius was suspended for life.[60] It would appear that Eustratius's opponents were moved by animosity not only towards him, but towards his friend and champion the Emperor.

Throughout the twelfth century both Church and Emperor continued to keep a watchful eye for heretical slips. There were a number of trials of well-known personalities, often church officials and scholars of standing accused on a definite issue, usually Trinitarian or Christological. In contrast to the more intangible problem of eradicating the widespread popular dualist sects such cases were in a sense easier to deal with, though synodal condemnation did not always end controversy.

Manuel's reign was particularly noticeable for problems of heresy. Like his grandfather Alexius and other predecessors on the imperial throne, Manuel was always ready to plunge into doctrinal discussion. In the 1150s a dispute arose out of a debate among the deacons of Hagia Sophia and others concerning the interpretation of the words in the liturgy 'Thou art He Who offers and is offered and receives'. The men named in the synodal enquiry were the learned deacon Soterichus Panteugenes, Patriarch-elect of Antioch, Eustathius, metropolitan of Dyrrachium, with Michael of Thessalonica and Nicephorus Basilaces, both deacons at Hagia Sophia and theological teachers at the patriarchal school. The point at issue was whether the eucharistic sacrifice was offered to the Father or to all three Persons of the Trinity. In 1156 the synod confirmed the latter as orthodox teaching and the opposite view was condemned.[61] But the question

[60] *GR* 1003; *DR* 1273; *DHGE*, 15 (Darrouzès); Gouillard, 'Synodikon', 68–71, 206–10; P. Ioannou, 'Eustrate de Nicée. Trois pièces inédites de son procès (1117)', *REB*, 10 (1952) 24–34; S. Salaville, 'Philosophie et théologie, ou épisodes scholastiques à Byzance de 1059 à 1117', *EO*, 29 (1930), 146–56.

[61] *GR* 1038; Gouillard, 'Synodikon', 210–15.

continued to be much debated and in a written dialogue Soterichus put the case for offering to the Father alone.[62] After further discussion under the presidency of Manuel, in the following year the synod anathematized Soterichus.[63] The anathema was formally entered in the Synodicon with the added statement that the Divine Liturgy was neither a mere memorial nor a distinct sacrifice but a daily renewal of the sacrifice on the Cross. Nicholas of Methone, who was fierce in defence of orthodoxy, wrote three tracts accusing Soterichus of Arianism and other heresies.[64] Soterichus who had sat on the board of enquiry as a Patriarch-elect was inevitably deprived of all office.

Another dispute in the intellectual circles of the capital during Manuel's reign had links with similar debates going on in western countries. Demetrius from Phrygian Lampe, a would-be theologian and a frequent ambassador to the West, came back to Constantinople from Germany in 1160 with criticism of the Latin interpretation of Christ's words 'My Father is greater than I' (John 14:28). The Latins held that the Son was both less than, and equal to, the Father. This was an old problem involving the human and divine natures of Christ and the hypostatic union and in Constantinople there were varying shades of interpretation. Manuel supported the western point of view. He was strongly pro-Latin and at that time had Italians in his service. Hugh Etherianus of Pisa, a western adviser of Manuel, was involved in the dispute and in the ensuing debates he put the Latin view. Manuel sent for Demetrius of Lampe but failed to win him over. Demetrius, who had considerable support, attempted to counter Manuel's efforts by defiantly circulating a written defence of his position. The controversy roused much discussion among the theologians in the City and the majority, moved by anti-Latin feeling as well as by their doctrinal arguments, were opposed to the Emperor. Manuel himself then approached the divided episcopate and those bishops suspected of supporting Demetrius were summoned individually to private interviews with him but without result. Then hearing that the dissident bishops were banding together against him, he resorted to the synod.[65]

[62] *PG* 140, cols. 140–8.
[63] *GR* 1041–3; *DR* 1412.
[64] Ed. A. Demetracopoulus, *Bibliotheca Ecclesiastica* (Leipzig, 1866), 321–59, see Beck, *Kirche*, 623–4.
[65] Nicetas Choniates, *De Man. Com.*, VII. 5 (*CB*, p. 276) and *Treasury of Orthodoxy*, *PG* 140, cols. 201–81; John Cinnamus, *Epitome*, VI. 2 (*CB*, pp. 251–7); P. Classen, 'Das Konzil von Konstantinopel 1166 und die Lateiner', *BZ*, 48 (1955), 339–68.

During 1166 several meetings of the synod were held. A statement confirming Manuel's position was drawn up and was inserted in the Synodicon. It was held that Christ's words referred to his human nature and it went on to anathematize those who maintained that Christ's suffering was only 'a fantasy'. It acclaimed those who held that the human nature of Christ by reason of the hypostatic union remained inseparable from God the Word and received like honour and adoration.[66] The entry in the Synodicon was prefaced by a tribute to the initiative taken by 'the divinely crowned, the most powerful, the theologian, the victor, the mighty Emperor, our born-in-the-purple autocrator Manuel Comnenus'. There was no mention of any individual offender. Manuel had four special marble tablets made and on these was engraved a long statement giving the accepted view. The tablets were set up inside Hagia Sophia, but as the patriarchal register shows the controversy lingered on and continued to provoke lively discussion. Statements had to be drawn up to which the episcopate had to give formal acceptance. Later on in Manuel's reign Constantine, metropolitan of Corfu, and the abbot John Eirenicus were condemned for their views on this subject.[67] Under the Angeli and even after 1204 the controversy went on and opinion seemed to swing against Manuel and the view he supported. Anti-Latin feeling was then growing even stronger than it had been in some quarters under the Comneni. As for Manuel himself there were many reasons why he should take a pro-Latin point of view. His personal preferences, his political ambitions, perhaps his western wife, his frequent contact with westerners living in his court or passing through Constantinople— these factors all enabled him to understand and develop a liking for a way of life that was rapidly becoming anathema to many of his subjects.

Towards the end of his reign Manuel went almost too far for his day, this time in another direction. Desiring to gain converts and perhaps moved by what for his generation was a rare understanding of the monotheism which Christianity and Islam held in common, he wished to omit the anathema against the God of Muhammad in the official abjuration required of converted Muslims. After fighting fiercely against tenacious opposition Manuel did manage to get some concession.[67a] In future Muslim converts were to abjure only Muhammad and his followers, but not his God.

[66] Text in Gouillard, 'Synodikon', 75–7; see also ibid. 217–26 for detail on the discussion of theological issues; *GR* 1059–67, 1075–7, and 1109–17.

[67] Gouillard, 'Synodikon', 77–81 (text).

[67a] See J. Darrouzès, *REB*, 30 (1972), 187–97.

Manuel's theological activities were in fact not always approved by his contemporaries. It was even thought (though not expressed until after his death) that he might have laid himself open to the charge of heresy over the Muslim abjuration. The historian Nicetas Choniates, who did not like Manuel, writing later on thought it safe to say then that the Emperor took too much upon himself, hating to take second place in the theological debates which were promoted so often, 'just as though he completely comprehended Christ himself and could therefore teach about Him more clearly and divinely'.[68]

Thus from the eleventh century onwards Byzantine intellectual life seemed to be characterized by an increasingly argumentative and less formal frame of mind. Perhaps the earlier period lacks evidence but it is undeniable that the attitude of a Leo VI, for instance, was very different from that of a Manuel I. In Byzantium there were always rhetorical and conventional pieces for special celebrations (as now on occasion in the Middle East). These are not entirely to western taste. But this difference of opinion should not obscure Byzantine achievement in both secular and religious spheres. Some years ago Herbert Hunger pointed out the vitality and variety of Comnenian literature.[69] The humour and wit, the satire, the secular romance, as well as the liveliness of religious dialogue and the pursuit of Platonic and Aristotelian traditions, these all characterized the twelfth, and to some extent the eleventh, centuries[70] and distinguished them from the earlier Byzantine world. It is hard to imagine a Nicetas of Nicomedia and Anselm of Havelberg publicly and courteously debating certain differences between the Churches of Rome and Constantinople in the atmosphere of acid superiority towards the West found in the tenth-century imperial court at the time of Liutprand's second visit.

Both eleventh and twelfth centuries saw men whose alertness and, in their own way, creativity, make it hard to see why it should ever have been suggested that the heresy trial of John Italus and others drove clerics, who were usually scholars as well, into a frame of mind described as 'elegant mandarinism'. Despite the

[68] Nicetas Choniates, *De Man. Com.* VII. 5 (*CB*, p. 275).

[69] H. Hunger, 'Die byzantinische Literatur der Komnenenzeit: Versuch einer Neubewertung', *Österreichische Ak. der Wiss.*, Phil. Hist. Kl., 1968, No. 3, pp. 59–76.

[70] Eleventh-century developments are reviewed in *TM*, 6 (1976).

example made of the philosopher John Italus and others, both philosophical studies and heresy trials continued throughout the Comnenian period. From time to time the study of philosophy seems to emerge, though with nothing like the brilliant and widespread reputation which it enjoyed in Psellus's day. Only twice do the actual names of the head or consul (hypatus) of the philosophers appear, Theodore of Smyrna who turns up in Hades in the satire Timarion, and Michael of Anchialus, later Patriarch Michael III (January 1170–March 1178). In his inaugural as hypatus, probably delivered in 1166 or 1167, Michael evidently thought it wise to make clear his views on philosophical studies. The errors of the philosophers, presumably the neoplatonists, had to be rejected, but he admitted that some of the ancient philosophers could be used to advantage. He himself meant to concentrate on Aristotle's study of the visible creation, believing that this could lead to knowledge of the invisible world.[71] Aristotle on the physical sciences was obviously safer than Plato. But the very fact of Michael of Anchialus's warning pointed to the continuing attraction of neoplatonism, especially Proclus. Nicholas of Methone (†*c.*1165) thought it necessary to write a full-scale refutation of Proclus's *Elements of Theology*, but evidently without much success. It was evident that whatever the official attitude the revival of neoplatonism by Psellus and his followers inaugurated a continuing (if prudently private) enjoyment of the officially suspect philosophers which continued to the days of Gemistus Plethon and beyond.[72] When Byzantines ran into doctrinal error because they applied syllogistic methods to religious mysteries, such as the Incarnation, it was understandable that they were condemned by the Church for spreading error and the root of the trouble was held to be the application of human reason to a supernatural mystery. Psellus would have said that the fault lay in the wrong use of human reasoning, for he maintained that its right use could only strengthen religious truth. It is true that the Byzantine Church never produced an Anselm of Canterbury, but its creative religious energy took other forms. It developed a theology and a spirituality in which there was place for a Gregory Palamas and a Nicholas Cabasilas, developing church doctrine and

[71] For the Greek text and commentary see R. Browning, 'A New Source on Byzantine-Hungarian Relations', *Balkan Studies*, 2 (1961), 173–214.

[72] See G. Podskalsky, 'Nikolaos von Methone und die Proklosrenaissance in Byzanz (11./12. Jh.)', *OCP*, 42 (1976), 509–23; Nicholas of Methone, *Refutation of Proclus' Elements of Theology*, ed. A. D. Angelou (Athens and Leiden, 1984).

embracing the religious life of all—monks, clergy, and the everyday laity.[73]

5. The dualist heresies

Individual heretics who had fallen into Christological error, often without meaning to, could be challenged and put right. The all-invasive dualist sects were far more insidious and consequently difficult to grapple with.[74] These sects were often particularly associated with Alexius I by reason of the confrontations during his reign so dramatically highlighted by Anna Comnena. But the dualist sects had a long history going back to the Gnostics and Marcionites in the early Christian Church and to the third-century Persian Mani and the Manichaeans. In the early middle ages a form of dualism was developed in the Armenian regions by a militant sect, the Paulicians.[75] Their stronghold was Tephrice in western Armenia. They were aggressive and constantly raided over the border and they had spread into Asia Minor. The Byzantines tried to root them out in their drive eastward though not very successfully. In the eighth century these Paulicians had gained a foothold in Europe. Along with Armenian and Syrian monophysites they had been transplanted to Thrace by the Byzantine Emperors Constantine V and Leo IV, the imperial purpose being the acquisition of first-rate soldiers for use in the wars against the Bulgars. Transplantation of this kind was normal Byzantine policy. The Paulicians kept their identity and were not converted to orthodoxy. It was also easy for them to infiltrate across the frequently changing frontier marches into Bulgaria.

Something of the Paulicians in the ninth century is known from Peter of Sicily who had first-hand knowledge of the sect because in

[73] See below pt. II, section 10.

[74] On heresies in general including the variant dualisms see J. Gouillard, 'L'Hérésie', 299–324, and M. Loos, *Dualist Heresy in the Middle Ages* (Prague, 1974). This section on the dualists, though carried through to the end of the middle ages, is placed here for convenience.

[75] For an indispensable guide in attempting to disentangle divergent evidence (and modern views) on the nature of the Paulician heresy see P. Lemerle, 'L'Histoire des Pauliciens d'Asie Mineure d'après les sources grecques', *TM*, 5 (1973), 1–144 (with 2 plates of the fortress Tephrice). See also N. G. Garsoïan, *The Paulician Heresy . . . in Armenia and the Eastern Provinces of the Byzantine Empire* (The Hague and Paris, 1967) and Lemerle's critique of this work, 'Histoire des Pauliciens', op. cit. 12–15.

869 he had been sent to Tephrice as imperial ambassador. He wrote an attack on these heretics calling his work a history of the Manichaeans, though it is clear that the two sects were not identical. The Byzantines often used the term 'Manichaean' as synonymous with 'Paulician'. Another source of information was the account of the 'recently revived' Manichaean heresy, a work attributed to 'Photius, the most holy archbishop of Constantinople'.[76] The essence of the Paulician belief appears to have been a distinction between two principles of good and evil. Matter was regarded as evil and hence the fundamental Christian belief in the Incarnation was rejected together with the sacraments and the hierarchy. There were many variations for, as John of Damascus was driven to confess of these and similar heresies, 'they differ among each other in utter confusion for their false teaching is divided up into innumerable factions'.[77] Some insight into what Paulicians thought—or rather what contemporary Byzantines believed them to think—is found in surviving forms of abjuration.[78] One non-doctrinal characteristic certainly seems to have distinguished the Paulicians and to have remained unaltered, that is their aggressive militancy and the close-knit nature of their communities. The movement had been strengthened in the tenth century by a further transplantation when John I Tzimisces moved a batch of Paulicians to the regions around Philippopolis, again in the hope of getting good recruits. But whatever form it took, this heresy was not eliminated and was still found in the Comnenian period.

The problem was further complicated both for the Byzantine Empire and for Bulgaria by the rise of yet another version of dualism in the Balkans in the tenth century.[79] This was Bogomilism, getting its name from its founder Bogomil ('loved of God') and closely linked to Messalianism. Mindful of the danger to orthodoxy (and to the establishment) the tenth-century Bulgarian tsar Peter (927–69) asked the Byzantine Patriach Theophylact (933–56) for advice in dealing with this form of what he described as 'Manichaeism mingled with Paulicianism'. Theophylact wrote

---

[76] See C. Astruc *et al.*, 'Les Sources grecques pour l'histoire des Pauliciens d'Asie Mineure; Texte critique et traduction,' *TM*, 4 (1970), 1–227.

[77] John of Damascus, *De Haeresibus*, PG 94, cols. 776–7.

[78] See C. Astruc *et al.*, 'Les Sources grecques', *TM*, 4 (1970), 185–207.

[79] For a general account see Obolensky, *Bogomils*; see also the more recent discussion in Obolensky, *Commonwealth*, 119–27.

two letters to him, one of which has survived. He laid down the ecclesiastical penalties for the different degrees of offence ranging from leaders (who if they repented had to be rebaptized) to the simple-minded who had no idea that they were participating in heresy. He pointed out that the civil penalty for obdurate heretics was death, but advised Peter to use persuasion and show clemency. The form of the anathema to be used set out the heretical doctrines under nine headings.[80]

This sect was attacked by a Bulgarian priest Cosmas in a treatise written in Old Church Slavonic.[81] He does not actually use the term Bogomil for the movement, this came later probably in the mid-eleventh century and it was found in Zigabenus's *Panoplia Dogmatica* which he wrote at Alexius I's request.[82] Unlike the Paulicians the Bogomils did not believe in two equal principles of good and evil but they made the Devil the elder son of God and a lesser force, and his brother was the younger son, the Logos-Son. The Devil was the creator of the world and it therefore followed that all material things were evil, including the sacraments. The Church and the priesthood were rejected; marriage was condemned; meat and wine were renounced. Certainly in their early days and until well on into the twelfth century the Bogomils seem to have had no regular church organization of their own. They did have leaders called 'apostles' and they followed their own way of religious life, holding prayer-meetings, using only the Lord's prayer and adopting a strict rule of fasting. They were less active and more contemplative than the warlike Paulicians and to outward appearances they must often have seemed to be simply orthodox monks leading devout and ascetic lives.

The Bogomils at first appealed mainly to the lower classes, the poor and oppressed peasantry and also to the lower clergy. That they were justified in their criticism of the established Church is borne out by Cosmas's plea for a higher standard among clerics and particularly monks whose behaviour, he maintained, contributed

---

[80] *GR* 788 and 789 (both undated, with summary of the heretical doctrines and the penalties to be imposed). The Patriarch's letter has been re-edited by I. Dujčev, 'L'epistola sui Bogomili del patriarca costantinopolitano Teofilatto', *Mélanges E. Tisserant*, II (*ST* 232, Vatican, 1964), 63–91.

[81] See H.-C. Puech and A. Vaillant, *Le Traité contre les Bogomiles de Cosmas le prêtre* (Paris, 1945), trans. and commentary, and ed. Ju. Begunov (Sofia, 1973), p. 297.

[82] *PG* 130, cols. 20–1360; tit. 27; cols. 1289–332 deals with the Bogomils.

towards the prevalence of the heresy of 'these wicked dogs'.[83] Cosmas also stressed another danger. The Bogomils had no respect for the established temporal regime, indeed they even encouraged disobedience towards those in authority such as the tsar or the great landowners. In a polity like Bulgaria, modelled closely on that of Byzantium, church and state stood together and the teaching of the Bogomils, if carried to its logical conclusion, would have undermined both.

With the final conquest of the Bulgarian kingdom by Byzantium in the early eleventh century the danger was brought still nearer home.[84] Already in the previous century the Bogomils had spread rapidly throughout the old Bulgaria, particularly in Macedonia. Then with the incorporation into the Byzantine Empire there was increased Hellenization of the unpopular upper hierarchy in the Bulgarian Church as well as the usual oppressive taxation and exacting landlords. This caused misery and discontent and on occasion revolt and the Bogomils, with their criticism of the establishment, understandably had a great appeal and gained many converts. Their influence was by no means confined to Bulgarian peasantry. It was entrenched in some of the other European provinces and reached the capital, while a form of the heresy was rampant in Asia Minor and in certain areas was found under the name of the Phundagiagitae. Contemporary concern is revealed in a letter of the monk Euthymius of the Peribleptos house in Constantinople written to fellow monks in Acmonia in Phrygia, a place which he himself knew personally. He was writing sometime after the year 1034. This letter contains valuable information on the teachings of the Bogomils at that time and brings out the heretics' emphasis on monastic life and their debt to neo-Messalianism.[85] Another critic of the eleventh century heresies was the author of a dialogue on demonology in which he censured a number of heresies, grouped together under the name 'Euchitae' and marked by some of the characteristics of both Bogomils and Messalians together with a good deal else, particularly demonology. But the

---

[83] See his *Advice to the Orthodox*, Puech and Vaillant, op. cit. 112–27.

[84] On Byzantine Bogomilism see Obolensky, *Bogomils*, 168–229.

[85] Text in G. Ficker, *Die Phundagiagiten: Ein Beitrag zur Ketzergeschichte des byzantinischen Mittelalters* (Leipzig, 1908); the letter is summarized in Obolensky, *Bogomils*, 176–83. 'Neo-Massalianism', 'comme il est prudent de l'appeler', is Gouillard's name for the revival of the tenth to twelfth centuries, 'L'Hérésie', 319.

demonology as expounded in this work was not really part of Bogomil teaching, though the Bogomils, partly influenced by the Messalians, did lay special emphasis on the role of demons inhabiting human beings.[86]

By Alexius Comnenus's day in the late eleventh century it was evident that Paulicians, Bogomils, Messalians, and other variants of dualist sects were well entrenched and widespread throughout the European and Asian provinces. Alexius's attacks on the two main groups are known in some detail from Anna Comnena. The Paulicians in Thrace (called Manichaeans by Anna) were subjected to long discussions with the Emperor himself lasting all day and far into the night. Alexius was then staying at Philippopolis in 1114 awaiting a Cuman attack from the north and was possibly apprehensive that the Paulicians might join the Turkic raiders. The three Paulician leaders, who were named by Anna, were unmoved, tearing Alexius's argument to shreds as though with sharp boars' teeth, so Anna said. But many appeared to yield to imperial persuasion. These were rewarded, the more important by 'great gifts' (unspecified) and the rest, farmers and labourers, were given arable land and vineyards and farm stock (which may have influenced their decision) and they were settled near Philippopolis at Neocastrum.[87]

On different occasions the Messalians and the Bogomils were attacked though without much real success. Anna correctly described the Bogomil doctrine as a mixture of Manichaeism ('which we also call the Paulician heresy') and Messalianism. The Bogomils and Messalians were a more tricky proposition than the Paulicians in that they went about looking like devout monks though inwardly ravening wolves, and their hold on the unwary was the greater since they pretended to conform to the Orthodox Church though in fact holding quite different tenets. They had even penetrated into some of the most important households in Constantinople. There is in fact a suggestion in Armenian sources that the formidable mother of Alexius Comnenus had succumbed to heresy. The fullest statement is in Matthew of Edessa but it is confused in detail and not conclusive. If Anna Dalassena did fall into heresy it would be one explanation why she faded out of her grand-

[86] *PG* 122, cols. 820–82 and ed. P. Gautier, *REB*, 38 (1980), 105–94 who argues against Psellus's authorship.
[87] Anna Comnena, XIV. 8–9.

daughter's history.[88] If she did err she presumably repented; she retired to the monastery of Christ the All-seeing which she had founded in Constantinople.[89]

Quite early in his reign Alexius tried to win over a Messalian or Enthusiast, Theodore of Trebizond (Blachernites, he had been a priest at the church of the Blachernae). The Emperor failed and the man was handed over to the synod and condemned to perpetual anathema.[90] Alexius's more spectacular effort was some time around 1110. He was evidently greatly stirred by the widespread notoriety and influence of the Bogomils. The leader of this sect, Basil, was invited to the imperial palace and under pretence of friendly discussion and possibly imperial conversion was induced to expound his heresy to the Emperor. The room was partitioned by a curtain and behind this was a secretary taking down the dialogue. The Senate, with military men and ecclesiastics, including the Patriarch Nicholas III, were also seated behind the curtain. Neither Basil nor his twelve 'apostles' could be won over either by persuasion or by imprisonment. Finally the synod decided that Basil, the chief heretic who remained defiantly unrepentant, should be burnt. This took place in the Hippodrome and is described by Anna Comnena in great detail and almost with relish.[91] It may have been at this time that the synod also drew up thirteen anathemas against the Bogomils and Messalians and heretics of a similar nature.[92]

But neither Alexius nor any other authority was successful in rooting out the heresy. In various forms the dualists persisted until the end of the middle ages. They turned up in widely separated regions of what had been the Byzantine Empire before 1204, and probably only a small proportion of those taken in by the heresy were detected. In the mid-twelfth century Michael Italicus, the archbishop of Philippopolis in Thrace, evidently complained to his old pupil Theodore Prodromus about heretics in his diocese and Theodore replied that they too had their troubles in

---

[88] S. Runciman, 'The End of Anna Dalassena', *Annuaire de l'Institut de Philologie et d'Histoire orientales et slaves*, 9 (1949 = *Mélanges H. Grégoire* I), 517–24; see also the criticism of J. Gouillard, *TM*, 1 (1965), 314, note 122.

[89] See Janin, *Églises et monastères*, III. 513.

[90] GR 946; Anna Comnena, X. 1.

[91] GR 988; Anna Comnena, XV. 9–10.

[92] GR 989.

Constantinople.[93] At the end of John II Comnenus's reign and the beginning of Manuel I's several cases came to trial in Constantinople. In 1140 the synod in the capital condemned the writings of Constantine Chrysomalus described perhaps unjustly as a mixture of Bogomilism and Messalianism. These works were apparently read with avidity by the monks of St Nicholas near the Hieron and were circulating in other monasteries. With Chrysomalus the monk Peter and the proedrus Pamphilus were named. Chrysomalus was anathematized and handed over to the civil authorities. The other two received only very light penalties as they admitted their error and said that they had not really understood the implications of the doctrines which they had accepted. The offending books were to be burnt.[94] Other offenders detected came from a far distant part of the Empire in Cappadocia. The bishops Clement of Sasima and Leontius of Balbissa were denounced to the metropolitan of Tyana and he deposed them from episcopal office and sent the case to the synod in Constantinople. The synodal document (1 October 1143) listed various practices and beliefs known to be Bogomil, some of which the defendants denied despite written evidence and witnesses from their dioceses. This did not seem to be such a clear-cut case as some. In the end the synod resorted to the commonly used precaution of confinement in isolation to prevent the spread of heretical views.[95] At the same time there was a case brought against a monk Niphon from Cappadocia who was accused of Bogomilism and pending investigation was kept in solitary confinement in the monastery of the Peribleptos. In 1144 he was condemned and excommunicated. In 1146 he was however let out of the monastery and leniently treated as a friend by the new Patriarch. This was Cosmas II Atticus (1146–7), described by the historian Cinnamus as a simple fellow whose indiscretion brought about his own deposition.[96] In the Macedonian provinces the various forms of the dualist heresy continued to flourish during Manuel's reign. As in Alexius's day in Thrace there seemed to be a mixture of 'Manichaeans'

[93] See R. Browning, 'Unpublished Correspondence between Michael Italicus, Archbishop of Philippopolis, and Theodore Prodromos', *Byzantino-Bulgarica*, I (1962), 279–97 (text and commentary).
[94] *GR* 1007 (May 1140); see Gouillard, 'L'Hérésie', 319–21, on certain apparent affinities between neo-Messalianism and some aspects of Orthodox spirituality.
[95] *GR* 1011, 1012, and 1014.
[96] *GR* 1013 and 1015; Cinnamus, *History*, bk. 2, ch. 10 (*CB*, pp. 63–6).

(presumably Paulicians), Bogomils (which often included, or were synonymous with, Messalians), and Armenians (monophysites). Such is the information in the life of Hilarion, bishop of Moglena in Macedonia during Manuel Comnenus's reign. The *Life* hinted that Manuel himself was drawn towards the heresies, which might reasonably be taken as only indicating the interest which was to be expected from the theologically-minded Emperor. The *Life* then went on to recount how Manuel urged the bishop to follow up his conversion of the monophysites and 'Manichaeans' by similar work among the Bogomils. Hilarion was said to have been successful both with these and with the monophysites and 'Manichaeans', though this is hardly borne out by later events.[97]

After 1204 the dualist heresy continued to flourish in early thirteenth-century Bulgaria, by now an independent kingdom. The tsar Boril (1207–18) made efforts to suppress it, as his Synodicon of 1211 showed. But Bulgarian dualism was not eradicated. As late as the second half of the fourteenth century Theodosius of Trnovo, monk and promoter of hesychasm in his country, thought it essential to warn his fellow countrymen first against the Bogomil and Messalian heresies, and then only secondly against the anti-Palamites.[98]

The dualist movement in the Second Bulgarian Empire had indeed from the outset repercussions because of Bulgaria's proximity to Thrace (and the newly formed Latin Empire and principalities). It was easy for the heresy to spread and even to become a pawn in the complicated political moves of that period. In what was left of the old Byzantine Empire dualism persisted, if it only occasionally came to the surface in the patriarchal registers or elsewhere. Patriarch Germanus II of Nicaea (1223–40) thought it necessary to send a warning to the inhabitants of Constantinople denouncing the Bogomils and Messalians and setting out the main points of their heresy; this letter was to be communicated to all the churches and read out on every Sunday and on each festival.[99] There was at that

---

[97] See the Slavonic life, cited by Obolensky, *Bogomils*, 223–6, and E. Kalužniacki, *Werke des Patriarchen von Bulgarien, Euthymius* (Vienna, 1901), 27–58.

[98] *Life*, ed. V. I. Zlatarski, *Sbornik za narodni umotvorenia, nauka i knizhina*, 20 (Sofia 1904), p. 16, 11 and p. 33, 20 and see M. Heppell, 'The Spiritual Testament of St Teodosi of Turnovo', *Sobornost*, 4 (1982), 202. On Bogomilism in the Second Bulgarian Empire see Obolensky, *Bogomils*, 230 ff.

[99] *GR* 1291 (undated); text in Ficker, *Phundagiagiten*, 115–125.

time no Orthodox Patriarch in Constantinople (which was in Latin hands) and Germanus, though of necessity seated in Nicaea, regarded himself as the Patriarch of the lost capital. The dangers of heresy featured in other surviving works of Germanus, such as his sermon on Orthodoxy Sunday and his *Contra Bogomilos*.[100]

The most spectacular episode in anti-dualist activity in the later middle ages in the Orthodox Church was the accusation of Messalianism and Bogomilism brought against the monks of Mount Athos by Barlaam in the mid-fourteenth century. Mount Athos had become a centre of Orthodox spirituality and churchmen of influence, such as Gregory Palamas, had often been monks on the Holy Mountain for a time. The opportunity for attack arose because of the hesychast stress on a contemplative inner life and a spiritual experience leading to knowledge of God. This had always been part of the monastic tradition in the Orthodox Church, but it received special emphasis and development in the fourteenth century when the hesychasts claimed that their methods led to a vision of the light of Tabor. The movement became the concern of a wide circle outside Mount Athos. It was also caught up in the various political cross-currents and animosities associated with Palamism.[101] Barlaam's accusation of 1341 was refuted and in fact counter-charges of a different kind brought against him.[102] There was however probably some ground for his attack. When in 1350 the hieromonk Niphon of Mount Athos was wrongly accused of the heresy he was cleared by a special letter to him from the synod, but in this letter mention was made of monks tainted with Messalianism who had been chased from Mount Athos.[103] It would appear that the heresy had penetrated the Holy Mountain. This was not unlikely in view of the comparative proximity of Thrace and Bulgaria, and if so it was a lapse which was evidently exploited by the anti-Palamites.

Thus the dualist heresy in all its variants was present in Byzantine life at every level. The Messalians and Bogomils were the most difficult to deal with because, unlike the militant and close-knit

---

[100] *In Restitutionem Imaginum* (Germanus works in a good deal on Bogomil errors), *PG* 140, cols. 660–76 and *In Exaltationem Venerandae Crucis et contra Bogomilos*, *PG* 140, cols. 621–44.

[101] See below, ch. VIII, section 7.

[102] *GR* 2210, 2211, 2213.

[103] *GR* 2317.

Paulician communities, they had perfected a technique of dissimulation. They also stressed an ascetic way of life which had on the surface some similarity with the contemplative practice of Orthodox monasticism. Amid concern with the pressures of external problems, and latterly of impending disaster, it is easy for the historian to overlook the insidious all-pervading nature of the dualist heresies. But occasional references in patriarchal registers and the sparse comments in other surviving sources reveal its prevalence and the rampant suspicions all too readily engendered, perhaps of a fellow monk or of a father or grandmother.[104] The provincial synodica string together the usual lists of dualist doctrines to be anathematized, but something of the pressing nature of the practical problem is shown in the synodicon of an Athenian suffragan where appeal was made for deliverance from 'the present' invasion of towns, villages, and whole settlements by these proselytizers who were unceasingly prowling round clothed in a 'pseudo-monastic habit', calling themselves 'Christians' and 'fellow-citizens of Christ', mixing freely with the orthodox and taking in the more simple minded.[105] It was easy for these false monks to pass from house to house, crossing frontiers in their peregrinations, perhaps even travelling westwards.[106] It was not for nothing that Balsamon in the late twelfth century could speak of 'whole fortresses and Bogomil villages surrendered to the heretics to be led astray by them'. He was commenting on the limitations of a heretic's civil rights as defined in earlier legislation (general councils, Justinian, *Basilics*).[107] Such legislation laid down standing penalties, for instance limiting rights of inheritance. In general with few exceptions the Byzantines in contrast to their contemporaries in the West, were comparatively lenient, usually resorting to excommunication, often with solitary confinement in a monastic house. Accusations, which were sometimes made out of malice, usually seem to have been fairly sorted out by the ecclesiastical authorities. It is possible that the synod under Patriarch Michael II Oxites had ordered Bogomils to be burnt but the only evidence seems to be Balsamon's

[104] *GR* 2084 (*c*.May, 1318).
[105] Gouillard, 'Synodikon', 63–9 (text); see his comments on the dualist sects, pp. 228–37.
[106] Contemporary western dualist movements and possible links with the East are not discussed here.
[107] *In Phot. Patr. Cp. Nomocan.*, tit. X, cap. 8, RP I. 242–6.

criticism of this action with the comment that it was not within the competence of ecclesiastical tribunals to inflict any kind of physical punishment against heretics; this was the responsibility of the civil power (ὁ πολιτικὸς νόμος).[108]

How sensitive the issue of the Bogomil and Messalian heresies had become in educated and monastic circles as early as the eleventh century is shown by the care with which the editor of Symeon the New Theologian's works tried to make sure that no taint of Messalianism attached to his master's words as when he substituted the harmless εὐαισθήτως for αἰσθητῶς (perceiving with the senses).[109] In fact Symeon probably did mean to speak of an actual sensible experience of the Holy Spirit working within a man. But he was nevertheless orthodox, believing as he did in θέωσις and the sanctification of matter. Unfortunately a sensible perception of the Holy Spirit was also part of the Messalian religious experience though for very different reasons. It is noticeable that later on in 1140 one of the synod's charges against Constantine Chrysomalus's mixture of Messalianism and Bogomilism was his claim that during the charismatic experience it was necessary to feel the Holy Spirit within oneself. The word used in the Greek document was αἰσθάνεται, precisely what the editor of Symeon had wished to avoid.[110]

Thus, fragmentary as the evidence is, it suffices to indicate the elusive nature of this dualism and the ease with which it could be confused, at least on the surface, with orthodoxy. It was never completely rooted out during the middle ages, though with the political decline of the Empire in the face of the Ottoman advance and the submission of the Balkan principalities less is heard of it. Increasingly large tracts of once dualist strongholds fell into Muslim hands or became tributaries. Their believers probably merged into the world of Islam, leaving only the curious massive carved tombstones with their strange symbols standing scattered in the Bosnian countryside as witness to this medieval dualism.

---

[108] GR 1020 (undated); *In Phot. Patr. Cp. Nomocan.*, tit. IX, cap. 15, RP I. 191.
[109] Symeon the New Theologian, *Catecheses*, I. 169.
[110] GR 1007, 'L'expérience sensible de l'Esprit opérant en lui', so Grumel translates it; RP V. 76 ff.

6. Relations with the West

The pattern of religious and political development in the twelfth and to some extent the eleventh centuries has been obscured by the overshadowing disaster of 1204. The setting up of the Latin Empire and principalities obviously introduced radical changes in the territorial extent of Byzantium as also in the ecclesiastical organization of the former Byzantine provinces. But changing relations between Franks and Greeks, between papacy and the Orthodox Church, were already apparent before the Fourth Crusade. From the mid-eleventh century onwards the pattern had been set which was to prevail until the final dissolution of the East Roman Empire. In fact in this respect the Comnenian and the Palaeologan periods are one.

Given the nature of the Byzantine polity with its accepted interdependence of church and state it was inevitable that politics should involve the Church. The situation was increasingly dominated by the relationship between the needs of the Empire and the attitude of the papacy. Ever since the inception of Constantinople, the New Rome, there had been recurrent friction between the papacy and the other patriarchates and as the authority of the three eastern patriarchs diminished under Muslim rule this meant Rome versus Constantinople. Usually differences had been resolved and Rome had always been given primacy of honour. But with the eleventh century increasing difficulties were encountered. Constantinople at first continued to act as it had done in the heyday of its tenth-century prestige, though in fact its political authority was being eroded both within and without. But in the western world the reformed papacy, supported by an upsurge of religious devotion finding its outlet both in monasticism and in the crusading movement, was gradually assuming an authority over the other four ancient patriarchates which was far removed from the primacy of honour which had been so willingly, and still was, accorded to Rome. Byzantium with its close association of Emperor and Church was all the more inclined to question papal claims in that up to the crusading movement Constantinople rather than Rome had in practice virtual control over the three eastern patriarchates then under Muslim rule. Its position and authority were very different from the fifth-century days when Antioch or Alexandria as well as Rome could stand up to the young patriarchate of New Rome. It continued to uphold traditional ecclesiastical government through the pentarchy and episcopal collegiality in the general council. But during the twelfth century Constantinople had to develop and defend its position in the face of a greatly strengthened papacy claiming universal authority and a very different situation in Syria and Palestine.

The hundred years spanning the first four crusades (1097–1204) proved to be a period of uneasy negotiation rather than the restoration of authority in Asia Minor, Syria, and Palestine which the Comneni had hoped for. As under the later Palaeologans, political and ecclesiastical relations between Constantinople and Rome were inextricably interwoven and characterized by a degree of urgency unknown in the earlier period. This was largely due to problems created by the western crusaders and by the ambitious Normans of South Italy. At the same time divergence in doctrine and discipline was constantly being brought to the fore in debate and in polemic, particularly as the reformed papacy continued to stress that the unity desired by Greek and Latin alike must be based on an acknowledgement of the papal claim to be the *ecclesia universalis*, the *mater et caput* of all Christian Churches. An analysis of relations between Byzantium and the West makes it clear that the Palaeologan period is simply the continuation of what had already begun under the Comneni and the Angeli, aggravated, as it were, by the results of the catastrophe of 1204. This is true in diplomacy, in polemic and in personal contacts between Greek and Latin.

It is against this background that Comnenian relations with the papacy must be seen. Alexius I, like Constantine IX before him, expected papal help against the Normans who were rapidly establishing themselves in the once Byzantine provinces in South Italy and were extending their ambitions to the Greek mainland. In his early days as Emperor Alexius had been excommunicated by the pro-Ducas Pope Gregory VII. But this ban was lifted by Urban II in 1089 and Alexius did not anticipate problems in ecclesiastical relations between Rome and Constantinople. When the papacy queried the omission of the Pope's name from the diptychs in 1089 Alexius and the Constantinopolitan standing synod invited Urban II to send his systatic letter and urged that papal representatives should then attend a council in Constantinople to dicuss any outstanding problems. In Alexius's eyes there should be no difficulty in commemorating the Pope in the liturgy provided normal procedure was followed.[111] Such an attitude could hardly accord with the views of the reformed papacy which as *mater et caput* rather than *primus inter pares* had probably already given up the ancient custom of the systatic letter (synodica) announcing election and containing the customary profession of faith.[112] Not unexpectedly Constantinople's suggestions to Urban II were not followed, but relations nevertheless were maintained and Alexius felt able to appeal to the West for help against the Turkic invaders then penetrating deep into Asia Minor. His plea for military aid to be under his control was answered in a quite different—and to Alexius unacceptable—fashion. Western concern at the increasing difficulty in gaining access to the Holy Places by pilgrims and growing devotion to the idea of a Holy War,[113] as well as economic motives, combined to channel towards Palestine a vast military undertaking bent on recapturing Jerusalem from the Muslims. This western crusading movement, though in part inspired by genuinely Christian ideals, was nevertheless motivated by certain political and personal ambitions and it changed the history of Byzantium.[114] From the start it ran counter to Byzantine needs and policy. Alexius and his immediate successors desired first to stem Turkic advances in Asia Minor and then gradually to push forward to regain their lost territory in Syria and Palestine, much of which, at least in Syria, had until recently been in Byzantine hands, including the key city of Antioch, the centre of an ancient patriarchate and only lost to the Muslims as late as 1084. In the event, the Byzantines found themselves fighting a losing battle, faced with the establishment (ineffective as it was to prove) of Latin crusader principalities in Syria and Palestine, and unjustly regarded by the West as traitors responsible for every Latin disaster. At the same time they were

[111] *GR* 954 (Sept. 1089 or soon after); see W. Holtzmann, 'Die Unionsverhandlungen zwischen Kaiser Alexios I. und Papst Urban II. im Jahre 1089', *BZ*, 28 (1928), 38–67 (with Greek texts).

[112] See F. Dvornik, *Photian Schism*, 326–8.

[113] This concept (which conflicted with Byzantine views) is developed by C. Erdmann, *Die Entstehung des Kreuzzugsgedankens* (Stuttgart, 1935).

[114] There is a vast literature on the crusades including several general surveys. See Setton, *Crusades* and Runciman, *Crusades*. P. Lemerle, 'Byzance et la croisade', *X Congresso Internazionale di Scienze Storiche, Relazioni 3* (Florence, 1955), 595–620, discusses the impact of the first four crusades on Byzantium and evaluates the Greek sources. For the effect of the crusades on the Orthodox patriarchates of Antioch and Jerusalem and on the separated eastern churches see Hamilton, *Latin Church in the Crusader States*.

living under the shadow of a threatened western attack on their capital itself and were menaced by the almost continuous hostilities of the Normans of Sicily.

The papacy was in an almost equally troubled situation. The crusading movement in Syria and Palestine constantly evaded its control. Urban II's avowed desire to free 'the eastern churches' (that is the Orthodox patriarchates of Antioch, Jerusalem, and Alexandria) remained unfulfilled in any sense acceptable to the Greek authorities, though the Orthodox faithful in the eastern Orthodox patriarchates generally managed to achieve some kind of *modus vivendi*.[115] In Italy the Pope was embroiled in the complicated rivalries of Sicily, the western Emperor, and the Italian cities. Of these last Venice, secure in the economic privileges wrested from Byzantium, was powerful enough to assume the dominating role which it was able to reinforce by setting up in the post-1204 years what was virtually an overseas empire.

Alexius, like his son John II and his grandson Manuel I, attempted to maintain normal contact with the papacy through the exchange of official embassies. The unfortunate appeal to Urban II for military aid was followed by attempts to negotiate with his successor Pascal II. Alexius hoped for papal help in controlling the crusaders in Syria and Palestine and the aggressive Normans of South Italy. Pascal for his part needed support against the German Henry V. But his political needs took second place to the assertion of papal authority in the Church. He was less of a diplomat than Urban II. Towards the end of 1112 he pressed Alexius to see that the papal primacy was recognized by the Patriarch of Constantinople and this primacy was defined as control over 'all the churches of God throughout the world'.[116] In papal eyes this was an essential preliminary before any political understanding between Emperor and Pope could be reached. Such a stipulation was to dominate all subsequent relations between Byzantium and the papacy and was the real stumbling-block to the union of the Churches. It was accompanied by constant papal failure to realize that there were limits beyond which imperial authority could not effectively intervene or command in the Orthodox Church. Michael VIII

---

[115] See below pp. 174–6 and Hamilton, *Latin Church in the Crusader States* for the widely differing and fluctuating relations between Franks and the Orthodox in the patriarchates of Antioch and Jerusalem.
[116] Ep. CDXXXVII, *PL* 163, cols. 388–9.

might submit at the council of Lyons II in 1274, John VIII with his higher clergy did likewise at Florence in 1438–9, but this was of no effect when adamantly opposed in Byzantium by the majority of the secular clergy, the monastic world, and the laity.

During the twelfth century the gulf between the Churches of Rome and Constantinople was only gradually recognized and then only by some. The three Comneni rulers all wished for ecclesiastical union and regarded this as a practical possibility. They were also aware of its political value. Alexius I had shown this in 1086 and later. In letters to the Romans and the Abbot of Monte Cassino in 1112 he deplored the treatment of Pascal II by the 'king' Henry V and to the Romans he put himself forward as protector of the Church, suggesting the revival of the old single Roman Empire with himself crowned by the Pope.[117] This conception of a single Empire under the East Roman ruler with a united Church, unrealistic as it was, continued to run through the policies of John II and Manuel I despite intermittent alliances between Byzantium and the German emperors.

John II, a statesman of high order and a realist, was aware of Balkan and Hungarian problems and the growing menace of the Sicilian Roger II. He also knew that his effectiveness in western and papal politics would be enhanced by successes in the East. Here he defeated the Muslim Danishmends of Melitene, the Christians of Lesser Armenia in the Taurus region, and the Normans of Antioch. It was at this point towards the end of his reign that he sent two letters to Pope Innocent II in 1139 and 1141.[118] The first speaks of church unity. It was in the second letter that John put forward his view of the two powers, the spiritual and the temporal, symbolized by the two swords, each distinct yet working in harmony within the terrestrial polity. This polity was interpreted as the universal Roman Empire under Byzantine rule. Writing in 1139 and 1141 John might reasonably feel that he had been sufficiently successful to consider implementing such overall control. It was in some respects perhaps not entirely out of keeping with western thought as reflected in Peter the Venerable's letters to John II and to the Patriarch of Constantinople, particularly if these can be dated to

---

[117] *DR* 1261 and 1262.
[118] *DR* 1302 and 1303. Dölger puts the letters in 1124 and 1126, but for the acceptance of the later dates see Lamma, I. 28–30, with discussion of the contents; see also Ostrogorsky, *History*, 385, note 1.

1138 when Lothair III was dead and Conrad III not yet crowned as western Emperor. Peter appeared to recognize Constantinople as the heir of the Old Roman Empire, though this may of course just have been a tactful preliminary to the specific favour which Peter begged of the Byzantine Emperor, that is, the restoration of the Cluniac house set up at Civetot at the time of the First Crusade.[119]

Manuel I's imperial policy and attitude towards Rome went even further than that of his father John Comnenus. He made use of papal difficulties to try to get help against the Normans in South Italy and here he also had the support of the German Emperor Conrad III with whom he was on the most friendly terms. In general he liked westerners, though realizing the menace to Byzantium from Roger II's ambitions and also from the Normans of Antioch. In the 1150s he did establish control over parts of South Italy but not for long. But he never gave up his own imperial ambitions, though with Frederick I Barbarossa's accession he had a formidable enemy. Overtures to the Pope continued, always with the bait of church union. The unbridgeable gap between reality and Manuel's conception of church and state was demonstrated in the imperial proposals probably made in an embassy to Rome towards the end of 1167. Manuel suggested to Alexander III that he should be recognized as the only Roman Emperor and should take possession of the city of Rome. In return he offered the union of the two Churches of Rome and Constantinople, suggesting that the Pope should hold the see of Constantinople (which was then vacant) as well as that of Rome. Alexander temporized knowing that such matters were difficult and complex. It was clearly impossible to telescope two major sees in this way. He simply asked that Constantinople should accept Roman primacy, commemorate the Pope in the diptychs, and recognize the right of appeal to Rome.[120] Such conditions were as unacceptable to Byzantium then as later on. But it is doubtful whether the opposition of the Patriach Michael of Anchialus was as violent as is often represented by some modern

[119] Lamma, I. 30–1, citing *PL* 189, bk. II, Epp. 39 and 40, cols. 260–2; *Letters*, ed. G. Constable (Cambridge, Mass., 1967), vol. I, Ep. 75 (to John II), pp. 208–9 and vol. II, pp. 148–9, and vol. I, Ep. 76 (to the Patriarch), pp. 209–10 and vol. II, p. 149, with the suggestion that they cannot be dated more closely than some time within Peter's abbacy and before John II's death, i.e. 1122–43.

[120] *Liber Pont.*, II. 415, 419–20 (*Vita Alex. III*); cf. Cinnamus, *History*, bk. VI, ch. 4 (*CB*, p. 262).

scholars.[121] They accept as genuine a colourful document attributed to Michael of Anchialus as well as an account of a synod in
which the Emperor Manuel I was said to have agreed to a total
repudiation of Roman demands. Furthermore it was implied that
the Romans were heretics. The document took the form of a
dialogue between Emperor and Patriarch in which the Patriarch
declared that he would prefer to be subject to the Turk rather than
the Pope since the one involved submission only in secular matters,
the other separation from the Orthodox faith and from God. He
then set out to attack papal claims to primacy and used the Photian
council to refute the filioque addition.[122] As long ago as 1903
Norden threw doubt on the attribution of these documents[123] and
in 1965 they were rejected as apocryphal by Darrouzès. He
maintained that George Tornices' letter of 1156 on the imperial
behalf,[124] the papal, imperial, and patriarchal correspondence of
1173, and the discourses of Eustathius of Thessalonica before 1175
all point to a courteous exchange of correspondence between
Manuel I, the Pope, and the Patriarch Michael of Anchialus. For these
and other reasons it would appear that the dramatic attack on the
papacy, in content and presentation so like later affirmations, could
more properly be assigned to the thirteenth century, possibly to the
reign of Michael VIII.[125]

With Byzantine reverses towards the end of Manuel I's reign and
during the troubled days of the Angeli imperial attempts at union
tended to peter out. Throughout the Comnenian period the
ecclesiastical situation had indeed been further complicated for
Byzantine rulers by reason of the Frankish intrusion of Latin

[121] e.g. Runciman, *Eastern Schism*, 121–2; Every, *Byzantine Patriarchate*, 169.

[122] *Dialogue*, ed. V. Loparov, VV, 14 (1907), 344–54; and L. Allatius, *De ...
Ecclesiae ... Consensione* (Cologne, 1648), bk. 2, ch. 5, pp. 555 ff. and ch. 12,
665 ff.

[123] Norden, *Papsttum*, 96; cf. GR 1121 and 1122.

[124] George Tornices, *Lettres et Discours*, ed. J. Darrouzès (Paris, 1970), Ep. 30,
pp. 324–35.

[125] J. Darrouzès, 'Les Documents byzantins du XII ͤ siècle sur la primauté
romaine', REB, 23 (1965), 69–82 and G. Hofmann, 'Papst und Patriarch unter
Kaiser Manuel I. Komnenos', EEBS, 23 (1953), 74–82 (text of papal and
patriarchal letters of 1173). Darrouzès's evidence in REB was to some extent
drawn from unpublished material thus emphasizing that the situation in the
twelfth century may have to be revised still further as more unexplored material
becomes available. A. Kazhdan, *People and Power* (Washington, DC, 1982), 157,
supports the attribution to Michael Anchialus but he does not appear to have
taken into account all Darrouzès's arguments, e.g. on the content of the Dialogue
and of the patriarchal letter edited by Hofman, op. cit.

patriarchs in Antioch. In the crusader principalities the Franks had found both the Orthodox Church and the various separated eastern Churches, mainly Armenian and Jacobite with some Nestorians and the small Maronite Church in Lebanon. Latin relations with the separated Churches were friendly and tolerant. In the thirteenth century the Maronites did in fact join Rome, keeping their own hierarchy and many of their usages. Relations between the Armenian Church in Lesser Armenia in south-east Asia Minor were to some extent politically motivated, as was the rather lukewarm union with Rome at the end of the twelfth century. The Jacobites (monophysites) and Nestorians were generally on good terms with the Latins. By the time of the crusades they were found in practice to differ little from the westerner, in contrast to the Orthodox with their tenaciously held doctrinal and ecclesiological differences. As a thirteenth-century Dominican observed, the Jacobites and Nestorians might have been named after heretics but this by no means implied that these 'men of simple and devout life' still held to old errors and if there were fools among them, well, even the Church of Rome was not free from such.[126] In fact relations between the separated eastern Churches and the Franks contrasted favourably with the injudicious and intolerant treatment which the former had often received from the Orthodox Church.

Relations between the Orthodox eastern patriarchates and the Latins varied and were on a rather different footing, since, unlike their separated neighbours, they were considered to be members of the same Christian Church as Rome, even though increasing doubts were felt about them as the century went on. Under Muslim rule from the seventh century onwards (except for the brief reoccupation of Antioch 974–1084) the three eastern patriarchates had given way to Constantinople in importance and were unable to play any major role in relations between Rome and Byzantium. Though subject to a non-Christian authority in secular matters, they had kept their hierarchy and in ecclesiastical matters were unmolested. This situation remained largely unchanged for the patriarchate of Alexandria since it did not come under the crusaders. It was otherwise with Jerusalem and Antioch. These came under the Franks who set up their own hierarchy and expected Greek

---

[126] Burchard of Mount Sion AD 1280, trans. A. Stewart (London, 1897), p. 107, cited by Hamilton, *Latin Church in the Crusader States*, 359.

ecclesiastics to recognize the authority of the Latin bishops. But Frankish rule did not greatly affect the middle and lower reaches. True they were ultimately under Latin ecclesiastical authority, but their faith and worship remained untouched, sometimes with Greek, more often with Syriac, as the liturgical language. In general tolerance was shown and there appear to have been no demands for specific submission to the papacy (though this was implied in recognition of Latin bishops). In any case there must have been a considerable language barrier between the Latins and the mostly Arabic-speaking Syrian Orthodox. They kept their churches, though not their cathedrals and they were for a time excluded from the greatly venerated Holy Sepulchre. In contrast to frequent practice in the thirteenth-century Latin Empire in the Aegean, the Greek monasteries in Syria and Palestine remained unmolested and continued to flourish, visited by Orthodox and Latin pilgrims alike. The kingdom of Jerusalem was on good terms with the Byzantines and Manuel I in particular gave generously to churches and monasteries there, even though some of the churches restored or embellished by him were in Frankish hands. The Latin church of the Holy Nativity in Bethlehem was even given mosaic decoration proclaiming the creed without the disputed filioque.[127] In Jerusalem itself Latin patriarchs were understandably appointed—in any case there were no Greek hierarchs there when the crusaders took the city and the Orthodox Patriarch in exile died in 1099. There seems to have been a line of titular Orthodox patriarchs of Jerusalem resident in Constantinople, but the existence of these shadowy figure-heads in the background did not disturb the amicable *modus vivendi* generally prevailing in the kingdom.

It was not so with Antioch. Here the Byzantines were constantly manœuvring to regain possession of what had so recently been part of their Empire. Whatever may have happened at a lower level where the Latin bishops were accepted and Frankish tolerance usually prevailed, the reinstatement of an Orthodox patriarch remained a constant Byzantine desideratum figuring in any treaties which the Comneni made with the Norman rulers of the

[127] H. Stern, 'Les Représentations des Conciles dans l'Eglise de la Nativité à Bethléem', *B*, 13 (1938), 421; cf. C. Walter, *L'Iconographie des conciles dans la tradition byzantine* (Paris, 1970), 160–1 and *passim*.

principality. The one occasion when political circumstances permitted Manuel I to restore an Orthodox patriarch to Antioch was hardly a success. Athanasius II came from Constantinople to his see in 1165, but was killed in an earthquake in 1170, after which the ousted Latin Patriarch of the city was able to return. As in the case of Jerusalem, titular Byzantine patriarchs of Antioch continued to be appointed, though they were of necessity almost always resident in Constantinople, the home of so many refugee prelates. This enforced exile did at least have the advantage of enabling them to take part in ecclesiastical matters under debate in the standing synod in the capital more easily than had been possible when they were resident in their eastern sees.

But apart from the sensitive problem of Antioch, the crusader ecclesiastical policy in the twelfth century seemed to have worked. It was not without significance that short-term western visitors to the Latin states sometimes considered the established Frankish colonists too tolerant and conciliatory towards the Muslim and non-Latin Christian population. For their part the Greeks too might well have taken exception to a *modus vivendi* in the Holy Land involving recognition of Latin bishops, a practice which was regarded as unacceptable by many Orthodox in Crete, Cyprus, and elsewhere during the following centuries.

Within the Empire many factors provided opportunity for greatly increased contact between Greek and Latin. It was not just the constant through traffic of pilgrims travelling to the Holy Places, or Franks going to join their families and try their luck in the crusader principalities, or members of various western religious orders going through to Syria, or the frequent embassies to Constantinople from the papal curia or some western court journeying along the Via Egnatia by way of Thessalonica. Western merchants were attracted by profitable economic openings in Constantinople and other imperial cities. The various trading quarters on the Golden Horn, ceded by treaty to the Venetians, the Pisans, and then the Genoese, also provided bases for Italian compatriots hoping for a career at the imperial court, or desiring to explore the intellectual resources of the Byzantine world. Thus the West flooded into the Empire in a way unknown to earlier generations.

This had particularly fruitful repercussions in the field of scholarship, particularly so far as the West was concerned. Links between the Greek and Latin worlds had long existed. There were Greek communities in Rome and monasteries there.[128] South Italy and Sicily had been Byzantine until the Arabs and Normans came and to some extent they retained both language and culture. There were many Greek monastic foundations on the 'Holy Mountain' in Calabria and elsewhere.[129] Some, as S. Niccolò di Casole near Otranto, or S. Salvatore di Messina, had particularly rich libraries. The Sicilian court from the late eleventh century onwards was a meeting place for Greek and western, as well as Arab, scholars. In Calabria and Sicily there were still traces of the Greek rite in the late 1940s. Then the resources, particularly of North Italy, were the more easily thrown open to Byzantium by reason of the establishment of expanding trading quarters with their churches and hospices within the City itself. These afforded a base for scholars and for members of religious orders as well as for merchants. The Pisan privileges were first granted in 1111 and it was this quarter which became particularly known for its scholars who had a mastery of Greek. This was valuable for visiting embassies or pilgrims. It also provided an expertise used to translate Greek works, both secular and ecclesiastical. Thus the western world became acquainted with such authors as Aristotle and Plato (in part) or with Galen. Particularly important for ecclesiastical issues were the translations of the Greek church fathers, the Cappadocians, John Chrysostom and John of Damascus (used to effect by Peter Lombard), though some of these had long been known to the West.[130] It surprised some of the Byzantine disputants that their Latin opponents could draw on what was the deeply valued heritage of the Orthodox Church. There was evidently a market for Latin translations of Greek works which in turn stimulated growing knowledge of the Greek language itself, though this did not come to any extent until after the twelfth century. But as early as the first half of the twelfth century Robert of Melun could bemoan the affectations of his

---

[128] See B. Hamilton, *Monastic Reform, Catharism and the Crusades (900–1300)* (Variorum, London, 1979), I—IV.

[129] See A. Pertusi, 'Rapporti tra il monachesimo italo-greco ed il monachesimo bizantino nell'alto medio evo,' *La chiesa greca in Italia dell'VIII al XVI secolo* (Atti del consegno storico interecclesiale. Bari, 1969; Padua, 1972), II. 473–500.

[130] See G. Bardy, *La Question des langues dans l'église ancienne* (Paris, 1948).

western contemporaries who peppered their writings with Greek phrases and used Greek theological terms.[31]

In Constantinople both the frequent western visitors and imperial inclination favoured the establishment of bilingual Italians at Manuel I's court. Two of his advisers were Pisan—the brothers Hugh Etherianus and Leo Tuscus. Both were scholars who could draw on the Greek patristic tradition. Hugh, 'imperialis aule interpres egregius', took part in a contemporary theological contro- versy, the Demetrius of Lampe affair. He was rushed to the palace and the matter was passionately debated until late in the night. On this occasion he supported the Latin side, as did the Emperor Manuel. He also wrote a work on the errors of the Greeks. His brother Leo (an interpreter in the imperial chancery) was able to satisfy the interests of those quite outside Byzantine theological circles. He translated the liturgy of St John Chrysostom for Raymond I of Tortosa, the seneschal of Barcelona who was in Constantinople on a mission and wanted to know more about the Greek rite.[132] Such men as these North Italian translators opened up to the West Greek patrology and Greek classics and much else while at the same time making available their expertise in Byzan- tium. But it was only later after 1204 that the Byzantines really got to know more of Latin classics and Latin theology.

The intense intellectual activity of the late eleventh and particu- larly the twelfth centuries and the presence of many westerners, both residents and visitors, favoured discussion of the differences between the two Churches. Both the political needs of the Empire for papal help and the reformed papacy's challenge to the East made these disputed theological issues of more than merely academic interest in intellectual circles. A few individual Byzantines were wise and tolerant. Such was the late eleventh-century Theophylact, archbishop of Ochrida. He thought that azymes could be allowed since the New Testament was not specific as to what was used at the Last Supper, and he maintained that divergence in custom and ritual

---

[131] See M. Anastos, 'Some Aspects of Byzantine influence on Latin Thought in the Twelfth Century', *Twelfth Century Europe and the Foundations of Modern Society*, ed. M. Clagett, G. Post, and R. Reynolds, 2nd edn. (Madison, Wisc., 1966), 132–4 (reprinted Variorum, London, 1979).

[132] A. Strittmatter, 'Notes on Leo Tuscus' Translation of the liturgy of St John Chrysostom', *Didascaliae: Studies in honor of A. M. Albareda*, ed. Sesto Prete (New York, 1961), 409–24; A. Jacob, 'La Traduction de la Liturgie de S. Jean Chrysostome par Léon Toscan', *OCP*, 32 (1966), 111–62.

was no cause for schism. He did consider the filioque to be a more serious problem, but he suggested that the unilateral western addition to the creed might possibly have been necessitated by the inadequacies of the Latin language. He did not however find that papal claims to primacy could justify ignoring patristic tradition and the seven general councils, though primacy of honour was certainly acknowledged. In Italy at about the same time the papacy held a council at Bari in 1098 at which Urban II showed a similar measure of tolerance towards the Greeks of South Italy and Sicily, now under Norman rule and Latin ecclesiastical jurisdiction. Anselm of Canterbury, then in exile and present at the council, like Theophylact, did realize that the filioque question raised serious difficulties but he did not speak of any schism, nor did Urban, and the South Italian Greeks kept their own ritual and usages, though now under Rome and not Constantinople, and there were only a few protests from higher clerics. Neither Theophylact nor Anselm of Canterbury had brought to the forefront the problem of primacy as now claimed by the reformed papacy. This was the real point at issue as subsequent discussions were to show.

In twelfth-century Byzantium there were notable debates between the two sides.[133] In 1112 the displaced archbishop of Milan, Grossolanus, was passing through Constantinople on pilgrimage. He was just possibly an unofficial member of an embassy from the Pope. Pascal II in his letter to Constantinople had expressed views unpalatable to the Orthodox Church. The situation was evidently openly discussed in the capital where Grossolanus took issue with a Byzantine theologian. Alexius I, always alive to theological problems, thought that the Byzantines could present a more effective defence. He pressurized seven Orthodox theologians into drawing up a collective reply in which justice would be done to the Greek point of view. This was translated into Latin for the guests. This Byzantine refutation of azymes, the filioque, and papal claims was probably presented by John Phournes, protos of the house on Mount Ganos. He was supported both by laymen, as the theologian Nicetas of Seides in Iconium, and by churchmen, such as Eustratius of Nicaea and four others. There was no dearth of theologically-minded Byzantine scholars, or of Italians from the Pisan colony on the shores of the Bosphorus near the Golden Horn

---

[133] Cf. Darrouzès, 'Documents byzantins', 42–88.

who could translate from Latin into Greek and vice versa. The debate was held in the presence of Alexius and the Patriarch with their lay and ecclesiastical officials.

One of the best-known public theological debates took place in John II's reign on the occasion of a German embassy to Constantinople when negotiations aimed at checking the South Italian Roger II were in process between Byzantium and the German Lothair III. On this occasion the ambassador Anselm, a Premonstratensian and bishop of Havelberg in north Germany, met Nicetas, metropolitan of Nicomedia. Nicetas had been one of the leading teachers of the patriarchal school and he was deputed to represent the Byzantine side. On arrival in Constantinople Anselm had already been questioned informally on many points before this public debate was suggested by the Emperor and Patriarch. Details of the two sessions have survived because when Anselm subsequently met Pope Eugenius III in Tusculum in 1144 he was asked to write a report on the debates. There is no independent account of the Greek side, but Anselm seems to represent the two points of view very fairly. He wrote three treatises of which the first (dealing with different views in the Church) does not concern the two actual debates.[134] Books II and III give the dialogue of the two conferences. The first turned on the filioque, the second mainly discussed Roman primacy, with some comment on liturgical differences, particularly azymes.[135]

As in the case of Grossolanus, there was wide interest among educated circles in Constantinople. The debates attracted an illustrious audience including Emperor and Patriarch and 'many Latins' as well as Greeks. The first conference was held in the Pisan quarter with North Italian scholars ready to translate (Moses of Bergamo was unanimously chosen for this) and notaries present to take down the debate. A second meeting was held a week later, this time in the apse of the Great Church itself. Various points emerge, above all the willingness and desire to explore each other's arguments in humility and charity. Twelfth-century Latin knowledge of Greek patristic

---

[134] *PL* 188, cols. 1141–60, text and trans. G. Salet (*SC* 118, Paris, 1966).

[135] *PL* 188, cols. 1163–248; Dialogue II, trans. P. Harang, 'Dialogue entre Anselme de Havelberg et Néchitès de Nicomédie sur la procession du Saint Esprit', *Istina*, 17 (1972), 375–425. Both Dialogues II and III are discussed by N. Russell, 'Anselm of Havelberg and the Union of the Churches', *Sorbornost*, 1 (2), 19–41 and 2 (1), 29–41. See also bibliography and comment in Darrouzès, 'Documents byzantins', 59–65.

resources seemed to surprise Nicetas who found Anselm's 'truly catholic' outlook a contrast to the Latin arrogance which he had met. 'You cite our doctors, but as you are a Latin do you believe them?' he asked and Anselm replied tactfully but ambiguously 'I would not deny the gift of the Holy Spirit to any Christian whether Greek or Latin'.[136] In the filioque discussion the two protagonists were very nearly in accord. Nicetas put forward the formula 'from (ἐκ) the Father and through (διά) the Son' for the procession of the Holy Spirit as other Greeks, Theophylact of Ochrida for instance, had done. 'We really think the same,' conceded Nicetas. But he considered that the Latin 'from the Son' could not be introduced unless sanctioned by 'a general council of eastern and western churches under the authority of the Holy Roman pontiff with the consent of the most devout Emperors' called to discuss the point. And only if there were a common resolution could the filioque be publicly accepted.[137]

But the discussion on the primacy, however courteously conducted, failed to resolve the differences. The debate explored two lines of approach, first the contention that the transference of the capital to Constantinople had conferred on the patriarchate authority and autonomy as defined in canon 28 of Chalcedon (which canon Rome however had not yet recognized) and secondly the Petrine position in the light of certain New Testament passages. Did Christ's mandate confer overall authority to Peter (Matthew 16:18–9 and Luke 22:32), or was this to be shared by all the apostles (John 20:23 and Matthew 18:18)?[138] The exegesis of these passages was to form a regular constituent of future polemic, including discussion of the claims of other apostles, John for instance, or other cities, such as Antioch or Jerusalem. Neither Anselm nor Nicetas conceded anything here, though courtesy may have to some extent concealed the gulf. But only a year after this in 1137 critical Greeks visiting Monte Cassino *en route* for Germany could declare to their hosts that the Roman bishop was in fact acting as an Emperor rather than a bishop.[139] In later exchanges mutual antagonism was continually coming to the surface. In 1155 papal envoys returning

---

[136] *PL* 188, ch. 24, cols. 1202–5; *Istina*, op. cit. 417–19.
[137] *PL* 188, ch. 26 and 27, cols. 1208–10; *Istina*, op. cit. 422–4.
[138] See *PL* 188, Dialogue II, especially chs. 7, 8, and 9.
[139] Peter of Monte Cassino, Chron., bk. 4, ch. 115, *MGH SS* VII. 833, cited Norden, *Papsttum*, 99–100.

from Constantinople presented Basil of Ochrida, metropolitan of Thessalonica, with a letter in which the Pope referred to the Greeks as 'the lost sheep' of the Gospel parable and made clear his claim to supreme authority in the Church. In replying to the Pope, Basil of Ochrida unequivocally rejected this.[140] The issue was clearly monarchical rule versus collegiality, albeit with primacy of honour for Rome. For the Byzantines it was not a relationship of mother and daughter but of sister Churches under the one shepherd Christ. For the Latins the Pope was the Vicar of Christ, exercising a *plenitudo potestatis* over the universal Church. Peter the Venerable might laud the orthodoxy of Byzantine Emperor and Patriarch (after all he was a suppliant for the restoration of the Cluniac monastery at Civetot), or Nicetas of Nicomedia and Anselm of Havelberg find grounds for agreement, but it was the paradox of the twelfth century that increasing, and often friendly, contacts between Latins and Orthodox seemed to run side by side with growing misunderstanding and a hardening of the differences between the two Churches.

There was at the same time an unfortunate blackening of character on either side largely for political, and also economic, reasons. This is evident from the literary sources. From the mid-twelfth century onwards Byzantine historians, Anna Comnena for instance or John Cinnamus, saw the Latin leaders as plundering barbarians. And it must be remembered that however excellent might be the relations between individual rulers, as Manuel I and Conrad III, the Empire had to suffer the passage of armies on the march to the Middle East as well as ruthless and often successful Norman raids on Byzantine provinces. For their part, the Latins, particularly the Normans, deliberately spread in the West a false story of Byzantine treachery in the early crusading cause, and later the French blamed the Greeks for the failure of the Second Crusade. The Byzantines knew quite well that the French, the Normans, the Germans, had come to consider the capture of Constantinople an essential preliminary to crusading success further East.

Thus during the twelfth century antagonisms and attendant polemic were building up in the political as well as the ecclesiastical field. But Greeks and Latins were not yet in schism, they did not

---

[140] J. Schmidt (ed.), *Des Basilius aus Achrida Erzbischofs von Thessalonich bisher unedierte Dialoge* (Munich, 1901); Darrouzès, 'Documents byzantins', 65–8.

normally regard each other as heretics. The double succession of patriarchs in the twelfth-century eastern churches in crusader principalities had little practical significance (except in so far as refugee prelates swelled the standing synod in Constantinople and could be used as pawns in ecclesiastical politics by Emperor or Patriarch). In the recurrent theological discussions either side seemed to hope that their own arguments might yet prevail. In the late twelfth century the soured and biased canonist Theodore Balsamon was much criticized in Constantinople and by other canonists for his fierce rigidity in insisting that captive Latins must formally accept Orthodox doctrine and usage before they could communicate in a Greek church, as well as for some of his other harsh rulings. It has been argued that the more significant antagonisms which inflamed Greek and Latin in the twelfth century arose out of political and economic pressures, perhaps provoked more by the West than by Byzantium.[141] The Latins desired increased trade and an enlarged market; they wanted more land which the western feudal system of primogeniture could not make available. Then on the Byzantine side there was the urgent need to come to terms with an impinging Muslim world (which was regarded as treachery by the West). It was almost as though religious problems only inflamed an already kindled fire. But this was not entirely true. The basic disagreement between the Latin and Orthodox Churches was present throughout, that is, the *plenitudo potestatis* versus collegiality and episcopal government. Byzantium kept to its age-long tradition and these religious issues were to take on a vital significance in the survival of Orthodoxy. No eirenic compromise could conceal the real implication of papal claims when after the catastrophe of the Fourth Crusade a Latin Patriarch and Latin bishops were appointed over the heads of the Byzantine hierarchy in Constantinople, as also in the conquered provinces. Thus the worst fears of a Balsamon or a John Camaterus were realized.

[141] See P. Lemerle, 'Byzance et la croisade', *Relazioni del X Congresso Internazionale di Scienze Storiche*, vol. 3, *Storia del medioevo* (Florence, 1955).

VII

THE EFFECTS OF THE FOURTH CRUSADE
1204–1261[1]

1. The patriarchate of Constantinople 1204–1261:
the Latins in occupation

On 13 April 1204 Constantinople fell to the Fourth Crusade. Its capture and the subsequent establishment of a Latin Empire and a number of virtually independent Latin principalities on former East Roman territory presented problems for the papacy as well as for the Byzantines and of course the crusaders themselves. Before the City had fallen the crusaders drew up a partition treaty laying down the division of the City and arranging a committee to apportion the lands still to be conquered. As had been clear from the outset of the expedition, Venice was the dominating power determined to direct affairs in her own interests. Thus the doge contrived to get a non-Venetian Emperor, Baldwin of Flanders and of Hainault, elected, leaving the appointment of the canons and Patriarch of Hagia Sophia to the Venetians. Thomas Morosini, a Venetian living in Venice, was elected. The Byzantine lands were partitioned among the Emperor, the Venetians, and the other leaders. Venice had special terms designed to exempt her from certain feudal obligations, to preserve the privileges which she already enjoyed under Byzantine rule and to exclude her rivals (such as Genoa and Pisa) from participation in the profits to come. Otherwise the feudal usages of the western world were to be transplanted to Greek soil. The foremost leaders owed homage to the Emperor (or were supposed to), and they in turn expected to exact homage from those to whom they granted out fiefs.

---

[1] In general for the Fourth Crusade and subsequent Latin Empire and principalities see Longnon; R. L. Wolff and H. W. Hazard (eds.), *History of the Crusades*, II (Madison and London, 1969); Runciman, *Crusades*, III; Setton, *Papacy and the Levant*, I (rich bibliography); Gill, *Byzantium and the Papacy*; Norden, *Papsttum*; Angold; Nicol, *Epiros*, I.

Thus conquest of the Byzantine Empire by western forces, already foreshadowed in the previous century, was substituted for the intended deliverance of Jerusalem (though this would follow, so it was alleged). The territorial division did not work out precisely as agreed, but the victorious westerners did succeed in setting up the Latin Empire (known as Romania) and in taking over many other Byzantine provinces. They spread out into Macedonia and Thessaly, through central Greece into the Peloponnese, and they took the Aegean islands and Crete, and the north-west fringe of Asia Minor. Cyprus had already fallen to the Latin Lusignans towards the end of the twelfth century. Venice and Venetian families seized the most strategic economic points, Modon and Coron in the south Peloponnese, useful ports of call *en route* for Crete which they also contrived to get, as well as Euboea and many of the Aegean islands. They did not however acquire the west coast of Greece which had originally been assigned to them. The conquest was accompanied by the establishment of western feudal usage in the Latin Empire of Romania and in the newly established fiefs as they were gradually acquired. And internal relations were complicated by the conflicting interests of the Franks and the Venetians (the two main parties) which had been in evidence from the outset.

The Byzantine government, which had shown obvious weaknesses during the twelfth century, could only put up a partial, and for a time an unfortunately divided, resistance. The capital had been lost and a succession of Greek emperors were either in flight or killed. But the 'crusaders' never gained the complete control which they had planned. Byzantine centres of resistance emerged in western Greece (Epirus and for a time Thessalonica) and in western Asia Minor (the Nicaean kingdom). There was also the Greek kingdom of Trebizond round the south-east shores of the Black Sea, set up by a branch of the Comnenian family just before the Fourth Crusade. Though by no means a negligible factor, Trebizond was not so deeply involved in the struggle to expel the intruding westerners, pursuing a more independent existence far from the contested lands and understandably more concerned with Turkish movements in Asia Minor.

Fortunately for the Latins during the early stages of their conquest Greek resistance did not emerge as a single united effort. Relations of the imperial Angeli family had fled to Asia Minor where Theodore Lascaris, the son-in-law of Emperor Alexius III, established what became known as the kingdom of Nicaea, though it was really concentrated more in the Smyrna-Nymphaeum region. Another Greek, also claiming Angeli-Comnenian ancestry, set himself up in Epirus as Michael Angelus Comnenus Ducas. Attempts to drive out the Latins were seriously hampered by acute rivalry between these two Greek kingdoms, each aspiring to take the lead in a revived imperial Byzantium centred in the capital. At the same time the rising Balkan principalities, Bulgaria in the thirteenth century, and Serbia in the following century, were bent on establishing themselves as heirs of the Greek imperial rulers of Constantinople and at the same time desired to assert the independence of their national Orthodox Churches.

Against this tangled and shifting background relations between the Greek and Latin Churches had to be sorted out. The problem was threefold. The Frankish and Venetian settlers needed their own Latin clergy and had to be provided for. Within the conquered territory the position of the Greek clergy, both higher and lower, had to be defined and the Greek laity, who for the most part remained *in situ*, could not be entirely deprived of their own pastors. Then there was the overriding question of the strained relations between Greek and Latin Churches. This long-standing issue, aggravated by the twelfth-century crusading movement, was brought into unavoidable prominence by the Fourth Crusade. This particular problem involved not only Greek ecclesiastics within the conquered provinces, but the independent Greek kingdoms of Nicaea and Epirus, and then eventually the partially restored Byzantine Empire under Michael VIII and his successors. From then onwards the question of union was to become a bargaining point in Byzantine diplomacy aimed at enlisting papal aid for Byzantium, first against further western aggression, and then against the advancing Ottoman Turks, the enemies of Greek and Latin alike.

Within the newly conquered Latin lands the establishment of a Latin patriarchate, Latin bishops, clergy, and monastic orders was inevitable.[2] From the outset the papal attitude was clearly expressed. Pope Innocent III condemned the looting of a Christian city by Christians. At the same time he hoped that the introduction of the Latin hierarchy would prove an effective step towards the

---

[2] For details on this (not the primary concern here) see Fedalto, *Chiesa latina*, I (2nd edn. essential) and II.

union of eastern and western Christendom and would then lead to the deliverance of Jerusalem which he so greatly desired. He seemed to think that the Greek clergy in the new Latin Empire would be willing to remain in office and would recognize the papal *plenitudo potestatis*, thus in effect being absorbed into the Roman Church. 'As the empire has been handed over (from the Greeks to the Latins), so must the rites of the priesthood be changed. Thus Ephraim having returned to Judah casts away the old leavened bread and is nourished on the unleavened bread of sincerity.'[3] So Innocent wrote on 15 May 1205 to the Emperor Baldwin I. It is true that he urged the Latins to show tolerance towards Greek rites and usages, provided there was recognition of papal primacy, but what he had in mind was the ultimate Romanization of the Greek Church. If the Byzantines did not fully appreciate, or at least allow for, the steady growth of papal claims from the eleventh century onwards, neither did the papacy understand the strength of Orthodox traditions and the tenacity with which these were guarded. Thus any *modus vivendi* in the Latin principalities was hardly on lines visualized by the Pope and in any case the wider aims of the papacy were never realized.

For Innocent III the situation was further bedevilled by the crusaders themselves and he had to assert his authority in order to prevent a secular take-over. The pre-conquest Latin partition treaty had stipulated that if a non-Venetian was elected Emperor, then the Venetians should have the right to appoint to Hagia Sophia. The able old Doge Enrico Dandolo scored a double trick in the election of the relatively harmless Baldwin of Flanders as Latin Emperor. He thus kept out the pro-Genoese Boniface of Montferrat from the imperial throne, and gained for Venice the control of the patriarchate. Without reference to Innocent fifteen Venetian canons were appointed (four of whom were illiterate) and they at once elected a Venetian patriarch.[4] When he learnt of this Innocent realized its implications. Either he had to make sure of his control over ecclesiastical affairs or be faced with a virtually independent authority which might well even assume the position of the former Byzantine patriarchate. When informed of Morosini's election as patriarch and asked to confirm this he wrote on 21 January 1205

---

[3] *PL* 215, col. 623, bk. 8, Ep. 55 (15 May 1205).
[4] See R. L. Wolff, 'Politics in the Latin Patriarchate', 225–303 for details on the patriarchate (with previously unpublished texts).

condemning lay action in church matters. He pointed out that the canons had been uncanonically instituted and he declared their election of the Venetian Morosini invalid. However not wishing to complicate further the already disturbed situation in Constantinople he then proceeded himself to appoint Morosini as patriarch.[5] He reserved the right to choose future patriarchs. Later in May 1205 he laid down procedure for the patriarchal election whereby the Venetian canons of Hagia Sophia had to act together with the praepositi of the conventual churches in Constantinople (there were about thirty of them and they were under French influence). In practice however the Pope had the controlling hand during the life of the Latin patriarchate (1204–61), and twice appointed directly. In any case the papacy had throughout to contend with a certain amount of Venetian hostility as well as a running battle between Frankish and Venetian interests.

One of Innocent's most severe criticisms was directed against the general Latin appropriation of Greek ecclesiastical property. The crusading agreement had laid down that, provided the clergy were decently provided for, church property would be secularized and shared out. The Byzantine Church was rich and the crusaders refused to return their spoils. In the end Innocent's protests effected a settlement whereby Latin clergy (and Greek who submitted) were granted one-fifteenth of all property in Romania outside the walls of Constantinople. Monasteries and their property were to remain untouched.[6] This rule of one-fifteenth was to apply to all future conquests and in addition the usual western annual tithe was to be paid. Later readjustments were made to provide a more just compensation for lost church property within the Latin Empire and fresh settlements, which now included the Venetians, awarded the Church first one-twelfth, and then one-eleventh of occupied lands.[7]

The Latin settlement meant the establishment of a Roman hierarchy if only to provide for the needs of those who were, at any rate to begin with, not Greek-speaking. In any case they could not be left to the care of schismatics (as the Greeks were regarded). The

---

[5] *PL* 215, col. 516, bk. 7, Ep. 203.

[6] On the fate of the Greek monasteries in Constantinople see R. Janin, 'Les Sanctuaires de Byzance sous la domination latine (1204–1261)', *EB*, 2 (1944), 134–84.

[7] See Wolff, 'Politics in the Latin Patriarchate', 262 ff, and texts in the Appendix.

prompt election of the Venetian Patriarch had shown the Greeks what to expect. Moreover they were in a dilemma because their own Patriarch, John X Camaterus, had fled from the sacked capital to Didymoteichum where he remained. He was old and seemed crushed by the disaster, and he gave no lead to his Church. He refused Theodore Lascaris' invitation to set up the Byzantine patriarchate in Nicaea, perhaps because he had family links with the ousted Emperor Alexius III. Had he gone to Nicaea he would almost certainly have been required to crown Theodore as Emperor. It is not clear whether he resigned before he died in mid-1206,[8] but until his death the Byzantine Church was virtually without its chief bishop and yet unable to proceed to a new election.

The papacy made various attempts to get the Greeks in Constantinople to recognize the Pope and the Venetian Patriarch Morosini and thus eliminate the awkwardness of a dual regime. It had yet to learn that the ease with which some rulers might promise union with the Holy See in no way indicated the attitude of the people or the monks. Several meetings were held in Constantinople during the years 1204–6. The first was under the guidance of the legate Peter Capuano. Towards the end of 1204 Peter and the higher Latin clergy met a group of Greek priests, monks, and laymen in Hagia Sophia. The Byzantines represented by John Mesarites, a leading figure in the monastic party, made it clear that papal supremacy was unacceptable and reminded the Latins that the Greeks had their own Patriarch (John Camaterus was still alive if inactive). The high-handed and threatening Peter Capuano got nowhere, and to begin with for a time he had not even got a papal mandate as he had come unsolicited from Syria. In 1205 Innocent replaced him with a more suitable legate having full authority to organize the Church throughout the Latin conquests.

Cardinal Benedict of Santa Susanna was a man of some tact and insight and his whole enterprise was more carefully planned and more far-reaching. He brought with him an interpreter from southern Italy, the monk Nicholas of Otranto, and a pile of Greek books. The bilingual Nicholas was a unionist who was used on various occasions in the negotiations between the Greeks and Latins, both in Constantinople and at the court of Nicaea. He recognized

---

[8] *GR* 1202, where his death is put in May 1206; cf. Gill, *Byzantium and the Papacy*, 34, who gives 20 June 1206.

Rome but had pro-Byzantine sympathies as his treatises on the filioque and the disputed Latin usages show.[9] Benedict travelled by way of Thebes, Athens, and Thessalonica. He seems to have made a point of inviting discussion with the Greeks.

In Thessalonica he was particularly impressed by 'the learned and holy men' with whom he conferred among whom was probably the displaced archbishop of Athens, Michael Choniates. But in Thessalonica the atmosphere was particularly favourable under the regency of Margaret of Hungary, widow of Boniface of Montferrat. When she had married Isaac II Angelus she had moved from the Latin Church of her upbringing to the Orthodox, and then on marrying the crusader ruler of Thessalonica she moved back again, though she retained a marked partiality for the Greek churchmen in the newly-founded Latin kingdom, even incurring (and apparently ignoring) Latin censure. The papal legate Benedict may have thought that some such accommodation might be reached with the Greek Church in general if only it would recognize papal supremacy and the Latin Patriarch of Constantinople. He may have been further encouraged by the submission of Theodore bishop of Euboea (Negroponte, then in Venetian hands). But events in the capital rapidly proved him wrong.

Three short meetings were held in 1206 in Constantinople in the patriarchal residence now occupied by Morosini. The first on 30 August turned on Morosini's demand for recognition and the papal primacy. In return for this he was prepared to allow the customary Byzantine veneration of one of their cherished icons (the Theotokos Hodegetria) which he had removed to Hagia Sophia—another instance of the perpetual friction engendered under the irritating Latin regime. The Byzantine spokesman on this occasion was Nicholas Mesarites, whose brother John had led the opposition to the Latins in the 1204 discussion with Peter Capuano. In fact it is Nicholas's funeral oration on his brother, who died in 1207, that supplies much of the information on the Greek point of view.[10] The Greek arguments were drawn from a treatise *Against those saying that Rome is the first see*, which had provided generation after

---

[9] On Nicholas's role in Byzantino-Latin relations see J. M. Hoeck and R.-J. Loenertz, *Nikolavs—Nektarios von Otranto Abt vonCasole* (Ettal, 1965).

[10] See A. Heisenberg, 'Neue Quellen zur Geschichte des lateinischen Kaisertums und der Kirchenunion', *Sitzungsb. der bayerischen Akademie der Wissenschaften. Philos.-philolog. und hist. Klasse* (Munich, 1922–3), I–III.

generation with material drawn from polemic on this issue.[11]

At the second meeting on 29 September Cardinal Benedict was present and was faced by a throng of monks not only from the capital but from the countryside round the sea of Marmora. As on other occasions, they were the unswerving supporters of the opposition. Their spokesman was John Mesarites. When faced by the legate's direct question 'Why do you not obey the Patriarch sent by the Pope who is the head of all churches' which of course implied commemoration in the liturgy, the reply was that until recently they had their own Patriarch and since his death they had no one to commemorate. This was followed by reiterating the arguments against the papal claim to universal jurisdiction maintaining that the true head of all the Churches was Christ. Even the usually equitable Benedict could not restrain his anger at the deadlock. He gave the Byzantines two days to think over the problem and on 2 October the third and final meeting was held. The result was unsatisfactory both to the legate and to Morosini. In fact Nicholas of Otranto writing about this meeting said that the Romans felt that it was useless to try to discuss points of dogma with the Byzantines. But it must have helped to clarify the issue for the Byzantines. First they again violently repudiated papal claims to universal jurisdiction and then significantly referred to those who had fled to join Theodore Lascaris in Nicaea, which was where the future for the Byzantines was to lie. According to Nicholas Mesarites the Byzantines were so moved that they declared it was even preferable to take refuge in the land of the Turks rather than to betray their true faith.

But before abandoning the capital one last effort was made. The Byzantines appealed to the Latin Emperor, Henry of Flanders, for help. He was liked and the Byzantines in Constantinople openly acknowledged him as their secular lord. They now asked him to allow them to elect their own Patriarch, but this was beyond Henry's competence, much as he wished to ameliorate the situation. They then wrote to Innocent III asking to elect their own Greek Patriarch and suggesting that this should be followed by a council in which the differences between the two Churches might be discussed. If they could elect their Patriarch they offered to acclaim the

[11] Its Photian origin has been questioned; see M. Gordillo, *OCP*, 6 (1940), 5–39.

Pope at the end of the liturgy (as for a secular ruler), pending the council, and hoped for union when his name could then be placed in the diptychs and commemorated in the anaphora. No reply was received from Innocent and the possibility of this *modus vivendi* was lost and did not recur. In any case it could hardly have been acceptable to Innocent. As might have been foreseen the patriarchal problem was solved otherwise in the rising Byzantine kingdom of Nicaea.

2. Ecclesiastical organization within the various Latin conquests

(i) Greece and the Cyclades

Most of the Byzantine bishops in the conquered lands shared the views expressed in the capital. Innocent's instructions were that bishops already consecrated were to be left undisturbed provided that they swore obedience to the papacy (which of course included the Latin metropolitans and Patriarch). The full Latin rite with unction was not to be insisted on for those already consecrated. When the Latin archbishop of Athens tried to impose this on the Greek Theodore of Euboea (who had submitted to Rome) he lost his case. But very few of the Greek prelates accepted papal primacy of jurisdiction. Most left their sees and either went to Byzantine centres, such as Nicaea and Epirus, or they drifted from place to place in comparative poverty, like the former archbishop of Athens, Michael Choniates, who wandered round and then lived for some years near Athens on the rather bleak island of Kea (which was in Greek hands). The archbishop of Patras seems for a time to have taken refuge in the inaccessible monastery of Megaspelaion high up in a steep ravine in the hills south of the gulf of Corinth. The metropolitans of Crete, Mitylene, and others went to Nicaea. Those in the Latin kingdom of Thessalonica were best off due to the pro-Greek policy of its rulers.

As the piecemeal occupation of central and southern Greece and the islands proceeded the Latins had to deal with the disturbed conditions created by the rift between the two branches of the Christian Church. At the higher level of diocesan organization this meant the appointment of Latin metropolitans and suffragans in the deserted sees and to some extent the rearrangement of the dioceses.[12] It meant making provision for the western religious orders who came flooding in, finding out where Greek monasteries had been deserted or could be taken over by the Latins and which Greek abbots had promised obedience to Rome, if only by lip-service, ascertaining where cathedral chapters could be filled with Latin nominees. Generally the Greek monasteries were left unharassed. For instance the former archbishop of Athens corresponded freely with houses in his old diocese, Kaisariani and St John the Hunter, both on the slopes of Mount Hymettus. But the deserted monastery of Daphni outside Athens was taken by the Cistercians, an order for which the lord of Athens, Otto de la Roche, had a special devotion. The canons regular of the Templars went to the metropolitan church in Athens, the famous Panagia Atheniotissa, the Parthenon of ancient Greece, and now the Latin cathedral of Notre Dame, following (so Innocent III hoped) the usages and customs of Notre Dame of Paris.[13]

It is clear that one crucial point in the early days of the ecclesiastical settlement was revenue and church property. From the very outset of the conquest this had been in dispute between the crusaders and the Church and it recurs again and again in Innocent's vast correspondence. In Romania church property had been secularized and for the most part restoration was virtually impossible. Further, some important sources of revenue were out of reach of the Latins. Hagia Sophia, for instance, had drawn considerable revenue from its properties in a region between Smyrna and Prinobaris, known for this reason as 'Hagiosophitike chora' and this was now part of the kingdom of Nicaea.[14] Whether the funds were simply taken over by the Byzantine Patriarch of Constantinople in Nicaea is not clear. With the establishment of a dual and often mutually hostile ecclesiastical system there must have been many instances of this kind.

The Greeks in what was now Latin territory were hardly in a

---

[12] See R. L. Wolff, 'The Organisation of the Latin Patriarchate of Constantinople, 1204–1261', *Traditio*, 6 (1948), pp. 48 ff., where the Latin *Provinciale* (*c.*1210 and 1228) is compared with the relevant Greek *Notitiae Episcopatuum*.

[13] *PL* 215, col. 1433, bk. XI, Ep. 113. For details on the Athenian Church (1204–1308) see Setton, *Papacy and the Levant*, I. 405 ff. and J. Longnon, 'L'Organisation de l'église d'Athènes par Innocent III', *Mémorial Louis Petit* (Bucarest, 1948) 336–40.

[14] H. Ahrweiler, 'La Région de Smyrne', *TM*, 1 (1965), 56–7.

position to protest at the wholesale plundering of ecclesiastical property but the Latin Church could do so. It was agreed by the Latins that some compensation should be made for the wholesale seizure in the first days of victory. A carefully worked-out procedure was laid down. The laity in Romania were to hand over to the Latin Church one-fifteenth of their property outside Constantinople and the same proportion in any lands not yet conquered. Laity were to pay the customary annual Latin tithe. Monasteries within and without the capital were to belong to the Church, presumably with their scattered and often wealthy property, though to ensure this must have meant endless work for the three-man commission set up to settle their disputes. This attempt to compensate and stabilize was agreed in March 1206 between the Church (the legate and Patriarch)[15] and the acting moderator Henry of Flanders (his brother Baldwin I had been captured by the Bulgarians in April 1205). It was subsequently modified, substituting one-twelfth, and then one-eleventh, for the one-fifteenth.

In the kingdom of Thessalonica and in the territory north of Corinth a different arrangement was made. At the Parlement of Ravennica in 1210 it was agreed, and it was possible, to restore church property. Churchmen were to be free from lay jurisdiction and impositions. But whether Latin or Greek they were to pay the *acrosticon* (*crustica*), the Byzantine land tax. The sons of ecclesiastics were subject to feudal military service unless they were ordained, and there were various regulations to meet the contingency of non-payment of the *acrosticon*. This concordat laid down what became the general practice in the feudalized Latin principalities.[16]

Such initial official arrangements needed a good deal of supplementation and in practice inevitably varied from place to place, and in some areas were constantly fluctuating. This was particularly so when territory changed hands, as when the Byzantines won back part of their lost lands. Success of this kind was followed by the immediate displacement of the Latin bishop by a Greek Orthodox ecclesiastic. The Latin bishop then became a titular and made what

---

[15] Confirmed by Innocent III; see *PL* 215, col. 967, bk. IX, Ep. 142 (5 Aug. 1206). See Wolff, 'Politics in the Latin Patriarchate', pp. 258 ff., on the haggling over the implementation of the agreement.

[16] Confirmed by Honorius III in 1219 and 1223 who cites the text of Innocent III's confirmation, *PL* 216, cols. 414–16; and C. A. Horoy (ed.), *Honorii III . . . Opera* (Paris, 1880), vol. 4, no. 10, cols. 409–16.

arrangements he could, often returning to the West. After the Byzantine recapture of Constantinople in 1261 the Latin Patriarch was turned out and eventually assigned in 1314 by Urban V to Venetian Euboea (Negroponte, with his see at Euripos) though also retaining his patriarchal title. Here he was in possession of a secure base until the Turkish occupation in 1470.[17] It was however in mainland Greece that land most frequently changed hands with inevitable ecclesiastical upheavals in the higher ranks as well as financial problems over rival claims to church property.[18]

Within areas dominated by Latins for all, or most, of the period before the Turkish conquest the measures of control over the Orthodox Church and the unofficially permitted degree of toleration largely depended on the policy of the ruling Latin authority and on local personalities and conditions. The principle of obedience to Rome had to be accepted which normally meant a Latin episcopate since with rare exceptions Greek bishops were not willing to conform, though a few seem to have paid lip-service to this ruling. The Greek rite was permitted with certain modifications, such as confirmation only by bishops, or Latin anointing on consecration. Within the general framework laid down by the papacy, and occasionally more liberally interpreted, as for instance in the more sympathetic approach of Innocent IV, different patterns emerged distinguishing the Peloponnese and Cyclades from the Venetian possessions and from Cyprus.[19]

The greater part of the Peloponnese (Morea) was in the hands of the Burgundian Villehardouin family until it passed to the Angevins in 1278. Here after initial resistance the Greek archons (the leading landowners and imperial officials) were integrated into the lower ranks of the western feudal hierarchy and there was a comparatively peaceful symbiosis since the conquerors needed the co-operation of the native magnates. In the ecclesiastical sphere many of the higher clergy left rather than accept papal primacy. The archbishop of

[17] See J. Koder, *Tabula Imperii Byzantini*, I, *Negroponte* ... (Vienna, 1973), 134 ff.

[18] On the administrative changes in Greek and Roman churches in central Greece under Latin rule see J. Koder, *Tabula Imperii Byzantini*, I, *Hellas und Thessalia* ... (Vienna, 1976), 83–9.

[19] See the brief survey by F. E. Thiriet, 'La Symbiose dans les états latins formés sur les territoires de la Romania byzantine (1202 à 1261): Phénomènes religieux', *Rapports, XVth International Congress of Byzantine Studies* (Athens, 1976).

Ochrida, Demetrius Chomatianus, spoke of many churchmen from the Peloponnese who had fled to Epirus[20] and others found a similar refuge in the Byzantine kingdom of Nicaea. But it is unlikely that there was a mass exodus of rural priests (papades) and monks from the villages and monasteries in the hilly regions of the Peloponnese. In fact attempts had to be made to limit the numbers of priests allowed to each group of households served. This was because certain exemptions from exactions were found to tempt men into the priesthood. The ecclesiastical problems recorded in the Peloponnese seem to have been largely disputes between higher members of the hierarchy and secular authorities and were often of a financial nature. It was possible for the more humble papas to follow age-long Orthodox tradition in matters of the Greek rite and everyday usage. In the second half of the fourteenth century the Greek version of the original French Chronicle of the Morea relates how the leaders (archontes) of the Morea obtained from Geoffrey Villehardouin in the previous century the promise that no Frank would force them to change their faith for the faith of the Franks or their custom and laws of the Romans.[21] This version was written by a Greek feudatory and its tone is friendly towards the Franks, illustrating the measure of tolerance which obtained and yet at the same time showing that there had been no complete integration, since there was evidently room for a Greek version to be read to an audience of Greek-speaking feudatories. The main barrier here, as elsewhere, was religion. It was extremely rare in the thirteenth and fourteenth centuries to find evidence of a Greek moving to the Latin rite, though there must have been some Latins who went to Greek churches since in 1322 this practice was fiercely condemned by Pope John XXII,[22] and there are instances during the fourteenth and early fifteenth centuries of conversions to Orthodoxy (mostly Italian names).[23]

In the Cyclades the islands were occupied by Italian families and here from the first there was little tension. The Latin Duchy of the

---

[20] Cited by A. Bon, *La Morée franque* (Paris, 1969), 90.

[21] *Chronicle of the Morea* (Greek version), ed. J. Schmitt (London, 1904), ll. 2093–4 (also ed. P. Kalonaros, Athens, 1940).

[22] Raynaldus, *Annales Ecclesiastici*, 24, anno 1322 (1 Oct.), cited by D. Jacoby, 'The Encounter of Two Societies: Western Conquerors and Byzantines in the Peloponnesus after the Fourth Crusade', *AHR*, 78 (1973), 898.

[23] See the *professiones fidei* cited in MM 2, e.g. pp. 8–9, 48, 84, 343, and *passim*.

Archipelago was under Marco Sanudo with his seat in Naxos. The conquerors were popular with the Greek islanders who welcomed protection from pirates and also from rapacious Byzantine tax-collectors and enjoyed growing economic prosperity under the new regime which did not succumb to the Ottomans until the sixteenth century. Their rulers were wisely tolerant in religious matters, though some ecclesiastical property and some local churches were inevitably taken over at the outset such as the small church of Aimamas at Potamia in the interior which after the Ottoman conquest stood crumbling into ruins in the gardens of what is still Latin church property. Oral tradition says that for long years a Greek priest used to go there once a year to say the Divine Liturgy. Under the Latins the capital moved from the interior to the new coastal seaport, the Chora, where on the summit of the steep hill above the harbour Marco Sanudo built the Venetian walled Castro and inside it an attractive little Latin cathedral now served by a priest and still used by the few surviving Roman Catholic families of the island. The original numbers of the conquerors must have been small and largely concentrated in the few splendid Venetian houses built within the Castro walls. Among the innumerable small Byzantine churches scattered over this fertile island there are some with double naves or additions built on in the nature of a small chapel or *parecclesion* but these appear to date from the post-Byzantine era[24] and it is impossible to say whether they were shared churches, as sometimes happened in occupied regions elsewhere in the late period.

(ii) Venetian conquests: Crete

In Byzantine lands directly occupied by Venice a rather different pattern emerged. The Commune was essentially a secular and non-feudal state.[25] It was primarily concerned in furthering the economic interests which it had been energetically pursuing in the East Mediterranean long before 1204. With this in mind it selected its share of the spoils and was powerful enough to hang on to some of its conquests for more than two hundred years after the fall of Constantinople. Crete was not finally lost until 1669. Venice was

[24] G. Dimitrokallis, Συμβολαὶ εἰς τὴν μελέτην τῶν βυζαντινῶν μνημείων τῆς Νάξου (Athens, 1972), 187; see also id., 'The Byzantine Churches of Naxos', *Am. Journ. Arch.*, 72 (1968), 283–6.
[25] On Venetian attitudes see F. Thiriet, *Romanie vénitienne.*

not particularly concerned with the Latinization of the Greek Church though it accepted certain papal rulings—nor did it give any priority to the promotion of the union of the two Churches. It had its own views on dealing with ecclesiastical problems within its conquered lands and its relations with the Roman Church were often strained, as its actions in Constantinople had shown from the outset. Beyond the bounds of the Latin Empire properly speaking Venice's most important acquisitions were Crete, and the two key posts of Modon and Coron in the south Peloponnese, and later in the 1380s Corfu, and Euboea (Negroponte) in 1390.

Crete affords a characteristic example of the Venetian attitude towards the Orthodox Church in its subject domains. The supreme authority was the Duke of Crete. The native landowners were virtually ignored, at any rate to begin with. Later some concessions were made to the archons with regard to their property but they were not given any share in the administration or allowed to marry into Venetian families. Venetian colonists were brought in to garrison the island and some of their castles still survive. In contrast to the Peloponnese there was a constant undercurrent of rebellion supported by the hardy rural population and the native Church and aided by the mountainous character of the island. A Latin hierarchy was set up under the archbishop of Crete with his seat at Candia. This was to some extent facilitated by the early departure of the Greek Archbishop Nicholas with three of his suffragans and some heads of monasteries who refused to recognize Roman primacy. They left the island and joined Theodore Lascaris in Nicaea. Venetian ecclesiastical policy was based on the elimination of any independent Orthodox Church. A Greek bishop would only be permitted if he were a uniate taking the oath of obedience to Rome.[26] What happened to all the original Greek hierarchy (there were ten bishops besides the archbishop) is not clear. It appears that at least one, possibly four bishops may have accepted the authority of the Latin Church.[27] Placed directly under the jurisdiction of the Latin archbishop were 130 Greek papades (priests) in parishes around Candia. The rest of the local Greek papades were under a

[26] The Orthodox see of the Venetian Coron in the Peloponnese was a curious exception due to unusual circumstances; the Greek bishop here was required to live seven kilometers outside the city; see Thiriet, *Romanie vénitienne*, 289 and 404.

[27] See J. Gill, 'Pope Urban V (1362–1370) and the Greeks of Crete', *OCP*, 39 (1973), 463.

Greek protopapas, or archpriest (archipresbyter), who was assisted by a protopsaltis or chief cantor. The number of Greek priests and monks was limited. Normally priests and monks could not enter or leave the island. New priests were ordained only to replace those who had died or were gravely ill. Ordination by an Orthodox bishop outside the island was forbidden. Presumably any Greek bishop who had submitted to Rome must have died by the early fourteenth century, for in 1326 John XXII spoke of the Greeks on Crete being without a Catholic Greek bishop and exhorted the Latin archbishop to appoint one. It sounds as though they were being ordained by non-Catholic bishops, for the Pope laid down that in future such functions might not be exercised in Crete by schismatic bishops.[28] Here the questions of language arose and in 1360 the examination of those seeking entry to the priesthood was entrusted to a Greek-speaking commission of four papades selected by the Venetian government to hold office for six months and not to be re-selected, nor were they to be drawn from the 130 Greek papades under the Latin archbishop.[29] The Byzantine rite and usages were freely permitted, subject only to the usual modifications in certain matters, such as the acceptance of minor orders, anointing, episcopal confirmation.[30] Monasteries were respected including those administering the property of houses outside the island, notably the two great foundations of St John on Patmos and St Catherine on Sinai both of whom relied on their Cretan land for food supplies which the Venetians allowed them to continue to export.

In practice the last word in ecclesiastical matters lay with the Venetian authorities and relations between the Commune and the Church were often uneasy. The Archbishop of Crete frequently complained that he was bypassed in decision-making and Urban V's comment that the Doge and Commune had more control over the Latins and Greeks in ecclesiastical matters than was usual was fully justified.[31] Increasing absenteeism and the divided authority

[28] *Acta Ioannis XXII*, A. L. Tăutu (Vatican, 1952) No. 81 (1 Apr. 1326), cited by J. Gill, 'Pope Urban V (1362–1370) and the Greeks of Crete', *OCP*, 39 (1973), 464–5.
[29] F. Thiriet, *Délibérations des Assemblées vénitiennes concernant la Romanie*, vol. I (Paris, 1966), nos. 668–9, pp. 247–8.
[30] See J. Gill, op. cit. 460–8.
[31] *Acta Urbani V*, ed. A. L. Tăutu (Rome, 1964), no. 153 (28 July 1368).

caused by the Schism in the Latin Church created further confusion
and provided an excuse for ignoring papal rulings and was certainly
a deterrent to union.[32] After the council of Florence Crete was
urged to implement decisions concerning the union of the two
Churches. The Commune saw the difficulties involved and realized
the advantages of its established policy whereby it controlled the
Greek majority, allowing them as much freedom in rite and usage
as was compatible with Venetian interests and papal rulings. As
elsewhere in lands of the Orthodox Church, the union of Florence
was not acceptable to the Greek majority. It is true that since 1204
many regions had been obliged, at least nominally, to accept
Roman primacy, but now there would be obligations which
seemed to touch them much more nearly, as for instance the
acceptance of the filioque in the creed. Opposition was strengthened
by the fifteenth-century flood of staunchly Orthodox refugees from
Byzantine and former Byzantine lands now being gradually overrun by the Ottomans.

Another fifteenth-century development added to Venetian problems. There were increasing signs that Venetians (castellani) garri-
soned throughout the island, and presumably by now often bilingual, were beginning to use the churches of the Greek rite. This
was partly because of a shortage of Latin priests and perhaps even
more because long years of coexistence had familiarized them with
the native religious life. This fraternizing was condemned by the
Venetian senate which urged the dispatch of Latin priests to the
castellanies and also forbade the erection of further Greek rite
churches.[33] All the same, as in Cyprus, this tendency pointed the
way to the increasing predominance of Orthodoxy which never
showed signs of succumbing to Latin influence. In contrast to the
strict segregation of the early years the late middle ages and after
saw the beginning of a symbiosis producing Veneto-Greek families
who were greatly to enrich Cretan life.

[32] See F. Thiriet, 'Le Zèle unioniste d'un Franciscain crétois et la riposte de
Venise (1414)', *Polychronion*, ed. P. Wirth (Heidelberg, 1966), 496–504.

[33] See F. Thiriet, 'La Situation religieuse en Crète au début du XVe siècle', *B*,
36 (1966), 201–12, and N. Tomadakis, 'La politica religiosa di Venezia a Creta
verso i Cretesi ortodossi dal XIII al XV secolo', in *Venezia e il Levante*, ed. A.
Pertusi (Florence, 1973), I(ii), 783–800.

(iii) Cyprus

Cyprus, another major Byzantine island which passed under Latin control, was rather differently situated. It had been captured from its Byzantine ruler by Richard I of England in 1191 at the time of the Third Crusade and in 1192 was acquired by the Poitevin Guy de Lusignan, the dispossessed king of Jerusalem (recently taken by Saladin). It remained in Lusignan hands for about three hundred years, closely linked with what was left of the kingdom of Jerusalem and much influenced by the Latin feudal customs established there. Finally through default of male heirs it came under Venetian control at the end of the fifteenth century until its conquest by the Ottomans in 1571. Cyprus had a predominantly Greek population but also, particularly as the Moslems advanced into the crusader states, it housed a number of other refugee communities, Syrians, Maronites, Jacobites, Armenians, certainly numerous enough to set up their own particular churches and to be specifically mentioned in various papal bulls directed towards the island. The Greek Orthodox Church in Cyprus differed from that in other parts of the Byzantine Empire in that it was autocephalous under an archbishop selected by the Emperor from the customary three names submitted to him, thus bypassing the Patriarch of Constantinople.[34]

Under western rule in 1196 a Latin hierarchy was set up under an archbishop at Nicosia and three suffragans. In contrast to Crete, the Greek hierarchy was also retained consisting of the archbishop at Famagusta and about fourteen sees scattered throughout the island. The secular administration, as in the kingdom of Jerusalem, was an adaptation on Latin feudal lines. The Lusignans left to themselves would probably have been more tolerant of the Greek Church than the papacy, and certainly the Cypriote Latin hierarchy, would permit. They and their barons did indeed resent the encroachments of the Latin clergy, particularly in matters of finance. Baronial payment of tithes to the Latin Church was a point in question which frequently intruded into conventions discussing ecclesiastical problems. The Latin hierarchy had in any case taken over the Greek

---

[34] For details on the Cypriot Church see J. Hackett, *A History of the Orthodox Church of Cyprus* (London, 1901, an amended Greek translation by C. A. Papaïoannou, 3 vols., Athens and Piraeus, 1923–32) and G. Hill, *A history of Cyprus* (Cambridge, 1948), III.

church property and was constantly improving its revenue from donations.[35]

The secular authority, then the Queen Mother Alice of Champagne, who was regent from 1218–25, would have left the Greek hierarchy as it was whether or not they took the oath of obedience to the Latin bishops, and by implication the papacy. But this was not in line with papal policy on the relations between the native, mostly Greek, population and the Latin conquerors. It was rejected in 1220 at a meeting in Limassol between the lay powers and the four Latin bishops. Obedience to Rome was insisted on and the numbers and movements of Greek priests and monks were restricted. Any plea for more flexibility was fiercely rejected by Pope Honorius in January 1222. On the contrary he went much further, pointing out that the anomaly of having two bishops in one see was uncanonical. He demanded obedience to the Latin hierarchy from Greek clergy and abbots. Bishops not conforming were to be expelled. Further discussion at Famagusta followed later in the year. This produced no alleviation for the Greeks. It defined the situation more closely, insisting on subordination to the Latin ordinary and restricting the Greek sees to four to correspond to the Latin hierarchy. Greek bishops taking the oath would in practice simply be acting under the Latin bishop of the diocese. The actual sees of the Greek bishops were removed to rural areas outside the main towns.[36]

In this way it was hoped to provide for the spiritual needs of the Greek majority while preserving Latin supremacy. But the conditions posed problems for the Cypriot bishops. The obedience to the Latin bishops required from all clerics, and particularly the oath of fealty which Greek bishops had to make to the Latin ordinary, placing their hands within his according to feudal usage, were found difficult to accept. The Greek archbishop Neophytus rejected these conditions and went into exile for a time. In such a situation the Cypriots in 1223 appealed for advice from the Byzantine Patriarch of Constantinople then resident in Nicaea. Germanus II was at first

---

[35] See the entries in J. L. La Monte, 'A Register of the Cartulary of the Cathedral of Santa Sophia of Nicosia', *B*, 5 (1929–30), 439–522; no.20 (8 Mar. 1222), states that 'the Latin clergy are to hold of right all properties which were previously held by Greek clergy . . .'.

[36] J. Hackett, op. cit. 470, gives a map of the Latin dioceses showing the four Orthodox episcopal sees.

inclined to permit 'economy' and acceptance as long as Orthodox rites and usages were preserved. But rioting and protesting anti-Latin extremists broke into the room where the Patriarch and his synod were debating and this decision was reversed, which was certainly more in keeping with Orthodox policy. Germanus then ruled that it was forbidden to take the feudal oath but it was permissible to get the consent of the Latin ordinary before taking office. He also agreed that laity and clerics should have the right of appeal from the Greek bishop to the court of the Latin metropolitan.[37]

There followed a confused period for the Greek Cypriots. During his exile Archbishop Neophytus was confirmed in his office by the Byzantine Emperor according to normal custom. He returned and evidently took the required oath followed by others. A strong protest was made against this by Patriarch Germanus in a letter of 1229 addressed to all the Orthodox in Cyprus both Greeks and Syrians. He commended all who had not submitted to Latin demands and exhorted them rather to worship at home. He made a bitter attack on the Latin Church and this only exacerbated the division within the Cypriot Orthodox community. Further Germanus was interfering in the affairs of an autocephalous Church, as Archbishop Neophytus pointed out when he appealed to the Byzantine Emperor to restrain the Patriarch.

An attempt to solve the unhappy state of the Orthodox in Cyprus was made during the pontificate of Innocent IV who had a more sympathetic attitude. First in 1246 he sent a Franciscan, Brother Lawrence, as legate to inquire into the problems in the East including Cyprus and to protect the Greeks who might have been oppressed by the Latins, which in itself was an admission that Latin policy in Cyprus was open to criticism. Then in 1248 the cardinal-bishop of Tusculum, Eudes, went to Cyprus and had discussions there with the Greek hierarchy. The Greeks sent their suggestions directly to the Pope. The tenor of their requests was a return to the pre-Latin diocesan organization of fourteen sees and the recognition of their own canon law in return for the promise of obedience which was to be made directly to the Pope or his legate, thus eliminating relations with the disliked Latin hierarchy. The Latin archbishop of Nicosia, Hugh of Fagiano, countered this move by

[37] GR 1250.

tightening the already restrictive requirements designed to promote
the Roman rite and usages. Innocent IV, through his legate Eudes,
responded by allowing the Greek bishops to elect their own
archbishop, Germanus, to fill the vacant see (1251). Thus Germanus
was granted unusual privileges which were to cease at his death.
Innocent also ruled that as far as possible the Greeks should retain
their own rite and customs.

But Innocent IV died in 1254 and his unusually sympathetic
approach ceased. His successor Alexander IV was either not tough
enough, or not willing, to maintain the measure of independence
from the detested Latin hierarchy which the Greek Cypriots so
greatly desired. The Latin Archbishop Hugh deeply resented the
concession and particularly the presence of a specially favoured
Greek archbishop. In the event, a running legal controversy over
Germanus ensued. The situation was clarified by Alexander IV's
bull which was amplified in Cyprus by synodal rulings embodied in
the Constitutio Cypria (1260). This was a return to four Greek
dioceses but no Greek archbishop (after Germanus' death). There
were certain minor concessions to the Greeks in matters of jurisdiction concerning their own people but in general subordination to
the Latin hierarchy was enforced.

This unhappy situation went on for about three hundred years
(1260–1571). The cartulary of the Latin cathedral of Santa Sophia in
Nicosia bears witness to continuing problems which split the two
Churches.[38] In ecclesiastical eyes the situation was aggravated by
the crown and barons who were often at loggerheads with their
own Latin hierarchy partly because of disputes over the payment of
tithes and partly because of the government's reluctance to stir up
resistance from the Greek majority. Thus in 1264 Urban IV had to
rebuke the Bailli for refusing to assist the archbishop of Nicosia in
enforcing orthodox (Latin) practices on the Greeks in the difficulties
which had arisen since Alexander IV's bull,[39] and in fact there were
ecclesiastical complaints of positive opposition to the Latin archbishop from the secular authorities.[40] Then there were increasing
difficulties in relations between the Greek and Latin hierarchies due
to some extent to declining standards and absenteeism in the Latin

[38] Conveniently summarized by J. L. La Monte, op. cit., *passim*; references
cited are to La Monte's numbering.
[39] La Monte, op. cit., no. 96 (1264).
[40] Ibid., no. 93 (1263).

Church. In 1472 Sixtus IV had to remind the four Greek bishops that they could not exercise jurisdiction outside the towns assigned to them.[41] During the fifteenth and following centuries there was evidence that there was more fraternization between Greek and Latin. In the early years of the fifteenth century an unsuccessful attempt to unite the Orthodox Church of Constantinople with the Greek Cypriots broke down on the grounds that the Cypriots were schismatics who went on occasion to Latin churches. On the other hand in 1438 the Latins in Cyprus were described by Aeneas Sylvius as being more Greek-minded than Roman.[42] Despite papal protests Latin women went to Greek services.[43] Greek bishops officiated in Latin dioceses. The decrees of the council of Florence were not put into practice. Irregularities and disorder seemed prevalent.

But behind the official testimony of papal bulls or cathedral records, all too often witnessing discord and failure, there is evidence of another kind telling of life on a different and more intimate level—that of the Latin families settled in the plains and mountains and the villages in the rural parishes of the island. These had their chapels and churches some of which still survive and are a living witness to the coming together of Greek and Latin Cypriots. Fragments of evidence point to shared churches, either double-naved or with a side chapel built on. The Panagia Angeloktistos at Kiti had a small Gothic chapel (late thirteenth or early fourteenth century) added for the Gibelet family, the French lords of Kiti with their Latin rite.[44] Similarly the church of Pelendri had a nave added for Latin use, as also the church of St John Lampadistis in Kalopanagiotis with its fifteenth-century frescoes of a Latin family whose two sons had Latin tonsures but wore the vestments of an Orthodox priest. The portraits of donors and families in the wealth of frescoes give a living presentation of late medieval life in Cyprus, with the mixed marriages and the changing fashions in dress and the mingling of the French and Greek languages.[45] Local co-operation and integration of this kind in Cyprus seems to have increased

---

[41] Ibid., no. 131 (1472).

[42] Cited by G. Hill, *History of Cyprus*, III. 1090.

[43] La Monte, no. 127 (1368).

[44] C. Enlart, *L'Art gothique et la renaissance en Chypre* (Paris, 1899), II. 440–1.

[45] A. and J. Stylianou, *The Painted Churches of Cyprus* (Cyprus, 1964), 109; see *passim* for other instances of the mingling of Greek and Latin usages and rites. See also id., 'Donors and dedicatory inscriptions, supplicants and supplications in the painted churches of Cyprus', *JÖB*, 9 (1960), 97–128.

during the last centuries of the Latin regime. The failure of the council of Florence, the fall of Constantinople in 1453, the anti-Latin anathemas of the Orthodox synod in Constantinople in 1483, all left untouched the amicable local relations witnessed by the village churches and noticed by travellers, such as the disapproving Felix Faber who when in Cyprus in the 1480s met a monk who 'on Sundays first said mass in the Latin church and consecrated the Host as do the westerners in unleavened bread. Then he went over to the Greek church and consecrated as the easterners do in leavened bread.'[46] The way was opening towards the mutual toleration which for a time was found in the former Byzantine lands in the Mediterranean[47] though that was not the view which was taken by Felix Faber and his contemporaries.

Thus in the conquered lands of the old Byzantine Empire the westerners imposed papal control and a Latin hierarchy. But though at local level a *modus vivendi* was to some extent achieved, the native Greeks were not won over to the Roman Catholic Church. When the westerners were ousted by the advancing Ottomans the Greeks threw off any forced recognition of papal primacy and under the rule of Muslim masters the Orthodox Church reverted to its normal life.

3. Thirteenth century rival Byzantine churches: Nicaea and Epirus

Not all of the East Roman Empire fell to the Latins in 1204 and for 250 years a brave attempt was made to maintain the Byzantine imperial tradition in church and state. An essential step was considered to be the recovery of the capital City which symbolized the imperial authority and in 1261 Constantinople was regained. Equally important in the minds of the majority was the Orthodox faith which together with the Hellenic tradition was in the long term all that was to survive Latin and Ottoman dominations. The maintenance of Byzantine continuity was at first bedevilled not only by Latin aggression but by rival Orthodox claimants to the

---

[46] Cited by C. D. Cobham, *Excerpta Cypria* (Cambridge, 1908), pp. 40–1 and *passim.*

[47] On such later relations between Roman Catholics and Orthodox see K. T. Ware, 'Orthodox and Catholics in the Seventeenth Century: Schism or intercommunion', in D. Baker (ed.), *Studies in Church History*, 9 (Cambridge, 1972), 259–76.

imperial succession, namely, the Greek rulers of Trebizond, Epirus, and Nicaea, as well as the rising Serbian and Bulgarian princes. Trebizond on the Black Sea was never a serious rival. The struggle really lay between Epirus and Nicaea, though the Balkan rulers were often powerful enough to turn the balance.

Nicaea however had certain advantages. Here in Asia Minor Theodore Lascaris, son-in-law of the dispossessed Alexius III, claimed to be the imperial successor to the Angeli and set up his court. To establish his position he needed patriarchal coronation and the support of the Orthodox Church. The old patriarch, John X Camaterus, refused to join him in Nicaea.[48] Theodore's opportunity came with the death of John in 1206 and the impasse in Constantinople when the Latins refused to allow the Greeks in the capital to elect a new Orthodox Patriarch of Constantinople. Then, as foreshadowed by Nicholas Mesarites in the fruitless discussion with the papal legate and the Venetian Patriarch, the frustrated Byzantines turned to Nicaea. Already a number of high Byzantine ecclesiastics and others had taken refuge here. Theodore prepared for the election by addressing himself to the bishops of the Empire, the higher clergy of Hagia Sophia, and the heads of the Constantinopolitan monasteries, summoning them to attend a synod in Nicaea in the third week of Lent 1208 to elect a new patriarch.[49] Michael IV Autorianus, a learned man, was duly elected on 20 March in time to consecrate the chrism on Maundy Thursday for the coronation of Theodore on Easter Sunday 1208,[50] three years after he had been acclaimed Emperor.[51] This gave Theodore the advantage of the customary imperial coronation as well as the support of the head of the Orthodox Church, though the archbishop was seated in Nicaea (temporarily it was hoped) and not in Constantinople.

From the outset the Patriarch worked closely with the Lascarids. There was no doubt about the value of his support for the Nicaean imperial claims. He issued a stirring letter exhorting the army to

---

[48] See P. Wirth, 'Zur Frage eines politischen Engagements Patriarch Johannes' X. Kamateros nach dem vierten Kreuzzug', *Byzantinische Forschungen*, 4 (1972), 239–52.

[49] *DR²* 1676a and 1676b (autumn 1207/before 2 Mar. 1208).

[50] See V. Laurent, 'La Chronologie des patriarches de Constantinople au XIII⁰ s. (1208–1309)', *REB*, 27 (1969), 129–33.

[51] *DR²*, vol. 3, p. 1.

stand by their monarch and granted absolution to those soldiers who fell in battle.[52] The tenor of the letter is a reminder of the initial struggles of Theodore who had to check the advance westward of the Greek Trebizond ruler, to keep back the Seljuks on his eastern border and to bargain with the Latin Emperor in Constantinople for the north-west coast of Asia Minor which was for a time in Latin possession. Further, his authority—and that of his Patriarch—was challenged by a formidable enemy in the rapidly expanding principality of Epirus in north-west Greece; and on the flanks were the two Balkan states, Bulgaria and, at this time the rather less dangerous, Serbia. Both Epirus and Bulgaria had in mind the recapture of Constantinople and with it the resumption of the imperial title now claimed by Nicaea.

While Theodore Lascaris was steadily building up his Nicaean kingdom as a base from which his successors were eventually to advance into the lost European provinces, his rivals in Epirus were cleverly expanding their territory. Theodore Angelus (1215–30), the most adventurous of the dynasty, successfully attacked the Latin kingdom of Thessalonica and captured its chief city. Here in 1224 he was crowned Emperor (basileus and autocrator) by Demetrius Chomatianus, the autocephalous archbishop of Ochrida, since the metropolitan of Thessalonica had refused to act. This coronation was a direct challenge to Theodore Lascaris. The weak and ineffective Latin Empire of Constantinople was unable to check either of its Greek opponents. It was indeed only the fierce antagonism between the two contestants for the imperial throne that enabled the Latin Empire to survive until 1261. Had the rulers of Epirus and Nicaea combined, the Latin Empire could hardly have resisted them, particularly had they won over the Bulgarian ruler to their side. As it was, the struggle between the Lascarids and Angeli had to be fought out and in so doing the Orthodox Church was split within itself.[53]

Both Epirus and Nicaea were firmly supported by their own ecclesiastics. Both were Orthodox, although Epirus, purely for political advantage, once or twice vacillated in the direction of Rome, and Theodore Lascaris, equally for political reasons, put out

---

[52] GR 1205, 1206, and 1207.

[53] For details of this contest see Nicol, *Epiros I* and A. D. Karpozilos, *The Ecclesiastical Controversy between the Kingdom of Nicaea and the Principality of Epíros (1217–33)* (Thessalonica, 1973).

feelers towards union with the Latin Church. The real root of the Epirote–Nicene trouble lay in political rivalry which, given the Byzantine view of Empire, inevitably involved the Church. For the Epirote Church to submit to the control of the Patriarch of Constantinople (temporarily in exile at Nicaea) was to admit the imperial claim of the Lascarids. From the outset difficulties of communication, Latin hostilities, towns captured from the Latins needing Greek bishops—all these factors provided an excuse for independent action. In 1213 the Epirote synod appointed to the sees of Dyrrhachium and Larissa, but the Patriarchs Michael IV, Theodore II, and Maximus II gave no approval. At this time the able Theodore Angelus was successfully advancing into Thessaly and Bulgarian Macedonia. Ecclesiastical problems in Macedonia were settled independently of Nicaea in a synod (1219) in which Demetrius Chomatianus played a leading part. He had been made autocephalous archbishop of Ochrida after Theodore Angelus had captured the city in 1217. This Bulgarian see claimed special privileges by reason of its link with the see of Justiniana and All Bulgaria and it was from here that Chomatianus, a distinguished canonist, became the driving force in the movement to set up an independent Epirote Church and to exercise some control over Serbia. Nicaea attempted to counter this by creating an autocephalous Church in Serbia where in 1220 Stephen II's brother Sabas was recognized as archbishop of Žiča and All Serbia.[54]

The growing independence of the Epirote ecclesiastics roused the Patriarch in Nicaea to make formal protest. In 1222 Manuel I tried to assert his authority. He did confirm the two irregular appointments under protest, but firmly stipulated that in future canonical procedure must be followed. Further, in an unconciliatory letter he unjustifiably stigmatized Demetrius Chomatianus as an uncultured foreigner,[55] which produced a fiery reply from John Apocaucus, the metropolitan of Naupactus. The rift had already been further widened by the Epirote refusal to take part in a meeting of the bishops of the four eastern patriarchates which Theodore Lascaris was planning to hold in Nicaea in 1220 to discuss an approach to Rome and church union.[56] Coupled with the refusal was the

---

[54] GR 1225.
[55] GR 1230.
[56] DR² 1704; see below p. 213.

suggestion that if such a meeting were held Epirus would be a more suitable venue, followed by a warning to Nicaea against over-fraternization with the Latins. The tone of the letter clearly indicated the attitude of Epirus.

The struggle came to a climax during the patriarchate of the determined and forceful Germanus II (4 January 1223–June 1240). Epirote bishops continued to be appointed and the Patriarch's nominees rejected. The special claims of the metropolitan of Ochrida were upheld. The Epirote episcopate firmly supported Theodore Angelus' imperial claims and his coronation by Choma-tianus. A synod held at Arta in 1225 made its position clear in a letter to Germanus. Epirus would choose its own bishops and it was hoped that the Patriarch in Nicaea would approve such appointments. The Patriarch's spiritual authority was recognized and his name was on the diptychs. But if he did not accept this situation, which had full imperial approval (a provocative addition), and send a reply within three months, then an approach to Rome might even be considered.

This double challenge to the authority of Patriarch and Lascarid Emperor was met. In a synodal letter drawn up after an emergency meeting of about forty bishops, apparently held in the vicinity of the imperial army quarters in Bithynia, Germanus swiftly called on Theodore Angelus to lay aside the imperial purple.[57] But the Patriarch's most stinging retort was reserved for Demetrius Cho-matianus, who had written to Germanus in an attempt to smooth over and justify the situation, stressing the well-being of the western Greek Church and the advantages to Orthodoxy of Theodore's successes against the Latins. What precedent was there, Patriarch Germanus asked, for a mere Bulgarian archbishop to crown a Roman Emperor? Why did he continue to undermine the unity of the Church? The Patriarch concluded by announcing the dispatch of an envoy, Nicholas Kaloethes, the metropolitan of Amastris, commissioned to rectify the situation.[58] The legate reached Thessalonica but achieved nothing. Schism ensued and the Patriarch's name was now no longer commemorated in the Divine Liturgy.[59] Correspondence however did not cease. The Epirote Church had able exponents of its cause. Both Demetrius Chomatianus and

[57] GR 1239.
[58] GR 1244.
[59] GR 1244 and 1248.

George Bardanes of Corfu eloquently defended their Emperor and Church, and Bardanes at least pleaded for a peaceful acceptance and compromise.

The rift was brought to an end by hard political facts. Theodore Angelus was defeated and blinded by the Bulgarians and Epirote power declined, while Nicaea under John III Vatatzes steadily ate into the European lands of the Latin Empire. Manuel Angelus (1230–7) found it expedient to turn to Nicaea, particularly in view of the danger of falling under the control of Bulgaria where the metropolitan of Trnovo had obtained autocephalous and patriarchal status,[60] thus diminishing the ecclesiastical authority of the archbishop of Ochrida and All Bulgaria. For a time Manuel Angelus had thought of getting papal protection and had approached Gregory IX in 1232, but when his Bulgarian father-in-law broke his country's alliance with Rome, he thought it prudent to call this off. However rather than submit to possible control by the Bulgarian (and Orthodox) Church he turned to Nicaea. The Patriarch's right to approve Epirote episcopal elections was accepted, though the hazardous nature of communications was also put forward as a reason for being allowed to continue making local appointments. Germanus however ridiculed Manuel's reasoning — the perils of travel are as difficult for us as for you. Then in 1233 he sent his legate Christopher, bishop of Ancyra with the title of the Exarch of the Western Church, to break down the wall between the two parts of the Byzantine Church and to set in order ecclesiastical affairs, including a close investigation into the status claimed by various monastic houses.[61]

4. The Nicaean Empire and Rome

Ecclesiastical relations between Epirus and Nicaea had been largely determined by politics. There was no underlying doctrinal controversy and once the rift had been closed the Orthodox Church and the Byzantine Empire (partially restored by the Lascarids and the Palaeologi) took their stand together as Byzantine tradition demanded. From 1204 onwards first the intrusion of westerners always eager to expand at the expense of Byzantium, and then

[60] *GR* 1282 and 1285.
[61] *GR* 1263 and 1265.

pressures from the eastern Muslim and Mongol worlds affecting both Latin and Greek, had introduced a new element into ecclesiastical diplomacy. For the Byzantines it rapidly became a matter of urgency to get the papacy to exert pressure to control Latin aggression in the Aegean world in return for the union of the two Churches. Every Emperor faced this problem. Could a union of the Roman and Orthodox Churches be achieved, to be followed by a crusade to win back the lost Jerusalem, a long cherished papal objective? And then as this objective grew more dim, it was a question of a united Christian effort to keep back the Ottomans and prevent the total dissolution of the Byzantine Empire. Thus the later middle ages saw a series of negotiations between Byzantium and the papacy in which the councils of Lyons II (1274) and Ferrara–Florence (1438–9) were only the highlights. The Byzantines may have initiated these discussions for political reasons, but in the course of debate doctrinal and ecclesiological differences inevitably arose and during the middle ages these proved irreconcilable. Any agreement was only temporary and was repudiated by the Byzantine majority. There was probably only one Emperor who might be said to have been a genuine convert and he was John V Palaeologus, though there were a certain number of high ecclesiastics and lay intellectuals who supported union or joined the Roman Church from conviction.

The Nicaean rulers all put out feelers to the papacy. Political circumstances alone made this inevitable, though the Lascarids and indeed most of the post-1204 Emperors would probably have welcomed ecclesiastical union, not at the dictation of the papacy, but on agreed terms. In the case of Theodore Lascaris his problem was exacerbated by the treatment of the Greek Orthodox in Constantinople during the early years of the Latin conquest.[62] On the one hand bitter complaints of especially harsh treatment from the papal legate Cardinal Pelagius of Albano reached Nicaea together with the steady stream of refugee monks and clergy. On the other hand some were won over by the tolerance and tact of the Latin Emperor Henry of Hainault. The Greek Patriarch, then Theodore II Irenicus (28 September 1214–31 January 1216), had no hesitation in stiffening resistance to Latin demands. He sent an encyclical to the Orthodox in Constantinople, counselling non-

---

[62] See above ch. VII, section 1.

acceptance of the uncompromising papal teaching and the rejection of the required oath of obedience.[63] Pelagius tried to find a way out of this impasse and discussions were arranged, first in Constantinople and then in the Nicaean kingdom. In both cases the Byzantine spokesman was Nicholas Mesarites, who had become metropolitan of Ephesus. He left an account of these meetings[64] and it is clear that his own critical attitude could hardly have promoted amicable relations. He found Latin protocol lacking in respect to the Byzantine envoy; he misunderstood the suburbicarian system of the Latin cardinal-bishops, casting aspersions on Albano; he criticized the royal purple of Pelagius's shoes, pointing to his own more humble usage (grey outside and scarlet lining concealed within). According to Mesarites, and there was only his own one-sided and lengthy discourse pronounced in Constantinople, the Latin contribution appears to have been confined to a brief expression of desire for unity (on Latin terms). On Mesarites' return to Nicaea with the cardinal's representative there was however a more genuine dialogue, mainly on the papal claim to primacy and on the filioque, both sides using the already familiar arguments. Again the result was a stalemate.

Towards the end of 1219 Theodore I, perhaps because ecclesiastical pacification particularly suited his general policy at that time, attempted to convene at Nicaea a pan-Orthodox council of the four eastern patriarchs (Constantinople, Alexandria, Antioch, and Jerusalem) in order to consider an approach to Rome. He was unsuccessful. His proposals were rejected out of hand by the Epirote Church then in an anti-Latin mood and critical of Theodore's marriage links with the reigning Latin house in Constantinople.

John III Vatatzes succeeded his father-in-law Theodore in 1222. By reason of both character and achievement he was the finest of the thirteenth-century Byzantine Emperors. His quality was recognized by his canonization and he is commemorated on November 4 as the Emperor St John the Merciful. He regained much of the lost territory in Europe, advancing at the expense of the Epirotes, the Bulgarians, and the Latins. For the papacy, already embroiled with the western Emperor, the Hohenstaufen Frederick II, the increasing weakness of the Latin Empire was an acute embarrassment.

At this point the initiative in the ecclesiastical sphere was taken by

[63] *GR* 1219.
[64] Ed. A. Heisenberg, *Neue Quellen*, III.

the vigorous Byzantine Patriarch, Germanus II, whose wide-ranging activities well illustrate the continuing strength of Byzantine influence despite political set-backs. Germanus had already ended the Epirote–Nicaean schism in favour of Nicaea and he had come to terms with the Bulgarian Church. Now in 1232 he approached Pope Gregory IX and the Roman cardinals urging a policy of unity.[65] He seemed to have been spurred on by the arrival in Nicaea of five Franciscans returning from a pilgrimage to the Holy Land. They had run into difficulties and had appealed to Nicaea for protection. They were able to take back to the West two letters from the Patriarch to the Pope and to the cardinals. Though warm in his praise of the friars Germanus could by no means contain his criticism of Rome. He reproached the papacy for Latin cruelty to the Greek Orthodox in Romania and for the recent martyrdom of thirteen Cypriot monks. He reminded the cardinals of the many different nations who followed the way of Orthodoxy. He admitted that there might have been faults on both sides, emphasizing that even the apostle Peter could do wrong but he did at least admit it. He argued a return to the unity of the Church by breaking down the wall of partition caused by Latin violation of the canons.

Gregory IX, whose reply to Germanus showed that he shared Innocent III's views on the Greek Church,[66] was hardly likely to yield any ground before such criticisms. Nevertheless he did arrange for a delegation to go to Nicaea and his envoys were two Dominicans and two Franciscans who took with them a further letter from the Pope.[67] The newly founded mendicant orders gave excellent service to the Latin Church and their members have been called 'the diplomats of the papacy' in the later middle ages. They were particularly useful in dealings with the Byzantines who admired their holy poverty and dedicated way of life.[68] They set up houses both in Constantinople—the Franciscans were in Pera by 1220—and elsewhere in Latin-occupied lands.[69] More important

---

[65] *GR* 1256 and 1257.

[66] A. L. Tăutu (ed.), *Greg. IX*, no. 179 (26 July 1232).

[67] See Golubovich, *Biblioteca*, II. 362–7; Tăutu, *Greg. IX*, no. 193 (18 May 1233).

[68] R. L. Wolff, 'The Latin Empire of Constantinople and the Franciscans', *Traditio*, 2 (1944), 213–37, discusses their role within the Latin Empire as well as their services in negotiating union.

[69] R. Loenertz, 'Les Établissements dominicains de Péra-Constantinople,' *EO*, 34 (1935), 332–49 (reprinted in his collected essays *Byzantina et Franco-Graeca*, I, Rome, 1970).

still, they were often bilingual and evidently acquired Greek theological works, valuable assets in debating with the Orthodox, though perhaps a somewhat one-sided advantage until later on when western expertise was matched by Greek scholars with knowledge of the Latin language and of Latin writings.

Gregory's delegation set out in 1233, arriving in Nicaea in January 1234. There is a Latin account of their mission.[70] The Greek point of view is provided by one of the main Byzantine protagonists, the theologian Nicephorus Blemmydes.[71] The Latin envoys were received in Nicaea with generous hospitality and there they met the Emperor John III Vatatzes and Patriarch Germanus II. Like Gregory IX the friars assumed that the schism had been caused by the Byzantine refusal to promise obedience to Rome. Discussions concentrated on the filioque, and Greek opposition to the addition to the creed was defended by Blemmydes. The friars attempted to refute the Byzantines by quoting in Greek a passage from Cyril of Alexandria—they had brought with them from Constantinople 'a considerable number of Greek books'—and they went on arguing far into the night by the light of candles and lanterns.[72] The friars also desired discussion on the azymes and the eucharist, but at the insistence of the Byzantine Patriarch this was postponed so that he could have time for consultation with the three eastern patriarchs and others. What Germanus really wanted was a full discussion in a general council but the friars had no authority to sanction this. Before they returned to Constantinople John Vatatzes asked them whether submission to Rome by the Byzantine Patriarch would be followed by the restitution of his rights (*restituet ei dominus Papa ius suum*),[73] which implied his return to Constantinople. If in a Christian spirit yet with marked ambiguity, the friars could only reply that the Lord Patriarch would receive greater mercy from the Pope and the whole Roman Church than he might think possible.

The visit in January 1234 which achieved nothing was followed up by pressing invitations from Emperor and Patriarch to further discussions at or near Nymphaeum in western Asia Minor, a place

[70] *Disputatio Latinorum et Graecorum* ..., ed. G. Golubovich, *Archivum Franciscanum Historicum*, 12 (1919), 428–70.

[71] N. Blemmydes, *Curriculum Vitae*, ed. A. Heisenberg (Leipzig, 1896) and J. A. Munitiz (Louvrain, 1984); P. Canart, 'Nicéphore Blemmyde et le mémoire adressé aux envoyés de Grégoire IX (Nicée, 1234)', *OCP*, 25 (1959), 310–25.

[72] *Disputatio*, op. cit., ch. 7, p. 434.

[73] *Disputatio*, op. cit., ch. 14, p. 445; Mansi, 23. 292.

much favoured by the Nicaean rulers.[74] The friars' reluctance to return was overcome by pressure brought to bear by political forces in Constantinople where Latin affairs were desperate and it was hoped that the envoys might persuade Vatatzes to hold off from attack if only for a short time. Despite the Greek desire to pursue further the filioque debate in the much larger synodal gathering in Nymphaeum, the friars insisted on discussing the controversial azymes as promised them at the previous meeting in Nicaea. Latins would have been willing to concede that both leavened and unleavened bread might be used in the eucharist. But they stuck to their teaching on the procession of the Holy Spirit from the Father and the Son, though conceding that if in agreement over Trinitarian doctrine the Greeks might omit the actual word filioque from the creed as was indeed done in the Greek liturgy in some Latin-occupied regions. The Greeks however repudiated the Latin use of unleavened bread and maintained the procession of the Holy Spirit from the Father alone. Both sides were outspoken and discussion grew more acrimonious, each condemning the other as heretical. The Emperor tried to mediate but realized the futility of this when he uttered the words 'This is not the way of peace'. The friars departed abruptly, harassed by the Greeks who wanted back the document they had drawn up on the liturgy and thus held up the conveyance of the friars' books—the friars themselves could only carry a few of the many tomes which they had brought with them and had so frequently consulted often to the discomfiture of the Greeks. Once again stalemate.

Innocent IV (1243–54), the near successor of Gregory IX (†1241) was more liberal in outlook than his predecessors. He showed this both in his awareness of the ecclesiastical problems of the Greeks living under Latin control[75] and in his dealings with the Nicaean Empire. Like John Vatatzes he was also a realist. Though he was not blind to the needs of the Latin Empire he was perceptive enough to see that it was becoming a hopeless liability. In addition he was alarmed at the alliance between Vatatzes and the Hohenstaufen Frederick II, 'the enemy of the Church'.[76] He therefore welcomed

---

[74] The friars were in fact invited to Leschera which would appear to have been near Nymphaeum where the discussions with the Emperor and clergy took place. See *GR* 1269–76 for correspondence and the debates on the filioque and azymes.

[75] See above pp. 203 ff.

[76] Nicholas of Curbio, ed. L. Muratori, *Rerum Italicarum Scriptores*, III, 1 (Milan, 1723), p. 592 k.

an advance from Nicaea when in 1248 John Vatatzes wrote to ask Innocent to send John of Parma, the Minister-General of the Franciscans, to reopen the question of union.[77] This Innocent willingly did, having no doubt politics as well as religion in mind for at that time the obstinate and dangerous Frederick II was still alive.

John of Parma with other 'learned men' went to Nymphaeum in 1249 and took part in a further debate on the filioque. He returned in 1250 with an imperial and patriarchal mission which reached the Pope in Perugia in 1251.[78] The envoys almost certainly brought with them a letter from the Patriarch Manuel II, a rather general exhortation to unity under Christ the only head of the Church. He avoided the word 'schism', preferring such synonyms as 'separation' (διάστασις). He referred to discussions to be held about a general council, the position of the Pope and 'our own just demands' and ended with a rather sweeping committal that the decisions of the conference would be accepted 'by us all'.[79] However nothing seems to be known with certainty about the outcome of this meeting and certainly no official action was taken then.

Negotiations with the papacy were reopened in 1253, this time with a quite different emphasis. The Byzantine Emperor made concrete and not impracticable suggestions and Innocent recipro-cated as far as he could. However Vatatzes believed that he had his clergy behind him. The Byzantine mission sent in 1253 reached the Pope, then in Anagni, in spring 1254. The imperial terms offered were—the replacement of the Pope's name in the diptychs and acknowledgement of his primacy (but no mention of any kind of oath of obedience with its feudal undertones); the Pope was to have appellant jurisdiction: he was to have first place in councils, speaking first and signing first; his judgements in council in questions of faith and in other matters were to hold good provided they did not contravene the gospels and canons; his decrees were to be binding if not in opposition to the canons. The filioque was specifically exempt from the clause on obedience in matters of faith,

---

[77] *DR*² 1795; the Byzantine Patriarch Manuel II wrote direct to John of Parma about this (*GR* 1311); on the embassy of John of Parma see Franchi, *La svolta*.

[78] *DR*² 1804 and *GR* 1313.

[79] G. Hofmann, 'Patriarch von Nikaia Manuel II. an Papst Innozenz IV.', *OCP*, 19 (1953), 59–70; he gives the text and dates the letter to 1250; he is followed by Gill, *Byzantium and the Papacy*, 90–1, 95; V. Laurent prefers the 1253 embassy (*GR* 1319).

which Innocent IV's successor, Alexander IV, thought unreasonable, though Innocent was willing to accept it provided that it was clear that the Greeks were at one with the Latins in their Trinitarian doctrine. After all the Greeks were conceding a good deal especially with regard to primacy and appellant jurisdiction. But in the other concessions there was a measure of safeguard in the insistence on conformity to the gospels and canons (a requirement likely to lead to endless argument). In return the Emperor demanded the restoration of Constantinople and the removal of the Latin Emperor as well as all Latin patriarchs, excepting only that the Patriarch of Antioch was to remain in office for his lifetime. The Greek patriarchs were to be restored to their rights.

Innocent IV accepted the proposals in matters of faith and discipline. Though not able immediately to effect the ejection of the Latin Emperor and the Latin Patriarch of Constantinople, he agreed in principle to Vatatzes' request, but pointed out that if his efforts at persuasion failed, then legal procedure should be applied.[80]

In substance the terms offered were very like those of Lyons II (1274) negotiated by Michael VIII Palaeologus, partly as a means of keeping off western attacks on Constantinople (by then in Byzantine hands). Here in the 1253–4 mission Vatatzes, very near to recapturing Constantinople himself, evidently meant to secure the same kind of safeguard. Whether the imperial proposals would ever have been formally accepted by the Byzantine Church as a whole remains unknown, despite evidence of support for Vatatzes. All three key figures died in 1254 before this could be put to the test— John III Vatatzes on 3 November and his Patriarch Manuel II in October,[81] Innocent IV on 7 December.

John III's son and successor, Theodore II Lascaris, had not got his father's statesmanship. He was particularly concerned with scholarship and theology. At some time before 31 March 1256 he reopened negotiations with the papacy and Innocent IV's successor, Alexander IV, sent as his envoy Constantine, bishop of Orvieto (already selected by Innocent IV for this office).[82] Constantine had full

---

[80] *DR*[2] 1816 a; the terms on either side are known from the letters of Innocent IV's successor Alexander IV to Theodore II Lascaris and to the papal legate Constantine, bishop of Orvieto.

[81] *GR*, fasc. IV, p. 111.

[82] See F. Schillmann, 'Zur byzantinischen Politik Alexanders IV.', *Röm. Quart.*, 22 (1908), 108–31.

powers and it was rather unfair of the new Byzantine Patriarch Arsenius Autorianus (November 1254–February/March 1260) to reproach Alexander IV for his legate's lack of authority. He wrote in the autumn of 1256 when Constantine had left, and he added that on the Byzantine side all decisions with regard to union really rested with the Emperor.[83] The one thing which the legate could not do was to hand over Constantinople to the Byzantine Emperor and evidently the negotiations got no further. It was left to Michael VIII to follow up Vatatzes' work for union.

[83] *GR* 1332.

VIII

CONTACTS: FAILURE AND ACHIEVEMENT 1258–1453

1. Michael VIII Palaeologus and the papacy: Byzantine doubts concerning union 1258–1274

The Lascarid Theodore II (†1258) left as his heir a minor, his son John IV. His plans for the regency were upset by discontented elements in the aristocracy and Michael Palaeologus seized control as guardian for the young Emperor. He rapidly became co-Emperor and was crowned either at the end of December 1258 or on 1 January 1259, having been raised on the shield earlier in December. He was able to profit from the astute work of John III Vatatzes who had consolidated the Byzantine position in Asia Minor and had expanded into Europe largely at the expense of Epirus and Bulgaria. By now the Latin Empire was negligible except as a pawn in papal and western policies, but strongly held and virtually independent Latin principalities, such as the Villehardouin lands in the Peloponnese, remained as obstacles to Byzantine expansion.

Michael Palaeologus was the last Byzantine Emperor to show any real signs of being equal to a situation of this kind and his career exemplified Byzantine policy at its best and at its worst. He was a tough general, an experienced and subtle diplomat and a ruthless and unscrupulous ruler. He had to justify his seizure of the throne. This he did partly by a drive against the alliance of Epirus, the Peloponnese, and the Hohenstaufen Manfred culminating in his victory at Pelagonia in 1259, partly by proceeding against Constantinople with the help of the Genoese. The capital was retaken on 25 July 1261 after the hasty flight of the Latin Emperor Baldwin II. This added to Michael's prestige in the short term but it did not win entirely unanimous approval since the far-sighted realized that there might be advantages in concentrating on Asia Minor and the defence of the eastern frontier. Such a view however ran counter to age-long tradition. On 15 August 1261 Michael Palaeologus entered the city to be re-crowned in Hagia Sophia, thus formally establishing his link with his imperial predecessors. But it was his own small son Andronicus who took his place as heir presumptive and not John IV. The young Lascarid was blinded on 25 December 1261 and imprisoned in Bithynia.

Michael VIII had earlier sworn fidelity to the Lascarid dynasty and this cruelty and perfidy roused violent protests from the pro-Lascarids and caused dissension within the Church. This opposition was led by the Patriarch Arsenius Autorianus who appears to have excommunicated Michael for his usurpation of the throne as early as 1259.[1] Arsenius was replaced for a brief period by Nicephorus II (*c*.March 1260–*c*.February 1261)[2] but returned in the summer of 1261 to the office again, this time not in Nicaea but in the newly regained Constantinople.[3] When early in 1262 he heard of the blinding of John Lascaris he again excommunicated Michael. Enmity between the Patriarch and Emperor came to a head when Arsenius refused to appear before Michael in the imperial palace in April 1264. He was deposed again and exiled to the island of Proconnesus.[4] Then in July 1265 Arsenius's successor Germanus III Markoutzas (28 May 1265–14 September 1266) excommunicated him by reason of his alleged implication in an anti-imperial plot.[5]

The cause of Arsenius attracted all manner of dissident elements from the politically motivated pro-Lascarids to the so-called 'zealots' or extremists. These latter extremists are to be found throughout Byzantine history in various contexts. Like the earlier Theodore the Studite, they sponsored views which seemed to undermine the long-established co-operation between Church and Emperor. The Arsenites considered censure of Michael Palaeologus's treatment of John IV Lascaris justified and the deposition of Arsenius invalid. Consequently they did not recognize the patriarchs succeeding him. The movement long survived the death of Arsenius in 1273 and was

---

[1] *GR* 1345; so Laurent, but see A. Failler, 'Chronologie et composition dans l'histoire de Georges Pachymère', *REB*, 38(1980), 45–53, who puts the case for Arsenius's retirement at the end of 1259, with Nicephorus succeeding him towards the end of December 1259 or 1 January 1260 until his death at the end of 1260. *PLP* (at present in progress) gives valuable information on ecclesiastical and other personalities of the period.

[2] But see Failler, op. cit.

[3] *GR* 1353.

[4] *GR* 1366 with discussion of the date.

[5] *GR* 1376.

to provide one more element in the later anti-unionist demonstrations following the council of Lyons (1274). Throughout Michael's reign it was a perpetual canker—or, as some would maintain, a salutary witness to Orthodoxy. Sponsored largely by monks and lower clergy, Arsenite opposition was fomented by the illusive underground activities of wandering agents described by the contemporary historian Pachymeres as 'men in sackcloth' (σακκοφόροι).[6] The movement had its genuinely convinced supporters but it did attract many malcontents and disreputable throwouts. It also appealed to an ignorant populace, always ready to follow a monastic lead and not always able to distinguish between a holy man and a subversive propagandist. It was not until 1310 under Andronicus II, who was considered more orthodox than his excommunicated father, that the Arsenites were finally brought within the Church.[7]

Against a background of increasing unease and resentment Michael VIII showed his quality and proceeded to lay the foundation of a dynasty which fought for 250 years against hopeless odds. In spite of the prestige given to the Palaeologus by the re-establishment of Byzantine government in the capital his position was precarious. He was well aware of his encirclement. He faced the ambitious Balkan kingdoms, the Latin principalities by now firmly rooted in Greek soil, the new western claimants to the Latin Empire of Baldwin II, lost only temporarily, so the West hoped. In addition there were disquieting uncertainties in the Asian world caused by Mongol turmoils and rising Turkish powers. Like his Lascarid predecessors, Michael VIII saw his best hope in coming to terms with the papacy. Here his bargaining power was in practice limited and his patient and often perceptive diplomacy was stretched to the utmost. In the last resort his moves were checkmated at every point by the immovable and unflinching opposition of the majority of his subjects who resisted any change in the doctrine and usages of their Church. The impression given by surviving imperial documents and papal registers and other sources is of intensive diplomatic activity in international circles.[8] and a dead weight of opposition

---

[6] Pachymeres, *De Mich. Pal.*, IV. 11 (*CB*, I, p. 277).

[7] *GR* 2003.

[8] For the diplomatic intricacies of the Byzantino-papal situation leading up to the council of Lyons and after see Setton, *Papacy and the Levant*, I, Roberg, *Union*; Geanakoplos, *Michael Palaeologus*; Runciman, *Sicilian Vespers*; and Franchi, *La svolta*.

from most ecclesiastics and laity at home. How far Michael himself had a genuine wish to promote the unity of Christendom is impossible to establish. Here the urgency of political problems may well have obscured personal feelings. Certainly the desire for reunion (on papal terms) represented the genuine wish of only a small minority of his Greek contemporaries.

From the outset Michael VIII had been in touch with the papacy. After the capture of Constantinople he approached Urban IV in 1262,[9] broaching the question of hostilities between Greeks and Latins, expressing the desire to restore the unity of the Church and asking for legates to be sent who should be peace-loving followers of Christ[10] and who would carry out the work of unity. He wisely did not embark upon dogmatic or liturgical discussion. His efforts were at first blocked by Urban's anti-Greek politics. Then, probably in 1263,[11] he put out an offer of union in general terms favourable to the papacy. He expressed the view, to some extent based on private discussions with the bilingual Bishop Nicholas of South Italian Cotrone, that 'The Roman Church of God does not differ from ours in the divine doctrines of its faith . . . but in almost everything is in agreement . . .' and all peoples, nations, patriarchal sees were subject to it. And he asked for legates to be sent to carry out the work of unity. The union was to be followed by the long-projected crusade. Evidently, as Michael wished, Urban was already considering holding a general council designed to settle outstanding problems.[12]

But on 2 December 1264 Urban IV died. His successor Clement IV took a much tougher line. Both Pope and the Palaeologus had to face a new situation caused by the rise to power of Charles of Anjou, a formidable opponent who by early 1266 had constituted himself heir to the defeated Hohenstaufen and was in process of establishing himself in South Italy, to be followed—an ominous development for Michael VIII—by advances in western Greece with an eye on Constantinople.

In 1266 and early 1267 Michael VIII was in contact with the Pope

[9] DR^2 1911.

[10] From Urban's reply to Michael, see J. Guiraud (ed.), *Reg. Urb. IV*, no. 295 (Paris, 1901); cf. the approach to Nicholas of Cotrone. (GR^2 1889[b]).

[11] DR^2 1918b, now dated spring/summer 1263, correcting Geanakoplos, *Michael Palaeologus*, 176, note 65, where part of the letter is translated.

[12] DR^2 1931b, c. summer 1264; from Clement IV's letter of 4 Mar. 1267 (=DR^2 1939a).

urging the recognition of the union of the two Churches in a general council to be followed by the crusade.[13] In return he expected Clement to condemn, or at least restrain, Charles of Anjou's threatening ambitions. As earlier in the thirteenth century during the Lascarid regime, the papacy now appeared willing to consider accepting the restoration of the Byzantines in Constantinople, a policy which carried with it a commitment to curb Charles of Anjou and provide the Byzantines with military aid. But at a price. Clement IV demanded immediate recognition of papal primacy and unconditional acceptance of Roman doctrine and usage not just by word of the Emperor but by clergy and people as well. Only after this would the question of a general council be considered, and then at a place of the Pope's choosing, to rectify and not to discuss. This demand differed greatly from the rather general though all-embracing promises already given by Michael VIII who seemed to have hoped to push through the union without provoking opposition on the home front by too much discussion of hotly debatable details. Michael stalled. So did Clement who continued to play off Charles of Anjou and the displaced Baldwin II against the Byzantine Emperor.

On Clement IV's death (23 November 1268) a quarrelsome interregnum intervened in the College of Cardinals with French and Italian candidates contesting the election to the papal see. In this situation Michael VIII chose to approach Louis IX in mid-1269 stressing the need for the union of the two Churches and pointing out the disruption in the Christian world likely to result if his brother Charles of Anjou chose to attack Constantinople.[14] But Louis died shortly afterwards on his unfortunate Tunisian crusade (25 August 1270) and Charles continued to go his way in western Greece and the Peloponnese. Michael was however saved by an alliance with the newly-elected Pope, an Italian, Tedaldo Visconti, who was enthroned on 1 September 1271 as Gregory X. Gregory stands out as one of the most spiritually minded of the later medieval popes and his quality was recognized by the contemporary Byzantine historian George Pachymeres who could not help contrasting him favourably with the Byzantine Emperor. Michael VIII, he wrote, only thought of church union because of the threat of Charles of Anjou, 'but Gregory and his followers desired this

[13] *DR*² 1939a and 1947.
[14] *DR*² 1968 (and *DR* 1971 to the College of Cardinals at Louis's suggestion).

peace for the sake of the good it would bring and for the unity of the Churches',[15] Gregory was concerned above all with his responsibilities as spiritual head of Christendom. He certainly had problems within the Latin Church—papal election procedure for example—but his greatest desire had always been to promote the recovery of the Holy Land and this, if only for practical reasons, implied the union of the Latin and Greek Churches.

Gregory therefore announced in March 1272 that a general council was to be convened for 1274. He evidently realized that he would have to deal with Charles of Anjou and his allies, if only temporarily, as the long desired recovery of Jerusalem would certainly not be served by antagonizing Michael VIII or by the setting up of another Latin Empire in Constantinople. While he was in Palestine at the time of his election in 1271 he was reported by Pachymeres to have written to the Byzantine Emperor to inform him of his plans.[16] Michael himself approached Gregory in the summer of 1272.[17] In a letter sent by hand of the trusted bilingual Greek-born Franciscan John Parastron he fervently assured the Pope of his desire for union. It was in answer to this that on 24 October 1272 Gregory replied telling Michael 'the illustrious Emperor of the Greeks', of his plans for a general council to open on 1 May 1274 and making clear the terms on which union was offered.[18] The Patriarch of Constantinople also received an invitation to attend the council.[19] The papal demands were those of Clement IV but the private instructions given to the legates, Parastron and four Franciscans, showed considerable sensitivity and understanding of Michael's difficult situation. The legates were empowered to offer the Emperor and the Byzantine clergy various different forms of submission, such as, 'We recognise and accept Roman primacy . . .', or 'We agree with the truth of the Catholic faith . . .', or 'We wish to recognise this faith . . .', thus softening the form of the total submission previously required by Clement IV, and repeated by subsequent popes whatever apparent modifications may have been offered by Gregory.

Michael sent back two of the friars with assurances of his ardent

---

[15] Pachymeres, *De Mich. Pal.*, V. 11 (*CB*, I, p. 370).
[16] Ibid., pp. 369–70.
[17] *DR*² 1986.
[18] J. Guiraud (ed.), *Reg. Grég. X* (Paris, 1892), no. 194.
[19] J. Guiraud (ed.), *Reg. Grég. X* (Paris, 1892), no. 196.

desire for union. He also pledged his support for the proposed crusade, though doubtless with an eye to consolidation in Asia Minor rather than the reconquest of the Holy Land, and he made it clear that for him a crusade was only a practical possibility if his enemies on the home front were kept in check. He asked for the safe conduct of his envoys and defended himself from any charge of failing to press for union, hinting at difficulties to be avoided if an even greater schism was to be averted.[20]

Perhaps the last words reflected Michael VIII's awareness of the gravity of this situation, aggravated as it was by conflicting ecclesiastical and political currents within the Empire. The council, involving public commitment to union, was now upon him and he had to persuade his Patriarch and bishops to give him some active support, hoping that. the majority of the general public would at least acquiesce. He took the line that the three papal claims— primacy, appellate jurisdiction, and commemoration in the liturgy—need mean very little in practice. They could be accepted in a spirit of expediency (the Byzantine *oeconomia*) in order to win papal co-operation in checking Byzantium's political enemies, notably Charles of Anjou. And of course the union of the two Churches was in itself a desirable objective. But it was not a simple situation in which the Emperor could easily impose his will. Up to a point he could compel but it was not within his power to convince. This was something which the papacy seemed never fully to appreciate, as is shown for instance by continual papal reproaches of imperial lukewarmness in failing to quash the continued and widespread Byzantine resistance to union after the council of Lyons II.

Something of the depth of Byzantine feeling and the far-flung anti-unionist propaganda is reflected in surviving documents and tracts of the period.[21] These provide ample justification for Michael's fear that the cause might be lost once his argumentative subjects became involved in polemic. He had so far tried to avoid doctrinal discussion. Such issues as the filioque, western usages (for instance unleavened bread), the doctrine of purgatory, the implications of the papal plenitude of power, were not brought into the

---

[20] *DR²* 2002 and 2002a; there appear to have been two letters around November 1273.
[21] Some of the key texts are given in *Dossier grec* (with French trans.).

open, at least not by Michael. He stressed the similarity of Greek and Latin belief. But he did not win over the synod. Indeed, the chartophylax Beccus, the chief archivist and chancellor of Hagia Sophia, went so far as to suggest that the Latins were in effect heretics, a charge which continued to be the contention of the anti-unionists.[22] For this Beccus was censured and imprisoned, probably towards the end of 1273.[23] Michael had a statement (*Tomos*) drawn up to support the unionists and to demonstrate the orthodoxy of the Latins, the text of which is known only by reference or quotation in the anti-unionist reply to it. This *Tomos* proved ineffective and Michael found that in addition to the continued hostility of the Arsenites on the Lascarid issue, he had the active opposition of the Patriarch Joseph, supported by a strong anti-unionist party drawn not simply from monastic extremists but including prominent laity, as the Emperor's sister Eulogia and certain of his leading generals.

A full and formal anti-unionist *Reply* (the *Apologia*) to Michael's *Tomos* was drawn up for the synod by a small group led by the uncompromising monk Job Jasites and including the historian Pachymeres. In its present form it contains some later additions, possibly Part III giving the historical and canonical reasons for rejecting the Latins, and it has been suggested that there was a shorter version, now apparently lost, which would have been read to the synod for its approval.[24] Familiar arguments are used to reject the filioque and support the Greek tradition of the fathers. The political argument for economy, or expediency, is rejected, since God chastens those whom he loves and in the past Rome has not shown itself conspicuously able to maintain peace. The Latins are regarded as heretics, and heretics should be avoided like mad dogs. To accept papal primacy would mean being faced with complete 'Latinismos'. In fact 'to gain the Pope ... I should lose myself'.[25] This uncompromising document contained the essence of the anti-unionist position.

The Patriarch Joseph, a monk in origin, seems to have been a kindly, peace-loving man, a non-intellectual, perplexed in the face

[22] GR 1399.
[23] On Beccus's career as J. Gill, 'John Beccus, Patriarch of Constantinople 1275–1282', *Byzantina*, 7 (1975), 253–66.
[24] Text and French trans. in *Dossier grec* where this problem is fully discussed; GR 1400.
[25] *Dossier grec*, p. 253 and *passim*.

of conflicting pressures but fiercely tenacious of Greek ecclesiastical tradition. In June 1273 he took what was in effect an oath not to subscribe to the union on the terms offered, pledging himself 'to keep inviolate the teaching of my Saviour'. He was not, he said, opposed to union as such and indeed fully supported it provided that the Old Rome would remove the cause of schism. How could Rome be commemorated in the liturgy as long as it maintained its innovations? To support Rome in such a situation would be to separate from the other three eastern patriarchates and he suggested holding a council with the eastern Churches 'to be convened by my Emperor', a thoroughly Byzantine point of view in keeping with imperial and ecclesiastical tradition.[26]

In June 1273 Joseph persuaded the synod to support him and sign an anti-unionist oath. Michael however did win one valuable ally when the imprisoned chartophylax John Beccus changed to the imperial side. While confined in the Tower of the Anema guarded by Varangians, Beccus who knew little if any Latin[27] was plied with mainly Greek patristic writings in support of the view that the Latin 'from' (ἐκ) and the Greek 'through' (διά) did not imply any doctrinal difference in the question of the filioque added to the creed by the Latins. On his conversion Beccus was released and resumed his office, supporting the Emperor's renewed efforts to get some kind of pro-union statement from the synod, the official ecclesiastical body, since the papal legates were waiting in Constantinople to take this back to Rome.

By October 1273 Michael, evidently despairing of mere verbal persuasion, frightened his bishops into acquiescence by his severe and humiliating treatment of the scholar and orator Manuel Holobolus, an obstinate opponent.[28] The bishops prepared to give in and asked for a statement giving precise definition of the terms of union. Michael VIII replied with a chrysobull issued on, or soon after, 25 December 1273.[29] In it the three terms are explicitly stated—primacy, appellate jurisdiction, and commemoration—but there is no mention of doctrinal issues. Further, Michael was careful to emphasize that, having agreed to the three claims, 'we must then

---

[26] GR 1401; text and trans. in *Dossier grec*, 134 ff.

[27] G. Hofmann, 'Patriarch Johann Bekkos und die lateinische Kultur', *OCP*, 11 (1945), 141–64.

[28] Pachymeres, *De Mich. Pal.*, bk. v, 20 (*CB*, I, pp. 391 ff.).

[29] *DR*[2] 2002b; text and trans. in *Dossier grec*, pp. 313 ff. and in Gill, 'Church Union', 12–19.

uphold all our other doctrines and rites'. In acknowledgement the synod drew up an address to the Emperor, stating that on these terms 'we have all come to the same conclusion as our God-crowned and mighty holy Lord and Emperor ...'[30] Thus by February 1274 a synodal letter to the Pope was produced explaining that after long deliberations the Emperor had won and 'we all agreed to the union'. But it was signed by only a minority with notable omissions, hardly reflecting any marked degree of unanimity.[31]

The Patriarch Joseph had pledged irrevocable opposition to union on the proposed terms and he therefore did not sign. It was clear that should the union go through he could hardly remain in office. The dilemma was temporarily solved by his withdrawal to the monastery of the Peribleptos pending the outcome of the council. He remained Patriarch however, retaining his revenues, patriarchal privileges, and commemoration in the liturgy, and he continued to direct patriarchal affairs.[32] Before he withdrew to Peribleptos on 11 January 1274 he made clear to the Emperor[33] and the bishops[34] that whether he would continue in the patriarchal office would depend on the conciliar decision brought back from Lyons by the imperial envoys. Further he granted the bishops of his eparchy permission to give their opinions as they wished in respect of the three papal demands. As for himself, he added, 'when the envoys have returned from there (Lyons), if indeed my soul shall acquiesce in what has been arranged by them, let me be still Patriarch; but if not, I shall surrender the throne to them that want it'.[35]

2. Michael VIII and the council of Lyons II (1274)

It was against this background of opposition, or at best unwilling co-operation, from the majority of the bishops and others that the

---

[30] Greek text and trans. in Gill, 'Church Union', 18–21; Latin text in Roberg, Union, Anhang I, No. 5, pp. 235–9, giving 44 archbishops and bishops with clergy of the Great Church and court officials.

[31] Cf. Gill, 'Church Union', pp. 8 ff.; A. L. Tăutu (ed.), Acta Urb. IV, and Greg. X (Vatican, 1953), no. 42, p. 125, par. 266. Figures vary slightly in the sources, but only 26 metropolitans signed.

[32] See GR entries for 1274.

[33] DR[2] 2004 and GR 1408.

[34] GR 1409; text and trans. in Gill, 'Church Union', 20–3.

[35] Text and trans. in Gill, 'Church Union', 23.

Byzantine envoys set out. The Patriarch of Constantinople had been invited but neither replied nor went. There were no representatives from the three eastern Patriarchs. There was however the former Patriarch of Constantinople, Germanus III, and one metropolitan of standing, Theophanes of Nicaea. The most authoritative figure was Michael VIII's chief minister, the grand logothete George Acropolites, described to the Pope by the friars accompanying the delegation as the 'primus secretarius imperatoris'. There were also two other senior officials, the finance minister Nicholas Panaretus and the head of the interpreters George Tzimisces Berriotes, together with the usual staff and suitably valuable presents. Unfortunately the boat containing a number of the staff and the gifts was caught off the southern Peloponnese in one of those sudden storms which plague the Aegean and foundered with almost total loss of life. The other vessel with the chief envoys reached Brindisi and with the help of the papal letters of safe conduct the delegates continued their journey by land and arrived at Lyons on 24 July 1274 in time to take part in the fourth session of the council.

Without waiting for the arrival of the Greeks the council (Lyons II, the Fourteenth general council in the Roman Church) had been formally opened on 7 May 1274 in the cathedral of St John. It was a splendid gathering, probably about 400 bishops[36] as well as other clergy and representatives of the rulers of six countries. King James I of Aragon came in person. Charles of Anjou was notably absent. Gregory X inaugurated proceedings with a sermon on the text 'With desire I have desired to eat this Passover with you' (Luke 22:15). He reminded his audience of the threefold purpose of the council. It had met to take part in the longed for union of the Greek and Latin Churches. This, though, greatly desirable in itself, was also an essential preliminary to the fulfilment of Gregory's dearest wish, the recovery of the Holy Land to be achieved by the crusade which the council would organize. Then, thirdly, there was the need to institute long-needed reforms within the Latin Church, including revised procedures for conducting and speeding up papal elections (it had taken three years for Gregory X to be elected).

The first three sessions (7 May, 18 May, and 4 June) were occupied with preliminaries, and more particularly the organization

---

[36] See Setton, *Papacy and the Levant*, I. 112–13, on the problem of estimating the precise numbers present.

and financing of the proposed crusade. It was however known, from a letter dispatched *en route* by Jerome of Ascoli (who was travelling with the delegation), that the Greeks were on their way and after the third session on 4 June the council was temporarily suspended pending their arrival.

The Byzantines reached Lyons on 24 June. They were escorted with due honours to the palace where the Pope was staying and with splendid ceremonial they received the kiss of peace from Gregory X. They clearly stated that they had come to express their obedience to the Holy See, and they had brought documents confirming this, a chrysobull from Michael VIII agreeing to the papal conditions and a similar profession of obedience from Michael's son, the co-Emperor Andronicus,[37] as well as the letter from the Greek clergy, though these did not commit themselves so specifically as the Emperor did. Michael had also sent a more personal note to the Pope, claiming that the union had been his dearest wish from youth onwards. He emphasized how he had pressed on to achieve this amid overwhelming administrative and military cares. After all, he maintained, Greek and Roman beliefs were really the same and controversy had only arisen by reason of misinterpretation of certain small words (*verbula*).[38]

To Gregory X this was a joyful occasion and on 29 June it was celebrated in the festal mass for St Peter and St Paul. As a sign of reconciliation the Gospel and Epistle were read in both Greek and Latin. The Latin creed was also followed by the Greek (with the filioque), intoned by the ex-Patriarch Germanus of Constantinople and other Greek-speaking clergy, mostly from Calabria, together with the Dominican William Moerbecke and the Franciscan John Parastron (who both knew Greek).

The formal submission and reunion took place during the fourth session of the council on 6 July with the Greek envoys seated to the right of the Pope.[39] It was emphasized that Greek acceptance of the papal terms had been freely undertaken without thought of temporal advantage, though this was regarded by some, if not most, as being exceedingly doubtful,[40] for the gravity of the Anjou threat

---

[37] *DR*[2] 2006, French trans. of Michael VIII's profession of faith in Wolter-Holstein, 276–80.
[38] *DR*[2] 2007.
[39] Franchi, *Concilio II di Lione*, 85.
[40] Ibid., 86, 'de quo multum dubitabatur'.

and Michael VIII's need for papal mediation must have been obvious. It was now that the statements from the Emperor,[41] his son Andronicus,[42] and the Greek clergy[43] were read in Latin translation. Except for its ending, Michael VIII's profession of faith was virtually identical with the contents of Clement IV's letter of 4 March 1267.[44] It began with the creed (with filioque), expressed belief in the seven sacraments, recognized Roman teaching on purgatory, the use of unleavened bread in the communion service and the differing Latin canon law on marriage. And freely and without compulsion he promised obedience to the Roman faith and above all accepted papal primacy, plenitude of power, and appellate jurisdiction. But he ended by pleading for the retention of Greek rites and usages.

We beg your Great Sanctity that our church should recite the holy creed as it has been recited from before the schism up to the present day, and that the rites which we used before the schism should be kept provided that they are not contrary to the faith which we have professed above, nor to the divine commandments, nor to the teaching in the Old and New Testament, nor to the doctrine of the holy general councils, nor to the holy fathers approved by the holy councils held under the spiritual leadership of the Church of Rome. This is not a matter of importance to your Great Sanctity nor contrary to usage. But it is a matter of difficulty for us because of the vast multitude of our people.[45]

This was in accordance with Michael VIII's frequent assurances to the Byzantine clergy that the proposed concessions to Rome would really mean very little in practice since Greek rites and usages would be retained, as indeed appeared to be the practice in the years immediately following the union of 1274. Something of this kind had in fact been suggested earlier on during negotiations between the papacy and John III Vatatzes.

Nevertheless the statement contained in Michael VIII's gold bull was on the face of it an impressive surrender to Rome. In the name of the Emperor, his plenipotentiary, George Acropolites, stood up

---

[41] *DR*² 2006; French trans. in Wolter-Holstein, 276–80.

[42] Tăutu, *Acta Urb. IV, Clem. IV and Greg. X* (Vatican, 1953), no. 44, pp. 130–1.

[43] Tăutu, op. cit., no. 42, pp. 124–7 (Latin); Roberg, *Union*, Anhang I, no. 5, pp. 235–9.

[44] Tăutu, op. cit., no. 23, pp. 61–9.

[45] Tăutu, op. cit., no. 41, p. 122 (Greek and Latin); Roberg, *Union*, Anhang I, no. 6, pp. 242–3 (Latin).

in the assembly and swore adherence to the complete profession of faith which had just been read. This he did for himself and for the Emperor whose 'full mandate' he had.[46] He had brought a letter of authorization from Michael VIII[47] and although later on the papacy raised problems because of the general character of this letter the good faith of the Emperor and his envoys was accepted by the council. Once George Acropolites had made his statement the union was considered to have been achieved. There was a striking absence of any discussion. Indeed the whole procedure simply consisted of the statements from the Byzantine Emperors and synod which were read, and then the official acceptance in the council when the plenipotentiary George Acropolites on oath affirmed these statements. In the papal view there was evidently no place for debate, for, as Clement IV had pointed out when he refused to consider Michael VIII's request for a general council to be held on Greek soil, Roman doctrine was 'pure' and 'the purity of the true faith' could not be the subject of any doubts.[48]

This somewhat authoritarian approach did not mean that the differences, apparent and real, between the Latin and Greek Churches had not been carefully considered over the years. The papacy had repeatedly tried to explain its doctrine and usages to the Byzantines, particularly through the good offices of the friars. Members of these new orders had proved invaluable papal agents in Constantinople and elsewhere, both during the Latin domination of the capital and particularly after 1261.[49] Some, such as the sympathetic and tolerant Franciscan John Parastron, who was greatly liked in Constantinople, went far towards understanding the Greek outlook. Parastron, who was equally at home in Greek or Latin, had tried to explain unfamiliar aspects of Roman belief to the Byzantines, such as its teaching on purgatory, a doctrine as yet unarticulated in the Greek Church. In his papal correspondence Michael VIII himself paid tribute to Parastron's efforts. Both from the Latin side and from the Greek unionists, considerable attempts were made to demonstrate that the Latin procession of the Holy Spirit from the

---

[46] Trans. in part in Setton, *Papacy and the Levant*, i. 117, and German trans. in Roberg, *Union*, 148.

[47] *DR*² 2008.

[48] 'verae fidei puritatem', Tăutu, op. cit., no. 23, p. 67.

[49] See Roncaglia, *passim*.

Father and the Son did not differ basically from Greek doctrine. In fact one of the main Greek objections to the filioque, forcibly presented in Patriarch Joseph's anti-unionist *Reply*, was the fear that this addition might imply two causes and two spirations for the Holy Spirit. This was emphatically denied by the West, as the council of Lyons II took the trouble to demonstrate in its first canon.[50]

Though in general the Roman point of view seemed somewhat inflexible, some effort was made in authoritative circles to understand how the schism had arisen and had been aggravated, and why the Greeks were, on the whole, so obstinately opposed to coming to terms with Rome. Perhaps one of the most perceptive analyses— from the Roman point of view—was offered by a former Master General of the Dominicans, Humbert de Romanis. In the second section of his work on the ecclesiastical problems of his day, known as the *Opus Tripartitum* and probably written in 1272–3, he discusses the schism with the Greeks.[51] He touches on doctrinal issues and he assumes the papal primacy but he discusses the practical and historical as well as the dogmatic reasons for this primacy which was unusual as the Latins usually kept to the argument from apostolicity and Christ's commission to St Peter. He also finds historical causes for Greek pride and assumption of superiority, going far back to Constantine the Great and beyond, as well as recognizing the aggravation of the post-1204 situation when the Byzantines were oppressed by the Roman Church and 'treated like dogs' by their Latin conquerors (this last point being something of an exaggeration once the Franks were established on Greek soil, witness relations in the Morea). He maintained that it was essential to foster understanding by mastering the Greek language and translating Latin works into Greek and by getting to know the Greek way of life. War must be avoided (a hit at Charles of Anjou perhaps) and the Latins 'should not demand full and entire obedience from the Greek Church, provided that its Patriarch is approved by the Pope and Roman legates received with honour'.

This was a more sensitive approach to the situation than many and in Humbert de Romanis's day there were already signs of a

---

[50] Cited Hefele, VI (1), 181–2; Roberg, *Union*, 247.
[51] Text ed. E. Brown, Appendix ad fasciculum ... (London, 1690), 207–28; French trans. in part in Wolter-Holstein, 268–72; see Roberg, *Union*, 85–95.

reciprocal linguistic movement which was to gather momentum in the fourteenth century. But the Greeks as a whole could not accept the Roman claims and the *Opus Tripartitum* has to be placed besides such writings as the anti-unionist *Reply* of Patriarch Joseph (probably composed by Job Jasites). The Byzantines claimed the sanction of ancient tradition and conciliar approval for their doctrine and church government. They found that the primacy of honour which was freely accorded to the bishop of Rome had in course of time developed into something different which undermined the position of the other four major patriarchates and overturned government by the pentarchy in the general council. Nor was appellate jurisdiction the normal practice of the four eastern patriarchates. Individual Byzantines did on occasion use it, but only when it suited them. Patriarch Joseph did not gloss over his concern, expressing his extreme views in somewhat unfraternal terms. 'Why' he asked 'should the Pope have any authority over us? We do not take part in electing him and he should not interfere in our affairs.'[52] 'According to the Gospel we have only one master and that is Christ.'[53] Joseph's views were those of the majority in Byzantium. The explanations offered by unionist advocates were unacceptable. In addition any signs of tolerance or of conciliatory minor concessions vanished as papal demands after Gregory X's death (1277) gradually grew more peremptory. The only achievement of Michael VIII's acceptance of the Roman faith was to win temporary papal support against Charles of Anjou.

3. Byzantine reaction to the union 1274–1282

The Byzantine envoys stayed in Lyons until the conclusion of the council at the end of July. They arrived back in Constantinople in the late autumn together with the papal legates and John Parastron. They announced the union. The papacy optimistically expected it to be acknowledged by clergy and people and it must be admitted that Michael VIII spared no effort to achieve this and fulfil his promise. He realized that it was essential to have the support of the Patriarch of Constantinople and in a sense the way was smoothed since the anti-unionist Joseph had threatened to resign if the

[52] *Dossier grec*, 228 ff.
[53] Ibid. 243.

reconciliation went through at the council of Lyons. In early January 1275 Joseph retired to the Lavra, a monastery near Anaplous at the Black Sea entrance of the Bosphorus (near enough to Constantinople to be within easy reach of his partisans). On 9 January the synod declared him deposed. On 16 January on the festival of St Peter in Chains in the imperial chapel in the palace of Blachernae the union was celebrated and the epistle and gospel read in Greek and in Latin. The bishop of Chalcedon was the celebrant and the papal envoys were present. As yet there was no Patriarch to take part in more formal ceremonies in Hagia Sophia. It was not until 26 May that a convert to union, the chartophylax John Beccus, was elected by the synod to the vacant office. Beccus was an individualist and a forceful character, a strong and intelligent upholder of his convictions, as his subsequent and often unhappy career showed.[54] He was not a man who could change from side to side as a matter of *oeconomia* or expediency. He came to accept the major Roman claims but he maintained that on patristic evidence the Greek and Latin views on the filioque could be reconciled. He apparently read little or no Latin and his views were mainly based on the Greek fathers, with translations of excerpts from only a few Latin works.[55] To call him 'Latinophron', pro-Latin, would be a misnomer. He was in fact passionately attached to the Byzantine way of life. 'It is the best interests of the Greek people which I have at heart,' he emphasized again and again, though this did not avail him much later on when the full storm of anti-unionist feeling burst out in the reign of Andronicus II.

Michael VIII had hoped that his recognition of the union (even if only in the imperial chapel), followed by his appointment of a unionist Patriarch, would satisfy the well-disposed Gregory X and suffice to stave off any papal support for a western attack on Constantinople. At the same time he himself did not cease to employ both force and diplomacy to regain lost Byzantine territory in Greece, somewhat to the neglect of the greatly reduced lands in Asia Minor, once a Lascarid stronghold. Michael was tough and determined—in contrast to his heir, the vacillating Andronicus—but in the end even he must have realized the difficulty of

[54] J. Gill, 'John Beccus, Patriarch of Constantinople 1275–1282', *Byzantina*, 7 (1975), 251–66.
[55] G. Hofmann, 'Patriarch Johann Bekkos und die lateinische Kultur', *OCP*, 11 (1945), 141–61.

maintaining the union in the face of the unrealistic stiffening of papal demands and the acute tension within his Empire. It was the tragedy of the union that it was superimposed on an already fiercely raging internal ecclesiastical controversy which also had marked political implications. The Patriarch Arsenius had a considerable following. He had been deposed for excommunicating Michael VIII for blinding and displacing the boy John IV Lascaris and his followers maintained that all subsequent elevations to the patriarch-ate were uncanonical. The Arsenite party, strengthened by a strong pro-Lascarid element, particularly in Asia Minor, was a threat both to internal harmony within the Byzantine Church and to the Palaeologan dynasty. A second party, the followers of the deposed anti-unionist Patriarch Joseph, also considered Beccus's appoint-ment irregular, and both Josephites and Arsenites, though not at one with each other, were against Michael VIII's unionist policy.

Further, outside these more specialized dissident circles there were many, some of them influential figures, who were anti-unionist mainly because they supported the traditions of the Byzantine Church and could not concur in papal claims to what amounted to supreme control of all Christian Churches. Among the most determined of these were certain members of Michael's own family (notably his sister Eulogia) and some of his top generals. These were in a position to intrigue with Michael's enemies outside his reconstructed Empire, such as the Balkan principalities, or Epirus and Thessaly, who seized the opportunity to pose as the protectors of Orthodoxy and were moreover in alliance with Charles of Anjou and Philip of Courtenay (who was then claimant to the Latin Empire of Constantinople). Then there were the lower classes, refugees from pro-Lascarid Asia Minor fleeing from the advancing Turks or those of Constantinople who remembered with hatred the Latin regime of the pre-1261 period. All these were ready to be inflamed by the anti-unionist and anti-Latin views poured forth by the monks. There was, too, much pamphlet propaganda,[56] as is evidenced by Michael VIII's severe penalties against this later on in his reign.

With the help of Beccus, Michael put up a good fight. An embassy went to Gregory X (†10 January 1276) and then to Innocent V (26 January 1276–22 June 1276) to announce progress

[56] See *Dossier grec*, p. ix and *passim*.

and to enquire after the proposed crusade. It also emphasized the need to control Anjou and Philip of Courtenay and to excommunicate the anti-unionist John Ducas of Thessaly. It was unfortunate for Michael that after Gregory X there were several short pontificates none of whose holders possessed Gregory's breadth of understanding of the Greek outlook. Nor did they fully take into account the particular Byzantine problems of the day, though these had certainly been explained by the friars who knew Constantinople well and travelled backwards and forwards between Rome and Constantinople.

With regard to the union, Innocent V desired Michael VIII, his son Andronicus, and the Greek clergy to swear personally that they accepted the Roman faith and primacy. This included reciting the addition of the filioque to the creed, and so would run contrary to Michael's assurance to his clergy that there would be no change in their accustomed usages if only they recognized the three main papal claims—primacy, jurisdiction, and commemoration. Innocent also pointed out that George Acropolites had no written authorization when he took the oath in Michael's name at Lyons in 1274. But, as in the case of Gregory X, Innocent gave his legation certain private instructions enabling them to moderate his demands if necessary.[57] Innocent died before his embassy reached Constantinople but his policy was swiftly taken up by his successor John XXI (mid-September 1276–20 May 1277) who sent similar letters to both Emperor and Patriarch. These were somewhat stiff in tone in that they stressed the need for Michael to make more effort and take a firmer line with his subjects. Whatever modifications were sanctioned in private instructions to the envoys, the detail of the actual demands marked a departure from the policy of Gregory X and made it even more difficult for Michael VIII to assure his bishops that all, or nearly all, could go on as before in the Byzantine Church. Stringent conditions were laid down to ensure that the Emperor, his son, and all the clergy should individually take an oath to abjure schism and accept the Roman faith, specifically including the filioque in reciting the creed. However, should this prove impossible the legates were instructed as before to get what recognition they could rather than to imperil the union by the rigidity of their demands. On the political issues John XXI was

[57] F. M. Delorme and A. L. Tăutu, *Acta ab Inn. V ad Benedictum XI (1276–1304)* (Vatican, 1954), nos. 3, 7–9, 11.

from the Byzantine point of view equally disappointing. Michael got no help against Epirus and Thessaly, who were in alliance with his Latin enemies, as both Innocent V and John XXI ruled this was a political and not an ecclesiastical matter and must therefore be dealt with by Michael. For obvious reasons the papacy preferred to remain neutral. Moreover Michael was urged to take steps to come to terms with his Latin enemies within five months.

Before John XXI's embassy reached Constantinople in the spring of 1277 Michael VIII and Beccus tried to gain control over a threatening situation and at least to give signs of active support for the union. On 19 February 1277 a synod was held at Blachernae and a document (a written statement, *tomographia*) was drawn up[58] and a copy was sent to the Pope with a letter signed by the bishops present.[59] The *tomographia* revealed the wide range of opposition to the union and explicitly condemned those schismatics who were refusing to accept the sacraments from unionist priests. Among the accused were 'some of royal blood and lineage, some members of the senate, some of the bench of bishops, of the church officials, of the status of monks and of the assemblage of layfolk, among whom there seem to be a large number of women (alas! for the evil guile of Satan . . .)'.[60] These, both lay and ecclesiastic, were then excommunicated and anathematized, and if a cleric also unfrocked. In addition to the bishops in synod, the *tomographia* was subscribed to by a long list of the great office-holders of Hagia Sophia,[61] amongst whom was Pachymeres, described as 'teacher of the Apostles'.[62] There was also a separate statement from the palace officials. This stressed the need to suppress the prevailing chaos in which streams of insults were insolently hurled around, each side calling the other schismatic,[63] a state of affairs most graphically described by Pachymeres.[64]

In April 1277 Michael VIII and his son agreed to John XXI's request that they should in person swear to the abjuration taken on their behalf at Lyons in 1274. This they did in a formal public

---

[58] *GR* 1341; text and trans. in Gill, 'Church Union', doc. V (3), pp. 22–9.

[59] Gill, op. cit., doc. VIII (2), pp. 34–41.

[60] Gill, op. cit., p. 25.

[61] Gill, op. cit., doc. VI (5), pp. 28–33.

[62] Gill, op. cit. p. 31, points out that the text should read 'Apostle', i.e. the liturgical lectionary giving the lessons from Acts and the Epistles.

[63] Gill, op. cit., doc. VII (4), pp. 32–5.

[64] Pachymeres, *De Mich. Pal.*, V. 23 (*CB*, I, p. 399 ff.).

session at the Blachernae palace in the presence of the papal envoys.[65] Beccus likewise expressed his renunciation of the schism and entire submission to the primacy of Rome.[66] Later in July 1277, Michael, in response to a papal reproach, attempted to arrange a truce with Anjou and Philip of Courtenay.[67] The unionist decisions of the February synod of Blachernae had been sent to Nicephorus of Epirus and John Ducas of Thessaly,[68] but they refused to accept them and it was well known that their courts were centres of anti-Palaeologan and anti-unionist intrigue. The Patriarch Beccus therefore took the step that the papacy had refused to do and the Epirotes were excommunicated on 16 July 1277.[69] They retaliated by convening a synod at Neopatras in December 1277 where they in turn excommunicated the 'heretics' Michael VIII and the other unionists.

The papacy now under the guidance of Nicholas III (25 November 1277–22 August 1280) was not reassured by the acts of the Blachernae council and thenceforth relations between Rome and Constantinople steadily worsened. Nicholas III in October 1278 prepared to send legates to demand the complete consummation of the union.[70] This included 'unity of faith' and the elimination of diversity, especially on the question of the filioque. Even more unacceptable to the Byzantines was the request that 'patriarch, prelates, clerics of every city, fortress, village or locality' should each individually swear by oath to accept the Roman faith and primacy. Legates were to visit throughout the land and collect up signed copies of the profession of faith to go to Rome. Worse still it was suggested that Michael VIII should ask for a cardinal-legate who would be resident in Constantinople. This last request was impossible from a Byzantine point of view. Even Nicholas III with his dreams of world-wide papal domination saw the difficulty ahead for there is evidence that he privately warned his envoys to move cautiously and do nothing to imperil the union.[71]

The embassy arrived in the spring of 1279. Michael VIII was faced with an exceptionally awkward situation, since not only were

---

[65] *DR*[2] 2028, 2029.
[66] *GR* 1433.
[67] Cf. Delorme-Tăutu, op. cit., no. 20, pp. 44–5; Roberg, *Union*, 201.
[68] *DR*[2] 2026a.
[69] *GR* 1435.
[70] J. Gay, *Reg. Nic. III* (Paris, 1938), no. 367.
[71] Gay, op. cit., nos. 376–7.

the papal terms totally unacceptable and the very opposite of what he had promised his bishops but he was in disagreement with his Patriarch. Beccus in his own way was as strong-minded as the Emperor and he had greatly annoyed Michael by his persistent pleas on behalf of the poor and the condemned. He also had personal enemies working against him. Bad feeling between them and mutual retaliation came to a head with Beccus's resignation from his office in early March 1279.[72] He did not leave the city but went to the monastery of Panachrantus. Michael had to coax him out of retirement to meet the papal envoys. At the same time the bishops had to be put into the right frame of mind before they heard what the envoys had to say. Michael therefore addressed the episcopate, warning them that Byzantine unionist policy had been grossly misrepresented to the papacy as a mere farce. He asked them to remain calm if he seemed rather too well-disposed towards the envoys, promising that the faith of their fathers would remain unaltered.[73] The bishops backed him up and he weathered the storm rather better than might have been expected. He tried to drive home the seriousness and firmness with which he was sponsoring the union by showing the envoys his prison where anti-unionists were miserably languishing. This was the occasion on which four dissident generals were exhibited, each chained in a corner of the same cell.

Beccus returned to the patriarchate on 6 August 1279. He found it impossible however to get the prelates to subscribe to papal demands, particularly with regard to the filioque, even though various other patristic terms more acceptable to the Byzantines could be found for the verb 'to proceed' (ἐκπορεύεσθαι) Michael and Andronicus again took the oath required[74] and Beccus replied to Nicholas III in September 1279, but Pachymeres reported that the episcopal signatures in the letter were greatly swollen by fictitious names attached to non-existent sees (all added in the same handwriting, but not necessarily implicating Beccus).[75]

In the imperial letter to Nicholas III Michael VIII makes no mention of any truce with his Latin enemies, as demanded by successive popes. Indeed throughout his reign he was engaged in

[72] GR 1443.
[73] Pachymeres, *De Mich. Pal.*, VI. 15 (*CB*, I, p. 458).
[74] DR² 2041, 2075.
[75] GR 1444; Pachymeres, *De Mich. Pal.*, VI. 17 (*CB*, I, p. 461).

military and diplomatic activity aimed at securing his position and extending his territory. After all, this only meant regaining what the Franks had seized when they disrupted the Empire from 1204 onwards. As the Palaeologus widened his field of activity—for instance by his negotiations with Peter III of Aragon—so the breach with the papacy widened. The contrasts of Michael VIII's reign were never more vividly demonstrated than in his last years. With increased cruelty he punished anti-unionists in all classes of society, but on 18 November 1282[76] he was himself excommunicated by the pro-Angevin Pope Martin IV as a schismatic and supporter of heretics,[77] an act repeated twice in the following year[78] and executed almost entirely for political motives. In contrast to his failure to achieve union must be set Michael's significant victory in March 1281 when he foiled the attempt of the invading Angevins to take Berat and thus open the way to Thessalonica and thence along the via Egnatia to Constantinople. Further, his diplomacy was rewarded by the crushing blow to Anjou when the Sicilian Vespers drove the Franks out of the island and brought in Michael's ally, Peter III of Aragon.

Whether he was genuinely converted to the Roman faith or not, Michael VIII had striven to uphold the union, and his rejection by Rome and his treatment after his death (11 December 1282) were both undeserved. Though he received the last unction and was buried, if quickly and quietly, later in 1285 he was denied the usual liturgical commemoration given to emperors.[79] The full anti-unionist reaction had set in and Andronicus was ruler with none of his father's quality. Perhaps Michael did err in retaking Constantinople. But even if he had renounced New Rome, Greece, and the islands it is doubtful whether he could have kept secure the Asia Minor kingdom in the face of western economic and dynastic ambitions and eastern pressures from the Turk.

[76] See Setton, *Papacy and the Levant*, I. 138, note 65.

[77] Raynaldus, vol. 22, ann. 1281, no. 25; see Geanakoplos, *Michael Palaeologus* 341–2 and Setton, *Papacy and the Levant*, I. 137–8.

[78] Members of the French School at Rome, *Reg. Martin IV*, fasc. 1–2 (Paris, 1901–13), no. 269 (7 May 1282) and no. 278 (18 Nov. 1282).

[79] GR 1489; and Geanakoplos, *Michael Palaeologus*, 370, note 12.

4 *Andronicus II: internal problems: Josephites and Arsenites: repudiation of the union*

With Michael VIII's strong hand removed, the early years of his son and successor the Emperor Andronicus II were characterized by marked anti-unionist reaction and also by confusion in ecclesiastical and political circles. The new Emperor was a less dominating figure than his father, and he was greatly tried during his troubled reign. Michael left him a legacy of an unacceptable union and heavy debts. He also inherited internal ecclesiastical strife, and then this was followed by family dissension and a rebellious grandson. Andronicus had certainly professed loyalty to the Roman faith, perhaps under pressure. But once the excommunicated Michael VIII had died Andronicus allowed himself to be swept along on the crest of anti-Roman feeling. He proved to be an excessively devout man, in some ways more monk than emperor, susceptible to monastic influence, and yet the friend of a learned humanist such as Theodore Metochites. He had no hesitation in repudiating the union with Rome. Towards the end of December 1282 the anti-unionists banned and penalized by Michael VIII were recalled.[80] This did not however bring tranquillity to Byzantium. It is true that there were still unionists, some moved by genuine conviction, such as Beccus, others, as the wealthy rural proprietors, seeing material advantages in being aligned with the West. But these were only a minority.

The greatest confusion was however caused by the bitter strife between two parties within the Byzantine Church—the Josephites and the Arsenites, both of whom were in schism as they had refused to recognize the establishment under Patriarch Beccus during Michael VIII's reign. Under Andronicus II the situation was not helped by some of the figures promoted to the patriarchal throne, so that the troubled polity was often deprived of stabilizing and guiding leadership. Even when an able man such as Gregory II the Cypriote became Patriarch, in the end he retired prematurely, as Beccus before him had tried to do under Michael VIII. As for John XII Cosmas and Niphon, they were not particularly suited for their high office. Athanasius in his two patriarchates at the turn of the thirteenth century was an exception. Strong-minded and with

[80] DR 2086.

excellent qualities, he showed that the Church could give a lead, though even his energetic resolution could not control or even stem the deteriorating situation and what was left of the Empire.

Of the two dissident parties facing Andronicus on his accession in 1282 the Josephites were the easiest to deal with. They were anti-unionists who resented the abdication of Patriarch Joseph in 1274 after the council of Lyons. They were joined by every kind of discontented element. Many of their followers were rampant vagrant monks who would no doubt have resented any kind of papal discipline had the union been consummated. They argued moreover that it was only because of their passionate championship of Orthodox traditions that Providence had been induced to save them by the Sicilian Vespers of 1282 (not realizing apparently that Providence used human agents, in this case the pro-unionist Michael VIII). They were now all set to repudiate any thought of alliance with Rome and were willing to end their schism with their own Church after the pro-unionist element had been ejected. And Andronicus seemed to be their willing tool.

It was the Arsenites however who presented the greater threat to Andronicus. They were the supporters of Patriarch Arsenius who, after some vacillation, had finally abdicated in protest at Michael VIII's blinding of the ousted young Emperor John IV Lascaris. Though Arsenius had died in 1273 the party remained in schism. It was strongly anti-unionist and equally strongly anti-Josephite, since its members refused to recognize the validity of Arsenius's abdication or of Joseph's election, and so, like the Josephites, if for different reasons, its followers were in schism with the ·Byzantine party not only in Constantinople but in what was left of Asia Minor where amid increasing harassment by the Turks old men could still remember the achievements of the Lascarid dynasty. Even after Michael VIII's death this opposition still continued to persist and Andronicus recognized the danger to himself and to his dynasty.

It was obviously in Andronicus's interests to placate the Josephites whom he now supported. After all it was the ex-Patriarch Joseph who had crowned him in November 1272 and to accuse Joseph of being uncanonically elected might well be to question the validity of his coronation. With the change of policy in 1282 the position of the Patriarch John Beccus clearly became untenable. The man who had so warmly upheld the union with Rome was the obvious scapegoat. At Andronicus II's request he left the patriarcheion for a monastery. On 31 December 1282 Joseph I was declared Patriarch for the second time. He was a dying man and authority was quickly seized by anti-unionist monks who in their fanaticism went to every extreme. Hagia Sophia was even considered to be unclean and had to be purified by one of the monks who had suffered under Michael VIII. Joseph, or rather, the monks acting in his name, declared Beccus deposed for usurping the patriarchal throne from Joseph and for professing unorthodox doctrine. Then the three official envoys who went to the council of Lyons, the metropolitan of Nicaea, Theophanes, the chartophylax Constantine Meliteniotes, and the archdeacon George Metochites, were also condemned, ostensibly because they were said to have taken part in a papal mass. In fact they had simply been present and as members of a diplomatic mission they could scarcely have done otherwise. And after all the same thing had happened in reverse in Constantinople when Latins had been present at the Orthodox liturgy without causing adverse comment. Bishops and clergy who had supported the union were suspended for three months,[81] though in the interests of ecclesiastical administration a certain number of dispensations, for instance in the case of Hagia Sophia, could not be long deferred.[82] Those of the laity who had supported Lyons were also penalized. All this was done in the name of the dying Patriarch.

Feeling within the City was further whipped up. Surrounded by an enflamed mob on the eve of Epiphany 1283 a synod of bishops sat in judgement on John Beccus. The Patriarch Joseph was too ill to attend and the Patriarch of Alexandria acted for him. Amid such turmoil any kind of reasonable trial was impossible and Beccus had no opportunity to defend himself. As he later pointed out in his *De depositione sua*,[83] he was harrassed beyond bearing and quite unable to state his case, so he temporized by renouncing unionist views, tacitly admitting that he had been overbold in writing about the mysteries of the Trinity.[84] In all probability it was only this that saved his life from the infuriated mob. He was condemned for heresy and exiled to Brusa, a spa with splendid marble baths, situated under the shadow of Mount Olympus in Bithynia. Here he had friends and relations and was not at first subjected to hardship.

[81] *GR* 1453.
[82] *GR* 1458.
[83] *PG* 141, cols. 964 D, 965 B.
[84] *GR* 1459.

In early March 1283 Joseph abdicated[85] and on 23 March he died. His place was speedily filled. On 28 March 1283 George of Cyprus became Patriarch as Gregory II. He was a scholar of some standing. Among his works he has left a brief *Autobiography*. He was a native of Cyprus, then being ruled by the western Lusignans. He left the island because he wished for his higher education to be Greek and not Latin. His attempt to study under Blemmydes in Ephesus met with a cursory rebuff and he then made his way painfully on foot via Nicaea to Constantinople. Here in the capital under George Acropolites' tuition he developed into a humanist in the early Palaeologan tradition as well as an able theologian with a wide circle of correspondents as his many letters show (no wonder that he bemoaned his lack of writing paper).[86] At first he supported Beccus and then after 1282 he renounced the union, but he was a partisan of neither the Josephites nor the Arsenites. Andronicus must have hoped that he would be able to stand above feuds and exercise control over the unruly elements in the capital. By now the Josephites had been to some extent placated. Their leader Joseph had come back to the patriarchate and in the end as a dying man had abdicated of his own free will (he could hardly do otherwise). He had even been swiftly canonized.[87] Moreover his followers had been allowed a free hand in their anti-unionist activities. It was far otherwise with the Arsenites who were still in schism and had been infuriated by the honour paid to the lately deceased Joseph.

Gregory continued to carry out anti-unionist measures. In April 1283 in Holy Week at the church of the Blachernae a synodal tome pronounced the deposition of all unionist bishops.[88] It was later made clear to the Dowager Empress that her deceased husband Michael VIII would not be permitted the liturgical commemoration normally accorded an Emperor on his anniversary.[89] It might well have been hoped that as far as the union went repudiation was complete and the matter could now rest. But this was not so. John Beccus had every intention of attempting to justify his position. In 1284 he was claiming the right to answer the charges brought

---

[85] *GR* 1459.
[86] *Ep.* 102, cited Hunger, *Literatur*, I. 231.
[87] *GR* 1461.
[88] *GR* 1463.
[89] *GR* 1489; Michael had at least been canonically buried, though not in Constantinople (see *GR.* IV, p. 279).

against him. To meet this challenge Patriarch Gregory appealed to the Emperor for support and a synod was convened at the beginning of 1285.[90] Beccus was condemned to solitary confinement in the 'Great Monastery' of Brusa.[91]

In February of the same year a second synod opened and this time there was some attempt at a debate. Beccus's later writings show how passionately he resented the suggestion that his views were heretical. His defence turned on his contention that the Greek fathers supported the procession from the Father and the Son, arguing that the prepositions ἐκ and διὰ had the same meaning. He cited a sentence from John of Damascus 'The Father is the emitter, or producer, of the Spirit through the Son'.[92] The matter seemed at the time to be unresolved and some of the anti-unionists put up a poor defence. George Moschabar, then the chartophylax, even went so far as to maintain that this passage in John of Damascus was spurious, for which he was rebuked by the grand logothete Theodore Muzalon. The synod dragged on for six months and then Beccus and his two unionist friends, Constantine Meliteniotes and George Metochites, were excommunicated and in the end sentenced to strict imprisonment in the fortress of St Gregory in the bay of Nicomedia off Bithynia. Beccus subsequently refused any kind of compromise even when Andronicus II made personal overtures to him, and he lived in hardship in St Gregory until he died in 1297. He continued to write in defence of the position which he had taken on the filioque, and he vehemently protested against the injustice of being regarded as either heretical or anti-Byzantine.[93] One of his near contemporaries, though an anti-unionist, warmly praised his theological acumen, maintaining that he was outstanding in doctrinal expertise.[94]

In spite of apparently fruitless discussions the synod which condemned Beccus and his associates did in fact have an outcome of importance for the development of Orthodox doctrine. Patriarch Gregory drew up a statement, or *Tomos*, on the filioque problem

---

[90] GR 1485.
[91] GR 1487; Janin, *Églises et monastères*, II. 175.
[92] *De Fide Orthodoxa*, bk. I, ch. 12, PG 94, col. 849 A; Kotter, II, p. 36, l. 48 (not found in all MSS as PG and Kotter note), ἐκ πατρὸς μὲν δι' υἱοῦ ἐκπορευομένη.
[93] See PG 141 for some of his treatises.
[94] Nicephorus Gregoras, *History*, bk. V, ch. 2 (*CB*, I, p. 129). Pachymeres, *De Mich. et Andr. Pal.* bk. V, 24 (*CB*, I, pp. 402–8 = *CFHB* 24/2, pp. 514–5).

which was signed by only relatively few bishops and official clerics.[95] This *Tomos* denied that the Father caused the Holy Spirit through the Son in the sense that the Holy Spirit received its existence from the Son as well as from the Father. Therefore the Spirit could not 'proceed', or get its existence, from both Father and Son. But it was eternally revealed or manifested through the Son.[96] This was further developed in Gregory's later writings on the procession of the Holy Spirit.[97] In distinguishing between eternal, uncreated, and unknowable existence and eternal, uncreated manifestation Gregory provided one more step forward in the development of the Orthodox tradition. In the fourteenth century it was to be taken further by Gregory Palamas's teaching on the uncreated essence of God and his uncreated energies.[98] Such doctrine was intimately connected with Orthodox belief in man's participation in Divinity, θέωσις, which lay at the root of Christian life in the Orthodox world and still does.

There was however clearly turmoil and dissension on religious matters as is reflected both by the small number of signatures to the *Tomos* and by the apparent freedom with which the views of the imprisoned Beccus and his friends could circulate. Unfortunately for Gregory one of his followers, the monk Mark, misrepresented his views by asserting that the Patriarch approved the statement, that the emission or way in which the Holy Spirit came into existence (ἐκπόρευσις) was the same as the Spirit's eternal revelation or manifestation (ἔκφανσις). This was the opposite of what Gregory had intended and he disavowed it.[99] But the episode had given his enemies a loophole. Led by the discredited George Moschabar, they rounded on him, also attacking the *Tomos*, though some of them had signed it. Gregory, who was at the time facing serious illness, protested bitterly to the Emperor about the hostile attacks. In May

---

[95] GR 1490.

[96] Cf. PG 142, col. 240 A, 'the manifestation through the Son of the Spirit which takes its existence from the Father'.

[97] See Gregory of Cyprus, *De processione Spiritus Sancti*, PG 142, cols. 269–300.

[98] See Meyendorff, *Introduction*, 25–30 and the analysis of Gregory II's views by O. Clément, 'Grégoire de Chypre "De l'ekporèse du Saint Esprit"', *Istina*, 17 (1972), 443–56.

[99] See his Ὁμολογία, PG 142, cols. 247–52; especially col. 250 A; he denounced Mark's words as foolish and nonsensical (φλύαρον χαρτίον), op. cit., col. 268 A); see also Meyendorff, *Introduction*, pp. 27–8.

1289 he wrote to one of his friends that he had never desired the office of patriarch and had accepted it only in the hope of bringing peace to a troubled Church. He added that he proposed to abdicate rather than be himself a cause of discord. This he did, probably about the beginning of June 1289.[100]

Up to a point Gregory II had eased the situation in the Byzantine Church even though he chose to resign in the face of pressure from his critics who attacked his theological position and resented his Cypriot origins. Brought up in a Latin-dominated island what could he know of the genuine Byzantine ecclesiastical tradition, asked his enemies? But he had however made his contribution to Orthodox doctrine and he is one of those to whom Gregory Palamas was indebted, as Acindynus recognized in the course of his attack on Palamas.[101]

5. Patriarch Athanasius I and his immediate successors

Gregory II's immediate successor, Athanasius I, who came to the patriarchate on 14 October 1289, was one of those specifically singled out when Palamas spoke of his predecessors in the spiritual life.[102] The monk Athanasius was the choice of the devout Andronicus II who was greatly attached to him and was always open to monastic influence. Andronicus, who certainly did not want an Arsenite patriarch, may have hoped that this undoubtedly holy man would be above criticism in the particularly difficult atmosphere of the day. With Gregory II's help the question of union with Rome had been scotched, at any rate temporarily. The Josephites had been placated. But there remained the discontented Arsenites. There was too increasing danger from Turkish encroachment in Asia Minor which necessarily meant some disruption of normal diocesan life. And there were evidently many lapses in clerical—and lay—standards.

Athanasius who in Palamas's words, 'adorned the patriarchate for a number of years' (1289–93 and 1303–9)[103] was by no means as ignorant as Nicephorus Gregoras would seem to imply when he

[100] *GR* 1513–18.
[101] See Meyendorff, *Introduction*, 29–30.
[102] Gregory Palamas, *Triad* I, 2, 12, p. 99 (ed. Meyendorff).
[103] Following the chronology of *GR*.

said that he was unlettered and uncultured.[104] Gregoras probably looked down on those who had not had the traditional higher education. Athanasius, who had early become a monk, had travelled widely from Athos to Jerusalem and to some of the outstanding monastic centres of Asia Minor, as Mount Auxentius. He spent eighteen years in the house of St Lazarus on Mount Galesius and his *Vita* described the rich library there which he voraciously devoured, reading through each book not once, as lazy creatures do, but three or four times.[105] He left more than 200 folios of his own writings, sermons, letters, canonical rulings, directives. These are in literary *koine* without much rhetorical embellishment which is a relief rather than otherwise. This corpus was certainly not the work of an ignoramus but of a clear thinker and a vigorous administrator.[106]

Athanasius had high standards and spared none. Bishops lingering in the capital were directed back to their dioceses. Monks were reminded of the rules of their chosen way of life. Even the Emperor was censured for allowing his officials to rob the islands of poultry and livestock and to drag off for his own use flocks of sheep meant for the slaughterhouses of Constantinople. Increasing resentment, particularly from the higher clergy and powerful laity, resulted in a stream of harassing complaints to the Emperor. Athanasius, perhaps desiring release from the heavy cares of his office as he envisaged it, left Constantinople for the monastery of Cosmidion just outside the city up the Golden Horn. Before going, he placed hidden in the capital of a pillar in the galleries of Hagia Sophia a document in which he defended himself and then excommunicated all his 'enemies' (without however explicitly naming them). He also sent the Emperor an unsigned copy of his abdication,[107] followed by further letters asking for protection from violence and speaking of the needs of the patriarchate.[108]

Andronicus II replaced Athanasius with another monk, John XII

---

[104] Nicephorus Gregoras, *History*, VI. 5 (*CB*, I, p. 180).

[105] *Vita*, ch. 8, cited Guilland, p. 121 (see note 106 below).

[106] GR draws at length on a number of Athanasius's letters cited from MS. Many of these have since been edited by A.-M. M. Talbot, *The Correspondence of Athanasius I Patriarch of Constantinople* (trans., text, and commentary, Washington, DC, 1975 = *CFHB*, VII). One of the best introductions to Athanasius is still R. Guilland, 'La Correspondance inédite d'Athanase ...', *Mélanges Charles Diehl* (Paris, 1930), I, 121–40.

[107] GR 1554.

[108] GR 1555–57.

Cosmas, hoping perhaps for less harassment. But during his years of office (1 January 1294–21 June 1303) John XII attempted to continue the work of his immediate predecessor, arousing the same opposition. The situation worsened. The poor were in terrible need, refugees continued to stream across the water from Asia Minor, and particularly heavy taxes were levied. John protested about the taxation, criticizing the Emperor himself. He even threatened to abstain from performing his office. Meanwhile Andronicus, suffering from characteristic scrupulosity, had been greatly upset by the discovery of Athanasius's hidden document anathematizing his false accusers and 'him who had been misled', presumably the Emperor. This had been brought to light by boys looking for pigeons' nests on the ledges of the capitals in the galleries of the Great Church.[109] Athanasius had to be restored to patriarchal office in order to get the implied ban lifted. Andronicus therefore took advantage of hostility to John. He may too have felt that John was unreasonably exacting in some of his criticisms, failing to appreciate the government's urgent need to raise funds. Athanasius meanwhile foretold an approaching disaster. Then in January 1304 the City was shaken by an earthquake and Athanasius's stock rose. After some debate in synod and some resistance from John (who was hostile to the former Patriarch), the way was clear for the reinstatement of Athanasius. John abdicated and for another six years Athanasius, regarded with awe as having the gift of prophecy, preached the Christian life, thundering triumphantly against the evils of his day, acting as the protector of the poor, the critic of the corrupt and powerful, both lay and ecclesiastic. Pachymeres, describing his austere domination, told how men were so afraid of his crippling penalties, including excommunication and imprisonment, that they even took refuge in the houses of the Latin friars across the Golden Horn in Pera.[110] Particularly important, at least in Andronicus's eyes, was Patriarch Athanasius's formal withdrawal of the general excommunication against his enemies during his first patriarchate, which he did with the admission that he had been in the wrong.

Many of Athanasius's letters belong to the second period of his patriarchate when the Empire was particularly hard hit by the Catalan threat as well as by the Turks. The situation was aggravated

---

[109] Pachymeres, *De And. Pal.*, bk. III, ch. 24 (*CB*, II, p. 249).
[110] Ibid., bk. VII, ch. 23 (*CB*, II, p. 616).

by bitterly cold winters, by famine and black market. The letters give a poignant picture of the Patriarch's struggles in widely differing spheres. His agonizing cry for firewood to keep his soup kitchens going in Constantinople is balanced by his grave concern for the higher affairs of state. Patriarchal responsibility in the later middle ages was all-embracing. The greater part of Athanasius's life had been spent in a monastic framework. But now he not only reminded the Emperor of his high office but he gave him instructions on such problems as dealing with the city defence or paying the army. He told him that the actions of his court officials would be scrutinized by the Patriarch himself (as indeed they were). He advised on foreign policy, urging avoidance of relations with the schismatic West, relying rather on repentant Orthodoxy and the return of the bishops to their Asia Minor sees. It was not without point that he ironically remarked in a letter that one of the few accomplishments of bishops lingering on in the capital was 'to depose patriarchs'.[111] He became increasingly unpopular, and the Arsenites, still in schism, increasingly vociferous. His enemies even set traps for him and for a second time he resigned, 'wearied by old age and illness, nor am I even in possession of my sight'.[112] In September 1309 he returned to his former house by Xerolophos in Constantinople.[113]

Perhaps more than any other fourteenth-century collection Athanasius's letters provide detail all too often unrecorded. Weighed down by the responsibility of his patriarchal office he was the protector of starving refugees and harassed citizens. And he did not hesitate to offer advice and admonition on higher problems of state and church. Asia Minor was virtually lost to the Turks. Dioceses went. Revenue ceased. Such disasters obviously affected the Christian population of Asia Minor now often pressurized to turn Muslim.[114] They also hit the Great Church in Constantinople and other ecclesiastical institutions having assets abroad. And as though these misfortunes were not sufficient, the Byzantine polity in the fourteenth century was torn by internal schism and intermittent civil wars.

[111] Ep. 30, ed. Talbot, p. 64.
[112] See Talbot, p. xxv and Ep. 112, p. 288.
[113] GR 1666.
[114] See Vryonis, *Decline, passim.*

Fully aware of dissension within the Church Athanasius in his farewell letter begged the bishops to assist the Emperor 'who cares for the Church more than anyone' and he expressed the hope that the right successor might be found to watch over the Christian flock.[115] Far from it. Niphon of Cyzicus (May 1310–April 1314) who succeeded Athanasius after a confused interval appeared to have few if any qualifications for his office. He was said to be illiterate and according to Nicephorus Gregoras was a luxury-loving gourmet, better suited to be a dealer in real estate than a patriarch.[116] No contrast could be more marked. But at least one thing was achieved, for it was during Niphon's patriarchate that the long drawn-out Arsenite schism within the Byzantine Church was at last resolved. Unlike the strongly anti-Arsenite Athanasius, Niphon was willing to compromise.

The Arsenites had long opposed the establishment and the hierarchy. They now modified their extreme demands which had included the election of an Arsenite patriarch. At a fantastic ceremony in Hagia Sophia on 14 September 1310 they were received back into the Church. Here the corpse of the dead Patriarch Arsenius was set up dressed in his patriarchal robes. The reigning Patriarch Niphon solemnly took from Arsenius's skeleton hand a document absolving all whom Arsenius had previously anathematized. This concession meant the recognition of the Palaeologan dynasty which was the main concern of the establishment. The Emperor Andronicus pronounced the terms of the agreement in a 'tome of union' and the liturgy for the Exaltation of the Holy Cross was then celebrated by former Arsenite and Orthodox bishops together.[117]

The feuding which had marked internal ecclesiastical relations during Andronicus II's reign to some extent now ceased. But other increasingly pressing problems thronged in as the patriarchal registers show. There was little continuity in the brief tenures of patriarchal office. After barely four years Niphon had to abdicate.

---

[115] Ep. 112, ed. Talbot, p. 288.

[116] Nicephorus Gregoras, *History*, bk. VII, ch. 9 (*CB*, I, p. 259).

[117] *DR* 2321; *GR* 2003 and 2004 and see V. Laurent, 'Les Grandes Crises religieuses à Byzance ...', *Bull. sect. hist. de l'acad. roumaine*, 26 (1945), 225–313 (with texts). Despite this reconcilation the die-hard Arsenites still continued to make trouble, e.g. concerning ordinations in the diocese of Myra (*GR* 2036, July–Sept. 1315).

His successor John XIII Glykys (May 1315–May 1319) was the patron and friend of the scholar and historian Nicephorus Gregoras. Though a layman and logothete at the time of his unanimous election he was admirably suited for high ecclesiastical office. But in 1319 at his own request he had to resign by reason of a grave progressive illness which made it impossible for him to celebrate the holy mysteries.[118] Much of his work had been concerned with administration and finance, showing how hopeless it was to struggle to maintain any kind of normal diocesan life particularly in the face of an Asia Minor virtually lost to the Turks.[119] John Glykys was succeeded by an imperial choice, Gerasimus I (March 1320–April 1321), the abbot of the Mangana monastery. He was greatly mocked by Nicephorus Gregoras who complained of his lack of learning and deafness (events however suggest that he could not have been totally deaf). Gerasimus died on the night of Easter Saturday (19 April 1321) at a time when hostilities between Andronicus II and his ambitious young grandson Andronicus III were coming to a head. A synod had been called by Andronicus II to excommunicate his grandson for rebellion. Gerasimus had apparently informed the young Andronicus of his grandfather's intention to restrain him and the young man had fled the capital with his followers.[120]

Whether or not this indicated that Gerasimus was pro-Andronicus III is unclear. It was at this time that the civil wars began, disrupting what was left of the Empire until almost the end of its political life in 1453. Already Gerasimus's action pointed the way to patriarchal partisanship in the coming bitter struggle for political power which rent the rapidly weakening state when Andronicus III forced his aged grandfather to abdicate in 1328. Patriarch Isaias (November 1323–May 1332) openly took his stand on the winning side but he was also the leading figure in mediating between the defeated old Emperor and his victorious grandson. And subsequent fourteenth-century patriarchs often played a key role in the troubles caused by the disputes between the Palaeologan John V and the co-Emperor John VI Cantacuzenus, as also with members of his rebellious and ambitious family.

[118] GR 2099.
[119] See GR *sub* John XIII Glykys, and Hunger, *Register* (Greek text and German trans.).
[120] GR 2103.

6. Renewed contacts with the West under Andronicus II and Andronicus III

Throughout Andronicus II's reign (1283–1328) violent anti-papal and indeed anti-western feeling persisted. Patriarch Athanasius for instance was as strongly opposed to union as his arch-foes the Arsenites and he castigated westerners as barbarous schismatics (he must have found Andronicus II's second marriage to Yolande-Irene of Montferrat highly unpalatable). But though Andronicus II had begun by repudiating the 1274 union with Rome he was inevitably in constant touch with Latin (as well as Slav) powers and the imperial registers show him bargaining through diplomatic channels for economic and territorial reasons.[121] This aspect of his diplomacy became even more important as Asia Minor slipped from Byzantine hands and Greek interests were now concentrated on extending control over central Greece and the Peloponnese. So much is freely admitted. But to imply that it was only at the very end of his reign that Andronicus II considered approaching the papacy over union is misleading. There was a constant awareness— at least at diplomatic levels—of the need to heal the rift between the two Churches, as is evident from surviving correspondence and other sources.[122] Though Andronicus II played for safety at the opening of his reign he had always realized the value of union as a bargaining counter. In 1311, when trying to arrange a marriage between his 'son' (perhaps his grandson Andronicus III) and Catherine of Valois, he apparently promised not only his own obedience to the Pope but that of his subjects.[123] Again in 1324 he started negotiations professing his readiness to become a Roman Catholic. From 1324 to 1327 the question of union was being discussed in papal and French circles,[124] while the well-informed Marino Sanudo Torsello expressed views on the possibility of a *rapprochement*, pointing out that in certain Byzantine quarters there was a strong desire to end the schism.[125] Andronicus II's hopes

---

[121] *DR passim.*

[122] This is well brought out by Laiou, *Andronicus II* (The Unionist Approach) where Norden's views on the reason for this unionist policy (i.e. fear of crusading attack on Constantinople) are convincingly challenged; see also Gill, *Byzantium and the Papacy*, 192–3.

[123] *DR* 2327.

[124] Cf. *DR* 2556 and 2564–6.

[125] e.g. Letter VII, ed. J. Bongars, *Gesta Dei per Francos* (Hanover, 1611), II. 299, cited Laiou, *Andronicus II*, 321.

however foundered with his abdication in 1328, forced on him by the victory of his grandson's party.

Whatever the majority of the populace and the monks might think, the desire to achieve union steadily persisted. A few years later in 1334 Marino Sanudo again remarked that not only the Emperor (then Andronicus III) but a number of priests and monks with whom he had talked were ready to acquiesce in union. Andronicus III's wife was the Italian Anne of Savoy and according to a Franciscan Chronicle the Pope's hope that she might convert her husband was fulfilled through the efforts of Frater Garcias, a Franciscan attached to the Empress's circle (she herself was said to have been a member of the Third Order of St Francis though she died an Orthodox nun.[126] It is impossible to know whether or not Andronicus was converted 'ad veram fidem et ecclesiae unitatem.[127] If so, this was understandably not made public. And in 1339 when addressing Pope Benedict XXII the Greek envoy Barlaam stated that if the Emperor's desire for union were generally known his life would be in danger.

Andronicus III certainly made a series of overtures to the papacy, sometimes making use of two Dominican bishops who travelled to and from the Crimea by way of Constantinople. In 1333 John XXII charged these two to explore the possibility of union and it was on the occasion of this visit to Constantinople that the Patriarch was pressed to arrange an open discussion. Nicephorus Gregoras records that he himself was urged to act as the Greek spokesman. He refused—he had rather an awkward personality—and he said that mysteries such as the Trinity were beyond human dialectic and he also pointed out that there was nothing for the Orthodox Church to debate since it had never deviated from the true faith.[128] At that time, Barlaam, a South Italian monk of the Greek rite who had settled in Constantinople, was a staunch supporter of the Greek Church and *persona grata* in influential Constantinopolitan circles. It is possible that he may have taken part in the proposed synodal

---

[126] See Gill, *Byzantium and the Papacy*, 297, note 57 and references and Gouillard, 'Synodikon', pp. 100–3; cf. Golubovich, *Biblioteca*, III. 291–303.

[127] Golubovich, *Biblioteca*, III. 294; see also U. V. Bosch, *Kaiser Andronikos III. Palaiologos* (Amsterdam, 1965), 120–1.

[128] Nicephorus Gregoras, *History*, bk. X, ch. 8 (*CB*, I, pp. 501–20).

discussions with the papal legates. It was during this period that he was writing anti-Latin tracts on the filioque.[129]

Later in his reign Andronicus III sent two embassies to the Pope led by Stephen Dandolo, one in 1337 to initiate further discussion[130] and a second in 1339 when Stephen was accompanied by Barlaam. The Latin record of the 1339 meeting at Avignon gives the full exposition of the Greek position as propounded by Barlaam.[131] He urged the value of generosity, pressing for immediate aid against the Turks before settling the question of union. Then he emphasized that it was only decisions taken in a general council which would be likely to win over the Greek majority. Like Marino Sanudo he pointed out that little could be gained by force. But on this occasion he never really faced the question of authority or the doctrinal issues and even suggested that in default of agreement each Church might retain its own views under 'a single shepherd'. In any case his over-simplification was rejected by the Pope, then Benedict XII, who took the line that instruction in Latin teaching was all that the orientals needed to convince them of the validity of the Roman faith. The mission failed but union still remained a living issue.

7. Palamite problems

This same Barlaam who put the Orthodox view to the papacy at Avignon had already opened a controversy in Byzantium which had far-reaching effects and at the same time revealed the vitality of Byzantine spirituality and theology. While defending the Orthodox Church during the 1333–4 union negotiations in Constantinople Barlaam had written on the filioque controversy. He asserted that the Latins could not prove their case by means of human

---

[129] GR 2170; there is some controversy as to whether the Greek texts refer to 1334–5 or to later discussions at Avignon in 1339; see C. Giannelli, 'Un progetto di Barlaam per l'unione delle chiese', *Misc. G. Mercati* (*ST* 123, Vatican, 1946), III. 157–208 and J. Meyendorff, 'Un Mauvais Théologien de l'unité au XIVe siècle: Barlaam le Calabrais', *1054–1954: L'Église et les églises* (Chevetogne, 1954), II. 47–64.

[130] DR 2830.

[131] Raynaldus, 25, ann. 1339, nos. 19–31; see also Giannelli, op. cit., Meyendorff, op. cit., and Gill, *Byzantium and the Papacy*, 196–9 (with trans. of extracts from Raynaldus).

reasoning since God in his essence was unknowable (which cut both ways in the controversy). He also took exception to practices which he found on Mount Athos. Here hermits living in asceticism and holy stillness (*hesychia*) claimed that repetition of the Jesus prayer and certain psychosomatic techniques helped them to experience the divine light which had shone round Christ on Mount Tabor, that is, they could know God while in this life. Barlaam's contention that God was in essence totally unknowable and his subsequent fierce condemnation of the Athonite hesychasts were challenged by a monk Gregory Palamas who had himself lived on Mount Athos. Palamas also took exception to Barlaam's view that non-Christian philosophers of antiquity might have had some 'enlightenment by God'.

Palamas wrote nine treatises arranged in groups of three and called *Triads*.[132] In these he defended and developed θέωσις, the deification of man. He maintained that, though the uncreated essence of God was unknowable, both here and in the next world man could share in God through uncreated energies bestowed by deifying grace. Barlaam took the offensive. He replied to Palamas's second *Triad* with a *Tract Against the Messalians* implying that hesychast practices were heretical. He then accused Palamas to the Patriarch John Calecas. A synod was held in Constantinople on 10 June 1341 at which Barlaam found himself condemned. The hesychasts had defended themselves in a hagioretic (monastic) *Tome* brought from Athos by Gregory Palamas and subsequent synodal sessions that year confirmed the Palamite position but further discussion was prohibited.[133] Barlaam returned to Italy, but within Byzantine circles the controversy continued.

At the same time following Andronicus III's death on 15 June 1341 civil war broke out. His heir John V was a minor and the regency of the Empress Mother Anne of Savoy and the Patriarch Calecas was successfully contested by the Grand Domestic John Cantacuzenus who was crowned as co-Emperor John VI in Constantinople in 1347. Cantacuzenus supported the Orthodox position of the Palamites and he deposed the Patriarch John XIV Calecas who had imprisoned Palamas for continuing the controversy contrary to the synodal ruling.[134] Isidore (May 1347–February/

---

[132] Gregory Palamas, *Triads*.
[133] GR 2210–13.
[134] GR 2270.

March 1350), a pro-Palamite and bishop-elect of Monembasia, was chosen patriarch and he soon afterwards appointed Palamas archbishop of Thessalonica.[135] It is clear that there was a body of opinion which followed Gregory Acindynus who had originally tried to mediate between Barlaam and Palamas. Acindynus's criticism was directed not to the hesychast techniques—this was a minor matter in the controversy—but to what he regarded as Palamas's wrong use of patristic writings. He saw him as 'an innovator' and not as a theologian building on a long-established tradition. Yet another synod was held in May–July 1351 in the Blachernae palace.[136] This is generally regarded as definitive in the Orthodox world. Palamite teaching was reaffirmed and anathemas against condemned opponents such as Barlaam and Acindynus were added to the Synodicon of Orthodoxy. Nicephorus Gregoras, who was certainly not pro-Latin, died in prison. He thought that the 'uncreated energies' implied more than one God. An Athonite monk Prochorus Cydones who took the Thomist view was excommunicated in 1368. Palamas (†1359) was canonized in this same year,[137] and one of the most notable fourteenth-century patriarchs, Philotheus Coccinus, wrote his encomium.[138]

Perhaps 'hesychast'—a word with various meanings—is an unfortunate description[139] of what was a development of significance both in the fourteenth century and in the continuing life of the Orthodox Church. This development in Orthodox teaching has on occasion been underrated or misunderstood by modern historians. In recent works which enjoy a high reputation it appears to be regarded as 'a purely domestic issue',[140] or worse still, 'a retreat into

[135] *GR* 2279.

[136] *GR* 2324.

[137] *GR* 2540 and 2541.

[138] There is a wealth of material on Gregory Palamas and his teaching. See bibliography and assessments in D. Stiernon, 'Bulletin sur le palamisme', *REB*, 30 (1972), 231–341 (not exhaustive on the Slav side); G. Podskalsky, *Theologie*, valuable, particularly on theological method (see the important section 'Die Methodenstreit im Humanismus und Palamismus'). On fourteenth-century Palamism, J. Meyendorff is the Orthodox guide; see his *Introduction*, collected articles in *Byzantine Hesychasm* (Variorum, London, 1974), and his articles 'Palamas' and 'Palamisme', *DS*, fasc. 76 (1983), cols. 81–107. There is a brief survey of recent views in *Eastern Churches Review*, 9 (1977); see also debates in *Istina*, no. 19 (1974).

[139] See J. Meyendorff, *Byzantine Hesychasm* (Variorum, London, 1974), Introduction, pp. 2–4 and his 'Mount Athos in the Fourteenth Century', *DOP*, 42 (1988), 156–65.

[140] Gill, *Byzantium and the Papacy*, 204.

an ivory tower of spiritual and cultural nationalism' under 'obscurantist Palamite leadership'.[141] This is to convey a wrong impression of what was in fact a development and reaffirmation of the spiritual experience of deification, the underlying basis of Christian life in the Orthodox Church. It is true that it came at a time of internal rivalries, patriarchal resignations and depositions, territorial contraction, and mass conversions to Islam, of gloom and pessimism in intellectual circles, all of which some scholars like to stress. Such a picture has to be balanced by an understanding of the long-term significance of fourteenth-century Byzantine spirituality (by no means confined simply to Palamite teaching). This is admirably brought out by J. Meyendorff's emphasis on the influence of Palamas and his theology on the Slav countries, particularly Russia.[142] The whole question did of course raise major issues, not only in its own day but for later generations, and the place of human reason in Christian epistemology is still being debated by western and Orthodox theologians.[143] But unlike some secular historians the theologians are at least more constructively assessing the significance of Palamite teaching. And deification, or divinization, is found in the western as well as the eastern tradition. It is implicit in the Offertory of the Roman Catholic mass, as well as in prayers and hymns in use in the West, all of which speak of 'sharing in', or 'being transformed into', the divinity of Christ. This is the 'participation' of which St Augustine spoke, meaning, as the Orthodox would say, participation through the grace of the Holy Spirit in the divine energies but not in the unknowable essence or *substantia* of God.[144]

8. John V Palaeologus and John VI Cantacuzenus: Constantinople and the West

Negotiations for union continued intermittently until they culminated in the council of Ferrara–Florence (1438–9), but in a some-

---

[141] Setton, *Papacy and the Levant*, I. 42 and 310, note 187.

[142] See Meyendorff, *Byzantium and the Rise of Russia*, especially 96–118, and *The Byzantine Legacy in the Orthodox Church* (New York, 1982), 143–9 and *passim*.

[143] Cf. the survey by G. Every, 'The Study of Eastern Orthodoxy: Hesychasm', *Religion*, 9 (1979), 73–91.

[144] Cf. *De Natura et Gratia*, 33 (37); I am grateful to Henry Chadwick for this reference to St Augustine.

what different atmosphere from that of the mid-thirteenth century. Politics still made western aid of first importance, but there was also a more genuinely religious feeling in the desire for union. Many factors had produced greater understanding of western thought and practice. Marriages in imperial circles, such as Irene of Montferrat and Andronicus II, or Andronicus III's wife Anne of Savoy with her Franciscan entourage, and indeed the increasing number of mixed marriages at every level (to the disapproval of papacy and Orthodox alike), as well as the proliferation of western ecclesiastics and religious orders, all contributed to familiarize fourteenth-century Byzantium with a different way of life. Many resented this, but some took the opportunity to explore a new world. It is noticeable that the private conversion of the Emperor John V Palaeologus to Roman Catholicism[145] caused little stir, something that could hardly have happened in Macedonian days. And the greatly admired Manuel II himself (contrary to views expressed by some modern scholars) showed no rigid hostility towards the Latins. After all, his intimate circle included men such as Demetrius Cydones.

John VI Cantacuzenus, who became senior co-Emperor in February 1347 after a struggle with the Empress Mother Anne of Savoy and the Patriarch Calecas, had been Andronicus III's Grand Domestic. He was committed to the cause of Palamas which was finally established in the synod of 1351. But he was equally anxious to found an acceptable basis for the union of the two Churches. Other factors, such as Aegean piracy, Turkish encroachment, and indeed the perilous position of all Christians in the East Mediterranean, were also in the forefront of Orthodox and papal negotiations. But pressing as such dangers were they could not obscure John VI's real concern with the ecclesiastical points at issue. As soon as he had secured his position as senior Emperor in 1347 he outlined his views to Bartholomew of Rome and sent envoys to the papal court, then in Avignon. Primacy he appeared to accord but doctrine was a matter for a general council.[146] Pope Clement VI temporized, promising to send his own envoys to Constantinople. He

---

[145] See O. Halecki, *Un Empereur de Byzance à Rome. Vingt ans de travail pour l'union des églises et pour la défense de l'Empire d'Orient: 1355–1375* (Warsaw, 1930) (full, but now needs some revision).

[146] R. J. Loenertz, 'Ambassadeurs grecs auprès du pape Clément VI (1348)', *OCP*, 19 (1953), 178–96 (Latin text and commentary).

delayed and in 1348 and 1349 John wrote several times to remind him of his promise.[147] Discussions with Franciscans and Dominicans continued and in his *History*[148] Cantacuzenus says that he was given to understand that Clement VI would support a general council (which seems improbable). Certainly when Clement did send envoys, a Franciscan and a Dominican bishop, there was no mention of a council.

Cantacuzenus and Clement VI's successor, Innocent VI, continued the dialogue. Then for a time politics intervened when John V Palaeologus, the junior co-Emperor and Cantacuzenus's son-in-law, successfully asserted his right to sole rule and in December 1354 John VI retired and entered a monastery as the monk Joasaph. He did not die until 1383 and he continued to exert considerable influence on affairs outside the monastery. It is impossible to say exactly why he abdicated. But he was a religious man, of a reflective nature, historian and theologian, and he spent much of his 'retirement' in writing.[149] He remained on excellent terms with the imperial household, said to have been regarded by all as their father, and he had a place in circles containing some of the finest minds of his day, such as Demetrius Cydones (despite differing views on Palamite and western theology), or Nicholas Cabasilas, or Manuel II the second son of John V. For Cantacuzenus, retirement to a monastery was not the refuge of a political failure or the last home of a dying man. It was probably a deliberate choice. He had for some time had the desire to place himself under the direction of the Patriarch Philotheus in a retreat of this kind, perhaps with like-minded friends. He went to St George of the Mangana, and then possibly to the fourteenth-century foundation of the Charsianeites house where he was said to have lived in the abbot's lodging.[150] His conception of the monastic vocation was flexible and as in Byzantium and elsewhere did not necessarily prevent continued service to the state.

Both Cantacuzenus and John V continued to keep in touch with the papacy whose aid was even more urgently needed in view of the

---

[147] *DR* 2937, 2942, 2943, 2957.
[148] Cantacuzenus, *History*, bk, IV, ch. 9 (*CB*, III, pp. 55 ff.).
[149] See D. M. Nicol, *The Byzantine Family of Kantakouzenos (Cantacuzenus) ca. 1100–1460* (Washington, DC, 1968), no. 22, for details on John VI.
[150] See H. Hunger, 'Das Testament des Patriarchen Matthaios I., 1397–1410', *BZ*, 51 (1958), 299.

Turkish capture of Gallipoli (1354) and subsequent Ottoman establishment in Europe, a threat to Slav and western powers as well as to Byzantium. John V took his own initiative with rather unusual proposals set out in a gold bull dated 15 December 1355[151] which was taken to Avignon by a Calabrian Greek, Paul, then archbishop of Smyrna, accompanied by Nicholas Sigerus. John promised obedience to Rome, both his own and that of his subjects (this latter to be brought about within six months), provided that the Pope should send an expedition against the Turks now settling in Europe. His eldest son Andronicus was to learn Latin, as were the children of the magnates, and his second son, the five-year-old Manuel, was to be sent to Avignon as a hostage presumably to be brought up in Latin ways. A papal legate was to be resident in Constantinople with the right of appointing Greek ecclesiatics to help promote the union. Much of this was quite unrealistic and does not say much for John V's political sense, though it is understandable that he himself was well disposed towards the Roman Catholic Church, as were certain of his subjects—and his mother was the Italian Anne of Savoy. Unlike Cantacuzenus he was therefore not harassed by doctrinal problems. It was however in keeping with imperial tradition that he asked for the prompt dispatch of military aid before the actual achievement of union. The Pope did send envoys one of whom was Peter Thomas, bishop of Patti and Lipari, later nominated Latin Patriarch of Constantinople. Peter Thomas stayed in the capital for some months in 1357. Though the Greeks did not follow their Emperor, Peter Thomas got a statement from John V affirming his complete submission to the holy Roman Church.[152] The other points in John's original proposal of 1355 do not seem to have been taken up. Manuel for instance did not go to the papal court. But John himself expressed the strong desire to visit the curia as indeed he did later on.

But defence against the Turks was, as always, hindered by inter-Christian feuds both political and religious, and the Pope's crusading plans achieved little. In 1365 in desperation John V, who had no inhibitions about travelling abroad as a suppliant, set off for Hungary with his two sons. He got little help. Then on his return he

---

[151] DR 3052.
[152] DR 3071 (Nov. 1357); see Philip of Mézières, *Vita S. Petri Thomae*, ed. J. Smet (Rome, 1954), 76–9.

was caught between the animosities of Catholic Hungary and Orthodox Bulgaria. He had to be rescued by the Green Count, his cousin Amadeo VI of Savoy, one of the few westerners to bring some effective aid to the beleaguered Empire. The Pope, then Urban V, hoped that with the goodwill of Louis of Hungary and the military expertise of Amadeo something might be achieved. John V, while he was staying in Hungary had again attested his acceptance of the Roman faith. Little came of the Pope's hoped-for expedition, except that Amadeo, acting independently, did have some success against the Bulgarians and Turks in 1366.

While travelling home through the Balkans John V continued discussions on union with Amadeo and with Paul, then the Latin Patriarch of Constantinople and a man familiar with Aegean problems. The dialogue was continued in Constantinople according to a surviving report.[153] John V (according to the document) stated that he was not capable of dealing with the question of the union of the Churches by himself but wished to act with 'the Emperor my father' (that is Cantacuzenus, then the monk Joasaph), the Patriarch, and bishops. He had certainly acted by himself in the past but he may have felt that the devout and learned Cantacuzenus was better able to sustain a public debate of this kind. He was present together with his wife Helena and two of his sons (Andronicus and Manuel—the latter left as hostage with Louis must have returned). Officials and clerics, including three metropolitans, were also present. The Byzantine Patriarch was then Philotheus (second patriarchate 1364–76), a friend of Cantacuzenus and though a Palamite not so rigidly anti-Latin as his predecessor Callistus I. He had to point out that he could not receive Paul officially as he had no written mandate from the Pope, but was willing to have informal friendly talks.

The discussion between Cantacuzenus and Paul took place in the Blachernae palace in early June 1367. To some extent the points made by Cantacuzenus and endorsed in part by Paul were similar to views which the ex-Emperor said that he had sent to the Pope in 1350 (according to his *History*). The two were agreed that arbitrary action would only exacerbate the situation (ch. 3). The tone of the report breathed reasonableness and a fraternal spirit and stressed the

---

[153] J. Meyendorff, 'Projets de concile œcuménique en 1367: Un dialogue inédit entre Jean Cantacuzène et le légat Paul', *DOP*, 14 (1960), 147–77 (Greek text, summary, and commentary).

oecumenical nature of the Church. Division was an evil (κακόν) which could only be removed, so Cantacuzenus argued, if Rome ceased to assume that the words of Peter's successor the Pope must be accepted as though they were the words of Christ. The settlement of differences must be through a catholic and oecumenical council to which all far and wide should be summoned. Why deepen the division by unilateral denial of the validity of our rites?[154] When Paul suggested that a general council was unnecessary because all decisions really rested with the Emperor whom he likened to a meat-spit—when he turned, all turned with him—this was rejected on the ground that obedience in matters of faith could not be forced (Michael VIII's failure was evidently not forgotten). In a sense the discussion as reported was somewhat imprecise, making no mention of certain specific points at issue, but offering a general protestation of willingness, offering to visit the Pope, even to kiss his feet (a curious custom thought Cantacuzenus), or to kiss the feet of his horse or the dust beneath him (ch. 20). To the assertion that surely papal aid would alleviate many ills for the Orthodox, Cantacuzenus replied with truth that they had managed to keep their faith even though some lived under infidel rule. Then after a short breathing space Paul was directly asked, 'Do thou think that what I have said is true and just?' and he agreed that it was, saying that he was in favour of a general council. Such a council was then fixed and was to be held in Constantinople between June 1367 and May 1369. There was to be free discussion on equal terms, 'and if we cannot agree, then let us each go our own way in peace', so ran Cantacuzenus's last words.

However well-intentioned, Paul had no official mandate for so firm an agreement which ran counter to papal policy, and still less to fix a date. But it was evidently regarded seriously by the Orthodox who took steps to implement the decision. Patriarch Philotheus wrote to inform the Bulgarian archbishop (later Patriarch) of the decision and invited him to Constantinople.[155] The Patriarchs of Jerusalem and Alexandria were in the capital at the time and together with Philotheus's envoys they were represented in an embassy which reached Viterbo in October 1367

---

[154] This was a reference to Louis of Hungary's alleged views on re-baptism; see here the cautionary comments of Gill, *Byzantium and the Papacy*, 216 and 303, note 53.
[155] GR 2524.

accompanied by Paul and Amadeo.[156] But papal letters of 6 November 1367 addressed to various Byzantine authorities made no reference to any projected general council. They did however refer to the Emperor John V's promised visit. Behind the more public discussions on union John V had evidently been pursuing his unilateral and personal policy and this must have been known to his immediate entourage and to Latin envoys such as Paul. It was Demetrius Cydones, the minister and friend of both Andronicus III and John VI Cantacuzenus, the translator of Aquinas, and himself a convert, who went to Viterbo in the summer of 1369 to announce to Urban V the promised arrival of John V.[157] The Emperor reached Rome in September and on 18 October was received into the Roman Church. His profession of faith followed the pattern laid down by Clement IV in 1267 and agreed to by Michael VIII, and the Greek and Latin text of the gold bull is preserved in the Vatican.[158]

The imperial conversion was a matter for rejoicing in curial circles but elsewhere it created a curious, and in some ways, an awkward situation. It meant that western powers, such as Venice, no longer had an excuse for hostility since John V was not now a schismatic as the Pope hastened to remind them. On the other hand, despite individual Byzantine conversions[159] and greater understanding of the Latin theological viewpoint, at any rate among individuals, the Orthodox Church remained in schism, as did the influential Cantacuzenus and John V's sons and grandsons. The Greek plea of 1367 for conciliar action remained unanswered until in 1370 a papal letter to the Greek clergy again specifically reiterated the usual refusal to hold a council of Greek and Latin prelates.[160] Within the Empire the conversion of John V seemed to have roused little, if any, comment, possibly because of the changed atmosphere due to the continued presence of Latin establishments and personnel and increased familiarity with individual conversions. Had John V attempted to enforce changes, as Michael VIII had done, it would have been different. John V lingered abroad, not entirely of his own will. After a stay of about five months in Rome he went on to

[156] DR 3115; cf. GR 2526.
[157] DR 3120.
[158] DR 3122.
[159] See Gill, *Byzantium and the Papacy*, 221–2.
[160] Tăutu, *Acta Urb. V* (Vatican, 1964), no. 184 (22 Feb. 1370).

Naples and then to Venice where he was virtually held captive pending payment of debts to the signoria. It was the autumn of 1371 before he got back to Constantinople.

9. Manuel II: the council of Ferrara–Florence and after

From this time on until the fall of the city in 1453 the Turks closed in, thus threatening all Aegean and Balkan powers. Endless rivalries, within the Palaeologan imperial family, with the Byzantine Church, and from 1378 the Great Schism in the papacy, as well as conflicting economic interests, seemed to rule out any united Christian front. From 1391–1425 John V's favourite son, Manuel II, struggled to keep control. Universally admired as a noble and generous Emperor, he presented in his personal fate all the conflicting currents and complexities besetting life in the last ages of the Empire. He was forced to become the vassal of the Ottoman ruler, yet he continually sought aid from the West against the Turk. Like his father he journeyed outside the Empire, a suppliant in European courts and everywhere greatly esteemed. Within his territory he suffered great hardship, aggravated by the curse of family feuds. Behind conventional rhetoric his writings show his agony of mind, as for instance at his brother Theodore's trials, as well as revealing the bitter physical deprivations which he had to endure.[161] Yet throughout he took comfort in close personal links with his friends, particularly Demetrius Cydones to whom he was greatly attached. He may have shared some of his anti-Palamite views, for in 1386 Cydones could write to Manuel of 'the arrows of the hesychasts which do not spare even an Emperor'.[162]

During the last years of the Empire the usual negotiations with the papacy continued, born of desperation. In September 1384 Patriarch Nilus wrote to Urban VI speaking of the unionist efforts of Frater William, bishop of Diaulia in Boeotia. He stressed, as Byzantines liked to do, that though they were being punished by the Turks for their sins, at least the infidels had left their ecclesiastical administration alone.[163] In 1385 Manuel sent an embassy to

---

[161] See Manuel II Palaeologus, *Funeral Oration on his brother Theodore*, ed. and trans. J. Chrysostomides (*CFHB* 26, Thessalonica, 1985), and Manuel II, *Letters, passim.*
[162] Ep. 327, ed. Loenertz, II. 258; trans. Dennis, *Manuel II in Thessalonica*, 147.
[163] *GR* 2773; MM, vol. 2, no. 379, p. 87.

Rome.[164] One of his envoys was ridiculed by Cydones who said that he could not think why Manuel had sent an ardent anti-Latin hesychast to Rome since he would find protocol and daily discussions difficult to sustain on an amicable basis, unless, added Cydones, like others, he might be converted to the Latin point of view.[165] In response to Manuel a papal embassy was sent to Constantinople in 1386 where, according to Cydones, it got a cold and critical reception. But, he went on, it was well received in Thessalonica (which Manuel was at that time (1382–7) trying to defend), 'and now our city is persuaded to give the same honours to the Son as to the Father'.[166] Cydones, already a convert to Roman Catholicism, was obviously quick to note any pro-Roman tendencies, but even so it is clear that they did exist, if only for the most part within a small educated circle.

The last years of the fourteenth century brought continuous failure to the Christians. The Serbs were defeated at Kossovo in 1389. A crusade led by Sigismund of Hungary was crushed at Nicopolis in 1396. Manuel II's 1400–3 tour of European cities, a noticeable political round which did not include a visit to Rome, brought no tangible result. It was followed up by the dispatch of the distinguished scholar and pro-Latin diplomat Manuel Chrysoloras on similar visits to western courts from 1407 onwards. But again without result. Manuel II's bitter disappointment is revealed in a letter to Chrysoloras probably dated 1409. He laments that Chrysoloras has not sent news of any help, the letter just received from him contains 'nothing of what we were hoping for'.[167]

The temporary relief afforded to Byzantium by the defeat of Bayazid at Ancyra in 1402 and the ensuing war between his sons (1402–13) might have provided opportunity for a concerted attack by all the Christian powers, but conflicting political interests ruled this out. In 1413 the Ottoman Mehmed I emerged victor, and for a time he preserved an uneasy peace with Manuel. The Emperor, under no illusions as to the real intent of the Ottoman, attempted to strengthen the position in the Morea, building the Hexamilion wall across the Isthmus, quelling Byzantine rebels in the Peloponnese and

---

[164] *DR* 3181a.
[165] Ep. 314, ed. Loenertz, II. 241, trans. in part, Dennis, *Manuel II in Thessalonica*, 137–8.
[166] Ep. 327, ed. Loenertz, II. 257, trans. Dennis, *Manuel II in Thessalonica*, 146.
[167] Manuel II, *Letters*, Ep. 55, pp. 154–57; also trans. Barker, *Manuel II*, 266–7.

making unceasing appeals for western assistance. Venice refused outright—it had its own problems of defence—but the Pope (by then Martin V) did at least grant an indulgence to Latins assisting with the wall. Though it could do little the papacy was fully aware of the threats both to the Greek Christians and to the Latins in the Aegean. Venice, for instance, still controlled considerable areas there and was under continual pressure.

Indeed during the early fifteenth century the papacy itself was hardly in a position to pressurize western powers, faced as it was by problems of heresy, need for internal reform of head and members, and above all the schism caused by rival popes. The council of Pisa (1409) only aggravated the situation by the election of what proved to be a third Pope, the Cretan-born Greek, Alexander V, who was recognized and congratulated by Manuel in a letter taken by John Chrysoloras.[168] The schism in the Church was however ended in the council of Constance (1414–18) with the repudiation of the three rival popes and the election of Martin V (1417). But the Pope himself still had to face a severe challenge to his authority in the attempt to assert the superiority of the general council.

During the council of Constance the union of the two Churches had been much in the minds of the delegates. Sigismund (later western Emperor) was a prominent figure in promoting the council. In response to his invitation Greek envoys had been sent to discuss union and the urgently needed aid against the infidel. To some Latins, Sigismund for instance, this aid was associated with the hope of launching a major crusade, not a very practical project in view of western antagonisms—England's war against France, or Sigismund's hatred of Venice. Nevertheless once the papal schism had been resolved, negotiations between Byzantium and the council were able to proceed. The Greeks throughout laid stress on the position of the papacy in the pentarchy, not that this meant compliance with all papal demands, but at least they made it clear that there had to be a single recognized Pope in the Latin Church, which had not been the case before 1417 because of the rival popes. The chief Greek envoy at Constance was the diplomat Nicholas Eudaimonoïoannes. The impression given to the conciliarists appeared to have been over-optimistic concerning Byzantine willingness to comply with papal demands. In the event, papal legates

---

[168] DR 3326.

went to Constantinople and a general council to be held in the capital was proposed. The Orthodox had always maintained there must be full discussion in an oecumenical council before any agreement could be reached, so that in their view this forthcoming council was no mere formality, a point which was evidently not appreciated by Rome. At first Martin V formally appointed a papal legate in 1420 in response to a Byzantine request. He was Cardinal Piero Fonseca, but his visit fell through. It was only in 1422 that a papal nuncio, the Franciscan Antonio da Massa, reached Constantinople. His experiences in the City illustrated the gulf between papal and Byzantine views. Even at this late date, just after the (temporary) siege of Constantinople by Murad II, Patriarch Joseph II stood his ground. Antonio had the papal position set out in nine statements or 'conclusiones' which were put to the Patriarch and to the co-Emperor John VIII (Manuel II was suffering from a stroke). In the third statement Antonio claimed that the Byzantine envoys to Constance had clearly said that the Greeks were ready to unite with the Latin Church in the faith which the Roman Church held and in obedience to that same Roman Church.[169] Therefore in Roman eyes the general council to be arranged was simply to confirm this. Not so, maintained the Patriarch, who then refuted all nine points along traditional Orthodox lines. He was supported by John VIII who stressed that his envoys to Constance had had no mandate to offer complete capitulation to Rome. The Emperor asked for a general council to be held in Constantinople, with papal responsibility for all expenses, since imperial poverty made this assistance essential. He added that enemy pressure was such that the council could not be arranged forthwith, but he undertook to inform the papacy as soon as this became practicable.[170]

Conditions did not improve for Byzantium. Nor did it for the papacy, harassed as it was by Italian warfare, the Bohemian heresy, the disasters suffered by Latin Cyprus, and the long-drawn-out struggle between conciliar and papal authority. Nevertheless negotiations on union continued. Since Constantinople as a site for a general council seemed unlikely, Martin V put forward a different

---

[169] See V. Laurent, 'Les préliminaires du concile de Florence: Les Neuf Articles du Pape Martin V et la réponse inédite du Patriarche de Constantinople Joseph II (Octobre 1422)', REB, 20 (1962), 5–60 (Greek and Latin text and trans.); cf. Syropoulos, Mémoires, II, 10–11, p. 112.
[170] DR 3406.

plan. He suggested that an Italian town, possibly on the Calabrian coast, perhaps Ancona, might be selected. He agreed to finance up to 700 Orthodox delegates and to guarantee their return expenses even if union were not achieved. Further he would contribute archers and galleys for the defence of Constantinople during John VIII's absence. Martin V died on 20 February 1431, but his proposals and promise of assistance were borne in mind in subsequent discussions and eventually proved the basis for the final agreement under Martin's successor Eugenius IV who was elected on 3 March 1431.

Meanwhile in accordance with western plans for reform another council had met in Basel in 1431. Here the new Pope Eugenius had to face endless opposition from the conciliarists. He tried to dissolve the council, but had to withdraw his bull for fear of provoking another schism. But throughout a series of unedifying Latin wrangles negotiations for the union of the Churches continued, both within and without the council. Realizing that to achieve the union of the two Churches would greatly enhance their prestige, both the anti-papal conciliarist majority and the Pope with his own supporters (a minority at Basel) put out various offers to the Byzantines. Anxious to take the matter further the council at first urged Eugenius to negotiate. Then it took action itself to get into touch with Constantinople. Its representatives returned from the capital in June 1434 with Byzantine envoys who agreed that the council should implement Martin V's proposals, but they adamantly refused to consider the conciliarists' desire that Basel should be the meeting-place for the forthcoming general council. Meanwhile Eugenius, unaware of this, had been conducting his own negotiations with Constantinople through his envoy Christopher Garatoni who suggested a change of plan so that the new council would be held in Constantinople (which would involve less papal expense). However the Pope then abandoned this and agreed to the proposals accepted at Basel and already ratified by the council's decree *Sicut pia mater*. Both council and Pope reproached each other for unilateral action and the council tried to coerce the Pope by cutting off his customary financial supplies. Support now began to rally round the Pope. At the same time the more extreme conciliarists made the mistake of continuing to refuse an Italian city as the meeting-place for the general council, hoping to get Basel accepted but also offering Avignon and Savoy which the Byzantines continued to refuse. Further embassies were exchanged. But it must have seemed to the Byzantines that the Latin Church had surmounted the Great Schism only to be faced with a still more dangerous situation in which the majority of the council at Basel and the papal party were at loggerheads and a serious attempt was being made to erode papal authority.

In the end the more moderate party and the Pope agreed in May 1437 to offer some Italian city (as in Martin V's original proposal). This was acceptable to the Byzantines. The extremists at Basel, who had feared to move to an Italian city, were however still optimistic and they sent a fleet to Constantinople to fetch the Orthodox delegates. The papal party had already done this and their ships arrived on 3 September 1437 a month ahead of the conciliarists' galleys. Taking their choice the Byzantines opted for the papal transport. They sailed on 27 November 1437. By the end of that same year the council of Basel had been transferred by papal bull to Ferrara. The extremists refused to move and remained in schism in Basel until 1449, but they could not prevent the general council of Ferrara–Florence (1438–9). The Byzantine choice of the papal rather than the conciliarist ships is understandable. It is true that they laid great stress on the authority of a general council, but it was a council in which the five senior 'patriarchs' (or their proxies) were present and of these five the doyen was the bishop of Rome. Moreover in this particular case (in contrast to the conciliarist party at Basel) it was Eugenius who promised to carry out all the conditions agreed upon with the Byzantines.

The Greek point of view, the endless and wearisome pre-conciliar discussions in Constantinople with the two contending parties from the West ('Spare me these meetings,' moaned Syropoulos), the decision to travel to Italy, the hazards *en route*, the experiences in Ferrara–Florence, are all movingly portrayed in the contemporary memoirs of the megas ecclesiarch Sylvester Syropoulos,[171] one of the high officials of the Great Church, who went with the contingent. His readable memoirs (not always entirely accurate and openly anti-unionist) give informal and revealing detail on what went on behind the scenes, as well as in public, in

[171] Syropoulos was edited (with a misleading Latin trans.) by R. Creyghton (The Hague, 1660) and references in older books are to this. It has now been completely superseded by V. Laurent's edition.

Byzantine circles. The old Patriarch Joseph II was shown as reluctant yet willing to go. He was nearly eighty and in wretched health, not a learned man but respected by many for his other qualities. He genuinely hoped for union and in his simplicity he thought that with goodwill and charity on either side a personal meeting with his brother the Pope could achieve it.[172] Joseph openly stated that the pure and radiant Orthodox doctrine would bring back the Latins to the true faith.[173] Despite the high, if unfounded, hopes of such as Joseph, the memoirs seem to reflect a general unwillingness to leave Constantinople and make the voyage. All were aware of the threat to the capital and this remained an underlying fear throughout the course of the council. They were driven by the overriding need to get the western military aid which it was hoped that the union would bring. But it is not true to assert, as is sometimes done, that this was the sole motive. The desire for union of simple-minded men such as the Patriarch Joseph, and indeed others, was genuine. There were also some who understood the Latin point of view and could see where Greek and Latins were expressing the same doctrinal truth in different ways. Such was Bessarion of Nicaea who was to be one of the Byzantine spokesmen at the council. Others were eventually to uphold only the Orthodox expression of Christian truths, though only Mark Eugenicus, metropolitan of Ephesus, resolutely refused to sign at Florence.

The Orthodox party numbered about 700. It included the Emperor and his officials, the Patriarch, and the leading dignitaries of Hagia Sophia (except for Theodore Agallianus, the hieromnemon, who had excruciating gout which vanished when the ships had sailed). There were a number of metropolitans and selected bishops, with hieromonks from important monasteries, clergy, and cantors (*psaltai*).[174] In addition there were certain distinguished laymen, such as George Scholarius and the revered and aged Gemistus Plethon. Other delegates, from Russia for instance, travelled separately by different routes. There were also envoys from Georgia and Moldo-Wallachia. The sacred vessels from the Great Church were taken for use in the liturgy. The Byzantines also

[172] Traversari, writing to Christophoro Garatoni, the papal referendarius, vol. 2, bk, III, Ep. 65, cols. 195–6 (= No. 140).

[173] Syropoulos, *Mémoires*, III, 25, p. 186.

[174] Many of the participants are listed in Gill, *Council of Florence*.

brought appropriate gifts, codices of Greek ecclesiastical and secular authors which were greatly valued by humanists in Italy.[175]

The anti-unionist Syropoulos took a gloomy view of the enterprise but he does provide many convincing details of the voyage. The Patriarch gave those travelling in his ship an improving talk on union but this did little to raise morale. There was acute congestion on board and the general tone was one of anxiety with continual controversy over proposed allocations of the papal subsidy as between the imperial and the patriarchal parties. The voyage was unspeakably wearing, protracted as it was by bad weather, delaying calms, and also by making stops whenever possible in order to afford a night's rest on land. It was said that the Emperor and the old Patriarch could only eat or sleep when on land. Even so disembarkments of this kind had their problems. At Methone (Modon), where the party put in, the Patriarch was at first only offered part of a ruined episcopal building then inhabited by pigs until the castelanus was finally persuaded to house him.

The Byzantines had sailed on 27 November 1437 but they did not reach Venice until 8 February 1438. Here in the flourishing and wealthy city they were accorded an impressive reception reminiscent of Byzantine standards in the long-past days of its splendour. In Venice the Byzantines were courted by both Pope and conciliarists remaining in Basel. The Emperor and the Patriarch chose to support Eugenius and Ferrara where the council had already opened on 8 January 1438. John VIII, followed by Patriarch Joseph, reached Ferrara in early March. Even before they had left Venice problems of etiquette and precedence had arisen. Some, like the tolerant Camaldolese Ambrogio Traversari who had a great liking for Joseph, understood the ingrained conservatism and pride of the Byzantines. In Venice he had urged the Latins not to take offence when hats were not removed, or when the Patriarch addressed the Pope as 'brother'. In Ferrara when it came to the western custom of kissing the Pope's foot, according to Syropoulos, the Patriarch refused this outright, condemning it as an innovation sanctioned neither by Scripture nor tradition. 'Did the apostles kiss the foot of St Peter?' he asked. He was ready to return to Constantinople if the Pope expected any more than a fraternal embrace. The Pope, anxious not to hinder the cause of union, gave in, but when the

---

[175] See I. Ševčenko, 'Intellectual Repercussions', 291–2.

Patriarch reached Ferrara he was accorded only a private instead of a public reception. Thus at the outset the Greeks stressed the equality of Rome and Constantinople and showed their conservatism in insisting on their ancient usage and tradition. It was difficult to reconcile the pentarchy and the papal monarchy. Problems also arose over seating arrangements at the inauguration of the council in the cathedral in Ferrara and later on in Florence. The age-long custom was for the Byzantine Emperor to convene and preside at general councils. But the Pope expected to take the seat of honour. He also upset the Byzantines by seeming to equate their Emperor with the western Emperor (though at the time the western seat was in fact vacant owing to the death of Sigismund). In the end the papal throne was placed on the Latin side of the cathedral but was raised above that of the Byzantine Emperor. The Patriarch was only given a seat opposite to the leading cardinals. Syropoulos was much put out to find himself with his fellow dignitaries (stauro-phoroi) from Hagia Sophia at the back of the church. Such conflicting currents of discontent were an added irritation to the inevitable problems of housing and maintenance, complicated by the papal difficulty in paying the promised subsidy to the visitors.

However the assembling of a general council where Greeks and Latins were at least prepared to discuss their differences was in itself an achievement. This was what Cantacuzenus had wanted. It was in marked contrast to the council of Lyons II (1274) which met only to receive the Byzantine, or at least the imperial, acceptance of Roman claims. Even so problems arose over the agenda. John VIII wished for a delay of four months in order to allow western powers, or their delegates, time to get to Ferrara. He had in mind the possibility of negotiating political aid against the Ottomans and his request for delay was allowed. But in the event he was to be disappointed since only few sent official envoys (Anjou and Burgundy). It was unfortunate that most western rulers at that time wished to remain neutral in the split between the more extreme conciliarists of Basel and the papacy and so did not cast in their lot with the general council at Ferrara.

The increasing impatience of both the Latin delegates and the Pope at the delay in debating the main points at issue finally persuaded the Emperor to agree to informal discussions before the four months were up. Small committees were formed and the Emperor nominated Bessarion and Mark Eugenicus to speak for the

Greeks. Cesarini was the chief spokesman for the Latins. Main dogmatic topics were ruled out and the subject of purgatory was chosen. In June 1438 Cesarini set out Roman teaching on this, fortified by many citations from the Greek and Latin fathers. Bessarion and Mark of Ephesus countered with a series of queries, particularly as to whether there was a middle state between death and the attainment of heaven during which the soul was purified by the fires of purgatory. No agreement was reached, nor was there unanimity on the Greek side.

These discussions during the summer were disrupted by the plague and many Latins left the city. For the Greeks remaining behind it was a period of acute anxiety and frustration, aggravated by rumours of Ottoman threats to Constantinople. In addition bitter rivalries between Italian cities and the Pope had brought the hostile Milanese-paid condottiere Nicholas Piccinino to the neighbourhood. The Byzantines rushed their valuables back to Venice for safety, including the liturgical vessels from Hagia Sophia, though they did keep their ceremonial vestments in the hope that these would be needed later on for the celebration of the union.

When formal discussions began in October on the much disputed topic of the filioque there was again disagreement. The Latins wanted to discuss the doctrinal implications of the addition or omission. The Greeks stood out for considering the authority whereby an addition might be made and they had their way. The Greek position throughout centuries of argument had remained unchanged: it was based on a canon of the council of Ephesus (431) which had prohibited any kind of alteration to the Nicene creed (it was taken that this meant the Nicene-Constantinopolitan creed). This ruling had been confirmed by subsequent general councils. The Latins argued that the words filioque were not an addition but a development and a clarification. They also maintained that it was open to a general council to add to the truth, though in fact the original addition had been unilateral on the part of the Latins, which was a further Greek criticism. The question of the legality of the addition continued at Ferrara through October up to 13 December 1438 with both sides still not in agreement, though Bessarion seemed to be won over to the Latin side. It looked as though any convincing answer must refer to Trinitarian doctrine and this led on to the main subject of debate, the doctrinal implications of the addition. The Latins now pressed for consideration of the dogmatic aspect of the filioque.

Meanwhile the Pope was in acute financial difficulties, the hostile Piccinino was in possession of neighbouring papal cities, as Bologna, the plague might flare up again, while the Greeks were only too anxious to return home. In fact two metropolitans tried to slip quietly away but were summoned back by the Emperor at the insistence of the Patriarch. During the late autumn there had been proposals to move the council to Florence, a safer venue and all the more acceptable in that the subsidies to the Greeks were more likely to be paid regularly in the city of the pro-papal and wealthy Medici. Indeed the Commune promised hospitality to all the Greeks, together with a fixed payment for a period of not more than eight months. After some persuasion this was agreed by the Greeks and on 10 January the council was formally transferred to Florence. It was here that the main debates and the union took place.

Florence was a city in which humanist studies were flourishing, as were art and architecture. Greek was eagerly learnt and both classic and patristic sources explored. Syropoulos thought that one point in favour of the transference to Florence was that there were likely to be more Greek books available there. This was important in a dispute in which so much seemed to depend on the authority of the church fathers. The Greeks had only been able to bring a limited number of codices, and these were not all ecclesiastical. John VIII for instance had included manuscripts of Plato, commentaries on Aristotle, and a Plutarch.[176] There was opportunity for informal meetings and philosophical discussions between Greeks and Latins.[177] The much revered Gemistus lectured on Plato. Interpreters and bilingual scholars such as Traversari were fully occupied. The Greeks as well could produce cultured men some of whom knew Latin. There were also available in Constantinople translations of Latin works, including Augustine's *De Trinitate* by Maximus Planudes, Aquinas's *Summa Theologica* by the Cydones brothers, and Boethius's *De Trinitate* by Manuel Calecas.[178]

But informal discussions at a high level did not necessarily help to bring agreement on the disputed doctrinal issues. The members of the council left Ferrara and they reached Florence during January 1439. In February they embarked on the doctrinal significance of the

[176] See I. Ševčenko, 'Intellectual Repercussions', 291–5.
[177] Syropoulos, *Mémoires*, V, 3, p. 258.
[178] On the translation of western theological works in the later middle ages see G. Podskalsky, *Theologie und Philosophie in Byzanz* (Munich, 1977), 173–80.

filioque. At the request of the Greeks this at first took place in private, but when nothing came of these meetings the Pope insisted on full public sessions which opened on 2 March. The Dominican Provincial of Lombardy and Mark of Ephesus were the main protagonists. Both sides sought proof from patristic sources. A good deal turned on the texts of Epiphanius and St Basil's *Adversus Eunomium* and his *Homily on the Holy Spirit*. Readings in the codices differed and some Greeks considered that passages which did not support them were corrupt. This was one of the main pillars of the Greek defence, though it was also admitted that it was possible that '*ek*' and '*dia*' might have the same meaning, that is, they allowed that the Spirit might proceed either 'from' (*ek*) or 'through' (*dia*) the Son. John of Montenero spoke at great length, citing both eastern and western fathers and arguing to prove his case that the Spirit is from the Father and Son and that these are one cause or principle. One of the Greek charges had always been that the filioque implied two causes for the Spirit. Mark of Ephesus consistently held that the procession was from the Father alone as had always been the teaching of the Orthodox Church.[179] By the end of March it looked as though stalemate had been reached. The Greeks refused to debate any further and complained bitterly about the Latin torrent of words. They frowned on the syllogistic method of arguing as applied to Christian mysteries. They were tired of hearing of Aristotle. Syropoulos overheard one of the Iberian (Georgian) delegates muttering 'Aristotle, Aristotle, why all this Aristotle when they should be quoting St Peter, St Paul, St Basil, Gregory the Theologian, Chrysostom, but not Aristotle'.[180]

During April and May endless informal talks went on to try and get the Greeks to accept the filioque. It was suggested that one way of breaking the deadlock was to agree that saints could not err in faith. Therefore the different expressions used by Greek and Latin saints must surely mean the same. Bessarion and Scholarius worked hard to try to bring home this truth. Mark of Ephesus was in agreement that saints could not err in faith; but this did not undermine his own belief because he thought that words in support of the filioque had been falsified. The Greeks then held a series of meetings in which opposing views were expressed. By the begin-

[179] Gill, *Council of Florence*, 180–226, gives a full account of the lengthy debates.
[180] Syropoulos, *Mémoires*, IX, 28, p. 464.

ning of June they had voted to accept union and the filioque but it was made clear that though they recognized the Latin addition they would not alter their own creed. The Patriarch Joseph, who had always hoped for union, was then gravely ill. Even so, he knew of the discussions and was sent one of the three copies of the *Tomos* embodying acceptance of the filioque. He died shortly after on 10 June and was buried in the church of Santa Maria Novella as one in communion with Rome. He was not an intellectual man but he had tenacity and strength of character and in spite of the infirmity of old age and a crippling illness he stood for the dignity of his office and acted as a peacemaker in the troubles of Ferrara and Florence. Men such as Traversari and John of Ragusa were impressed by his qualities and by the depth of his spiritual life.[181]

Between Joseph's death and 26 June at the Pope's urgent insistence certain other outstanding differences between the two Churches were dealt with. These included the use of leavened or unleavened bread, the azymite controversy which had been left undecided at Ferrara, and whether the sacrament of the Eucharist was effected by the dominical words of institution, 'This is my Body', or by the prayer of the epiclesis, the calling down of the Holy Spirit, as in the Greek liturgy. There was too the fundamental question of the papal primacy. The Emperor insisted to the Pope that he was having no more long debates. With some difficulty a statement was agreed on. The Latins conceded the addition of certain reservations though these were too vague to afford any real limitation on papal power. On 6 July the final form of the definition was pronounced at Latin mass in the cathedral church, now Santa Maria del Fiore, in Greek by Bessarion, in Latin by Cesarini. After emphasizing the papal primacy throughout the whole world, the document spoke of Christ having handed down to the Pope plenary power according to the manner and deeds of the oecumenical councils and holy canons. It mentioned the other venerable patriarchates in the traditional order, adding that they were to have all their privileges and rights.[182] Then came the signatures headed by John VIII followed by the names of the oriental patriarchates and their procurators, and then the rest of the Greek bishops, the Hagia Sophia dignitaries and the hieromonks. Except for two names.

---

[181] See Gill, *Personalities*, 15–34.
[182] *Greek Acta*, 464; the Latin text of the bull *Laetentur coeli* is in Gill, *Council of Florence* and it is translated in Gill, *Conciles*.

Isaiah, metropolitan of Stauropolis in Caria, had left Florence unseen. Mark of Ephesus refused. Neither the Emperor nor the Pope could make him change. The Pope wanted to have him tried and condemned in Italy, but fearing something of this kind Mark had already got the Emperor to promise him a safe return to Constantinople.

Rather unsuccessful attempts were made by the Byzantines to test the reality of the union. John VIII wanted to have the Latin mass followed by a celebration of the Greek liturgy, but the Latins demurred, saying that they were unfamiliar with the Greek service and would like to try it out in private first. Some of the Greek metropolitans thought that the Latins in Greek sees in Crete and other islands should now be withdrawn from the dioceses 'which they have snatched from us'. They sent a deputation to the Pope but without any effective result.[183]

In spite of their desire to return home the Byzantines did not get away from Venice until October 1439. On their journey back the union met with a mixed reception when they put in at various stops and evidence tends to conflict depending on whether the writer is anti-unionist or not. Syropoulos' rather sour account of events in Modon does not tally with that of one of the *Shorter Chronicles* which says that Latin and Orthodox bishops celebrated in the church of St John the Theologian with mixed congregations on 23 and 24 November 1439. 'On 24 November the Byzantine bishop ('Ρωμαῖος is the word used), Kyr Joseph, celebrated in St John the Theologian and all the clergy and people from the district were there and they received the blessed bread (*antidoron*) and the castelanus and all the archons were present as well as the Byzantines ('Ρωμαῖοι).'[184] And Garatoni, who went back to Constantinople with the Byzantines, could write to Eugenius and speak of 'the willing recognition of the union' in places where they stopped, mostly still Venetian possessions.[185] There had indeed already been evidence of some unofficial fraternization in dioceses in Latin hands where there were Orthodox as well as Latin clergy (though often all too few of the latter).

The returning ships reached Constantinople on 1 February 1440.

---

[183] Syropoulos, *Mémoires*, X, 21–2, pp. 506–8.
[184] Schreiner, *Kleinchroniken*, vol. 1, Chronicle 104, no. 4, p. 662 and vol. 2, *Commentary*, p. 457.
[185] *Ep. Pont.*, ed. G. Hofmann, III, Doc. 243 (Rome, 1946).

It was only then that the Emperor learnt from his mother (no one else dared tell him) of the death of his wife, Maria Comnena, a Trebizond princess, to whom he was greatly attached. Inconsolable in his grief, for a time he seemed unable to turn his mind to ecclesiastical affairs and he did not publish the decree of union. A mixed reception was given to the union. Some who had signed at the council now repudiated it. Mark of Ephesus actively engaged in anti-unionist propaganda and his prestige stood high because from the start he had resolutely refused to support union on the terms offered and had not signed. But the Emperor, if somewhat inactive in the cause, was not opposed to union and the Patriarch chosen on 4 May 1440 to fill the vacant office was a unionist, Metrophanes II. He commemorated the Pope's name in the diptychs, but expressly affirmed that the union made no difference to Orthodox usage or to the Divine Liturgy and the creed. He was however in bad odour with Rome because he wrote to the Pope and to the cardinals as to equals and continued to call himself 'oecumenical' Patriarch.

Thus in Constantinople there was a sharp rift between unionist and anti-unionist. The latter refused to take part in unionist services. The Patriarch Metrophanes twice tried to compel the Emperor to take active measures by himself retiring to a monastery and refusing to function unless the union was enforced. Then just before both parties were due to meet in the standing synod the Patriarch died (1 August 1443) and nothing was done. The new Patriarch, Gregory III[185a] had already attempted to defend the unionist position before his election which was probably in the summer of 1445. By that time his main protagonist, Mark Eugenicus, had himself died.[186] In August 1444 the Pope, alarmed at the delay in public recognition of the union and concerned with the drive against the Ottomans, sent a legate to Constantinople. The subsequent defeat of the Christian forces at Varna in November 1444 was a blow not only to the Pope and to Constantinople, but to the unionist party, for the anti-unionists were all too ready to point out the weakness of Latin help and the well-deserved punishment inflicted on those who betrayed their Orthodox faith. Nevertheless debates between the two sides, at which the papal legate was present, continued to be held between September 1444 and November 1445. The unionists were represented by the Dominican

185a On Gregory III, see *PLP* 4591.
186 On these dates see Gill, *Council of Florence*, 365–6.

Bartholomew Lapacci, the anti-unionists by George Scholarius. Originally Scholarius had been a strong supporter of union and he was a learned man. He had been won over by Mark of Ephesus and he now led the opposition.[186a] But further discussions were really a pointless exercise, merely repeating the arguments of Florence and certainly not convincing any anti-unionists.

With John VIII's death on 31 October 1448 and the accession of his younger brother Constantine XI (as he had wished), the situation grew more tense. As Ottoman pressure increased Constantine took more active steps in support of union, and he evidently had strong backing from official circles, including Luke Notaras. The anti-unionists were intransigent. They wrote to the Pope repudiating Ferrara–Florence and suggesting a new council in Constantinople. They caused trouble in the capital and in spite of the Emperor's unionist views things became so difficult that in August 1451 the Patriarch Gregory left Constantinople for Rome. With Muhammad closing in and Rumeli Hissar rising on the European shores of the Bosphorus even more urgent pleas for western help went out, and still more bitter became the unionist controversy. On 12 December 1452 union was solemnly celebrated in Hagia Sophia and the Pope's name formally included in the diptychs. Thus the bull 'Let the heavens rejoice' was accepted, by some in good faith, by others perhaps with 'economy', and by many not at all. Nevertheless there was no general uprising against it by the populace. Perhaps the shadow of the Turkish army in the countryside beyond the walls made men feel that their last hope lay in throwing in their lot with the West. But this was not the view of the hard-core anti-unionists.

Modern writers take different views concerning the rapid breakdown of the union, sometimes understandably influenced by their own religious convictions or otherwise.[187] The two main points at issue between the Orthodox and the Latin Churches were doctrinal and ecclesiological, that is, the Trinity with the related deification (*theosis*) of man and the uncreated energies, and then church

[186a] T. N. Zèsès, *Γεννάδιος Β′ Σχολάριος* (Thessalonica, 1980).

[187] See the different views expressed by D. J. Geanakoplos, 'The Council of Florence (1438–1439) and the problem of union between the Greek and Latin Churches', *Church History*, 24 (1955), 324–46 (reprinted with revisions in *Byzantine East and Latin West*, Oxford, 1966), Gill, *Council of Florence*, and 'The sincerity of Bessarion the unionist', *JTS*, n.s. 26 (1975), 377–92, and Ševčenko, 'Intellectual repercussions'.

government by papal monarchy. Trinitarian differences were discussed under the filioque problem but there the most that can be said is that both sides finally agreed that they expressed themselves differently while holding the same truth. *Theosis*, sometimes misunderstood in the West, was not formally touched on, but there may be a hint of western criticism in the reference in the final statement on purgatory to the way in which God is known after death.[188] Similarly there was little real consideration of the basic question of papal primacy. The Roman claims were stated in the bull and were presumed aş agreed by all. On the Orthodox side this must have been with many mental reservations, for papal primacy as Rome then understood it was not accepted by the Orthodox Church.

It may be asked why the Byzantine delegates almost all signed a decree which in certain respects ran counter to their long-established tradition. It has been argued that they were worn down by prolonged absence from home in precarious and uncomfortable conditions and were under pressure from the Emperor John VIII and the Patriarch Joseph. Moreover they were fully aware of the dangers facing Constantinople and the urgent need for western aid which it was hoped would come as the result of union. It was understandable that there was overwhelming desire to return home, as well as bitter frustration at being continually out-argued by the Latins to no effect. But it is hardly true that they had been prevented by the Emperor from freely stating their case as they saw it. His nomination of Mark of Ephesus and Bessarion as the two chief Byzantine spokesmen showed a desire that both points of view should be heard. But after so many months of often fruitless discussion both Pope and Emperor did feel that some decision must be taken and perhaps to that extent pressure might be said to have been brought to bear. The majority of the delegates were not learned prelates. Apart from their weariness and strong desire to get home they may have been influenced at the time by a small group of more intellectual men who were genuinely convinced by the theology and ecclesiology of Rome. Such were Bessarion of Nicaea and Isidore of Kiev, and at the time of the council George Scholarius. For some years there had been in Constantinople an

[188] Gill, *Council of Florence*, 414, Decree of Union, '... intueri clare ipsum deum trinum et unum, sicuti est ...'. Gill, ibid., 285, comments that this was added to the decree 'to counter Greek palamitic theology', presumably the Greek distinction between essence and energies.

intellectual élite who were familiar with some of the works of such western thinkers as Augustine, Boethius, Aquinas, and in some cases had themselves been converted to Roman Catholicism. For more than two hundred years Aegean lands had been overrun with Frankish settlers and Latin clergy. Western religious houses had been established. Dominicans and Franciscans had become familiar and often respected figures in Constantinople and had acted as interpreters and envoys. So that the Greek Orthodox world was aware of the best in Roman Catholicism. At the same time at a much more homely level Greek and Latin priests and congregations in the countryside for lack of clergy or of buildings had perforce occasionally to fraternize much to the disapproval of both papacy and some Byzantine canonists. It is therefore no surprise that men such as Bessarion may well have thought that the union might work.

Mark Eugenicus knew better. He was the one learned Byzantine bishop at the council who had consistently supported Orthodox teaching and Orthodox views on church government. When he returned to Constantinople he found himself the leader of the many anti-unionists. But he had to work hard with his propaganda in the face of a small but by no means negligible unionist party which included the Emperor John VIII and the Patriarch Metrophanes II (the Emperor's choice). John VIII had been brought up in circles which were not rigidly anti-Latin. His grandfather had become a Roman Catholic. His father Manuel II counted among his close friends some of the learned Byzantine scholars who had been converted, such as Demetrius Cydones whose letters Manuel carefully preserved in a special book. On the other hand Manuel was equally aware of the best in the Orthodox world as his close ties with Nicholas Cabasilas showed. Contrary to the opinion of some modern scholars Manuel was not fanatically anti-Latin. In his oft-cited (and as yet unpublished) treatise on the filioque written during his stay in Paris he specifically stated that he was not writing to attack the Latins (as is usually assumed) but only in order to explain the Greek point of view to them.[189] Nevertheless the advice he was said to have given to his son John VIII was that of a realist. Drag out discussions on union but never actually agree to it. Thus you will

---

[189] Cod. vat. gr. 1107, f. 1. I am indebted to J. Chrysostomides for access to the microfilm of this manuscript.

keep the Turk in a state of suspense fearing lest Byzantium and the West unite. Moreover, added Manuel, any real union would prove impossible in view of the disposition of our people. Sphrantzes reported that on being given this advice John said nothing and walked out of the room in silence.[190] As events showed, he disagreed with his father. Syropoulos affirmed that at the council John declared that his father wanted the union but did not live to achieve it, leaving this task to his son, 'and so it is his work which I myself am carrying out as he commanded'.[191] This may have been wishful thinking on John's part: it does not accord with Manuel's advice to his son. Events seemed to prove that Manuel showed the sounder judgement in realizing that the Orthodox Church of his day could not be won over. But it must be admitted that the unionists' chances of success were never really tested since the political regime supporting them collapsed with the fall of the City in 1453.

The weight of ordinary public opinion in both lay and monastic circles was anti-unionist, which suited the new Ottoman rulers. George Scholarius, who had turned against the Latins, influenced by Mark Eugenicus, later became the first Patriarch under the Turks and was known by his monastic name of Gennadius. The well-known words which Ducas (probably wrongly) attributed to Luke Notaras about preferring the Turkish turban to the Latin mitre[192] may reflect a common charge made against the anti-unionists, namely, that they were pro-Turkish because they refused to come to terms with the Latins. But distrust of the Franks engendered by regrettable political circumstances did not necessarily mean that Byzantines were actively pro-Turkish. Before the actual fall of the City prophecies were circulating concerning the end of the world and the miraculous salvation of Constantinople, and many believed these. It followed that surrender to the Latin Church would not be needed.[193] In the event Patriarch Gennadius and the Byzantines with him accepted the inevitable but without any betrayal of Orthodoxy. The traditional majority thus survived, holding to the

---

[190] Sphrantzes, *Chronicon Minus*, ed. V. Grecu (Bucharest, 1966), Mem. XXIII, 5–6, pp. 58–9, *PG* 156, cols. 1046 D–1047 A.
[191] Syropoulos, *Mémoires*, IX, 15, p. 448.
[192] Ducas, *Historia byzantina*, ch. 37, 14–16 (*CB*, p. 264) and ed. V. Grecu, (Bucharest, 1958), ch. 37, 10, p. 329.
[193] See Ševčenko, 'Intellectual Repercussions', 296–300.

pentarchy and the seven general councils and the fathers, but by no means static as the hesychast movement had shown.

Apart from theological and ecclesiological issues the anti-unionists had one weighty ally which helped to nullify pro-unionist pressures. The Byzantines had long learnt to fear western ambitions as well as papal claims in the East Mediterranean and they had suffered much at the hands of the Latins. The most deadly reproach which they could utter was 'You have become a Frank'. This was deeply ingrained in the popular mind and was fomented by many of the monks, particularly in the capital. While some educated circles might stress the importance of cultural links between the West and the Greeks, this was more than countered by a widespread fear of becoming 'Latinized'. Manuel II had correctly gauged the strength of public feeling when he said that his people were not of a disposition to unite with Rome. The hasty excommunications of 1054 have now been annulled by Rome and Constantinople (1965). But it is significant that in 1971, more than 500 years after the council of Florence, Archbishop Jerome of Athens could be reported as saying to Cardinal Willebrands that it would still need much time before the faithful of the Church of Greece could forget the past unfraternal activities of Rome and be ready to take part in any movement towards Christian unity.[194]

10. The authority of the Byzantine Church in the later middle ages (c.1334–1453)

The drama of the struggle for imperial survival dominated the Aegean in the later middle ages and inevitably the Byzantine Church was closely involved in two respects. As has been shown, it had to attempt to make good the disruption to ecclesiastical life caused by the Latin conquests, and then it took part in the proposals for ending the schism with Rome. The union however broke down. The Ottoman took over the East Roman Empire. But such disasters should not be allowed to convey unmitigated failure at this time. Other more important activities were taking place within the Orthodox world which were to strengthen the Church and enable it to survive and act as a vitalizing force for Greeks, the Balkan principalities, and Russia. During a period when official documents,

[194] Secretariat for Promoting Christian Unity, Information Service, 15, 11.

polemic, and debate on the differences between Orthodox and Latin Churches seem almost to monopolize some modern treatments of the subject, the contemporary patriarchal registers provide a corrective. Selecting at random the first term of office of John XIV Calecas (February1330–2/8 February 1347), one sees at once that patriarchal activities—apart from a demanding and wide-ranging everyday administrative routine—include directives to bishops in dioceses under Turkish rule and exhortation to the faithful in such regions, condemnation of the Emperor of Trebizond's second marriage, a ruling to the metropolitan of Russia, elevation of the bishop of Galicia to the rank of metropolitan and assignment to him of suffragan bishops, the confirmation of the ordination of Gerasimus as Patriarch of Jerusalem, as well as involvement in the hesychast problems. Such entries give a lead to some of the more important developments within the Byzantine Church at the time—hesychasm and the spiritual renewal, relations with the Slav churches, arbitration in disputes and conduct within the Orthodox world whether concerning ecclesiastics or laity. In addition the patriarchs were frequently involved in political issues. This was inevitable at a time when support or otherwise of a particular religious issue, that is, hesychasm, was linked to a political party. The retention of the office of Patriarch did largely depend on imperial support and during the period of civil war between John V and Cantacuzenus, and again among the sons of John V, it was almost impossible to remain neutral. Hence various depositions and reinstatements. Such occurrences should not necessarily reflect on the Patriarch concerned.

The Orthodox monastic revival in the later middle ages was stimulated by the hesychast or contemplative way of life. As earlier, Byzantine monastic traditions greatly influenced south-east Europe and Russia, particularly through Mount Athos.[195] Then Bulgarian Paroria founded by Gregory of Sinai in the 1330s also became for a time another international centre in the Orthodox world, attracting disciples to the spiritual life of prayer, likewise Kilifarevo in the Balkan Mountains near Trnovo founded in the mid-fourteenth century by Theodosius of Trnovo with the support of the Bulgarian tsar. Serbia already had its splendid royal foundations, cenobitic, but not untouched by hesychasm. Late in the fourteenth century houses

[195] Obolensky, *Commonwealth*, 301–8 and *passim*.

were set up in Wallachia inspired by Nicodemus, an Athonite who was half Serb, half Greek, who knew the Byzantine hesychast and Patriarch Philotheus. In Russia, again under Byzantine influence, both cenobitic houses and eremitic groups flourished. Sergius of Radonezh (*c.*1314–92) founded the Great Lavra of the Trinity at Zagorsk near Moscow (still in existence). Though he himself had for a time lived an eremitic life, at Philotheus' request he adopted for his foundation the cenobitic rule of the Studite house in Constantinople. According to his *Life* the house was in touch with the Patriarchs of Constantinople.[196] Further south in the harassed and disputed lands of northern Greece a group of eremitic and cenobitic settlements, the spectacular Meteora, developed on the high isolated peaks of north-west Thessaly. The founder of the Great Meteoron, Athanasius, had become a monk while on Mount Athos where he was inspired by Gregory of Sinai. He also knew Isidore and Callistus (later Patriarchs of Constantinople) who were then living a hesychast life in a hermit settlement dependent on the house of Iviron and were directed by Gregory. Athanasius left the Holy Mountain after being attacked by Turkish raiders and found his refuge on top of one of the peaks of the curious rock formations near Kalambaka.[197]

Thus at every stage the significant role, particularly of Mount Athos, and to a lesser extent and for a limited time the Paroria, emerges. Almost all those who inspired the fourteenth-century monastic revival had received at least some of their training at one of those centres, or in some cases both, perhaps starting in a cenobitic house, and then becoming a member of a lavra, or living as a more isolated hermit. Many of these men were by no means uneducated and, as surviving *Lives* show, were often widely travelled and experienced in the spiritual life. Some left their own writings[198] and they translated from Greek into Slavonic such spiritual guides as the *Ladder* of the seventh-century John Climacus or the contemporary works of Gregory Palamas. Often they turned out to be excellent administrators, both as abbots and in the higher ranks of the clergy, as Patriarch Philotheus Coccinus, who was also something of a diplomat as well as being distinguished for his

[196] See Meyendorff, *Byzantium and the Rise of Russia*, 134.
[197] Nicol, *Meteora*, 88–105.
[198] On Calistus's writings see D. B. Gones, Τὸ συγγραφικὸν ἔργον τοῦ Οἰκουμε-νικοῦ Πατριάρχου Καλλίστου Aʹ (*Athens, 1980*).

liturgical work. This fourteenth-century movement was marked by a strongly international character, at least as far as the Orthodox world was concerned, but it owed much of its impetus to the traditions of Greek spirituality. It built up a spiritual powerhouse on which the Orthodox Church could draw during the long struggle against the Turk—and also against the Latins, for there was a deep attachment to traditional Orthodox teaching and in many ways feeling against the claims of the Roman Church was quietly strengthened. Thus when writing to the monks of Trnovo about their own patriarch, Callistus I made it clear in passing that his patriarchate was not in communion with Rome.[199]

The majority of the patriarchs in the fourteenth century were monks in the hesychast tradition. Isidore I (17 May 1347–1 March 1350) was an Athonite, Callistus I (10 June 1350–15 August 1353; beginning 1355–August 1363) had been the hegumenus of Iviron on Mount Athos, Philotheus Coccinus (end August 1353–November/ end 1354; 8 October 1364–summer 1376) had been head of the Great Lavra of Athos. Likewise monks were also among their successors. John XIV Calecas (February 1334–2/8 February 1347) was an exception; he had been chaplain to John Cantacuzenus during Andronicus III's reign and then one of the palace clergy.[200]

From the 1340s onwards two issues particularly touched the Byzantine patriarchate: its relation to the Palamites and its own position in the wider Orthodox world. Union which so dominated certain diplomatic circles (and also modern textbooks) was not to the forefront except on occasion by express imperial wish. The question of Palamite teaching, which was recognized as Orthodox by the standing synod in Constantinople in 1347 or 1351, was at first closely bound up with the two parties in the civil war between John V Palaeologus and John VI Cantacuzenus, hence the changes in the patriarchate varying with the fortunes of either party. Calecas, who turned against John Cantacuzenus, was deposed. Callistus suffered a similar setback, alternating with Philotheus. Rebuffs of this kind were frequent in Byzantine politics, witness Photius or Athanasius I, and did not necessarily reflect on the quality of the man, or his work for the Byzantine polity.

---

[199] *GR* 2442.
[200] Dates from *GR*; cf. Darrouzès, *Registre synodal* and Hunger, *Register*, on patriarchal activities.

More important than the ups and downs of office for imperial reasons were the wider influence and claims of the patriarchs during the latter years of the Empire. At a time when the imperial position was being constantly eroded by the Ottoman advance and Latin military aid being implored, the Orthodox Church went its own way, strengthened in its spiritual life and emphasizing its own powers of jurisdiction and moral authority, thus in a way unconsciously preparing for its role under Turkish domination and elsewhere. Byzantine rulers had long lost any real political control over the Balkan principalities, the Mongols were dominating north-east Russia and the pagan principality of Lithuania was supreme in the once Kievan lands. Yet the patriarchate of Constantinople could still successfully assert its ecclesiastical authority, a striking tribute to its standing. And not only in Balkan and Russian lands, for it still took the lead in the long greatly weakened eastern patriarchates and to some extent had undermined the old conception of a pentarchy of equals.

A pressing concern of the Patriarch was the reorganization and the institution of metropolitanates and bishoprics. He also had to combat as far as possible the claims to independence made by comparatively recently formed Balkan patriarchates. Serbia was a force to be reckoned with particularly in the mid-fourteenth century. In 1346 the imperialist-minded Stephen Dushan had converted the archbishopric of Peć into a patriarchate giving its head the provocative title 'Patriarch of the Serbs and Greeks'. This was disputed by Constantinople though the documentation is not always clear,[201] particularly concerning the agreement finally reached. After Dushan, Serbia tended to split up. The ruler of Serres came to terms with Constantinople in 1375 recognizing its authority.[202] Peć may have continued to use the title 'patriarch' but its head was referred to as 'archbishop' and not 'patriarch' in the Constantinopolitan chancery.[203]

In Rumanian lands north of the Danube metropolitanates were set up in the emerging principalities in Wallachia ('Ungrovlachia') at Argeş (1359)[204] and in Moldavia ('Moldovlachia') at Suceava

---

[201] See *GR* 2444 where it is pointed out that the excommunication of Dushan is based on a suspect text.
[202] Cf. M. Lascaris, *Mélanges Diehl* I (Paris, 1930), 171–5.
[203] *GR* 2663.
[204] *GR* 2411.

later in the century,[205] both recognizing Constantinople. Their metropolitans were Greek, appointed by the Great Church. In thus throwing in their lot with the Orthodox world they could act as a bulwark against Roman Catholic Hungary. They drew on Byzantine traditions through Slav channels and though ethnically outside the Slav world for some time they used a liturgy in Church Slavonic. They had close links with Mount Athos. Chariton, one of the metropolitans of Wallachia, had been the hegumenus of the Kutlumus monastery and then protos of Mount Athos. They were familiar with hesychasm through their contacts with Paroria and Kilifarevo as well as the Holy Mountain. Tismana, one of the best-known early Rumanian monastic houses, was founded by Nicodemus of Greek and Serbian parentage and formerly a monk in the Serbian house of Chilandari on Mount Athos, thus demonstrating once more the international character of Orthodox monasticism in the late middle ages.[206]

The Russian Church owed its origin to Byzantine sources and was under the patriarchate of Constantinople. Since 1250 the metropolitan of Kiev and all Russia appeared to have alternated between a Greek and a native Russian.[207] In the fourteenth century drastic territorial changes were taking place. The old Kievan principality was being absorbed into the Grand Duchy of Lithuania. In the centre and north-east the Mongols of the Golden Horde were now dominant and under their tolerant overlordship the principality of Moscow was growing in importance. These changes in the balance of power were reflected in ecclesiastical problems of organization. Originally there had been a single metropolitan of Kiev and all Russia. But with political changes and the expansion of Lithuania in the west the metropolitan had moved, first to Vladimir in 1300, and then in 1328 to Moscow, though keeping his title 'of Kiev and all Russia'. Two problems arose. The emergent duchies of Lithuania and Moscow both aspired to have the see of the Russian metropolitan, the primate of the whole region, or failing this, Lithuania claimed the right to its own metropolitan. Then there was

---

[205] V. Laurent, 'Aux origines de l'église de Moldavie', *REB*, 5 (1947), 158–70.

[206] See A. Elian, 'Byzance et les Roumains à la fin du Moyen Âge', *Proceedings of the Thirteenth International Congress of Byzantine Studies 1966* (Oxford, 1967), 195–203.

[207] D. Obolensky, 'Byzantium, Kiev and Moscow: A Study in Ecclesiastical Relations', *DOP*, 11 (1957), 21–78.

the complication of imperial politics, the desire to see the still partly pagan Lithuania attracted into the Orthodox and not the Latin world, though not at the cost of losing the goodwill of Moscow which looked as though it might get the better of the Mongols (as it eventually did). Further, from the ecclesiastical angle in the changing patriarchal circles there was some difference of opinion as to whether it was wiser to promote centralization or diversity. Philotheus was usually for the former, Callistus for the latter.

The situation was complicated in the mid-fourteenth century by the presence in Constantinople of a strong Lithuanian party of whom the disgruntled anti-Palamite Nicephorus Gregoras was a keen supporter. Lithuania wanted its metropolitan to have the title 'of Kiev and all Russia' and claims of this kind were made when in 1355 Patriarch Callistus again became Patriarch and set up Roman as metropolitan for Lithuania, in opposition to the Muscovite Alexius appointed by Philotheus in 1354. Eventually it was made clear that Roman's authority was limited to Lithuania and after his death his metropolitanate lapsed. But in the 1360s and 1370s the bitter struggle between Lithuania and Moscow led Philotheus to establish a metropolitanate of Galicia (1371), since complaints were made that the Muscovite metropolitan never visited western regions. This was followed in 1375 by the appointment of a Lithuania candidate, Cyprian, as metropolitan of Kiev and all Russia although this title was already held by Alexius, the metropolitan in Moscow. This was not well received by Moscow, though after Alexius's death in 1378 Cyprian moved to Moscow and was accepted, even so not without set-backs. The attempts of Lithuania to get the advantage in the Orthodox Church were halted in 1386 when Jagiello, the son of the pagan ruler Olgerd became a Roman Catholic and married the young queen of Poland. Henceforth Lithuania was linked to a Latin country and did not look towards Constantinople.

Cyprian's two terms of office (1379–83; 1389–1406) were notable. His activities were far-ranging. He travelled widely in his vast metropolitanate. He found himself involved in plans for joining with Poland and Hungary against the Turks—as in Constantinopolitan circles, the Turkish problem could not be ignored even in Muscovy. He specially fostered monasticism and the hesychast tradition and he himself copied works by such Byzantine guides to the spiritual life as John Climacus. In addition he was instrumental in the compilation of various Russian chronicles. In his copy (1397) of the liturgical book, the *Euchologion*, there is mention of the Byzantine Emperors in the diptychs. This raises the relation between the Muscovite ruler and the Byzantine Emperor. It became known in Constantinople that prince Basil I of Moscow (1389–1425) had opposed the metropolitan's inclusion of the imperial name in the diptychs. The Byzantine Patriarch, then Antony IV (1389–90; 1391–7), wrote to 'the king of Moscow' reproaching him, 'It is not good that you say "We have a Church, but not an Emperor, nor is this a matter for concern to us" ', and he continued 'It is not possible for Christians to have a Church and no Emperor, for the Empire and the Church have great unity and fellowship and they cannot be separated one from the other.'[208] And he continued at length on the oecumenical sovereignty of the basileus and autocrator of the Romans.[209]

That the late fourteenth century was a time of fast diminishing political power in certain respects made no difference to the Byzantines. The Emperor could still attempt to assert his personal authority in many fields in spite of reduced financial and military resources, though it may have been quietly ignored as in the case of some Muscovite rulers. John V Palaeologus thought it worth while to get synodal confirmation of nine articles defining his authority in exercising control over high ecclesiastical and lay personnel. In most cases he was probably only reasserting what had long been imperial practice but there were one or two additions, for example the right to nominate high officials (archons) in the Great Church and the right of veto in the election of metropolitans who had to promise loyalty to the Emperor (this was probably due to awkward episcopal partisanship during civil war, or even co-operation with the Turk). The Emperor was defined as 'defensor' of the Church and the canons.[210] But he did not exercise his rights within the patriarchate of Constantinople unchallenged, otherwise he would not have taken the trouble to call a special synod in the Studite house to confirm and further define these. He could still control

---

[208] MM, vol. 2, no. 447, pp. 190–1; GR 2931 (dated here Sept.–Oct. 1393); trans. E. Barker, *Social and Political Thought in Byzantium* (Oxford, 1957), 194–6.

[209] On the tangled Byzantino-Russian relations see Meyendorff, *Byzantium and the Rise of Russia*.

[210] GR 2699; V. Laurent, 'Les Droits de l'empereur en matière ecclésiastique: L'Accord de 1380/1382', *REB*, 13 (1955), 5–20 (with text and trans.).

patriarchal appointments. The fourteenth century is filled with patriarchal depositions and reinstatements dictated by the political needs of the moment which were often vital in a century of civil wars.

Patriarchs might go in and out of office at imperial will but certainly in the second half of the fourteenth century they had no hesitation in affirming their authority in terms which seemed to run as contrary to the long-held Orthodox theory of the pentarchy and collegial responsibility as did the papal claim to universal primacy. Patriarch Philotheus, addressing the princes (*reges*) of all Russia in 1370, wrote 'Since God has appointed Our Humility as leader of all Christians found anywhere on the inhabited earth (οἰκουμένη), as solicitor and guardian of their souls, all of them depend on me, the father and teacher of them all'.[211] In his letter to prince Basil of Moscow Patriarch Antony IV stressed that he was occupying the throne of Christ and was acting for him.[212] And, as he pointed out, the Byzantines might have lost many places and lands, but in contrast Christianity was being preached everywhere, and here he must surely have been thinking of the wide diffusion of Orthodoxy.

[211] GR 2580; MM, vol. 1, no. 266, p. 521, trans. Meyendorff, *Byzantium and the Rise of Russia*, 283–4. This may of course have been a traditional use of 'oecumene'.

[212] MM, vol. 2, no. 447, p. 189.

PART II

ORGANIZATION AND LIFE OF THE ORTHODOX CHURCH IN BYZANTIUM

1. Collegiality: the emergence of the pentarchy; the position of Constantinople

Originally the Christian Church grew up within the Roman Empire, sometimes persecuted, sometimes tolerated, one of many religions, officially frowned on because it did not subscribe to emperor-worship. Faith and tenacity enabled it to survive. When in the early fourth century it was recognized by the Roman Emperor Constantine I it had already taken root in the cities of the Empire, spreading out into the countryside around. Its organization was based on that of the civil administration and it was the bishops of the great cities who took the lead in church affairs—Rome, Alexandria, and Antioch—and this they could do openly from the days of Constantine onward. With the foundation of Constantine's capital, Constantinople, a different situation was created. As 'New Rome' and the centre of the eastern half of the Empire it emancipated itself from the ecclesiastical jurisdiction of the metropolitan of Heracleia in Thrace and claimed second place in the hierarchy next to Old Rome. In 381 this was recognized by the second general council, Constantinople I, thus displacing powerful Alexandria. By the end of the fourth century Christianity had become more than a tolerated faith as it had been under Constantine I, for Theodosius proscribed all non-Christian religions. Thus strengthened the Church sought to define its beliefs. The vital theological issues and the rivalries of the fifth and sixth centuries are outside the scope of this book. But by the early seventh century, though some doctrinal problems still remained unresolved, ecclesiastical organization had taken shape and the pentarchy had emerged, consisting of the bishops of five cities, the Pope of Rome, and the Patriarchs of Constantinople, Alexandria, Antioch, and Jerusalem. The first four were of political as well as apostolic significance. Jerusalem was given its position by reason of its special association with the life of Christ on earth.

When in the seventh century the Muslims conquered the lands of the Roman Empire in North Africa, Egypt, Syria, and Palestine the situation changed and church government took on its medieval pattern. The Patriarchs of Alexandria, Antioch, and Jerusalem lived on but were under a non-Christian regime, outside the contracted bounds of the Roman Empire and this orthodox Church now found itself side by side with the separated non-Chalcedonian Churches, either monophysite or Nestorian (these latter were largely in Persian territory). Although the three eastern patriarchs continued when possible to take part in conciliar and other discussions, clearly they were not of anything like the same importance in the Christian world as Rome and Constantinople. Further, in the course of the fifth to the eighth centuries the political situation in what had been the western half of the Roman Empire radically altered. The sixth-century efforts of Justinian I had failed to regain for the Roman Empire its western provinces which were settled by immigrant Germanic peoples and out of the wanderings of Lombards, Franks, Visigoths, there grew up the independent principalities of western medieval Europe. Italy long remained a bridgehead and East Rome struggled, in the end unsuccessfully, to contest the claims of Lombard, Frank, and Muslim, as well as those of the papacy which had been endowed with temporalities by gift of the victorious Carolingians. It was not however until the late eleventh century that Byzantium was finally evicted from Italian lands. From then onwards the Byzantine Empire, which had to some extent reasserted itself on its eastern reaches, had to give way before a threefold attack: ambitious vigorous western feudatories, a new wave of Turkic peoples in the east, and pressure from the young principalities in the Balkans.

Against this background Byzantium reached its greatest strength in the tenth and early eleventh centuries, after that it slowly lost ground to its Latin and Muslim rivals and was finally integrated into the fifteenth-century Ottoman Empire. In contrast the Orthodox Church did not succumb. As already described in Part I, it held its own in the face of continuing and increasing challenge from the Latin Church. Like the medieval East Roman Empire, the Orthodox Church was not static during the five hundred years from the seventh to the mid-fifteenth centuries nor, as one modern western medievalist would have it, can it be described as 'the Greek Church in a state of slow decline'. It has to be thought of in terms of the patriarchate of Constantinople, since historical circumstances meant that it was only this branch which could take the lead, though the three eastern patriarchates continued their rather shadowy life, unable to take any effective initiative in the ecclesiastical world and in practice virtually subordinate to Constantinople.

The jurisdiction of the patriarchate of Constantinople as shown in the various episcopal lists[1] extended over the provinces within the Empire, and over the countries it converted to Christianity, such as the Balkans, at times provinces of the Empire and at times independent principalities, or the various Russian principalities, never politically integrated into Byzantium. Thus through the medieval centuries the patriarchate of Constantinople gradually expanded or contracted. The annexation of South Italy and Illyricum, the recapture of Crete, added metropolitans and bishops to the list, as did the new Balkan episcopates. On the other hand with the eleventh-century Norman conquests in South Italy, the Greek monasteries and churches increasingly recognized Latin jurisdiction, though keeping their own usages. And Muslim inroads into Byzantine territory in Asia Minor meant that many bishops fled to Constantinople or to Nicaea (from 1204–61) or to Epirus thus deserting their dioceses. Fluctuating fortune in the later middle ages often made it difficult to know who was in charge of a diocese.

Throughout these changes the Orthodox Church under the leadership of Constantinople maintained that ecclesiastical decisions on major issues must be made by a pentarchy of the original five leading sees supported by episcopal consensus in a general council and it became increasingly difficult to reconcile with papal claims to universal primacy.

2. The patriarchate of Constantinople and the Emperor

Such fluctuations in the territorial extent of the patriarch of Constantinople were in a sense peripheral to the life and development of the medieval Church within the Byzantine Empire and in no way lessened its claims to authority. It accepted limitations of time and space without sacrificing either its belief or its spirituality and it was in no sense 'a department of state' as some modern scholars would have it. It was an integral part of the East Roman polity and as such had a special relationship with the Emperor, the Christian ruler who was regarded as the vicegerent of Christ. Both

[1] See below, *Notitiae Episcopatuum*, section 4, pp. 310–12.

Graeco-Roman and Jewish traditions had accorded religious authority to the ruler. The Christian Emperor was not worshipped as divine as in the Hellenistic world (this is what the Christians had objected to), but he did have a special and indeed unique position as the representative of Christ responsible for the good government of the Empire. This was assumed from Constantine I's day and is clearly stated by Justinian I in his novels. The Christian polity was made up of the priesthood (*sacerdotium*) and the Empire (*basileia*) and they should work together, the one promoting orthodoxy, the other regulating human affairs.[2] But the Emperor had an overall responsibility for both civil and canon law. 'If we make every effort to enforce civil laws, how much more should we not try to enforce the canons and the divine laws designed for the salvation of our souls?'[3] The position accorded to the Byzantine Emperor thus reflected the integration of non-Christian and Christian elements. He was an autocrator whose absolute authority was tempered by his ultimate responsibility for good government in all spheres of the Christian life.

The Emperor's position was emphasized in the elaborate ritual of his public life which was shared by church dignitaries, officers of state, and members of the court and imperial household. Protocol was strictly observed and much of its detail can be found in the tenth-century *Book of Ceremonies* which Constantine VII drew up for his son. The procedures thus described did not leap into being, ready made. They date from various periods and resulted from gradual changes in practice over the centuries moving from pagan to Christian and reflecting an increasing predominance of the religious elements.[4] There seems to have been an increased emphasis on the religious element in the late sixth and early seventh centuries. For instance the God-given Emperor of the acclamations for the fifth century Leo I—'God gave you to us. God will guard you'[5]—

---

[2] *Corpus*, III, Nov. 6, Praef., pp. 35–6.

[3] *Corpus*, III, Nov. 109, Epilogue, pp. 519–20.

[4] Cf. E. Kitzinger, 'The Cult of the Images in the Age before Iconoclasm', *DOP*, 8 (1954), 121–8 and A. Cameron, 'Images of Authority: Élites and Icons in late Sixth-Century Byzantium', *Past and Present*, 84 (1979), 3–25; reprinted in *Byzantium and the Classical Tradition*, ed. M. Mullett and R. Scott (Birmingham, 1981).

[5] *De Cerimoniis*, I. 91 (*CB*, I, p. 411).

was originally crowned in the imperial palace, but by the early seventh century this took place in a church, soon to be established as the patriarchal Great Church of Hagia Sophia and accompanied by an elaborate liturgy stressing the divine nature of the appointment. Whatever part may have been played by army, senate, and people, it was God who placed power in imperial hands and set up the Emperor as autocrator. There was no intermediary between God and the Emperor, but a resolute Patriarch could impose certain limitations on imperial activities or demands if he disapproved of these. Such was Polyeuctus's refusal to accord the status of martyr to Nicephorus II's troops who fell in battle.

The position of the Emperor in the civilized world, the *oecumene*, and his direct link with God were stressed in the elaborate ceremonial at receptions, banquets, and audiences in the vast halls of the Great Palace, particularly the Golden Hall (*chrysotriclinus*), the main throne room. The same emphasis characterized the festivals of the Christian year celebrated in Hagia Sophia and in other churches in the capital, often accompanied by processions to particularly venerated shrines, as the Blachernae church which housed the robe of Theotokos. Secular and religious elements were closely integrated. Ambassadors were formally received in the main throne room where in the post-iconoclast period Christian themes associated with the Empire were stressed, as in the icon of Christ in majesty above the imperial throne and the Theotokos standing as the protector of the City. Thus at every turn figural art stressed the link between the heavenly and the earthly kingdom.[6] It was the same with the ritual and responses in the liturgy. And in the festivals linked with episodes in the life of Christ the Emperor had a special role. Everything stressed his unique and sacred character though he never had the authority of the priesthood. Within Hagia Sophia there was (as in the imperial palace) a special porphyry rota where the Emperor stood to pray before entering the sanctuary at special times. Ritual was laid down whereby he met the Patriarch in the narthex at the Royal Door. The procession, imperial guards, court, clergy, then entered the cathedral, before the people crowding the outer narthex and atrium were admitted. Further details can be

[6] Grabar, *Iconoclasme*, 34 and *passim*, illustrates the widespread use of figural representation to further imperial prestige.

found in the Emperor Constantine VII's *Book of Ceremonies*, supplemented by the fourteenth-century Pseudo-Codinus. It was an elaborate procedure, difficult if not impossible to maintain to the full in the disordered years after 1204, though the very existence of the Pseudo-Codinus points to the tenacity with which the Byzantines held to all that their ceremonial symbolized even in the late middle ages. But the Pseudo-Codinus also reflects changes which had come about since the tenth century, such as the permanent establishment within the capital and across the Golden Horn of various privileged foreign groups, particularly the Genoese, who had to be accorded a place in such ceremonial as was possible.[7]

The precise authority of the Emperor in ecclesiastical affairs has been much disputed and certainly often misunderstood through failure to realize the nature of the Byzantine polity and the close integration of imperial and ecclesiastical interests. On the threshold of the medieval era the fifth-century Pope Leo I made it clear that it was the imperial duty to promote orthodoxy, but not in the sense of determining faith which fell to an episcopal general council. The imperial role was to summon the general council and to confirm and promulgate its decisions. Throughout the medieval period this remained the imperial position though it was on occasion infringed, as in the seventh century and in the iconoclast period. Certainly the Emperor was responsible for implementing conciliar decisions. He also legislated freely in disciplinary and administrative matters affecting the Church, and on occasion against the will of Patriarch and metropolitans. He was closely concerned with the suppression of heresy. In fact almost at every turn it seemed to be chance whether the Emperor or the Church took the initiative in providing good ecclesiastical government or in protecting orthodox tradition, matters in which they both had a common interest. The Byzantines themselves did not always agree on the nature of imperial authority. The twelfth-century canonist Balsamon sometimes went as far as to imply that the Emperor was above canon law. Certainly long before Balsamon he was called the 'living' or 'animate law' (*empsychos nomos*), an oriental and Hellenist legacy embodied in Justinian I's novel 105.[8] The thirteenth-century canonist Demetrius Chomatianus called him the epistemonarches, meaning the super-

---

[7] Cf. Pseudo-Codinus, ch. 4, pp. 234–5.
[8] *Corpus*, III, Nov. 105, 2, 4, p. 507.

visor or director in divine matters.[9] This was generally interpreted as the guardianship of orthodoxy rather than the right to initiate or innovate in doctrinal matters, whatever his prerogative in other affairs. All the same it will at once come to mind that during the 800 years or so from the seventh to the fifteenth century there were instances of imperial attempts to solve doctrinal issues, such as monotheletism or iconoclasm. Their interventions might take the form of pronouncements, as the Type of Constans II, but more generally they sought to fortify themselves with conciliar support. In the long run if Emperors were considered to have deviated from true doctrine, their rulings were repudiated and the orthodox faith re-established by a council, as in the case of iconoclasm and Nicaea II (787), the last general council recognized by the Orthodox Church. After this there were no major doctrinal issues in which the Emperor was personally involved and few clashes between Emperor and Church, the exceptions being Lyons II (1274) and Ferrara–Florence (1438–9) both of which were to some extent called forth by reason of dire Byzantine need for western military aid, however much there was a genuine desire on both sides for the reunion of the Churches.

An occasional fierce monastic voice might exhort the Emperor to confine himself to purely secular affairs. Such was the view of the redoubtable Theodore Studites, but his understandable outburst was evoked in the heat of the iconoclast controversy when imperial policy was attacking orthodoxy and in general his views were not shared. Given the medieval Roman Empire, it was appropriate that its ruler should have a special function within the Christian polity. Thus the political theory of East Rome developed on different lines from that of contemporary western kingdoms. In the Latin world there was a more clear-cut division between church and state and its 'patriarch', the Pope, occupied a relatively detached position *vis-à-vis* various rulers such as the Capetians or Angevins, and his closer association with the would-be 'Roman' emperors, the Carolingians and their successors, bore little if any resemblance to the relationship between the Patriarch of Constantinople and the genuine successors of the Caesars in New Rome.

---

[9] *PG* 119, col. 949B, to Const. Cabasilas, Resp. 1; and Pitra, *Analecta Sacra*, vol. 6 (Paris-Rome, 1891), Resp. 4, col. 634; RP V, p. 429.

3. Canon law: the nomocanons

The exceptional executive position of the Emperor and the implicit limitations on his authority were exemplified in the rulings governing the Church. The distinction between doctrine and discipline is at once apparent. In one of his *Dialogues* between a Greek and a Latin the twelfth-century Basil of Ochrida, Archbishop of Thessalonica, began with the pronouncement 'We have no doubt as to the foundations of our belief—the Gospels, the apostolic and patristic traditions and the canons of the holy general councils'.[10] In addition certain local councils of the fourth and fifth centuries as well as the 'Photian' councils of Constantinople 859–61 and 879–80 were accepted. The council in Trullo[11] or Quinisextum (691–2) was regarded as a supplement to the Fifth and Sixth general councils. It was held that a general council should produce both dogmatic and disciplinary acta, and the Quinisextum supplied the disciplinary canons missing from the Fifth and Sixth councils. These 102 canons were particularly important for the Orthodox Church, but they were not accepted by the West. The 'apostolic tradition' meant the eighty-five 'Apostolic' Canons dating from the pre-Nicaean period, but not of apostolic origin. These dealt with church order and were formally recognized by the Quinisextum which however rejected an apocryphal collection, the 'Apostolic Constitutions'. Only fifty of the Apostolic Canons, translated in the fifth century by Dionysius Exiguus, found their way into the Latin tradition. The 'patristic tradition' was varied and could be contradictory. In general it implied the late third to fifth-century fathers, men such as John Chrysostom and the Cappadocian churchmen, particularly the often quoted St Basil the Great. The later eighth-century St John of Damascus was also revered. As Basil of Ochrida said, these sources formed the basic tradition of the canon law of the Orthodox Church. But they were supplemented in various ways.

The most important additional source was imperial legislation on ecclesiastical matters. On occasion Emperors made doctrinal pronouncements, for instance during the monophysite and monothelite controversies, but such decisions were confirmed (or rejected) by general councils. The iconoclast rulings were rejected by the council

---

[10] J. Schmidt, *Des Basilius aus Achrida, Erzbischofs von Thessalonich, bisher unedierte Dialoge* (Munich, 1901), p. 41.
[11] So called from the domed hall in which it was held.

of Nicaea II. Matters of heresy came within the purview of the ecclesiastical authorities, but the Emperor was also closely involved. He and his officials could be present at the standing synod in Constantinople which after the ninth century was considered the appropriate body to deal with such matters. Byzantine Emperors were also much addicted to theology and took part in, or themselves arranged, informal and even formal, discussions on disputed doctrinal topics before the matter reached the synod for debate and official pronouncement.[12] The heresies condemned could, if the synod so decided, be added to the Synodicon of anathemas read out in church each year on the first Sunday of Lent. The criteria for dealing with basic Trinitarian and Christological questions to which most heresies could be related, had already been laid down in the seven general councils, supplemented by the patristic writings. Here the Emperor did not have the final word.

It was different in disciplinary matters where decisions often (but not always) had to be implemented by the civil authorities. Here the Emperor pronounced on innumerable topics, particularly in the earlier middle ages, as is evidenced by Justinian's novels. After his time care for ecclesiastical organization continued to be regarded as an integral part of imperial responsibilities.[13] Later Emperors, as Leo VI, or Nicephorus II, issued edicts or codes in which for instance marriage laws, or monastic houses, were regulated. There were innumerable special cases in which immunities were granted to individuals or to a monastic house by imperial edict. Ecclesiastical organization was another field for imperial regulation, promotion from bishop to metropolitan, or the fusing of two dioceses, or creation of new ones. Action of this kind did not always go unchallenged by the ecclesiastical authority, usually the standing synod in Constantinople, as in Alexius I's reign. But in general the imperial right to share in the regulation of the Church in disciplinary matters was accepted.

Thus there were two sources of canon law, imperial and ecclesiastical, and they were not always in accord either within themselves or with each other. They were brought together in collections known as nomocanons in which the two classes of rulings (νόμοι

---

[12] See above, ch. VI *passim*.
[13] On the imperial position see H.-G. Beck, 'Nomos, Kanon und Staatsraison in Byzanz', *Österreichische Ak. der Wiss.*, Philosoph.-Hist.Kl., Sitzungsberichte 384 (Vienna, 1981).

and κανόνες) were set out. The most important of these was the *Nomocanon in XIV Titles* put together by the Anonymous II in the seventh century. This was not the only ecclesiastical code. There was also a sixth-century collection of fifty titles, later expanded in the ninth century. But the *Nomocanon in XIV Titles* was probably the most widely used during the middle ages.[14] It continued to be supplemented by additions or explanations both from imperial and ecclesiastical sources. The legal codes of the iconoclasts, the *Basilics*, the *Epanagoge*, the novels of Leo VI, all contained rulings which concerned the Church. Though never an official handbook, it was the *Epanagoge* which defined the inseparable bonds binding church and state, Emperor and Patriarch. There were too the rulings of the patriarchs and of the standing synod. When problems arose reference would be made to the canons of the general councils or the patristic writings or the 'apostolic' tradition, as well as to the imperial codes of Justinian, and then to the *Basilics* of the early Macedonian period and subsequent imperial and patriarchal rulings.

There were not only inconsistencies within the body of commentaries. Contradictory opinions might be found within the works of the same church fathers. Often circumstances very different from those of the early Empire had to be reckoned with. It was in the intellectually active twelfth century that three distinguished canonists, urged on by the Comnenian Emperors, made a major attempt to clarify some of the conflicting and complicated rulings of canon law. These canonists were John Zonaras, Alexius Aristenus, and Theodore Balsamon, and like the canons on which they commented they did not always agree in their interpretations.

Zonaras, noted as a historian as well as a canonist, had been in imperial service. Under Alexius I he was commander of the imperial guard and head (protoasecretis) of the imperial chancery. He ended his life as a monk on one of the Princes Islands. He commented at length on the Apostolic Canons, the synods, and the church fathers. His balanced judgements were used by later commentators (sometimes without acknowledgement).

His successor in this field was Alexius Aristenus who had been nomophylax and orphanotrophus, and then oeconomus of the

---

[14] On these basic codifications and the subsequent stream of commentaries and minor legal writings see Beck, *Kirche, sub* Kanonisches Recht; H. Scheltema, 'Byzantine Law', *CMH* IV (2), and *DDrC* 2, 'Byzantin: Droit canonique' (C. de Clercq); see also the Vatican series issued by the *Codificazione Canonica Orientale, Fonti*, fasc. 8.

Great Church. He was asked by John II Comnenus to provide a commentary on the *synopsis canonum*, a collection attributed to Symeon Metaphrastes. Aristenus was later used by Balsamon. His work was also of considerable influence in the Slav Balkans.

The best known of the twelfth-century canonists was the learned Theodore Balsamon who was active under Manuel I Comnenus and Isaac II Angelus. He became one of the leading deacons of the Great Church and he held the key office of chartophylax. He regarded this office as being of supreme importance, 'the gateway to the secretariat', and he wrote a discourse on the subject.[15] At some time between 1184 and 1191 under Isaac Comnenus he was elected Patriarch of Antioch but he never went to live in his see. He was essentially a man with interests rooted in the capital and he liked to enlarge on the effects of the alleged Donation of Constantine and the so-called translation of power to New Rome. He was bitterly opposed to the growing claims of the Latins whom he regarded as heretics.

It was at the request of Manuel I (well known for his theological interests) and Patriarch Michael III of Anchialus that he set about commenting on the vast canonical collections, the accumulation of nearly a thousand years. It was a gigantic programme and taxed all the resources of Balsamon's extensive legal knowledge. He also had to deal with the special problem posed by the omission of some of Justinian's ecclesiastical legislation from the later code, the *Basilics*, which raised the question of the validity of Justinian's legislation. There were also the many ecclesiastical and imperial rulings made after *Basilics*.[16] Where differences appeared to be irreconcilable Balsamon seemed to prefer the canonical ruling.[17] As chartophylax Balsamon was also responsible for drawing up one of the two extant versions (probably the final one) of the replies which the standing synod had made to queries raised by Mark, Patriarch of Alexandria, when he was in Constantinople. Mark was worried by problems which were constantly arising in a minority patriarchate set amid non-Chalcedonians in a Muslim-governed land.[18]

---

[15] 'On the offices of chartophylax and protecdicus', RP IV. 530 ff.

[16] On Balsamon and his programme see *DDrC* vol. 2, cols. 76–83 (E. Herman); cf. H. Scheltema, op. cit., for comments on the legal background to Balsamon's work.

[17] Tit. I, cap. 2, schol. 2, RP I. pp. 37–8.

[18] See V. Grumel, 'Les Réponses canoniques à Marc d'Alexandrie, leur caractère officiel, leur double rédaction', *EO*, 38 (1939), 321–33.

Balsamon was an arrogant man with an inflated idea of the office of chartophylax. He was rigid and harsh in his attitude towards the non-Chalcedonians. 'Do not throw holy things to the dogs' was his uncompromising beginning when considering them. He ruled that Latin prisoners could not be given communion in Orthodox churches unless they had totally repudiated Latin dogma and usages. Churches, he continued, may not be shared with heretics, that is Latins, Nestorians, Jacobites. Anathema to those who associate with them.[19] Balsamon was certainly a major influence in Orthodox canon law in the later middle ages, but some of his views did not go unchallenged. In the thirteenth century in reply to the query raised by Constantine Cabasilas, metropolitan of Durazzo, 'Must we adhere to Balsamon's rulings in canon and civil law?' it was stressed that Balsamon was not always right, a view 'which I heard many legal experts in Constantinople expressing during Balsamon's lifetime.'[20]

The tolerant and humane Demetrius Chomatianus was less well known than Theodore Balsamon and in the long run probably far less influential. He pursued legal studies in Constantinople in the late twelfth century and would have known Theodore Balsamon. He became chartophylax in Ochrida in Bulgaria and then in 1217 archbishop. He had close links with the rulers of the Greek kingdom of Epirus. Unlike Balsamon sitting in Constantinople before the catastrophe of 1204, Chomatianus had to live with the effects of the Latin occupation. It was a time of uncertain and constantly changing boundaries and posed queries concerning ownership and use of churches calling for the tolerance of a Theophylact of Bulgaria (whom Chomatianus was fond of citing). In response to queries from Constantine Cabasilas, metropolitan of Durrazzo, an attitude very different from that of Balsamon was shown. It was pointed out how much Greeks and Latins had in common, the Scriptures, music, preaching, icon veneration, adoration of the Holy Cross, though at the same time without forgetting real differences, as the filioque and to a lesser extent unleavened bread.[21] The surviving works of Chomatianus[22] show him dealing with

[19] *PG* 138, col. 965.
[20] *PG* 119, cols. 981–4 (here attributed to John, bishop of Kitros, but probably by Demetrius Chomatianus).
[21] *PG* 119, cols. 960–4.
[22] Listed by L. Stiernon, *DHGE* 14, cols. 201–5 (with bibliography).

both secular and ecclesiastical problems arising in the Macedonian countryside as well as further afield. The frequency with which he was asked to adjudicate in all manner of secular, even economic problems as well as ecclesiastical contingencies points both to his own reputation and to the extent to which the Church was increasingly regarded as the stable factor in a disintegrating society. Problems referred to him range from a plea for help in countering a conspiracy to murder in which it was planned to dump the victim into a deserted stretch of sea (the boat was ready waiting) to the relations between Greek and Latin clergy in the border regions, and here in direct contrast to Balsamon Chomatianus found it permissible to enter Latin churches. He was confronted with every kind of marriage problem—the rival claims of legitimate and illegitimate children, or of a mistress whose claim to a vineyard and an ox was challenged by angry relations on the ground that she had bought these out of the housekeeping money. He was consulted by his fellow ecclesiastics of Jannina and Anactoropolis. A Greek monk Gregory travelled from Athos to appeal for his ruling, since the Greek monks living in Iviron were troubled as to whether they could communicate with the Georgian monks in the house who, under pressure from the Latin authorities in Thessalonica, had submitted to Rome.[23] As with Balsamon, though in a very different spirit, Chomatianus's rulings were of value both from the strictly legal aspect and as reflecting situations for which there was little if any precedent. In the case of Chomatianus his activities were marked by an involvement in secular cases which was to increase among churchmen during the later middle ages.[24]

It was the work of a fourteenth-century canonist that was most used in the later middle ages and after. Matthew Blastares[25] was a hieromonk from Mount Athos who settled in Thessalonica. In 1335 he produced his *Syntagma*. This set out a summary of ecclesiastical

---

[23] For Chomatianus's rulings and letters see Pitra, *Analecta Sacra*, 6, *passim*. This collection affords rich and graphic material for social and economic as well as ecclesiastical affairs.

[24] Extracts from the twelfth-century canonists and Chomatianus on ecclesiastical problems can be found in Latin translation in *Codificazione Canonica Orientale, Fonti*, serie II, fasc. 5, *Textus Selecti ex Operibus Commentatorum Byzantinorum Iuris Ecclesiastici*, ed. I. Croce with introduction by E. Herman (Vatican, 1939).

[25] See *DDrC* 2. 920–5 (E. Herman); most of his writings are in RP VI and PG 144.

law (both canon and civil) arranged alphabetically. It relied on the *Nomocanon in XIV Titles* and gave the gist of the comments of Zonaras and Balsamon. Much of the civil law was taken from the *Basilics*. The merit of this compendium was its conciseness and convenient alphabetical arrangement. It rapidly attained popularity particularly in the Balkans and Russia. In Serbia it was translated into the Slav language in the mid-fourteenth century. It was also used by later Greek canonists and was long regarded as authoritative.

The other late medieval canonist of note was Constantine Harmenopoulus. He belonged to Thessalonica and became nomophylax and a General Judge. He was best known for his *Hexabiblos* which dealt only in part with canon law. He also produced an *Epitome* of the canons which was much used.[26]

It was the leading twelfth-century jurists, Zonaras, Aristenus, and particularly Balsamon, who contributed the most important work on canon law in the later period. Their commentaries and sifting broke the ground by interpreting the old rulings to meet conditions in a rapidly changing society. But in this field as elsewhere there were marked differences in attitude. Balsamon's rigidity and intolerance towards the westerners could only make for difficulties in an Empire where the presence of Latins even in the twelfth century was becoming a fact of everyday life. A different point of view was shown by Demetrius Chomatianus. Unlike Balsamon he was faced with the full consequences of a partial political conquest. He was more constructive in his approach both to an alien society and to the ecclesiastical problems posed by the presence of two Churches often inadequately served in respect of buildings and priests.

4. *The* Notitiae Episcopatuum: *the higher clergy and imperial ceremonial*

Whatever may be argued to the contrary, there is plenty of evidence to show that as far as the upper reaches were concerned, there was in Byzantium a strong sense of order ($\tau\acute{\alpha}\xi\iota\varsigma$). Anyone of rank or office whether lay or clerical had his own fixed place in the hierarchy. This was set out in official lists and a glance at these lists

---

[26] *Hexabiblos*, ed. W. E. Heimbach (Leipzig, 1851) and K. Pitsakes (Athens, 1971) and for his other works see *PG* 150; see also Hunger, *Profanliteratur*, II, 474f. and *PLP* 1347.

shows how extensive a range was covered particularly for the imperial household and for civil and military administration. They did also indicate the geographical distribution of the sees. The four eastern patriarchates each had their own list, though the vicissitudes of the middle ages (Muslim and sporadic Frankish conquests) meant that the Constantinopolitan *Notitia* became the most important list for Byzantium.[27]

Precise dating of the tweny-one *Notitiae Episcopatuum* edited by Darrouzès appears difficult to fix but the lists seem to have been revised at irregular intervals, under Leo VI, in the late twelfth century, and then, after the confused diocesan organization in the troubled Frankish conquests, in the mid-fourteenth century, while *Notitia 20*, the *Ecthesis Nea*, comes from the end of the fourteenth century. Lists (like the Church itself) continued under Turkish rule; *Notitia 21* is from the end of the fifteenth century. Changes in the order of metropolitans or episcopal sees often reflected expansion or contraction of imperial territory. The eighth-century acquisition of the dioceses of South Italy, Sicily, and Illyricum meant that these now came under the jurisdiction of Constantinople, thus bringing in Thessalonica, one of the most important cities of the Empire. In the eastern regions names continued to appear on the list, though the territories in question were under Muslim rule and their bishops often refugees in Constantinople. Changes in the list might come about through the elevation of a suffragan bishop to the rank of metropolitan, as in Alexius I's reign when it was considered that the Emperor should not have acted without consulting the standing synod. Sees might be doubled up as in Asia Minor whither Christian inhabitants had fled before the Turks or been converted to Islam and episcopal resources were almost nil. Another feature of later *Notitiae* was the creation of a number of sees in the near vicinity of Constantinople. This had its repercussion on ecclesiastical politics since the additional prelates could swell the numbers of the standing synod and if necessary provide support for Emperor or Patriarch against the powerful office-holders of the Great Church.

The *Notitiae Episcopatuum* were of practical value. They determined the order in which bishops appended their signatures to

---

[27] The definitive text with trans. and commentary is now J. Darrouzès, *Notitiae Episcopatuum Ecclesiae Constantinopolitanae* (Paris, 1981); see also Beck, *Kirche*, 148–88, and 188–99 for the *Notitiae* of Alexandria, Antioch, and Jerusalem.

conciliar acta. They were used when bishops took part in imperial ceremonies and the current list would often be found appended to the *Tactica*. The best known of the *Tactica* are the ninth- and tenth-century lists and the much later fourteenth-century Pseudo-Codinus.[28] These set out the order of precedence of dignitaries and functionaries in imperial ceremonial, such as audiences or banquets or ceremonies connected with the festivals of the Christian year or the holding of synods. They are relevant here because high ecclesiastics were an integral part of the polity. They appear in the *Tactica* as 'the metropolitans', or 'the archbishops' and the current *Notitia* would be consulted to determine the order of each particular group.

Imperial protocol for formal occasions was almost always linked to the Church's calendar, though on occasion traces of pagan festivals, as the Brumalia, still lingered on. The various *Tactica* describe the splendid processions across the City, the rich clothes appropriate to each grade and occasion, the accompanying entertainments, the organ and singing by the cantors and by the orphans, thus bringing to life the ritual and symbolism of the imperial way of life which so impressed foreign visitors. Many classes participated in this. The Epiphany celebrations were particularly resplendent and those present included the priests, deacons, subdeacons, readers, and cantors from the Palace and Great Church and the Nea, as well as the clergy of the patriarchal secretariat (papades) and selected poor. And though not guests, the populace at large could at least enjoy the processions just as crowds still enjoy public spectacles. Such ecclesiastical occasions demonstrated the indissoluble link between church and state.

5. *The oecumenical Patriarch and his election*

The Church, like the secular government, had its own institutions and administrative departments. These were marked by conservative adherence to tradition. There was also change in emphasis and detail. But intermittent and scanty sources make it difficult to follow the development of such changes. Circumstances seemed to

---

[28] See N. Oikonomides, *Les Listes de préséance byzantines des IXe et Xe siècles* (text, trans. and full commentary, Paris, 1972); Pseudo-Codinos; Philotheus's protocol for ceremonies (dated 899) was included in the *De Cerimoniis*.

have been met as they arose; in a sense this was living by 'economy', adaptability, despite efforts at strict adherence to hierarchical status as laid down in the (occasionally revised) *Notitiae Episcopatuum* or the imperial handbooks on protocol. Moreover Byzantine ecclesiastical history was riddled with conflicts over authority spurred on by a passion for debate.

In the post-sixth-century period the final choice of a patriarch rested with the Emperor. Initially the metropolitans met in the standing synod in Constantinople and selected three names. Only they could vote, but as in other synodal business, views could be expressed unofficially by others outside the metropolitan circle, such as the leading officials of the Great Church. The three names were submitted to the Emperor who could either select one of these or a fourth candidate of his own choice. The *De Cerimoniis* describes in detail how the announcement (μήνυμα) and investiture (πρόβλη- σις) were made by the Emperor in the Magnaura palace in the presence of senate and clergy. The Patriarch was then escorted to his own palace, the patriarcheion adjoining Hagia Sophia. He was enthroned in the Great Church on the following Sunday after receiving the patriarchal insignia from the Emperor and he was consecrated by the metropolitan of Heracleia.

Thus in practice the Emperor could put in his own man. He was similarly influential in bringing about deposition or resignation. Only rarely did he choose one of his own family: it was Leo VI and Romanus I in the tenth century who did this. There were obvious reasons why an Emperor (or an Empress) might want a man with a particular outlook, such as the statesmanlike Tarasius who cleared up iconoclast problems, or there might be a desire to further political ends, as in the appointment of the unsuitable monk Eustratius Garidas, the protégé of Anna Dalassena who was thus won over to accept an unpalatable Ducaena as daughter-in-law. And the fourteenth-century hesychast controversies, as well as family rivalries, saw a prolonged see-saw of resignations and reappointments according to the views of the dominant Emperor. But in spite of certain unfortunate appointments this system by no means produced a series of sycophants or weaklings—Nicephorus I, Tarasius, Photius, Nicholas Mysticus, and most of the eleventh-century patriarchs were among those who upheld the dignity of their high office. They were enlightened and educated men, often originating from a lay or non-monastic milieu. Normally they were priests on their election, but one or two were actually laymen, as Photius and Nicephorus. During the latter middle ages many were monks, appointed for their views for or against union with Rome, or in the fourteenth century for their hesychast or anti-hesychast associations, men who in addition to their patriarchal activities often left a body of writings, Callistus I for instance, or Philotheus Coccinus also important for liturgy. This move towards monastic appointments is in keeping with the significant role of the monastic world in general during the later middle ages. The Church's awareness of its own authority and its desire to stress this is also reflected in the fifteenth-century work of archbishop Symeon of Thessalonica on ordinations. He said that the formal pronouncement of the election of a new patriarch was made by both 'our powerful and sacred ruler' and by 'the sacred and holy synod', and though he allowed the imperial right of selection he specifically emphasized that the choice was really that of the metropolitans.[29] In the case of resignations whatever pressure might have been brought to bear on various patriarchs their resignations had to be accepted by the synod, as the patriarchal registers show, and they were not always automatically endorsed without question. And in reverse the synod could not depose without imperial confirmation.

6. Patriarchal administration: the major officials of the Great Church

The patriarchal palace was conveniently connected with the south gallery of Hagia Sophia. Its extensive rooms provided departmental offices, a library, rooms for tribunals and the standing synod, chapels and reception rooms in which the Emperor and his entourage could be offered refreshments after the liturgy or where visitors could be given audience. The work of the Patriarch had a double aspect. His responsibilities included the Great Church and his own immediate sphere as well as supervision of the metropolitans throughout the patriarchate. But this authority was further extended to include certain Orthodox Churches which in the course of time came within his jurisdiction, as Russia, Bulgaria, Serbia, though in practice the extent of his authority might vary with changing political circumstances, particularly in the Balkan princi-

---

[29] De Sacris Ordinationibus, *PG* 155, cols. 440B–C; see also Bréhier, II. 480 and *Miscellanea G. Mercati* (*Studi e Testi* 123, Vatican, 1946), III. 368–72.

palities. The content of his normal activities covered a wide range. Of prime importance was the maintenance of orthodoxy and the stamping out of heresy. Then there were pastoral and disciplinary duties and liturgical problems, the administration of extensive church property and of stauropegial foundations (held directly from him), as well as considerable jurisdictional activities for he was the final court of appeal in ecclesiastical cases. He had too a special relationship with the Emperor and his family, officiating at coronations and on such occasions as marriages and baptisms, this latter being particularly important with its traditional cutting of a lock of the infant's hair which was regarded as authentication of his legitimacy. The Patriarch might also be drawn into the government of the day, as was the case with the tenth-century Nicholas Mysticus, or, though less officially, the early fourteenth-century Athanasius I or later John Calecas.

All this demanded delegation and an extensive secretariat with numerous departments, some of which concentrated on patriarchal business while others dealt more specifically with the administration of the Great Church. In these patriarchal and cathedral activities there was both overlap and development. In a period lasting from the seventh to the fifteenth century change was inevitable, particularly with the added disruption caused by the Fourth Crusade and the Latin settlements and the temporary exile of the Byzantine Emperors to their restricted Nicaean kingdom. It is only gradually that the history of the major ecclesiastical officials and the administration over so long and so stormy a period is being reconstructed as the sparse and often intractable evidence is brought to light. Even so there still remain wide gaps.[30]

The archons, or officials of the Great Church, were usually in orders and their administrative post had nothing to do with the conferment of their order. Symeon of Thessalonica called their office an 'external service' (ἔξω διακονία). The leading administrators in Hagia Sophia were normally deacons. They were the first five (called a *pentas*) and in importance they were rather like the cardinal deacons of Rome. The provinces and dioceses also had their officers appointed by the metropolitan or suffragan bishop. In

---

[30] In the brief comments which follow I am much indebted to the work of Jean Darrouzès; see particularly his *Offikia, Registre*, and *Documents inédits*. Bréhier, II gives a brief account but since he published in 1949 understandably he is rarely able to give change and development as Darrouzès does.

Constantinople appointment would be by the Patriarch or very exceptionally by the Emperor as was the case for a time with the oeconomus who might then be a layman. In Hagia Sophia the five, at times increased to six, leading officials divided between them the main administrative work. They are mentioned in an imperial *prostagma* of 1094 as the exokatakoiloi (a name the meaning of which seems uncertain[30a]). Four of them had the title 'megas', and in the later middle ages other titles were somewhat arbitrarily given them without any but an honorary significance.

The great oeconomus had financial responsibilities and was concerned with certain, but not all, of the temporalities of the Great Church. Inevitably he had contacts with the officials of the imperial fisc. Though he did not deal with metropolitanates or stauropegial monasteries, his activities were far-reaching since the Great Church owned property throughout the Empire and from 1204 onwards financial claims and counter-claims must have been particularly complex, quite apart from the break caused by the Nicaean exile. Church property passed from Greek to Latin hands and back again with bewildering frequency. In the post-1261 period the authority of the oeconomus seemed to wane. Patriarchs made increasing use in financial matters of special officials, exarchs, thus bypassing the oeconomus, a move perhaps designed to favour the patriarchal privy purse in times of increasing financial stringency, and it no doubt also reflected the perennial struggle between bishop and cathedral over the division of temporalities. By the fourteenth century the name of the oeconomus of the Great Church had ceased to appear on official lists. For instance it is not found in the rulings of Patriarch Matthew drawn up at the end of the fourteenth century.

The great sceuophylax was a high-ranking sacristan who supervised liturgical matters, the sacred vessels, vestments, ceremonies, and chant, and accordingly his activities were concerned with the Great Church, a heavy responsibility in view of the elaborate ritual and established protocol which embellished the daily services and the festivals of the Christian year.

The great sacellarius, who appeared at the time of Patriarch Nicholas III, was charged with monastic supervision in Constantinople and in Pera across the Golden Horn. Outside this the Patriarch appointed special exarchs to visit diocesan monasteries.

The sacelliou, not known before the eleventh century, supervised

---

[30a] But cf. Darrouzès, *Offikia*, 60 and 540–1.

parish churches and also those in private hands to see that there was a proper liturgical standard and due maintenance of the fabric.

The protecdicus, an official found as early as the mid-fifth century, had by the late twelfth century become the 'sixth finger' in the hand directing patriarchal administration and was by then one of the major cathedral officials with his own tribunal, responsible for ecclesiastical discipline and charged with the registration of marriage certificates, and with such problems as the right of sanctuary or the instruction of repentant apostates or foreign converts.

The great chartophylax and the patriarchal chancery. The great chartophylax became the most important of the leading archons of Hagia Sophia. Originally in the seventh century he had been an archivist and secretary, and was then not so important as the archdeacon or syncellus or protonotary. As the authority of the archdeacon and the syncellus (originally the close associate of the bishop or patriarch) decreased, so the importance of the chartophylax grew from the ninth century onwards until he became the leading figure in the patriarchal chancery and in the absence of the Patriarch was chairman of the standing synod. But he was not a judge (whatever Balsamon might say). In many respects he acted for the Patriarch and he controlled a large secretariat. Under his supervision the secretaries drafted patriarchal letters with all their careful variation of style, dignified and rhetorical in tone to other patriarchs, simpler and more popular in foreign letters, to Russia for example, with the opening *prooimion* always stressing the divine source of the patriarchal authority and its link with the apostolic succession.[31] If the patriarch was not present the chartophylax presided over elections in the standing synod, though without the right to vote or debate. His secretaries drew up the minutes and registered the acta. But he did not have overall control of patriarchal administration and there were other patriarchal secretariats. Balsamon himself had been chartophylax before he was elected Patriarch of Antioch and he attributed to the office powers which it did not in fact possess, including the right to judge in ecclesiastical cases. This was not so and would have infringed the rights of the court of the ecdiceion. But Balsamon was notorious among his contemporaries for his sense of his own importance and he liked to claim that he was 'the patriarchal cardinal', 'the mouth and hand' of the Patriarch.

[31] See H. Hunger, 'Zum Stil und zur Sprache des Patriarchatsregister von Konstantinopel. Rhetorik im Dienste der orthodoxen Hierarchie', *Studien*, 11–60.

The survival of the fourteenth-century register of the patriarchal chancery affords insight into Byzantine diplomatic and illustrates the range of chancery work during the years 1315–1404 (Patriarchs John XIII–Matthew).[32] It also shows a certain disarray in the somewhat haphazard ordering of the entries, perhaps reflecting the particularly troubled conditions of the post-1204 period.[33] The register lists both official and private acts varying in importance. The formal *prostagma* of Andronicus III setting up the metropolitanate of Serres (1329) contrasts with the simple promise of the priest ecclesiarch of the Great Church not to beat his wife. Some patriarchal acts, as distinct from those made in the synod, can scarcely be classed as diplomatic, such as the homily on the conversion of the professional magician Amarantina. There are instructions to specially appointed patriarchal eparchs who were ousting the sacellarius in monastic supervision. They had to deal with patriarchal rights over metropolitans and monasteries and churches. Some entries record administrative or judicial decisions taken jointly by Patriarch and synod.

7. *The patriarchal synod: the metropolitans*

The synod *endemousa*, the standing synod,[34] often referred to in registers and other sources, was a patriarchal committee which came to have legislative, administrative, and judicial functions. It was in existence in the early middle ages and presumably met when required, but it comes into greater prominence and more regular use from the tenth century. Despite innate conservatism like much in Byzantine institutional life it had an *ad hoc* side to it, adapting itself as circumstances required. It had nothing like the authority of the general council, though instances of its decisions were of special importance in the Orthodox Church, as for instance the Palamite synods of 1347 and 1351. It became an indispensable element in the administration of the patriarchate, and the patriarchal secretariat seemed at times to merge into the synod. The evidence of the tenth-century Anonymous showed the synod concerned with the daily

[32] See MM 1–2, Darrouzès, *Registre*, Hunger, *Register* and *GR*, vols. 5–6.
[33] Documents did get lost; John V had to apply to Venice for copies of certain treaties as his own had got lost. See J. Chrysostomides, 'Venetian Commercial Privileges . . .', *Studi veneziani*, 12 (1970), 273.
[34] See R. Potz, *Patriarche und Synode in Konstantinopel . . .* (Vienna, 1971).

problems of the three dioceses of Asia, Pontus, and Thrace and at the same time dealing with ecclesiastical affairs of a more general nature since the metropolitans were present in the city.

According to late eleventh-century evidence (Nicetas of Ancyra) the synod met three times a week to deal with routine matters. It was held in the rooms or offices (*secreta*) of the patriarcheion, presumably with reasonable access to the library and archives. It was served by the chancery whose notaries would be present though not members. The cathedral archons had to be there and they were responsible for the preparation of the agenda and the minutes and the circulation of decisions taken. The high dignitaries sat by the Patriarch, the others behind. Cases were introduced by the appropriate great archon. Metropolitans who happened to be in the capital attended if they wished and like the great deacons could speak to the case in hand. Others could only express their views through the Patriarch. The kind of cases regularly dealt with can be seen from the registers, increasing in scope and number through the years.

The synod also dealt with extraordinary needs and special problems Such might be the trials of well-known public figures for heresy, John Italus or the twelfth-century cases. Then the Emperor would be concerned and would convoke the synod at such times that he and his imperial judges would also be present and perhaps the senate, thus demonstrating the close link between the secular and ecclesiastical authorities.

The synod had the right to elect the Patriarch in the sense of presenting three names for imperial choice, likewise if it was the election of a metropolitan or autocephalous archbishop the three names were submitted to the Patriarch. At a special meeting to elect a patriarch the Emperor or his representatives might be present. Procedure was laid down: the declaration of the vacancy, the consideration of the candidates and then the notification of the three agreed names to the chairman. If these were all rejected a new session was required. If the election of a patriarch was in question, then the imperial nomination of a fourth name pleasing to the Emperor had to be accepted. Once elected and enthroned the Patriarch would circulate to the other patriarchs and the bishops his *synodica* (*grammata*), that is, the announcement of his election and his profession of faith, which despite its title had nothing to do with the synod and was a personal statement.

Similarly metropolitans came to be elected, not by the suffragans and 'neighbours' (leading men) of their province (Sardica, can. 6), but in the Constantinopolitan synod. On such an occasion the metropolitans and archbishops present in the capital would be summoned. Voting was in person, unless there was a valid reason for absence. As the senior ecclesiastic and archbishop, the Patriarch convoked the meeting but did not take part in the discussions or vote, though no doubt he could make his views known. He selected from three names presented to him by the electoral body and he had the right of consecration. It was even argued that the metropolitans were the suffragans of the Patriarch, consecrated by him in the capital, and that he should therefore have a greater share in their election. The Emperor had no part in these elections (in contrast to the patriarchal election), though he did once or twice make attempts to intervene, as Nicephorus II,[35] or in 1071 when Romanus IV's request was refused by the synod.[36] Balsamon, who was by no means consistent or always in tune with tradition, did on occasion accord this right, claiming that the Emperor was above the canons.[37] But in practice the synod and Patriarch evidently managed to retain their rights, though no doubt the Emperor could be useful in bringing pressure to bear on recalcitrant victims such as John Mauropous or Theophylact of Ochrida who after enjoying the amenities of the capital did not want to be relegated to a provincial backwater (as they saw it) in Asia Minor or Bulgaria. But canonically the Patriarch had the final word in the election of metropolitans.

Evidence ranging over the tenth (possibly earlier) to the eleventh centuries does not give a continuous history of ecclesiastical administration but it does at least underline both change and conflict.[38] This was inevitable. Conservative as the Church might be in some respects, it found that the rulings of the early fathers and the canons of the general councils could not provide for all later contingencies nor could they forestall every clash of interest. Hence the need for authoritative comment on the application of the old accepted general principles and this was the work of the twelfth-century

[35] DR 703 (c.964) and DR 726 (repudiation by John I Tzimisces on his accession, Dec. 969).
[36] GR 900 (Nov. 1071, though Romanus had by then been deposed).
[37] PG 138, col. 93 BC (Carthage, can. 16); RP III. 349.
[38] See Darrouzès, Documents inédits; see also the comments of P. Karlin-Hayter, 'Notes sur quatre documents d'ecclésiologie byzantine', REB, 37 (1979), 249–58.

canonists. During the years from the tenth century to the break-up of the Empire in 1204, quite apart from routine patriarchal business, the standing synod increased in importance, dealing independently with problems such as heresy which in the early middle ages had usually been resolved in a general council. Now relations with Rome were uneasy and the eastern patriarchates negligible. At the same time an underlying tension between the Patriarch and the metropolitans developed. This had been evident in the tenth century when the metropolitans tried to take advantage of the inexperienced young Patriarch Theophylact who often seemed to be indifferent to administrative needs. According to the writings of the Anonymous and Nicetas of Amasea[38a] they would have liked to retain decision-making in their own hands, reducing the role of the Patriarch to that of an executive. This however failed. The rights of the Patriarch as chief archbishop in his patriarchate were maintained despite the fact that he was perpetually subject to external pressures, especially from the Emperor.

A further complication particularly affecting the Patriarch and synod was introduced in about the mid-eleventh century and was to continue until the end of the middle ages. This was the influx of refugee ecclesiastics, metropolitans, autocephalous archbishops and suffragans, from enemy-occupied lands. Sojourn in the capital had always been attractive. In the early tenth century Nicholas Mysticus had had to push off the bishop of Alania to his distant see and from time to time injunctions to bishops to return to their dioceses appear in both patriarchal and imperial registers. But now clergy came as refugees and had some excuse for staying in Constantinople. Their presence posed a twofold problem. Finance was a serious hazard. It is not clear how far funds could come through to Constantinople from lands lost to the Empire. Many fees would inevitably be lost, but revenue belonging to a particular see or monastery now under enemy rule might well be drawn from its often widespread property still in Byzantine-held territory. It is difficult to say whether such revenue did reach either the original see (where there were presumably still cathedral clergy to be supported) or whether it got to bishops in exile in the capital. With the additional hazard of Latin occupation after 1204 and further changes in the Middle East such property would be at risk. But no general principle can be

[38a] See Darrouzès, *Documents inédits* (with text and trans.), 116 ff.

applied. For instance in the early fourteenth century the monastery of St Catherine on Mount Sinai still seemed to have some of its property in Venetian-held Crete. When Athanasius the Patriarch of Alexandria was driven out by the Mamluks he took refuge in Constantinople (where he was involved in various ecclesiastical disputes—he was an anti-unionist) and then in the early fourteenth century he apparently was able to go to a *metochion* in Crete belonging to St Catherine of Sinai.[39] In the thirteenth century bishops in the Nicaean kingdom probably came off best. But that did not last and the general contraction and indeed the uncertainty of Byzantine boundaries was reflected in the frequent requests in the patriarchal registers for some kind of aid (*epidosis*) for refugee clergy. This bore heavily on foundations within the capital whose own resources, often drawn from the mainland and the islands, were likely to be equally straitened.

Another problem posed by the presence in the capital of increasing numbers of metropolitans was a matter of diplomacy, since such a group could form a powerful lobby in ecclesiastical politics and could exert its influence on occasions when the standing synod had to consider questions of policy. An instance of this kind occurred in the last quarter of the eleventh century. It resolved itself into a struggle between the metropolitans and the great deacons of Hagia Sophia. These deacons, the staurophoroi, were a powerful group. As deacons they could marry, though they would have to renounce their wives should they be elected to a metropolitanate, which often happened. A deacon of the Great Church might in fact be promoted in the hope of removing a too forceful personality from the capital, and should he become metropolitan of a nearby province he would have no excuse for lingering in Constantinople apart from synodal business. Such moves were however countered by obtaining the right to refuse 'promotion' if this was so desired. It is easy to visualize the influence which these deacons could exercise, linked, as they often were, with the leading families in the capital. The Emperor knew where strength lay and in Alexius I's reign he aligned himself with the officials of Hagia Sophia against Patriarch and 'visiting' metropolitans. The point then at issue was the imperial right to promote a bishop to the status of metropolitan. During the second half of the eleventh century there had been an

[39] See A. Failler, 'Le Séjour d'Athanase II d'Alexandrie à Constantinople', *REB*, 35 (1977), 44.

imperial upgrading of the bishops of Madyta and Basileion to the fury of their respective metropolitans. In a long drawn-out dispute the Patriarch and metropolitans opposed this move but without success. The Emperor Alexius finally got his way, backed by the officials of the Great Church who stood to gain financially to the loss of the indignant metropolitans of Heracleia and Ancyra from whom the suffragans had been filched.[40]

With the fall of Constantinople in 1204 the two groups in the capital, the bureaucracy of the Great Church and the metropolitans in the City, were necessarily broken up. Some clergy certainly stayed, for instance monastic inmates and lower clergy, including some from Hagia Sophia though the church itself was no longer in their hands. Patriarch Germanus's records show him receiving back a repentant deacon from the Great Church who had misguidedly accepted Latin jurisdiction, and from Nicaea he exhorted the Orthodox in Constantinople and elsewhere not to recognize foreign pastors. Some of the clergy of Hagia Sophia when they failed to set up a new Orthodox Patriarch there found a home in Nicaea where traditional ecclesiastical government was re-established though on a greatly reduced scale. In 1208 a synod in Nicaea elected the new Patriarch. The Lascarid Emperors in exile were anxious to continue what they considered to be normal imperial practice. They exercised their right to raise suffragans to metropolitan status, modifying diocesan organization in order to give increased authority to sees now more important than previously (Pontic Heracleia and Philadelphia). They used imperial influence to provide when possible for refugee bishops (in this way the exiled bishop of Mitylene got a vacant bishopric).[41] But to some extent pressure of this kind was lightened because exiles could also take refuge elsewhere, for instance in the kingdom of Epirus.

The patriarchal register for 1208–61 illustrates the scope of central ecclesiastical administration during the Nicaean period.[42] As previously in Constantinople, much work on the various patriarchal rulings lay with the chartophylate. It was a period of activity for the metropolitans composing the synod (that is, any who happened to be present in Nicaea or wherever the synod was held). The work of the synod involved relations with Orthodox Churches outside the

---

[40] See *GR* 904 and *DR* 1117.
[41] *DR*[2] 1701.
[42] *GR* 1203 ff.

territorial bounds of Nicaea, as Cyprus or Serbia, as well as the disputed jurisdiction of Nicaea over Epirus and the perennial problem of relations with Rome.[43] The Church was also called upon to participate in imperial trials. A metropolitan might be among a panel of judges. The Patriarch and other ecclesiastics might be present and consulted at a trial, but did not pass judgement which rested with the Emperor (on one such occasion Blemmydes protested that normal legal procedure should have been followed).[44] There is a haphazard quality about extant entries in the registers; similar problems, for instance monastic difficulties, are dealt with sometimes by patriarchal, sometimes by synodal, ruling. At the same time patriarchal control was being exercised over episcopal administration by the use of supervisory exarchs, sometimes metropolitans, sometimes other ecclesiastics, as was Patriarch Germanus II's practice.

In the post-1261 period the oecumenical work of the patriarchate in the general or 'international' sense which had been evident under the Nicaeans, particularly as far as the Slav countries were concerned, continued. At the same time there was increasing internal tension between Patriarch and metropolitans, as also between Patriarch and Emperor. Patriarch Athanasius I evidently disliked large numbers of metropolitans in the capital and urged them (and the suffragans) to return to their sees. He even thought of a synod of abbots in which case metropolitans would have no excuse for lingering in Constantinople (and abbots were often excellent administrators). Patriarch Philotheus put the metropolitans under a patriarchal vicar and made inroads on their power (and finance) by forbidding them to set up stauropegial monasteries. On the other hand in 1279 the Emperor Michael VIII tried to limit the Patriarch's authority by putting stauropegial houses under the appropriate bishop and withdrawing all monasteries from patriarchal jurisdiction;[45] later there was a strong protest from Patriarch Antony IV. The various elements—Emperor and Patriarch, metropolitans, suffragans, and leading cathedral officials—continued to struggle to gain the ascendancy and thus to secure the means whereby they could increase their meagre resources in times of acute financial

---

[43] See also above, pt. I, ch. VII.
[44] See Angold, 168–9 for instances of this kind.
[45] *DR*[2] 2040.

stringency. What is however of far greater significance was the spirituality found in the monastic world and the authority of the patriarchate shown not only in assistance given to the government (the General Judges for instance) but in its high standing in the Orthodox world quite outside the rapidly vanishing Empire.

8. Secular clergy in the provinces (eparchies) and in the dioceses[46]

The bishops and their congregations constitute the Orthodox Church and basically, whatever the rank, the episcopal office was the same. There was nevertheless a clearly marked episcopal hierarchy. In the patriarchate of Constantinople this was headed by the oecumenical Patriarch or archbishop. Then there were the leading bishops with the title of metropolitan, whose sees were the centres of the eparchies or provinces. Occasionally a metropolitan would be called an 'archbishop', as in the case of Athens, but he was obviously in a different class from the archbishop of Constantinople. The highest ranking metropolitan was given the title of 'protothronus', and similarly the highest suffragan in each province. Order of precedence was laid down in the *Notitiae Episcopatuum*.[47] Under the metropolitan were his suffragan bishops, each with their own diocese. The autocephalous archbishop was a special case. Originally the metropolitan see was the chief city in a civil province, but should the government divide this province so that a second city gained this status, then its bishop considered that he should be raised to the rank of metropolitan. This was opposed by the existing metropolitan in the original province (on grounds of loss of prestige and finance) and a solution was then found in giving the newly created metropolitan a purely honorary rank as an independent or autocephalous archbishop holding directly from the Patriarch and without any suffragans.[48] This kind of archbishop is found throughout the middle ages and is distinct from such as the autonomous archbishop of Cyprus who had suffragans and was virtually independent of the Patriarch of Constantinople.

[46] Further details are given by E. Herman, 'The Secular Church', *CMH* IV (2); in general this chapter still holds, though it was in fact written in the late 50s before the appearance of much of Darrouzès's work.
[47] See above pt. II, section 4.
[48] Chalcedon, can. 12; see E. Chrysos, 'Zur Entstehung ... der autokephalen Erzbistümer', *BZ*, 62 (1969), 263–86.

The election of a metropolitan came to take place in the synod in Constantinople (as described above) and not in his province. This was more practical when metropolitans were so often in the capital. Their responsibilities within their diocese followed much the same pattern as those of their suffragans, though their absence meant that these had to be increasingly delegated. Procedure for the election of a bishop was laid down by canon law as early as Nicaea I (can. 49). The metropolitan had to convoke the suffragans of his province (eparchy); three would constitute a quorum. They were to select three names. The metropolitan took no share in this, but he had the right to choose one of the three names submitted and he then proceeded to consecrate the newly-elected bishop with the obligatory assistance of two or three suffragans. Those absent from the meeting could vote and affirm by letter and the majority were to prevail. In filling the vacant see there was to be a delay of not more than three months. It is possible that Justinian I favoured the participation of clergy and leading citizens, but the sole right of the bishops was reaffirmed by Nicaea II, can. 3. But in this as in other cases, the rulings of the canons had come to be modified owing to altered circumstances, and the twelfth-century canonists were not unanimous in their interpretations. In the case of episcopal elections the practical difficulty which arose was the frequent presence in Constantinople of the metropolitans and the problems created for the diocese should there be a long delay in filling the vacant see, apart from contravening the three months' limit. Ninth-century evidence points to episcopal elections in Constantinople and by the mid-eleventh century it was sufficiently frequent for Patriarch Michael Cerularius to attempt to stop the practice. He failed and in 1072 Patriarch John Xiphilinus sanctioned the election of bishops in Constantinople. This clearly continued and Balsamon thought such elections illegal, but he is misleading for the practice was regarded as normal. In the course of a synodal enquiry in 1143 criticizing the consecration of bishops by the metropolitan alone the actual election of two bishops in Constantinople was spoken of as usual procedure.[49]

By canon law episcopal office was incompatible with secular

---

[49] *GR* 1011; N. A. Oikonomides, 'Un décret synodal inédit du patriarche Jean VIII Xiphilin concernant l'élection et l'ordination des évêques', *REB*, 18 (1960), 55–78.

office.[50] This did not debar a bishop from participation in non-ecclesiastical affairs, but he was considered to be acting in an advisory capacity for moral reasons. In this respect he had many obligations often of an informal kind as for instance the letters of the eleventh-century humanist Archbishop John of Euchaita show. A bishop might be charged with watching over local officials, supervising prisons, and in times of need giving encouragement to those resisting enemy attack. His more specifically ecclesiastical duties included pastoral care (preaching on Sundays and festivals though not in other bishops' dioceses), and watching out for signs of heresy. His administrative duties covered supervision of monasteries and charitable institutions (unless these were specifically exempt by their *typicon* or by stauropegial foundation). He was responsible for such divergent duties as overall care for liturgical offices and for the diocesan temporalities. In this he was assisted by officials attached to his cathedral church who had the same duties as those serving the Great Church though on a much smaller scale and without certain obligations peculiar to the patriarchal clergy in the capital. By canon law the appointment of a financial officer, the oeconomus, was obligatory.[51] This was extended to cover all churches and monasteries. And it became necessary at the outset of each episcopate to make clear what was the bishop's personal property which could be claimed by his heirs at his death. Outside his diocese the bishop had to attend his metropolitan's synod held at least once a year, though central synodal duties as well as a certain predilection for Constantinople often meant that the metropolitan was not in his province. And increasing enemy inroads, not to say Latin occupation, must have frequently resulted in the absence of the bishop too, as well as disruption of cathedral and diocesan life. Translation from one see to another was normally forbidden though this did occur, increasingly so with the loss of territory to the Muslims.

One of the bishop's main duties was jurisdictional. By reason of his position he had always been regarded as a natural arbiter. This responsibility developed into a recognized and defined authority to act as judge in his court in certain cases. Guide-lines on this subject were laid down before the seventh century especially by the legislation of Justinian I. This bishop might be appealed to by laity

[50] e.g. Chalc., can. 3 and 7.
[51] Chalc., can. 26, Nicaea II, can. 11.

in matters involving moral issues. He had authority over his clergy
who were forbidden to seek redress in the secular courts (Chalc. can.
9 and later rulings).[52] If laity brought civil suits against the clergy of
Constantinople these were to be heard by the Patriarch or his
delegate, so Heraclius ruled in 629.[53] Similarly such cases in the
provinces or dioceses were judged by the metropolitan or the
bishop assisted by his leading officers. His deputy and chairman of
the court (as in Constantinople) would be his chartophylax. Marriage problems were originally dealt with by both secular and
ecclesiastical courts and indeed often by patriarchal ruling as the
entries in the registers show. Civil and canon law differed on this
subject, but the views of the Church on the indissoluble nature of
the marriage union tended to prevail. In 1084 Alexius I supported
the ecclesiastical claim to sole jurisdiction in this field,[54] but not
with entire success. It was an intricate subject riddled with problems, particularly concerning the prohibited degrees of kindred and
affinity.

Various penalties could be imposed by the Church such as
suspension from office or excommunication or relegation to a
monastery. In cases of very serious crime involving a penalty of
exile or death the cleric would be unfrocked and handed over to the
secular authority for punishment. Alexius I tried to insist that in
civil cases between laity and clergy the defendant must be tried in
his own court,[55] that is, if a cleric was bringing an accusation against
a layman the case would be tried in the secular court, a practice
which was criticized by canonists. Appeal was from bishop to
metropolitan and his synod composed of all the bishops of the
province, and then failing this to the Patriarch. Charges against
metropolitans, or by a metropolitan against one of his suffragan
bishops or other clergy came to the Patriarch and the standing
synod in Constantinople. There was no appeal against the Patriarch
even though this might be the court of first instance. There were
isolated cases of appeal to the Pope but this was extremely rare.
Balsamon seems to deny that appeal could be made from the
Patriarch to the Emperor, though this would appear to conflict with

[52] As by Patriarch Alexius I in 1028 (GR 835); cf. 1 Cor. 6: 1–8.
[53] DR 199.
[54] DR 1116.
[55] DR 1071 (1081).

his opinion that the Emperor was above the canons, not that he was consistent in this view of imperial authority.

The secular clergy as a whole were divided into major orders (bishops, priests, and deacons) and minor orders (subdeacons, readers, exorcists, cantors, and doorkeepers). There were also deaconesses, though these declined in importance during the later middle ages. As already shown, bishops varied in status though their ecclesiastical order was the same, that is, there were metropolitans, autocephalous archbishops, and suffragan bishops.[56] Certain conditions governing age, character, and minimum education were laid down by canon law. These were occasionally modified, sometimes by imperial ruling. Canon 14 of the Quinisextum council (691) said that a man however worthy could not be ordained priest before he was thirty years old, and similarly a deacon had to be twenty-five and a deaconess forty. All clergy except bishops could be married provided that this had taken place before they were ordained subdeacon, though certain women, such as actresses or prostitutes or widows, were ruled out and so were second marriages. Bishops if already married had to separate from their wives. From time to time the disciplinary canons of the councils reminded all ranks of clergy (from bishops downwards) of the conduct expected of them in matters of dress and behaviour. They were warned against gambling, haunting racecourses, taverns, and theatres, or taking part in unseemly festivities after a marriage ceremony,[57] but it does not of course follow that all were addicted to such practices.

A certain standard of education was required, particularly from bishops who were expected to be in the habit of reading with care the canons and the Scriptures and should know the Psalter by heart (Nicaea II, can. 2). The great ecclesiastics of Hagia Sophia were often highly educated and were among the scholars of their day. But these were comparatively few in number. At the beginning of the twelfth century the Emperor Alexius I evidently found resources available for pastoral work in the capital inadequate for he instituted a special salaried grade for clergy and even monks and laity who were to be trained as didaskaloi to carry out such teaching duties.[58] During the twelfth century there was certainly

---

[56] 'Suffragan' is used in the sense of a bishop with a diocese under the metropolitan of the province in which his diocese was situated.
[57] Cf. Quinisextum, cans. 9, 24, 50, 51, or Nicaea II, can. 16.
[58] DR 1236, see also Darrouzès, *Offikia*, 72–5.

opportunity for men and boys to attend ecclesiastical teaching establishments in the capital and probably elsewhere in large towns such as Thessalonica, Athens, or Corinth. Modern scholars sometimes speak only of an 'intellectual élite' thus giving an incomplete picture. Surviving textbooks used in teaching subjects such as reading and writing, grammar, and geography,[59] point to the demand for at least a moderate standard which must have profited many who did not at the time know that they were going to join the ranks of the clergy. Ecclesiastical, like state, administration was highly organized with its various departments, and to a lesser extent this was also the case in the provinces and dioceses. Such administration could not have functioned without a personnel with a reasonable standard of literacy and numeracy, though there may well have been very few in the top flight. Nor could the educational standard of the country clergy have been entirely negligible. It was essential for them to have had some education in order to perform their part in the liturgy and this applied not only to the priest but also to the deacon and the reader who both had a special role in the service. Often it was the country papas who provided elementary education in the village and the psalms were always favourite material in teaching children to read. Monasteries had their schools though intended primarily not for the outside public but for boys meaning to take monastic vows. The ninth-century Studite house in Constantinople had a special teacher for its children. In the mid-eleventh century on the far eastern borders of the Empire Eustathius Boilas expected the clergy of his church of the Theotokos to give instruction to boys on his estate with a view to their serving the church. Evidence, scattered as it is, suggests that education at a modest level was generally available and the Church profited from this.

The numbers of the clergy at any given time cannot be assessed even approximately, but both literary and archaeological evidence during the 800 years covered by this book point to continual foundations of churches, and particularly monasteries, each of which would have had one or more of its own churches (as at Hosios Loukas in Phocis). It is only necessary to look through the two volumes of Janin listing the churches and monasteries of Constantinople and certain provinces,[60] or the *Tabula Imperii*

[59] Cited and discussed by Wilson, *Scholars*.
[60] Janin, *Églises et monastères*, II and III.

Byzantini which includes sections on the Church,[61] to realize the continuous activity of Christians in the East Roman Empire. Constantinople with its opportunities for ambitious churchmen as well as laity and its obvious cultural amenities has all too often overshadowed life in the provinces which needed its clergy as much as did the capital. Some figures can however be known. The approximate numbers of the various ranks of the episcopate can be calculated from the *Notitiae Episcopatuum*. The clergy attached to Hagia Sophia, including the pentades (the leading officials in nine groups of five), appeared to have been more than 600 in the seventh century when, at the instigation of the Patriarch Sergius, the Emperor Heraclius decreed that the Great Church was overstaffed. He laid down the maximum number for each order from priest to doorkeeper. Even then the total was more than a hundred in excess of the number permitted by Justinian I who had tried to deal with the same problem. At the same time Heraclius also issued a ruling about the clergy serving the church of St Mary at Blachernae.

Churches and chapels in each diocese were under the control of the bishop. They fell into two main classes. The 'catholic' (καθο-λικαί) churches were parish churches for general use and there were not many of them. Then there were the chapels, oratories, and churches to be found in monasteries or in the private houses of the wealthy, or on country estates, or indeed built by the villagers themselves for their own use. These private buildings were by far the greater number. The position of the 'catholic' or public churches was clear. Their clergy were appointed by the bishop of the diocese and they administered the main sacraments as of right. Private churches, which proliferated often in conjunction with a monastic foundation, appointed their priests subject to the bishop's approval; they were supposed to get episcopal consent for performing baptisms and marriages as well as for the celebration of the liturgy. This seems to have been an attempt to safeguard the rights of parish priests in the towns and proved to be a continuing battle. In the private category there were very diverse kinds of church or chapel. The oratories in a rich man's house evidently attracted priests from provincial dioceses, hence Nicaea II, can. 10, which forbade clergy to go into other dioceses particularly the diocese of

---

[61] *Tabula Imperii Byzantini*, I (general ed. H. Hunger), J. Koder and F. Hild, *Hellas und Thessalia* (Vienna, 1976, the series is in progress); J. Koder, *Negroponte* ... (Vienna, 1973, publication of the *Commission für die Tabula Imp. Byz.*).

this imperial city and 'live with princes and celebrate the divine liturgy in their chapels' unless sanctioned by their own bishop and by the Patriarch. Very different were the two private churches of the Theotokos and St Barbara (the mortuary chapel) built by the eleventh-century Eustathius Boïlas on his eastern estate and carefully provided for in his will.[62] Presumably without his church of the Theotokos his tenants would not have had the services of a priest. Such churches on a country estate were not likely to be in competition with a 'catholic' church and fulfilled a genuine need. But it might well be otherwise in a city where there was an increasing tendency to establish private chapels and to found monasteries in which some of the family fortune was invested in the form of an endowment. In practice this permanently withdrew financial resources from episcopal control, and in some cases also from the state, as more than one Emperor was quick to perceive but failed to prevent.[63]

The finances of the Church were complicated and the subject of conciliar and imperial legislation, and the guide-lines had been laid down before the seventh century.[64] The responsibility for private churches and chapels rested with the founder as was made clear in ecclesiastical legislation (for example Nicaea II, can. 17). The vast complex of the Great Palace had its own churches and chapels which were served by the imperial clergy, a much sought-after office carrying with it a sum on appointment and a regular salary. Less exalted private foundations also made their own arrangements. The main body of the Church, the Patriarch, and the bishops and the clergy under them, derived their income from donations given by the faithful. These might include modest offerings in kind, but the vast bulk of ecclesiastical revenue came from property which steadily accumulated over the centuries. This was inalienable, though the Church sometimes had to struggle to preserve its rights over property which had either been leased out, or, more rarely, directed to imperial need in times of crisis.

---

[62] See Lemerle, 'Le Testament d'Eustathius Boïlas (Avril 1059)', *Cinq études,* 15–63.

[63] See section 9 below on monasteries. This characteristic proliferation of pious foundations in towns is commented on by Dagron, 'Le Christianisme dans la ville byzantine'.

[64] Details are given by E. Herman, 'Die kirchlichen Einkünfte des byzantinischen Niederklerus', *OCP,* 8(1942), 378–442.

Bishops and clergy were originally not supposed to claim fees or regular obligatory offerings for their services. This was explicitly forbidden in pre-eleventh-century canons, but was evidently a common practice. In any case there was probably a very thin line between a precise fee and a customary 'gift', perhaps after a marriage or baptism or an ordination. During the eleventh century payments to the bishop were admitted and regulated by imperial and patriarchal legislation. The *canonikon* was an annual tax levied on villages and varying in proportion to the number of families there and calculated in terms of what they were supposed to be able to afford. In the twelfth century some could not manage the usual 'gift'. 'Then be content with what you are offered' was the advice of Balsamon to Mark Patriarch of Alexandria when he brought up this point.[65] Priests of 'catholic' churches had to make an annual payment of one *nomisma* to their bishop and this became extended to private churches and monastic foundations. The longstanding 'gifts' made to the bishop by an ordinand were also regulated during the eleventh century. A bishop got three *nomismata* for ordaining a priest or deacon, and one for a reader.[66] Likewise at a lower level priests received certain fees. At the top imperial bounty expended large sums on special occasions such as a coronation. The *De Cerimoniis* mentions the sum of 100 pounds of gold for the clergy of Hagia Sophia. There were also from time to time suggestions that the higher clergy of the Great Church lived in too lavish a style. In the early fourteenth century Patriarch Athanasius thought that they could well cut down their income. He was no doubt mindful of the want and penury being suffered at that time by the flood of refugees from Turkish-occupied Asia Minor.

But most clergy were not of episcopal rank or leading office-holders at Hagia Sophia. Those deputed by the bishop to serve the comparatively few 'catholic' churches in a town might be granted an allowance or *diaria* paid in money or kind, or in the later middle ages they were allotted *klerikata*, that is, property from which they enjoyed the proceeds as a lessee, the Church retaining ownership. There were far more private than 'catholic' churches especially in the countryside and the owner, that is, the founder or his heirs,

[65] RP IV. 471–3 (Resp. 31), cited by Herman, *CMH* IV (2), 125 (= *PG* 138, col. 980, Resp. 28).
[66] GR 851.

sometimes paid a salary to the priest as provided for in the foundation charter. Many such priests would also work like other small farmers on the estate thus living partly off their produce. Work of this kind in order to make a living was sanctioned by the Church, but there were repeated prohibitions on holding lucrative offices or engaging in money-making occupations such as banking or running an inn.[67] It would be rash to generalize about the economic position of parish priests. Evidence from the thirteenth century onwards, from sources such as Chomatianus's rulings, Athos archives, patriarchal registers, shows considerable variation in their material circumstances. In both city and countryside there were instances of wealthy parish clergy as well as others living on the poverty line. There was also variation in function. Being familiar with local problems they might be called in to help resolve disputes, perhaps concerning property, or to act as witnesses to charters and wills, or even to perform marriages which offended against canon law, in which case they were called to account by the patriarchal synod.[68]

The acceptance of secular offices by the clergy was prohibited, though there were frequent instances of the violation of this rule, as for example Michael Psellus who began his career as teacher and politician, then became a monk, and finally succeeded in emerging from monastic life (though not without censure) to resume his political career. In the later middle ages, when the Empire was in process of disintegrating, churchmen took office in the interests of the state and acted for instance as General Judges. One profession however remained strictly forbidden. In no circumstances were clergy allowed to take life or fight and this prohibition was adhered to throughout the middle ages and the penalties were severe. In the West it is true that episcopal tenants-in-chief had to retire from the royal council when it came to taking life and limb, but on occasion they certainly fought in battle, notably during the crusades, thus rousing the astonishment and indeed the bitter criticism of the Orthodox. Thus in some ways the secular clergy in the East Roman Empire were in contrast to those of the Latin Church. They did not feature in Byzantine society as a separate entity or 'estate'. There

[67] See E. Herman, 'Le professioni vietate al clero bizantino', *OCP*, 10 (1944), 23–44.
[68] See B. Ferjančić, 'Ogled o parohijskom sveštenstvu u poznoj vizantiji' ('On Parish Clergy in Late Byzantium'), *ZRVI*, 22 (1983), 59–115.

were no powerful prince-bishops as in Germany, no great ecclesiastical feudatories. Orthodox clergy had the special rules or *nomocanons* appropriate to their needs and calling, but there were no
ecclesiastical tenants-in-chief to sit as of right in the senate or the
imperial council. In this respect within its conservative framework
Byzantine society was much more loosely woven than in the West.
This does not imply that the secular clergy were not conscious of
their place in the patriarchate and in the Church. It was this which
sustained them. From the political angle when Michael VIII
recaptured Constantinople he was attempting an impossible task
and the rot set in. But not so in the life of the Church. To the secular
clergy the Great Church was the traditional centre of the patriarchate and its re-establishment there in 1261, even though in difficult
and frequently changing circumstances, was welcomed. While the
state ran down, the patriarchate maintained and increased its
authority.

9. *Monks and monasteries*

In its origins in the late third and early fourth centuries Christian
monasticism was concentrated in Egypt closely followed by settlements in Palestine. This withdrawal from the everyday world was
motivated by a desire to pursue a disciplined life of extreme
asceticism almost amounting to a form of voluntary martyrdom. It
was believed that the purging of unworthy thoughts and actions
and unceasing prayer would lead to a knowledge of God. The
movement spread throughout Christendom though eventually its
development in the Latin world differed in some respects from that
of the East Mediterranean. In Egypt and in the Judaean wilderness
from the start there was every shade of ascetic dedication. The
solitary isolation of the desert hermit Antony contrasted with the
large cenobitic establishments of the converted soldier Pachomius at
Tabennisi near the Nile. Likewise the way of life of the solitary
cave-dwellers, sometimes living in groups called Lauras and meeting only on Saturdays and Sundays, differed greatly from a
community such as was found in the Palestinian house of St Sabas.
The Egyptian movement has had a rather better press than that of
Palestine. This was partly because of the popularity, in the West as
well as in the East, of the various collections of the sayings or
precepts of the Egyptian desert fathers. But it is in fact possible that

Palestinian monasticism may have had a greater influence on the eastern movement, situated as it was in a land which had special associations for Christians and was constantly visited by pilgrims.[69]

One of the formative figures of the early movement had been the fourth-century Basil of Caesarea, himself a bishop and aware of the problems which monasticism could cause in a diocese. He realized that a disciplined way of life within a community was best suited to meet the needs of most monks certainly during the early stages of their new life. The way of the solitary was not excluded by St Basil but it was for the disciplined and more experienced monk. But St Basil left no rule and founded no order. He did however provide answers to questions about problems likely to arise in a cenobitic house, some comparatively slight, some quite basic such as the framework of daily worship or the position of the abbot and the obligation of unquestioning obedience. His advice was frequently referred to by later monastic leaders. But the contrast between St Basil's *Ascetica* (consisting of questions and answers) and the *Regula* attributed to St Benedict of Nursia is striking. Though it was some time before the *Regula* became widespread and authoritative in the West, it did provide a concise and ordered statement on the conduct of a monastic community, at the same time clearly setting out its ideals and goal, a rule which was to afford guidance through the centuries to the present day. St Basil covered only a rather random presentation of problems of widely differing importance, though he was in agreement with the *Regula* as to the monk's goal and the aims of cenobitic life.

The rapid and widespread adoption of monastic life throughout the Empire from the fourth century onwards posed problems for both ecclesiastical and secular authorities. The movement took many forms and though this may have been a source of strength to those dedicated to this life it often proved to be a trial to the secular Church since it made effective supervision of monks difficult. The state was concerned with the withdrawal of manpower and the reduction of productivity on monastic lands. The Church saw the need to regulate the conduct of both institutions and individuals within each diocese. Then cutting across such policies were two

[69] The case for Palestinian monasticism is well put by D. J. Chitty, *The Desert a City: An Introduction to the Study of Egyptian and Palestinian Monasticism under the Christian Empire* (Oxford, 1966).

complicating and very different factors—the widely venerated charismatic monk who was often a law unto himself (though not necessarily a solitary), and on the other hand the widespread desire of the laity both high and low to invest in a monastic foundation.

Churchmen like Basil of Caesarea and his successors realized the need to control the movement and up to a point the Church got its way. In the early middle ages when there was acute theological controversy the general councils were also aware of the danger of uncontrolled roving monastic partisans. By the seventh century it had been made clear that monks, though they might refuse ordination, were nevertheless under the bishop of the diocese. Conciliar decisions, patriarchal and episcopal rulings, imperial legislation, all upheld diocesan control while approving and emphasizing the life of prayer, individual poverty, and obedience.[70]

Throughout its history in the East Mediterranean the monastic movement was marked by great flexibility. It is not possible here to do more than mention the main types of monastic life, with the more important developments which grew up at different times and in different regions, often with ensuing problems. As in the early days of the movement, throughout the middle ages monasticism expresses itself in various ways. There were cenobitic houses of all sizes varying from the large imperial foundations such as the twelfth-century Pantocrator of John II Comnenus to the very small house set up by villagers. The minimum number of monks required to constitute a house was three and it has been suggested that ten to twenty was an average number[71] but this can only be a tentative estimate owing to incomplete evidence, and it may well have been much less. Then there were groups of monks living for most of the week independently in their own separate cells, meeting together on Saturdays and Sundays, and accepting the guidance of a more experienced monk. Such groups were like the original lauras and were known as *kellia*. A number of these *kellia* might accept a common spiritual director and form a *skete* directly linked to a

---

[70] The best introduction to the intimidating multitude of regulations governing Byzantine monasticism is to be found in the *Codificazione canonica orientale, Fonti*, ser. II, fasc. 10, *De monachico statu iuxta disciplinam byzantinam*, ed. P. de Meester (Vatican, 1942) which cites many of the relevant sources (with Latin trans.); see F. Dölger's review, *BZ*, 45 (1952), 82–4.

[71] P. Charanis, 'The Monk as an Element of Byzantine Society', *DOP*, 25 (1971), 72.

cenobitic house. In addition there were completely solitary hermits living entirely on their own, a life considered suitable only for the more experienced. All forms might be found in the vicinity of a cenobitic house, even within its surrounding walls. In the late middle ages a further monastic association developed in which several monks were grouped into families, living together and owning private property. They were under a superior and normally the different groups met only for services in the chapel. This system was called idiorhythmic, that is, it was based on a private individual routine.

Rather more evidence has survived for monasticism than for the diocesan life of the secular clergy. In the East there were never orders or congregations in the western sense. Despite wide differences in the kind of life adopted which might range from the eremitic to the large cenobitic house, Byzantine monasticism might be said to form a single 'ordo' in that it had a common purpose of leading an ascetic and celibate life of prayer and individual poverty withdrawn from the secular world. Many solitaries adopted this isolation only for part of their monastic life. As they became more experienced they would withdraw from the common life of their house, perhaps to a cell in the grounds, or to some distant island, or mountain cave such as abounded on Mount Athos. This was a recurrent feature of Orthodox monasticism. For every grand foundation described in a surviving charter, or from the extensive records preserved on Mount Athos, there were hundreds of smaller houses, perhaps known only from a saint's life or from some passing reference in other sources. Such was the little house founded in Asia Minor in the eleventh century known only from the writings of John Mauropous. Some houses have survived to the present day, such as the monastery of Hosios Meletios (†1105) situated on a spur of Mount Cithaeron in Boeotia. This last is a good example of what a fairly well-off house might once have been. It still stands with its encircling outside wall and imposing gateway, its stables, refectory, kitchen, and bakehouse, its rows of little cells along two walls with their arcading, and its *kellia* outside the walls, remains of which can still just be discerned, its free-standing church with its side chapel in the centre of the courtyard. When Leake visited the house in 1805 its lands grazed 3,000 sheep and goats, so the abbot told him as he called out to the shepherd to bring in the best beast for Leake's meal.

In 1978 the house was being cared for by about six nuns and it was still the objective of pious pilgrimage.[72]

Normally in the case of a cenobitic house the rights of the diocesan bishop were recognized. His consent was necessary when making a new foundation. Conditions of entry for postulants, the length of the noviciate, the solemn frocking of the novice, were all set out in one of the liturgical books, the *Euchologion*. The method of electing the hegumenus, or superior, might vary in accordance with the founder's wishes, but the choice when made had normally to be confirmed by the bishop. The superior was supreme within the house and was responsible for the spiritual well-being of his monks and for the ordering of the daily round. Prayer both in community and in private was the most important part of the monk's life. Corporate worship took place in the monastic church (the *catholicon*)[73] where the main offices and the liturgy were said. The lesser offices, terce, sext, and none, might be said while performing household or agrarian duties, or even excused for those working in the scriptorium as being likely to hinder their concentration on their allotted tasks. Administrative details might vary from house to house but certain duties were essential in any foundation. The daily routine of manual work in the house and on the estate provided for the needs of the community and this was controlled by the various officers appointed by the superior. The writings of Theodore Studites and his followers laid down wise guidance in the many problems of internal administration in a cenobitic house. Theodore even wrote short poems in classical metre on some of the officers in his house and their duties, as the cellarer, the choirmaster, the doorkeeper, the general overseer. He also addressed a poem to a passing visitor who was enjoined to refrain from imparting frivolous gossip from the secular world to the monks while enjoying their hospitality.[74]

---

[72] There is an excellent account of the layout of Byzantine monasteries in A. K. Orlandos, Μοναστηριακὴ Ἀρχιτεκτονική, 2nd edn. (Athens, 1958); this is based on surviving monuments including Hosios Meletios. For the history of the house see A. Orlandos, "Ἡ μονὴ τοῦ Ὁσίου Μελετίου καὶ τὰ παραλαύρια αὐτῆς", Ἀρχεῖον τῶν Βυζαντινῶν Μνημείων τῆς Ἑλλάδος, 5 (1939–40), 34–118.

[73] Not to be confused with the *catholicon* or general church served by secular clergy.

[74] See P. Speck, *Theodoros Studites: Jamben auf verschiedene Gegenstände* (= *Supplementa Byzantina*, 1, Berlin, 1968), text, trans. and commentary.

In a large house, such as the Studite monastery in Constantinople,[75] the library and scriptorium were specially important. This was not for any intellectual purpose but for liturgical and devotional use in the community. The complicated service books were needed. Monks had to read suitable works, homilies, and aids to progress in the contemplative life, such as the early fathers or the much valued *Ladder* of John of Mount Sinai or later the addresses and meditations of Symeon the New Theologian and many of the saints' lives. Reading was obligatory and was strictly controlled by the librarian with provision made for getting books back on time. Theodore himself was said to have been an excellent calligrapher and he well understood the problems and temptations of the copyist ranging from gross inaccuracy to making off with other scribes' pens.[76] From such inventories as have survived it would appear that few secular works were to be found in a monastic library, and those perhaps only by chance. In the fourteenth century Theodore Metochites, the lay patron of the monastery of the Chora in Constantinople, wrote anxious letters from exile about the care of the books which he had placed in its library, which presumably would not all have been religious, but he was something of an exception. All houses had to have some liturgical books and wealthy founders provided splendidly decorated and illustrated copies. The larger important houses, as on Mount Athos or the monastery of St John the Divine on Patmos, had fairly extensive collections, if somewhat limited in scope. By 1201 Christodoulos's house on Patmos, founded towards the end of the eleventh century, had built up a library of 330 books of which the catalogue survives. Of these 168 at least were biblical or liturgical and little more than a dozen were secular in content. Fourteen volumes, mainly lectionaries, had superbly ornamented covers enriched with gold and silver decoration. Some items of this fine collection still survive but about 200 manuscripts have disappeared.[77]

[75] Variously known as 'the monastery of Studius' or incorrectly as 'the Studium', this was the monastery of St John Baptist in the district of Studius; see Janin, *Églises et monastères*, III, 430 ff. and Dagron, 'Le Christianisme dans la ville byzantine', 8–9.

[76] See Lemerle, *Humanisme byzantin*, 121–8.

[77] The library catalogue and subsequent history of the library was analysed by C. Diehl, 'Le Trésor et la bibliothèque de Patmos au commencement du 13ᵉ siècle', *BZ*, 1 (1892), 488–525 (with text of the 1201 inventory); much work on the Patmos archives has since been done by members of the Hellenic Research Centre, see E. L. Vranousi *et al.*, Σύμμεικτα, I (Athens, 1966), *passim*; and E. L. Vranousi, Τὰ ἁγιολογικὰ κείμενα τοῦ ὁσίου Χριστοδούλου . . . (Athens, 1966). On the inventory see now C. Astruc, *TM*, 8 (1981), 15–30.

During the course of the middle ages certain centres or houses attained considerable prestige and influence. In the eighth century Mount Olympus rising up behind Brusa in Bithynia had a vigorous monastic colony. It was here that Theodore Studites began his early career. He was well known as the consistent opponent of the iconoclasts and as the fierce denouncer of imperial intervention in church affairs. But more important still was his outstanding work as a monastic leader. After the disturbances of the iconoclast movement there was widespread need to restore order in the disrupted daily life of monastic houses. Theodore was a wise spiritual director as was shown by his much used addresses to monks known as the *Greater and Lesser Catecheses*. He was a firm and humane abbot and an able administrator. The Studite Constitution based on his work laid down detailed instructions for a temperate regime exacting obedience but avoiding 'both extremes and inadequacy'. As the Constitution admitted, the way of life which he advocated was only one of many rules for monasteries, but it could justly claim to be the most widely used and approved way, 'the royal rule'. In basic principles it was very like the Benedictine rule. One of the best descriptions of daily routine in a Studite house is to be found in an address given by Symeon the New Theologian (†1022).[78] He began his stormy monastic life in the Studite house in Constantinople and then left under the cloud of insubordination to become abbot of St Mamas, another house in Constantinople. Here standards had evidently slipped. Like Theodore, Symeon gave addresses to his monks and these homilies continued to be used by later generations; in fact a special edition of them was prepared for general use and with this in mind certain personal touches were cut out. They offered practical guidance in the spiritual life and they dealt with the many small trials of everyday relationships and conduct in a community. They were in fact so painfully penetrating that Symeon's monks evidently found it hard to sit through them and on at least one occasion there was a riot in protest at his regime.

Theodore Studites, who was liturgist and hymnographer as well as abbot and administrator, continued to exercise far-reaching influence. His character though forceful was more balanced than that of the fiery and passionate Symeon, 'the most enthusiastic zealot', who went to such extreme lengths in urging on his monks. Theodore was used and quoted from San Salvatore of Messina in Sicily and Patir di Rossano in South Italy to the Pečersky house in

[78] Symeon the New Theologian, *Catecheses*, vol. III, no. 26, pp. 68–97.

Kiev. For instance Sicilian and Calabrian *typica* stipulated that at certain appointed times all monks had to leave their work and assemble in church to hear the *Catecheses* of Theodore Studites being read.[79] The Studite St John Baptist monastery in Constantinople remained a leading house during the middle ages and in the early fifteenth century was described as richly decorated with mosaics with its seven altars and its chapels to the Theotokos, but thereafter the church was converted to Muslim use and the monastery left to fall into ruins and disappear.[80] The foundations on Bithynian Mount Olympus which had come under the control of the Studite house in Constantinople, together with many other monasteries in the region, were still flourishing in the eleventh and later centuries. But eventually Muslim inroads and the unsettled state of Asia Minor took their toll.[81]

Another source of strength to monastic life was found in northern Greece on the peninsula of Mount Athos, a spectacular setting with its stark cliffs and well-wooded hills rising to the high peak at the southern end. Even before the tenth century there were monks and a foundation on the Holy Mountain and from Basil I onwards there had been imperial interest in the Athonites. It was in 963 under imperial auspices that the Great Lavra, the most important of the cenobitic houses, was founded by Athanasius, the confessor of the Emperor Nicephorus II Phocas. Settlements with their dependencies grew and were international in character including not only Greek foundations but those of other races—Serbian, Georgian, Russian, and for a time Italian. The tenth-century settlements found it expedient to have a common council which provided a useful representative committee. Their meeting place was at Karyes on the central western side of the peninsula where the hegumeni sat under a protos.[82] Thus a kind of federal system was set up and in course of time the Great Lavra became the dominating house. Surviving libraries and archives of these houses contain

---

[79] On the strength of Greek influence in South Italy see A. Pertusi 'Rapporti tra il monachesimo italo-greco ed il monachesimo bizantino nell'alto medio evo', *La chiesa greca in Italia dall'VIII al XVI secolo* (*Atti del convegno storico interecclesiale*, Bari, 1969; Padua, 1972), II. 473–500.

[80] See Janin *Églises et monastères*, III. 430–40.

[81] See Janin, *Églises et monastères*, II, section VI, *passim*.

[82] On the early settlements and the development of the central assembly see *Actes de Protaton*, ed. D. Papachryssanthou (= *Archives de l'Athos*, 7, Paris, 1975), *passim*.

priceless printed books and manuscripts, often liturgical, and much valuable material dealing with internal administration or with relations between the different houses, sometimes disputes over their land boundaries. Many of the documents also inevitably concern involvement with outside authorities, problems arising over donated property, mostly in northern Greece and the islands, or appeals to the Emperor on questions of fiscal immunities.[83]

Despite many complications over property and disputes over financial exactions, all of which are so often detailed in its archival material, Athos was intended to offer a life dedicated to prayer and contemplation and as far as possible disturbing factors were excluded. Besides banning every form of female life it did strive to exclude lay intruders, such as villagers seeking to graze their herds on the land of the peninsula. Though fully recognizing the obligation of hospitality, its charters did not make specific provision for services to the laity such as occur in some *typica*.

The monastic federation of Athos was particularly well known but there were many other establishments. Another group which, like Athos, has survived if precariously, was that of the Meteora. These houses were founded in the fourteenth century on inaccessible peaks rising up near Kalambaka in Thessaly. For long the only approach was by means of a net winched up the sheer cliff. But with unfortunate 'modernization' of access the houses have become show pieces and monastic life was, and is, threatened by tourist inroads, so that after enduring the rigours of the Second World War and after[84] some of the few monks left have been driven to take refuge on the Holy Mountain, though even here made-up roads and timber lorries have penetrated, displacing the age-long tracks. Many other houses have long since disappeared, or, like the Cappadocian rock monasteries in Asia Minor hollowed out of the vast peaks, remain uninhabited, virtually in ruins and sometimes mutilated with only fading frescoes or even a refectory table and benches carved out of the limestone, to point to their life before the Turks came. Some monasteries are known only from surviving

[83] This indispensable body of material is now in process of being edited in the series *Archives de l'Athos, Actes*. See *Actes de Lavra*, I—IV (= Archives 5, 8, 10, 11, Paris, 1970–82); *Actes de Saint Pantéléèmon* (= Archives 12, Paris, 1982), ed. P. Lemerle *et al.* and other volumes.

[84] See the firsthand experiences of Hammond, *The Waters of Marah*; who lived in northern Greece in the early 1950s, and D. M. Nicol, *Meteora*, 2nd ed. (London, 1975).

charters (*typica*), or from isolated references in saints' lives, or from imperial and patriarchal registers. At its best, to make a foundation was an edifying deed pleasing to God and might also provide for specified services to the sick or old or poor,[85] but this was not the primary aim and sometimes did not figure at all, as in the charter which the monk Christodoulos of Patmos obtained in 1081 from the Emperor Alexius I, though there was usually the customary alms-giving. Charters drawn up by laity would ensure a burial place for the founder and his family and their perpetual commemoration in the prayers of the community. Attempts were made to ensure the independence of the house including freedom from molestation by various fiscal agents. Christodoulos tried to safeguard his island from tax-collectors and requisitioners by laying down an amazingly detailed list of protected items, in fact everything on the island ranging from brood mares and mules to rabbits and 'anything on four feet', from peacocks to ducks and any kind of egg. He also specified that no exiles were to be planted on the island. Charters gave instructions for the administration of the house, the election of future abbots, the permitted number of monks, the role of the founder and his descendants, and the endowments were carefully listed. Foundations could be a means of investing capital in an inalienable property and often of ensuring a home for the founder in old age. Alexius I's wife, Irene Ducaena, arranged quarters for herself in her foundation in Constantinople. The fourteenth-century minister Theodore Metochites had the same in mind for himself when he built up the library in the monastery of the Chora for use in his old age.

Houses were founded by various classes and races. The eleventh-century Michael Attaliates (originally having some link with Attalia on the southern Asia Minor coast) was a Constantinopolitan lawyer of means who used his property to found an almshouse in Raidestus and a small church in Constantinople. Christodoulos, a refugee monk (also originally from Asia Minor), gained a grant of the island of Patmos and became head of the now famous and still flourishing monastery of St John the Divine. Gregory Pacurianus, a wealthy Georgian, provided for monks who spoke and wrote Georgian though his foundation was in northern Greece near Philippopolis.

---

[85] The many monastic services to those outside the house are discussed by D. J. Constantelos, *Byzantine Philanthropy and Social Welfare* (New Brunswick, 1968).

What is striking about these charters is their attempt to ensure protection from outside authority (and the almost certain rapacity of tax officials) and to prevent alienation of endowments, stressing the authority of the founder and his descendants in the case of laity.[86] For lay founders it was a kind of family insurance policy motivated by the very human desire to provide security in this world as well as the next. The foundation was not necessarily on any site connected with some special event or miracle but on property owned by the founder. It was often only a small family affair enjoying none of the publicity of the grand foundations whose *typica* have survived. Nevertheless these many lesser houses were of supreme importance in Byzantine social and economic life, particularly in the town. Financial resources donated to a monastery could not be drawn on by the fisc and they could prove economically productive if well handled thus providing a kind of annuity for the founder and his family.[87]

The coveted independence of a monastic foundation was always a vexed question. It cut across diocesan and often patriarchal authority and it had financial implications, such as the payment of the usual *canonicon* tax to the bishop. There was moreover no guarantee that standards would be maintained, and it might not always be possible to carry out the arrangements in the charter, perhaps through lack of descendants, though a resourceful founder like Gregory Pacurianus appointed the Studite house to act in the last resort in the election of the abbot. From time to time particularly from the eleventh century onwards efforts were made by the Church to exercise control through the supervision of patriarchal officials.

The continued proliferation of monastic houses brought other problems. Deeply rooted in Byzantine society as it was, the monastic way of life itself was not challenged, but attempts at a high level were made to regulate it. The tenth-century Emperor Nicephorus II was certainly not anti-monastic. But while specifically

---

[86] See Lemerle, *Cinq études*, on Gregory Pacurianus and Michael Attaliates; for Patmos see E. Vranousi, above, note 77. For Pacurianus's Typikon now see P. Gautier, *REB*, 42 (1984), 5–145.

[87] For the effect on towns of these pious foundations and the economic implications see Dagron, 'Le Christianisme dans la ville byzantine': see also Dagron's comments on A. Failler's paper 'Le Monachisme byzantin aux XIᵉ et XIIᵉ siècles: Aspects sociaux et économiques', *Cahiers d'histoire*, 20 (1975), 299–301.

praising the more eremitic monks living in cells and lauras he tried to prevent new cenobitic foundations at a time when houses already founded were falling into ruins. In the long run he was unsuccessful. Not only did Basil II repeal his legislation but the urge to make a new foundation remained strong. Saints' lives sometimes relate how their hero came across a monastery in ruins which he then built up. This tendency was never eradicated in the middle ages and even as late as the twentieth century the abandonment of buildings left to decay seemed endemic in Asia Minor.

Troubles also arose in the reverse direction. In the legislation of the same Nicephorus II it was emphasized that the unseemly accumulation of property by some foundations ran counter to the tenets of genuine monastic life. It is true that this accumulation was partly due to pious donations or to the 'dowry' brought by those entering monastic life but there is also evidence that there was sometimes a deliberate policy of land acquisition.[88] This frequently resulted in under-productivity which affected the finances of the state. To remedy this a practice was evolved whereby a monastery was given into the charge of another authority, lay or ecclesiastical. If lay this was originally for one or two lifetimes. The translation was called a 'gift' ($\delta\omega\rho\epsilon\acute{a}$) and the beneficiary was the charisticar- ius.[89] The procedure may have been of long-standing practice but surviving evidence is mainly from the tenth century onwards. The tirade directed against this practice by John Oxites, Patriarch of Antioch during Alexius I's reign, as also that of the twelfth-century Eustathius of Thessalonica, are both well known. John Oxites had many grievances and this was one of them, no doubt well founded in certain cases where the monastery was starved of essential means to the benefit of the charisticarius. Worse still, said Oxites and

---

[88] See P. Charanis, 'The Monastic Properties and the State in the Byzantine Empire', *DOP*, 4 (1948) 53–118. On the general legal aspects of monastic property see J. M. Konidares, *Τὸ δίκαιον τῆς μοναστηριακῆς περιουσίας ἀπὸ τοῦ 9ου μέχρι τοῦ 12ου αἰῶνος* (Athens, 1979).

[89] Commonly referred to in modern usage as a charisticarium, but see P. Lemerle, 'Un Aspect du rôle des monastères à Byzance: Les monastères donnés à des laïcs, les charisticaires', *Compte rendu à l'Acad. Inscript. et Belles Lettres* (Paris, 1967, reprinted Variorum, London, 1978), pp. 9–28; H. Ahrweiler, 'Le Charisti- cariat et les autres formes d'attribution de couvents aux Xe–XIe siècles, '*ZRVI*, 10 (1967), 1–27 (reprinted Variorum, London, 1971); on the charisticium in general see E. Herman, 'Ricerche sulle istituzioni monastiche bizantine ...' *OCP*, 6 (1940), 293–375 and in *DDrC*, 3 (1942), cols. 611–17.

Eustathius, the practice led to an infiltration of laity into the monastery thus almost converting it into a secular establishment. The charisticarius might intrude laymen or even go to live in the house himself with his family. Any development of this kind which turned a monastery into a secular dwelling was forbidden by canon law (Chalc. can. 24; Quinisextum, can. 19). Presumably the Empress Irene's separate quarters in her foundation did not count as secularization of the house as such.

Abuse of the system affected not only the inmates of the monastery but the ecclesiastical authorities. Legislation during Alexius I's reign shows the difficulty of keeping track of the possessions of a house granted out. Patriarch Nicholas III with the support of Alexius I made an evidently not very successful attempt to get possessions registered in the patriarchal chancery in a detailed inventory in order to prevent charisticarii from selling or otherwise disposing of them at will.[90] From the late eleventh century onwards there was an increasing need to conserve all financial resources of the patriarchate. These were in any case being diminished by enemy inroads and at the same time there was the added burden of providing for the refugee clergy flooding into Constantinople.

Authorities (including Balsamon) did not condemn the practice of the charisticium though aware of its abuses. Its faults were an obvious target for critics, but little publicity was given to any who cared for the welfare of the houses entrusted to them, as Psellus sometimes did.[91] At its best the system afforded protection to the house and provided estate management which was beyond the resources of the monks. How burdensome monastic property could become is well illustrated by the surviving archives of the Athos houses. Athos itself was somewhat outside normal practice and had to cope with its own problems. But particularly during the latter middle ages the advantages of protection for an ordinary house were recognized and a system of *ephoreia* was practised. An ephor or guardian of some eminence would be nominated by the Emperor, or the house would be put in the care of a larger and well-known establishment, such as John II's house of the Pantocrator. Not that

[90] *GR* 931; *DR* 1115; see J. Darrouzès, 'Dossier sur le Charisticariat', *Polychronion: Festschrift F. Dölger* (Heidelberg, 1966), 150–65.

[91] From his Letters Psellus had an interest in various houses in the Mount Olympus region and made some efforts on their behalf; see Janin, *Églises et monastères*, II. 161 and 167.

this last was anything new. The Bithynian houses were connected with the family of Theodore Studites and were closely linked with his house in Constantinople; Michael Attaliates did something of the same with his foundations; and in her charter of 1115 the Empress Irene expressly rejected anything of the kind and forbade that her house should ever be given as 'dorea or epidosis or ephoreia', thus showing that arrangements of this sort were then being practised.[92]

It may be asked what monastic 'withdrawal from the world' really meant in the life of East Rome. Many surviving sources seem to point to an almost restless quality like that of the urge to the *peregrinatio* of the Celtic monks. This comes out in the extensive travelling which occupied the lives of many monks and which gave the lie to suggestions of any inevitable barrier between East and West. The late ninth-century St Blaise (†c.910) went from Constantinople to a house on the Aventine in Rome for eighteen years, then back to the Studite house for another four years before setting off for Athos where he founded a community. Pirates, brigands, and warfare deterred Byzantine monks no more than they did nineteenth-century British travellers in the Aegean. Palestine, Mount Sinai, Cyprus, the monasteries on the western side of Asia Minor, were all visited by the fourteenth-century St Sabas.[93]

This was not tourism but a quest. In some cases such as the missions to the Slavs (like the English St Boniface to the Germans) the results were tangible. Though often not. But 'withdrawal', as spiritual directors pointed out, was a withdrawal of the mind, an interior process. In a monastic house where conditions might be thought to favour a spiritual life there were still contacts with fellow humans with all the attendant annoyances and problems, as Symeon the New Theologian knew only too well. Even withdrawal to a cell or cave might not ensure complete isolation. Symeon the New Theologian is regarded as one of the greatest of Orthodox contemplatives, but it should be added that although he did have a

[92] MM 5. 332. 'Epidosis' was the handing over of a house to the charge of another monastery or to an ecclesiastic who drew the revenue; it is often referred to in sources of the later middle ages when the maintenance of refugee bishops was a problem.
[93] For examples of far-flung monastic travel see A. E. Laiou-Thomadakis, 'Saints and Society in the late Byzantine Empire', *Charanis Studies: Essays in Honor of Peter Charanis*, ed. A. E. Laiou-Thomadakis (New Brunswick, 1980), 84–114.

period of isolation he was for the most part a man with an active public life. As a young man he was engaged in violent altercation with the abbot of his house, then he became the vigorous head of his own monastery, embroiled in public debate with the churchman Stephen of Nicomedia, condemned by the synod for insisting on publicly pursuing the unauthorized cult of his own spiritual director, exiled but still in touch with many families in Constantinople, persistent in his refusal of the synod's peace overtures (understandably as he had no wish to become an archbishop as was suggested to him). His life was no exception though perhaps more stormy than most. Monks were closely knit into the fabric of Byzantine life. They did not always live up to their ideals and like other members of Byzantine society were satirized. But they cannot be judged simply by the prohibitions of conciliar, synodal, or imperial rulings. The defects which these reveal are more than balanced by positive achievement, the pursuit of a Christian way of life which included major contributions to Orthodox spirituality and to the development of one significant aspect of that spirituality, the liturgy.

10. The spiritual life of the Orthodox in Byzantium

It may be asked what was the nature of the Christian life within the Church just described, a Church marked by long, sustained, and usually unsuccessful, dialogue with its Latin neighbours, as well as by its often constructive missionary work, though it failed with Islam, and latterly was hampered by innumerable difficulties in maintaining everyday diocesan life in a splintered Empire. In dealing with so vital an aspect of Byzantine society as the Church it would be odd (though not unknown) to fail to emphasize the significance of its religious life, if only briefly, and also tentatively, since historians are not usually experts on liturgy and theology, music, art, and architecture, all of which are relevant in assessing Byzantine religious life during the long medieval period which saw change as well as conservation.[94]

It was well understood in the East Roman Empire that Christians were members of a Church marked by a supra-natural character. By means of its sacraments, or mysteries as they were called, special

---

[94] There is no satisfactory, detailed and comprehensive survey of the Byzantine Church known to me; see below pp. 369 ff.

graces were conferred on members of this society through the Holy Spirit. These sacraments were not always pinned down to seven as in the Latin Church, though this number came to be usually accepted. Baptism, together with confirmation or *chrismation* (so called from the anointing with chrism or oil) which was conferred at the same time as baptism, marked the infant's entry into the Church. It was an important occasion and could be accompanied by elaborate ceremonial. Once baptized and therefore a full member of the Church the baby could receive the consecrated bread and wine in the sacrament of the eucharist. This sacrament was known in the Orthodox Church as the liturgy, or the Divine Liturgy.[95] Other sacraments were marriage, holy orders, penance, anointing of the sick. There were also rites not found in the West, such as the blessing of waters at Epiphany, which if not regarded as sacraments were thought to have a sacramental character. Great emphasis was placed on baptism (with *chrismation*) and the eucharist, and it is understandable that these form the core of the fourteenth-century classic of Byzantine spirituality, Nicholas Cabasilas's *Life in Christ*.

Besides the eucharist there were also other services, or offices, offering daily prayer and praise to God in monasteries, cathedrals, and churches. In 528 Justinian I ordered all clergy in every church to say the main daily offices, that is, orthros[96] and vespers, for he thought that it was quite wrong that laity should so zealously flock into churches to perform their part in the psalmody while the clergy shirked their own obligations.[97] The monastic offices were seven or eight in number, depending on whether the midnight service was counted separately or reckoned in with orthros which immediately followed it. These offices were midnight, orthros, prime (the first hour counted from sunrise, about six a.m. but varying with the season), terce, sext, none, vespers, and compline. Of these orthros and vespers were the most important and had the more elaborate services.

Anyone who has been present at vespers or orthros in an Orthodox monastery in the East Mediterranean may well have wondered at the pile of large black books carried by the entering

[95] The word 'liturgy' has a double meaning; it can stand either for the eucharistic service or for church services in general.

[96] Modern writers sometimes use 'matins', sometimes 'lauds', for this dawn service, so for clarity the Greek 'orthros' is used here.

[97] *Corpus*, II, *Codex*, I, 3, 41 (42), p. 28.

monks. These are usually the Venetian-printed liturgical books needed for the office of that particular day and season.[98] The eucharist and the daily offices had certain fixed prayers and litanies, readings, canticles, and responses. But there were also special additions depending on the day of the year and on the Church's season. Of the twelve major festivals some had a fixed date, such as Christmas (25 December) or the Annunciation (25 March), others depended on the date of Easter which was on the Sunday following the first full moon after the Spring equinox and therefore varied from year to year. Seasons, such as Lent, or the coming of the Holy Spirit at Pentecost, took their timing from the date of Easter. In addition each day of the year commemorated a growing list of saints, or some special occasion. Further there were books for the different melodies, called modes or tones, allotted to each week, or for special days, and used for the sung portions of the office. It was because of this rich variety of worship in the Church's year that so many different books were needed for all the daily services.

So complicated a system did not spring into being ready made, and a good deal could happen between the second and the fifteenth centuries. As in other spheres of Byzantine life conservatism was tempered by creativeness and change. By the seventh century morning and evening prayers and the commemoration of the Lord's Supper of the very early period had developed into services whose basic structure corresponded to the daily worship which was found in the medieval Orthodox Church and later.[99] But during the middle ages there was both further development and clarification particularly with regard to the eucharist and the daily offices of orthros and vespers. In fact one of the significant achievements of the medieval period was the splendid hymnody which at its best

---

[98] The sixteenth-century Venetian press was the first to print Orthodox liturgical books and it reprinted them at intervals. They continue to be used in many East Mediterranean monasteries. There are also some more modern editions, see the *Festal Menaion*, p. 12. The question of the redaction used in Venice is examined by A. Raes, 'Les Livres liturgiques grecs publiés à Venise', *Mélanges E. Tisserant*, III (*ST* 233, Vatican, 1964). He shows how individual 'correctors' could determine content, change the rubric, and add or delete, often without the authorization of the Great Church, though in fairness it should be added that changes were not so drastic as to affect the Orthodox liturgical tradition.

[99] For a brief survey of the early period up to the seventh century see H. Chadwick, *The Early Church* (London, 1967), ch. 18.

was marked by poetic quality as well as spiritual content and was indissolubly linked to the music to which it was sung.[100] At the same time it was necessary to draw up service books providing the material appropriate to the calendar and seasonal cycles of the liturgical year. Here a debt is owed to the authors of the hymns, often monks, and to certain monastic houses, notably St Sabas in Palestine and the Studite house in Constantinople, whose practices set the pattern for some of the service books perfected during the middle ages and still in use today, if with some modification particularly in small monasteries and at parish level.

Originally the sung (*asmatikos*) service of cathedrals and large secular churches was not identical with the monastic offices though in course of time each borrowed from the other.[101] For instance they had different ways of distributing the psalter, of dealing with the biblical canticles and of introducing the canons. Also the cathedral practice demanded more singers and priests and deacons than the monastic usage. The early fifteenth-century Symeon, archbishop of Thessalonica (†1429), lamented that after the breach in 1204 the splendid cathedral ceremonies had almost entirely fallen out of use.[102] Not altogether though, to judge from archimandrite Ignatius of Smolensk's description of the coronation of Manuel II and his Serbian wife Helena Dragaš in 1392 in Hagia Sophia. He told of the rich and colourful clothes and embroidered coats of arms of the multinational congregation, the women in the galleries behind silk curtains able to view without being seen and the equally splendid ecclesiastics with the magnificently garbed cantors. Then there were the all-night services climaxing the next day in the coronation and the eucharist with the chanting of the *cherubikon* and the consecration prayer. Despite Symeon of Thessalonica's lament it would appear that even in the last days of the Empire something of its former glory was possible.[103]

The basic elements in vespers and orthros were psalms, readings from the Scriptures, prayers, verses, and responses, together with

[100] See Wellesz, *Byzantine Music and Hymnography.*
[101] See O. Strunk, 'The Byzantine Office at Hagia Sophia', *DOP*, 9–10 (1956), 175–202.
[102] *De Sacra Precatione, PG* 155, col. 556.
[103] See R. Salomon, 'Zu Ignatij von Smolensk', *Beiträge . . . Theodor Schiemann* (Berlin, 1907), 260–5 (German trans.), and S. P. Khitrovo, *Itinéraires russes en Orient* (Geneva, 1889), 143–7 (French trans., needs revision).

the commemorations which at orthros would include a brief description of the saint's life taken from the appropriate *Menaion* or month book which gave the hymns, responses, and account of the saint or saints for each day of that particular month. It is not proposed here to set out all the service books[104] or to discuss the extensive work in progress on the medieval offices and Divine Liturgy.[105] But it is possible to indicate some of the main changes introduced, particularly in orthros with the development of the canon and its accompanying music.

The complexity of the daily services can be seen by looking at the structure of the offices, particularly orthros.[106] In the monastic offices the whole psalter, divided into twenty sections each called a *kathisma*[107] was covered in a week unless there were other arrangements as was the case at special times such as the Lenten fast. In addition to the psalms, prayers, litanies, and readings, by the sixth century there were many single sung verses or stanzas (*troparia*) interpolated into Palestinian practice if the account of the abbot of St Catherine on Mount Sinai's reported disapproval of this can be credited. Monastic communities and anchorites at this time seem to have thought that such practices undermined the proper austerity of the office. Thus by the mid-sixth century it would appear that the biblical canticles with other songs or hymns had been introduced.[108] Some hymns, as 'O gladsome light' (Φῶς ἱλαρόν) sung

---

[104] These are listed in Wellesz, *Byzantine Music and Hymnography*, and in the *Festal Menaion* which also gives definitions of technical terms used in Orthodox services, as does D. Touliatos-Banker, 'The Byzantine Orthros', *Byzantina*, 9 (1977), 351–7.

[105] Much is being done by the Pontifical Institute of Oriental Studies and a glance through its periodical *OCP* and its publications in the *OCA* will indicate work examining in detail the development of Orthodox offices and liturgy. There is also a good brief general survey in *DS*, 11 (1982), 'Office divin byzantin' (M. Arranz), cols. 710–20, though this does in effect give more on the monastic office of the Sabaite tradition than cathedral services.

[106] See D. Touliatos-Banker, 'The Byzantine Orthros' *Byzantina*, 9 (1977), 325–50 and *Festal Menaion*, 'Plans of the Services'.

[107] *Kathisma* also has the meaning of a verse (*troparion*) at the end of a section (also called a *kathisma*) of the psalter and in the *Festal Menaion* this is translated as 'sessional hymn'.

[108] The biblical canticles were songs usually in praise of some special occasion, such as Moses' hymn of victory after the crossing of the Red Sea (Exod. 15) or the Magnificat (Luke 1). In the Middle Ages they were usually counted as nine, the ninth and tenth being taken together (Magnificat and Benedictus). They are listed in Wellesz, *Byzantine Music and Hymnography*, 38.

at vespers, were of great antiquity. Others which came to be added were creations of the middle ages. The sixth-century Syrian-born Romanus, influenced by Syriac poetry, wrote superb and dramatic hymn-sermons known as *kontakia*. These consisted of a number of verses, all written to the same metre, which was based on syllable and stress, not quantity as in classical metre, and they were sung with a refrain. Romanus may perhaps have been the author of most of the great *Akathistos* (that is 'sung standing') *kontakion* still used in the Orthodox Church—all of it is sung on the Saturday of the fifth week in Lent.[109] Its opening verses referring to the protection of the capital by the Theotokos in a time of great danger must have been added later, probably in the early seventh century.

But the *kontakion* hymn was not to remain a feature of the office. From the late seventh century onwards a new form of hymn, the canon, was developed, said to have been invented by a Palestinian monk Andrew who became bishop of Crete (†*c*.740). Some of the best-known canons were from monastic circles, particularly St Sabas in Palestine (John of Damascus and Cosmas, bishop of Maiuma) and in the ninth century the Studite house in Constantinople (Theodore Studites and Joseph the hymnographer). The canon became a feature of the office of orthros. Though it tended to displace the reading or singing of the biblical canticles it remained closely related to these songs. It consisted of nine hymns or odes each of which was linked to a different biblical canticle and reflected its content. There was an acrostic running through the various verses of the odes which makes it possible to tell when the original canon has been shortened, which sometimes happened. The second ode, being based on a penitential biblical canticle, was usually omitted. The climax came with the ninth ode which was in honour of the Theotokos and linked to the Magnificat and Benedictus. Each ode was prefaced by its mode (ἦχος) which gave the starting note. This was followed by the *hirmus* or verse which set the metre for each ode and for which the melody was composed. As the number of canons increased the different pattern verses were collected in a service book, the *Hirmologion*, and the melodies were written above each line of the pattern verse. Poets then just put the first two or three words of their selected model at the beginning of each of their eight odes (the second being omitted) together with the mode.

109 See *Lenten Triodion*, 419. On the authorship cf. C. Trypanis, *Fourteen Early Byzantine Cantica* (Vienna, 1968).

The singers would at once know the melody and the starting note.

The writing of canons was not confined to the famous monastic centres and they were produced by laity as well as monks and clergy. Many canons never got into the service books. There are whole collections often in sets of eight, one for each mode, each set dedicated to Christ or to a saint. Such collections might have been used as supplementary hymn-books or perhaps may have simply expressed religious devotion. There are for instance 151 canons attributed to the eleventh-century John Mauropous almost all of which are still in manuscript.[110]

By the eleventh century there was not much room in the already full liturgical round. Still sanctity did not abruptly dry up from the eleventh century onwards, nor did ecclesiastical problems cease. Some additions were made, as for the fourteenth-century canonized Gregory Palamas. Then there was the late eleventh-century institution of the festival of the three fathers, Chrysostom, Basil, and Gregory of Nazianzus, for which commemoration John Mauropous, archbishop of Euchaita, was said to have written the canons for orthros found in the *Menaion*. And from time to time condemnation of some heresy was added to the Synodicon read on Orthodoxy Sunday at the beginning of Lent. There were also offices which did not get into the regular service books, as that for Symeon the New Theologian in manuscript on Mount Athos and printed in this century as a pamphlet by a local press at Volos.

In setting out directions and in providing additional material for the various parts of the services the Studite house was an important centre particularly in the formative period from the ninth century onwards. It was responsible over the years for the *Triodion*, a liturgical book for the Lenten fast, so called because the eight odes of the orthros canons were reduced to three,[111] and also for the *Pentecostarion* for the period from Holy Saturday evening, that is from the beginning of Easter rejoicing. Theodore Studites and others of his house did much to expand and beautify the monastic office so that the Constantinopolitan usage, widely followed elsewhere, as on Athos or in Russia, gradually became less austere. With an increasingly full calendar it was necessary to provide direction

---

[110] See J. M. Hussey, 'The Canons of John Mauropous', *JRS*, 37 (1947), 70–3, and E. Folieri, *Giovanni Mauropode, metropolita di Eucaita, otto canoni paracletici a N. S. Gesù Cristo* (Rome, 1967).

[111] Much of this is translated in the *Lenten Triodion*.

for the conduct of the services and for this purpose *typica* were drawn up.[112] They varied in their rubrics for as in other respects there were many differences in usage.[113]

Music came to have an important place in the Orthodox services and in some cases, for instance the canons, words and music went together. This close relation of words to melodic formulae is well demonstrated by Wellesz who gives examples of the words and music of some of the outstanding Byzantine hymns, as John of Damascus's canon for Easter day.[114] The elucidation of Byzantine musical notation has made much progress during the last fifty years and it is now possible to transcribe the eight modes. The Byzantines used plain chant and had no instruments in their churches (it was otherwise with imperial court ceremonial). A reproduction of the *Hirmologion*, the book which gives music and metrical patterns for the canons, can be seen in the splendid series *Monumenta Musicae Byzantinae*. The principle of the eight modes had already been set out in an earlier musical handbook for more general purposes, the *Little Octoechus*. This is said to have been the work of John of Damascus and others at the monastery of St Sabas. It gives the mode and words of the sung pieces for each week beginning with the Saturday evening of Easter week. During what is known as the middle period of Byzantine music (twelfth to fifteenth centuries) melodies, particularly for the *stichera* (stanzas), were remodelled, introducing ornamentation subtly related to the word stress. Those who have heard this music will probably agree that it equals, perhaps even surpasses, the plain chant of the Latin Church.

Byzantine religious life derived strength from the daily offices, but its mainspring was the eucharistic service, the celebration of the Last Supper. This was not normally every day except in some of the larger monastic houses. The early eleventh-century Symeon the New Theologian certainly speaks of daily communion which contrasts with fourth and fifth-century monastic usage. Running through the life of the Church from its very inception was the belief that man was destined to be made divine, here only in part, but wholly in the next world. This could come about through indivi-

---

[112] The word *typicon*, also used of a monastic foundation charter, has the general meaning of 'direction' or 'rulings'.

[113] Monastic offices according to the *Typicon* of St Sabas are set out in *DS*, 11, cols. 716–19.

[114] Wellesz, *Byzantine Music and Hymnography*, ch. 9.

dual response to the grace of the Holy Spirit (synergy). Such active participation in divinity, or deification (θέωσις), did not mean sharing the unknowable essence of God but participation in the divine and uncreated energies. Palamas had emphasized this, though it was evident from the earliest days of the Church and was an integral part of the teaching of both eastern and western fathers. It constantly recurs in medieval Orthodox writings. The seventh-century Maximus the Confessor, writing of the mystery of deification, like others before him, stressed that God had become man that man might be deified. Those, he said, who communicate in a right disposition can with grace become gods and be called as such.[115] It followed that the eucharist was the centre of Orthodox religious worship and that the gift only became operative when the recipient's daily life made him worthy to receive it, a point stressed by spiritual directors such as Symeon the New Theologian.

The Orthodox eucharist, like the daily offices, existed in several versions. The most commonly used was the Liturgy of St John Chrysostom (not however written by this father). Others were the Liturgies of St Basil and of St James. The Liturgy of the Pre-sanctified belonged to certain times in Lent and had no consecration of the gifts in its service, but used the Bread and Wine consecrated at the previous Sunday eucharist. The eucharist service is a dramatic one with its two processions, the Little Entrance preceding the Gospel reading, the Liturgy of the Word, and then the Great Entrance when the bread and wine, the gifts, are brought to the altar. In some places, Constantinople for instance, in the earlier period the gifts were brought from a building or sacristy (*skeuophy-lakion*) outside the church. The climax of the service was the eucharistic prayer of consecration with its invocation (epiclesis) of the Holy Spirit. This was followed by the communion of the faithful, the blessing and dismissal.

During the period of more than a thousand years the simple communion rite of the second century was filled with prayers, litanies, chants, to accompany the rites and to meet the needs of various developments.[116] The extent and complexity of this filling out can be seen from the instructions for the patriarchal eucharist

---

[115] *Orat. dom. exp.*, PG 90, col. 905D; *Mystagogia*, 21 PG 91, cols. 696D–697A.

[116] See R. Taft, 'How Liturgies grow: The Evolution of the Byzantine "Divine Liturgy"', *OCP*, 43 (1977), 355–78; see also his 'Mount Athos: a Late Chapter in the History of the Byzantine Rite', *DOP*, 42 (1988), 179–94.

according to the rite of the Great Church as celebrated in the eleventh century and set out in a *Diataxis* (a *Typicon* or rubric book).[117] Then in some big cities, as Constantinople (it was the same in Rome too) on certain days the services were held at other churches called 'stations' and served by the clergy of Hagia Sophia. The Patriarch, clergy, and laity would go in procession to these stations and accompanying chants and prayers had to be produced for such occasions.

The action of the eucharist service was held to have symbolical meaning. And not only the sacramental rites but the church building, the mosaics and frescoes on the walls, the icons—all these were closely linked to the Christian interpretation of the Divine economy, or plan, for the cosmos. This is reflected in the actual post-iconoclast layout of the building and in the iconography. Here Nicaea II and the victory over iconoclasm were significant for architecture and representational art. The long-naved basilica, such as St Demetrius of Thessalonica, well suited to the earlier processions of clergy and laity gave way to the more centralized cross-in-square church with a single-spaced interior covered by the main cupola, with the ambo, a tall pulpit which in Hagia Sophia had steps leading up to it and room for the cantors underneath it. There was a solea or passage-way from the ambo to the sanctuary, and then beyond the body of the church the sanctuary itself into which no layman might go, save only the Emperor at certain times. The *prothesis* and *diaconicon*, small rooms either side of the sanctuary, appeared to take the place of the outside *skeuophylakion* or sacristy where such had existed, as in Constantinople. There were many different local and provincial variations, but surviving Byzantine churches, whether the resplendent Hagia Sophia (now a museum), the minute Athenian churches, or the modest monastic *catholica*, as Hosios Loukas and Nea Mone on Chios, do on the whole illustrate the cross-in-square principle and the iconography of the later eleventh-century churches shows an enrichment contrasting with the more austere decoration of the immediate post-iconoclast period. The emphasis of the iconography changed too, becoming less imperial and more sacerdotal, reflecting the power of the clergy

[117] R. Taft, 'The Pontifical Liturgy of the Great Church according to a Twelfth-Century Diataxis in Codex British Museum Add. 34060', *OCP*, 45 (1979), 279–307 and 46 (1980), 89–124.

and stressing the eucharist, as in the frescoes of Christ and the communion of the apostles.[118]

The interpretation of the eucharistic rite and the church in which it took place was considered in commentaries written at widely differing intervals. These works also throw light on the development of the eucharistic rite during the course of the middle ages. The best known are the *Mystagogy* of Maximus the Confessor, the *Historia Ecclesiastica*, the first version of which is attributed to Patriarch Germanus I (eighth century), and the *Explicatio* of Nicholas Cabasilas (fourteenth century). There were also the *Protheoria* written for a bishop and his clergy in the late eleventh century and then the very late works of Symeon, archbishop of Thessalonica in the fifteenth century.[119] Maximus the Confessor's was the first medieval attempt to explain the symbolism of the eucharist and he wrote (with a distinct Alexandrian bias) more for monastic than for lay circles. It was otherwise with Patriarch Germanus writing for laity with an Antiochene historical emphasis stressing the connection between the eucharistic rites and the earthly life of Christ. Together they laid the foundation for the symbolism which was to develop in the post-iconoclast period.

The church building, the cross-in-square, was the whole cosmos dominated by Christ the Pantocrator looking down from the centre cupola. Beneath and grouped round him on the vaults and walls were the heavenly host, angels, and saints, with the Theotokos in the apse above the sanctuary. On the walls was pictured the life of Christ, and then of the Theotokos, the Dormition often on the west wall and scenes from her life on the narthex walls. Thus clergy and congregation would be conscious of their unity with the celestial world pictured around them: together they were the Church. As the *Historia Ecclesiastica* put it, 'The Church is heaven on earth',[120] to be echoed more than five hundred years later by Nicholas

---

[118] See T. F. Mathews, *The Early Churches of Constantinople: Architecture and Liturgy* (London, 1971); O. Demus, *Mosaic Decoration: Aspects of Monumental Art in Byzantium* (London, 1948); C. Mango, *Byzantine Architecture* (New York, 1976), and C. Walter, *Art and Ritual of the Byzantine Church* (London, 1982).

[119] The best guides to these commentaries are Bornert, *Commentaires*, and H.–J. Schulz, *Die byzantinische Liturgie: Glaubenszeugnis und Symbolgestalt*, 2nd edn. (Trier, 1980); there is a good general introduction by R. Taft, 'The Liturgy of the Great Church: An Initial Synthesis of Structure and Interpretation on the Eve of Iconoclasm', *DOP* 34–5 (1980–1).

[120] The passage is cited by R. Taft, op. cit. 72–3.

Cabasilas, 'Angels and men form one Church, a single choir because of the coming of Christ who is both of heaven and of earth'. Within the church everything symbolized some aspect of the Divine economy. The altar was Christ's tomb; the sanctuary stood for the unseen heavenly sanctuary; the bishop's throne in the apse behind the altar was where Christ sat with the apostles and it prefigured his coming again in glory (the *parousia*). In this way the whole history of salvation was symbolized and not only for the church and its contents. The *Historia Ecclesiastica* goes on to explain the sacramental rites in terms of Christ's plans for man's redemption. This *Historia* was the most widely used and probably the most important of the medieval commentaries on the symbolism of the eucharist and it existed in various versions revised to meet changing needs. For instance the development of the prothesis rite, the preparation of the gifts, brought changes of emphasis and increased stress on Christ present in the elements.

It was not until the mid-fourteenth century that another influential treatise of this kind was written, this time by a layman and a master of the spiritual life, Nicholas Cabasilas. His *Explicatio* or *Commentary on the Divine Liturgy*[121] came late into the medieval Orthodox Church. It was closely linked to, and in some respects supplemented, the fourth book on the sacraments of his *Life in Christ*. As with earlier mystagogical interpretations, every part of the eucharistic rite was stressed as being central to Christian belief and linked to the redemptive plan of Christ and to the deification of each human being, and in Cabasilas's case there was a strong eschatological emphasis. It is only after this life that full blessings come to the perfect.[122] The heir of the earlier commentators, yet he reflected the problems of his own age—such as hesychasm, or concern with the omission of the epiclesis from the Latin words of institution in the mass. The freshness and clarity and insight of his approach in presenting the traditional teaching of his Church have commended his commentary on the Byzantine eucharist to succeeding generations, both Orthodox and Roman Catholic alike. He was highly lauded at the Council of Trent.

Cabasilas was not the last to write on the symbolism of the

---

[121] Trans. S. Salaville, 2nd edn. with R. Bornert *et al.* (*SC*, 4 bis, Paris, 1967) and J. M. Hussey and P. A. McNulty, *Commentary on the Divine Liturgy* (London, 1960 and 1978).

[122] See Nicholas Cabasilas, *Commentary*, ch. 1, p. 28 and ch. 45, p. 102.

eucharistic rite. Symeon, archbishop of Thessalonica, continued this tradition up to the eve of the fall of his city to the Turks. Comparatively little known, though there are signs of more interest in him, he left a bulky corpus on a variety of topics, historical as well as liturgical.[123] His liturgical writings cover the seven sacraments and certain other ceremonies and rites, as the consecration of a church. In his two treatises on the Church and the Holy Liturgy he followed Maximus the Confessor (and the Pseudo-Dionysius) and thus favoured the Alexandrine tradition.[124] Apart from interpretation of the rites, Symeon's writings are of special value for their exposition of pontifical liturgy as he knew it. He also touches on the *prothesis*, the preparation of the bread and wine, which Philotheos Coccinus had sorted out in his *Diataxis* (book of rubrics). Like his predecessors Symeon found in the eucharistic rites symbolism for the different actions in the life of Christ. For instance the Little Entrance with the gifts symbolized the coming of the Incarnate Christ. To the different parts of the church he assigned the traditional symbolism and again the unity of the Church was emphasized. 'There is only one Church above and below', and the eucharist is the cosmic (παγκόσμιον) sacrifice[125] and he stressed that the foundation of the faith was the episcopacy and the ancient and excellent traditions of the Church.[126] Thus to the very end the tradition was maintained to be handed on after 1453 to succeeding generations in the Orthodox Church.

The commentaries on the symbolism and meaning of the Divine Liturgy, too often overlooked, are a salutary reminder that this mystery was the mainspring of Orthodoxy for all—laity, monks, and clergy. It was moreover stressed that great preparation and a right disposition were necessary before approaching the eucharist. Thus Christian life had a twofold aspect. There was the remembrance of the Divine purpose, of the life of Christ and of the saints, all set out in the liturgical year and recalled in the cycle of the

---

[123] See D. Balfour, *Politico-historical works of Symeon Archbishop of Thessalonica (1416/17–1429): Text and commentary* (Vienna, 1979) and Ἔργα Θεολογικά ('Ανάλεκτα Βλατάδων, 34, Thessalonica, 1981); Symeon's liturgical works are being edited by J. M. Phountoules, I, Εὐχαὶ καὶ Ὑμνοι (Thessalonica, 1968); see also *PG* 155.

[124] See Bornert, *Commentaires*, 248–63.

[125] *PG* 155, *De Sacro Templo*, ch. 131, col. 340 A.

[126] *PG* 155, *Expositio de divino templo*, ch. 86, col. 700D–701B.

services, crowned by participation in the eucharist. Then linked to this was the constant struggle to practise personal asceticism, to eliminate impure thoughts and actions. Thus through the synergy, the working together with the Holy Spirit through the grace implanted at baptism, it would be possible to progress towards knowledge of God through participation in the uncreated divine energies. As Basil the Great said, 'We affirm that we know God through his energies, but we do not presume to approach his essence.'[127]

The medieval Church had its outstanding—and well-known—classics of the spiritual life.[128] The fourth-century Cappadocians, the two Gregories and Basil, were followed by a succession of distinguished Christian thinkers. As well as Maximus the Confessor and John of Damascus, both of whom explored the problems of Christian doctrine and spirituality, there were others whose writings were widely used particularly in monastic circles. Evagrius of Pontus (fourth century) though condemned for Origenist tendencies left writings on the spiritual life which managed to creep into monastic circles under cover of other names. Pseudo-Macarius (fourth to fifth century) was not the fourth-century Egyptian monk as used to be thought, but probably lived in Mesopotamian reaches surrounded by Messalian influences which he challenged.[129] He had links with Basil and Gregory of Nyssa and like Mark the Monk (fourth to fifth century)[130] stressed that grace through the Holy Spirit must be actively experienced. Diadochus, bishop of Photice in Epirus (fifth century),[131] wrote *capita* on the spiritual struggle which were highly valued—they together with Mark the Monk's

---

[127] Basil, Ep. 234 (edn. Loeb, III, p. 372).

[128] To examine the differing approaches of individual spiritual writers is outside the scope of this work. Guidance may be found in the *Dictionnaire de spiritualité* (bibl.) and many texts have appeared in the *Sources Chrétiennes* (with French trans.); see also Beck, *Kirche* (bibl. to about 1957).

[129] See V. Desprez, ed. and trans., *Pseudo-Macaire, Œuvres Spirituelles* I (*SC* 275, Paris, 1980 with bibl.).

[130] Sometimes known as Mark the Hermit, but see K. T. Ware, 'The Sacrament of Baptism and the Ascetic Life in the Teaching of Mark the Monk', *Studia Patristica*, X, ed. F. L. Cross (Berlin, 1970), 441–52. See also H. Chadwick, 'The Identity and Date of Mark the Hermit', *ECR* 4 (1972), 125–30 and O. Hesse, 'Was Mark the Monk a sixth-century Higumen near Tarsus?' *ECR* 8 (1976), 174–8.

[131] See Diadoque de Photicé, *Œuvres spirituelles*, ed. and trans. E. des Places (*SC* 5 bis, Paris, 1955).

works were given to the young Symeon the New Theologian by his spiritual director. John of Sinai (sixth to seventh century) wrote a *Ladder* giving the thirty steps whereby progress might be made in the spiritual life,[132] a work which was vividly illustrated in surviving manuscripts; it was pored over by Symeon the New Theologian who found a copy in the library of the family home in Paphlagonia. Isaac of Nineveh (seventh century)[133] writing in Syriac was translated into Greek in the ninth century by monks of St Sabas, and his translators took care to replace any citation of Evagrius with the name of an acceptable orthodox substitute. Evagrius's work on prayer for example circulated under the name Nilus of Sinai. The sober homilies of Theodore Studites (ninth century) formed daily reading in many cenobitic houses. The abbot Symeon the New Theologian (†1022) left a fiery and passionate collection of sermons and poems instructing his monks and describing his own agonizing struggles and his rewarding experiences.[134] All these were formative influences, often not mentioned by name but clearly recognizable. Symeon's flaming and fanatical love for the brothers in his charge—'I am a most enthusiastic zealot'—reflects Isaac of Nineveh's same emphasis, 'I am become mad for the sake of my brothers' profit'. Thus often without open acknowledgement earlier work was integrated into a common tradition and this continued throughout the middle ages, and was reinforced by later medieval teachers such as Gregory of Sinai and others associated with the hesychast movement.

Some spiritual directors, as Evagrius of Pontus or Maximus the Confessor, thought in clearly marked stages, but this is not always the case as Symeon's writings show. In general there was agreement that the body must be brought under control by constant fasting and prayer, by mourning, repentance, and tears, thus inducing a state of *apatheia* which was not simply the elimination of passions, but an active state of charity and perpetual turning towards God. From the days of the New Testament onwards the exhortation to

---

[132] Trans. Lazarus Moore (London, 1959).

[133] Eng. trans. from P. Bedjan's edn. of the original Syriac (Paris, 1909) by A. J. Wensinck, *Mystic Treatises of Isaac of Nineveh* (Amsterdam, 1923, re-ed. Wiesbaden, 1967).

[134] There are critical editions in the *SC* of Symeon the New Theologian's works (with trans.) by J. Darrouzès (*Theological and Ethical Treatises*), B. Krivocheine (*Catecheses*), and J. Koder (*Hymns*).

pray without ceasing had been stressed and there was endless teaching on this and the form which such prayer might take varied. Diadochus advocated increasing invocation of the words 'Lord Jesus', or simply 'Jesus', and there were many other forms. Words very like, or similar to, the later standard form 'Lord Jesus Christ, Son of God, have mercy on me', as used by Gregory of Sinai (†1346), can be found in sixth-century works, but this was not then general, nor were any special physical methods then advocated to accompany such a prayer in order to induce complete withdrawal, as later with the hesychasts.[135]

Once the initial stages in spiritual progress had been mastered the state of *apatheia* was reached and this was maintained by withdrawal into holy quiet or *hesychia*. This spiritual silence, this peace of heart, was in its highest form a state of wordless prayer. Isaac of Nineveh said that all must stand still, 'for the master of the house has come'. This was the goal. But to describe it as a 'vision' is perhaps misleading in that it conceals the essential nature of the experience and indeed of Orthodox spirituality. Originally there had been some difference of interpretation. This turned on the relation between mind and matter, soul and body. Was knowledge of God something which only illuminated the mind, almost a platonic illumination of the intellect, or did it deify the whole human being? The suspicion with which the fourth-century Evagrius of Pontus was sometimes regarded, or the condemnation (perhaps unjustly) of the eleventh-century scholar John Italus for supposed Platonic teaching, emphasized the Church's realization that any dualist separation of mind and body would deny the reality of the Incarnation of the second Person of the Trinity, Christ, true God and true man. It was only because God became man that men could become gods. The reality of sharing in God was repeatedly emphasized. It was an actual physical consciousness of the indwelling Christ. The body became divine. Thus, wrote Symeon, my members are Christ and if they offend it is an offence against the Godhead. The most direct expression of this is in Symeon's Hymn 15. This is the Hymn from which Pontanus expunged certain passages on the ground that they would cause scandal.[136] But the implications of Orthodox teaching on deification are as Symeon

[135] See K. Ware, 'The Jesus Prayer in St Gregory of Sinai', *ECR* 4 (1972), 3–22.
[136] See *PG* 120, cols. 531–2, note 19.

stated. Its essence was that it fully involved mind, soul, and body. But if the experience came it could not be sustained in this life. The soul sank back into despair and had to renew its struggles.

This experience seemed to require no hierarchy, no mediator. It raised the question of the powers of the specially holy man and his place in the Church. In Byzantium as elsewhere the saintly man, whether ordained or not (usually not) had always been specially reverenced; the authority derived from his particular charismata was unquestioned. Some, as Symeon the New Theologian, went further and seemed to endow the spiritually gifted but unordained monk with some of the functions of the priesthood, and even denied unworthy priests the right to perform the sacraments. Problems of this kind had been experienced from the very early days of monasticism, when monks wished to be exempt from normal ecclesiastical discipline and in some cases were regarded as having special powers. But such situations were met and to some extent resolved by the common sense of monastic leaders and the judicious rulings of church councils. The strength of the Orthodox Church lay in its wisdom in not forcing the issue. For instance it allowed some latitude in the matter of spiritual direction and confession. It was able to accept and use the outstanding goodness of a holy man without having to weave sociological theories of explanation.

Spiritual directors often wrote for solitaries and cenobites. But not always as Nicholas Cabasilas's *Life in Christ* showed. In many cases it was made clear that a high degree of perfection could be attainable in all walks of life. In the early days of monasticism the desert fathers could recall and praise the spiritual achievement of a doctor toiling away at his profession in Alexandria. Ascetic discipline and inward activity did not exclude manual or intellectual work. Indeed, as Macarius said, while walking or talking or eating a Christian should always have in mind 'the memory of God'. It might be thought that the rigorous demands made by spiritual directors were beyond all but the most dedicated solitary or cenobite. But deification was not the preserve of a select minority. In practice monks themselves rarely had a secluded life. If in a community they came into contact with its other members as well as with laity through hospital or community services, and monasteries frequently had essential outside business. Anchorites might withdraw to isolated places, yet their solitude was often disrupted by devout visitors and suppliants. Moreover it was clear that all were exhorted to look to the needs of their brethren. Thus progress towards knowledge of God was shared by all. No one had more exacting standards than Symeon the New Theologian and he included everyone in the passionate plea which marked his last hymn (no. 58). In this he addressed all men, emperors and rulers, monks and laity, metropolitans, bishops, and priests, castigating them all, yet appealing to all. In a calmer spirit in his *Life in Christ* Nicholas Cabasilas made the same call to men in every sphere, whether working in the city or the countryside.

Despite the insistence that Christian life could be lived to the full by all it is difficult to assess how far this was so. Evidence so often records sins and omissions, the survival of pagan rites and the prevalence of magic. Superstition was widespread and not confined to Christians. Muslims for instance tried to get their babies baptized just to be on the safe side. But there is also evidence of the careful instruction of children of the servants on a country estate or in the villages. And in daily life, in baptism, in marriage, and in death, the humblest Christian necessarily had contact with the Church. There was too the weekly liturgy, if not always morning and evening offices. In a large city like Constantinople it is known that there were crowded services in Hagia Sophia. On the many festal days there were processions of clergy and people going on foot from the cathedral to celebrate at the various stations, the civil officials on horseback, as also the Emperor, though he sometimes went by boat, and the Patriarch if old would join the procession nearer the stational church.[137] The village as well as the city had its celebrations, its panegyria which have survived to the present day. Such events may have been an occasion for spectacular festivities, but they were motivated by the desire to testify to events or saints remembered by the Church with gratitude and they had the liturgy and special chants appropriate to the day. To some degree the thronging crowd would have been aware of this. Within the church the inarticulate majority may well have felt something of the transcendental spirituality of the liturgy, as foreign visitors did. In some respects it is possible that Orthodox worship at the end of the middle ages did not differ in essentials from what was found during the present century in villages and monasteries of Greece and on

[137] See R. Janin, 'Les Processions religieuses à Byzance', *REB* 24 (1966), 69–88.

Mount Athos.[138] Those who have taken part in the splendid festal services in a church such as Thessalonican Hagia Sophia or in the simpler weekly liturgy of a village church will have some understanding of what Orthodoxy meant in the middle ages.

In certain ways the legacy from the middle ages left problems. Some Byzantines (as also some Latins) thought that religious differences between the Orthodox and the West were not insuperable and had in fact been over-emphasized. Nevertheless considerable prominence over a long period was given to the controversies between the two Churches, partly because of increasing involvement with pressing political needs particularly in the later period, and this did seem to underline the differences between Rome and Orthodoxy each convinced of the validity of its own position, a point of view lasting into modern times and hardly a constructive background to any oecumenical efforts. Then there is the question of national Orthodox Churches, rather a divisive element in the modern world-wide expansion of Orthodoxy.[139] It is true that this was a development which had been aggravated by modern secular states, but it was certainly found in embryo in the middle ages, though kept in check by the medieval conception of an Orthodox 'commonwealth'.

But there is much on the credit side. Orthodoxy had its beginnings in the days of the early Church but it was shaped during the middle ages. The medieval Orthodox Church owed a particular debt to the guardianship of the Byzantine Empire. The capital, Constantinople, provided a focus for Orthodoxy during a period when the three eastern members of the original pentarchy, Alexandria, Antioch, and Jerusalem, were no longer able to contribute anything in the way of leadership, though Jerusalem remained the objective of devout pilgrimage and was for a time a factor in Christian crusader politics. Byzantine missionary work, though

---

[138] See the experiences of P. Hammond, *Waters of Marah*; and there is a firsthand description of life on Mount Athos in the 1950s by C. Cavarnos, *Anchored in God: An inside Account of Life, Art, and Thought on the Holy Mountain of Athos* (Athens, 1959). There is a good introduction to the thought and practice of the Orthodox Church in P. Evdokimov, *L'Orthodoxie* (Neuchâtel and Paris, 1959); see also the brief comments in T. Ware, *The Orthodox Church* (London, 1963), pt. II and J. Meyendorff, *Byzantine Theology: Historical Trends and Doctrinal Themes* (London and Oxford, 1975), pt. II.

[139] Cf. J. Meyendorff, *The Byzantine Legacy in the Orthodox Church* (New York, 1982), 225–9.

unsuccessful with Islam and with the Jews, was however significant, mainly because it brought Christianity to the South Slavs and Russia, and with it knowledge of the East Roman world. The capital always had many religious links outside its frontiers, as for instance with Georgia, or with Mount Sinai, and it was a kind of international clearing-house. Orthodox monks moved freely throughout the Middle East and elsewhere. Its Church was sustained by a body of writings which in their profundity offered— and continue to offer—spiritual guidance not only to the Orthodox but to Christians of other beliefs. And it was within the Empire that Christian dogma was hammered out in the general councils. But perhaps the greatest gift of the East Romans to the Orthodox Church was the creativeness which fostered the growth of the liturgy. It was not that Constantinople was in any way exclusively responsible for the many different elements which conditioned the development of the liturgy, but it did provide a framework within which the spiritual life of the Church could grow during a thousand years and more. It is possible that the presentation of the great sacramental mystery with its dignified ritual may have been influenced by the feeling for ceremony so deeply rooted in imperial life. Like the icons and the figures and scenes in mosaic and fresco on the church walls, the drama of the rite, the music and responses gradually added over the years, all had their place in conveying to the faithful however unlettered the events of the Christian dispensation and an awareness of their participation in the 'mystery of faith' and in the cosmic unity of all believers. When Constantinople fell the Emperor and his ministers vanished, but the bishop, the core of each local Christian community, remained and the Church, strengthened by the liturgical tradition built up during the middle ages, lived on.

BIBLIOGRAPHICAL NOTE

THIS book makes no attempt to provide a comprehensive bibliography. In general, works in Slav and non-European languages are not cited here. Much valuable work has been, and is being, done by scholars in the Balkans and in Eastern Europe and reference to this can usually be found in the bibliographical sections of international periodicals especially the *Byzantinische Zeitschrift* or *Byzantinoslavica*.

Certain books have been reprinted unaltered and such reprints have not generally been noted. Some bibliographical references will be found in appropriate footnotes in the text, but for readers wanting a first-time quick survey suggestions are added here giving a few secondary authorities with some reference books and collections of sources.

GENERAL WORKS

The best short account of the general historical background (with notes on the sources) is G. Ostrogorsky, *History of the Byzantine State*, 2nd English edn. based on the 3rd German edn. of 1963 with a few bibliographical additions (Oxford, 1968). L. Bréhier, *Le Monde byzantin*, 3 vols. (Paris, 1947–50), covers the whole range of Byzantine life; the second volume (*Institutions*) has a section on the Church and has its uses but does not bring out the element of change and now needs some revision. The *Cambridge Medieval History*, vol. IV, pts 1 and 2 (Cambridge, 1966–7), covers most aspects of Byzantine history and life including chapters on ecclesiastical topics; it has detailed bibliography to about 1966. H. Ahrweiler, *Byzance et la mer* (Paris, 1966) covers a good deal more than the title would suggest and has a running commentary on the course of Byzantine history. Among more recent general treatments are A. Guillou, *La Civilisation byzantine* (Paris, 1974) and A. P. Kazhdan, *Byzanz und seine Kultur* (Berlin, 1973), both useful for discussion of social, economic and cultural factors, if only partially adequate on the Church. Kazhdan finds Guillou's treatment of the Church 'logical and harmonious', 'the church is plucked from its mystical haze and dumped into the thick of administrative life'. R. Browning, *The Byzantine Empire* (London, 1980) provides a brief introduction but is better on literature than the Church. Other personal interpretations are put forward by H.-G. Beck, *Das byzantinische Jahrtausend* (Munich, 1978) and C. Mango, *Byzantium: The Empire of New Rome*

(London, 1980). A good introduction to the influence of Byzantium and its Church on the Balkan peoples and Russia is found in D. Obolensky, *The Byzantine Commonwealth* (London, 1971). For general comments on the early medieval background see J. Herrin, *The Formation of Christendom* (Blackwell, 1987). A selection of sources is given by C. Mango, *The Art of the Byzantine Empire 312–1453* (Englewood Cliffs, N.J., 1972, reprinted Toronto, 1986).

One of the best descriptions of the impact of Christianity on the Byzantine Empire is given by H. Hunger, *Reich der neuen Mitte: Der christliche Geist der byzantinischen Kultur* (Graz, Vienna, and Cologne, 1965). H. Jedin (gen. ed.), *Handbuch der Kirchengeschichte* (Freiburg, Basel, and Vienna), II, 2 (1975) and III, 1 and 2 (1966–8) contains chapters on the Byzantine Church by H.-G. Beck, but these have now been superseded by H.-G. Beck, *Geschichte der orthodoxen Kirche im byzantinischen Reich* (Göttingen, 1980). Jedin has a full bibliography but this is inconveniently split between the different volumes; volume I has much that is relevant to the later period. The older A. Fliche and F. Martin, *Histoire de l'église depuis les origines jusqu'à nos jours* (Paris, 1934 ff.) still retains some value (see Bréhier and Amann in vols. 5–7). G. Every, *The Byzantine Patriarchate 451–1204*, 2nd edn. (London, 1962) presents a stimulating if sometimes controversial discussion of the historical setting but only to 1204. There is a good, if exceedingly brief, survey by D. Knowles and D. Obolensky, *The Christian Centuries*, II, *The Middle Ages* (London, 1969), giving both the eastern and western points of view.

ATLASES, GEOGRAPHY AND TOPOGRAPHY

See the *Cambridge Medieval History*, IV, General bibliography II, to which should be added: R. Janin, *La Géographie ecclésiastique de l'empire byzantine*, pt. I, vol. 2, *Les Églises et monastères des grands centres byzantins* (Paris, 1975) and vol. 3, *Les Églises et monastères: Constantinople* (Paris, 1953, 2nd edn., 1969); *Tabula Imperii Byzantini*, I, J. Koder and F. Hild, *Hellas und Thessalia* (Vienna, 1976), II, F. Hild, *Das byzantinische Strassensystem in Kappadokien* (Vienna, 1977) and F. Hild and M. Restle, *Kappadokien* [*Kappadokien, Charsianon, Sebasteia und Lykandos*], III, P. Soustal in co-operation with J. Koder, *Nikopolis und Kephallenia* (Vienna, 1981), IV, K. Belke and M. Restle, *Galatien und Lakonien* (Vienna, 1984); the series is in progress. See also H. Ahrweiler, 'L'Histoire et la géographie de la région de Smyrne entre les deux occupations turques (1080–1317) particulièrement au XIIIᵉ siècle', *Travaux et Mémoires*, 1 (1965), 1–204. Useful atlases with ecclesiastical maps are K. von Spruner—T. Menke, *Hand-Atlas ... 3rd edn. (Gotha, 1880); K. Heussi and M. Hermann, *Atlas zur Kirchengeschichte*, 2nd edn. (Tübingen, 1919); J. Martin, ed., *Atlas zur*

Kirchengeschichte (Freiburg, 1970, 2nd edn. 1987); J. Engel, *Grosser Historischer Weltatlas*, Pt. 2, Mittelalter, 2nd edn. (Munich, 1978).

A. Guillou, *La Civilisation byzantine*, is one of the few general books to give a section on the geography of the empire (with good illustrations and a separate bibliography).

CHAPTERS 1–5 (c. 600–c. 1025)

There is no satisfactory detailed work covering the whole of this period. J. B. Bury, *History of the Later Roman Empire . . . (395–800)*, 2 vols. (London, 1889; new edn. going only to 565, London, 1923), and his *History of the Eastern Roman Empire . . . (802–867)* (London, 1912), still remain valuable. R. Jenkins, *Byzantium: The Imperial Centuries A.D. 610–1071* (London, 1966) briefly presents a point of view but needs revision especially on the Church. Studies on individual emperors include A. Rambaud, *L'Empire grec au dixième siècle: Constantin Porphyrogénète* (Paris, 1970); A. J. Toynbee, *Constantine Porphyrogenitus, and his World* (London, 1973), uneven and not at his best on religion; S. Runciman, *The Emperor Romanus Lecapenus and his Reign: A Study of Tenth-century Byzantium* (Cambridge, 1920). G. Schlumberger's old and monumental but readable four volumes on the years 963–1057, *Nicéphore Phocas* (Paris, 1890) and *L'Épopée byzantine* (Paris, 1896–1905) contain a vast wealth of information (it is not always immediately apparent where it comes from). It needs revision; H. Grégoire was somewhat critical of Schlumberger (see his chapter on the Macedonians in the *Cambridge Medieval History*, vol. IV, pt. 1).

One profitable approach to the tenth century would be through the sources where reliable and accessible editions exist, as the *Vita Euthymii Patriarchae Cp.*, ed. and trans. P. Karlin-Hayter (Brussels, 1970), teeming with information on Leo VI's reign. There are also the informative letters of his contemporary Patriarch Nicholas I, ed. and trans. R. J. H. Jenkins and L. G. Westerink (Washington, DC, 1973). G. Moravcsik's edition of Constantine Porphyrogenitus, *De Administrando Imperio*, trans. R. J. H. Jenkins, 2nd edn. (Washington, DC 1967) with a separate full commentary by Jenkins *et al.* (London, 1962) shows the Byzantine attitude towards its neighbours. The *De Cerimoniis*, ed. in part and trans. by A. Vogt (Paris, 1935, 1939–40), provides detail on the year-long ceremonies at court.

Particular episodes falling within this period which are obvious subjects for treatment are the iconoclast controversy and the Photian troubles.

A good deal has appeared on the controversial subject of iconoclasm. Some bibliography is given (pp. x–xi) in *Iconoclasm*, ed. A. Bryer and J. Herrin (Birmingham, 1977), but this collection of papers read at a symposium in 1975 is uneven in quality and in spite of the title does not cover all the ground. The general survey by E. J. Martin, *A History of the Iconoclastic Controversy* (London, 1931) should be used with caution if at all. An introduction and some discussion of the first phase of the controversy may be found in A. Grabar, *L'Iconoclasme byzantin: Dossier archéologique* (Paris, 1957) and S. Gero, *Byzantine Iconoclasm during the Reign of Leo III* (Louvain, 1973) and his *Constantine V* (Louvain, 1977) both with special attention to the oriental sources. The second phase in the ninth century can be approached through P. Alexander, *The Patriarch Nicephorus of Constantinople: Ecclesiastical Policy and Image Worship in the Byzantine Empire* (Oxford, 1958). The aftermath of the iconoclast controversy is examined in the definitive work by J. Gouillard, 'Le Synodikon d'Orthodoxie: Édition et commentaire', *Travaux et Mémoires*, 2 (1967), 1–316. This deals not only with the more immediate state of affairs after 843 but provides a running commentary on later heresies all of which were in due course added to the condemnations in the Synodicon.

An essential introduction to the career of the scholar and Patriarch Photius and relations between Rome and Constantinople in the later ninth century is F. Dvornik, *The Photian Schism: History and Legend* (Cambridge, 1948) in which he shows that western condemnation of Photius as an arch-heretic was a late and unfounded charge. But see also the examination of the controversy by D. Stiernon, *Constantinople IV* (*Histoire des conciles œcuméniques*, 5, Paris, 1967), who gives commentary, texts (French trans.) and a critical bibliography. Some of Photius's homilies have been translated with comments by C. Mango (Cambridge, Mass., 1958).

Intellectual life is covered in one of the most memorable publications of recent years, P. Lemerle, *Le Premier Humanisme byzantin. Notes et remarques sur enseignement et culture à Byzance des origines au Xe siècle* (Paris, 1971).

CHAPTER 6 (C. 1025–1204)

(*Note*: The division is not entirely satisfactory, but 1204 is at least significant in that it marks the intrusion of the greatly resented Latin hierarchy into Byzantine dioceses.) There is no single detailed work bringing out the contrast between a flourishing intellectual and economic life, the failure to deal with the challenge of the advancing Turk and the encroaching Latin crusaders and the increasing problems of the Church. Schlumberger, op. cit., to the mid-eleventh century and Chalandon on the three Comnenian rulers (1081–1180) reveal nothing of the present ferment of discussion on the nature of Byzantine life in the eleventh and twelfth centuries. F. Chalandon, *Les Comnènes* ... I, *Alexis Comnène*; II, *Jean II Comnène* ... *et Manuel I Comnène*, 2 vols. (Paris, 1900–13) concentrates on political history and is solid but hardly stimulating, in fact it was said (I think by Diehl, probably by others too) that Chalandon had 'killed off' the Comnenian period as a subject for research for at least a generation or more. The last years before the Fourth Crusade (1180–1204) have more recently been covered by C. M. Brand, *Byzantium Confronts the West* (Cambridge, Mass., 1968) but very much from the political angle.

The ingredients for a reconsideration of the eleventh and twelfth centuries are now emerging. One constructive introduction to the period would be through P. Lemerle, 'Byzance au tournant de son destin', *Cinq études sur le XIᵉ siècle byzantin* (Paris, 1977) and the papers in *Travaux et Mémoires*, 6 (1976), *Recherches sur le XIᵉ siècle*. A lively antidote to Chalandon can be found in A. Kazhdan, *Studies on Byzantine Literature of the Eleventh and Twelfth Centuries* (Cambridge, 1984).

For an introduction to relations between Constantinople, Rome, and the western crusaders see P. Lemerle, *L'Orthodoxie byzantine et l'œcuménisme médiéval: Les Origines du 'schisme' des Églises (Bulletin de l'Association Budé*, 1965). A reference work on the crusades is the *History of the Crusades*, gen. ed. K. M. Setton, (1955– , in progress). There is an enormous amount of literature on these topics and there are many other approaches.

CHAPTERS 7–8 (C.1204–1453)

The 250 years of the splintered Empire are complex and difficult to deal with in a short note, and in any case from the point of view of the Church there is no single, detailed and well-balanced presentation. Works covering this period (including monographs on individual Emperors) often tend to be orientated towards relations between Constantinople and the West. J. Gill, *Byzantium and the Papacy 1198–1400* (New Brunswick, 1979) does just this with success even if slightly biased towards the West. K. M. Setton, *The Papacy and the Levant (1204–1571)* (Philadelphia, 1976–1981) gives full and readable detail with rich bibliography but is also rather more concerned with western than Byzantine reactions. The two general councils of the period have been fully treated. Here the best guides are: for Lyons II, B. Roberg, *Die Union zwischen der griechischen und der lateinischen Kirche auf dem II. Konzil von Lyon (1274)* (Bonn, 1964); and H. Wolter and H. Holstein, *Lyon I et Lyon II (Histoire des conciles œcuméniques*, 7, Paris, 1966); and for Ferrara–Florence see J. Gill, *The Council of Florence* (Cambridge, 1959) and his *Constance et Bâle–Florence (Histoire des conciles œcuméniques*, 9, Paris, 1965). There is a racy firsthand account of what went on behind the scenes on the occasion of the Ferrara–Florence council by a high official from Hagia Sophia, *Les 'mémoires' du Grand Ecclésiarche de l'Église de Constantinople Sylvèstre Syropoulos sur le concile de Florence (1438–1439) (Concilium Florentinum: Documents et Scriptores*, set. B, 9, Rome, 1971), ed. and trans. V. Laurent. Some insight into the attitude of one of the more understanding Byzantine emperors towards union is seen in John VI Cantacuzenus's discussion with the papal legate Paul, edited by J. Meyendorff, *Dumbarton Oaks Papers*, 14 (1960), 147–77 (Greek text, summary, and commentary).

In the first half of the thirteenth century the situation was complicated by rivalry between the two Greek kingdoms of Epirus and Nicaea which is briefly described by D. M. Nicol, *The Despotate of Epiros* I & II (Oxford, 1957; Cambridge, 1984) and M. Angold, *A Byzantine Government in Exile* (Oxford, 1970), not particularly full on the Church. There is a vivid account of the experiences of a delegation of friars to negotiate on union with John III Vatatzes of the Nicene Empire, *Disputatio Latinorum et Graecorum* ... ed. G. Golubovich, *Archivum Franciscanum Historicum*, 12 (1919), 428–70, not however a book easy to come by. The prominence often given to the negotiations on union should be balanced by probes into regional activities. For instance on the structure of society in the Peloponnese see D. Jacoby, 'The Encounter of Two Societies: Western Conquerors and Byzantines in the Peloponnese after the Fourth Crusade', *American Historical Review*, 78 (1973), 873–906. Or on the measure of symbiosis between Greeks and Latins in Cyprus see A. and J. Stylianou, *The Painted Churches of Cyprus* (Cyprus, 1964). Conditions in Asia Minor outside the control of either Greek or Latin are revealed by S. Vyronis, *The Decline of Medieval Hellenism in Asia Minor* ... (Los Angeles and London, 1971). Similar probes could be made in other regions, e.g. the Cyclades or Crete, see the references given in chapter VII above. The differing attitudes of Greek and Latin to theological problems are discussed by Podskalsky, *Theologie und Philosophie in Byzanz* (Munich, 1977), but he is often not easy reading; he gives a note on Latin theological works translated into Greek.

The Greek church re-established in Constantinople in 1261 had its internal problems. On hesychasm see as a start J. Meyendorff, *Introduction à l'étude de Grégoire Palamas* (Paris, 1959, also trans. later into English (London, 1962) but less full). Poverty and other economic difficulties are described in *The Letters of Patriarch Athanasius I*, ed. A.-M. M. Talbot (Washington, DC, 1975). This should be balanced by the less well publicized but important work by N. Oikonomides, *Hommes d'affaires grecs et latins à Constantinople (XIIIe–XVe siècles)* (Montreal and Paris, 1979). A salutary reminder that 1453 did not mean the end of the Orthodox patriarchate (any more than 1054 marked a definite schism) can be found in S. Runciman, *The Great Church in Captivity* (Cambridge, 1968).

PART II. ORGANIZATION AND LIFE OF
THE ORTHODOX CHURCH

General

A full and reliable account of the Orthodox Church in the Byzantine Empire has yet to be written. In fact this is probably not yet possible because evidence is still in process of emerging, so that only interim reports can be presented, although there were certain basic tenets which remained unchanged throughout the period. There are several very brief general accounts usually from the Orthodox point of view, e.g. T. Ware, *The Orthodox Church* (London, 1963); J. Meyendorff, *Byzantine Theology* (London and Oxford, 1975) and his *The Orthodox Church* (New York, 1981), which goes up to the present day. A good exposition though exceedingly brief is 'The Byzantine Church' by J. Meyendorff in *The Byzantine Legacy in the Orthodox Church* (New York, 1982). A somewhat more detailed presentation is found in H.-G. Beck, *Geschichte der ortho-doxen Kirche im byzantinischen Reich* (with bibliography) (Göttingen, 1980).

Political theory: relations between church and state

Discussions on this topic occur *passim* in most general Byzantine histories, but are sometimes misleading and treat the problem out of context. A short balanced assessment may be found in S. Runciman, *The Byzantine Theocracy* (Cambridge, 1977). H. Ahrweiler, *L'Idéologie politique de l'Empire byzantin* (Paris, 1975) presents a point of view showing how emphasis in imperial ideology varied. O. Treitinger, *Die oströmische Kaiser- und Reichsidee* (Darmstadt, 1956) offers a massive collection of evidence (rather solid reading). A. Grabar, *L'Empereur dans l'art byzantin* (Paris, 1932), shows differing attitudes towards the Emperor as evidenced by representational art. F. Dvornik, *Early Christian and Byzantine Political Philosophy*, 2 vols. (Washington, DC, 1966) is important but unfortunately hardly gets to Byzantium properly speaking.

Administration

There is no full and compact account of either central or diocesan administration, though there are valuable detailed studies on particular aspects (see J. Darrouzès cited in pt. II above). The best brief introduction is probably E. Herman, 'The Secular Church', *Cambridge Medieval History*, vol. IV, pt. 2. L. Bréhier, *Le Monde byzantin*, II (*Institutions*) is fuller but was published in 1949 before a good deal of fresh material became available. There are two short studies on the synod in Constantinople, the sometimes misleading J. Hajjar, *Le Synode permanent (σύνοδος ἐνδημοῦσα) dans l'église byzantine des origines au XIᵉ siècle* (OCA 164, Rome, 1962) and R. Potz, *Patriarche und Synode in Konstantinopel. Das Verfassungsrecht des ökumenischen Patriarchates* (Vienna, 1971) which deserves to be better known. Instances of the various ways in which the canons had to be modified and *ad hoc* directives given to meet changing circumstances can be found in the rulings of Theodore Balsamon in Rhalles and Potles (see below under Reference Works) and more particularly revealing are those of Demetrius Chomatianus in J.-B. Pitra, *Analecta Sacra et Classica*, VI (Paris and Rome, 1891). Many examples of everyday practical problems can be seen by looking through the patriarchal and imperial registers (see below).

Religious life

Theology. The basis of Orthodox teaching was hammered out in the general councils, two of which (by Orthodox reckoning) fell within this period, i.e. Constantinople III (680) and Nicaea II (787). The vital Trinitarian and Christological problems were constantly coming to the surface. An introduction to these problems in their historical setting is given by H.-G. Beck, *Kirche und theologische Literatur im byzantinischen Reich* (Munich, 1959), pt. 3; this is an indispensable reference book and pt. 4 contains notes on theologians and theological literature of the middle ages.

An introduction to the seventh century can be found in H. A. Wolfson, *The Philosophy of the Church Fathers*, vol. 1, 3rd edn. (Cambridge, Mass., 1970). The theological teaching of Orthodoxy in Byzantium is outlined by J. Meyendorff, *Byzantine Theology: Historical Trends and Doctrinal Themes*, 2nd edn. (New York, 1979), pt. II, *Doctrinal Trends*; like some other theologians (but unlike Lossky) he has reservations on the supposed influence of Pseudo-Dionysius on Orthodox teaching, cf. V. Lossky, *The Mystical Theology of the Eastern Church* (London, 1957; 2nd edn., New York, 1975).

Problems connected with Orthodox teaching abounded in the middle ages, e.g. iconoclasm (see above), or dualist heresies, see the general survey by M. Loos, *Dualist Heresy in the Middle Ages* (Prague, 1974). The best introduction to Byzantine heresies is J. Gouillard, 'L'Hérésie dans l'empire byzantin des origines au XIIe siècle', *Travaux et Mémoires*, 1 (1965), 299–324.

Liturgy. Orthodox theology found its expression in the public worship of the Church; its theology is reflected in the liturgy, both the eucharist and the daily offices. The best introduction on its development is R. Taft, 'How Liturgies grow: The Evolution of the Byzantine "Divine Liturgy"', *Orientalia Christiana Periodica*, 43 (1977), 355–78. The eucharist itself was a complex service and in some respects it varied with the day and season of the Church's year. There are various translations of the immovable part of the liturgy, e.g. Athenagoras Kokkina, *The Liturgy of the Orthodox Church*, Greek text and English trans. (London and Oxford, 1979). For the additions proper to certain festivals or periods of the year see the translations of Mother Mary and K. Ware, *The Festal Menaion* (London, 1969) and *The Lenten Triodion* (London and Boston, 1978). E. Wellesz gives an excellent introduction to the music and hymns used in the services in *A History of Byzantine Music and Hymnography*, 2nd edn. (Oxford, 1961). The Orthodox liturgy is not easy to follow but the constructive course is to abandon an armchair approach and be present at the actual services.

Discipline of the interior life. The best approach is twofold. First through the advice given on leading a spiritual life. Many writers are published (with trans.), some in the series *Sources Chrétiennes*, e.g. Pseudo-Macarius, or Symeon the New Theologian, writing for monastic circles, or, writing for a wider circle, Nicholas Cabasilas, *Life in Christ*, trans. C. J. de Catanzaro (New York, 1974), significantly linked to his work on the liturgy. Then, secondly, much can be gained from the lives of the saints which reflect the impact on ordinary laity of monks trying to put this spiritual discipline into practice. There are a number of lives translated, e.g *St Peter of Atroa*, ed. and trans. V. Laurent (Brussels, 1956), or the seventh-century John the Almsgiver, in *Three Byzantine Saints*, trans. E. Dawes and N. H. Baynes (Oxford, 1948). See also relevant comments on different aspects of religious life in *The Byzantine Saint*, ed. S. Hackel (London, 1981). The *Philokalia*, a collection of spiritual texts widely used in the Orthodox world, has been translated from the Greek by G. E. H. Palmer, P. Sherrard, and K. Ware (London, 1979–84).

Monasticism. The regulations governing monastic life are comprehensively dealt with by P. de Meester (see under reference works), but it needs a good deal of reconstruction to get a satisfactory picture of monastic life from his formidable detail. A better initial approach would be by way of D. J. Chitty, *The Desert a City* (Oxford, 1966) as background introduction, then passing on to consider one or two cenobitic houses as revealed in their foundation charters. See P. Lemerle, *Cinq études sur le XIe siècle byzantin* (Paris, 1977) on the well-endowed houses of Pacurianus and Attaliates. See also Pacurianus's *typicon*, ed. and trans. P. Gautier, *REB*, 42 (1984), 5–145. On the spiritual targets aimed at see above on the interior life. There is no single work satisfactorily covering the whole period. In a sense Orthodox monasticism is more difficult to deal with since unlike the Latin Church it did not differentiate into distinct orders but knew only a single ordo or way of life, and this was flexible in that monks often moved freely from community to eremitic life and sometimes back again. This comes out clearly in the saints' lives; in this respect the *Life of Symeon the New Theologian*, ed. I. Hausherr and G. Horn (Rome, 1928) is particularly instructive.

Collections of sources

Two of the main collections of sources for Church history are found in J. P. Migne, *Patrologiae Cursus Completus, Series Graeco-Latina* (Paris, 1857–66) and the *Corpus Scriptorum Historiae Byzantinae* (Bonn, 1828–97). These are being gradually superseded by new editions, chiefly in the *Corpus Fontium Historiae Byzantinae*. The older collection of the councils is J. D. Mansi, *Sacrorum Conciliorum nova et Amplissima Collectio* (Florence and Venice, 1759–98). See also *Conciliorum Oecumenicorum Decreta*, ed. J. Alberigo *et al.* (Freiburg, 1962) and P. P. Joannou, *Discipline générale antique*, I, *Les Canons des pères grecs* (*Pont. Comm. per la redaz. del Cod. di diritto can. orient. Fonti*, fasc. 9, Grottaferrata, 1962). Some of the canons which concern the Orthodox Church are given with translation and commentary by H. J. Schroeder, *Disciplinary Decrees of the General Councils* (St Louis, Mo., and London, 1937) and there are translations by H. R. Percival, *A Select Library of Nicene and Post-Nicene Fathers of the Christian Church*, 2nd ser., 14 (Oxford and New York, 1900). C. J. Hefele–H. Leclercq, *Histoire des conciles* (Paris, 1907–) contains some texts and comments but needs revision.

Patriarchal activities and the canonists are included in F. Miklosich and J. Müller, *Acta et Diplomata Graeca Medii Aevi*, 6 vols. (Vienna, 1860–90), and G. A. Rhalles and M. Potles, Σύνταγμα τῶν θείων καὶ ἱερῶν κανόνων, 6 vols. (Athens, 1852–9). Miklosich–Müller is in part superseded by H. Hunger and O. Kresten (ed.), *Das Register des Patriarchats von Konstantinopel* (*Corpus Fontium Historiae Byzantinae* XIX, Vienna 1981) giving text and translation covering the period 1315–31.

For hagiographical material see the Bollandists' *Acta Sanctorum* (Brussels, 1643–) and other publications of this Society. The writings of many Orthodox churchmen and monks can be found in the series *Sources Chrétiennes* (text and translation).

REFERENCE WORKS

Further detail on sources and secondary material can be found in G. Moravcsik, *Byzantinoturcica*, 2nd edn. (Berlin, 1958, the '3rd edn.' is a reprint), which covers a wide range of Greek source material; H.-G. Beck, *Kirche und theologische Literatur im byzantinischen Reich* (Munich, 1959); H. Hunger, *Die hochsprachliche profane Literatur der Byzantiner*, 2 vols. (Munich, 1978); F. Halkin, *Bibliotheca hagiographica graeca*, 3rd edn., 3 vols. (Brussels, 1957). These works have now largely taken the place of

K. Krumbacher, *Geschichte der byzantinischen Litteratur (527–1453)*, 2nd edn. (Munich, 1897) who listed and discussed the whole range of Byzantine sources available in his day. Guidance on specific points is found in F. Dölger, *Regesten der Kaiserurkunden des oströmischen Reiches*, pts. 1–5 (Munich and Berlin, 1924–65), pt. 3, 2nd edn. by P. Wirth (Munich, 1977); and for the patriarchate see *Les Regestes des Actes du Patriarcat de Constantinople*, V. Grumel, fasc. 1–3 (Paris, 1932–47), fasc. 1, 2nd edn. (Paris, 1972), fasc. 2–3, 2nd edn. J. Darrouzès (Paris, 1989); V. Laurent, fasc. 4 (Paris, 1971); and J. Darrouzès, fasc. 5–6 (Paris, 1977–9, in progress). On monastic regulations see P. de Meester (ed.), *De monacho statu iuxta disciplinam byzantinam* (Vatican, 1942). On canon law see the handbook of N. Milaš, *Das Kirchenrecht der morgenländischen Kirche*, 2nd edn. (Mostar, 1905).

The French ecclesiastical dictionaries (some still in progress) contain valuable material, especially the *Dictionnaire de droit canonique* (Paris, 1935–65), the *Dictionnaire de spiritualité* (Paris, 1937–), the *Dictionnaire de théologie catholique* (Paris, 1905–50), and the *Dictionnaire d'histoire et de géographie ecclésiastiques* (Paris, 1912–). All these should be supplemented by bibliography to date which is found in the annual international periodicals, especially *Byzantinische Zeitschrift* and *Byzantinoslavica*.

Addendum to Chapter 6:

M. Angold, *The Byzantine Empire 1025–1204* (London, 1984), which reached me after this book was in the press, gives a brief introduction to life under the later Macedonians, the Comneni and the Angeli.

GLOSSARY

This gives some of the terms used in the text. In the field of administration if can only be an approximate guide since titles and functions changed during middle ages. Some of the chief ecclesiastical offices are described in Part II and a detailed guide to their development can be found in *De Offikia.*

Antidoron	The blessed (not the consecrated) bread which is offered to all after the close of the Liturgy
Apocrisíarius	A papal or patriarchal legate
Azymes	Unleavened liturgical bread
Castellani	Governors or commanders of fortresses or strongholds especially in Venetian-occupied territory
Despot	In the later period a title bestowed by the emperor on an honorary, an imperial prince or a virtually independent ruler
Diaconicon	The part of the sanctuary to the right of the altar; it was used as a sacristy where vessels and vestments were kept
Diptychs	Two-sided tablets on which the names of those commemorated during the Liturgy were written
Domestics	A wide range of imperial and ecclesiastical officials; the title 'Domestic' was followed by a description of the particular office, as Domestic of the Great Church or Domestic of the Cantors (the protopsaltes); the Grand Domestic was the commander-in-chief of the imperial army
Ecdiceion	An ecclesiastical tribunal with a wide range of duties, dealing with questions such as sanctuary, slaves, marriages; its terms of reference came to be much disputed, but it was not a judicial court
Exarch	An imperial provincial governor; a patriarchal visitor or representative
Grand ecclesiarch	Title conferred on a leading official of the Great Church (late)

Great Church, the	Commonly used by the Byzantines for Hagia Sophia in Constantinople
Hegumenus	Head of a monastery
Hieromonk	Monk who was also a priest
Hieromnemon	Ecclesiastical official with liturgical functions; he took part in ordinations
Hypatus ton philosophon	Title (consul) given to the head of the philosophical faculty in Constantinople
Koine	The form of the Greek language which was generally used in the Mediterranean from late Hellenistic times onward; it should be distinguished from the more formal style which sought to reproduce classical Attic
Logothete	Originally a financial official but the term came to be applied to a variety of offices; the Logothete of the Drome was in charge of communications and foreign affairs (middle period); the Grand Logothete was the highest imperial minister (late period)
Nomocanons	Collections of ecclesiastical rulings together with imperial laws (nomoi) bearing on church affairs
Nomophylax	Title ('guardian of the laws') given to the head of the law faculty set up in Constantinople in the eleventh century, and in the late period to certain patriarchal officials
Novel	Imperial law
Papas (pl. papades)	A parish priest, often the village priest
Phiale	A paved and terraced courtyard or square with a fountain in the centre
Praepositi	Term often applied to chief functionaries; used of the heads of the conventual churches in Constantinople under the Latins, or (after 1204) to refugee bishops in respect of a diocese other than their own from which they drew revenue
Proedrus	President, applied to various positions as for instance 'President of the senate' (eleventh century)
Protoasecretis	Head of the imperial chancery
Protecdicos	Head of the ecdiceion (*q.v.*)

Prothesis	The part of the sanctuary to the left of the altar where the bread and wine for the Liturgy is prepared
Protospathar	Chief sword-bearer
Stauropegial	A monastery which came directly under the Patriarch; the 'cross-fixing' took place at the time of the foundation ceremony
Staurophoros	A very late title ('cross-bearing') applied to the leading officials of the Great Church
Syncellus	Originally the close associate of a bishop or Patriarch (lit. 'cell-companion'), then it became a title and fell out of use after the eleventh century
Theme	Originally a military division, then an administrative region or province
Varangians	Scandinavians or Northmen serving in Byzantium as mercenaries who formed a special imperial guard

INDEX

abbots 324, 341

Abgasia, Georgian province 91, 116

Accusation, by Psellus 137

Acindynus, Gregory, anti-Palamite 249, 259

Acmonia in Phrygia, monks in 159

Acropolites, George, grand logothete 230, 232-3, 238, 246

acrosticon (crustica), Byzantine land tax 194

Ad Constantinum Caballinum 43

Aegean: Latins in 175, 185, 212, 284
  piracy in 261

Aemilianus, bishop of Cyzicus 56

Aeneas Sylvius, on Latins in Cyprus 205

Africa, North 18, 19, 21, 31, 62, 298

Agallianus, Theodore, hieromnemon 273

Agatho, chartophylax 24

Agatho, Pope 22

Akathistos kontakion 354

Alans, Alania 91, 140
  bishop of 91, 321
  metropolitan of 116

Albano, *see* Pelagius of Albano

Alexander, Emperor 106

Alexander III, Pope 172-3

Alexander IV, Pope 204, 218-19

Alexander V, Pope 269

Alexandria 59, 167, 213, 367
  under Muslim rule 10, 28, 46, 174, 298, 322
  patriarchs 16, 22, 245, 265, 307, 322
  and Photian controversy 73, 76, 80
  monophysites in 11, 33 n. 8, 130
  and Maximus the Confessor 359, 361
  see also pentarchy, eastern patriarchates

Alexius I Comnenus, Emperor 125, 140, 141, 306, 344, 346
  relations with papacy 168-71, 179-80
  relations with church 146-8, 305, 311, 322-3, 328, 329, 347
  fight against heresy 142-6, 148-51, 156, 160-1, 162

Alexius II Comnenus, Emperor 141

Alexius III Angelus, Emperor 185, 189, 207

Alexius Studites, Patriarch of Constantinople 112, 127-9, 130

Alexius, metropolitan in Moscow 292

Alice of Champagne, regent of Cyprus 202

Amadeo VI, count of Savoy 264, 266

Amorium, in Phrygia 60, 62
  bishop of 47

Amphilochia of Photius 88-9

Amphilochius, metropolitan of Cyzicus 88

Analytics of Aristotle 150

Anastasius I, Emperor 12

Anastasius, Patriarch of Constantinople 38, 39

Anastasius III, Pope 104

Anastasius the Librarian 46

Anatolia, *see* Asia Minor

Anatolicon theme 55

Ancona, in Calabria 271
  bishop of 83

Ancyra (Angora, Ankara) in Asia Minor
  see of 47, 323; battle of 268

Andrew, bishop of Crete 354

Andronicus I Comnenus, Emperor 141

Andronicus II Palaeologus, Emperor 221, 242, 243, 250-4, 255
  and council of Lyons 231-2, 236-41 *passim*
  and Josephites and Arsenites 222, 243-6, 252-3

Andronicus III Palaeologus, Emperor 254, 255-7, 258, 266, 289, 318

Andronicus IV Palaeologus, Emperor 263, 264

Andronicus, brother of Michael VII 144

Angeli family 141, 153, 168, 173, 185-6, 207, 208
  see Isaac II, Alexius III

Angevins 195, 242, 275, 303
  see Charles of Anjou

Ani, district of Armenia 115-16, 130, 139

Anjou, *see* Angevins

Anna Comnena, historian 140, 145, 146–7, 149–50, 156, 160–1, 182

Anna Dalassena, mother of Alexius I Comnenus 140, 142, 160–1, 313

Anna, wife of Vladimir of Kiev 118

Anne of Savoy, wife of Andronicus III 256, 258, 261, 263

anointing 195, 199

Anonymous II, seventh-century canonist 306

Anonymous, tenth-century writer 318, 321

Anselm, archbishop of Canterbury 155, 179

Anselm, bishop of Havelberg 154, 180–2

antidoron 280

Antioch 115, 122, 129, 170, 181, 213, 359
    patriarchate 20, 22, 151, 167, 175–6, 218, 307, 346 and *see* pentarchy, eastern patriarchates
    under Muslim rule 10, 28, 46, 169, 174, 298
    under crusaders and Normans 147, 169, 171–2, 175–6
    and Photian controversy 73, 76, 80
    and Cerularius 130, 134

Antonio da Massa, Franciscan, papal nuncio 270

Antony I Cassimatas, Patriarch of Constantinople 61

Antony II Cauleas, Patriarch of Constantinople 102–3

Antony IV, Patriarch of Constantinople 294, 324

Antony of Cyzicus 73

Antony, hermit in Egypt 335

apatheia 363–4

apocrisiarius 19, 27, 60

Apostle (teacher of Epistles) 146

Apostolic Canons 304, 306

Apostolic Constitutions 304

Apulia, Byzantine province in South Italy 127, 132

Aquinas, Thomas, western theologian 266, 277, 284
    Thomism 259

Arabic 35, 175

Arabs 9, 18, 22, 34–6, 51, 52, 88, 92, 94; in Palestine 16; North Africa 21; Sicily 127, 177

archbishops 325

autocephalous 208, 319–20, 321, 325, 329; of Cyprus 201, 325; in Serbia 209

archdeacon 317

Archipelago, Latin Duchy of the 196–7

architecture 99, 277, 349, 358–9

archives, archivists 24, 227, 319, 334, 342

archons 195, 198, 293, 315, 317, 319

archpriest (archipresbyter) 199

Arethas, archbishop of Caesarea in Cappadocia 89–90, 104 and n. 5

Argeş, in Wallachia, metropolitanate 290–1

Argyrus, Lombard in Byzantine service 131–2, 133, 134

Arianism 152

Aristenus, Alexius, canonist 27 n. 34, 306–7, 310

Aristotle 143, 150, 154, 155, 177, 277, 278

Armenia, Armenians 90, 97 n. 91, 125, 139
    monophysite church 14, 15, 130–1, 138, 149–50, 163, 174
    against Chalcedon and Quinisextum councils 18, 26, 28, 129
    and Paulicians 33, 156
    migrations 115–16, 122, 156, 201 and *see* Lesser Armenia

Armenian sources on Leo III and Comneni 35, 160

army 47, 110, 207–8, 252, 271
    and iconoclasm 41, 50, 51, 55, 62, 67
    and Paulicians 54, 156
    changes in system 125, 194

Arsas, George, of Alexandria 15

Arsenites 221–2, 227, 237, 243–4, 246, 252–3, 255

Arsenius Autorianus, Patriarch in Nicaea and Constantinople 219, 221, 237, 244, 253

art 67, 119, 143, 277, 349, 358–9

Arta, in Epirus, synod at 210

Artabasdus, brother-in-law of Constantine V 39

Ascetica of St Basil 336

asceticism 336, 338, 362, 365

Asia, diocese of 319
    Asian provinces 14, 42, 43
    trade-routes 92

Asia Minor:
    under attack 9, 53, 125–6, 129, 156, 169, 185, 299

themes 14, 43, 116
revolt against Michael II 62
Latins in 208
Lascarids 236–7, and *see* Nicaea, kingdom of
under Turkish rule 252, 254, 255
iconoclasm 36–7, 59
monophysites 116
Bogomilism 159
bishoprics 311, 320
monasticism 348, and *see* Bithynia
asmatikos (sung service) 352
Athanasius I, Patriarch of Constantinople 243–4, 249–53, 255, 289, 315, 324, 333
letters 110, 251–3
Athanasius II, Patriarch of Antioch 176
Athanasius, Patriarch of Alexandria 322
Athanasius, Jacobite Patriarch 139
Athanasius, founder of the Great Lavra on Mt Athos 342
Athanasius, founder of the Great Meteoron in Thessaly 288
Athens 190, 193, 330
suffragan bishop of 165
archbishops of 286, 325, and *see* Choniates, Michael
Latin archbishop of 192
churches 193, 358
Athos, Mount, centre of monasticism in northern Greece 66, 70, 100, 287, 338
foundations 113, 122, 288, 291, 342, 348
and hesychasm 164, 258, 288–9
archives and books 334, 340, 342–3, 347, 355
Attaliates, Michael, lawyer 344, 348
Augusta, imperial title 105, 113
Augustine of Hippo, western theologian 30, 68, 260, 277, 284
Auxentius, Mount, in Bithynia 42, 250
Avars 14, 22
Avignon, residence of popes 257, 261, 263, 271
azymes, *see* unleavened bread

Baanes, patrician 80
Bacchus 26
Baghdad 88
Baldwin I, Latin Emperor of Constantinople 184, 187, 194
Baldwin II, Latin Emperor of Constantinople 220, 222, 224

Balkans:
inflow of Slavs 9, 18, 32, 91, 94
Christianity in 98, 100, 299
ecclesiastical jurisdiction 67, 73, 76
nationalism and independence 127, 141, 222, 237, 298
under Ottomans: importance of Orthodox Church 166, 286, 290
see also Bulgaria, Croatia, Illyricum, Serbia
Balsamon, Theodore, Patriarch of Antioch, canonist 165–6, 183, 306–10, 317, 326, 333, 347
on Emperor 302, 328–9
on vernacular in liturgy 96–7.
baptism 98, 101, 104, 117 and n. 19, 158, 315, 331, 350, 366
Baradaeus, Jacob, bishop 11, 14
Bardanes, George, metropolitan of Corfu 211
Bardas, brother of Empress Theodora (wife of Theophilus) 63, 70–1, 72, 78
Bari, council of 179
Barlaam of Calabria 164, 256–9
Bartholomew of Rome 261
Basel, council of 271–2, 274, 275
Basil I the Macedonian, Emperor 78–82, 83–5, 342
Basil II, Emperor 112, 119–20, 121, 122, 124, 127, 346
and Kiev 101, 118
religious toleration 115, 129
Basil I, prince of Moscow 293–4
Basil, Bogomil leader 161
Basil the Great of Caesarea, church father 113, 278, 304, 336–7, 355, 362, and *see* Cappadocians
liturgy of 357
Basil, bishop of Gortyna in Crete 27
Basil of Ochrida, archbishop of Thessalonica 182, 304
Basil, bishop of Pisidian Antioch 40
Basilaces, Nicephorus, deacon at Hagia Sophia 151
Basileion, bishop of 323
basileus 54, 208, 293
basilicas 358
Basilics, legal code 165, 306, 307, 310
Bayazid I, Ottoman Sultan 268
Beccus, chartophylax, *see* John XI Beccus, Patriarch
Benedict of Nursia 336

Benedict of Santa Susanna, cardinal 189–91
Benedict XII, Pope 256–7
Benedictine rule 341
Benjamin, Coptic Patriarch of Alexandria 16
Berat, in Albania, attacked by Angevins 242
Berengar, north Italian ruler, vassal of Otto I 120, 121 n. 24
Beser, renegade Syrian 35
Bessarion, archbishop of Nicaea 273, 275–6, 278–9, 283–4
Biblotheca (Myriobiblon) 88–9
bishops 52, 326–9, 339
Bithynia, centre of monasticism 42, 348, and *see* Olympus
Bizna in Bithynia 31
Bizya, in Thrace 21
Blachernae, church of St Mary in Constantinople 39, 64, 161, 246, 301, 331
    palace 149, 236, 240, 264
    iconoclast council 57
    synods 239–40, 259
Blaise, St 348
Blastares, Matthew, canonist 309–10
Blemmydes, Nicephorus, theologian 215, 246, 324
Boethius 277, 284
Bogomil heresy 126, 142, 157–66
Bohemia 94, 98
    Bohemian heresy 270
Boilas, Eustathius, landowner 330, 332
Boniface, English missionary to Germans 348
Boniface of Montferrat 187, 190
Boril, Bulgarian tsar 163
Boris I, Bulgarian khan 77, 81–2, 99, 126
Bota, pagan festival 26
Brumalia, pagan festival 26, 312
Brusa, in Bithynia 93, 245, 247, 341
Bulgaria, Bulgars:
    conflict with Byzantium 51–5, 106, 119, 213, 220 and *see* Symeon, tsar
    Byzantine province 118, 125, 159; themes, 122; claim to imperial succession 186, 207, 208
    Great Bulgaria 94
    Second Bulgarian Empire 163
Bulgaria, church in:
    adoption of Christianity 74, 77–8, 91–2, 94–101

quarrel over jurisdiction 81–2, 83–5, 87
dualist heresies 156–9, 163, 164
organisation and clergy 209, 211, 214, 265, 314, 320
monasticism 287–8, 291
Burgundians 195–6, 275

Caballinus, *see* Constantine V, Emperor
Cabasilas, Constantine, metropolitan of Durazzo 308
Cabasilas, Nicholas 155, 262, 284, 350, 359–60, 365
Caesarea, metropolitan of 139
Calabria, under Greek jurisdiction 46, 73, 127, 177, 231, 342
Calecas, *see* John XIV Calecas, Patriarch
Calecas, Manuel, scholar 277
Callistus I, Patriarch of Constantinople 264, 288, 289, 292, 314
canon, form of hymn 352–6
canon law 70, 74–5, 81, 112, 203, 279, 304–10, 326–9, 347
    on marriage 51, 139, 232, 328
    and Emperor 300, 302, 328–9
    and *see* Chalcedon, Ephesus, Nicaea I and II, Quinisextum, Sardica
canonikon, annual tax 333, 345
canticles 352, 353, 354
cantors (*psaltai*) 199, 273, 312, 329, 352, 358
Capetians, French rulers 303
Capitulare de Imaginibus 49–50
Cappadocia, region in Asia Minor 116, 162
    rock monasteries 42, 59, 343
Cappadocians 10, 177, 304, 362, *see* Basil the Great, Gregory of Nazianzus, Gregory of Nyssa
Carolingians 50, 54, 67, 85, 120, 126, 298
Carthage, debate on monothelitism at 18
castellanies 200
catacombs 30
Catalans 251
Catecheses of Theodore Studites 341, 342
Catherine of Valois 255
catholicon: general parish church 339 n. 73
    the principal church of a monastery 339, 358
Caucasus 15, 22, 87, 91–2, 116
cellarer 339
Celtic monks 348
ceremonial 301–2, 312, 316, 350, 356, 361, 368

Ceremonies, Book of, see De Cerimoniis

Cerularius, *see* Michael I Cerularius, Patriarch

Cesarini, Julian, cardinal 276, 279

Chalcedon, council of 10–12, 13, 16–17, 20 and Leo III, 34–5
  canons 27, 69, 181, 328, 347
  non-Chalcedonians 15, 127, 129, 138, 307, 308; in Armenia 15, 129, 131; and *see* Jacobites, monophysites, Nestorians
  bishop of Chalcedon 236

chancery 72, 317–18, 319, 347

charisticarius 346–7

charitable institutions 53, 139, 252, 327, 344

Chariton, metropolitan in Wallachia 291

Charlemagne, Frankish ruler 49–50, 54, 62, 120, 126
  coronation 52, 53

Charles of Anjou 223–6, 230, 231–2, 234, 235, 237, 240

chartophylax 24, 227, 245, 247, 307–8, 317, 323, 328

Cherson, in south Russia 21, 93, 97, 116, 118

cherubikon 352

Chilandari, Serbian monastery on Mt Athos 291

choirmaster 339

Chomatianus, Demetrius, archbishop of Ochrida 196, 208–11, 302–3, 308–9, 310, 334

Choniates, Michael, archbishop of Athens 190, 192, 193

Choniates, Nicetas, historian 152 n. 65, 154

Chora, seaport in Naxos (Cyclades) 197

Chora, the, monastery in Constantinople 340, 344

chrismation (confirmation) 195, 199, 350

Christ the All-seeing, monastery in Constantinople 161

Christodoulos of Patmos, monk 340, 344

Christology 9–29, 30, 32–4, 38–9, 58, 66, 151, 152–3, 156, 305

Christopher, bishop of Ancyra 211

Chrysoloras, John 269

Chrysoloras, Manuel, scholar and diplomat 268

Chrysomalus, Constantine 162, 166

Chrysostom, *see* John I Chrysostom, Patriarch

chrysotriclinus, hall in imperial palace 67, 301

church treasure 147–9

Cilician Gates, mountain pass in south-east Asia Minor 115

Cinnamus, John, historian 152 n. 65, 162, 182

Cistercians 193

Cithaeron, Mount, in Boeotia 338

civil law 139, 166, 300, 310, 328

classical studies 88–90, 143–4, 150, 178, 277

Clement, bishop of Sasima 162

Clement of Ochrida 99–100

Clement I, Pope 97

Clement IV, Pope 223–4, 225, 232, 233, 266

Clement VI, Pope 261–2

Cletorologion of Philotheus 65

Climacus, John, of Mount Sinai 288, 292, 340, 363

Cluniac monastery at Civetot 172, 182

Commonitorium of Pope John VIII 84

Comnenian period 65, 126, 141, 153, 167, 168, 171, 173, 175, 306
  literature 154–5
  heresies 155, 157
  Comneni in Trebizond 185; in Epirus 186; *see* Alexius I and II, John II, Manuel I, Adronicus I, Emperors

confession 365

confirmation, *see* chrismation

Conon, Pope 24

Conon, *see* Leo III, Emperor

Conrad III, Western Emperor 172, 182

Constance, council of 269, 270

Constans II, Emperor 18, 21–2, 303

Constantia, Empress 31

Constantine I the Great, Emperor 47, 49, 90, 234, 297, 300

Constantine III, Emperor 18

Constantine IV, Emperor 22

Constantine V, Emperor, iconoclast 34, 36, 38–44, 49, 56, 58, 66
  marriage 92
  military affairs 50, 54–5, 156

Constantine VI, Emperor 36, 44, 49, 51–2, 53, 55

Constantine VII Porphyrogenitus, Emperor 104, 106, 108, 109, 112, 113 and *see De Cerimoniis* and *De Administrando*

Constantine VIII, Emperor 112

Constantine IX Monomachus, Emperor 124, 128, 138, 168

Constantine IX Monomachus—*contd.*
  and Armenia 116, 131
  and Cerularius 130, 132–4
Constantine X Ducas, Emperor 131, 138, 139
Constantine XI Palaeologus, Emperor 282
Constantine, son of Basil I 84
Constantine, son of Michael VII Ducas 140
Constantine II, Patriarch of Constantinople 39
Constantine III Lichudes, Patriarch of Constantinople 138
Constantine I, Pope 28
Constantine, bishop of Orvieto 218–19
Constantine (Cyril), apostle of the Slavs 92–7, 99
Constantine of Nacoleia, bishop 36–7, 43
Constantine, metropolitan of Corfu 153
Constantinople:
  foundation and transfer of capital from Rome 9, 167, 181, 297
  attacks and threats 31–2; from Russians 101, 118; Turks 129, 276; the west 141, 182, 236; Balkan states 141; Epirus and Bulgaria 109, 208
  capture by crusaders (1204) 184
  under Latin rule 164, 188, 191, 212–13, 218–19
  retaken by Michael VIII (1261) 195, 220–1, 242, 335
  taken by Ottomans (1453) 197, 206, 285, 368
  refugees in 147, 175–6, 183, 321
  foreigners 153, 177–8, 214, 302, and *see* friars, Genoese, Pisa
  iconoclasm in 59, 62; Bogomilism 160; trials for heresy 21–2, 162, 164, and *see* Italus
  poorhouse 53
Constantinople, churches:
  Latin, closed by Cerularius 132
  conventual 188
  and *see* Blachernae, Hagia Sophia, Holy Apostles, St Irene
Constantinople, councils and synods:
  general councils: I (381) 297; II (553) 12, 13, 24; III (680–1) 15 n. 5, 22–4
  others, IV (868–9) 84; 64, 133–4 and *see* Quinisextum *and s.v.* iconoclasm and Photius
  standing synod, *see synodos endemousa*

Constantinople, monasteries:
  see Christ the All-seeing, Cosmidion, the Chora, Mangana, Panachrantus, Pantocrator, Peribleptos, Psamathia, St Mamas, Studite
Constantinople, patriarchs: *see* patriarchate
Constitutio Cypria 204
Contra Bogomilos of Germanus II 164
converts to Bogomilism 159; to Greek Church 114, 153, 317; to Islam 260; to Roman Catholicism 261, 266, 268, 284
Copronymus, *see* Constantine V, Emperor
Copts 14, 16
Corfu, taken by Venetians 198
Corinth 27, 330
  gulf of 192
  isthmus of 268
Coron, in Peloponnese, taken by Venetians 185, 198
coronation 301, 315, 352
  of Leo V 55; John I Tzimisces 113; Theodore I 207
  of Charlemagne 49, 52, 54; Otto I 120
  of Theodore Angelus of Epirus 210
Cosmas, bishop of Maiuma 354
Cosmas, Bulgarian priest 158–9
Cosmas I (of Jerusalem), Patriarch of Constantinople 140, 142, 145
Cosmas II Atticus, Patriarch of Constantinople 162
Cosmidion, monastery outside Constantinople 250
cosmology 10
councils, general (oecumenical) 165, 179, 181, 275, 279, 286, 302–3, 304, 337, 365, 368, and *see* Nicaea I and II, Constantinople I, II and III, Chalcedon, Ephesus
  proposals for further general councils 265–6, 270–1
  other councils, *see* Basel, Constance, Constantinople, Ferrara-Florence, Florence, Frankfurt, Hieria, Lateran, Lyons, Pisa, Quinisextum, Trent, *and s.v.* iconoclasm, Photius
Crescentii family in Rome 111, 120–1
Crete:
  taken by Muslims 62
  under Venetians 185, 197–200, 322
  Greek clergy 27, 192, 299

Latin clergy 176, 198–9, 280
Crimea 91–3, 117
Croatia 100, 126
crusades, crusaders 120, 126, 136, 141, 167–70, 182, 186, 334, 367
First 172; capture of Antioch 147
Second 182
Third 201
Fourth 99, 167, 183, ch. VII *passim* 315
later projects 212, 223–6, 230, 263
Tunisian crusade 224
Sigismund of Hungary 268, 269
crusader principalities 174–5, 176, 183, ch. VII *passim*
crustica, see *acrosticon*
Cumans 126, 142, 160
Curcuas, John, general 114
Cyclades 37
under Latin rule 195, 196–7
Cydones, Demetrius 261, 262, 266, 267–8, 277, 284
Cydones, Prochorus, monk of Athos 259, 277
Cyprian, metropolitan of Kiev and all Russia 292–3
Cyprus 42, 325, 348
under Latin rule 176, 185, 195, 200, 201–6, 214, 270, 324
Cyril, Patriarch of Alexandria 11–13, 215
Cyril, *see* Constantine (Cyril)
Cyrillic script 96
Cyrus of Phasis, Patriarch of Alexandria 13, 15, 16, 20, 23

daily offices 350–2, 366
Dalmatia, Slavonic liturgy in 98
Dandolo, Enrico, doge of Venice 184, 187
Dandolo, Stephen, *see* Stephen
Danishmends of Melitene 171
Daphni, monastery near Athens 193
deaconesses 329
deacons 329, 333
of Hagia Sophia 148, 151, 315, 319, 322
De Administrando of Constantine VII 117
De Cerimoniis (*Book of Ceremonies*) of Constantine VII 64–5, 300, 302, 313, 333
De depositione sua of John XI Beccus, Patriarch 245
De haeresibus et synodis 37–8
Definition (*Horos*) 40–1, 48–9, 57–8, 84–5

deification (theosis) 12, 68, 166, 248, 258, 260, 282–3, 357, 360, 364–5
Demetrius from Phrygian Lampe 152, 178
Demosthenes 88
Deusdedit, cardinal 74
Deusdedit of Cagliari, bishop 20
diaconicon 358
Diadochus, bishop of Photice in Epirus 362–3, 364
dialectic 144–5, 150–1
diaria, clergy allowance 333
diataxis, rubric book 358, 361
didaskaloi 329
Didymoteichum, town in Thrace 189
Digenes Acritas, epic poem 114
Dionysius Exiguus 26, 304
Dominic of Grado 135 n. 21
Dominicans 174, 214–16, 231, 234, 256, 262, 281, 284
Provincial of Lombardy 278
Donation of Constantine 307
Donatus, bishop of Ostia 80
doorkeepers 329, 331, 339
dorea 346, 348
dualism 87, 122, 126, 142, 148, 150, 151, 156–66
Ducas, Andronicus 104
Ducas, Constantine, son of Michael VII 140
Ducas family 137–8, 140, 142, 144, 148, 168, 186
Ducas, John, of Thessaly 240
Durazzo, *see* Dyrrachium
dyophysites 11, 12, 16
dyothelite doctrine 23
Dyrrachium (Durazzo) 151, 209, 308

eastern patriarchates:
in Muslim territory 39, 167, 174, 290
absence from councils 39, 45–6, 48, 230
Ferrara-Florence 279
and Photius, 78, 83, 87, 122; Cerularius 134
and Leo VI 105, 107
papal claims 136
and Greeks in Nicaea 209, 215; Michael VIII 228
see Alexandria, Antioch, Jerusalem, pentarchy
ecclesiarch 272, 318
ecdiceion, court of 317

Ecloga, legal code 43–4, 96
Ecthesis 17–18, 19, 20
Ecthesis Nea, list of bishops 311
Edessa, in Mesopotamia 12, 31, 115
education 66, 93, 109, 130, 329–30, 366
  Law School 138, 308
  patriarchal schools 89, 146, 151, 180
Edict of Union, *see Henoticon*
Egypt:
  monasticism 335
  monophysites 11, 16
  paganism 33
  attacked from east 14, 18
  taken by Muslims 91, 297
elections:
  papal 230
  patriarchal 312–14, 319
  of metropolitans 326
Elements of Theology of Proclus 155
Elvira, synod of 33
Emperor 44, 300, 302
  relations with church 300–3, 306, 312,
    313–14, 316, 319, 322–5
  and canon law 304–6
empsychos nomos, appellation of Emperor
  302
Enthusiasts 161
Epanagoge, legal code 87, 102, 306
eparchies 325–6
Ephesus 32, 40, 140, 246
  canon of council of 276
ephoreia 347–8
epiclesis 279, 357, 360
epidosis 348 and n. 92
Epiphanius, bishop of Salamis in
  Cyprus 30, 33, 278
Epiphanius, patriarchal official 40
Epiphany 56, 71, 104, 245, 312, 350
Epirus, kingdom of 185–6, 192, 196, 207,
  220, 237, 239, 299, 308, 323
  Epirote church 209, 213, 324
  excommunication 240
  schism with Nicaea 208–11, 214
epistemonarches 303
Epitome of Harmenopoulos 310
Ethiopia 90
Euboea (Negroponte) 185, 190, 195, 198
eucharist 26, 41, 215, 350–2, 356–62 *passim*
Euchologion 293, 339
Eudaimonoïoannes, Nicholas, diplo-
  mat 269

Eudes, cardinal-bishop of Tusculum 203
Eudocia Baïane, third wife of Leo VI 104
Eudocia, wife of Constantine X and Roma-
  nus IV 139
Eugenius I, Pope 22
Eugenius III, Pope 180
Eugenius IV, Pope 271–2, 274–82
Eugenius, bishop of Ostia 83
Eulogia, sister of Michael VIII 227, 237
Euripos, seat of Latin Patriarch 195
Eusebius of Caesarea, historian 30–1, 33,
  88
Eustathius, Patriarch of Constantino-
  ple 116, 122
Eustathius, archbishop of Thessalonica 88,
  173, 346–7
Eustathius, metropolitan of Dyrra-
  chium 151–2
Eustratius Garidas, Patriarch of Constanti-
  nople 140, 142, 145, 148, 313
Eustratius, metropolitan of Nicaea 150–1,
  179
Euthymius I, Patriarch of Constanti-
  nople 103–6, 107
Euthymius, monk from Mt Olympus 104
Euthymius, of Peribleptos monastery in
  Constantinople 159
Evagrius of Pontus 13, 362–4
exarch 211, 316
  of Ravenna 19, 21
  of North Africa 21
exokatakoiloi 316
exorcists 329
Explicatio (*Commentary on the Divine
  Liturgy*) of Nicholas Cabasilas 359–60
Ezra, Catholicos of Armenia 15

Faber, Felix, traveller in Cyprus 206
Famagusta 202
  archbishop of 201
fasting 26–7, 131, 132, 158
Ferrara-Florence, council of 212, 260,
  272–85, 303
feudal system 183, 184–5, 195, 201, 202–3,
  217
  military service 194
filioque:
  introduction into creed 20, 78, 84–5, 87,
    97
  controversy over 135, 150, 173–81, 200,
    213–18, 226–41 *passim*, 276–9, 308

treatises on 122, 190, 257, 284
finance 332–4
Florence 277
  council of 171, 200, 205–6; and *see* Ferrara-Florence
florilegia 20, 55–7, 61, 64
Fonseca, Piero, Cardinal 270
forgeries 15, 135
Formosus of Porto, Pope 81, 86
Fount of Knowledge of John of Damascus 143
Franciscans:
  based in or near Constantinople 225, 231, 233, 251, 256, 261, 284
  as papal envoys 203, 214–16, 262, 270
  Franciscan Chronicle 256
Frankfurt, council of 50, 62
Franks 39, 76, 109, 132, 167, 298
  in Middle East 173–6, 284, 311
  missionaries in Bulgaria 78; Great Moravia 87, 94–8; Hungary 98
  see also Angevins, Carolingians, Charlemagne, French, Germany, Latin Church, Latin Empire
Frederick I Barbarossa, Western Emperor 172
Frederick II, Western Emperor 213, 216
French 182, 188, 205
frescoes 68, 205, 343, 358–9, 368
friars, *see* Dominicans and Franciscans

Galacrenae, near Chalcedon in Asia Minor, monastery in 105
Galen 177
Galesius, Mt, monastic centre north of Ephesus 250
Galicia, Russian principality 287, 292
Gallipoli 139, 263
Ganos, Mt, in Gallipoli 139, 179
Garatoni, Christopher 271, 273 n. 172, 280
Gelasius I, Pope 77
Gemistus Plethon, philosopher 155, 273, 277
General Judges 310, 325, 334
Gennadius II Scholarius, Patriarch of Constantinople, *see* Scholarius, George
Genoese 142, 176, 184, 187, 220, 302
George I, Patriarch of Constantinople 22–4

George of Cyprus, *see* Gregory II the Cypriote, Patriarch
George of Cyprus, supporter of icons 40
George Tzimisces Berriotes, interpreter 230
Georgia, Georgians (Iberians) 90, 273, 278, 342, 344, 368
Gerasimus I, Patriarch of Constantinople 254
Gerasimus, Patriarch of Jerusalem 287
Germaniceia, *see* Marash
Germanus I, Patriarch of Constantinople 35, 36–8, 39–40, 45, 66, 359
Germanus II, Patriarch in Nicaea 163–4, 202–3, 210–11, 214–15, 323–4
Germanus III Markoutzas, Patriarch of Constantinople 221, 230, 231
Germanus, archbishop of Nicosia 204
Germany, Germans (East Franks) 94–5, 98, 121, 126–7, 152, 182, 335, 348
Géza, Hungarian ruler 98
Gibelet family 205
Glaber, Rudolf, western historian 122
Glagolitic script 96, 100
Gnostics 156
Golden Horde 291
Golden Horn 176, 179, 250, 302, 316
Goths 91
Grand Domestic 258, 261
Great Church, *see* Hagia Sophia in Constantinople
Great Lavra of the Trinity, near Moscow 288
Great Lavra on Mt Athos 342
Great Palace in Constantinople 37–8, 64, 105, 301, 312, 332
Greece, Greeks 32, 366–7
  in Moravia 94
  in Rome 177
  Greek language 95, 100, 175, 177–8, 250
  Greek churches in Italy 135
  under Latin Empire 185, 192–6
Greek Anthology 67
Green Count, *see* Amadeo VI, count of Savoy
Gregoras, Nicephorus, historian 249–50, 253–4, 256, 259, 292
Gregory II the Cypriote, Patriarch of Constantinople 243, 246–9
Gregory III, Patriarch of Constantinople 281–2

Gregory VII, Pope (Hildebrand) 131–2, 168

Gregory IX, Pope 211, 214–16

Gregory X, Pope 224–5, 230–5, 236, 237–8

Gregory Asbestas, archbishop of Syracuse 70–1, 72, 76

Gregory, bishop of Caesarea 40

Gregory, exarch of North Africa 21

Gregory of Nazianzus (the Theologian), church father 12, 278, 355, 362, and *see* Cappadocians

Gregory of Nyssa, church father 30, 362, and *see* Cappadocians

Gregory of Sinai 287–8, 363–4

Grossolanus, Peter, archbishop of Milan 150, 179, 180

Grottaferrata, monastery near Rome 120

Guiscard, Robert, Norman duke of Apulia 139–40, 145

Guy de Lusignan 201

Hadrian I, Pope 45–50, 52

Hadrian II, Pope 80, 82, 97

Hagia Sophia, church in Thessalonica 367

Hagia Sophia (Holy Wisdom), the Great Church, in Constantinople:
synods and meetings 57, 61, 80, 84, 180, 189
special services 56, 64–5, 366
enthronements 53, 71, 313
coronations 113, 221, 301
ritual for Emperor 301–2
splendour of liturgy 119, 312, 358
architecture and decoration 67, 153, 190, 301, 358
distribution of charity 139
clergy and officials 147, 148, 151–2, 207, 239, 273, 279, 293, 311, 314–18, 322–3, 331, 333
assets abroad 193, 252
appointment of metropolitans 291, 293
deposition of *Ecthesis* 17, 19; of papal bull 133; hidden document 250–1
during Latin Empire 184, 187–8
now a museum 358

Hagiosophitike chora 193

Hall of the Nineteen Divans 38

Harmenopoulos, Constantine, canonist 310

Hauteville, Norman family in south Italy 131

Hebrew 93, 95

hegumenus 95, 339, 342

Helen, daughter of Robert Guiscard 140

Helena, wife of Emperor Constantine I 49

Helena, wife of Constantine VII 117

Helena, wife of John V Palaeologus 264

Helena Dragaš, wife of Manuel II 352

Hellas 27
Helladic theme 37

Hellenic civilization, Hellenism 9, 89, 119, 206, 300, 302

Henoticon (Edict of Union) 12

Henry of Hainault (Flanders), Latin Emperor of Constantinople 191, 194, 212

Henry III, German Emperor 131–2, 133

Henry V, German Emperor 170–1

Heracleia in Thrace, metropolitans of 112, 150, 297, 313, 323

Heraclius, Emperor 14–18, 328, 331

hermits, anchorites 25, 335, 338, 365–6

hesychasm 164, 258–60, 267, 268, 286–9, 314, 360, 363
in Bulgaria and Balkans 163, 287, 291
in Russia 287, 292

Hexabiblos of Harmenopoulos 310

Hexamilion wall across Isthmus of Corinth 268–9

Hieria, imperial palace on Bosphorus near Chalcedon: iconoclast council 39, 45, 56 and n. 64, 57–8

hieromnemon 273

hieromonks 164, 273, 279, 309

Hierotheus, bishop of Turkia (Hungary) 98

Hilarion, bishop of Moglena in Macedonia 163

Hildebrand, *see* Gregory VII, Pope

Hincmar of Rheims 78

Hippodrome 161

Hirmologion, hirmus 354, 356

Historia Ecclesiastica, commentary on the liturgy 359–60

Hohenstaufen 213, 216, 220, 223

Holobolus, Manuel, scholar 228

Holy Apostles, church in Constantinople 46, 73, 74

Holy Cross 14, 30, 308

Holy Epiphany, monastery at Kerasontus in Cherson 116

Holy Land, *see* Palestine

Holy Mountain in Calabria 120, 177

Holy Mountain, *see* Athos
Holy Nativity, church in Bethlehem 175
Holy Places 141, 169, 176
Holy Sepulchre 175
Holy Spirit 122, 166, and *see* filioque
Holy Wisdom, *see* Hagia Sophia
Honorius I, Pope 16 n. 10, 17, 18, 23
Honorius III, Pope 202
Horos, see *Definition*
Hosios Loukas, monastery in Phocis 330, 358
Hosios Meletios, monastery in Boeotia 338
Hugh Etherianus of Pisa 152, 178
Hugh of Fagiano, Latin archbishop of Nicosia 203–4
humanism, humanists 89–90, 143, 243, 246, 274, 277
Humbert, cardinal-bishop of Silva Candida 132, 133–6
Humbert de Romanis, Master General of Dominicans 234–5
Hungary, Magyars 92, 94, 98–9, 126, 171, 291, 292
   visited by Emperor John V 263–4
Hunnic peoples 32, 91
Hylilas, John, *see* John VII the Grammarian, Patriarch
Hymettus, Mt, near Athens 193
hymnody, hymns 341, 351–6, 364, 366
hypatus 143, 155
Hypatius of Ephesus, bishop 32

Ibas of Edessa 12
Iconium, in Asia Minor:
   Muslim kingdom 126
   bishop of 47
iconoclasm, iconoclasts ch. II *passim* 87
   councils 38, 39–41, 56, 73, 74
   imperial rulings 302–3, 304–5
   legal codes 306
iconodules, *see* iconophiles
iconophiles ch II *passim*
icons ch. II *passim* 84, 149, 190, 301, 308, 368
   iconography 358–9
idiorhythmic 338
Ignatius, Jacobite metropolitan of Melitene 139
Ignatius of Smolensk, archimandrite 352
Ignatius, Patriarch of Constantinople 70–6, 79–82, 83, 86, 102

Illyricum:
   under papal jurisdiction 21, 27
   under patriarchal jurisdiction 46, 52, 299, 311
   papal claims on 73–4, 75, 132
Incarnation 10, 17, 66, 94, 144, 155, 157
Innocent II, Pope 171
Innocent III, Pope 186–9, 191–2, 193, 214
Innocent IV, Pope 195, 203–4, 216–18
Innocent V, Pope 237–8, 239
Innocent VI, Pope 262
in Trullo, *see* Quinisextum council
Irene Ducaena, wife of Alexius I 140, 142, 313, 344, 347, 348
Irene, Empress, mother of Constantine VI 44–6, 49, 50, 51–2, 55, 57
Irene of Montferrat, wife of Andronicus II 255, 261
Isaac I Comnenus, Emperor 124, 130, 136–8, 141
Isaac II Angelus, Emperor 190, 307
Isaac of Nineveh 363–4
Isaiah, metropolitan of Stauropolis in Caria 280
Isaias, Patriarch of Constantinople 254
Isauria, district of south-east Asia Minor 34
Isidore I, Patriarch of Constantinople 258–9, 288, 289
Isidore of Kiev, metropolitan of Russia 283
Islam 22, 34, 43, 114, 153, 166, 260, 311, 368
Italus, John, philosopher 140, 148, 150
   trial for heresy 142–6, 149, 154–5, 319, 364
Iviron, Georgian monastery on Mt Athos 288, 289, 309

Jacobites, Syrian monophysites 14, 34, 115, 116, 174
   in Cyprus 201
   charged with heresy 129, 139, 308
Jagiello, son of Olgerd of Lithuania 292
James I, king of Aragon 230
Jannina, clergy of 309
Jerome, archbishop of Athens 286
Jerome of Ascoli 231
Jerusalem 181, 213, 297–8, 367
   in infidel territory 10, 14, 16
   and crusades 169, 170, 174–6, 185, 187, 201, 212, 225, 367
   patriarchs 175, 176, 265, 287

Jerusalem—*contd.*
  and councils and synods 20, 22, 46, 80–1, 265
  approached by Theodore Studites 59; and Photius 73, 76, 80
  see also pentarchy and eastern patriarchates
Joannices, monk, of Mt Olympus near Brusa 63
Joasaph, *see* John VI Cantacuzenus
Job Jasites, monk, anti-unionist 227, 235
John I Tzimisces, Emperor 112, 113–14, 115, 118, 119, 121, 124, 157
John II Comnenus, Emperor 141, 162, 170–2, 180, 307, 337, 347
John III Vatatzes, Emperor in Nicaea 211, 213–19, 220, 232
John IV Lascaris, Emperor in Nicaea 220, 221, 237, 244
John V Palaeologus, Emperor 212, 254, 258, 261, 262–4, 266–7, 287, 289, 293
John VI Cantacuzenus, Emperor 254, 258, 261–6 *passim*, 275, 287, 289
  retirement as monk Joasaph 262
John VIII Palaeologus, Emperor 171, 270–82, 283, 284–5
John I Chrysostom, Patriarch of Constantinople 177, 178, 278, 304, 355
  liturgy of 88, 96, 357
John VII the Grammarian (Hylilas), Patriarch of Constantinople 55, 57, 62, 63
John VIII Xiphilinus, Patriarch of Constantinople 138–40, 143–4, 326
John IX, Patriarch of Constantinople 150
John X Camaterus, Patriarch of Constantinople 183, 189, 207
John XI Beccus, Patriarch of Constantinople 227–8, 236–41, 243, 244, 246–7
John XII Cosmas, Patriarch of Constantinople 243, 250
John XIII Glykys, Patriarch of Constantinople 254, 318
John XIV Calecas, Patriarch of Constantinople 258, 261, 287, 289, 315
John IV, Pope 18
John VII, Pope 28
John VIII, Pope 82, 83–6, 102
John X, Pope 107
John XII, Pope 120
John XIX, Pope 122–3
John XXI, Pope 238–9
John XXII, Pope 196, 199
John the Almsgiver, bishop 15
John Apocaucus, metropolitan of Naupactus 209
John VIII Bar Abdoun, Jacobite Patriarch 129
John of Damascus, church father:
  champion of icons 36, 39–40, 42–3, 48, 66, 68
  against imperial interference 56, 66
  writings 48, 143, 157, 247, 304, 362
  translated 99, 177
  hymns 354, 356
John Eirenicus, abbot 153
John of Jerusalem, opponent of iconoclasm 35–6, 43
John, bishop of Kitros 308, n. 20
John Mauropous, archbishop of Euchaita 320, 327, 338, 355
John of Montenero 278
John the Orphanotrophus 127–8
John V Oxites, Patriarch of Antioch 147–8, 346–7
John of Parma, Minister-General of Franciscans 217
John Phournes, protos of monastery on Mt Ganos 179
John of Ragusa 279
John of Sinai, *see* Climacus, John
John, syncellus of Antioch 46
John of Synnada, metropolitan 36–7
John, bishop of Trani in Apulia 132
Joseph I, Patriarch of Constantinople 227–9, 234–7, 244–6
Joseph II, Patriarch of Constantinople 270, 273–9, 283
Joseph, priest 51, 53–4
Joseph the hymnographer, Studite monk 354
Josephites, anti-unionist party 237, 243–4, 246
Judaism, Jews 25, 26, 119, 300, 368
  and iconoclasm 35–6, 43
  and Khazars 92–4, 117
Justin I, Emperor 13
Justinian I, Emperor 31, 91, 298
  interest in church affairs 11, 12, 326, 331, 350
  legislation 165, 305–7, 327
  conception of imperial office 300, 302
Justinian II, Emperor 24–8, 35, 92
Justiniana and All Bulgaria, see of 209

Kaisariani, monastery on Mt Hymettus 193
Kakig, ex-king of Ani 139
Kalambaka in Thessaly, *see* Meteora
Kanikleion palace in Constantinople 63
Karyes on Mt Athos 342
kathisma, section of psalter 353
kellia 337, 338
Khazars, Khazaria:
 missions to 87, 91–2, 97
 adoption of Judaism 92–4, 117
Kiev, principality of 94, 290, 291
 Greek influence on 101, 117–19, 122
 metropolitan of 291
Kilifarevo, monastic centre in Bulgaria 287, 291
klerikata, property leased to clergy 333
kontakia 354
Kossovo, battle of 268
Krum, Bulgar leader 53
Kutlumus, monastery on Mt Athos 291

Lachanodracon, Michael, governor of Thracesian theme 43
Ladder of John Climacus 288, 340, 363
Lapacci, Bartholomew, Dominican friar 281
Larissa, Epirote see of 209
Lascarids 211, 224, 323
 their supporters 221, 227, 237
 and *see* Theodore I and II and John IV, Emperors
Lateran:
 council of 649, 15 n. 5, 19–20, 21–2
 palace 28
Latin Church in east (after 1204) 183, 186–92, 218, 284, 309
 in Greece and Cyclades 192–7
 in Crete 197–200
 in Cyprus 201–6
Latin Empire (Romania) 163–4, 167, ch. VII *passim*, 220, 222, 234, 237, 286, 308, 310, 315, 321, 327
Latin language 77, 95, 179, 215, 263
Lavra, monastery near Anaplous on Bosphorus 236
Lavra, on Mt Athos, foundation of 113
law, study of 138, 143, 308
 translations into Slavonic 96, 119
Lazi, Caucasian people won over by Justinian I 91
Lazica, in Caucasus 15, 22

Lebanon, Maronite church in 174
Legatio of Liutprand 121
Lent 26–7, 28, 132, 351, 355
 first Sunday in (Orthodoxy Sunday) 144, 355
Leo I, Emperor 301, 302
Leo III, Emperor:
 iconoclasm 34–8, 39, 42, 43–4, 58
 military campaigns 36, 50
Leo IV, Emperor 44, 45, 55, 156
Leo V the Armenian, Emperor 55–60, 61, 69
Leo VI the Wise, Emperor 107–8, 154, 311, 313
 and Photius 82, 86
 fourth marriage 102–6, 107
 legal codes 305–6
Leo I the Great, Pope 23, 77, 302
Leo III, Pope 54, 60
Leo IX, Pope 131–2, 134
Leo, ambassador in Rome 76
Leo, archbishop of Ochrida 132
Leo, metropolitan of Chalcedon 148–9
Leo the Mathematician 89
Leo Tuscus of Pisa, scholar 178
Leontius, bishop of Balbissa, in Cappadocia 162
Lesser Armenia, in south-east Asia Minor 116, 131, 171, 174
Lexicon of Photius 88
Liber Pontificalis 27–8
libraries:
 monastic 177, 250, 340, 342–3, 344
 patriarchal 93, 314, 319
 private 363
Libri Carolini 49–50
Life in Christ of Nicholas Cabasilas 350, 360, 365
Limassol, in Cyprus 202
Lithuania 290, 291–2
liturgy 152, 180, 349–50, 357, 361, 368 *and see* eucharist
 liturgical languages 95
 translations into Slavonic 96–100, 119; Syriac 175; Latin 178
 in Armenian church 131
Liutprand, bishop of Cremona, ambassador in Constantinople 121 and n. 24, 126, 154
logothete 230, 247, 254
Lombards 13, 31, 39, 50, 120, 131, 298
Lothair III, Western Emperor 172, 180

Louis I, king of Hungary 264
Louis II, Frankish ruler 78
Louis the Pious, Western Emperor 61–2
Louis IX, king of France 224
Lusignans 185, 201, 246
Lyons, second council of 171, 212, 218, 222, 226, 229–35, 238, 275, 303
  opposition to 235–42, 244, 245

Macarius, Patriarch of Antioch 22–3
Macedonia 27, 95–6, 100, 209, 309
  Bogomils in 159, 162
  Latins in 185
Macedonian period 62, 65, 112, 119–20, 121, 124, 128, 136, 306
Madyta, bishop of 323
magic and the occult 25, 36, 130, 137, 159–60, 318, 366
Magnaura Palace in Constantinople 45, 49, 313
Magyars, *see* Hungary
Mamluks 322
Manfred, king of Sicily 220
Mangana, St George of the, monastery in Constantinople 138, 254, 262
Maniaces, George 124
Manichaeans 54, 87, 156–7, 160, 162–3
Mansur, *see* John of Damascus
Manuel I Comnenus, Emperor 98–9, 141, 151–4, 162–3, 170–8 *passim*, 182, 307
Manuel II Palaeologus, Emperor 261, 262, 263, 264, 267–70, 284–5, 352
  Ottoman threat 267, 268
Manuel I, Byzantine Patriarch in Nicaea 209
Manuel II, Byzantine Patriarch in Nicaea 217–18
Manuel Angelus, ruler of Epirus 211
Marash (Marcaš, Germaniceia), in North Syria 34–5, 115
Marcionites 156
Margaret of Hungary, regent of Thessalonica 190
Maria, Alan princess, wife of Michael VII 140
Maria Comnena, wife of John VIII 281
Marinus (I), deacon, legate and pope 80, 86
Mark Eugenicus, metropolitan of Ephesus, spokesman at council of Ferrara-Florence 275–6, 278, 283

opposed to union with Rome 273, 280, 281–2, 284, 285
Mark, Patriarch of Alexandria 97 n. 91, 307, 333
Mark the Monk 248, 362–3
Maronite church 174, 201
marriage 305, 309, 315, 317, 328, 331, 350
  and canon law 51, 139, 232, 334
  of clergy 26–7, 322, 329
  mixed 129, 205, 261
  second or more: Constantine VI 51–2; Leon VI 103–6; Zoe 128; Nicephorus III 140; Emperor of Trebizond 287
  divorce 51
Martin I, Pope 19–21, 22
Martin IV, Pope 242
Martin V, Pope 269–71, 272
Mary the Paphlagonian, wife of Constantine VI 51
Matthew I, Patriarch of Constantinople 316, 318
Matthew of Edessa, chronicler 160
Maximus II, Greek Patriarch in Nicaea 209
Maximus of Aquileia, bishop 20
Maximus the Confessor 11, 16, 18, 31, 363
  defence of Orthodoxy 19–22
  writings 14–15, 357, 359, 361, 362
Medici family 277
Megaspelaion, monastery south of gulf of Corinth 192
Mehmed, *see* Muhammad
Melitene, in Mesopotamia:
  monophysites in 115, 129, 139
  defeat of Muslims at 114, 171
Meliteniotes, Constantine, chartophylax 245, 247
menaion 353, 355
Menas, Patriarch of Constantinople 15
mercenaries 118, 125
Mesarites, John, monk opposed to Latin Patriarch 189, 190–1
Mesarites, Nicholas, metropolitan of Ephesus 190–1, 207, 213
Mesopotamia 15, 115, 125, 129, 362
Messalianism 157, 159–66, 258, 362
  neo-Messalianism 159
Meteora, group of monasteries near Kalambaka in Thessaly 288, 343
Methodius, apostle of the Slavs 93–8, 99
Methodius I, Patriarch of Constantinople 59, 61, 63–5, 67, 69–71, 102

Methone, *see* Modon

Metochites, George, archdeacon 245, 247

Metochites, Theodore, humanist and imperial minister 243, 340, 344

Metrophanes of Smyrna, supporter of Patriarch Ignatius 73, 86

Metrophanes II, Patriarch of Constantinople 281, 284

metropolitans 290–3, 305, 311–15, 318–29 *passim*

Michael I Rangabe, Emperor 51, 53–4, 70

Michael II, Emperor 60–2, 63–4

Michael III, Emperor 62, 65, 67, 70–1, 73, 76–8, 92, 95

Michael IV the Paphlagonian, Emperor 128, 130

Michael VI, Emperor 130, 136

Michael VII Ducas, Emperor 139–40, 144–5

Michael VIII Palaeologus, Emperor 173, 186, 243, 245, 246, 324
   work for union with Rome 219, 220–9, 235–42, 244, 265, 266
   and council of Lyons 170–1, 218, 229–35
   recapture of Constantinople 220–1, 242, 335

Michael I Cerularius, Patriarch of Constantinople 87, 129–38, 326

Michael II Oxites, Patriarch of Constantinople 165

Michael III of Anchialus, Patriarch of Constantinople 155, 172–3, 307

Michael IV, Greek Patriarch in Nicaea 207–8, 209

Michael I, ruler of Epirus 186

Michael Italicus, archbishop of Philippopolis 161–2

Michael of Thessalonica, deacon 151

Michael the Syrian, monophysite Patriarch of Antioch, historian 41, 138

missionaries 82, 85, 87, 90–101, 116–17, 348, 367–8
   western 78, 82, 126

Mitylene, metropolitan of 192
   exiled bishop of 323

Modon, in Peloponnese (Methone) 185, 198, 274

moechian controversy 51

Moerbecke, William, Dominican friar 231

Moldavia (Moldovlachia) 290

Moldo-Wallachia 273

monenergism 13–15, 23–4

Mongols 212, 222, 290, 291–2

monks, monasticism Part II, section 9
   monastic party and relations with authority 50, 51, 53–6, 69–70, 144, 305
   opposition to iconoclasm 42–3, 55, 56, 63, 66
   opposition to union with Rome 171, 189, 191, 237, 245, 314
   abuses 113, 128, 130
   involved in heresy 149–50, 158–9
   under patriarchal supervision 211, 316, 318, 324, 327
   schools 330
   in Italy and Sicily 120, 177; Russia 292
   monophysites in east 115
   under Latin Empire 175, 188, 193–4, 198–9
   see Athos, hesychasm, Olympus, Studite monastery, Theodore Studites

monophysites 11, 13, 15, 33, 40–1, 87, 114, 130, 304
   in Egypt 14, 16, 18
   among Syrians 14, 115, 156
   among Armenians 116, 122, 131, 149–50, 156, 163, 174
   persecuted 138–9
   in Muslim territory 24, 298

monotheism 153

monotheletism 13, 16–20, 22–4, 31, 303, 304

Monte Cassino, monastery in Italy 120, 181
   abbot of 171

Moravia, Great Moravia 87, 94–101 *passim*

Morea, *see* Peloponnese

Morosini, *see* Thomas Morosini, Latin Patriarch of Constantinople

mosaics 37, 67–8, 175, 342, 358, 368

Moschabar, George, chartophylax 247–8

Moscow 288, 291–2

Moses of Bergamo, Italian scholar 180

Muhammad the Prophet 9, 153

Muhammad (Mehmed) I, Ottoman Sultan 268

Muhammad (Mehmed) II the Conqueror, Ottoman Sultan 282

Murad II, Ottoman Sultan 270

music 39, 308, 312, 349, 351–6, 358, 368

Muslims 9–10, 20, 62, 114–15, 119, 124, 171, 183, 212, 342

Muslims—*contd.*
in Asia Minor 126, 252, 299; in Balkans 166; Crete 62; Egypt 91, 297; North Africa 31, 62, 298; Palestine 176, 297; Sicily 62, 120; Spain 31, 62; Syria 91, 297
theologians 93–4
attitude to icons 34–5
superstition 366
converts to Christianity 114, 153–4
Christians in Muslim territory 16, 24, 39, 129 *and see* Alexandria, Antioch, Jerusalem
see also Arabs, Islam, Ottomans, Seljuks
Mutawakkil, Caliph 93
Muzalon, Theodore, grand logothete 247
Myra, in Lycia, bishop of 47
Myriobiblon, see Bibliotheca
Mystagogia of Photius 87
Mystagogy of Maximus the Confessor 359

national churches 131, 186, 367
nationalism 125, 127, 131
Naum, missionary to the Slavs 99, 100
navy 125, 271
Naxos (Cyclades), centre of Latin duchy 197
Nea Mone, monastery on Chios 130, 358
Negroponte, *see* Euboea
Neocastrum, in Thrace, settled by Paulicians 160
Neopatras, synod at 240
Neophytus, archbishop of Cyprus 202–3
neoplatonists 143, 150, 155
Nestorians 11, 12, 14, 24, 40, 174, 298, 308
Nicaea, general councils:
    I 10; canons 20, 326; Nicene creed 276 *and see* filioque
    II, on icons 33, 35–7, 40, 43, 45–50, 149, 303, 305; aftermath 51, 55; annulment 57, 60; restoration 64, 67, 84; canons 329, 331, 332
Nicaea, kingdom of 185–6, 193, 196, 198, 299, 315, 316, 323–4
    struggle with Epirus 208–11, 324
    relations with Rome 211–19, 324
    patriarchs in 163–4, 189, 191–2, 207–8, 323–4
Nicephorus I, Emperor 51, 52, 53–4
Nicephorus II Phocas, Emperor 112–13, 115, 118, 126, 301, 305, 320, 342, 345–6

Nicephorus III Botaneiates, Emperor 140
Nicephorus I, Patriarch of Constantinople 47, 53–4, 69–70, 313–14
    opposed to iconoclasm 55–61, 66
    writings 35, 48
Nicephorus II, Greek Patriarch in Nicaea 221
Nicephorus I, despot of Epirus 240
Nicetas, archbishop of Nicomedia 154, 180–2
Nicetas, metropolitan of Heracleia 150
Nicetas of Amasea 321
Nicetas of Ancyra 319
Nicetas of Seides in Iconium, theologian 179
Nicetas, Studite monk 133
Nicholas I Mysticus, Patriarch of Constantinople 86, 89, 111, 313
    and Leo VI's fourth marriage 103–8
    in politics 108–10, 315
    missionary work 91, 116, 321
    letters 110, 112
Nicholas III, Patriarch of Constantinople 147, 148, 149, 161, 347
Nicholas I, Pope 73–8, 79, 80, 85, 97
Nicholas III, Pope 240–1
Nicholas, metropolitan of Alania 116
Nicholas, bishop of Cotrone 223 and n.10
Nicholas, archbishop of Crete 198
Nicholas Kaloethes, metropolitan of Amastris 210
Nicholas of Methone 152, 155
Nicholas of Otranto, monk 189, 191
Nicodemus, Athonite monk in Rumania 288, 291
Nicomachean Ethics of Aristotle 150
Nicomedia, in Bithynia 28, 154
Nicopolis, battle of 268
Nicosia in Cyprus, Latin archbishop of 201, 204
Nilus of Rossano, monk 120
Nilus of Sinai, pseudonym 363
Nilus, Patriarch of Constantinople 267
Nilus the Calabrian, monk 149–50
Niphon I Cyzicus, Patriarch of Constantinople 243, 253
Niphon, hieromonk of Mt Athos, accused of heresy 164
Niphon, monk from Cappadocia, accused of Bogomilism 162
nomocanons 305–6, 310
nomophylax 138, 306, 310

Normans 139–40, 145, 182
  in Italy 127, 131–3, 135, 141, 168, 172, 177, 179, 299
  in Sicily 141, 170, 177, 179
  in Antioch 171–2, 175
Northmen 117, 127
  see also Varangians
Notaras, Luke 282, 285
Notitiae Episcopatuum 310–12, 313, 325, 331
Notre Dame, Latin cathedral in Athens 193
Nouthesia, by George of Cyprus 40
nuns 25, 106, 128, 256
Nymphaeum, town near Smyrna in Asia Minor 186, 215–16, 217

Ochrida, in Bulgaria 100
  archbishop of 211; *and see* Leo and Theophylact
Octoechus, Little, musical handbook 356
oeconomus 46, 306–7, 316, 327
oecumene 91, 133, 301
Olga, Russian princess 101, 117–18
Olgerd, pagan ruler of Lithuania 292
Olympiodorus, historian 88
Olympius, exarch of Ravenna 21
Olympus, Mt, monastic centre in Bithynia 51, 93, 102, 104, 138, 245, 341, 342
  and iconoclasm 59, 63, 66
  and Psellus 143, 347 n. 91
Onogurs 94
Opus Tripartitum of Humbert de Romanis 234–5
Origen 10, 13, 21, 362
orphanotrophus 306
Orthodoxy Sunday 63–5, 164, 355
orthros, daily office 65, 350–51, 352–4, 355
Otranto, in south Italy 59, 121
Otto I, German Emperor 117–18, 120–1
  and n. 24
Otto II, German Emperor 121
Otto III, German Emperor 121
Otto de la Roche, lord of Athens 193
Ottomans:
  attacks on Byzantine Empire 166, 186, 200, 206, 212, 275, 276, 281–2, 290
  in Greek islands 197
  in Cyprus 201
  in Europe 263
  relations with Manuel II 267, 268
  final victory 124, 286–7, 298

Oxeia, island in sea of Marmora 147

Pachomius, monk in Egypt 335
Pachymeres, George, historian 222, 224–5, 227, 239, 251
Pacurianus, Gregory 344–5
paganism in Byzantine Empire 25–6, 28, 30, 33–4, 300, 312, 366
  in Balkans 100
  in Kiev 118
  in Lithuania 290, 292
  pagan philosophy 143
Palaeologan period 65, 142, 167, 211, 237, 253, 267; *see* Michael VIII, Andronicus II, III and IV, John V and VIII, Manuel II, Constantine XI, emperors
Palamas, Gregory, archbishop of Thessalonica 155, 164, 248–9, 258–60, 261, 288, 355, 357
Palamites, Palamism 164, 260, 262, 264, 289
  anti-Palamites 163, 164, 267, 292
  synods 318
Palestine (Holy Land) 15–16, 19, 31, 176, 348
  influx of Arabs 18
  Muslim conquest 297
  and crusades 169–70, 175, 225–6, 230
  monasteries 59, 335–6, 353
Pamphylia, bishops in 40, 61
Panachrantus, monastery in Constantinople 241
Panagia Angeloktistos, church at Kiti in Cyprus 205
Panagia Atheniotissa, metropolitan church in Athens 193
Panaretus, Nicholas, finance minister 230
Pannonia 94, 97
Panoplia Dogmatica of Zigabenus 158
Pantocrator monastery, founded by John II Comnenus 337, 347
papades (parish priests) 196, 198–9, 330
  patriarchal secretariat 312
Paphlagonia 128, 363
Parastron, John, Franciscan friar 231, 233, 235
parecclesion 197
Paroria, monastic centre in Bulgaria 287–8, 291
Parthenon 193
Pascal I, Pope 60, 64
Pascal II, Pope 170–1, 179

Patir di Rossano, monastery in Calabria 341
Patmos 199, 340, 344
Patras, archbishop of 192
patriarchate 290, 294, *and see* pentarchy
of Constantinople 299, 325, 335
relationship to Emperor 300–303, 313–14
election 312–14, 319
jurisdiction 15, 328–9, *and see* Bulgaria (church in), Illyricum, South Italy
finance 347
patriarcheion 56, 63, 313, 314, 319
Paul, archbishop of Thessalonica 21
Paul, bishop of Ancona 83
Paul II, Patriarch of Constantinople 18, 19, 20, 23
Paul IV, Patriarch of Constantinople 45
Paul, Latin archbishop of Smyrna 263–6
Paul the One-eyed, monophysite bishop 15
Paulicians 33, 54, 156–7, 158, 160, 163, 165
Pečersky monastery in Kiev 341–2
Pechenegs 117, 126, 142
Pelagius of Albano, cardinal-bishop, papal legate 212–13
Pelagonia, battle of 220
Pelendri church in Cyprus 205
Peloponnese (Morea) 255, 268–9
Slavs in 94, 100
Latins in 185, 195–6, 198, 220, 224, 234
Chronicle of the Morea 196
pentarchy 81, 108, 134–5, 168, 235, 269, 275, 286, 290, 294, 297, 299, 367
pentas, pentades 315, 331
Pentecostarion 355
Pera, across Golden Horn, friars and monks in 214, 251, 316
Peribleptos monastery in Constantinople 159, 162
Persia 14, 15, 31, 156, 298
Perugia 217
Peter, Patriarch of Constantinople 23
Peter III, Patriarch of Antioch 134–5
Peter the Fuller, Patriarch of Antioch 12
Peter III, king of Aragon 242
Peter I, Catholicus of Armenia 131
Peter, abbot of St Sabas in Rome 46, 49
Peter, arch-priest, oeconomus 46, 49
Peter, Bulgarian tsar 157—8
Peter Capuano, papal legate 189, 190
Peter, cardinal-priest 83

Peter Lombard, theologian 177
Peter, metropolitan of Alania 116
Peter of Sicily 156–7
Peter the Venerable 171–2, 182
Peter Thomas, bishop of Patti and Lipari 263
Petronas, brother of Empress Theodora (wife of Theophilus) 63
phiale, courtyard behind Hagia Sophia 139
Philadelphia, see of 323
Philip of Courtenay, son of Baldwin II 237, 240
Philippopolis, in Thrace 150, 157, 160, 344
philosophy, study of, *see* Aristotle, Plato, neo-platonists
Philotheus, author of *Cletorologion* 65
Philotheus Coccinus, Patriarch of Constantinople 259, 262, 264, 265, 288–9, 292, 294, 314, 324, 361
Photius, Patriarch of Constantinople 67, 72–9, 83–90, 101, 102–3, 122, 129, 289, 313–14
out of office 79–82
Photian councils and synods 76, 78, 80, 84, 173, 304
humanist and scholar 75, 88–9, 143, 157
Phrygia, in Asia Minor 36, 60, 152, 159
Phundagiagitae, Bogomils 159
Piccinino, Nicholas, condottiere 276–7
pirates 197, 261
Pisa, Pisans 152, 178, 184
on Golden Horn 176–7, 179–80
council of 269
Pisidia bishop of 47
Planudes, Maximus, scholar 277
Plato, abbot of Saccudium in Bithynia 47, 51
Plato, platonism 143–4, 154, 155, 177, 277, 364
plenitudo potestatis 182, 183, 187, 226, 232, 279
Plutarch 88, 277
Poland 98, 292
Polychron, monastery 95 and n. 88
Polyeuctus, Patriarch of Constantinople 112–13, 121, 301
Pontanus 364
Pontus, district of Asia Minor on the Black Sea 116
diocese of 319
Pontic Heracleia 323
Potamia, in Naxos 197

prayer 363–5
  Jesus prayer 258, 364
pre-Gregorian reformers 127, 131
Premonstratensian 180
Pre-sanctified, Liturgy of the 357
Preslav, in Bulgaria 99, 100
priests 329–35
Princes Islands in sea of Marmora 70, 113, 306
Principo, island in sea of Marmora 71
Prinobaris, in Asia Minor 193
Proclus, neoplatonist 143, 150, 155
Proconnesus, island in sea of Marmora, place of exile 221
Prodromus, Theodore 161–2
proedrus 138, 162
Prote, island in sea of Marmora 113
protecdicus 317
Protheoria, treatise on eucharist 359
prothesis 358, 360, 361
protoasecretis 45, 72, 89, 306
protonotary 317
protopapas 199
protopsaltis 199
protos, of Mt Athos 342
protospathar 27
protosyncellus 130
protothronus 325
protovestiarius 138
psaltai, *see* cantors
Psalter 96, 146, 329–30, 352, 353
Psamathia, monastery in Constantinople 105
Psellus, Michael, scholar, historian, teacher, politician 128, 130, 136–7, 155, 160 n. 86, 334, 347
  and Xiphilinus 138, 139, 143–4
  and John Italus 142, 145
Psephos of Sergius I, Patriarch 17
Pseudo-Codinus, writer on ceremonial 302, 312
pseudo-Cyrillic work 150
Pseudo-Dionysius the Areopagite 15, 16 and n. 9, 17, 23, 32, 361
Pseudo-Macarius, writer on spirituality 362
Pyrrhus, Patriarch of Constantinople 15, ·17–19, 20, 23

Quinisextum council (in Trullo) 24–9, 304
  canons 32–3, 304, 329, 347

Radoald, bishop of Porto 73–6, 81

Rastislav, ruler of Great Moravia 95–6, 97
Ravenna 13, 18, 27
  exarchs of 19, 21
Ravennica, Parlement of 194
Raymond I of Tortosa, seneschal of Barcelona 178
readers, an ecclesiastical order 72, 329, 333
Refutatio et Eversio of Patriarch Nicephorus I 57–8
relics 30, 38, 41, 49, 97
reliquaries 38
Reply (Apologia), anti-unionist document 227, 234–5
rex 49, 54, 120, 294
Rhetor 146
Rhodes, bishop of 47
Richard I, king of England 201
Robert of Melun 177–8
Roger II, king of Sicily 171, 172, 180
Roman Church: claim to primacy 10, 27, 77, 133–6, 167–73, 179–83, ch. VII *passim*
  (after 1204) 224, 225, 227–9, 240, 294
  at council of Lyons 232–5, 238
  under John VI 261; John VIII 279, 283
  primacy of honour 61, 81, 108, 126, 179
Roman, metropolitan for Lithuania 292
Romania, *see* Latin Empire
Romanus, hymnographer 354
Romanus I Lecapenus, Emperor 106–7, 108–10, 111, 313
Romanus II, Emperor 112
Romanus IV Diogenes, Emperor 124, 125–6, 139, 141, 320
Rome, city of:
  Greeks in 13, 59, 63, 75, 97, 120, 177, 348
  visit by patriarch 18; by emperor 266
  councils: Lateran 19–22; Photian 84
Ros, *see* Rus
Rossano, in south Italy 120
Rumania 290–1
Rumeli Hissar, Ottoman fort on European bank of the Bosphorus 282
Rus (Ros) 87, 92, 117
Russia:
  conversion of 114, 117–19, 124, 368
  and Orthodox Church 122, 273, 286–7, 290, 291–4, 299, 314
  monasticism 260, 287–8, 342, 355
  use of vernacular 100–1, 310
  Russian *Primary Chronicle* 101, 119

Sabas, archbishop of Žiča and All Serbia 209
Sabas, St 348
Saccudium, monastic house in Bithynia 47, 51
sacellarius 316, 318
sacelliou 316–17
sacraments 349, *and see* eucharist
St Catherine, monastery on Mount Sinai 199, 322, 353
St Demetrius of Thessalonica:
 basilica 358
 icon of 31
St Gregory, fortress off Bithynian coast 247
St Irene, church in Constantinople 72
St James, Liturgy of 357
St John the Divine, monastery on Patmos 199, 340, 344
St John the Hunter, monastery on Mt Hymettus 193
St John Lampadistis Kalopanagiotis, church in Cyprus 205
St Lazarus, monastery on Mt Galesius 250
St Mamas, monastery in Constantinople 341
St Paul, apostle 10, 278
St Peter, apostle 10, 44, 181, 214, 278
St Sabas, Greek monastery in Rome 46, 59
St Sabas, monastery in Palestine 335, 352, 354, 356, 363
Saladin 201
Salzburg, archbishop of 95
Samandar, in Khazaria 92
San Niccolò di Casole, monastery near Otranto 177
San Salvatore di Messina, monastery 177, 341
Santa Sophia, Latin cathedral in Nicosia 204
Santorin (Thera) 37
Sanudo, Marco 197
Sanudo Torsello, Marino 255–6, 257
Saracens 83
 Saracen-minded 40, 42
Sardica, canons of 75, 320
Savoy 271
Saxons 120, 126
Scandinavians 94, 117
 see also Northmen and Varangians
sceuophylax 316
Schemarium, fortress in Caucasus 22
schism between Rome and Constantinople 122, 130, 136, 179, 182–3, 214–17, 226ff., 234–5, 255, 266, 286
 between Epirus and Nicaea 208–11, 214
 in papacy (Great Schism) 200, 267, 269, 272
 Josephites and Arsenites 243–6, 252–3
Scholarius, George (Gennadius II, Patriarch) 273, 278, 282, 283, 285
Scriptor Incertus de Leone Bardae Armenii filio 56
scriptorium 339–40
Scylitzes Continuatus, chronicle 138
secreta 319
Seljuk Turks 126, 208
Serbia 186, 207, 208
 church in 186, 209, 290, 314, 324
 monasticism 191, 287, 342
 vernacular culture 100, 310
 defeat at Kossovo 268
Sergius I, Patriarch of Constantinople 14–15, 16 n. 10, 17, 20, 23, 331
Sergius II, Patriarch of Constantinople 122
Sergius I, Pope 27
Sergius of Radonezh, monk 288
Serres, in Macedonia, ruler of 290
 metropolitanate of 318
Severus, monophysite Patriarch of Antioch 33 and n. 8
Sicily 22, 47
 under Greek jurisdiction 46, 52, 67, 73, 311
 under Latin 179
 Muslims (Arabs) in 62, 119–20, 127, 177
 Normans in 127, 141, 170, 177, 179
 Sicilian Vespers 242, 244
 influence of Theodore Studites 341–2
Sigerus, Nicholas 263
Sigismund, king of Hungary, later Western Emperor 268, 269, 275
silentium (imperial council) 38
simony 52, 133
Sinai, Mount 199, 322, 340, 348, 368
Sirmium, see of 97
Sisinnius, bishop of Perge in Pamphylia 40
Sisinnius II, Patriarch of Constantinople 116, 122
Sixtus IV, Pope 205
skete 337–8
skeuophylakion 357, 358
slavery 98, 115
Slavonic 95–101 *passim*, 119, 122, 288, 310
 Old Church Slavonic 96, 158, 291

Slavs:
and Christianity 9–10, 94–100, 114, 260, 307, 348, 368
penetration of Byzantine empire 14–24 *passim*, 31 39, 91, 124
in Balkans 32, 126
see also Bulgaria, Russia, Serbia
Slovakia, part of Great Moravia 94
Smyrna 73, 86, 186, 193
solea 358
Sophronius, Patriarch of Jerusalem 16–17, 33 n. 8
Soterichus Panteugenes, Patriarch-elect of Antioch 151–2
soteriology 10, 12
South Italy:
Greeks in 13–14, 119–21, 122–3, 127, 131–2, 179
monasticism 42, 120, 177
iconoclasm in 59
ecclesiastical jurisdiction 52, 67, 127, 131–2, 179, 311
Arabs in 177; Normans 141, 168, 170, 172, 177, 179–80, 299; Charles of Anjou 223
Sozopolis, on Black Sea 149
Spain 31, 33, 62, 85
Sphrantzes, George, historian 285
spirituality 164, 260, 289, 299, 349–68
stauropegial foundations 315, 316, 324, 327
staurophoroi 275, 322
Stephen I, Patriarch of Constantinople 86, 102
Stephen II of Amasea, Patriarch of Constantinople 111
Stephen V, Pope 60
Stephen VI, Pope 86
Stephen, bishop of Nepi 80
Stephen Dandolo 257
Stephen, first king of Hungary 98
Stephen of Nicomedia 349
Stephen the Younger, *Life* of 39, 42
Stephen II of Serbia 209
Stephen IV Dushan, king of Serbia 290
stichera (stanzas) 356
Strymon, region near Thessalonica 93
Studite monastery in Constantinople 66, 102, 127, 140, 342, 348
opposition to iconoclasm 43 *and see* Theodore Studites
to imperial marriages 51, 53–4
anathematised 69

synod in 293
cenobitic rule 288
teaching 330
library 340
monastic offices 352, 354, 355
Stylianus of Neocaesarea opposed to Photius 86, 102
Stylianus Zaoutzes, minister under Leo VI 102, 103
subdeacons 72, 329
Suceava, in Moldavia, metropolitanate 290–1
Suda, dictionary 88
suffragans 315, 320, 321, 324, 325–6, 328–9
in Latin churches 192
Svatopluk, ruler of Great Moravia 97–8
Svyatoslav, prince of Kiev 117–18
Syllaeum, in Pamphylia, bishop of 61
Sylvester II, Pope 98
symbolism 359–61
Symeon, archbishop of Thessalonica 314, 315, 352, 359, 361
Symeon, Bulgarian tsar 99, 108–10, 118
Symeon Metaphrastes 307
Symeon the New Theologian 133, 348–9, 356–7, 363, 364–6
writings 166, 340, 341, 355
hymns 364, 366
syncellus 38, 317
synergy 357, 362
synodica (*grammata*), systatic letter, synodical 45, 53, 60, 73, 134, 168–9, 319
Synodicon of anathemas 65, 144, 151–3, 163, 165, 259, 305, 355
synodos endemousa, standing synod in Constantinople 57, 71, 128, 133–4, 168, 183, 307, 311, 317, 318–22, 328
condemnation of heresies 13, 144, 305
choice of patriarch 70, 86, 313–14
synopsis canonum 307
Syntagma of Matthew Blastares 309–10
Syracuse 22, 70
Syria:
north Syrian emperors 34, 41, 50, 55
monophysites in 11, 14, 115, 138, 156
monasteries in 175
attacked by Persia 14; by Arabs 18; by Turkic tribes 125, 138, 169
lost to Muslims 91, 297
crusaders in 169–70, 176
refugees from 129; in Cyprus 201, 203
Syriac 35, 175, 354, 363

systatic letter, *see synodica*
Syropoulos, Sylvester, megas ecclesiarch 272–5, 277, 278, 280, 285

Tactica 312
Taormina, bishop of 71
Tarasius, brother of Photius 88–9
Tarasius, Patriarch of Constantinople 45, 53, 72, 313
  and second council of Nicaea 37, 45–9, 51–2, 84
  criticised 57, 69–70
Tarsus, city in Cilicia in south-east Asia Minor 19, 115
Taurus region, mountain range in south-east Asia Minor 171
taxation:
  civil 113, 125, 159, 194, 251
  immunities 343
  tax-collectors 197, 344, 345
  ecclesiastical 345, *and see* tithes
Teilhard de Chardin, modern theologian 68
Templars 193
Tephrice, in Armenia, Paulician stronghold 156–7
Terebinthus, island in sea of Marmora 71
Tessaracontapechys, legendary figure 35–6
tetragamy, of Leo VI 103–8, 110
themes 14, 37, 43, 55, 115–16, 122
Theoctistus, logothete of the drome 62–4, 71
Theodora, eleventh-century Macedonian Empress 128, 130, 136
Theodora, Empress, wife of Theophilus 62–5, 67, 70–1, 72
Theodora, Empress, wife of John I Tzimisces 113
Theodora, Empress, wife of Justinian I 11
Theodore I Lascaris, Emperor in Nicaea 185–6, 189, 191, 198, 207–9, 212–13
Theodore II Lascaris, Emperor in Nicaea 218–19, 220
Theodore II Irenicus, Byzantine Patriarch in Nicaea 209, 212–13
Theodore, Pope 18–19
Theodore Angelus, despot of Epirus and Emperor of Thessalonica 208–11
Theodore, bishop of Euboea (Negroponte) 190, 192
Theodore, bishop of Pharan in Sinai 15, 20

Theodore, brother of Manuel II Palaeologus 267
Theodore of Mopsuestia, theologian 12
Theodore of Smyrna 155
Theodore of Tarsus, archbishop of Canterbury 19, 22
Theodore of Taurianum (Taormina), bishop 48
Theodore of Trebizond (Blachernites), heretic 161
Theodore Santabarenus, metropolitan of Euchaita 86
Theodore Studites, abbot of Studite monastery 51, 53–4, 63, 339–41, 348
  defence of icons 38, 43, 48, 66, 341
  against imperial intervention 50, 56, 221, 303
  writings 58–61, 69–70, 339, 341, 363
  hymns 354, 355
Theodoret, theologian 12
Theodosius I, Emperor 297
Theodosius, archbishop of Caesarea in Bithynia 21
Theodosius, bishop of Ephesus 40
Theodosius of Trnovo, monk and hesychast 163, 287
Theodote, second wife of Constantine VI 51
Theodotus Mellissenus Cassiteras, Patriarch of Constantinople 57, 59–61
Theognostus, abbot, pro-Ignatian 72 n. 11, 76, 86
theopaschism 12
Theophanes, chronicler 35, 37
Theophanes, metropolitan of Nicaea 230, 245
Theophano, first wife of Leo VI 103
Theophano, wife of Constantine VII 112, 113
Theophano, wife of Otto II 121
Theophilus, Emperor 45, 62, 64
Theophylact, Patriarch of Constantinople 98, 111–12, 157–8
Theophylact, archbishop of Ochrida in Bulgaria 135, 178–9, 181, 308, 320
Theophylact, chief notary 20
theosis, *see* deification
Theostericus, author of *Vita Nicetae* 56, n. 56
Thera (Santorin) 37
Thessalonica 93, 95, 190, 268
  archbishops of 21, 27

under jurisdiction of Constantinople 73, 311

under protection of St Demetrius 31, 32

on route from west to Constantinople 176, 242

resistance to Latins 185

Latin kingdom of 192, 194

taken by Theodore Angelus 208

schools 330

Thessaly 185, 209, 237, 239

monasteries in 288, 343

Thomas Morosini, Latin Patriarch of Constantinople 184, 187–8, 189, 190–1, 207

Thomas of Claudiopolis, bishop 36–7

Thomas, priest, deposed for conducting Leo VI's marriage 105

Thomas, syncellus of Alexandria 46

Thomas the Slav, leader of revolt 62

Thomism, *see* Aquinas

Thrace 47, 156, 160, 162, 163, 164

diocese of 319

Thracesian theme 43

Three Chapters, censured by Justinian I 12

Tiberias, in Palestine 36

Timarion, satire 155

Tismana monastery in Rumania 291

tithes 188, 194, 201, 204

Tome of Union 107

tomographia (written statement) on church union 239

Tomos of Michael VIII Palaeologus 227

of Patriarch Gregory II 247–8

of Ferrara-Florence 279

Tornices, George 173

trade 92, 117, 125, 142, 176–7, 183

translations 180

from Greek into Latin 26, 49, 99, 132, 177, 178

into Slavonic 96–7, 98, 100, 288

from Latin into Greek 17, 46, 84, 134, 234, 266, 277

from Syriac into Greek 363

travel 250, 256, 348

by land 176, 190

by sea 28, 116, 230, 272, 274

Traversari, Ambrogio, scholar 273 n. 172, 274, 277, 279

Trebizond, Greek kingdom of 185, 207, 208, 281, 287

Trent, council of 360

Triads of Gregory Palamas 258

tribute, payment of 109, 118, 166

Trinity, doctrine of 10, 17, 151–2, 216, 218, 245, 256, 282–3, 305

Triodion, liturgical book 100, 355

Trisagion (Sanctus) 12

Trnovo, in Bulgaria

metropolitan of 211

monastery near 287, 289

troparia, stanzas 353

Trypho, Patriarch of Constantinople 111

Turkia, bishop of 98

Turkic peoples:

drive westwards 9, 91, 94, 131, 138, 160, 298

in Asia Minor 125, 169

in Bulgaria 99

see Cumans Magyars (*s.v.* Hungary), Pechenegs

Turks 191, 195, 257, 267, 292

advances westward 129, 142, 222, 237, 242, 251, 261

in Asia Minor 185, 244, 252, 254

in Europe 263

checked by Amadeo of Savoy 264

see also Onogurs, Seljuks, Ottomans

Tusculum 180

house of 120

Tyana, metropolitan of 162

Type (Rule of faith) 19, 20–1

of Constans II 303

typicon 327, 342, 343, 344–5, 356, 358

Ungrovlachia 290

union of Greek and Roman churches:

attempts at 148, 168, 170–2, 187, 192, 209, 212–19, ch. VIII sections 1–3, 255–7, 261, ch. VIII section 9, 314

and John V 263–4, 266

opposition to 189, 243–7, 281–6, 322

unleavened bread (azymes) 132, 135, 150, 178, 180, 206, 226, 232, 279, 308

in Armenian church 131

view of friars 215–16

Urban II, Pope 168–9, 170, 179

Urban IV, Pope 204, 223

Urban V, Pope 195, 199, 264, 266

Urban VI, Pope 267

Varangians 117, 118, 228

Varna, battle of 281

vassals 120, 135, 267

veneration of icons 48–9, 62, 64, 149, 190
opposition to 56, 58, 59, 61 *and see* iconoclasm
Venice, Venetians 96, 98, 266–7, 269, 274, 276, 280
expansion of trade 125, 141–2, 170, 176
Fourth Crusade and after 184–90 *passim*, 195
in Crete 197–200, 322
in Cyclades 197
in Cyprus 201
Versinicia, battle of 54
vespers 350–1, 352–4
Via Egnatia 176, 242
Vigilius, Pope 12, 15
Vikings 92, 94
Villehardouin family 195, 220
Villehardouin, Geoffrey 196
Visconti, Tedaldo, *see* Gregory X, Pope
Visigoths 298
Vita Constantini 93–5
Vita Euthymii 104–6, 108
Vita Nicephori 56, 58
Vitalian, Pope 22
Viterbo 265–6
Vladimir, in north-east Russia 291
Vladimir, prince of Kiev 101, 118–19

Wallachia 288, 290
Willebrands, cardinal 286
William, bishop of Diaulia in Boeotia 267

Xerolophos, district in Constantinople 252
Xiphilinus, *see* John VIII Xiphilinus, Patriarch

Yazid II, Muslim ruler 35–6
Yolande-Irene, *see* Irene of Montferrat

Zacharias, bishop of Anagni 73–6, 81
Zacharias, protospathar 27, 29
Zagorsk, near Moscow, monastery at 288
Zaoutzes, *see* Stylianus
Zeno, Emperor 12
Zeta, Serbian principality 126
Žiča in Serbia, archbishopric of 209
Zigabenus, Euthymius, author of *Panoplia Dogmatica* 158
Zoe Carbonopsina, fourth wife of Leo VI 104–6, 108–9
Zoe, Macedonian empress 121, 124, 128, 130
Zoe, second wife of Leo VI 103
Zonaras, John, canonist and historian 306, 310

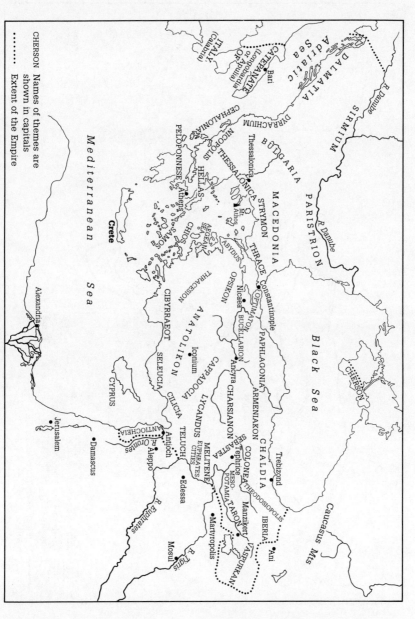

MAP I. The Byzantine Empire c. 1025

Mediterranean Sea

Black Sea

Adriatic Sea

Aegean Sea

ITALY (Longobardia) (Calabria)

CATEPANATE (to Longobardia or APULIA)

Bari

DALMATIA

SIRMIUM

R. Danube

R. Danube

PARISTRION

BULGARIA

DURRACHIUM

CEPHALONIA

NICOPOLIS

Thessalonica

THESSALONICA

PELOPONNESE

Athens

HELLAS

CHIOS

SAMOS

Mt. Athos

MACEDONIA

STRYMON

THRACE

THRACESION

ABYDUS

OPSIKION

Constantinople

OPTIMATON

BUCELLARION

Nicaea

PAPHLAGONIA

Ancyra

CHARSIANON

ARMENIAKON

CHALDIA

Trebizond

Caucasus Mts

CHERSON

Crete

CIBYRRAEOT

ANATOLIKON

Iconium

CAPPADOCIA

LYCANDUS

SELEUCIA

CILICIA

TELUCH

EUPHRATES CITIES

MELITENE

SEBASTEA

COLONEA

Tephrice

MESO POTAMIA

THEODOSIOPOLIS

IBERIA

Ani

VASPURKAN

Manzikert

TARON

Martyropolis

Mosul

R. Tigris

Edessa

R. Euphrates

Aleppo

R. Orontes

Antioch

ANTIOCHEIA

Damascus

Jerusalem

Alexandria

CYPRUS

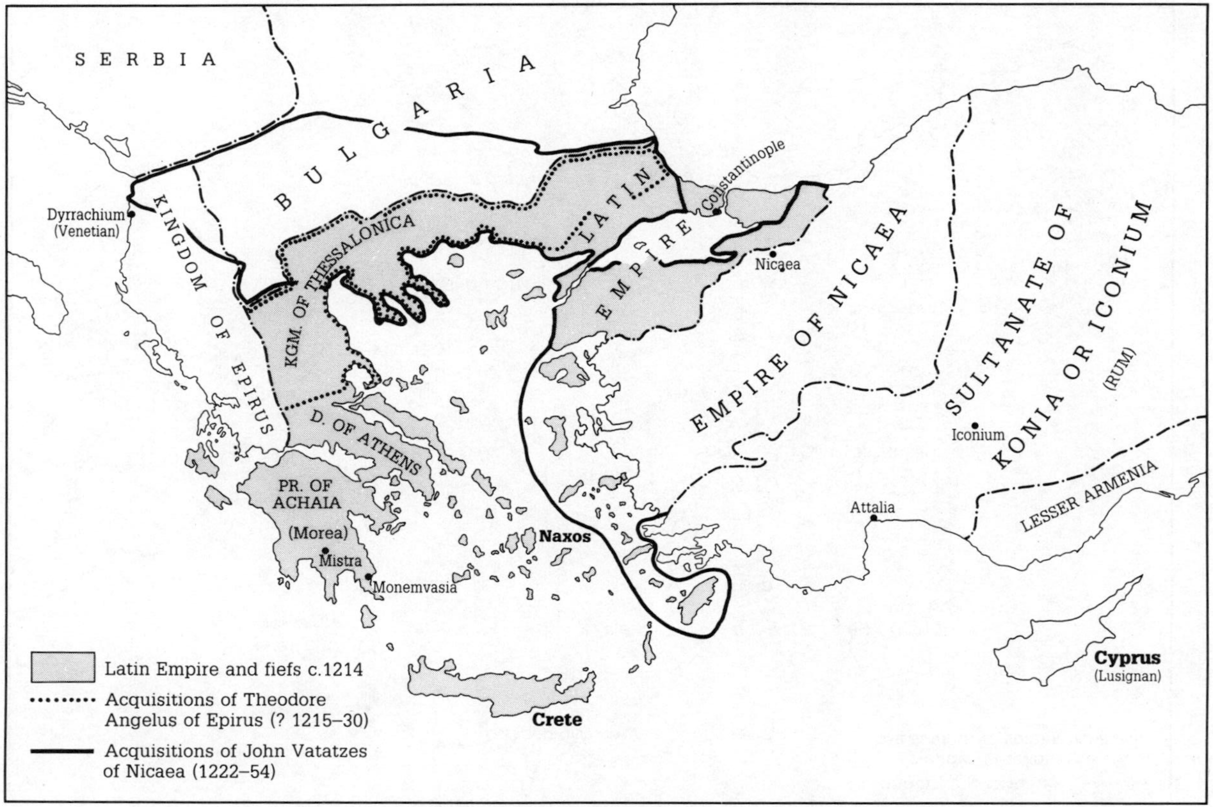

MAP 2. The Aegean World *c.* 1214–1254

SERBIA

BULGARIA

KONIA OR ICONIUM

SULTANATE OF

(RUM)

LESSER ARMENIA

Cyprus
(Lusignan)

EMPIRE OF NICAEA

Iconium

Attalia

Nicaea

Constantinople

LATIN EMPIRE

KINGDOM OF EPIRUS

Dyrrachium
(Venetian)

KGM. OF THESSALONICA

D. OF ATHENS

PR. OF ACHAIA
(Morea)

Naxos

Mistra

Monemvasia

Crete

Latin Empire and fiefs c.1214

Acquisitions of Theodore
Angelus of Epirus (? 1215–30)

Acquisitions of John Vatatzes
of Nicaea (1222–54)

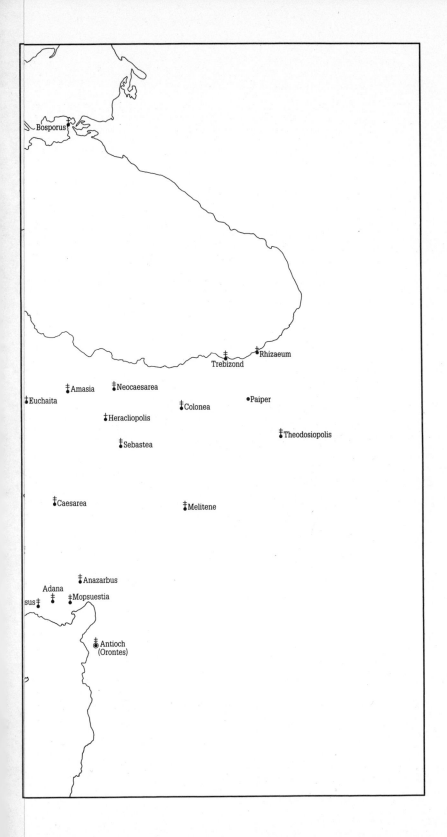

Bosporus

‡Trebizond ●Rhizaeum

‡Amasia ‡Neocaesarea

‡Euchaita ‡Colonea ●Paiper

‡Heracliopolis

‡Theodosiopolis

‡Sebastea

‡Caesarea ‡Melitene

‡Anazarbus

Adana

sus‡ ‡ ‡Mopsuestia

‡Antioch
(Orontes)